T0200993

# EVOLVING INTELLIGENT SYSTEMS

**Books in the IEEE Press Series on Computational Intelligence**

*Introduction to Evolvable Hardware: A Practical Guide for Designing Self-Adaptive Systems*
Garrison W. Greenwood and Andrew M. Tyrrell
2007    978-0471-71977-9

*Evolutionary Computation: Toward a New Philosophy of Machine Intelligence, Third Edition*
David B. Fogel
2006    978-0471-66951-7

*Emergent Information Technologies and Enabling Policies for Counter-Terrorism*
Edited by Robert L. Popp and John Yen
2006    978-0471-77615-4

*Computationally Intelligent Hybrid Systems*
Edited by Seppo J. Ovaska
2005    978-0471-47668-4

*Handbook of Learning and Appropriate Dynamic Programming*
Edited by Jennie Si, Andrew G. Barto, Warren B. Powell, Donald Wunsch II
2004    978-0471-66054-X

*Computational Intelligence: The Experts Speak*
Edited by David B. Fogel and Charles J. Robinson
2003    978-0471-27454-2

*Computational Intelligence in Bioinformatics*
Edited by Gary B. Fogel, David W. Corne, and Yi Pan
2008    978-0470-10526-9

*Computational Intelligence and Feature Selection: Rough and Fuzzy Approaches*
Richard Jensen and Qiang Shen
2008    978-0470-22975-0

*Clustering*
Rui Xu and Donald C. Wunsch II
2009    978-0470-27680-8

# EVOLVING INTELLIGENT SYSTEMS
## Methodology and Applications

EDITED BY

Plamen Angelov
Dimitar P. Filev
Nikola Kasabov

IEEE Computational Intelligence Society, *Sponsor*

 **IEEE Press Series on Computational Intelligence**
David B. Fogel, Series Editor

A JOHN WILEY & SONS, INC., PUBLICATION

Published by John Wiley & Sons, Inc., Hoboken, New Jersey.
Published simultaneously in Canada.

For general information on our other products and services or for technical support, please contact our Customer Care Department within the United States at (800) 762-2974, outside the United States at (317) 572-3993 or fax (317) 572-4002

Wiley also publishes its books in a variety of electronic formats. Some content that appears in print may not be available in electronic formats. For more information about Wiley products, visit our web site at www.wiley.com

*Library of Congress Cataloging-in-Publication Data:*

Evolving intelligent systems : methodology and applications / Plamen Angelov, Dimitar P. Filev, Nik Kasabov.
    p. cm.
  Includes index.
  ISBN 978-0-470-28719-4 (cloth)
  1.  Computational intelligence. 2.  Fuzzy systems. 3.  Neural networks (Computer science)
  4.  Evolutionary programming (Computer science) 5.  Intelligent control systems.
  I. Angelov, Plamen.  II. Filev, Dimitar P., 1959-  III. Kasabov, Nikola K.
  Q342.E785 2009
  006.3–dc20

                                              2009025980

Printed in the United States of America.

10 9 8 7 6 5 4 3 2 1

# CONTENTS

# PREFACE

One of the consequences of the information revolution is the ever-growing amount of information we are surrounded with and the need to process this information efficiently and extract meaningful knowledge. This phenomenon was termed "digital obesity" or "information obesity" by Toshiba Ltd. One of the specifics of this phenomenon is that the information not only is presented in huge quantities, but also is dynamic, presented in a form of streams of data. The latter brings new challenges to the established approaches to processing data, usually in an offline and stationary form. To address the new challenges of extracting highly interpretable knowledge from streams of data, online techniques and methodologies have been developed, so that a higher level of adaptation, compared to conventional *adaptive systems* known from *control theory* (Astrom & Wittenmark, 1989), is achieved. These new modeling methods are also principally different from the *classical system identification theory* (Ljung, 1988). They differ also from the traditional *machine learning* and *statistical learning* methods (Hastie et al., 2001), where the processes are usually assumed to have Gaussian distribution and random nature. *Evolving intelligent systems (EISs)* are based on fuzzy and neuro-fuzzy techniques that allow for the structure and the functionality of a system to develop and evolve from incoming data. They represent a fuzzy mixture of locally valid simpler systems, which in combination are highly nonlinear and non-Gaussian. They can be considered fuzzy mixtures of Gaussians, but these mixtures are not pre-fixed and are adapting/evolving to capture the real data density distribution (Angelov & Zhou, 2008).

A computer, engineering, or any other system that possess features of computational intelligence is commonly called an *intelligent* system. Many intelligent products such as camcorders, washing machines, games, and so on have reached the market. Once created/designed, however, most of them do not continue to learn, to improve, and to adapt. This edited volume aims to bring together the best recent works in the newly emerging subtopic of the area of computational intelligence, which puts the emphasis on lifetime self-adaptation, and on the online process of evolving the system's structure and parameters. Evolving systems can have different technical or physical embodiments, including intelligent agents, embedded systems, and ubiquitous computing. They can also have different computational frameworks, for example, one of a fuzzy rule-based type; one of a neural network type; one of a multimodel type. The important feature that any EIS possesses is the ability to:

- Expand or shrink its structure, as well as to adapt its parameters, and thus to evolve
- Work and adapt incrementally, online, and, if necessary, in real time

The newly emerging concept of dynamically *evolving* structures, which was to some extent already applied to neural networks (Fritzke, 1994), brought powerful new concepts of *evolving fuzzy systems* (Angelov, 2002; Angelov & Filev, 2004; Angelov and Zhou, 2006) and evolving neuro-fuzzy systems (Kasabov, 2002; 2007), which together with some other techniques of computational intelligence and statistical analysis are considered to be EIS (Angelov & Kasabov 2006; Yager, 2006). EIS combines the interpolation abilities of the (neuro-)fuzzy systems and their flexibility with the adaptive feature of the online learning techniques. Evolving fuzzy systems (EFSs), in particular, have the additional advantage of linguistic interpretability and can be used for extracting knowledge in the form of atomic information granules (linguistic terms represented by fuzzy sets) (Angelov, 2002; Pedrycz, 2005; Zadeh, 1975) and fuzzy rules. Neuro-fuzzy systems have also a high degree of interpretability due to their fuzzy component (Kasabov, 1996; Wang & Mendel, 1992).

One can formulate EIS as a synergy between systems with expandable (evolvable) structures for information representation (usually these are fuzzy or neuro-fuzzy structures, but not necessarily) and online methods for machine learning (Lima et al., 2006; Yager, 2006). The area of EIS is concerned with nonstationary processes, computationally efficient algorithms for real-time applications, and a dynamically evolving family of locally valid subsystems that can represent different situations or operating conditions. The overall global functioning of an EIS is a result of much simpler local subsystems implementing the philosophical observation by the British mathematician Alan Turing, who said, "The Global order emerges from the chaos of local interactions." EISs aim at lifelong learning and adaptation and self-organization (including *system structure evolution*) in order to adapt to unknown and unpredictable environments. EISs also address the problems of detecting temporal *shifts* and *drifts* in the data patterns, adapting the learning scheme itself in addition to the evolution of the structure and parameters of the system.

This new topic of EIS has marked a significant growth during the past couple of years, which has led to a range of IEEE-supported events: symposia and workshops (IEEE IS2002, EFS06, GEFS08, NCEI2008/ICONIP2008, ESDIS2009, EIS2010); tutorials; special sessions at leading IEEE events (FUZZ-IEEE/IJCNN 2004, NAFIPS 2005, WCCI2006, FUZZ-IEEE2007, IJCNN2007, IEEE-SMC2007, SSCI 2007, FUZZ-IEEE2007, IPMU2008, IEEE-IS2008, EUSFLAT/IFSA 2009, IPMU2010, WCCI-2010), and so forth. Numerous applications of EIS to problems of modeling, control, prediction, classification, and data processing in a dynamically changing and evolving environment were also developed, including some successful industrial applications. However, the demand for technical implementations of EIS is still growing and is not saturated in a range of application domains, such as: autonomous vehicles and systems (Zhou & Angelov, 2007); intelligent sensors and agents (Kordon, 2006); finance, economics, and social sciences; image processing in CD production (Lughofer et al., 2007); transportation systems; advanced manufacturing and process industries such as chemical, petrochemical, and so on. (Macias-Hernandez et al., 2007); and biomedicine, bioinformatics, and nanotechnology (Kasabov, 2007).

The aim of this edited volume is to address this problem by providing a focused compendium of the latest state-of-the-art in this emerging research topic with a strong emphasis on the balance between novel theoretical results and solutions and practical industrial and real-life applications. The book is intended to be the one-stop reference guide for both theoretical and practical issues for computer scientists, engineers, researchers, applied mathematicians, machine learning and data mining experts, graduate students, and professionals.

This book includes a collection of chapters that relate to the methodology of designing of fuzzy and neuro-fuzzy evolving systems (Part I) and the application aspects of the evolving concept (Part II). The chapters are written by leading world experts who graciously supported this effort of bringing to a wider audience the progress, trends, and some of the major achievements in the emerging research field of EIS.

The first chapter is written by Ronald Yager of the Machine Intelligence Institute of Iona College, New Rochelle, New York, USA. It introduces two fundamental approaches for developing EIS. The first one, called the *Hierarchical Prioritized Structure(HPS)*, is based on the concept of aggregation and prioritization of information at different levels of hierarchy, providing a framework for a hierarchical representation of knowledge in terms of fuzzy rules. The second approach, the *Participatory Learning Paradigm(PLP)*, follows from the general learning model that dynamically reinforces the role of the knowledge that has been already acquired in the learning process. The participatory concept allows for expanding the traditional interpretation of the learning process to a new level, accounting for the validity of the new information and its compatibility with the existing belief structure. Both methodologies provide a foundation for real-time summarization of the information and evolution of the knowledge extracted in the learning process.

Chapter 2, *Evolving Takagi-Sugeno Fuzzy Systems from Streaming Data (eTS + )*, is authored by Plamen Angelov of Lancaster University, Lancaster, UK. The author emphasizes the importance and increased interest in online modeling of streaming data sets and reveals the basic methodology for creating evolving fuzzy models that addresses the need for strong theoretical fundamentals for evolving systems in general.

The chapter provides a systematic description of the eTS (evolving Takagi-Sugeno) method that includes the concept of density-based estimation of the fuzzy model structure and fuzzy weight recursive least squares (wRLS) parameter estimation of the model parameters. This chapter also discusses the challenging problem of real-time structure simplification through a continuous evaluation of the importance of the clusters that are associated with dynamically created fuzzy rules. The author also proposes some interesting extensions of the eTS method related to online selection and scaling of the input variables, applications to nonlinear regression and time series approximation and prediction, and soft sensing.

The third chapter, *Fuzzy Models of Evolvable Granularity*, is written by Witold Pedrycz of University of Alberta, Edmonton, Canada. It deals with the general strategy of using the fuzzy dynamic clustering as a foundation for evolvable information granulation. This evolvable granular representation summarizes similar data in the incoming streams by snapshots that are captured by fuzzy clustering. Proposed methodology utilizes the adjustable Fuzzy C-Means clustering algorithm to capture the data dynamics by adjusting the data snapshots and to retain the continuity between the consecutively discovered structures. It monitors the evolution of the clusters from one data snapshot to another and tracks successive splits or mergers of the corresponding information granules. The level of information granularity is continuously adapted through a reconstruction criterion that monitors and quantifies an error resulting from pattern granulation and de-granulation.

The fourth chapter, *Evolving Fuzzy Modeling Using Participatory Learning*, is authored by Elton Lima, Michael Hell, Rosangela Ballini, and Fernando Gomide of the University of Campinas (Unicamp), Campinas, Brazil. This chapter elaborates on the role of the Participatory Learning Paradigm (PLP) as a tool for real-time learning of the structure of the Takagi-Sugeno model. The authors follow the framework of the eTS model learning, providing a novel interpretation of the problem of online learning of the model structure. PLP is introduced as an alternative to the process of density estimation that reveals the input–output space clusters and corresponding rules. Participatory learning rate is driven by the similarity between the current data and the existing cluster centers. Similarity between the cluster centers guides the decision for creation of new clusters and effectively controls the granularity of the model and automatically eliminates redundant clusters.

The fifth chapter, *Toward Robust Evolving Fuzzy Systems*, is written by Edwin Lughofer of the Johannes Kepler University, Linz, Austria. This chapter presents a methodology for developing evolving systems that includes vector quantization and adaptive resonance theory (ART)-based learning of the model structure and recursive wRLS type estimation of rule consequent parameters. Besides the systematic description of the main algorithms (FLEXFIS—applicable for real-time modeling, and FLEXFIS-Class—applicable for building up evolving fuzzy classifiers for online classification), the author focuses on issues related to the robustness and stability during the learning process and hence achieving higher performance of the evolved models. Discussion of the problems of robustness, stability, performance, and convergence of the evolving techniques goes well beyond the particular algorithms and can generically apply to most of the known methods for developing evolving systems. The main theoretical contributions of this chapter are demonstrated and analyzed in three real-world examples.

The sixth chapter, *Building Interpretable Systems in Real Time*, is authored by José Ramos, Carlos Pereira, and António Dourado of University of Coimbra, Coimbra, Portugal. This chapter discusses two alternative methods for developing fuzzy models. The first one is a version of the eTS method; the second approach deals with a kernel-based incremental learning technique. The focus of the authors is on the interpretability of the obtained models—a challenging problem that is related to online implementation of the mechanisms for merging membership functions, rule-based simplification, reduction of rule redundancy, and overall complexity of the models. They also analyze the sensitivity of the model interpretability, complexity, and precision of some of the most important design parameters that are common in almost all methods for learning evolving models—the radii of the clusters and the similarity threshold between fuzzy sets.

Chapter 6 concludes the set of methods for developing evolving fuzzy systems. The next four chapters are dedicated to the problem of designing neuro-fuzzy evolving systems.

Chapter 7, *Online Feature Extraction for Evolving Intelligent Systems*, is authored by Seiichi Ozawa of Kobe University, Kobe, Japan, and S. Pang and Nikola Kasabov of Auckland University of Technology, Auckland, New Zealand. This chapter introduces an integrated approach to incremental (real-time) feature extraction and classification. The incremental feature extraction is done by two alternative approaches. The first one is based on a modified version of the Independent Principle Component Analysis (IPCA) method. It is accomplished through incremental eigenspace augmentation and rotation, which are applied to every new training sample. The second feature-extraction approach, called the Chunk IPCA, improves the computational efficiency of the ICPA by updating the eigenspace in chunks of grouped training samples. The incremental feature-extraction phase is blended with an incremental nearest-neighbor classifier that simultaneously implements classification and learning. In a smart learning procedure, the misclassified samples are periodically used to update the eigenspace model and the prototypes. The combination of feature extraction, classification, and learning results forms an adaptive intelligent system that can effectively handle online streams of multidimensional data sets.

Chapter 8, *Stability Analysis for an Online Evolving Neuro-Fuzzy Recurrent Network*, is authored by José de Jesús Rubio of Autónoma Metropolitana University, Azcapotzalco, Mexico. This chapter deals with an evolving neuro-fuzzy recurrent network. It is based on the recursive creation of a neuro-fuzzy network by unsupervised and supervised learning. The network uses a nearest-neighbor-type algorithm that is combined with a density-based pruning strategy to incrementally learn the model structure. The model structure learning is accompanied by an RLS-type learning method. The chapter also includes a detailed analysis of the numeric stability and the performance of the proposed evolving learning method.

The ninth chapter, *Online Identification of Self-Organizing Fuzzy Neural Networks for Modeling Time-Varying Complex Systems*, is authored by Girijesh Prasad, Gang Leng, T. Martin McGinnity, and Damien Coyle of University of Ulster. The focus of this chapter is on a hybrid fuzzy neural learning algorithm, in which a fuzzy paradigm is used to enhance certain aspects of the neural network's learning and adaptation performance. The algorithm is exemplified by a self-organizing model, called the Self-Organizing Fuzzy Neural Network (SOFNN), that possesses the ability to self-organize its structure along with associated premise (antecedent) parameters. The self-organizing neural network creates an interpretable hybrid neural network model, making effective use of the learning ability of neural networks and the interpretability of fuzzy systems. It combines a modified RLS algorithm for estimating consequent parameters with a structure-learning algorithm that adapts the network structure through a set of new ellipsoidal-basis function neurons. The result of the proposed architecture and learning is a method that is computationally efficient for online implementation.

Chapter 10, *Data Fusion via Fission for the Analysis of Brain Death*, is authored by Ling Li, Y. Saito, David Looney, T. Tanaka, J. Cao, and Danilo Mandic of Imperial College, London, UK, and addresses the problem of continuous analysis of time-series signals, such as EEG, in order to detect an abnormal state such as brain death. The chapter proposes that the signal is first decomposed into its oscillatory components (fission) and then the components of interest are combined (fusion) in order to detect the states of the brain.

The following three chapters are focused on the methodology for evolving clustering and classification.

Chapter 11, *Similarity Analysis and Knowledge Acquisition by Use of Evolving Neural Models and Fuzzy Decision*, is authored by Gancho Vachkov of Kagawa University, Kagawa, Japan. This chapter presents an original evolving model for real-time similarity analysis and granulation of data streams. Two unsupervised incremental learning algorithms are proposed to compress and summarize the raw data into information granules (neurons). This way, the original, *raw* data set is transformed into the *granulation* (compressed) model and represented with a small number of neurons. The author introduces two characteristic features—Center-of-Gravity Distance and Weighted Average Size Difference—to adequately describe individual granules. The similarity analysis is based on a fuzzy rule-based model that uses the two characteristic features to analyze the similarity of the granulated data. The resulting computationally effective algorithm can have numerous potential applications in problems that relate to fast search through a large amount of images or sensory information, for proper data sorting and classification.

Chapter 12, *An Extended Version of the Gustafson-Kessel Algorithm for Evolving Data Stream Clustering*, is written by Dimitar Filev of Ford Research & Advanced Engineering, Dearborn, Michigan, USA, and Olga Georgieva of Bulgarian Academy of Sciences, Sofia, Bulgaria. The authors make the case for a new, evolving clustering method, called the *evolving GK-Like(eGKL)* algorithm that resembles the Gustafson-Kessel (GK) clustering algorithm as a general tool for identifying clusters with a generic shape and orientation. The chapter discusses the methodology for recursive calculation of the metrics used in the GK algorithm. It also introduces an original algorithm that is characterized with adaptive, step-by-step identification of clusters that are similar to the GK clusters. The algorithm is based on a new approach to the problem of estimation of the number of clusters and their boundaries that is motivated by the identified similarities between the concept of evolving clustering and the multivariate statistical process control (SPC) techniques. The proposed algorithm addresses some of the basic problems of the evolving systems field (e.g., recursive estimation of the cluster centers, inverse covariance matrices, covariance determinants, Mahalanobis distance type of similarity relations, etc.).

Chapter 13, *Evolving Fuzzy Classification of Nonstationary Time Series*, is by Yevgeniy Bodyanskiy, Yevgeniy Gorshkov, Illya Kokshenev, and Vitaliy Kolodyazhniy of the Kharkiv National University of Radio-Electronics, Kharkiv, Ukraine. The authors present an evolving robust recursive fuzzy clustering algorithm that is based on minimization of an original objective function of a special form, suitable for time-series segmentation. Their approach is derived from the conjecture that the estimates that are obtained from a quadratic objective function are optimal when the data belong to the class of distributions with bounded variance. The proposed algorithm learns the cluster centers and the corresponding membership functions incrementally without requiring multiple iteration and/or initial estimate of the number of clusters. One of the main advantages of this novel algorithm is its robustness to outliers. The algorithm can be carried out in a batch or recursive mode and can be effectively used in multiple evolving system applications (e.g., medical diagnostics and monitoring, data mining, fault diagnostics, pattern recognition, etc.).

The second part of the book is comprised of four chapters discussing different applications of EIS.

Chapter 14, *Evolving Inferential Sensors in Chemical Process Industry*, is authored by Plamen Angelov of Lancaster University, Lancaster, UK, and Arthur Kordon of the Dow Chemical Company, Freeport, Texas, USA. The chapter defines an interesting and promising area of evolving system applications—design of inferential sensors. Inferential (soft) sensors are widely used in a number of process-monitoring and control applications as a model-based estimator of variables that are not directly measured. While most of the conventional inferential sensors are based on first-principle models, the concept of evolving systems offers the opportunity for online adaptation of the models that are embedded in the inferential sensors when measured data is made available. The authors provide a detailed discussion on the theory and the state-of-the-art practices in this area—selection of input variables, preprocessing of the measured data, addressing the complexity/accuracy dilemma, and so on. They also justify the use in the inferential sensors of the Takagi-Sugeno model as a flexible nonlinear mapping of multiple linear models. Further, they make the case for the eTS as an effective approach for developing self-organizing and adaptive models as a foundation of a new generation of highly efficient inferential sensors, called *e-Sensors*. The idea of evolving inferential sensors is demonstrated in four case studies from the chemical process industry.

Chapter 15, *Recognition of Human Grasp by Fuzzy Modeling*, is written by Rainer Palm, Bourhane Kadmiry, and Boyko Iliev, of Orebro University, Orebro, Sweden. This chapter provides another example of the potential of the evolving models for addressing real-world practical problems—the evolving approach is applied to the problem of modeling and quantification of human grasp in robotic applications. The authors analyze three alternative algorithms for human grasp modeling and recognition. Two of those algorithms are based on evolving Takagi-Sugeno models that are used to describe the finger joint angle trajectories (or fingertip trajectories) of grasp primitives, while the third one is a hybrid of fuzzy clustering and hidden Markov models (HMM) for grasp recognition. The authors experimentally prove out the advantages (recognition rate and minimal complexity) of the first algorithm, employing an evolving TS model approximating the minimum distance between the time clusters of the test grasp and a set of model grasps.

Chapter 16, *Evolutionary Architecture for Lifelong Learning and Real-Time Operation in Autonomous Robots*, is by Richard J. Duro, Francisco Bellas, and José Antonio Becerra of University of La Coruña, Spain. This chapter focuses on the robotic applications of the evolving system concept. It discusses the fundamentals of the evolvable architecture of a cognitive robot that exhibits autonomous adaptation capability. The robot continuously adapts its models and corresponding controls (behaviors) to the changing environment. The kernel of the robot intelligence is a general cognitive mechanism that is associated with its *multilevel Darwinist brain*, including short- and long-term memories and a unique Promoter-Based Genetic Algorithm (PBGA) combining neural and genetic learning algorithms.

The final chapter, *Applications of Evolving Intelligent Systems to Oil and Gas Industry*, is written by José Juan Macías Hernandez of CEPSA Tenerife Oil Refinery and University of La Laguna, Tenerife, Spain, and Plamen Angelov of Lancaster University, Lancaster, UK. This chapter reviews the opportunities for application of evolving systems to different process-control problems in oil refineries and in process industry in general. Special attention is given to the evolving model-based industrial (indirect) inferential sensors. The authors introduce an interesting e-Sensor version of the eTS algorithm as an adaptive inferential sensor that is employed for product quality monitoring. They also demonstrate how the Takagi-Sugeno modeling technique can be expanded to the problem of automatic selection of a subset of important input variables that are used to predict estimated process characteristics. Practical aspects of the design and implementation of evolving inferential sensors, including initialization, calibration, prediction, and performance under different operating modes, are also presented.

To view supplemental material for this book, including additional software for downloading, please visit http://www.lancaster.ac.uk/staff/angelov/Downloads.htm.

In closing, the editors would like to express their gratitude to all contributors and reviewers for making this volume a reality. We hope that this book will be a useful tool and inspiration for better understanding of the philosophy, theoretical foundations, and potential of practical applications of the EIS.

The Editors,
*Lancaster, UK*
*Dearborn, Michigan, USA*
*Auckland, New Zealand*
*February 2010*

## REFERENCES

Angelov, P. (2002). *Evolving Rule-Based Models: A Tool for Design of Flexible Adaptive Systems.* Heidelberg, New York, Springer-Verlag, ISBN 3-7908-1457-1.

Angelov, P., D. Filev (2004). "An Approach to On-line Identification of Takagi-Sugeno Fuzzy Models." *IEEE Trans. on System, Man, and Cybernetics: Part B—Cybernetics*, Vol. 34, No. 1, pp. 484–498, ISSN 1094-6977.

Angelov, P., N. Kasabov (2006). "Evolving Intelligent Systems, eIS," *IEEE SMC eNewsLetter*, June 2006, pp. 1–13.

Angelov, P., X. Zhou (2006). "Evolving Fuzzy Systems from Data Streams in Real-Time." *Proc. 2006 International Symposium on Evolving Fuzzy Syst.*, Ambleside, UK, September 7–9, 2006, IEEE Press, pp. 29–35, ISBN 0-7803-9719-3.

Angelov, P., X. Zhou (2008). "On-Line Learning Fuzzy Rule-Based System Structure from Data Streams." *Proc. World Congress on Computational Intelligence, WCCI-2008*, Hong Kong, June 1–6, 2008, IEEE Press, pp. 915–922, ISBN 978-1-4244-1821-3/08.

Astrom, K. J., B. Wittenmark (1989). *Adaptive Control.* Reading, MA: Addison-Wesley.

Domingos, P., G. Hulten (2001). "Catching Up with the Data: Research Issues in Mining Data Streams." *Workshop on Research Issues in Data Mining and Knowledge Discovery*, Santa Barbara, CA.

EC (2007). NMP-2008-3.2-2: Self-Learning Production Systems—Work Programme on Nanosciences, Nanotechnologies, Materials, and New Production Technologies. Available online at ftp://ard.huji.ac.il/pub/251/NMP_Fiche_small__2008_02.pdf.

Fritzke, B. (1994). "Growing Cell structures: A Self-Organizing Network for Unsupervised and Supervised Learning," *Neural Networks*, Vol. 7, No. 9, pp. 1441–1460.

Hastie, T., R. Tibshirani, J. Friedman (2001). *The Elements of Statistical Learning: Data Mining, Inference and Prediction*. Heidelberg, Germany: Springer-Verlag.

Kasabov, N. (1996). *Foundations of Neural Networks, Fuzzy Systems and Knowledge Engineering*. MIT Press.

Kasabov, N. (2002). *Evolving Connectionist Systems: Methods and Applications in Bioinformatics, Brain Study and Intelligent Machines*. Springer-Verlag.

Kasabov, N. (2007). *Evolving Connectionist Systems: The Knowledge Engineering Approach*. Springer-Verlag.

Kasabov, N., Q. Song (2002). "DENFIS: Dynamic Evolving Neural-Fuzzy Inference System and Its Application for Time-Series Prediction." *IEEE Trans. on Fuzzy Systems*, Vol. 10, No. 2, pp. 144–154.

Kordon, A. (2006). "Inferential Sensors as Potential Application Area of Intelligent Evolving Systems." *International Symposium on Evolving Fuzzy Systems*, EFS'06.

Lima, E., F. Gomide, R. Ballini (2006). "Participatory Evolving Fuzzy Modeling." *Proc. 2006 International Symposium on Evolving Fuzzy Systems EFS'06*, IEEE Press, pp. 36–41, ISBN 0-7803-9718-5.

Ljung, L. (1988). *System Identification: Theory for the User*. Englewood Cliffs, NJ: Prentice-Hall.

Lughofer, E., P. Angelov, X. Zhou (2007). "Evolving Single- and Multi-Model Fuzzy Classifiers with FLEXFIS-Class." *Proc. FUZZ-IEEE 2007*, London, UK, pp. 363–368.

Macias-Hernandez, J. J., P. Angelov, X. Zhou (2007). "Soft Sensor for Predicting Crude Oil Distillation Side Streams Using Takagi Sugeno Evolving Fuzzy Models." *Proc. 2007 IEEE Intern. Conf. on Systems, Man, and Cybernetics*, Montreal, Canada, pp. 3305–3310, ISBN 1-4244-0991-8/07.

Pedrycz, W. (2005). *Knowledge-Based Clustering: From Data to Information Granules*. Chichester, UK: Wiley-Interscience, pp. 316.

Wang, L., J. Mendel (1992). "Fuzzy Basis Functions, Universal Approximation and Orthogonal Least-Squares Learning." *IEEE Trans. on Neural Networks*, Vol. 3, No. 5, pp. 807–814.

Yager, R. (2006). "Learning Methods for Intelligent Evolving Systems." *Proc. 2006 International Symposium on Evolving Fuzzy Systems EFS'06*, IEEE Press, pp. 3–7, ISBN 0-7803-9718-5.

Zadeh, L. A. (1975). "The Concept of a Linguistic Variable and Its Application to Approximate Reasoning, Parts I, II and III," *Information Sciences*, Vol. 8, pp. 199–249, 301–357; Vol. 9, pp. 43–80.

Zhou, X., P. Angelov (2007). "An Approach to Autonomous Self-Localization of a Mobile Robot in Completely Unknown Environment Using Evolving Fuzzy Rule-Based Classifier." *First 2007 IEEE Intern. Conf. on Computational Intelligence Applications for Defense and Security*, Honolulu, Hawaii, USA, April 1-5, 2007, pp. 131–138.

# 1

# LEARNING METHODS FOR EVOLVING INTELLIGENT SYSTEMS

Ronald R. Yager

**Abstract:** In this work we describe two instruments for introducing evolutionary behavior into intelligent systems. The first is the hierarchical prioritized structure (HPS) and the second is the participatory learning paradigm (PLP).

## 1.1 INTRODUCTION

The capacity to evolve and adapt to a changing environment is fundamental to human and other living systems. Our understanding of the importance of this goes back to at least Darwin [1]. As we begin building computational agents that try to emulate human capacities we must also begin considering the issue of systems that evolve autonomously. Our focus here is on knowledge-based/intelligent systems. In these types of systems, implementing evolution requires an ability to balance learning and changing while still respecting the past accumulated knowledge. In this work we describe two instruments for introducing evolutionary behavior into our intelligent systems. The first is the *hierarchical prioritized structure (HPS)* and the second is the *participatory learning paradigm (PLP)*. The HPS provides a hierarchical framework for organizing knowledge. Its hierarchical nature allows for an implicit prioritization of knowledge so that evolution can be implemented by locating new knowledge in a higher place in the

*Evolving Intelligent Systems: Methodology and Applications,* Edited by Plamen Angelov, Dimitar P. Filev, and Nikola Kasabov

hierarchy. Two important aspects of the structure are considered in this work. The first is the process of aggregating information provided at the different levels of the hierarchy. This task is accomplished by the hierarchical updation operator. The other aspect is the process of evolving the model as information indicating a change in the environment is occurring.

The participatory learning paradigm provides a general learning paradigm that emphasizes the role of what we already know in the learning process. Here, an attribute about which we are learning is not viewed simply as a target being blindly pushed and shoved by new observations but one that participates in determining the validity of the new information.

Underlying both these instruments is a type of nonlinear aggregation operation that is adjudicating between knowledge held at different levels. Central to this type of aggregation is a process in which the privileged knowledge is deciding on the allowable influence of the less-favored knowledge.

## 1.2 OVERVIEW OF THE HIERARCHICAL PRIORITIZED MODEL

In [2–5] we described an extension of fuzzy modeling technology called the hierarchical prioritized structure (HPS), which is based on a hierarchical representation of the rules. As we shall subsequently see, this provides a rich framework for the construction of evolving systems. The HPS provides a framework using a hierarchical representation of knowledge in terms of fuzzy rules is equipped with machinery for generating a system output given an input. In order to use this hierarchical framework to make inferences, we needed to provide a new aggregation operator, called the *hierarchical updation (HEU)* operator, to allow the passing of information between different levels of the hierarchy. An important feature of the inference machinery of the HPS is related to the implicit prioritization of the rules; the higher the rule is in the HPS, the higher its priority. The effect of this is that we look for solutions in an ordered way, starting at the top. Once an appropriate solution is found, we have no need to look at the lower levels. This type of structure very naturally allows for the inclusion of default rules, which can reside at the lowest levels of the structure. It also has an inherent mechanism for evolving by adding levels above the information we want to discard.

An important issue related to the use of the HPS structure is the learning of the model itself. This involves determination of the content of the rules as well the determination of the level at which a rule shall appear. As in all knowledge-based systems, learning can occur in many different ways. One extreme is that of being told the knowledge by some (usually human) expert. At the other extreme is the situation in which we are provided only with input–output observations and we must use these to generate the rules. Many cases lie between these extremes.

Here we shall discuss one type of learning mechanism associated with the HPS structure that lies between these two extremes, called the *DELTA* method. In this we initialize the HPS with expert-provided default rules and then use input–output observations to modify and adapt this initialization. Taking advantage of the HPS we are able to introduce exceptions to more general rules by giving them a higher priority, introducing them at a higher level in the hierarchy. These exceptions can be themselves rules or specific points. This can be seen as a type of forgetting mechanism that can allow the implementation of dynamic adaptive learning techniques that continuously evolve the model.

## 1.3 THE HPS MODEL

In the following, we describe the basic structure and the associated reasoning mechanism of the fuzzy systems modeling framework called the hierarchical prioritized structure (HPS).

Assume we have a system we are modeling with inputs $V$ and $W$ and output $U$. At each level of the HPS, we have a collection of fuzzy *if-then* rules. Thus for level $j$, we have a collection of $n_j$ rules:

$$\text{If } V \text{ is } A_{ji} \text{ and } W \text{ is } B_{ji}, \text{ then } U \text{ is } D_{ji} \quad i = 1, \ldots, n_j$$

We shall denote the collection of rules at the $j$th level as $R_j$. Given values for the input variables, $V = x^*$ and $W = y^*$, and applying the standard fuzzy inference to the rules at level $j$, we can obtain a fuzzy subset $F_j$ over the universe of $U$, where

$$F_j(z) = \frac{1}{T}\sum_{i=1}^{n_j}\lambda_{ji}D_{ji}(z) \text{ with } \lambda_{ji} = A_{ji}(x^*)\wedge B_{ji}(y^*) \text{ and } T = \sum_{i=1}^{n_j}\lambda_{ji}. \text{ Alternatively, we}$$

can also calculate $F_j(z) = \text{Max}_i[\lambda_{ji}\wedge D_{ji}(z)]$. We denote the application of the basic fuzzy inference process with a given input, $V = x^*$ and $W = y^*$, to this sub-rule base as $F_j = R_j \bullet$ Input.

In the HPS model, the output of level $j$ is a combination of $F_j$ and output of the preceding level. We denote the output of the $j$th level of the HPS as $G_j$. $G_j$ is obtained by combining the output the previous level, $G_{j-1}$, with $F_j$ using the hierarchical updation (HEU) aggregation operator subsequently to be defined. The output of the last level, $G_n$, is the overall model output $E$. We initialize the process by assigning $G_0 = \varnothing$.

The key to inference mechanism in the HPS is the HEU aggregation operator $G_j = \gamma(G_{j-1}, F_j)$, where

$$G_j(z) = G_{j-1}(z) + (1-\alpha_{j-1})F_j(z)$$

Here, $\alpha_{j-1} = \text{Max}_z[G_{j-1}(z)]$, the largest membership grade in $G_{j-1}$. See Figure 1.1.

Let us look at the functioning of this operator. First we see that it is not pointwise in that the value of $G_j(z)$ depends, through the function $\alpha_{j-1}$, on the membership grade of elements other than $z$. We also note that if $\alpha_{j-1} = 1$, no change occurs. More generally, the larger $\alpha_{j-1}$ the less the effect of the current level. Thus, we see that $\alpha_{j-1}$ acts as a kind of choking function. In particular, if for some level $j$ we obtain a situation in which $G_j$ is normal, and has an element with membership grade one, the process of aggregation stops.

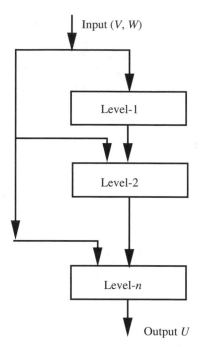

**Figure 1.1.** Hierarchical prioritized structure.

It is also clear that $G_{j-1}$ and $F_j$ are not treated symmetrically. We see that, as we get closer to having some elements in $G_{j-1}$ with membership grade one, the process of adding information slows. The form of the HEU essentially implements a prioritization of the rules. The rules at the highest level of the hierarchy are explored first; if they find a good solution, we look no further at the rules.

Figure 1.2 provides an alternative view of the HPS structure.

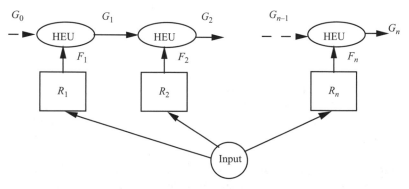

**Figure 1.2.** Alternative view of HPS.

## 1.4 AN EXAMPLE OF HPS MODELING

We shall illustrate the application of this structure with the following example

**Example :** Consider a function $W = F(U, V)$ defined on $U = [0,10]$ and $V = [0,10]$. Refer to Figure 1.3 for the following discussion. We shall assume that in the white areas the value of the function is *small* and in the black areas the value of the function is *large*. The figure could, for example, be representative of a geospatial mapping in which $W$ is the altitude and the black areas correspond to a mountain range.

We can describe this functional relationship by the following three-level HPS structure:

**Level-1:** If U is *close to five*, then W is *small*.      (Rule 1)

**Level-2:** If $((U-5)2 + (V-5)^2)^{0.5}$ is *about two*, then W is *large*.      (Rule 2)

**Level-3:** If $U$ and $V$ are *anything*, then W is *small*.      (Rule 3)

For our purposes, we define the underlined fuzzy subsets as follows:

$$Small = \left\{ \frac{0.3}{5}, \frac{0.6}{6}, \frac{1}{7}, \frac{0.6}{8}, \frac{0.3}{9} \right\} \text{ and } Large = \left\{ \frac{0.3}{21}, \frac{0.6}{22}, \frac{1}{23}, \frac{0.6}{24}, \frac{0.3}{25} \right\}$$

$$close\ to\ five(U) = e^{\dfrac{-(U-5)^2}{0.25}} \text{ and } about\ five(r) = e^{-(r-2)^2}$$

Let us look at three special cases.

1. $U = 5$ and $V = 6$. Here rule one fires to degree 1. Hence the output of the first level is $G_1 = \left\{ \frac{0.3}{5}, \frac{0.6}{6}, \frac{1}{7}, \frac{0.6}{8}, \frac{0.3}{9} \right\}$. Since this has maximal membership grade equal to one, the output of the system is $G_1$.

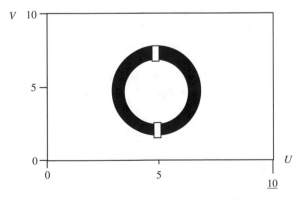

Figure 1.3. Structure of F(U, V).

2. $U = 6$ and $V = 6$. Here the firing level of Rule 1 is 0.02 and the output of the first level is $G_1 = \{\frac{0.2}{5}, \frac{0.2}{6}, \frac{0.2}{7}, \frac{0.2}{8}, \frac{0.2}{9}\}$ and has maximal firing level 0.2. Applying the input to Rule 2, we get a firing level of 1. Thus $F_2 = \{\frac{0.3}{21}, \frac{0.6}{22}, \frac{1}{23}, \frac{0.6}{24}, \frac{0.3}{25}\}$. Thus $G_2(z) = \{\frac{0.2}{5}, \frac{0.2}{6}, \frac{0.2}{7}, \frac{0.2}{8}, \frac{0.2}{9}, \frac{0.24}{21}, \frac{0.46}{22}, \frac{0.8}{23}, \frac{0.46}{24}, \frac{0.24}{25}\}$ and therefore $\alpha_2 = 0.8$. Applying the input to Rule 3 three we get firing level 1. Thus $F_2 = \{\frac{0.3}{21}, \frac{0.6}{22}, \frac{1}{23}, \frac{0.6}{24}, \frac{0.3}{25}\}$. Since $G_3(z) = G_2(z) + (1 - 0.8) \; F_3(z)$ we get $G_3 = \{\frac{0.26}{5}, \frac{0.312}{6}, \frac{0.4}{7}, \frac{0.312}{8}, \frac{0.26}{9}, \frac{0.24}{21}, \frac{0.46}{22}, \frac{0.8}{23}, \frac{0.46}{24}, \frac{0.24}{25}\}$.
Defuzzifying this value we get $W = 16.3$.

3. $U = 9$ and $V = 8$. In this case, the firing level of Rule 1 is 0; thus $G_1 = \varnothing$. Similarly, the firing level of Rule 2 is also 0, and hence $G_1 = \varnothing$. The firing level of Rule 3 is one, and hence the overall output is *small*.

## 1.5 HIERARCHICAL UPDATION OPERATOR

Let us look at some of the properties of this hierarchical updation operator $\gamma$. If $A$ and $B$ are two fuzzy sets of $Z$, then we have $\gamma(A, B) = D$, where $D(z) = A(z) + (1 - \alpha) B(z)$ with $\alpha = \text{Max}_{z \in Z}(A(z))$. This operator is not pointwise as $\alpha$ depends on $A(z)$ for all $z \in Z$. This operator is a kind of disjunctive operator; we see that $\gamma(A, \varnothing) = A$ and $\gamma(\varnothing, B) = B$. This operator is not commutative $\gamma(A, B) \neq \gamma(B, A)$. An important illustration of this is that while $\gamma(Z, B) = B$, we have $\gamma(A, Z) = D$, where $D(z) = A(z) + (1 - \alpha)$. The operator is also nonmonotonic. Consider $D = \gamma(A, B)$ and $D' = \gamma(A', B)$, where $A \subseteq A'$. Since $A(z) \leq A'(z)$ for all $z$, then $\alpha \leq \alpha'$. We have $D'(z) = A'(z) + (1 - \alpha') B(z)$ and $D(z) = A(z) + (1 - \alpha) B(z)$. Since $A \subseteq A'$, monotonicity requires that $D'(z) \geq D(z)$ for all $z$. To investigate the monotonicity of $\gamma$ we look at $D'(z) - D(z) = A'(z) - A(z) + B(z)(\alpha - \alpha')$.

Thus, while $A'(z) - A(z) = 0$, we have $(\alpha - \alpha') \leq 0$, and therefore there is no guarantee that $D'(z) \geq D(z)$.

We can suggest a general class of operators that can serve as hierarchical aggregation operators. Let $T$ be any $t$-norm and $S$ be any $t$-conorm [6]. A general class of hierarchical updation operators can be defined as $D = \text{HEU}(A, B)$, where $D(z) = S(A(z), T(1 - \alpha, B(z))$ with $\alpha \geq \text{Max}_z(A(z))$.

First, let us show that our original operator is a member of this class. Assume $S$ is the bounded sum, $S(a, b) = \text{Min}[1, a + b]$ and $T$ is the product, $S(a, b) = ab$. In this case, $D(z) = \text{Min}[1, A(z) + \bar{\alpha}B(z)]$. Consider the term $A(z) + \bar{\alpha}B(z)$. Since $\alpha = \text{Max}_z[A(z)]$, then $\alpha = A(z)$ and therefore $A(z) + \bar{\alpha}B(z) \leq \alpha + (1 - \alpha) B(z) \leq 1$. Thus $D(z) = A(z) + (1 - \alpha) B(z)$, which was our original suggestion.

We can now obtain other forms for this HEU operator by selecting different $S$ and $T$. If $S = \text{Max}(\vee)$ and $T = \text{Min}(\wedge)$, we get

$$D(z) = A(z) \vee (\bar{\alpha} \wedge B(z))$$

If $S$ is the algebraic sum, $S(a, b) = a + b - ab$ and $T$ is the product, then

$$D(z) = A(z) + \bar{\alpha}B(z) - \bar{\alpha}A(z)B(z) = A(z) + \bar{\alpha}\bar{A}(z)B(z)$$

If we use $S$ as the bounded sum and $T$ as the Min, we get

$$D(z) = \text{Min}[1, A(z) + \bar{\alpha} \wedge B(z)]$$

Since $\alpha \geq A(z)$, then $A(z) + \bar{\alpha} \wedge B(z) \leq \alpha + (1 - \alpha) \wedge B(z) \leq \alpha + (1 - \alpha) \leq 1$; hence we get

$$D(z) = A(z) + \bar{\alpha} \wedge B(z)$$

More generally, if $S$ is the bounded sum and $T$ is any $t$-norm, then

$$D(z) = \text{Min}[1, A(z) + T(\bar{\alpha} \wedge B(z))]$$

Since $T(\bar{\alpha} \wedge B(z)) \leq \bar{\alpha} = 1 - A(z)$, then

$$D(z) = A(z) + T(\bar{\alpha}, B(z))$$

## 1.6 THE DELTA METHOD OF HPS LEARNING

In the preceding, we have described the inference mechanism associated with the hierarchical prioritized structure. We have said nothing about how we obtained the rules in the model. The issue of the construction of the HPS model is an important one. The format of the HPS model allows many different methods for obtaining the model.

In this section we shall outline a dynamic learning approach for the construction of an HPS that allows the system to continuously learn and evolve. We call this the *default-exception-learning-that's-adaptive (DELTA)* method for HPS. In this approach we initialize the HPS by providing a default representation of the relationship we are trying to model. With this default relationship we allow the system builder to provide an initial model of the system that will be augmented as we get more data about the performance of the actual system. This default model can be as simple or as complex as the designer's knowledge of the system can support. In this approach the augmentation of the model will be one in which we add specific observations and rules to the HPS. The addition of knowledge to the structure will be driven by observations that are exceptions to what we already believe the situation to be. The exceptions will be captured and stored at the top level of the hierarchy. Groups of exceptions shall be aggregated to form new rules, which will stored at the next level of the hierarchy.

We shall use a three-level HPS model as shown in Figure 1.4. For ease of explanation we shall assume a model having a single input. The extension to multiple inputs is straightforward.

The construction of the structure is initialized with the first and second levels being empty. The third level is initialized with our default information about the structure of the relationship between the input and output variables $V$ and $U$. In particular, the third level

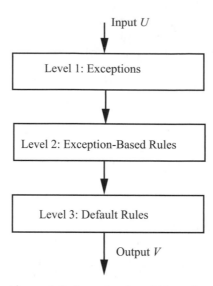

Input $U$

Level 1: Exceptions

Level 2: Exception-Based Rules

Level 3: Default Rules

Output $V$

**Figure 1.4.** Exception-based hierarchy.

contains default rules of the form

$$\text{If } V \text{ is } A \text{ then } U \text{ is } f(V)$$

In the above, $f(V)$ is some prescribed functional relationship and $A$ is a fuzzy subset indicating the range of that default rule. The knowledge in the default can be any manifestation of the prior expectation of the system modeler. It could be a simple rule that says $U = b$ for all values of $V$, a linear relationship that says $U = k_1 + k_2 V$ for all values of $V$, or a collection of more complex rules based on some partitioning of the input space.

The HPS model will evolve based on observations presented to it, especially observations that are exceptions to what we already believe. In particular, the information in levels 1 and 2 will be obtained from the observations presented to the model. As we shall see, level 1 will contain facts about individual observations that are exceptions to what we already believe. Level 2 shall contain rules that aggregate these exceptions. The aggregation process used here is very much in the spirit of the *mountain clustering method* [7–10] introduced by Yager and Filev.

In Figure 1.5, we provide a flow diagram of the basic learning mechanism used in this approach. In the following, we describe the basic mechanism for the construction of this type of HPS. An observation $(x, y)$ is presented to the HPS model. We calculate the output for the input $x$, and denote this $y^*$. We then compare this calculated output with the desired output. If $y$ and $y^*$ are close to each other, we can disregard this data and assume it doesn't provide any learning. If $y$ and $y^*$ are not close, we use this data to modify the HPS. More specifically for the pair $(y, y^*)$ we calculate the value $Close(y, y^*) \in [0,1]$ indicating the degree of closeness of the observed value and the calculated value. If $Close(y, y^*) \geq \alpha$, a threshold level, we disregard the data. If $Close(y, y^*) < \alpha$, we use this data to update the model. We denote for this observation $\mathcal{P} = 1 - Close(y, y^*)$ as a measure of this

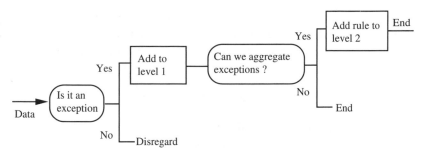

Figure 1.5. Schematic of learning process.

observation's ability to count as an exception, its strength of exception. We add to the top level of the current HPS model this observation in the form of a point rule,

$$\text{If } V \text{ is } x, \text{ then } U \text{ is } y$$

For simplicity, we shall denote this rule as the ***point***$(x, y)$. We further associate with this rule a value $M$, which we initialize as $\mathcal{P}$, its strength of exception. As we shall see, this $M$ value will be used in the same way as the mountain function is used in the mountain method to help in the aggregation of point exceptions to form exception rules. We next update the $M$ value for all the other exception rules in the top level of the HPS. For any point rule, if $V$ is $x_i$, then $U$ is $y_i$, in the top level we update $M_i$ as

$$M'_i = M_i + \mathcal{P}e^{-\text{Distance}((x,y)-(x_i,y_i))}$$

Thus we see that as a result of experiencing an observation that is considered an exception we add this observation to a current model and modify the $M$ value of all other exceptions by adding to them a value proportional to the strength of the current exception modulated by its distance to the current exception.

We next check to see whether the addition of this new exception has caused a accumulation of the exceptions that can be gathered to form an exception rule; here we use the $M$ values.

Specifically, we find the data point in the top level that now has the highest $M$ value. Let us denote this value as $\hat{M}$ and assume it occurs for the point $(\hat{x}, \hat{y})$. If $\hat{M} \geq \beta$, $\beta$ being a threshold value for exception rule formation, we create a new rule of the form

$$\text{If } V \text{ is about } \hat{x}, \text{ then } U \text{ is about } \hat{y}$$

where, as we have noted above, $\hat{x}$ and $\hat{y}$ are the coordinates of the data point with the largest $M$ value. This new rule is added to the second level of HPS. Thus we see that a collection of exceptions close to each other focused at $(\hat{x}, \hat{y})$ form an exception rule at the second level. We emphasize that it is with the aid of the $M$ function that we measure the power of a exception point in the first level to be the nucleus of an exception rule in the second level.

The final step is the cleansing and reduction of the top level by eliminating the individual exception rules that are now accounted for by the formulation of this new rule at the second level. We first modify our function $M$ at each point $(x, y)$ in the top level to form $M'$, where

$$M'(x, y) = M(x, y) - \hat{M} e^{-\text{Distance}((x,y) - (\hat{x}, \hat{y}))}$$

We next eliminate all point rules for which $M'(x, y) \leq 1 - \alpha$.

Further, we let $\hat{A}$ and $\hat{B}$ be the fuzzy subsets about $\hat{x}$ and $\hat{y}$. For each exception point in the top level, we calculate $\hat{A}(x_i)$ and $\hat{B}(y_i)$ and let $t_i = \text{Min}(A(x_i), B(y_i))$. We then eliminate all exceptions for which $t_i \geq \lambda$, a threshold for exception cleansing.

It should be noted that the above procedure has a number of parameters affecting our actions. In particular we introduced $\alpha$, $\beta$, and $\lambda$. It is with the aid of these parameters that we are able to control the uniqueness of the learning process. For example, the smaller we make $\alpha$, the more rigorous our requirements are for indicating an observation as an exception; it is related to our sensitivity to exceptions. The parameter $\beta$ determines openness to the formulation of new rules. The choice of these parameters is very much in the same spirit as choice of the learning rate used in the classical gradient learning techniques such as back propagation. Experience with the use of this exception-based machinery will of course sharpen our knowledge of the effect of parameter selection. At a deeper level the selection of these parameters should be based on how we desire the learning to perform and gives us a degree of freedom in the design of our learning mechanism, resulting, just as in the case of human learning, in highly individualized learning.

It is important to emphasize some salient features of the DELTA mechanism for constructing HPS models. We see this has an adaptive-type learning mechanism. We initialize the system with current user knowledge and then modify this initializing knowledge based on our observations. In particular, as with a human being, this has the *capability* for continuously evolving. That is, even while it is being used to provide outputs it can learn from its mistakes. Also we see that information enters the systems as observations and moves its way down the system in rules very much in the way that humans process information in the face of experience.

## 1.7 INTRODUCTION TO THE PARTICIPATORY LEARNING PARADIGM

Participatory learning is a paradigm for computational learning systems whose basic premise is that learning takes place in the framework of what is already learned and believed. The implication of this is that every aspect of the learning process is effected and guided by the learner's current belief system. Participatory learning highlights the fact that in learning we are in a situation in which the current knowledge of what we are trying to learn participates in the process of learning about itself. This idea is closely related to Quine's idea of *web of belief* [11, 12]. The now-classic work by Kuhn [13] describes related ideas in the framework of a scientific advancement. With the

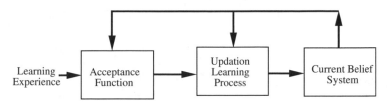

**Figure 1.6.** Partial view of a prototypical participatory learning process.

participatory learning paradigm we are trying to bring to the field of computational intelligence some important aspects of human learning. What is clear about human learning is that it manifests a noncommutative aggregation of information; the order of experiences and observations matters. Typically, the earlier information is more valued. Participatory learning has the characteristic of protecting our belief structures from wide swings due to erroneous and anomalous observations while still allowing the learning of new knowledge. Central to the participatory learning paradigm is the idea that observations conflicting with our current beliefs are generally discounted.

In Figure 1.6, we provide a partial systemic view of a prototypical participatory learning process that highlights the enhanced role played by the current belief system. An experience presented to the system is first sent to the acceptance or censor component. This component, which is under the control of the current belief state, decides whether the experience is compatible with the current state of belief; if it is deemed as being compatible, the experience is passed along to the learning components, which use this experience to update the current belief. If the experience is deemed as being too incompatible, it is rejected and not used for learning. Thus we see that the acceptance component acts as a kind of filler with respect to deciding which experiences are to be used for learning. We emphasize here that the state of the current beliefs participates in this filtering operation. We note that many learning paradigms do not include this filtering mechanism; such systems let all data pass through to modify the current belief state.

Because of the above structure, a central characteristic of the PLP (participatory learning paradigm) is that an experience has the greatest impact in causing learning or belief revision when it is compatible with our current belief system. In particular, observations that conflict too much with our current beliefs are discounted. The structure of the *participatory learning system* (*PLS*) is such that it is most receptive to learning when confronted with experiences that convey the message "What you know is correct except for this little part." The rate of learning using the PLP is optimized for situations in which we are just trying to change a small part of our current belief system. On the other hand, a PLS when confronted with an experience that says "You are all wrong; this is the truth" responds by discounting what is being told to it. In its nature, it is a conservative learning system and hence very stable. We can see that the participatory learning environment uses sympathetic experiences to modify itself. Unsympathetic observations are discounted as being erroneous. Generally, a system based on the PLP uses the whole context of an observation (experience) to judge something about the credibility of the observation with respect to the learning agent's beliefs; if it finds the whole

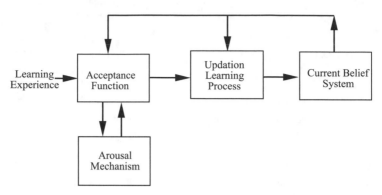

Figure 1.7. Fully developed prototypical participatory learning process.

experience credible, it can modify its belief to accommodate any portion of the experience in conflict with its belief. That is, if most of an experience or observation is compatible with the learning agent's current belief, the agent can use the portion of the observation that deviates from its current belief to learn.

While the acceptance function in PLP acts to protect an agent from responding to "bad" data, it has an associated downside. If the agent using a PLP has an incorrect belief system about the world, it allows this agent to remain in this state of blissful ignorance by blocking out correct observations that may conflict with this erroneous belief model. In Figure 1.7, we provide a more fully developed version of the participatory learning paradigm that addresses this issue by introducing an arousal mechanism in the guise of a critic.

The arousal mechanism is an autonomous component not under the control of the current belief state. Its role is to observe the performance of the acceptance function. If too many observations are rejected as being incompatible with the learning agent's belief model, this component arouses the agent to the fact that something may be wrong with its current state of belief; a loss of confidence is incurred. The effect of this loss of confidence is to weaken the filtering aspect of the acceptance component and allow incoming experiences that are not necessarily compatible with the current state of belief to be used to help update the current belief. This situation can result in rapid learning in the case of a changing environment once the agent has been aroused. Essentially, the role of the arousal mechanism is to help the agent get out of a state of belief that is deemed as false.

Fundamentally, we see two collaborating mechanisms at play in this participatory learning paradigm. The primary mechanism manifested by the acceptance function and controlled by the current state of belief is a conservative one; it assumes the current state of belief is substantially correct and requires only slight tuning. It rejects strongly incompatible experiences and doesn't allow them to modify its current belief. This mechanism manifests its effect on each individual learning experience. The secondary mechanism, controlled by the arousal mechanism, being less conservative, allows for the possibility that the agent's current state of belief may be wrong. This secondary mechanism is generally kept dormant unless activated by being aroused by an accumulation of input observations in conflict with the current belief. What must be emphasized is that the arousal mechanism contains no knowledge of the current beliefs; all knowledge resides in the belief system. It is basically a scoring system calculating how the current belief system is performing. It essentially does this by noting how often the system has encountered incompatible observations. Its effect is not manifested by an individual incompatible experience but by an accumulation of these.

## 1.8 A MODEL OF PARTICIPATORY LEARNING

As noted in the preceding, participatory learning provides a paradigm for constructing computational learning systems; as such, it can used in many different learning environments. In the following, we provide one example of a learning agent based on the PLP to illustrate some instantiation of the ideas described above [14]. While this is an important example of learning in a quantitative environment, we note that the PLP can be equally useful in the kind of symbolic learning environments found in the artificial intelligence and machine learning community.

In the illustration of PL that follows, we have a context consisting of a collection of variables, $x(i)$, $i = 1$ to $n$. Here we are interested in learning the value of this collection of variables. It is important to emphasize the multidimensionality of the environment in which the agent is doing the learning. Multidimensionality, which is present in most real-world learning experiences, is crucial to the functioning of the participatory learning paradigm since the acceptability of an experience is based on the compatibility of the collection of observed values as a whole with the agent's current belief. For simplicity we assume that the values of the $x(i) \in [0,1]$. The current state of the system's belief consists of a vector $V_{k-1}$, whose components $V_{k-1}(i)$, $i = 1$ to $n$, consist of the agent's current belief about the values of $x(i)$. It is what the agent has learned after $k - 1$ observation. The current observation consists of a vector $D_k$, whose components $d_k(i)$, $i = 1$ to $n$, are observations about the variable $x(i)$. Using a participatory learning type of mechanism, the updation of our current belief is the vector $V_k$ whose components are

$$V_k(i) = V_{k-1}(i) + \alpha \rho_k^{(1-a_k)}(d_k(i) - V_{k-1}(i)) \tag{I}$$

Using vector notation, we can express this as

$$V_k = V_{k-1} + \alpha \rho_k^{(1-a_k)}(D_k - V_{k-1}) \tag{Ib}$$

In the above, $\alpha \in [0,1]$ is a basic learning rate. The term $\rho_k$ is the compatibility of the observation $D_k$ with the current belief $V_{k-1}$. This is obtained as

$$\rho_k = \left(1 - \frac{1}{n}\sum_{i=1}^{n}|d_k(i) - V_{k-1}(i)|\right)$$

It is noted that $\rho_k \in [0,1]$. The larger $\rho_k$, the more compatible the observation is with the current belief. One important feature that needs to be pointed out is the role that the multidimensionality plays in the determination of the compatibility $\rho_k$. The system is essentially looking at the individual compatibilities as expressed by $|d_k(i)-V_{k-1}(i)|$ to determine the overall compatibility $\rho_k$. A particularly notable case is where for most of the individual variables we have good compatibility between the observation and the belief but a few are not in agreement. In this case, since there is a preponderance of agreement we shall get a high value for $\rho_k$ and the system is open to learning. Here, then, the system has received a piece of data that it feels is a reliable observation based on its current belief and is therefore open to accept it and learn from the smaller part of the observation, which is not what it believes. We shall call such observations *kindred* observations. The agent's openness to kindred observations plays an important part in allowing PL-based systems to rapidly learn in an incremental fashion [15].

The term $a_k$, also lying in the unit interval, is called the *arousal rate*. This is obtained by processing the compatibility using the formula

$$a_k = (1-\beta)a_{k-1} + \beta(1-\rho_k) \tag{II}$$

Here $\beta \in [0,1]$ is a learning rate. As pointed out in [14], $\beta$ is generally less than $\alpha$. We see that $a_k$ is essentially an estimate of the negation, one minus, the compatibility. Here we note that a low arousal rate, small values for $a_k$, is an indication of a good correspondence between the agent's belief and the external environment. In this case, the agent has confidence in the correctness of its belief system. On the other hand, a value for $a_k$ closer to one arouses the agent to the fact that there appears to be some inconsistency between what it believes and the external environment.

We see from equation (Ib) that when $a_k \approx 0$, the learning from the current observation $D_k$ is strongly modulated by $\rho_k$, the compatibility of $D_k$ with the current belief $V_{k-1}$. If the compatibility $\rho_k$ is high, we learn at a rate close to $\alpha$; if the compatibility $\rho_k$ is low, we do not learn from the current observation. On the other hand, when $a_k \approx 1$, and therefore the agent is concerned about the correctness of its belief, the term $\rho_k^{(1-a_k)} \approx 1$ is independent of the value $\rho_k$ and hence the agent is not restrained by its current belief from looking at all observations.

We note that the updation algorithm (I) is closely related to the classic *Widrow-Hoff learning rule* [16].

$$V_k(i) = V_{k-1}(i) + \alpha(d_k(i)-V_{k-1}(i)) \tag{W-H}$$

The basic difference between (I) and (W-H) is the inclusion of the term $\alpha\rho_k^{(1-a_k)}$ instead of simple $\alpha$. This results in a fundamental distinction between the classic leaning model (W-H) and the PL version. In the classic case, the learning rate $\alpha$ is generally made small in order to keep the system from radically responding to erroneous or outlier observations. In the PL version, the basic learning rate $\alpha$ can be made large because the effect of any observation incompatible with the current belief is repressed by the term $\rho_k^{(1-a_k)}$ when $a_k$ is small. This effectively means that in these PL systems, if a relatively good model of the external environment is obtained, the system can very rapidly tune itself and converge. On the other hand, the classic model has a much slower rate of convergence.

An often-used strategy when using the classic learning algorithm (I) is to let $\alpha$ be a function of the number of observations $k$. In particular, one lets $\alpha$ be large for low values of $k$ and then lets it be smaller as $k$ increases. In the PLP, it would seem that here we should treat the learning parameter $\beta$ in a similar manner.

What we emphasize here is that we determined the acceptability of an observation by using the pointwise compatibilities of the features of the observation with the agent's current belief about the values of the features. More complex formulations for the determination of acceptability can be used within the PLP. For example, in many real learning situations the internal consistency of the features associated with an observation (experience) plays a crucial role in determining the credibility of an observation. The knowledge of what constitutes internal consistency, of course, resides in the current belief systems of the learning agent. When a person tells us a story about some experience he had, a crucial role in our determining whether to believe him is played by our determination of the internal consistency of the story. At a more formal level, in situations in which we are trying to learn functional forms from data, it would appear that the internal consistency of the data in the observation could help in judging whether an observation should be used for learning.

## 1.9 INCLUDING CREDIBILITY OF THE LEARNING SOURCE

Let us consider the nature of a learning experience. Generally, a learning experience can be seen to consist of two components. The first is the *content of the experience*; we have been dealing with this in the preceding. The second is the *source of the content*. Information about both these components is contained in the agent's current belief system.

In order to decide on the degree of acceptability of a learning experience and its subsequent role in updating the current belief, a participating learning-based system must determine two quantities. The first is the *compatibility of the content* of the experience with the system's current belief system. The second is *the credibility of the source*. The information needed to perform these calculations is contained in the agent's current belief system. A point we want to emphasize is that information about the source credibility is also part of the belief structure of a PL agent in a similar way as information about the content. That is, the concept of credibility of source is essentially a measure of the congruency of the current observation's source with the agent's belief of what are good sources.

Generally, compatible content is allowed into the system and is more valued if it is from a credible source rather than a noncredible source. Incompatible content is generally blocked, and more strongly blocked from a noncredible source than from a credible source.

As we have pointed out, a learning experience consists of content as well as an indication of its source. We noted that the credibility of the source should play a role in the learning process. In the model previously presented we paid no attention to the source. We were implicitly assuming that the source had complete credibility. Let us now consider including information about the source credibility in our learning model based on the participatory learning paradigm.

Here we shall begin to look at ways of including source credibility in the learning process. We assume we have a collection of possible sources of content, $S = \{S_1,\ldots,S_n\}$. In this situation, we associate with each source a value $C(j) \in [0,1]$ indicating the agent's current belief about the credibility of content provided by source $S_j$. This information is stored in the belief system of the agent doing the learning. We can denote this as a vector $\mathbf{C}$.

Consider that now we are in a situation in which the $k$th observation is provided by source $S_j$. We now provide a form for our updation algorithm (I) that takes into account the learner's perceived credibility of this source, $C(j)$. Here

$$V_k = V_{k-1} + \alpha\, C(j)\rho_k^{(1-a_k)}\left(d_k(i) - V_{k-1}(i)\right) \tag{Ic}$$

We see that a source with zero credibility has no effect, $V_k = V_{k-1}$. On the other hand, in the case when $C(j) = 1$, we get our original model.

The process of updating the arousal, $a_K$, associated with the model is also affected by the credibility of the source. In these cases, we must modify (II) to take into account the credibility of the source. We first note that the original arousal-level updation algorithm was

$$a_k = (1-\beta)a_{k-1} + \beta(1-\rho_k)$$

or equivalently

$$a_k = a_{k-1} + \beta(\bar{\rho}_k - a_{k-1})$$

where

$$\bar{\rho}_k = 1 - \rho_k$$

Modifying this to take into account the credibility of the source, we get

$$a_k = a_{k-1} + C(j)\beta(\bar{\rho}_k - a_{k-1}) \tag{IIc}$$

Again we see that sources with zero credibility do not affect our degree of arousal; on the other hand, for those with credibility one, we get the original model.

We note that formula (IIc) can be expressed as

$$a_k = (1 - C(j)\beta)a_{k-1} + C(j)\beta\bar{\rho}_k$$

Implicit in our inclusion of the credibility of the sources has been an assumption that a source's credibility, $C(j)$, is fixed. More generally, the agent using the PLP will learn and update its belief about the credibility of the sources as a result of its learning experiences in a manner similar to the way it learns content. Before providing this generalization, we shall more usefully denote the credibility of source $S_j$ as $C_k(j)$, indicating the credibility of $S_j$ after the $k$th learning experience.

In the following, we shall provide a formula to allow the updation of the source credibility. In expressing this formulation we shall find it convenient to use the term $M_{jk}$

defined such that $M_{jk} = 1$ if $S_j$ is the source of the $k$th observation, and $M_{jk} = 0$ if $S_j$ is not the source of the $k$th experience. Using this notation we express our algorithm for modifying the source credibility as

$$C_k(j) = C_{k-1}(j) + M_{jk}\lambda \bar{a}_{k-1}(\rho_k - C_{k-1}) \qquad \text{(III)}$$

where $\bar{a}_{k-1} = 1 - a_{k-1}$ and $\lambda \in [0,1]$ is a base learning rate. We note that if $S_j$ is not the source of the $k$th learning experience, then $M_{jk} = 0$ and $C_k(j) = C_{k-1}(j)$. Thus, in this case we do not make any changes in our credibility. If $M_{jk} = 1$, then

$$C_k(j) = C_{k-1}(j) + \lambda \bar{a}_{k-1}(\rho_k - C_{k-1}(j)) = (1 - \lambda \bar{a}_{k-1})C_{k-1}(j) + \lambda \bar{a}_{k-1}\rho_k$$

Here we see $\lambda \bar{a}_{k-1}$ is an effective learning rate; it is the product of our base learning rate and the negation of the arousal level. Essentially $\bar{a}_{k-1}$ is the confidence in the current model. Thus, if $\bar{a}_{k-1} = 1$, then $C_k(j) = C_{k-1}(j) + \lambda \bar{a}_{k-1}(\rho_k - C_{k-1}(j))$. Here $\rho_K$ is being used to calculate the current degree of performance of the source.

We make some observations about the learning-updation model for the $C_k(j)$, First, we note that if there exists only one source $S = \{S_1\}$, then we will get $C_k(1) = 1 - a_k$. That is, the credibility of the agent is the negation of the arousal level. Since $1 - a_K$ is essentially the credibility of the model, we see that the credibility of a sole source and the credibility of the resulting model are equivalent.

We note that in the source credibility updation algorithm (III) we can have different base learning rates for each source. Thus we can have $\lambda(j)$ instead of $\lambda$, where $\lambda(j)$ is the base rate of learning the credibility of the $j$th agent. Further, if $\lambda(j) = 0$, then $C_k(j) = C_{k-1}(j)$ for all $k$. This implies a fixed assigned credibility for the $j$th source.

## 1.10 TYPES OF LEARNING SOURCES

In the following, we shall try to identify and classify some types of sources of content that are involved in learning experiences. The first type of source is *direct sensory experiences*. These are related to observations we make with our own sensory organs. Examples of this are seeing an auto accident, being at a baseball game and watching the Yankees win, smelling alcohol on somebody's breath, or hearing John tell Mary "I love you."

The second type we shall denote as an *authority*. Examples of learning experiences from an authority are being told something by another person, reading something in a book or obtaining it from the Internet, and hearing news on the radio or seeing it on TV. The basic idea is that the contents have been processed by some other *cognitive* agent. For these types of sources the content can be subject to "interpretation" by the processing agent.

A third source of content is *electromechanical sensor* data. This is data obtained through some electromechanical device such as the speedometer on your car, a thermometer, or the types of screens air traffic controllers use. Numerous other types of devices can be listed. Here the contents have been processed by a neutral *physical* device.

Another source of content is what we shall call *reflection*. Here we mean the conscious rational manipulation of information already in an agent's belief system that brings to the agent's awareness knowledge that is implicit in the current belief system. Deduction, induction, and reasoning are examples of this source. It can be seen as a kind of reorganization of knowledge in the agent's belief system. An interesting example occurs when the agent becomes aware of a conflict in his system. This source of content here is clearly distinct from the preceding three in that in the first three the source of the new content comes from outside the agent. In the case of reflection, the source of the content is internal to the agent. An additional aspect of what we have in mind with this reflective source of information that we want to emphasize without getting too deep into philosophical issues is the conscious *rational* aspect of this process.

Another source of content for our learning experiences is what we shall denote as *mystic*. Examples of this would be information coming from the subconscious, dreams, hallucinations, being told by God, and what some people call *gut feeling*. What we want to point out here is that for the most part this can be considered as *internally sourced* information; however, for some of these, such as being told by God, it is not clear whether it is from external or internal sources. Further, for some people, this type of content can be considered as "empty." However, for others, this is a valid type of learning experience. This category of learning is becoming an increasingly important one in our time since one objective of many security systems is to try to understand, predict, and manipulate the actions of terrorists, many of whom are religious fundamentalists who construct their belief system using this type of source.

We feel that various types of agents can be modeled by formalizing the credibility that they attach to these different categories of sources of learning experiences.

## 1.11 CONCLUSION

In this work we described two instruments for introducing evolutionary behavior into intelligent systems. The first was the hierarchical prioritized structure (HPS) and the second was the participatory learning paradigm (PLP). We saw that underlying both these instruments is a type of nonlinear aggregation operation that is adjudicating between knowledge held at different levels. Central to this type of aggregation is a process in which the privileged knowledge is deciding on the allowable influence of the less-favored knowledge.

## 1.12 REFERENCES

1. Darwin, C., *The Origin of the Species*, London, 1859.
2. Yager, R. R., "On a Hierarchical Structure for Fuzzy Modeling and Control." *IEEE Trans. on Systems, Man and Cybernetics* 23, 1189–1197, 1993.
3. Yager, R. R., "On the Construction of Hierarchical Fuzzy Systems Models." *IEEE Trans. on Systems, Man and Cybernetics Part C: Applications and Reviews* 28, 55–66, 1998.

4. Rozich, R., T. Ioerger, R. R., Yager, "FURL—A Theory Revision Approach to Learning Fuzzy Rules." *IEEE World Congress on Computational Intelligence*, Honolulu, Hawaii: *Proceedings of Conference on Fuzzy Systems*, 791–796, 2002.

5. Yager, R. R., "Organizing Information Using a Hierarchical Fuzzy Model." In *Systematic Organisation of Information in Fuzzy Systems* ( P., Melo-Pinto, H., Teodrescu, T., Fukuda, eds.), NATO Science Series. IOS Press: Amsterdam, 2003, pp. 53–69.

6. Klement, E. P., R. Mesiar, E., Pap, *Triangular Norms*. Dordrecht, Kluwer Academic Publishers, 2000.

7. Yager, R. R., D. P., Filev, "Approximate Clustering via the Mountain Method." *IEEE Trans. on Systems, Man and Cybernetics* 24, 1279–1284, 1994.

8. Yager, R. R., D. P., Filev, "Generation of Fuzzy Rules by Mountain Clustering," *Journal of Intelligent and Fuzzy Systems* 2, 1994, pp. 209–219.

9. Rickard, J. T., R. R. Yager, W., Miller, "Mountain Clustering on Non-uniform Grids Using p-Trees," *Fuzzy Optimization and Decision Making* 4, 2005, pp. 87–102.

10. Yager, R. R., D. P., Filev, "Summarizing Data Using a Similarity-Based Mountain Method," *Information Sciences* 178, 2008, pp. 816–826.

11. Quine, M.V.O., "Two Dogmas of Empiricism," *Philosophical Review* 60, 1951, pp. 20–43.

12. Quine, M. V. O., *From a Logical Point of View*. Cambridge: Harvard Press, 1953.

13. Kuhn, T. S., *The Structure of Scientific Revolutions*. University of Chicago Press: 1962.

14. Yager, R. R., "A Model of Participatory Learning." *IEEE Trans. on Systems, Man and Cybernetics* 20, 1990, pp. 1229–1234.

15. Yager, R. R., D. Z., Zhang, "Effective Suggestion Based on Participatory Learning," *Expert Systems: Research & Applications* 7, 1994, pp. 423–432.

16. Widrow, B., M. E., Hoff, "Adaptive Switching Circuits," *IRE Western Electric Show and Convention Record*, Part 4, 1960, pp. 96–104.

# 2

# EVOLVING TAKAGI-SUGENO FUZZY SYSTEMS FROM STREAMING DATA (eTS+)

Plamen Angelov

## 2.1 BACKGROUND AND MOTIVATION

It is a well-known fact that nowadays we are faced not only with large data sets that we need to process quickly, but with huge data streams (Domingos & Hulten, 2001). Special requirements are also placed by the fast-growing sector of autonomous systems, where systems that can retrain and adapt on-the-fly are needed (Patchett & Sastri, 2007). Similar requirements are enforced by the advanced process industries for self-developing and self-maintaining sensors (Qin et al., 1997). Now, they even talk about *self-learning industries* (EC, 2007). All of these requirements cannot be met by using offline methods and systems that can merely adjust their parameters and are linear (Astrom & Wittenmark, 1989). These requirements call for a new type of system that assumes the structure of nonlinear, nonstationary systems to be adaptive and flexible.

The author of this chapter started research work in this direction around the turn of the century (Angelov, 2002; Angelov & Buswell, 2001), and this research culminated in proposing with Dr. D. Filev the so-called *evolving* Takagi-Sugeno (eTS) fuzzy system (Angelov & Filev, 2003). Since then, a number of improvements of the original algorithm have been made, which require a systematic description in one publication. In this chapter an enhanced version of the eTS algorithm will be described, which is called

*Evolving Intelligent Systems: Methodology and Applications,* Edited by Plamen Angelov, Dimitar P. Filev, and Nikola Kasabov

*eTS+*. It has been tested on a data stream from a real engine test bench (data provided courtesy of Dr. E. Lughofer, Linz, Austria). The results demonstrate the superiority of the proposed enhanced approach for modeling real data streams in precision, simplicity, and interpretability, and the computational resources used.

## 2.2 FUZZY SYSTEM STRUCTURE IDENTIFICATION FROM STREAMING DATA

### 2.2.1 MIMO Structure

The structure of fuzzy systems is defined by fuzzy rules, input variables, fuzzy sets, linguistic connectives, and the inference mechanism. The *Takagi-Sugeno (TS) fuzzy systems* usually have consequent parts of linear form and the overall system is of the *multi-input–single-output (MISO)* type. Evolving TS fuzzy systems can, in general, be of the *multi-input–multi-output (MIMO)* type (Angelov et al., 2004):

$$Rule^i :\ IF(x_1\ is\ close\ to\ x_1^{i*})AND\ldots AND(x_n\ is\ close\ to\ x_n^{i*})$$

$$THEN\left(y_1^i = a_{01}^i + \sum_{j=1}^{n} a_{j1}^i x_j\right)AND\ldots AND\left(y_m^i = a_{0m}^i + \sum_{j=1}^{n} a_{jm}^i x_j\right) \tag{2.1}$$

See Figure 2.1.

The antecedents are usually described by Gaussians:

$$\mu_j^i(x_k) = e^{-\frac{\left(x_j^{i*}-x_{kj}\right)^2}{2(\sigma_j^i)^2}}\ ;\ i = [1, R];\ j = [1, n];\ k = 1, 2, \ldots \tag{2.2}$$

where $\mu_j^i$ denotes the membership of the current input, $x_k$ to the $j$th fuzzy (linguistic) set of the $i$th fuzzy rule; $x_j^{i*}$ is the focal point of the $j$th fuzzy set of the $i$th fuzzy rule; and $\sigma_j^i$ is the projection of the zone of influence of the $i$th cluster on the axis of the $j$th input variable, $x_j$.

The association degree of the input to a particular fuzzy rule, known as the *activation degree*, is defined by a $T$-norm (Yager & Filev, 1994), which is usually represented by the product operator:

$$\tau^i(x_k) = \mathop{T}_{j=1}^{n} \mu_j^i(x_k) = \prod_{j=1}^{n} \mu_j^i(x_k) = \mu_1^i(x_k) \times \ldots \times \mu_n^i(x_k) \tag{2.3}$$

Figure 2.1. A graphical representation of a MIMO system.

Each fuzzy rule approximates the output in a local region centered at the focal point and defined in a fuzzy way (the degree of truth and influence of this local approximation depends on the distance to the focal point and is represented by the membership function (2.2)). Thanks to the fuzzily defined antecedents, any nonlinear system can be approximated by a set of fuzzily coupled locally linear subsystems (Wang & Mendel, 1992).

## 2.2.2 Neural Network Implementation of eTS+

It is well known that the TS fuzzy system can be represented as a neural network (Jang, 1993). The network-like structure enables the flexibility and parallelism and the development of effective learning techniques. The confluence of neural networks as structure framework with the power of fuzzy systems as knowledge granule models leads to neuro-fuzzy constructs. eTS+ can also be represented as a six-layer neuro-fuzzy system (Figure 2.2), which is similar to the fuzzy basis-function networks (Wang & Mendel, 1992).

The first layer takes the inputs, $x_k$ and feeds the second layer, which has neurons with activation functions determined by the membership functions $\mu^i_j(x_k)$ defined in (2.2). In this way, the second layer acts as the granulation of the input universes. The third layer

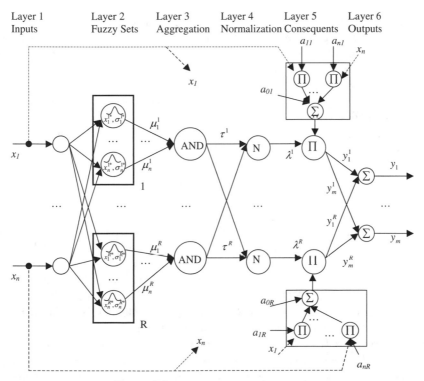

Figure 2.2. eTS+ as a neural network.

of the network aggregates the degrees of satisfaction of particular fuzzy sets per input variable and performs the *T*-norm (usually product operation). It gives as output the degree of activation of each particular fuzzy rule $\tau^i(x_k)$ defined in (2.3). Further, in layer 4, the activation levels are normalized in order of the contributions of the rules to the overall output to sum up to 1 (or 100%). The first four layers represent the *antecedent* part of the fuzzy system. The remaining layers, 5 and 6, are responsible for the *consequent* part, and they are therefore linked to the antecedent part through links from layer 1 in order to feed the inputs into layer 5 (bold lines in Figure 2.2). This layer also gets parameter values and multiplies them by the inputs to produce the local output of the linear subsystem. Finally, layer 6 sums together the local outputs by first cross-multiplying each one of them by the normalized activation level, $\lambda^i(x_k)$, and produces the *m* outputs.

### 2.2.3 Unsupervised Learning Antecedents by Recursive Density Estimation

Historically, first came the assumption that the structure of the fuzzy systems is defined *a priori* based entirely on expert knowledge (Zadeh, 1975). Later, it was demonstrated that the structure can be developed based on partitioning the entire data space into *axes-orthogonal hyper-boxes* along the linguistic variables and assigning membership functions to each box (Sugeno & Kang, 1988). Methods for automatic fuzzy systems design (e.g. using genetic algorithms) were also developed (Angelov & Buswell, 2002; Roubos et al., 2003). However, all these methods are applicable for batch, offline modes of providing the data. For the case when the data are streaming, novel online methods for fuzzy system structure identification are required. One effective online technique proposed in Angelov and Filev (2003) is based on partitioning the data space into overlapping local regions through *recursive density estimation* (*RDE*) and associating clusters (respectively fuzzy sets) to them.

The density of the data space can be estimated by the *mountain* function (Yager & Filev, 1994):

$$M(v) = \sum_{i=1}^{K} e^{-\frac{|v-z_i|^2}{2\sigma^2}} \tag{2.4}$$

where *v* denotes the centre of a grid; $z_i$ is the current data point (for the purpose of fuzzy system identification *z* is considered to be an input/output pair, $z = [x^T, y^T]^T$; $\sigma$ is the radius of the cluster; and *K* is the number of data points.

This concept borrows from the Parzen windows (Hastie et al., 2001) and Gaussian kernel-based estimators, KDE (Elgammal et al., 2002). It is taken further in the subtractive clustering (Chiu, 1994) where the need of the grid is replaced by using each data point as a prototype of a cluster focal point. An alternative clustering method that was also used for data space partitioning aiming at fuzzy systems design is *participatory learning* (Silva et al., 2005). All of the above methods, however, rely on the use of thresholds to decide whether a new cluster should be formed. *eClustering*, proposed in Angelov (2004), is a principally different approach in that it applies to *streaming* data and is *one-pass* (noniterative), and in its current version, called *eClustering +*, it does not rely on user- or problem-specific thresholds. It estimates the density at a data point using a Cauchy function:

$$D_t(z_t) = \frac{1}{1 + \dfrac{1}{t-1}\displaystyle\sum_{i=1}^{t-1}\sum_{j=1}^{n+m}(z_{tj}-z_{ij})^2}$$

(2.5)

$$D_1(z_1) = 1; t = 2, 3, \ldots$$

where $D_t(z_t)$ is the density of the data evaluated around the last data point of the data stream provided to the algorithm $z_t$; $n$ denotes the dimension of the inputs vector; $m$ is the dimension of the outputs vector; and $t$ denotes the number of points for which information about $z$ is available.

In eClustering the density, $D_t(z_t)$ is evaluated recursively and the whole information that concerns the spatial distribution of all data is accumulated in a small number $(n + m + 1)$ of variables ($b_t$ and $c_{tj}$; $j = [1, n+m]$):

$$D_t(z_t) = \frac{t-1}{(t-1)\left(\displaystyle\sum_{j=1}^{n+m}z_{tj}^2 + 1\right) + b_t - 2\displaystyle\sum_{j=1}^{n+m}z_{tj}c_{tj}}$$

(2.6)

$$D_1(z_1) = 1; t = 2, 3, \ldots$$

where $b_t = b_{t-1} + \displaystyle\sum_{j=1}^{n+m}z_{(t-1)j}^2$; $b_1 = 0$; $c_{tj} = c_{(t-1)j} + z_{(t-1)j}$; and $c_{1j} = 0$.

Note that while $t$ can grow large, both $n$ and $m$ are usually small and finite numbers.

The recursive density estimator (RDE) (2.6) has broader application areas than online evolving fuzzy clustering and fuzzy systems design. In Angelov et al. (2008a) it was applied for detecting novelties in video streams. RDE proved to work faster than the well-established KDE approach by an order of magnitude. In Angelov et al. (2008c), RDE was used to generate a passive method for collision avoidance in uninhabited aerial systems. Both applications are very important for the emerging market of autonomous and robotic systems.

RDE is the cornerstone component of eClustering + (which itself is used for the online design of eTS + ). RDE provides a computationally efficient technique to estimate online in one-pass the generalization capability and the representativeness of a particular data point. Obviously, data points with high density are good candidates to be cluster focal points (respectively, focal points of antecedents of fuzzy rules). If a data point is selected to be a cluster focal point, its density determined at the moment when it becomes a focal point by equation (2.6) will be kept in memory and updated. The update is necessary due to the online nature of the algorithm and because any new data point coming from the data stream will influence the data density (seen in the summation over $i$ in equation (2.5)). The density around cluster focal points can also be recursively updated

(Angelov, 2004) by:

$$D_t(z^{i*}) = \frac{t-1}{t-1+(t-2)\left(\frac{1}{D_{t-1}(z^{i*})}-1\right) + \sum_{j=1}^{n+m}(z_{tj}-z_{(t-1)j})},$$

$$D_1(z^{i*}) = 1, t = 2, 3, \ldots \tag{2.7}$$

where $i^*$ denotes the focal points of the $i$th fuzzy rule.

The aim of the data space partitioning used in fuzzy systems design, however, differs from the aim of the conventional clustering (Duda et al., 2000). The latter aims to find natural groupings in such a way that the data points in a certain cluster are *compact* and clusters are well *separable*. When data space partitioning is used for the purpose of forming a fuzzy rule base, the clusters normally overlap and are not necessarily mutually exclusive. Therefore, the second objective (well-separable clusters) is not so important when the partitioning is used for the design of a fuzzy system. In this case, the aims of data space partitioning can be formulated as.

- Form *representative* clusters with high generalization capability.
- *Coverage*—ensure that the membership functions of the fuzzy sets that are formed around cluster focal points cover the entire data space.
- Determine the *number of clusters* from data distribution alone.
- Avoid user- and problem-specific *thresholds*.
- *Simplify the structure* by removing least representative clusters as the data pattern evolves.

The first aim is achieved by selecting the data points with the highest value of $D$. The second aim is formally satisfied if the membership functions are of Gaussian type.

In practice, however, the values of the membership functions outside the so-called $2\sigma$ zone (Hastie et al., 2001) are negligibly small. Let us denote the number of *outer* data points (points that do not lie inside the $2\sigma$ zone of any of the clusters) at the $t$th time instant (after $t$ data samples are read) by $N_t$. That is:

$$N_t \leftarrow N_t + 1; \ \left|z_{jt}^i - z_j^{i*}\right| > 2\sigma_{jt}^i \ \text{for} \ \forall i = [1, R] \ \text{and} \ \forall j = [1, n+m] \tag{2.8}$$

The first aim of the data space partitioning as described above (forming representative clusters) can be achieved by forming clusters around focal points that have high density,

$$\text{Condition } A_1: \ \eta D_t(z_t) > \max_{i=1}^{R} D_t(z_t^{i*}); \ \eta = \begin{cases} 1 & \mu_j^i(x_t) > e^{-2}, \forall i, \forall j \\ \dfrac{N_t - 3}{\log t} & \text{otherwise} \end{cases} \ ; t = 2, 3, \ldots$$

where $\eta$ is the normalized number of "outer" points (Figure 2.3); obviously, the higher $\eta$, the easier it is to create a new cluster.

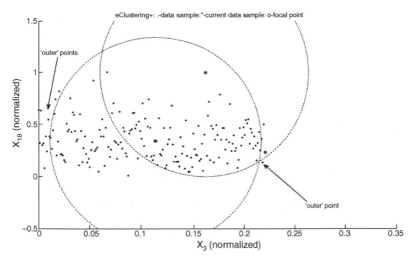

Figure 2.3. "Outer" data points ($N_t = 12$; $t = 185$; $\eta = 1.724$) in the NOx test problem.

Note that the factor $\eta$ plays a role only after several (at least 5) outer points. In Angelov et al. (2004b), an alternative form of Condition A was proposed:

$$\text{Condition } A_2: \quad D_t(z_t) > \max_{i=1}^{R} D_t(z_t^{i*}) \quad OR \quad D_t(z_t) < \min_{i=1}^{R} D_t(z_t^{i*})$$

Condition $A_2$ is more "agile," and its second part ensures a very good coverage, but it is more susceptible to an influence from outliers that can become cluster focal points (see the focal point in the upper-right corner of Figure 2.3). They can be removed or replaced later using quality indicators described in subsection 2.2.5, but this leads to more changes in the rule-based structure. Condition $A_1$, on the other hand, may have problems with detecting newly emerging clusters in a distant area (Figure 2.4).

To avoid redundancy and to control the level of overlap, Condition B is also introduced (Angelov & Zhou, 2006), which is instrumental for removing highly over-lapping clusters:

$$\text{Condition } B: \quad IF\left(\exists i, i = [1,R] : \mu_i^j(x_t) > e^{-1}, \forall j,j = [1,n], t = 2,3,\dots\right) THEN(R \leftarrow R-1)$$

If Condition B is satisfied, that means the new candidate cluster focal point describes any of the previously existing cluster focal points to a certain degree. The previously existing focal point(s) for which this condition is satisfied are being removed.

Finally, the antecedent part of the fuzzy rule-based system can be formed using the cluster focal points that were identified by eClustering + and it will have the following form:

$$Rule^i: \quad IF(x_1 \text{ is close to } x_1^{i*})AND(x_2 \text{ is close to } x_2^{i*})AND\dots AND(x_n \text{ is close to } x_n^{i*})$$

$$(2.9)$$

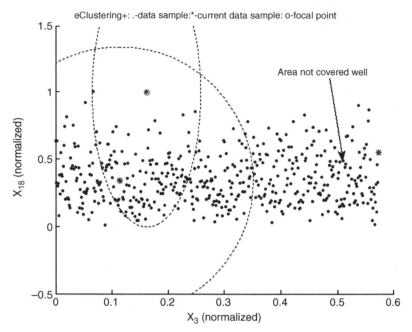

Figure 2.4. Forming new clusters based on Condition $A_1$ is not very agile.

### 2.2.4 Fuzzy Inference (Rules Cooperation or Competition)

It was mentioned that the aim of typical clustering approaches differs from the aim of data space partitioning for the purposes of fuzzy system structure identification. The clusters that are associated with the antecedent parts of fuzzy systems tolerate significant overlap. The reason is that the fuzzy rules in a rule base are not competitive, but rather collaborative. This mechanism can be compared to the proportional voting system. Mathematically, this is expressed through the *center of gravity (CoG)* aggregation mechanism (Yager & Filev, 1994):

$$y = \sum_{i=1}^{R} \lambda^i y^i; \ \lambda^i = \frac{\tau^i}{\sum_{l=1}^{R} \tau^l} \tag{2.10}$$

where $\tau^i$ is the activation level of $i$th fuzzy rule and $\lambda^i$ is the normalized activation level of the same rule; and $R$ is the number of fuzzy rules.

CoG performs weighted averaging of the outputs of individual fuzzy rules to produce the overall output. It makes use of the ability of fuzzy systems to cope with uncertainties and has a cooperative nature. An alternative is presented by the *winner-takes-all (WTA)* mechanism of inference, which has a competition-like nature and can be compared to the majority voting system:

$$y = y^i, i = \arg \min_{l=1}^{R} \lambda^l \qquad (2.11)$$

The WTA inference mechanism is usually used in classification problems. In cases when data distribution is such that relatively distant clusters with little dependency between each other exist, WTA inference will lead to emphasizing the most important cluster and completely ignoring the impact of the distant, more dispersed clusters. This might be a better strategy in such cases.

Finally, the WTA approach has also a "softer" version called *few-winners-take-all* (*fWTA*):

$$y = \sum_{i=1}^{W} \lambda^i y^i; \ \lambda^i = \frac{\tau^i}{\sum_{l=1}^{W} \tau^l} \qquad (2.12)$$

where $W$ denotes the number of winners ($W < R$); without loss of generality one can assume $W = \begin{cases} R/2 & \text{for even } R \\ \dfrac{R-1}{2} & \text{for odd } R \end{cases}$

In a case like the one described above, fWTA inference will lead to selecting the most influential clusters, which is better than selecting just the winner, but also ignores the most dispersed clusters.

## 2.2.5 Online Monitoring of the Quality of the Clusters/Antecedents

Once clusters are generated (by assigning the current data sample to be the focal point of the cluster), then quality can be constantly monitored. The quality of the clusters can be described by:

- Their *support*—the number of data samples associated to the cluster (Angelov & Filev, 2005):

$$S_t^i = S_{t-1}^i + 1, i = \arg \max_{i=1}^{R} \tau^i(x_t), t = 2, 3, \dots, \qquad (2.13)$$

*Support* indicates the generalization power that the specific fuzzy rule provides.
- Their *age*—an accumulated relative time tag (Angelov & Filev, 2005; Angelov & Zhou, 2006):

$$A_t^i = t - \frac{\sum_{l=1}^{S_t^i} I_l}{S_t^i}, i = [1, R], t = 2, 3, \dots \qquad (2.14)$$

where $I_l$ denotes the index (time tag) of the $l$th data sample of the $i$th cluster in respect to the whole data stream.

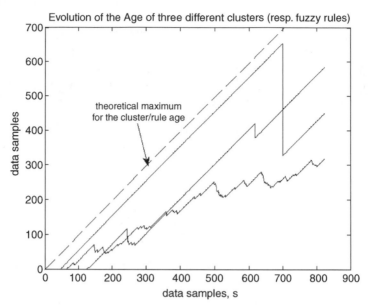

**Figure 2.5.** Evolution of the *age* of the clusters/fuzzy rules for the NOx estimation problem.

The age indicates how up-to-date the information that is generalized by a certain fuzzy rule is. Based on the age, one can simplify the fuzzy rule-based system online by removing *old* rules. Based on the age dynamics (measured by the derivative of the age) one can also detect *shift* and *drift* of the concept (Angelov & Zhou, 2008). Figure 2.5 demonstrates the evolution of the age of fuzzy rules (respectively clusters).

- *Utility*—the accumulated relative firing level of a particular antecedent (Angelov, 2006):

$$U_t^i = \frac{\sum_{l=1}^{t} \lambda^l}{t - I^{i*}}, \ i = [1, R], \ t = 2, 3, \ldots \tag{2.15}$$

where $I^{i*}$ denotes the index (time tag) of the data sample that was used as a focal point of the *i*th fuzzy rule (in other words, it indicates *when* a fuzzy rule was generated).

The utility indicates how much a certain fuzzy rule was used after it was generated—its variability represents the nonstationarity. Figure 2.6 demonstrates the evolution of the utility of the fuzzy rules for the same problem.

- *Zone of influence* (radius), which can be adaptively updated (Angelov & Zhou, 2006) and will be described in the next section.

- *Local density*, which is another measure of the generalization power:

$$L_t^i(z_t) = \frac{1}{1 + \sum_{j=1}^{n+m} (v_{jt}^i)^2}, \ L_1^i(z_1) = 1, \ i = [1, R], \ t = 2, 3, \ldots \tag{2.16}$$

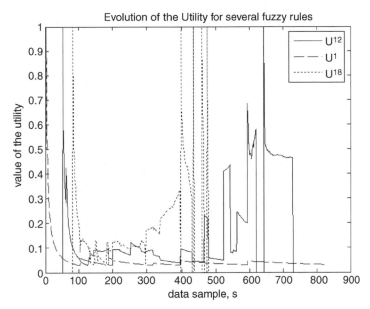

Figure 2.6. Evolution of the *utility* of the clusters/fuzzy rules for the NOx estimation problem.

where $(v_{jt}^i)^2 = \frac{1}{S_t^i-1}\sum_{l=1}^{S_t^i-1}(z_j^{i*} - z_{lj})^2$ denotes the local scatter (Angelov & Filev, 2005).

It is obvious that the only difference between the global density given by (2.5) and the local density (2.16) is the number of data points that are taken into account—in the local density, only the points that *support* a particular cluster are taken into account, whereas the global density is in respect to *all* data points read so far. Also it is obvious that the local scatter can be updated recursively (Angelov & Zhou, 2006).

In data-driven models, the importance of the fuzzy rules can be evaluated by these quality measure indicators, which also assist the evolution process.

## 2.2.6 Online Structure Simplification (Marginal Rules Removal)

The structure of the evolving fuzzy system is open—the rule base can grow by generating new fuzzy rules but it can also shrink by removing rules that are:

- Outdated (old, that is with high *age*).
- With low *support*, that is, with low generalization power (in order for a rule to be established, its focal point must have high generalization power *at the moment of its generation*, but this may change later due to the online nature of the process).
- With low *utility*, that is, the data pattern shifted away from the focal point of that rule.

Any of these cases may lead to disabling a fuzzy rule by assigning zero to the normalized firing level:

$$\text{Condition } C_1: \quad IF \ \left(U_t^i < \bar{U}_t - \hat{U}_t\right) \quad THEN \quad (R \leftarrow R-1) \tag{2.17}$$

$$\text{Condition } C_2: \quad IF \ \left(A_t^i > \bar{A}_t + \hat{A}_t\right) \quad THEN \quad (R \leftarrow R-1) \tag{2.18}$$

$$\text{Condition } C_3: \quad IF \ \left(S_t^i < 3\right) \quad AND \quad (t \geq I^{i*} + 10) \quad THEN \quad (R \leftarrow R-1) \tag{2.19}$$

where $\bar{U}_t$ denotes the *mean utility* after $t$ data are read; $\hat{U}_t$ denotes the *standard deviation* of the *utility* after $t$ data are read; $\bar{A}_t$ denotes the *mean age* at moment $t$; $\hat{A}_t$ denotes the *standard deviation* of the *age* after $t$ data are read.

As an alternative to Condition $C_1$, Angelov and Filev 2005 proposed to use a threshold, $\eta$ (suggested values are [0.03; 0.1]), in the following way:

$$\text{Condition } C'_1: IF \quad (U_t^i < \eta) \quad THEN \quad (R \leftarrow R-1) \tag{2.17a}$$

Based on these principles, and satisfying the remaining aims, the algorithm, called eClustering +, is proposed.

---

**Pseudocode of eClustering +**

*Algorithm eClustering +*

```
Begin eClustering+
      Read the input-output pair, z_t
      IF (t = 1) THEN (Initialise)
      ELSE
             Calculate recursively the data density around by
                 (2.6);
             Update recursively the density of the focal points
                by (2.7);
             IF (Condition A) THEN (form a new focal point, R ←R+1;
                z^i*←z_t; D(z^i*)←1; I^i*←1) ;
             IF (Condition B) THEN (remove the rule for which
                it holds)
             Assign the current data sample to the nearest cluster
                (to the rule it satisfies most);
      END IF
      Repeat the procedure until end of the data stream or
         external request to stop
END eClustering+
```

Notes:

1. Initialize includes initialization (if possible) or assigning the input part of the first available data point to become the focal point of the first cluster ("starting from scratch"): $x^{1*} \leftarrow x_1$; $R \leftarrow 1$; $D(x^{1*}) \leftarrow 1$, $b_1 \leftarrow 0$; $c_1^j \leftarrow 0$.
2. Condition A may be realized as $A_1$ or $A_2$.

## 2.3 PARAMETER IDENTIFICATION BY fwRLS METHOD

Once the structure of the evolving fuzzy system eTS + is defined and established, the problem of parameter identification becomes important. It takes place *only* when there are real/measured outputs (let us have $t$ measured outputs out of $k$ data samples in total; that is, for $(k - t)$ of the data samples we know the inputs only, $t \leq k$). One can use supervised learning for these instances. In eTS +, we assume that real outputs may not always be provided. When this is the case, eTS + produces output as an offline system and no update and evolution takes place. When real/measured outputs are provided (we denote them by $\bar{y}_t$), they are used to:

- Tune (optimize) the consequent parameters of the locally linear subsystems, as will be described below.
- Calculate the potential of the input–output pair to form a new cluster (respectively fuzzy rule) or to replace an existing one.
- Update the cluster (respectively fuzzy rule) quality indicators and, if necessary, remove clusters/rules that are *old*, with low *utility* and *support*.

Equation (2.10) can be transformed into a vector form (Angelov & Filev, 2004):

$$y = \psi^T \theta \tag{2.20}$$

where $y = [y_1, y_2, \ldots y_m]^T$ is the $m$-dimensional output of the MIMO eTS +; $\psi = [\lambda_1 \bar{x}^T, \lambda_2 \bar{x}^T, \ldots, \lambda_n \bar{x}^T]^T$ denotes the fuzzily weighted extended inputs vector, $\bar{x} = [1, x_1, x_2, \ldots, x_n]^T$; $\theta = [(\gamma^1)^T, (\gamma^2)^T, \ldots, (\gamma^R)^T]^T$ is the vector of parameters of the rule base; and $\gamma^i = \begin{bmatrix} a_{01}^i & \cdots & a_{0m}^i \\ \cdots & \cdots & \cdots \\ a_{n1}^i & \cdots & a_{nm}^i \end{bmatrix}^T$ denotes the matrix of consequent part parameters (parameters of the $i$th linear local subsystem) assuming $m$ outputs. Note that if use fWTA (2.12), the same expressions will take place but $R$ will have to be substituted for by $W$. Note also that the time index is dropped for clarity (e.g., $y = \psi^T \theta$ instead of $y_k = \psi_k^T \theta_t$).

### 2.3.1 Local or Global Optimization

Learning and evolving eTS + from data streams combines structure and parameter identification, unsupervised data partitioning, and supervised consequent parameters learning (Figure 2.7).

Each time the real/target outputs $\bar{y}_t$ are provided, the consequents' parameters can be updated recursively using one of the two forms of fwRLS (Angelov & Filev, 2004)—locally or globally optimal. Both have different computational requirements and give somewhat different results. The error function in global terms can be

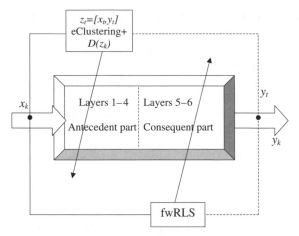

**Figure 2.7.** A schematic representation of eTS+ identification as a two-stage process (the dashed line illustrates that the output values are fed back to eTS +, not necessarily at each step ($t \leq k$); when the output is not fed back, eTS + works in prediction mode, only providing $y_k$).

defined as:

$$E_G = \sum_{l=1}^{t} \left( \bar{y}_l - \psi_l^T \theta_l \right)^2 \rightarrow \min \tag{2.21}$$

That is, the fuzzy weights $\lambda$ are redistributed between the fuzzy rules and implicitly represented through $\psi$. Thus, a compensatory (collaborative) effect of the fuzzy aggregation takes place and the overall result is possibly a lower error overall, but a lower transparency and higher errors locally. This problem has been discussed elsewhere (Yen et al., 1998). The alternative is to apply a locally optimal error criterion:

$$E_L^i = \sum_{l=1}^{t} \lambda^i(x_l) \left( \bar{y}_l - \bar{x}_l^T \gamma_l^i \right)^2 \rightarrow \min \tag{2.22}$$

Note that the local criteria are given per rule. To get the overall error criterion, we sum them together, $E_L = \sum_{i=1}^{R} E_L^i$. The fuzzy weights are outside the error per rule factor and thus are not distributed between rules. This leads fuzzy systems designed using local optimization criteria to have higher interpretability locally. When using the vector form, these criteria can be rewritten as:

$$E_G = \left( Y - \Psi^T \Theta \right)^T \left( Y - \Psi^T \Theta \right) \tag{2.21a}$$

where $Y$ is an $(m \times t)$-dimensional, $\Psi$ is an $R \times (n + 1) \times t$-dimensional, and $\Theta$ is a $R \times (n + 1) \times m \times t$-dimensional matrix formed by the instantaneous values of $y_l, l = [1, t]$, where $y_l = [y_{1l}, y_{2l}, \ldots y_{ml}]^T$ is an $m$-dimensional output vector, $\lambda_l^i, i = [1, R], \bar{x}$, and $\theta$.

$$E_L^i = \left(Y - X^T \Gamma^i\right)^T \Lambda^i \left(Y - X^T \Gamma^i\right), i = [1, R] \qquad (2.22a)$$

where $X$ is an $(n + 1) \times t$-dimensional, and $\Gamma$ is an $(n + 1) \times m \times t$-dimensional matrix formed by the instantaneous values of $\bar{x}$ and $\gamma$.

Solutions to the optimization problems formulated with either of the two criteria (2.21a) or (2.22a) can be sought by using the *recursive least squares* (*RLS*) estimation technique (Ljung, 1988). A direct application of RLS, however, may lead to nonconvergence because the original RLS algorithm is designed under the assumption of a fixed system structure. In eTS + we not only have fuzzily coupled linear subsystems and streaming data, but we also have system *structure* evolution, as described in the previous section. It is true that the structural changes are much less frequent than the sampling rate, but they still do not permit using RLS directly. This led to the introduction of fwRLS (Angelov & Filev, 2004), which has two versions; one of them is for the global case and the other one is for the local optimization case. We consider here only the local version of fwRLS (L-fwRLS) and will give the reasons why. L-fwRLS gives the optimal update of the parameters of the $i$th local linear subsystems:

$$\gamma_{t+1}^i = \gamma_t^i + C_t^i \bar{x}_t \lambda_t^i \left(\bar{y}_t - \bar{x}_t^T \gamma_t^i\right), \ \gamma_1^i = 0 \qquad (2.23)$$

$$C_{t+1}^i = C_t^i - \frac{\lambda_t^i C_t^i \bar{x}_t \bar{x}_t^T C_t^i}{1 + \lambda_t^i \bar{x}_t^T C_t^i \bar{x}_t}, \ C_1^i = \Omega I_{(n+1) \times (n+1)} \qquad (2.24)$$

where $I = \begin{bmatrix} 1 & 0 & \dots & 0 \\ 0 & \dots & \dots & \dots \\ \dots & \dots & 1 & 0 \\ 0 & \dots & 0 & 1 \end{bmatrix}_{(n+1) \times (n+1)}$ a denotes a $(n+1) \times (n+1)$ unitary matrix, and $\Omega$

denotes a large number (usually $\Omega = 1000$).

Generally, the set of parameters that satisfy the global optimization criteria (2.21a) differ from the set of parameters that satisfy the local criteria (2.22a). The effect that adding a new fuzzy rule or removing one from the structure will have on the convergence of the L-fwRLS is significantly smaller than in G-fwRLS, because this effect is expressed only through the fact that the values of the normalized activation levels $\lambda$ change. More importantly, the covariance matrixes $C^i$, $i = [1, R]$ do not change, because they are not coupled as in the global case (Angelov & Filev, 2004). Therefore, when adding a new fuzzy rule, a new covariance matrix is initiated, $C_t^{R+1} = I\Omega$. Globally optimal parameters require a more complicated update (Angelov & Filev, 2004) and the covariance matrix is of size $R(n + 1) \times R(n + 1)$ while the size of the covariance matrix in the locally optimal case is just $(n + 1) \times (n + 1)$. There are, indeed, $R$ of these local covariance matrixes (per rule), but the memory required is still less by a factor of $R$. In the local case the covariance matrixes are updated independently. Parameters of the new rules that are formed online can be either initialized as shown in (2.23) or approximated from the parameters of the existing $R$ fuzzy rules, using them as a fuzzy rule base

(Angelov & Filev, 2004):

$$\gamma_t^{R+1} = \sum_{i=1}^{R} \lambda^i \gamma_{t-1}^i \qquad (2.25)$$

Parameters of all other rules can be inherited from the previous time step when the output was provided:

$$\gamma_t^i = \gamma_{t-1}^i, i = [1, R] \qquad (2.26)$$

When a fuzzy rule is replaced by another rule due to Condition B, the focal point of the new rule is close to the focal point of the rule to be replaced (this is the very reason it is being replaced) and therefore the parameters and the covariance can be inherited by the fuzzy rule being replaced (Angelov & Filev, 2004):

$$\gamma_t^{R+1} = \gamma_{t-1}^{i*}, \mu_j^{i*}(x_t) > e^{-1}, \forall j, j = [1, n] \qquad (2.27a)$$

$$C_t^{R+1} = C_{t-1}^{i*}, \mu_j^{i*}(x_t) > e^{-1}, \forall j, j = [1, n] \qquad (2.27b)$$

It is interesting to note that whereas the expectation is for the globally optimal parameters to ensure a lower error as compared with the locally optimal parameters, which have the advantage of higher interpretability (Yen et al., 1998), the test results indicate that this is not always the case. Several benchmark problems were tested (courtesy of Mr. X. Zhou, who performed the tests) using both local and global optimality criteria. Figure 2.8 presents the results of the test in which both models start learning "from scratch," learning during the whole data stream ($t = k$, there is no separate validation data set, and after each sample a prediction is made and at the next time step the true value of the output is used for updating the eTS + ).

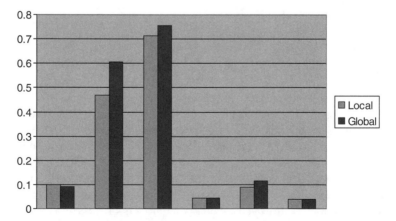

Figure 2.8. RMSE using global and local optimization of the parameters (from left to right: Six different data streams are presented—Mackey-Glass, Box-Jenkins, NOx, HVAC, AutoMPG, Polypropylene).

The same number of fuzzy rules were generated in both cases (this is not unexpected because the structure identification in both cases is the same). It was also noticed that the computation time of the locally optimized version is significantly lower compared to the alternative case.

Note that when local optimization criteria are used for parameter identification, the removal of a rule from the rule base does not affect the $R - 1$ covariance matrixes of the remaining rules in the rule base, each one of which has dimension $(n + m) \times (n + m)$. It does, however, affect the optimality of the parameters that were adapted using the fuzzily weighted RLS method, but this damage can be considered as noise with which the fwRLS can cope. If a global optimization criteria is used (Angelov & Filev, 2004), the covariance matrix combines the cross-effect of all rules and is much bigger (of size $R(n + m) \times R$ $(n + m)$) and a removal of a rule leads to deletion of $(n + m)$ columns and rows from it. Analyzing the process we can conclude that the local optimization of parameters provides a simpler (using significantly smaller covariance matrixes) and more stable and robust solution (changes affect only one of the $R$ covariance matrixes compared to a change in the dimension of a large covariance matrix by adding or removing a number of columns and rows), which is more interpretable, and in a number of practical cases is also more precise.

Additionally, the removal of marginal rules (Condition C) does affect the local version of the algorithm to a much smaller degree (through $\lambda$ only) than the global version, where the covariance matrix C is also being affected. Therefore, while having both versions in eTS + the local optimization of parameters will be considered as the default.

## 2.3.2 Adaptation of the Cluster Radius (Zone of Influence)

The (usually Gaussian) membership function was defined by equation (2.5). The cluster radius $\sigma$ is an important parameter that affects the results because it is part of the membership function and thus of the activation level of the fuzzy set. It also defines the spread of the linguistic variable that might be assigned to the projection of the cluster on the axes. In eClustering (Angelov, 2004), the radius was assumed to be predefined in the same way as in mountain (Yager & Filev, 1994) and subtractive clustering (Chiu, 1994) approaches. In (Angelov & Zhou, 2006) a variable radius was introduced, which learns the data distribution:

$$\sigma_{jt}^i = \alpha \sigma_{jt}^i + (1-\alpha)\nu_{jt}^i, \ \sigma_{j1}^i = 1, j = [1, n+m] \qquad (2.28)$$

where $\alpha$ is a learning constant (the value of $\alpha = 1$ is assumed without loss of generality).

It has to be noticed that the absence of problem-specific parameters is an obvious advantage in any algorithm (this is especially true for online algorithms). Whereas the parameter $\alpha$ is suitable for all problems, the value of the radius is to a great extent problem specific (although suggested values in range [0.3;0.5] for normalized data are also relatively problem independent, it can be demonstrated that it does affect the results). Figure 2.9 illustrates the evolution of the radius in eTS + .

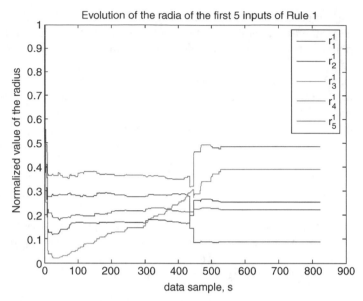

**Figure 2.9.** Evolution of the radius.

From Figure 2.9 one can see that the radii of all the clusters converge to a stable value pretty quickly.

### 2.3.3 Online Input Variables (Features) Selection

So far we have assumed that the number of input variables $n$ is predefined and fixed. This is very often the case because the factors that affect the output are usually known from the *prior* knowledge. In many problems, however, there is a large number of (often) correlated inputs, and input variable selection (also known in classification literature as *feature selection* (Duda et al., 2000)) is a very important problem. This is especially true for *inferential* (*intelligent*) sensors (Fortuna et al., 2007; Kordon et al., 2003). This problem is usually considered in offline mode as a part of the preprocessing and is usually approached using principal component analysis (PCA) (Li et al., 2000), GA (Smits et al., 2006), partial least squares (PLS) (Fortuna et al., 2007), and sensitivity analysis (Hastie et al., 2001).

It is often difficult to obtain representative data of dynamic and nonstationary systems that will permit extracting the best subset of input variables. Therefore, it is important to develop a method that enables automatic input variable selection on-the-fly. Having such a technique, the starting fuzzy rule-based system may encompass all available inputs and can automatically trim the structure in all directions:

- Horizontally (online input variables selection, Condition D)
- Vertically (adding or removing fuzzy rules by eClustering+, age, utility, Conditions B and C for shrinking the rule base, and Condition A for expanding the rule base)

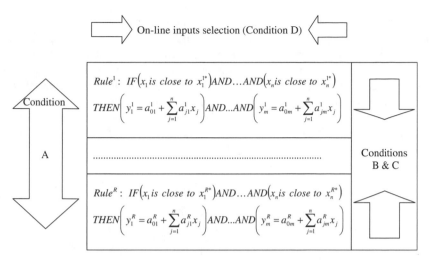

On-line inputs selection (Condition D)

$Rule^1$:  $IF\left(x_1 \text{ is close to } x_1^{1*}\right)AND...AND\left(x_n \text{ is close to } x_n^{1*}\right)$

$THEN\left(y_1^1 = a_{01}^1 + \sum_{j=1}^{n} a_{j1}^1 x_j\right)AND...AND\left(y_m^1 = a_{0m}^1 + \sum_{j=1}^{n} a_{jm}^1 x_j\right)$

Condition

A

........................................................................

$Rule^R$:  $IF\left(x_1 \text{ is close to } x_1^{R*}\right)AND...AND\left(x_n \text{ is close to } x_n^{R*}\right)$

$THEN\left(y_1^R = a_{01}^R + \sum_{j=1}^{n} a_{j1}^R x_j\right)AND...AND\left(y_m^R = a_{0m}^R + \sum_{j=1}^{n} a_{jm}^R x_j\right)$

Conditions
B & C

**Figure 2.10.** Horizontal and vertical evolution in eTS+.

- Internally (adapting the radius affecting the membership functions and cluster shapes, (2.28); adapting the consequents' parameters by fwRLS, (2.23) for the local case)

This is illustrated in Figure 2.10.

The idea (Angelov, 2006) for automatic input variable selection is based on the online monitoring and analysis of the consequents' parameter values. If the values of the parameters $a_{jlt}^i$, $i = [1,R]$, $l = [1,m]$ are negligibly small across the rules for a certain input (feature) $j \in \{1,n\}$ and certain output $l \in \{1,m\}$ for the data points seen so far, one can conclude that this particular input/feature $j$ is not contributing significantly toward the overall output and this input variable (feature) is a candidate for removal. This can be mathematically represented by the accumulated sum of the consequent parameters for the specific $j$th input/feature in respect to (normalized by) all $n$ inputs/features (Angelov, 2006):

$$\omega_{jlt}^i = \frac{\pi_{jlt}^i}{\sum_{r=1}^{n} \pi_{jlt}^i}, \ i = [1,R]; \ j = [1,n], \ l = [1,m] \qquad (2.29)$$

where $\pi_{jlt}^i = \sum_{r=1}^{t} \left|\gamma_{jlr}^i\right|$ denotes the accumulated sum of parameter values.

The values of $\pi_{jlt}^i$ indicate the contribution of a particular input/feature that can be monitored. The values of $\omega_{jlt}^i$ indicate the ratio of the contribution of a particular input/ feature compared with the contributions of all features, $P_{lt}^i = \sum_{r=1}^{n} \pi_{rlt}^i$, or with the contribution of the "most influential" feature, $\bar{\pi}_{lt}^i = \max_{r=1}^{n} \pi_{rlt}^i$, $l = [1,m]$, $i = [1,R]$, $t = 1,2,...$.

An extensive empirical study (Angelov & Zhou, 2008) indicates that, whereas the former is more appropriate for problems with high dimensional input (e.g., more than 10), for problems with a smaller dimension of the input (number of features) (e.g., 10, which is very often the case), the latter is more appropriate because it is more representative. When the number of features is large, the sum of contributions $P$ becomes a large number on its own and masks the effect of a particular feature. Therefore, the comparison in this case is with the feature that contributes most, $\bar{\pi}$. Finally, the following condition for removal of less relevant inputs (features) and thus for horizontal adaptation of the fuzzy system is proposed (Angelov, 2006):

$$
\text{Condition D}_1 : \quad
\begin{array}{l}
IF\left(\exists j^*|\omega^i_{j^*lt} < \varepsilon P^i_{lt}\right) \; AND(n \leq 10) \quad THEN(remove\, j^*) \\[4pt]
where \; i = [1, R], \; l = [1, m], \; t = 2, 3, \ldots
\end{array}
\tag{2.30a}
$$

$$
\text{Condition D}_2 : \quad
\begin{array}{l}
IF\left(\exists j^*|\omega^i_{j^*lt} < \varepsilon \bar{\pi}^i_{lt}\right) \; AND(n > 10) \quad THEN(remove\, j^*) \\[4pt]
where \; i = [1, R], \; l = [1, m], \; k = 2, 3, \ldots
\end{array}
\tag{2.30b}
$$

where $\varepsilon$ denotes a coefficient (suggested values are [0.03;0.1]).

Note that a removal of a feature leads to a change in the dimension (shrinking) of a number of variables (e.g., the vector of inputs $x$; the vector of focal points $x^*$; recursive variables $b$ and $c$; and more importantly, the covariance matrix, $C$, parameters, $a$, $\gamma$).

The role of the online selection of input variables is very important in the *inferential* or *intelligent* sensors (Angelov et al., 2008). It also adds to the arsenal of tools for autonomous evolution of fuzzy systems.

## 2.3.4 Online Scaling of the Input Values

The problem of treating all of the data equally is very important, especially for an online automatic self-developing system such as eTS + that deals with streaming data. The values of different input variables need to be in comparable ranges in order for the coefficients of the consequent part and in the covariance matrixes not to have extremely high values. There are two techniques that are widely used for dealing with this problem—*normalization* and *standardization* (Duda et al., 2000). Both of these can be applied to the data stream online (in a recursive manner) before feeding the data to eTS + as detailed in Angelov and Filev (2005) for standardization and in Angelov et al. (2007) for normalization. When comparing online normalization to the online standardization one can conclude that the online normalization is exact because it treats all data points equally despite the fact that the range of data may change. However, it brings instability, because any new data point that is outside of the range so far extends it. Standardization, on the other hand, is much more robust because the mean and standard deviation accumulate the effects of all the data and do not change suddenly and drastically. Therefore, by default, in eTS + online standardization is applied, which confines over 95% of the standardized data into the range [−2; 2] (Duda et al., 2000).

The standardization is based on the subtraction of the mean and normalizing by the standard deviation of the data (Duda et al., 2000):

$$\hat{z}_{jt} = \frac{z_{jt} - \bar{z}_{jt}}{\zeta_{jt}}, \, j = [1, n], \, t = 2, 3, \ldots \tag{2.31}$$

where $\hat{z}_{jt}$ denotes the standardized value of the $j$th input variable (feature) at the $t$th time instant; $\bar{z}_{jt} = \frac{1}{t} \sum_{l=1}^{t} z_{jl}, \, j = [1, n], \, t = 2, 3, \ldots$ denotes the mean per input variable (feature); and $\zeta_t^j$ denotes the standard deviation of the $j$th input/feature calculated based on $t$ data samples.

Both the mean and the standard deviation can be updated recursively (Angelov & Filev, 2005) by:

$$\bar{z}_{jt} = \frac{t-1}{t} \bar{z}_{j(t-1)} + \frac{1}{t} z_{j(t-1)}; \, \bar{z}_{j1} = 0, \, j = [1, n+m], \, t = 2, 3, \ldots \tag{2.32a}$$

$$\zeta_{jt}^2 = \frac{t-1}{t} \zeta_{j(t-1)}^2 + \frac{1}{t-1} \left( z_{jt} - \bar{z}_{j(t-1)} \right), \, \zeta_{j1} = 0, \, j = [1, n+m], \, t = 2, 3, \ldots \tag{2.32b}$$

In order to simplify the notations we assume that the input–output vector $z$ has been standardized and will use $z$ having in mind $\hat{z}$. In order to return to the original scale, the following transformation has to take place:

$$z_{jt} = \hat{z}_{jt} \zeta_{jt} + \bar{z}_{jt}, \, j = [1, n+m], \, t = 2, 3, \ldots \tag{2.33}$$

## 2.4 NONLINEAR REGRESSION AND TIME-SERIES PREDICTION USING eTS +

The TS fuzzy system with evolving structure (as described in Section 2.2) and adaptive parameters learned online (as described in the previous section) is a very flexible construct that can be applied to a range of problems, such as:

- Regression models of the type $y_k = f(x_k)$. Note that only a subset of the outputs are supposed to be measured, $\bar{y}_t; \, t \leq k$.
- Time-series prediction or filtering, for example, $\hat{y}_t = f(x_{t-1}, \ldots, x_{t-Nx}, y_{t-1}, \ldots, y_{t-Ny})$, which is also known as *nonlinear autoregression with exogenous input (NARX)* or as *nonlinear output error (NOE)*, when the past *predictions* are used instead of the *actual* data.
- Classification, when the output is the class label that is implemented in the eClass0 approach (Angelov et al., 2007), or when the classification surface is approximated by eTS+, which is implemented in eClass1 and eClassM (Angelov & Zhou, 2008b).

- Clustering or novelty detection (Angelov et al., 2008).
- Control (Angelov, 2004b).

The flowchart of the eTS + algorithm is given in Figure 2.11.

One particular application of eTS + for regression is its implementation as an inferential sensor, called *eSensor* (Angelov et al., 2008), which is schematically represented in Figure 2.12.

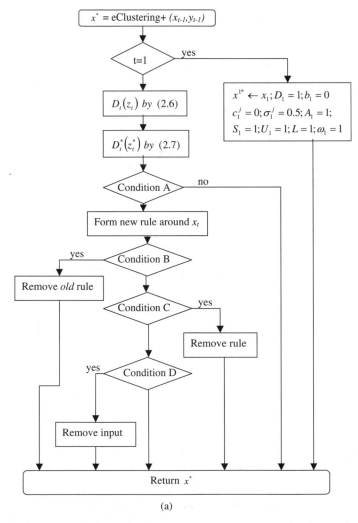

(a)

**Figure 2.11.** a. Flowchart of the eClustering + part of eTS +. b. Flowchart of eTS +.

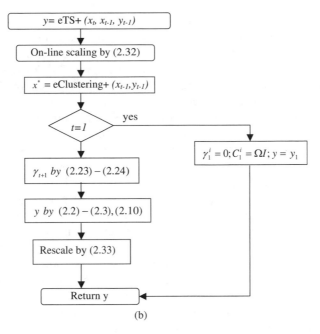

$$y = eTS+ (x_t, x_{t-1}, y_{t-1})$$

On-line scaling by (2.32)

$$x^* = eClustering+ (x_{t-1}, y_{t-1})$$

$t=1$    yes

$$\gamma_1^i = 0; C_1^i = \Omega I; y = y_1$$

$\gamma_{t+1}$ by (2.23) – (2.24)

$y$ by (2.2) – (2.3), (2.10)

Rescale by (2.33)

Return y

(b)

**Figure 2.11.** (*Continued*)

## 2.5 APPLICATION OF eTS+

In this section we use a data stream generated by conventional sensors mounted on car engines subjected to tests (courtesy of Dr. E. Lughofer, University of Linz, Austria). In this experiment, initially 180 different physical variables were measured using conventional (hard) sensors. Most of these potential inputs to the regression model are the same physical variables (such as pressure in the cylinders, engine torque, rotation speed, etc.) measured at different time instances (different time delays). The aim is to evaluate the

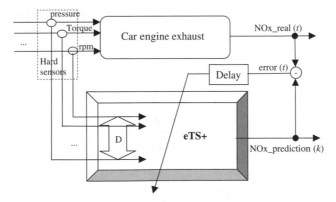

**Figure 2.12.** eSensor for the NOx emissions (D denotes online inputs selection using Condition D; $t \leq k$).

content of NOx in the emissions from the exhaust automatically, possibly in real time and adaptively. The proposed method, eTS +, is used to generate automatically and evolve a nonlinear regression model from the input data streams. The performance was compared with alternative methods (Kasabov & Song, 2002; Lughofer, 2005) and with the original version of eTS (Angelov & Filev, 2003), which is using global optimization and fixed radius ($r = 0.3$) for all inputs/features.

The problem of selecting a small subset of the highly correlated inputs is not easy and is usually done subjectively, based on the *prior* knowledge, experience, or offline methods. In Angelov and Lughofer (2008), five inputs were used. Using eTS + one can start processing all 180 inputs and automatically select the best subset online. This horizontal evolution leads to a removal of 122 different inputs. If the online input selection (Condition $D_2$) is applied together with the *utility*-based marginal rules removal (Condition $C_1$), the structure simplifies to 4 inputs and 4 well-interpretable fuzzy rules only! All the results are tabulated in Table 2.1 (the default values for $\eta$ and $\varepsilon$ of 0.1 were used for conditions C and D respectively). One can see that the prediction error is lower with the model that has inputs selected automatically and the time needed for calculation is reduced significantly. Note that FLEXFIS and one of the implementations of the original eTS algorithm have been applied to 5 preselected (using *prior* knowledge and offline preprocessing) inputs/features. Despite the features being preselected offline, the precision is not higher than using eTS +, which selects the features online.

The online input variables selection process is illustrated in Figure 2.13. It is interesting to notice from Table 2.1 that removing marginal rules helps reduce the number of inputs selected at the end. This can be explained by the fact that Condition D is

**T A B L E  2.1.** Performance of Different Versions of eTS on the NOx Emissions Estimation Problem and a Comparison with Other Evolving Fuzzy Systems Approaches

| Method | #inputs | #rules | RMSE | Correlation | Comput. time[1], s |
|---|---|---|---|---|---|
| DENFIS[2] | 180 | 413 | 0.17 | 0.917 | 96 |
| eTS (original[3]) | 180 | 22 | 0.19 | 0.839 | 59.32 |
| eTS (original[4]) | 5 (preselected) | 3 | 0.17 | 0.915 | 0.76 |
| FLEXFIS[4] | 5 (preselected) | 5 | – | 0.911 | 3.16 |
| Feedforward NN[5] | 180 | 2 hidden layers 15 neurons each | 0.15 | 0.934 | 1.8 |
| exTS[6] | 180 | 22 | 0.17 | 0.914 | 0.282 |
| eTS + (D only)[7] | 58 | 40 | **0.14** | **0.943** | 0.134 |
| eTS + (C$_1$ only)[7] | 180 | 7 | 0.15 | 0.929 | 0.158 |
| eTS + (D & C$_1$)[7] | **4** | **4** | 0.14 | 0.939 | **0.026** |

[1] Simulations were carried out using Matlab® on a laptop equipped with memory 1 GB and Intel® U2500CPU.
[2] (Kasabov & Song, 2002).
[3] (Angelov & Filev, 2004).
[4] (Angelov & Lughofer, 2008).
[5] Using Matworks®.
[6] (Angelov & Zhou, 2006).
[7] Introduced first in Angelov (2006).

TABLE 2.2. Test with Mackey-Glass Time Series[1]

| Method | #rules | RMSE | NDEI[2] | Computational time, s |
|---|---|---|---|---|
| DENFIS | 27 | 0.102 | 0.404 | 1.4 |
| eTS (original, r = 0.25) | 9 | 0.094 | 0.373 | 0.473 |
| Feedforward NN | 2 × 15 neurons | 0.122 | 0.441 | 7.6 |
| Kalman filter[3] | **1** | 0.117 | 0.462 | 0.24 |
| exTS | 12 | **0.080** | **0.320** | 0.83 |
| eTS + ($C_1$ only) | **8** | 0.111 | 0.438 | **0.08** |
| eTS + (D & $C_1$) | 10 | 0.099 | 0.392 | 0.09 |

[1] More details about this benchmark problem can be found in Asuncion and Newman (2007); conditions of the test are the same as for the previous experiment.
[2] Nondimensional error index—described in more detail for example, in Angelov and Filev (2004).
[3] Kalman (1960).

checked for each rule one by one, rather than on all rules as a whole. Dropping a marginal rule leads to removal of some inputs, which causes the relevant inputs to also drop out.

The Mackey-Glass chaotic time series is generated from the Mackey-Glass differential delay equation defined by Asuncion and Newman (2007):

$$\frac{dM}{dt} = \frac{0.2M(t-\tau)}{1+M^{10}(t-\tau)} - 0.1M(t) \tag{2.34}$$

The aim is to use the past values of $x$ to predict some future value of $x$. We assume $x(0) = 1.2$, $\tau = 17$ and the value of the signal 85 steps ahead $x(t + 85)$ is predicted based on the values of the signal at the current moment, 6, 12, and 18 steps back:

$$y = M_{t+85}; \quad x = [M_{t-18}; M_{t-12}; M_{t-6}; M_t]^T \tag{2.35}$$

The training data set consists of 3000 data samples and the validation data set of 500 data samples. The *nondimensional error index* (*NDEI*) is defined as the ratio of the root mean square error over the standard deviation of the target data (Kasabov & Song, 2002). Note that this particular benchmark data set (Mackey-Glass time series) has four inputs only and condition D is not particularly necessary, and the number of fuzzy rules generated is not excessively large by applying the original (Angelov & Filev, 2004) and extended (Angelov & Zhou, 2006) versions of eTS, and, therefore, the effect of the improvements eTS + brings is primarily in the smaller time required for computations because of the use of local learning. Note that eTS + can also work in global learning mode.

## 2.6 CONCLUSION AND OUTLOOK

In this chapter a new and enhanced version of the popular evolving Takagi-Sugeno approach (Angelov & Filev, 2004) is introduced, called eTS + . It builds on the strengths of the original eTS; namely, it is also fully recursive (thus suitable for online applications

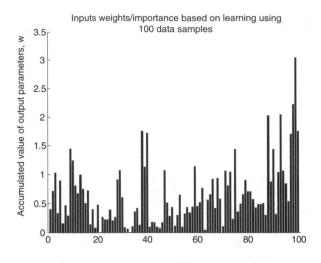

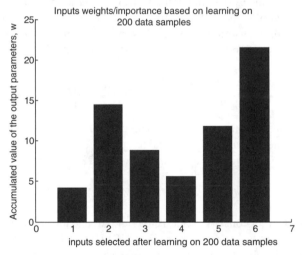

Figure 2.13. Online input variables selection (Condition D) for the NOx test problem; top plot—a snapshot after 100 data samples have been read; second plot—a snapshot after 200 data samples have been read; third plot—a snapshot after 300 data samples have been read; bottom plot—the finally selected features.

and computationally light), robust, flexible, and autonomous (can start from scratch and does not use thresholds or user-specific parameters). It has, however, additional advantages—namely, alternative mechanisms that allow shrinking of the rule base as well as its growth based on age and utility of the rules; online input variables selection (horizontal evolution); and alternative conditions for forming rules. It does not necessarily assume that each data sample will have real/target output. It also has a variable zone of influence of the clusters that are used to form fuzzy rules, and can have multiple outputs (MIMO structure). It has been demonstrated on the test example using real data

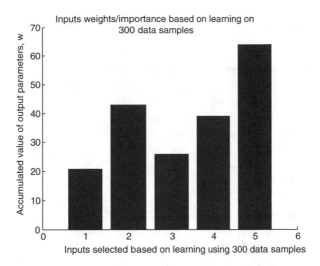

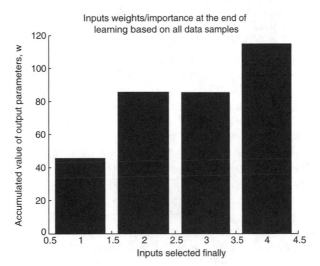

Figure 2.13. (*Continued*)

that the proposed improvements, which are subject to a pending patent (Angelov, 2006), lead to significantly improved results of eTS + . A wide range of industrial and research applications of eTS + are currently under investigation.

## 2.7 ACKNOWLEDGMENTS

The author would like to extend thanks to Mr. Xiaowei Zhou, for assistance in tests and experiments, to Dr. Edwin Lughofer, for providing the data for the NOx problem, and to Prof. Fernando Gomide, for useful feedback on the manuscript.

## 2.8 REFERENCES

Angelov, P., R. Buswell (2001). "Evolving Rule-Based Models: A Tool for Intelligent Adaptation." *Proc. 9th IFSA World Congress,* Vancouver, BC, Canada, July 25–28, 2001, pp. 1062–1067.

Angelov, P. (2002). *Evolving Rule-Based Models: A Tool for Design of Flexible Adaptive Systems.* Heidelberg, New York; Springer-Verlag, ISBN 3-7908-1457-1.

Angelov, P., R. Buswell (2003). "Automatic Generation of Fuzzy Rule-Based Models from Data by Genetic Algorithms," *Information Sciences,* Vol. 150, No. 1/2, pp. 17–31.

Angelov, P., D. Filev (2003). "On-line Design of Takagi-Sugeno Models," In: *Lecture Notes in Computer Sci.,* Vol. 2715, *Fuzzy Sets and Systems,* IFSA2003 ( T. Bilgiç, B. De Baets, O. Kaynak, eds.), pp. 576–584.

Angelov, P. (2004). "An Approach for Fuzzy Rule-Based Adaptation Using On-line Clustering," *Int. Journal of Approximate Reasoning,* Vol. 35, No. 3, pp. 275–289.

Angelov, P. P. (2004b). "A Fuzzy Controller with Evolving Structure," *Information Sciences,* Vol. 161, pp. 21–35, ISSN 0020-0255.

Angelov, P., D. Filev (2004). "An Approach to On-line Identification of Takagi-Sugeno Fuzzy Models." *IEEE Trans. on System, Man, and Cybernetics, Part B—Cybernetics,* Vol. 34, No. 1, pp. 484–498, ISSN 1094-6977.

Angelov, P., C. Xydeas, D. Filev (2004a). "On-line Identification of MIMO Evolving Takagi-Sugeno Fuzzy Models." *Proc. International Joint Conference on Neural Networks and International Conference on Fuzzy Systems, IJCNN-FUZZ-IEEE,* Budapest, Hungary, July 25–29, 2004, pp. 55–60, ISBN 0-7803-8354-0.

Angelov, P., J. Victor, A. Dourado, D. Filev (2004b). On-line Evolution of Takagi-Sugeno Fuzzy Models. *Proc. 2nd IFAC Workshop on Advanced Fuzzy/Neural Control, Oulu, Finland, September 16–17, 2004,* pp. 67–72.

Angelov, P., D. Filev (2005). "Simpl_eTS: A Simplified Method for Learning Evolving Takagi-Sugeno Fuzzy Models." *2005 IEEE Int. Conference on Fuzzy Systems, FUZZ-IEEE,* Reno, Nevada, May 22–25, 2005, pp. 1068–1073, ISSN 0-7803-9158-6/05.

Angelov, P. (2006). Machine Learning (Collaborative Systems) Patent ( WO2008053161, priority date—November 1, 2006; international filing date October 23, 2007).

Angelov, P., X. Zhou (2006). "Evolving Fuzzy Systems from Data Streams in Real-Time." *Proc. 2006 Int. Symposium on Evolving Fuzzy Syst.,* Ambleside, UK, September 7–9, 2006, IEEE Press, pp. 29–35, ISBN 0-7803-9719-3.

Angelov, P., X. Zhou, F. Klawonn (2007). "Evolving Fuzzy Rule-Based Classifiers." *2007 IEEE Int. Conference on Computational Intelligence Applications for Signal and Image Processing,* Honolulu, Hawaii, April 1–5, 2007, IEEE Press, pp. 220–225.

Angelov, P., E. Lughofer (2008). "A Comparative Study of Two Approaches for Data-Driven Design of Evolving Fuzzy Systems: eTS and FLEXFIS." *Int. Journal on General Systems,* Vol. 37, Issue 1, February 2008, pp. 45–67.

Angelov, P., X. Zhou (2008a). "On Line Learning Fuzzy Rule-based System Structure from Data Streams." *Proc. World Congress on Computational Intelligence, WCCI-2008,* Hong Kong, June 1–6, 2008, IEEE Press, pp. 915–922, ISBN 978-1-4244-1821-3/08.

Angelov, P., X. Zhou (2008b). "Evolving Fuzzy Rule-Based Classifiers from Data Streams." *IEEE Transactions on Fuzzy Systems,* Vol. 16 (6), Special Issue on Evolving Fuzzy Systems, pp. 1462–1475.

Angelov, P., R. Ramezani, X. Zhou (2008a). "Autonomous Novelty Detection and Object Tracking in Video Streams Using Evolving Clustering and Takagi-Sugeno Type Neuro-Fuzzy System." *World Congress on Computational Intelligence,* Hong Kong, June 1–6, 2008, pp. 1457–1464, ISBN 978-1-4244-1821-3/08.

Angelov, P., A. Kordon, X. Zhou (2008b). "Evolving Fuzzy Inferential Sensors for Process Industry." *Proc. 3rd International Workshop on Genetic and Evolving Fuzzy Systems,* Witten-Bomerholz, Germany, March 4–7, 2008, IEEE Press, pp. 41–46, ISBN 978-1-4244-1613-4.

Angelov, P., C. D. Bocaniala, C. Xydeas, C. Pattchet, D. Ansell, M. Everett, G. Leng (2008c). "A Passive Approach to Autonomous Collision Detection and Avoidance in Uninhabited Aerial Systems" *Proc. 2008 EUROSIM,* Emanuel College, Cambridge, UK, April 1–3, 2008, pp. 64–69.

Astrom, K. J., B. Wittenmark (1989). *Adaptive Control.* Reading, MA: Addison-Wesley.

Asuncion, A., D. Newman (2007). "UCI Machine Learning Repository", http://mlearn.ics.uci.edu/MLRepository.html.

Chiu, S. (1994). "Fuzzy Model Identification Based on Cluster Estimation," *Journal of Intelligent and Fuzzy Systems*, Vol. 2 (3), pp. 267–278.

Domingos, P., G. Hulten (2001). "Catching Up with the Data: Research Issues in Mining Data Streams." *Workshop on Research Issues in Data Mining and Knowledge Discovery,* Santa Barbara, CA, 2001.

Duda, R. O., P. E. Hart, D. G. Stork (2000). *Pattern Classification—Second Edition.* Chichester, West Sussex, England: Wiley-Interscience.

EC (2007). "NMP-2008-3.2-2—Self-Learning Production Systems." Work Programme on Nanosciences, Nanotechnologies, Materials and New Production Technologies, available online at ftp://ard.huji.ac.il/pub/251/NMP_Fiche_small__2008_02.pdf.

Elgammal, A., R. Suraiswami, D. Harwood, and L. Davis (2002). "Background and Foreground Modeling Using Non-parametric Kernel Density Estimation for Visual Surveillance KDE," *Proc. 2002 IEEE*, Vol. 90, No. 7, pp. 1151–1163.

Fortuna, L., S. Graziani, A. Rizzo, M. G. Xibilia (2007). "Soft Sensor for Monitoring and Control of Industrial Processes. In *Advances in Industrial Control Series* ( M. J. Grimble, M.A. Johnson, eds.). Berlin, Springer-Verlag.

Hastie, T., R. Tibshirani, and J. Friedman (2001). *The Elements of Statistical Learning: Data Mining, Inference and Prediction.* Heidelberg: Springer-Verlag.

Jang, J. S.R. (1993). "ANFIS: Adaptive Network-Based Fuzzy Inference Systems." *IEEE Trans. on SMC*, Vol. 23, No. 3, pp. 665–685.

Kalman, R. (1960). "A New Approach to Linear Filtering and Prediction Problems." *Trans. of the ASME—Journal of Basic Engineering*, Vol. 82, pp. 35–45.

Kasabov, N., Q. Song (2002). "DENFIS: Dynamic Evolving Neural-Fuzzy Inference System and Its Application for Time-Series Prediction." *IEEE Trans. on Fuzzy Systems*, Vol. 10, No. 2, pp. 144–154.

Kordon, A., G. Smits, A. Kalos, and E. Jordaan (2003). "Robust Soft Sensor Development Using Genetic Programming." In *Nature-Inspired Methods in Chemometrics* (R. Leardi, ed.). Amsterdam: Elsevier, pp. 69–108.

Li, W., H. H. Yue, S. Valle-Cervantes, and S. J. Qin (2000). "Recursive PCA for Adaptive Process Monitoring." *Journal of Process Control*, Vol. 10 (5), pp. 471–486.

Ljung, L. (1988). *System Identification, Theory for the User.* Englewood Cliffs, NJ: Prentice-Hall.

Lughofer, E., E. Klement (2005). "FLEXFIS: A Variant for Incremental Learning of Takagi-Sugeno Fuzzy Systems," *Proc. FUZZ-IEEE 2005,* Reno, Nevada, pp. 915–920.

Patchett, C., V. Sastri (2007). "Decision Architectures for Uninhabited Autonomous Aerial Systems." *EuroSim 2007,* Ljubljana, Slovenia, September 9-13, 2007.

Qin, S. J., H. Yue, and R. Dunia (1997). "Self-Validating Inferential Sensors with Application to Air Emission Monitoring," *Industrial Engineering Chemistry Research*, Vol. 36, pp. 1675–1685.

Roubos, J., M. Setnes, J. Abonyi (2003). "Learning Fuzzy Classification Rules from Data." *Information Sciences*, Vol. 150, pp. 77–93.

Silva, L., F. Gomide, R. R. Yager (2005). "Participatory Learning in Fuzzy Clustering." *Proc. 24th IEEE International Conference on Fuzzy Systems, FUZZ-IEEE,* Reno, Nevada, May 22–25, 2005, pp. 857–861, ISSN 0-7803-9158-6/05.

Smits, G., A. Kordon, E. Jordaan, C. Vladislavleva, M. Kotanchek (2006). "Variable Selection in Industrial Data Sets Using Pareto Genetic Programming," In *Genetic Programming Theory and Practice III.* (T. Yu, R. Riolo, B. Worzel, eds.). New York: Springer, pp. 79–92.

Sugeno, M., K. T. Kang (1988). "Structure Identification of Fuzzy Model." *Fuzzy Sets and Systems*, Vol. 28, No. 1, pp. 15–23.

Takagi, T., M. Sugeno (1985). "Fuzzy Identification of Systems and Its Applications to Modeling and Control." *IEEE Trans. on Systems, Man and Cybernetics*, Vol. 15, No. 1, pp. 116–132.

Wang, L., J. Mendel (1992). "Fuzzy Basis Functions, Universal Approximation and Orthogonal Least-Squares Learning." *IEEE Trans. on Neural Networks*, Vol. 3, No. 5, pp. 807–814.

Yager, R., D. Filev (1994). "Approximate Clustering via the Mountain Method." *IEEE Trans. on Systems and Cybernetics*, Vol. 24, No. 8, pp. 1279–1284.

Yen, J., L. Wang, C. W. Gillespie (1998). "Improving the Interpretability of TSK Fuzzy Models by Combining Global and Local Learning," *IEEE Trans. Fuzzy Syst.*, Vol. 6, pp. 530–537.

Zadeh L. A. (1975). "The Concept of a Linguistic Variable and Its Application to Approximate Reasoning: Parts I, II, and III," *Information Sciences*, Vol. 8, pp. 199–249, 301–357; vol. 9, pp. 43–80.

# 3

# FUZZY MODELS OF EVOLVABLE GRANULARITY

Witold Pedrycz

In real-world scenarios, we are often faced with nonstationary phenomena whose parameters or even structures change over time and/or space. The underlying systems evolve. Subsequent models of such phenomena, including fuzzy models, describing these phenomena have to evolve so that they stay relevant. Considering the inherent granularity present in fuzzy modeling, the objective of this study is to endow fuzzy models with an important feature of evolvable granularity—granularity whose level mirrors the varying dynamics and perception of the data/system. Depending on the architecture of the fuzzy models, the changes in granularity can be directly translated into the number of rules, local models, number of fuzzy neurons, and so on. As information granularity is positioned in the center of the design of such fuzzy models, we develop a concept of dynamic data granulation realized in the presence of incoming data organized in the form of *data snapshots*. For each of these snapshots we reveal a structure by running fuzzy clustering. The proposed algorithm of *adjustable Fuzzy C-Means* exhibits a number of useful features associated with the dynamic nature of the underlying data: (1) The number of clusters is adjusted from one data snapshot to another in order to capture the varying structure of patterns and its complexity, and (2) continuity between the consecutively discovered structures is retained—the clusters formed for a certain data snapshot are constructed as a result of evolving the clusters discovered in the predeceasing snapshot. The criterion used to control the level of information granularity

---

*Evolving Intelligent Systems: Methodology and Applications,* Edited by Plamen Angelov, Dimitar P. Filev, and Nikola Kasabov

throughout the process is guided by a reconstruction criterion that quantifies an error resulting from pattern granulation and de-granulation. The proposed design strategy being focused on the evolution of information granules implies further detailed developments of local models (e.g., those forming conclusions of the associated rule-based architecture).

## 3.1 INTRODUCTORY NOTES

In a number of scenarios of data analysis, we encounter collections of data being generated over time or over space. Banking data, supermarket data, weather recordings, sensor data, customer reports, customer segmentation, data streams and the alike—all of them are examples of data generated over either time or space. Models describing such phenomena need to be endowed with significant evolvable capabilities. In fuzzy modeling we have witnessed an emergence of a new category of fuzzy models that address the dynamics of the changes, referred to as *evolvable fuzzy models* [1, 2]. An outstanding feature of models that supports their *evolvability* comes with a model's modularity. In this study, to offer a sound focus we concentrate on rule-based architectures of the form

$$\text{If } A_i, \text{ then } f_i(x, \mathbf{a}_i) \tag{3.1}$$

where $A_i$ are information granules (fuzzy sets defined in the multivariable input space) and $f_i$ stand for the conclusion part. In essence, the form of the conclusion could be very diversified. We could encounter fuzzy sets, linear functions, polynomials, and neural networks. The vector of parameters of the conclusion part is denoted by $\mathbf{a}_i$. In particular, those could be the parameters of the polynomials or the connections of the neural network.

The construction of fuzzy rule-based models has been a topic of intensive design studies and we have witnessed a great deal of important developments [12, 13, 18, 19, 21]. Particularly discussed were various issues dealing with multiobjective developments of fuzzy models involving a satisfaction of criteria of accuracy and interpretability. The design of rule-based topologies is naturally split into two phases:

1. Formation of the condition parts of the rules
2. Development of the conclusions of the rules

The number of rules is directly associated with the granularity of the fuzzy model—a unique feature of the class of rule-based architectures. The higher the number of the rules, the higher the granularity of the model and the more details are captured. Quite commonly, the condition parts of the rules are constructed with the use of fuzzy clustering, which produces a collection of information granules—clusters formed in the input space. Various clustering techniques have been exploited as a generic design framework for the design of fuzzy sets and partition the input space. The development of the conclusion part is quite standard, as in many cases it boils down to the linear estimation problem with some eventual enhancements.

The fuzzy model evolves continuously by being faced with incoming data to capture the essence of the system that undergoes changes. Such changes could be either continuous or abrupt. In the case of continuous changes, the model may adapt to such modifications through the corresponding changes made to the parameters of the model. In situations where we encounter more radical changes, the structure of the model needs to be modified in a structural manner. In the context of fuzzy rule-based systems, the parametric changes can be quite directly translated into continuous updates of the parameters of the local models standing in the conclusions of the rules. In the case of linear models, we can see here a recurrent format of the updates of the parameters that is well documented in the literature. The structural changes are more sophisticated and their realization is associated with the varying number of the rules. In the presence of dynamically collected data, information granules move around, and become more refined or generalized—all of these effects are driven by the nature of the data being collected and their continuous changes.

In this study we will concentrate on this facet of evolvability of the fuzzy models. We develop a general strategy, using which the number of rules (viz. the number of fuzzy clusters) becomes modified dynamically (either reduced or extended) depending on the current dynamics of the data (phenomenon). Once the dynamic clustering offers this interesting opportunity of modifying the granularity of the model, in the developed strategy we also strive for the maintenance of *continuity* of the information granules, meaning that when revising the granularity of the model, we refine or generalize the clusters starting from the configuration of information granules encountered in the past. This algorithmic aspect is of particular relevance when dealing with iterative schemes of fuzzy clustering (e.g., Fuzzy C-Means, FCM) where the results are affected by the initial conditions (say randomly initialized partition matrix) the method starts with.

The chunks (sets) of data that we use to form information granules and describe their dynamics are referred to as *data snapshots*. In particular, the problem of segmentation of temporal data [3–5, 9] falls under the same rubric as one of the possible scenarios of dynamic clustering.

Fuzzy clustering [6, 12, 15, 18] can be regarded as a viable alternative to consider when dealing with dynamic data granulation; however, its generic version does require some essential changes to address the dynamics of the available data. Our ultimate objective is to revisit and redevelop Fuzzy C-Means (FCM) so that the generic algorithm could be efficiently used in the framework of dynamic data analysis. In particular, we will be interested in dynamically adjusting the number of clusters for each temporal segment of the data (the number could be decreased so some clusters could be merged; the number of clusters could be also increased, leading to the split of some clusters). Further, we consider a weighted distance function being optimized as a part of the FCM optimization (which leads to the selection of the relevant attributes-features).

In what follows, to illustrate the essence of the problem, we consider that the datasets are available at some data snapshots (say, temporal, spatial, or spatio-temporal segments $\Omega_1, \Omega_2, \ldots, \Omega_\Pi$) as illustrated in Figure 3.1. The clusters are formed for $\Omega_1$ and then, when the next snapshot becomes available ($\Omega_2$), the clustering is run again starting from some initial configuration that has been *inherited* from $\Omega_1$.

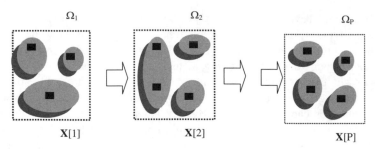

**Figure 3.1.** Data snapshots (Ω) of multivariable data **X**[1], **X**[2],…, **X**[P] and the ensuing clustering activities along with the adjustment of the number of clusters through their splitting or merging.

As illustrated in Figure 3.1, the clustering activities are focused on data positioned within the individual data snapshots. What is interesting is the way the clusters are built dynamically and carried over from one data snapshot to another. The computational facets of the problem associated directly with the FCM are outlined in more detail in Figure 3.2. Here, two aspects of dynamic behavior of the clusters are of interest. While the prototypes can migrate between data snapshots (which is a desirable effect as it contributes to the continuity of the overall process of data analysis), it is interesting to observe the changes in the number of the clusters themselves. The number of clusters is not fixed in advance but could fluctuate from one data snapshot to another depending on the structure of data themselves and the complexity of the underlying dynamics of the data (that is, the underlying phenomenon generating the data).

Referring to Figure 3.2, let us elaborate in more detail on the process of clustering. We start with the first data snapshot, run the FCM on the data present there by producing a collection of the prototypes $v_1[1]$, $v_2[1]$, …, $v_c[1]$ (the number in the square bracket denotes that those prototypes are built on the basis of the data coming from the first segment **X**[1]). The number of clusters is determined by the acceptable level of the predetermined optimization criterion. We elaborate on the computational details later on. When running the FCM on the second data snapshot **X**[2], we proceed with the

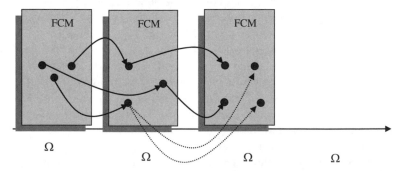

**Figure 3.2.** The concept of dynamic clustering—progression of the FCM constructs (prototypes and partition matrixes) in successive data snapshots and dynamic adjustments of the number of the clusters (prototypes) through cluster merging and cluster split.

prototypes that were formed for $\mathbf{X}[1]$ and use them as the starting point when running the FCM for $\mathbf{X}[2]$. Inevitably, when iterating FCM, the prototypes change their location as a result of revealing the topology of the actually processed data. Once done, it could well be that a certain clustering quality indicator (performance index) produced there could exceed some required threshold or could assume values that are far lower than this threshold. In both cases, the number of clusters needs to be dynamically adjusted. In the first case, it must be increased—we could do that by splitting the most heterogeneous (diversified) cluster. In the second case, the number of clusters could be too high (capturing too many unnecessary details) and some merging process could be of interest.

There have been some developments along the line of dynamic fuzzy clustering. The reader may refer to [7] as this paper offers a certain way of adjusting the granularity of findings through successive modifications of the number of clusters. Some other studies have been reported in [8, 9] predominantly in the setting of data segmentation and dynamic clustering, in which data streams dealt with involved patterns whose processing must be realized in order of their appearance.

The problem of adjustable fuzzy clustering shares some similarities with a suite of algorithms known as *data stream mining* and *time series clustering* [3, 14, 20]; however, there are also some evident differences. In terms of similarities, we are concerned with data that are accumulated successively and whose processing (i.e., structure determination) is carried out in an incremental fashion. There are several meaningful differences. First, in time series we are concerned with the factor of time, in this study the data could be arranged timewise (as a time sequence), but this is one of the possibilities exercised in the proposed approach. Second, the data within a scope of a data snapshot are not affected by the time variable but are treated en bloc.

The organization of the study is the following. Given the formulation of the problem already covered in this section, we concentrate on the fundamental design aspects, namely (1) splitting and merging criteria, (2) assessment of quality of clusters that could be directly used when controlling the dynamics of the clusters and deciding on the change of the number of clusters themselves, and (3) optimization capabilities of fuzzy clustering (FCM), which could be exploited upfront when running the algorithm.

## 3.2  FUZZY C-MEANS AS AN OPTIMIZATION ENVIRONMENT FOR THE DESIGN OF INFORMATION GRANULES

Fuzzy C-Means (FCM) [6, 16, 17] is one of the commonly encountered algorithms being used in the formation of information granules—fuzzy sets [22]. The conceptual aspects are well reported in the literature. The method comes with a wealth of refinements and algorithmic investigations. There are numerous case studies. We definitely do not intend to reiterate all of those; however, we believe that there are two points worth stressing. The first one concerns the parametric flexibility of the algorithm (which helps induce geometry of the clusters formed in this manner). The second one elaborates on the issue of quality of clusters and brings forward a concept of the reconstructability criterion, using which we assess a way of moving from numeric data to information granules (referring to it as *granulation*) and back to numeric quantities (*de-granulation*).

In this section, to avoid notational clutter, we abstract from the concept of data snapshots; we will consider a data set $\mathbf{X} = \{\mathbf{x}_1, \mathbf{x}_2, \ldots \mathbf{x}_N\}$ where $\mathbf{x}_k$ is defined in the $n$-dimensional space of real numbers and $c$ stands for the number of clusters. As a distance function $\|.\|$, we consider a weighted Euclidean distance of the form $\sum_{j=1}^{n} \dfrac{(a_i - b_j)^2}{\sigma_j^2}$, where $\sigma_j$ is a standard deviation of the $j$th variable (feature) and $\mathbf{a}$ and $\mathbf{b}$ are n-dimensional vectors of real numbers.

### 3.2.1 Fuzzification Coefficient as an Optimization Mechanism of the FCM

The objective function minimized in the FCM algorithm is a sum of distances of patterns $\mathbf{x}_1, \mathbf{x}_2, \ldots, \mathbf{x}_N$ from the prototypes $\mathbf{v}_1, \mathbf{v}_2, \ldots, \mathbf{v}_c$:

$$Q = \sum_{i=1}^{c} \sum_{k=1}^{N} u_{ik}^{m} \|\mathbf{x}_k - \mathbf{v}_i\|^2 \qquad (3.2)$$

where $c$ is the number of the clusters. The optimization is realized with respect to the structure, that is, the prototypes and the partition matrix $U = [u_{ik}]$. The fuzzification coefficient $(m)$ that assumes values greater than 1 implies directly the resulting geometry of the fuzzy clusters. Values close to 1 (say 1.05) imply a Boolean nature of the clusters, so most of the entries of the partition matrix are practically equal to 0 or 1.

Typically, as commonly shows up in the literature, the fuzzification coefficient $(m)$ assumes a value of 2.0. In this case, the membership functions resemble a Gaussian membership function. For higher values of $m$, say 3 or higher, the membership functions start to become quite "spikey," with the membership grade equal to 1 for the prototype, and then rapidly decrease to zero. The average membership for each cluster is equal to $1/c$. By selecting the value of $m$ we can control the shape of the membership functions and select the most suitable one in light of some predefined criterion.

### 3.2.2 Reconstruction Criterion in the Assessment of Quality of Clusters

The number of clusters is another important design feature of the clustering algorithm. There have been a number of *cluster validity indexes* [10, 11], which are geared to assess the most "suitable" number of clusters that are supposed to correspond with the "true" structure in the data. The inherent problem with them is that quite often one gets several conflicting suggestions depending on which cluster validity index has been selected. In this study, we follow a different path, which could be referred to as a *granulation–de-granulation strategy* [17, 18]. In essence, once the information granules have been formed by the FCM, we use the prototypes to represent each pattern in the form of information granules by computing the corresponding membership degrees. At the next step, we complete a de-granulation, which is to estimate the pattern on the basis of the prototypes and the membership degrees. Ideally, we would expect that the result of such de-granulation should return the original pattern. While this is quite unlikely, we may consider the distance between the original pattern and its de-granulated version to constitute a viable measure of quality of obtained reconstruction. Let us move to the technical details, which provide some required formal description of the strategy. Denote by $\mathbf{X}_i$ the data whose membership in the $i$th cluster is the highest, that is,

$$\mathbf{X}_i = \{\mathbf{x}_k \in \mathbf{R} | i = \arg_k \max u_k(\mathbf{x})\} \tag{3.3}$$

The reconstruction error for the $i$th cluster is computed as the following sum of distances between $\mathbf{x}_k$ and its de-granulated version $\hat{\mathbf{x}}_k$:

$$V_i = \sum_{\mathbf{x}_k \in \mathbf{X}_i} \|\mathbf{x}_k - \hat{\mathbf{x}}_k\|^2 \tag{3.4}$$

where

$$\hat{\mathbf{x}}_k = \frac{\sum_{i=1}^{c} u_{ik}^m \mathbf{v}_i}{\sum_{i=1}^{c} u_{ik}^m} \tag{3.5}$$

The maximal value of $V_i$, $V_{\max} = \max_i V_i$, can serve as a suitable measure describing the reconstructibility aspects provided by the information granules. By varying the number of the clusters ($c$) we can affect the values of $V_i$ and in this way focus on selecting the most suitable structure in the data set.

## 3.3 DYNAMIC FORMATION OF FUZZY CLUSTERS—SPLITTING AND MERGING MECHANISMS

In what follows, we discuss the mechanisms of splitting and merging clusters. Before moving into details, we note that the objective function minimized by the FCM for the first data snapshot exploits the standard sum of distances

$$Q[1] = \sum_{i=1}^{c[1]} \sum_{\mathbf{x}_k \in \mathbf{X}[1]} u_{ik}^m \|\mathbf{x}_k - \mathbf{v}_i[1]\|^2 \tag{3.6}$$

(here $Q[1]$ concerns the first data snapshot). Let us also note that the number of clusters, say $c[1]$, may be selected on the basis of the assumed threshold level $V_{\max}$. For the first data snapshot, we choose such $c[1]$ for which the reconstruction error does exceed some predefined threshold level, that is, $V_{\max} < \varepsilon$; with the value of $\varepsilon$, $\varepsilon > 0$ is given in advance. Here we may adjust the number of the clusters so that the required inequality is satisfied. The choice of the threshold level can be realized by observing how much the reconstructability criterion is affected by the number of clusters; it might well be that $V$ exhibits a visible kneelike relationship when varying the number of clusters. We select the minimal value at $c$ at which is observed a radical reduction in the values of the performance index under consideration. Subsequently, this particular value of $\varepsilon$ becomes associated with the corresponding value of $V$. With respect to the number of clusters, one may consider the use of any of the *cluster validity indexes* (partition coefficient, partition entropy, etc.), which can navigate our search for the number of clusters, that is, the granularity of findings. A certain drawback associated with these validity indexes is that each of them might eventually point at a different number of clusters (which might be quite confusing), or some indexes could exhibit a fairly monotonic character that prevents us from using them as a reliable indicator of the preferred level of granularity of the structure.

### 3.3.1 Splitting Mechanism of the Clusters

If the reconstruction criterion of the clustering completed for some data snapshot does not meet the assumed requirement by exceeding the assumed threshold $\varepsilon$, then some clusters need to be split. Intuitively, this split could involve the cluster characterized by the highest level of variability, that is, the one for which the index $V_i$ attains a maximum among all the clusters. Let this cluster's index be denoted by $i_0$. The split is realized by conditional clustering [15] of the data falling under the realm of the elements belonging to the $i_0$-th cluster, that is, $\mathbf{X}_{i_0}$. Denote the set of indexes of these patterns by $\mathbf{I}_0$. The formulation of the problem is given in the form

$$\min \sum_{i=1}^{2} \sum_{k \in I_0} f_{ik}^{m} \|\mathbf{x}_k - \mathbf{z}_i\|^2 \tag{3.7}$$

subject to the constraint

$$\sum_{j=1}^{2} f_{jk} = u_{i_0 k} \tag{3.8}$$

In essence, by minimizing (3.6) we invoke a computing process in which we split the $i_0$-th cluster into two clusters, maintaining a balance of the membership grades of the original cluster. Here $\mathbf{z}_i$ are the prototypes and $F = [f_{ik}]$ denotes a partition matrix that satisfies constraint (3.7), meaning that the split is driven by the data and membership grades of the most diversified cluster. The term *conditional clustering* comes from the fact that we require that the resulting membership degrees $f_{ik}$ are distributed according to the membership values available for the cluster to be split. The detailed calculations of the partition matrix $F$ and the two prototypes $\mathbf{z}_1$ and $\mathbf{z}_2$ are carried out iteratively according to the two formulas

$$f_{ik} = \frac{u_{i_0 k}}{\sum_{j=1}^{2} \left( \dfrac{\|\mathbf{x}_k - \mathbf{z}_i\|}{\|\mathbf{x}_k - \mathbf{z}_j\|} \right)^{1/(m-1)}} \tag{3.9}$$

and

$$\mathbf{z}_i = \frac{\sum_{k \in I_0} f_{ik}^m \mathbf{x}_k}{\sum_{k \in I_0} f_{ik}^m}$$

$$i = 1, 2; \mathbf{x}_k \in \mathbf{X}_{i_0} \tag{3.10}$$

The detailed derivations of these expressions are presented in [15].

The general tendency is that with more clusters, the values of the reconstruction criterion are getting lower. If required, further splits of the clusters could be completed until the point the reconstruction criterion has been satisfied.

### 3.3.2 Merging Mechanism of the Clusters

If the objective function for the number of the clusters is lower than the predefined level $\varepsilon$, then the number of the clusters could be reduced, meaning that some original clusters could be combined together (merged). The way of doing that would be to merge two prototypes that are the closest to each other. Consider that these two are indexed by $s$ and $l$, that is $\mathbf{v}_s$ and $\mathbf{v}_l$. The new prototype $\mathbf{v}^\sim$ results from the minimization of the following expression with respect to it; the new prototype $\mathbf{v}^\sim$ results from the minimization of the following performance index:

$$Q = \sum_{k=1}^{N} (u_{sk} + u_{lk})^m \|\mathbf{x}_k - \mathbf{v}^\sim\|^2 \to \text{Min } Q \text{ with respect to } \mathbf{v}^\sim \tag{3.11}$$

If for this reduced number of clusters the resulting reconstruction criterion is still lower than the critical value, we can move on with another reduction of the number of the prototypes. The process could be repeated by reducing the number of the clusters by one.

Let us rewrite the performance index (3.11) in a coordinate-wise fashion:

$$Q = \sum_{k=1}^{N} (u_{sk} + u_{lk})^m \|\mathbf{x}_k - \mathbf{v}^\sim\|^2 = \sum_{k=1}^{N} \sum_{j=1}^{n} (u_{sk} + u_{lk})^m (x_{kj} - v_j^\sim)^2 / s_j^2 \tag{3.12}$$

We make the derivative of $Q$ equal to zero, $\nabla_{v^\sim} Q = \mathbf{0}$, and this leads to the new prototype

$$\mathbf{v}^\sim = \frac{\sum_{k=1}^{N} (u_{sk} + u_{lk})^m \mathbf{x}_k}{\sum_{k=1}^{N} (u_{sk} + u_{lk})^m} \tag{3.13}$$

### 3.3.3 Processing Interaction between Results of Processing of Data Slices

Given the underlying mechanisms of merging and splitting information granules, an overall flow of computing is displayed in Figure 3.3.

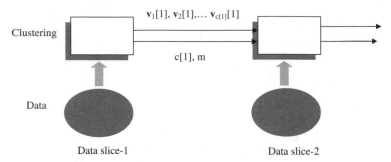

**Figure 3.3.** An overall flow of processing. Note that the processing leads to a more abstract description of data slices represented in the form of information granules.

In the structure shown here, we have underlined the successive nature of processing where the results produced at one data slice are made available at the consecutive slice, where the most generic communication is realized in terms of the collection of the prototypes $\{\mathbf{v}_i[ii]\}$ and the number of the clusters. At the initial data slice, we determine the optimal value of the fuzzification coefficient ($m$) whose value is afterward kept unchanged when moving through consecutive data slices. The choice of the threshold level $\varepsilon$ used in conjunction with the reconstruction criterion is also made when dealing with the first data slice. It is worth noting that at this point we engage the user to convey his or her preferences, which are used in further exploitation of data forming in successive data slices.

## 3.4 CHARACTERIZATION OF STRUCTURAL DYNAMICS OF THE FAMILIES OF CLUSTERS

The structure of clusters changes from one data slice to another. It is of interest to characterize these changes at some general level so we could learn about the dynamics of the structural changes of the evolvable model. There are several possible alternatives we can consider in describing the evolvable structure.

### 3.4.1 Granularity of Structure

The number of clusters $c[1]$, $c[2]$, ... reported in the consecutive data slices can be viewed as the simplest and most concise structural characteristics one could think of. The increasing sequence of these numbers is indicative of the growing structural complexity (which manifests in the increasing number of the clusters one has to construct to deal with it). This does not tell us, however, at all about the relationships between the prototypes produced in two neighboring data slices.

### 3.4.2 Relationships between Information Granules

To capture more detailed structural relationships, we take a different detailed path whose crux is the following. Given the prototype $\mathbf{v}_i[ii + 1]$, we express it in terms of the

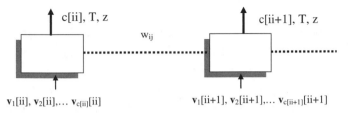

**Figure 3.4.** Expressing relationships between information granules through describing information granules in terms of the granules obtained for the previous data slice.

prototypes $v_j[ii]$ available at the $ii$th data snapshot. More specifically, we obtain degrees of membership of the $i$th prototype expressed by $v_j[ii]$, which are determined in a standard manner:

$$w_{ik} = \frac{1}{\sum_{j=1}^{c[ii]} \left( \frac{||v_i[ii+1]-v_k[ii]||}{|v_i[ii+1]-v_j[ii]|} \right)^{2/(m-1)}} \tag{3.14}$$

where $i = 1, 2, \ldots, c[ii + 1]$ and $k = 1, 2, \ldots, c[ii]$. This representation is schematically captured in Figure 3.4.

If all these values are either close to 0.0 or close to 1.0, this becomes indicative of a sound representation of the prototypes in terms of the structure we have revealed so far. On the other hand, if the values of $w_i$ tend to be close to $1/c[ii]$, we may talk about a high level of uncertainty when expressing the prototypes in the language of the already-available structure. More formally, we can quantify the structural diversity by introducing a functional $\varphi$ defined on the set of membership degrees such that $\varphi(0) = \varphi(1) = 0$, which is increasing over $[0,1/c[ii])$, attains the maximal value at $1/c[ii]$, and then monotonically decreases to zero. The sum of the following form

$$T = \sum_{i=1}^{c[ii+1]} \varphi(w_i) \tag{3.15}$$

serves as a concise indicator of the uncertainty of structural differences observed from one data slice to another.

The collection of connections $[w_{ij}]$ formed by the elements computed by (3.14) can be used to construct a relational model of structural relationships. Consider the $i$th element (prototype) observed in the $(ii + 1)$th data slice. It is described by the prototypes present in the $ii$th data slice whose activation levels are $w_{i1}, w_{i2}, \ldots, w_{ic[i]}$. The same occurs for any other prototype available in the $(ii + 1)$th data slice. This gives rise to the following collection of input–output pairs of data:

1st prototype $\quad y(1) = [w_{11}w_{12}\ldots w_{1c[ii]}] \qquad\qquad z(1) = [1\,0\,0\,0\ldots.0]$
2nd prototype $\quad y(2) = [w_{21}w_{22}\ldots w_{2c[ii]}] \qquad\qquad z(1) = [0\,1\,0\,0\ldots.0]$
$c[ii+1]$ prototype $\quad y(c[ii+1]) = [w_{c[ii+1]1}\,w_{c[ii+1]2}\ldots w_{c[ii+1]c[ii]}] \quad z(c[ii+1]) = [0\,0\,0\,0\ldots.1]$

Given this structure of data, we arrive at the estimation problem in which the output is expressed by means of the activation levels $w_{ij}$. In general, we can formalize the relationship as a certain set of fuzzy relational equations

$$\mathbf{z}(k) = \mathbf{y}(k) \bullet R$$

$k = 1, 2, \ldots, c[ii + 1]$, where $\bullet$ stands for a certain relational operator, such as max-min, min-max, or their generalized versions of max-$t$ and min-$s$ with $t$ and $s$ being the corresponding $t$-norm or $t$-conorm. The fuzzy relation $R$ is to be determined and one could consider using one of the estimation methods (which might lead to exact or approximate solutions to the problem). One can also describe the $i$th prototype in terms of the prototypes obtained for the $ii$th data slice by considering the following combination:

$$\hat{\mathbf{v}}_i[ii+1] = \sum_{j=1}^{c[ii]} w_{ij}^m \mathbf{v}_j[ii] \qquad (3.16)$$

The quality of reconstruction (or expressability) of the prototypes in consecutive data slices can be quantified in terms of the global error

$$\sum_{i=1}^{c\{ii+1\}} \|\hat{\mathbf{v}}_i[ii+1] - \mathbf{v}_i[ii+1]\|^2 \qquad (3.17)$$

This error tells us about the ability of compatibility of the prototypes in successive data slices.

Altogether we can envision the three measures of structural relationships and their quality, that is, (1) number of clusters, (2) specificity (3.15), and (3) reconstructability (3.17).

## 3.5 EXPERIMENTAL STUDIES

In what follows, we illustrate the functionality of the dynamic clustering by considering some synthetic two-dimensional data. The series of synthetic two-dimensional data is composed of a mixture of Gaussian distributions where the number of distributions as well as their location varies from one data set to another. We note that the dynamics of the clusters from data to data vary (Figure 3.5). In the first case, we see three well-delineated clusters. In the second snapshot of data, in Figure 3.5b, we see that the clusters evolve into three groups. The number of data in each data snapshot is different; we have 450, 850, and 1,450 patterns, respectively.

The starting phase of dynamic clustering relies on the use of the first data snapshot, using which we set up the parameters of the clusters. Given the structure of data, we consider $c = 3$ clusters as being representative of the structure visible in this data snapshot. The optimization involves the choice of the value of the fuzzification coefficient ($m$). Here we sweep through a range of possible values of the coefficient

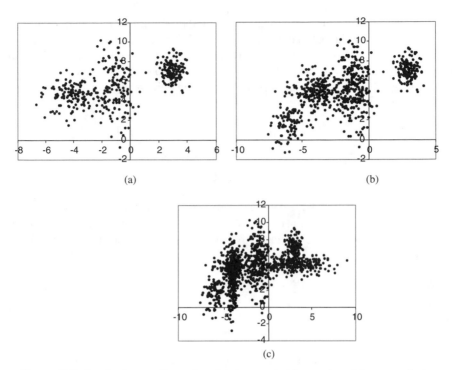

Figure 3.5. Synthetic two-dimensional data reported in a series of four snapshots.

by starting from 1.1 (in which case the partition matrix resembles the Boolean one where almost all of its entries are close to 0 or 1) and increasing the values to 3.0, where the average membership in each cluster is getting close to $1/c$. The plot of the resulting reconstruction criterion (where we report the highest value of this criterion obtained for all clusters) is included in Figure 3.6.

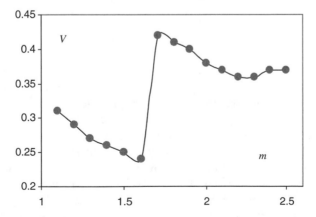

Figure 3.6. The values of the reconstruction criterion as a function of fuzzification coefficient ($m$).

This relationship exhibits a strongly delineated minimum for the values of $m$ around 1.5; more precisely, the optimal value is equal to 1.6. In the clustering of the next data snapshots we will be using this particular value of the fuzzification coefficient. The value of the reconstruction criterion is equal to 0.2411. The prototypes obtained after running the FCM algorithm for 40 iterations (with the starting point being a randomly initialized partition matrix) are as follows:

$$\mathbf{v}_1 = [2.35 \; 7.17]$$
$$\mathbf{v}_2 = [-1.63 \; 3.46]$$
$$\mathbf{v}_3 = [-3.63 \; 5.11]$$

which, when compared with the data in Figure 3.5a, reflects the location of the clusters. Use these prototypes as an initial condition for clustering the second data snapshot while running the method for the same number of clusters as before (3.3). The obtained prototypes are now equal to

$$\mathbf{v}_1 = [2.44 \; 7.13]$$
$$\mathbf{v}_2 = [-2.57 \; 5.06]$$
$$\mathbf{v}_3 = [-5.69 \; 1.53]$$

The value of the reconstruction criterion obtained for these clusters equal to 0.362 exceeded the threshold value (viz. the one obtained for the starting phase), which triggered the process of splitting the cluster with the highest value of the reconstruction criterion. Here it is the second cluster identified in this way. After splitting this cluster, we lowered the value of the reconstruction criterion to 0.199, which terminated further splitting. The new prototypes obtained as a result of the split are

$$\mathbf{v}_1 = [2.44 \; 7.13]$$
$$\mathbf{v}_2 = [-5.69 \; 1.53]$$
$$\mathbf{v}_3 = [-3.05 \; 5.88]$$
$$\mathbf{v}_4 = [-1.97 \; 4.19]$$

Proceeding with the four clusters and handling clustering of the next data snapshot we continue with four clusters that give rise to the reconstruction criterion with the value below the threshold value. This triggers an attempt to merge the two closest clusters; however, as a result of this the reconstruction criterion exceeds the threshold level, which in turn causes the merge of these two clusters to be revoked.

The dynamics of the clusters formed in successive data snapshots—with the groups illustrated in Figure 3.7—is well captured by the results of the algorithm.

The second data snapshot is more complex as far as its structure is concerned and this led to the increased number of clusters to capture the topology of the data. The refinement of the second cluster ($\mathbf{v}_2$) could have been expected as we see more data in the neighboring regions whose structure required two more detailed clusters. The next data

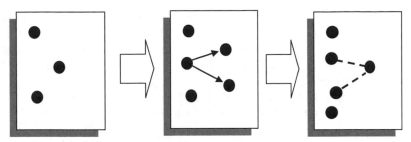

**Figure 3.7.** The dynamics of the clusters formed in consecutive data snapshots; dotted lines indicate that the merging of the clusters has been revoked.

snapshot shows the same number of clusters as before; however, they look far more condensed and because of their compactness we witness the attempt to merge the clusters.

## 3.6 CONCLUSION

In this study, we have introduced the concept of fuzzy dynamic clustering. Its outstanding features include: (1) The structure is constructed on the basis of data snapshots that capture the data falling within some time limits, and reflect physical distribution of data collection, and (2) there is a granular continuity of the clustering process in the sense that the clusters obtained for one data snapshot are used as the starting point of clustering realized for the next snapshot. In this sense, we can monitor changes (evolution) of the clusters from one data snapshot to another and record successive splits or mergers of the corresponding information granules. The dynamic fuzzy clustering discussed here is different from dynamic fuzzy segmentation and clustering in the sense that in the data falling within a given data snapshot we do not consider the factor of time.

The model of dynamic clustering presented in this study could be also used as a fundamental machinery to build *dynamic* fuzzy models, that is, the models in which we encounter a variable and adjustable level of granularity of the local models—an effect that is of particular relevance in fuzzy rule-based models [12, 13, 19, 21]. Here a fuzzy model—a collection of rules—is formed for each data snapshot and the individual rules evolve, in terms of both their conditions and the conclusion parts as well as the overall number of rules.

## 3.7 ACKNOWLEDGMENTS

Support from the Natural Sciences and Engineering Research Council of Canada (NSERC) and Canada Research Chair (CRC) is gratefully acknowledged.

## 3.8 REFERENCES

1. P. Angelov, "A Fuzzy Controller with Evolving Structure," *Information Sciences*, 161, 1–2, 2004, 21–35.

2. P. Angelov, "An Approach for Fuzzy Rule-Base Adaptation Using On-line Clustering," *International Journal of Approximate Reasoning*, 35, 3, 2004, 275–289.

3. B. Babcock, S. Babu, M. Datar, R. Motwani, J. Widom, "Models and Issues in Data Stream Systems." Proc. of 21st *ACM Symposium on Principles of Database Systems (PODS 2002)*, Madison, Wisconsin, 2002, 30–45.

4. S. Bandyopadhyay, C. Giannella, U. Maulik, H. Kargupta, K. Liu, S. Datta, "Clustering Distributed Data Streams in Peer-to-Peer Environments," *Information Sciences*, 176, 2006, 1952–1985.

5. J. Beringer, E. Hullermeier, "Online Clustering of Parallel Data Streams," *Data & Knowledge Engineering*, 58, 2006, 180–204.

6. J. C. Bezdek, *Pattern Recognition with Fuzzy Objective Function Algorithms*. New York: Plenum Press, 1981.

7. F. Crespo, R. Weber, "A Methodology for Dynamic Data Mining Based on Fuzzy Clustering," *Fuzzy Sets & Systems*, 150, 2005, 267–284.

8. S. Guha, A. Meyerson, N. Mishra, R. Motwani, "Clustering Data Streams: Theory and Practice." *IEEE Trans. on Knowledge and Data Engineering*, 15, 2003, 515–528.

9. Y. P. Huang, C. C. Hsu, S. H. Wang, "Pattern Recognition in Time Series Database: A Case Study, on Financial Database," *Expert Systems with Applications*, 33, 2007, 199–205.

10. A. K. Jain, R. C. Dubes, *Algorithms for Clustering Data*. Englewood Cliffs, NJ: Prentice-Hall, 1988.

11. A. Jain, M. Murt, P. Flynn, "Data Clustering: A Review," *ACM Computing Surveys*, 31, 1999, 264–323.

12. S. Mitra, Y. Hayashi, "Neuro-Fuzzy Rule Generation: Survey in Soft Computing Framework." *IEEE Trans. on Neural Networks*, 11, 3, 2000, 748–768.

13. C. Molina, L. Rodríguez-Ariza, D. Sánchez, M. Amparo Vila, "A New Fuzzy Multidimensional Model." *IEEE Trans. on Fuzzy Systems*, 14, 6, 2006, 897–912.

14. N. H. Park, W. S. Lee, "Cell Trees: An Adaptive Synopsis Structure for Clustering Multidimensional On-line Data Streams," *Data & Knowledge Engineering*, 63, 2007, 528–549.

15. W. Pedrycz, "Conditional Fuzzy Clustering in the Design Of Radial Basis Function Neural Networks." *IEEE Trans. on Neural Networks*, 9, 1998, 601–612.

16. W. Pedrycz, *Knowledge-Based Clustering: From Data to Information Granules*. Hoboken, NJ: John Wiley & Sons, 2005.

17. W. Pedrycz, K. Hirota, "Fuzzy Vector Quantization with the Particle Swarm Optimization: A Study in Fuzzy Granulation–Degranulation Information Processing," *Signal Processing*, 87, 2007, 2061–2074.

18. W. Pedrycz, F. Gomide, *Fuzzy Systems Engineering*. Hoboken, NJ: John Wiley & Sons, 2007.

19. T. Takagi, M. Sugeno, "Fuzzy Identification of Systems and Its Application to Modelling and Control." *IEEE Trans. on Systems, Man, and Cybernetics*, 15, 1985, 116–132.

20. D. Tasoulis, M. Vrahatis, "Unsupervised Clustering on Dynamic Databases," *Pattern Recognition Letters*, 26, 13, 2005, 2116–2127.

21. J. Yen, L. Wang, C. Gillespie, "Improving the Interpretability of TSK Fuzzy Models by Combining Global Learning and Local Learning." *IEEE Trans. Fuzzy Systems*, 6, 4, 1998, 530–537.

22. L. A. Zadeh, Towards a Theory of Fuzzy Information Granulation and Its Centrality in Human Reasoning and Fuzzy Logic," *Fuzzy Sets and Systems*, 90, 1997, 111–117.

# 4

# EVOLVING FUZZY MODELING USING PARTICIPATORY LEARNING

E. Lima, M. Hell, R. Ballini, F. Gomide

**Abstract:** This chapter introduces an approach to developing evolving fuzzy rule-based models using participatory learning. *Participatory learning* assumes that learning and beliefs about a system depend on what the learning mechanism knows about the system itself. Participatory learning naturally augments clustering and gives effective unsupervised fuzzy clustering algorithms for online, real-time domains and applications. Clustering is an essential step to construct evolving fuzzy models and plays a key role in modeling performance and model quality. Recursive approach to estimate the consequent parameters of the fuzzy rules for online modeling is emphasized. Experiments with the classic *Box & Jenkins benchmark* is conducted to compare the performance of the evolving participatory learning with the evolving fuzzy systems modeling approach and alternative fuzzy modeling methods. The experiments attest the efficiency of the evolving participatory learning to handle the benchmark problem. The evolving participatory learning method is also used to forecast the average hourly load of an electricity generating plant and to compare with the evolving fuzzy systems modeling using actual data. The results confirm the potential of the evolving fuzzy participatory method to solve real-world modeling problems.

*Evolving Intelligent Systems: Methodology and Applications,* Edited by Plamen Angelov, Dimitar P. Filev, and Nikola Kasabov

## 4.1 INTRODUCTION

Fuzzy rule-based models are a highly modular and easily expandable form of fuzzy models. They support the principle of locality and the distributed nature of modeling as each rule can be viewed as a local descriptor of a system regime [25]. Fuzzy rule-based models effectively combine and interpolate different operating regimes to describe general behavior [15]. One of the major difficulties in developing rule-based models is the proper, adequate, and expedient generation of their structure, especially the rule base, rule semantics, membership functions, and parameters.

A trend until the early 1990s was to rely on existing expert knowledge and to tune fuzzy membership function parameters using gradient-based methods or genetic algorithms (GAs) using problem-specific data [1]. During the late 1990s, data-driven rule/ knowledge extraction methods were intensively investigated and developed [5, 13, 14]. Data-driven methods attempt to identify model structure and model parameters based on data and uses expert knowledge as complementary information. The main techniques used during this period include clustering, linear least squares, and nonlinear optimization to fine tune rule antecedent and consequent membership function parameters [13, 14]. As the modeling complexity increases, however, the information required to develop fuzzy rule bases may not be easily available and experts may be unable to extract all relevant knowledge. Genetic fuzzy systems appeared during the past few years as one of the few techniques capable of developing complex fuzzy system models [24]. Genetic fuzzy systems constitute a powerful approach to the design of fuzzy models. Basically, these are fuzzy systems augmented by learning mechanisms based on genetic algorithms. Essentially, genetic fuzzy systems approaches use evolutionary techniques to adjust the components of fuzzy models. Evaluation of complete solutions is one of the features of traditional evolutionary approaches.

In contrast with evolutionary approaches, incremental or growing algorithms developed local models using heuristic search for rule antecedents and corresponding rule consequents optimized by local weighted least-squares technique [11, 23].

Fuzzy neural networks with evolving structures have been developed as an alternative to fuzzy rule-based modeling [22]. This modeling approach constitutes evolving connectionist systems whose structure and functionality are continuously adapted using incoming information [17]. They adopt different mechanisms for network updating, but basically parameter learning and self-organization are based on clustering and error of previous steps. Evolving connectionist systems learn local models from data using clustering and a local output function for each cluster [6].

The concept of evolving fuzzy systems introduced the idea of gradual self-organization and parameter learning in fuzzy rule-based models [2]. Evolving fuzzy systems uses information streams to continuously adapt the structure and functionality of fuzzy rule-based models. The basic learning mechanisms rely on online clustering and parameter estimation using least squares algorithms. Online clustering is based on the idea of data potential or data density. The evolving mechanism ensures greater generality of the structural changes because rules are able to describe a number of data samples. Evolving fuzzy rule-based models include mechanisms for rule modification to replace a less informative rule with a more informative one [2]. Overall, evolution guarantees gradual change of the rule-base structure inheriting structural information. The idea of parameter adaptation of rules antecedent and consequent is similar in the framework of evolving connectionist systems [19] and evolving Takagi-Sugeno (eTS) models and their variations [2–4]. In particular, the eTS model is a functional fuzzy model in Takagi-Sugeno form whose rule base and parameters continually evolve by adding new rules with higher summarization power and modifying existing rules and parameters to match current knowledge.

The original eTS approach is rooted in a recursive evaluation of the information potential to cluster new data and the focal points of the fuzzy rules [7]. The eTS algorithm continuously evaluates the relationship between potentials and dynamically updates the number of rules and their antecedent parameters. This process is followed by a recursive least-squares procedure to update the rule consequent parameters. A simplified version of the eTS learning algorithm [4] reduces the complexity of the original eTS. The *simpl_eTS* replaces the notion of information potential with the concept of scatter and provides a similar but computationally more effective algorithm. Simpl_eTS uses Cauchy membership functions, instead of Gaussians, and the notion of *rules/clusters age* to improve computational and modeling performance.

This chapter suggests a distinct approach, namely, evolving fuzzy participatory learning (ePL) to develop evolving fuzzy rule-based models. The approach joins the concept of participatory learning (PL) [31] with the evolving fuzzy modeling idea [2, 3]. In evolving systems the PL concept is viewed as an unsupervised clustering algorithm [28] and is a natural candidate to find rule-base structures in evolving fuzzy modeling. Here we focus on functional fuzzy (TS) models. Similar to eTS and simpl_eTS, structure identification and self-organization in ePL means estimation of the focal points of the rules, the antecedent parameters, except that ePL uses participatory learning fuzzy clustering instead of scattering, density, or information potential. With the antecedent parameters fixed, the remaining TS model parameters can be found using least-squares methods [13]. Instead of using data potential as in eTS, the evolving fuzzy participatory learning captures the rule-base structure at each step using convex combinations of new data samples and the closest cluster center, the focal point of a rule. Afterward, the rule-base structure is updated and, similarly to eTS and simpl_eTS, the parameters of the rule consequents are computed using the recursive least-squares algorithm.

Computational experiments with the classic Box & Jenkins benchmark are performed to compare the performance of the evolving fuzzy participatory learning (ePL) with the evolving fuzzy system modeling (eTS, simpl_eTS, xTS) and neural fuzzy modeling methods. The experiments show that the ePL performs satisfactorily for this benchmark problem. The ePL method is also used to forecast the average hourly load of an electricity generating plant and to compare further with eTS, xTS, neural network modeling, and neural fuzzy modeling using actual data. The results confirm that evolving fuzzy participatory learning is a promising method to solve real-world problems.

The chapter proceeds as follows. Section 4.2 briefly reviews the idea of evolving fuzzy rule-based modeling and the basic eTS method. The next section introduces the concept of participatory learning, the features of the evolving fuzzy participatory learning (ePL) method, and its computational details. Section 4.4 considers the classic

Box & Jenkins benchmark to analyze and compare ePL against eTS, simpl_eTS, xTS, and neural network and neural fuzzy models. Actual electrical load data of a major power plant are used in Section 4.5 to forecast the average hourly loads for a one-day period.

## 4.2 EVOLVING FUZZY SYSTEMS

When learning models online, data are collected and processed continuously. New data may confirm and reinforce the current model if data are compatible with existing knowledge. Otherwise, new data may suggest changes and a need to review the current model. This is the case in recurrent models and dynamic systems where operating conditions modify, fault occurs, or parameters of the processes change.

In evolving systems, a key question is how to modify the current model structure using the newest data sample. Evolving systems use incoming information to continuously develop their structure and functionality through online self-organization.

The rule-based models whose rules are endowed with local models forming their consequents are commonly referred to as *fuzzy functional models*. The Takagi-Sugeno (TS) is a typical example of a fuzzy functional model. A particularly important case is when the rule consequents are linear functions. The evolving Takagi-Sugeno (eTS) models and their variations [3] assume rule-based models whose fuzzy rules are as follows:

$$\mathfrak{R}_i : \textit{IF } x \textit{ is } \Gamma_i \textit{ THEN } y_i = \gamma_{i0} + \sum_{j=1}^{p} \gamma_{ij} x_j$$

$$i = 1, \ldots, c^k$$

where

$\mathfrak{R}_i = i$th fuzzy rule
$c^k = $ number of fuzzy rules at $k; k = 1, \ldots$
$x \in [0, 1]^p = $ input data
$y_i = $ output of the $i$th rule
$\Gamma_i = $ vector of antecedent fuzzy rules
$\gamma_{ij} = $ parameters of the consequent

The collection of the $i = 1, \ldots, c^k$ rules assembles a model as a combination of local linear models. The contribution of a local linear model to the overall output is proportional to the degree of firing of each rule. eTS uses antecedent fuzzy sets with Gaussian membership functions:

$$\mu = e^{-r\|x^k - v_i\|} \tag{4.1}$$

where $r$ is a positive constant that defines the zone of influence of the $i$th local model and $v_i$ is the respective cluster center or focal point, $i = 1, \ldots, c^k$.

Online learning with eTS needs online clustering to find cluster centers, assumes gradual changes of the rule base, and uses recursive least squares to compute the consequent parameters. Each cluster defines a rule.

The TS model output at $k$ is found as the weighted average of the individual rule contributions as follows:

$$y^k = \frac{\sum_{j=1}^{c^k} \mu_j y_j}{\sum_{j=1}^{c^k} \mu_j} \qquad (4.2)$$

where $c^k$ is the number of rules after $k$ observations and $y_j$ the output of the $j$th rule at $k$.

The recursive procedure for online rule-based models evolution is summarized by algorithm 1 [3].

---

## Algorithm 1: eTS Procedure

*Input:* data samples, $x^k \in [0, 1]^p, k = 1, \ldots$
*Output:* model output

1. Initialize the rule base structure and parameters.
2. Read new data.
3. Compute the potential of the new data recursively.
4. Update the potentials of old cluster centers recursively.
5. Modify or update the rule-base structure.
6. Compute the rule consequent parameters recursively.
7. Compute eTS model output.

---

Clustering starts with the first data point as the center of the first cluster. The procedure is a form of *subtractive* clustering, a variation of the Filev and Yager *mountain* clustering approach [30]. The capability of a point to become a cluster center is evaluated through its potential. Data potentials are calculated recursively using Cauchy function to measure the potential. If the potential of new data is higher than the potential of the current cluster centers, then the new data become a new center and a new rule is created. If the potential of new data is higher than the potential of the current centers, but it is close to an existing center, then the new data replace the existing center. See [2] and [3] for more details. Current implementation of eTS adopts Cauchy functions to define the notion of data density evaluated around the last data of a data stream, and monitor the clustering step, and contains several mechanisms to improve model efficiency, such as online structure simplification. See Chapter 1 for updated coverage and computational details of the current implementations.

## 4.3 EVOLVING FUZZY PARTICIPATORY LEARNING

Evolving fuzzy participatory learning (ePL) modeling adopts the same scheme as eTS. After the initialization phase, data processing is performed at each step to verify whether a new cluster must be created, an old cluster should be modified to account for the new data, or redundant clusters must be eliminated. Cluster centers are the focal point of the rules. Each rule corresponds to a cluster. Parameters of the consequent functions are computed using the local recursive least-squares algorithm. In this chapter we assume, without loss of generality, linear consequent functions.

The main difference between ePL and eTS concerns the procedure to update the rule-base structure. Differently from eTS, ePL uses a fuzzy similarity measure to determine the proximity between new data and the existing rule-base structure. The rule-base structure is isomorphic to the cluster structure because each rule is associated with a cluster. Participatory learning assumes that model learning depends on what the system already knows about the model. Therefore, in ePL, the current model is part of the evolving process itself and influences the way in which new observations are used for self-organization. An essential property of participatory learning is that the impact of new data in causing self-organization or model revision depends on its compatibility with the current rule-base structure, or equivalently, on its compatibility with the current cluster structure.

## 4.3.1 Participatory Learning

Let $v_i^k \in [0, 1]^p$ be a variable that encodes the $i$th $(i = 1, \ldots, c^k)$ cluster center at the $k$th step. The aim of the participatory mechanism is to learn the value of $v_i^k$, using a stream of data $x^k \in [0, 1]^p$. In other words, $x^k$ is used as a vehicle to learn about $v_i^k$. We say that the learning process is participatory if the contribution of each data $x^k$ to the learning process depends on its acceptance by the current estimate of $v_i^k$ as being valid. Implicit in this idea is that, to be useful and to contribute to the learning of $v_i^k$, observations $x^k$ must somehow be compatible with current estimates of $v_i^k$.

In ePL, the objects of learning are cluster structures. *Cluster structures* are characterized by their cluster centers (prototypes). More formally, given an initial cluster structure, a set of vectors $v_i^k \in [0, 1]^p, i = 1, \ldots, c^k$, updates in ePL proceed using a compatibility measure, $\rho_i^k \in [0, 1]$, and an arousal index, $a_i^k \in [0, 1]$. Whereas $\rho_i^k$ measures how much a data point is compatible with the current cluster structure, the arousal index $a_i^k$ acts as a critic to remind when the current cluster structure should be revised in front of new information contained in data. Figure 4.1 summarizes the main constituents and functioning of the participatory learning.

Due to its unsupervised, self-organizing nature, the PL clustering procedure may at each step create a new cluster or modify existing ones. If the arousal index is greater than a threshold value $\tau \in [0, 1]$, then a new cluster is created. Otherwise, the $i$th cluster center, the one most compatible with $x^k$, is adjusted as follows:

$$v_i^{k+1} = v_i^k + G(x^k - v_i) \tag{4.3}$$

where

$$G_i^k \, \alpha \, \rho_i^k \tag{4.4}$$

$\alpha \in [0, 1]$ is the learning rate, and

$$\rho_i^k = 1 - \frac{||x^k - v_i||}{p} \tag{4.5}$$

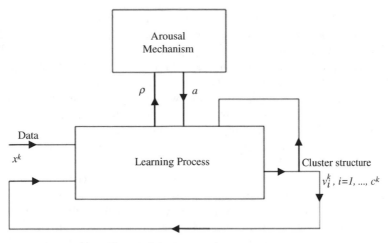

**Figure 4.1.** Participatory learning.

with $\|.\|$ a norm, $p$ the dimension of input space, and

$$i = \arg \max_{j} \{\rho_j^k\} \tag{4.6}$$

Notice that the $i$th cluster center is a convex combination of the new data sample $x^k$ and the closest cluster center. Similarly to (4.3), the arousal index $a_i^k$ is updated as follows:

$$a_i^{k+1} = a_i^k + \beta(1 - \rho_i^{k+1} - a_i^k) \tag{4.7}$$

The value of $\beta \in [0, 1]$ controls the rate of change of arousal: The closer $\beta$ is to one, the faster the system is to sense compatibility variations.

The way in which ePL considers the arousal mechanism is to incorporate the arousal index (4.7) into (4.4) as follows:

$$G_i^k = \alpha(\rho_i^k)^{1-\alpha_i^k} \tag{4.8}$$

When $a_i^k = 0$, we have $G_i^k = \alpha\rho_i^k$, which is the PL procedure with no arousal. Notice that if the arousal index increases, the similarity measure has a reduced effect. The arousal index can be interpreted as the complement of the confidence we have in the truth of the current belief, the rule-base structure. The arousal mechanism monitors the performance of the system by observing the compatibility of the current model with the observations. Therefore, learning is dynamic in the sense that (4.3) can be viewed as a belief revision strategy whose effective learning rate (4.8) depends on the compatibility between new data and the current cluster structure, and on model confidence as well.

Notice also that the learning rate is modulated by compatibility. In conventional learning models, there are no participatory considerations and the learning rate is usually set small to avoid undesirable oscillations due to spurious values of data that are far from cluster centers. Small values of learning rate, while protecting against the influence of noisy data, slow down learning. Participatory learning allows the use of higher values of learning rate; the compatibility index acts to lower the effective learning rate when large deviations occur. On the contrary, when the compatibility is large, it increases the effective rate, which means speeding up the learning process.

Clearly, whenever a cluster center is updated or a new cluster added, the PL fuzzy clustering procedure should verify whether redundant clusters are created. This is because updating a cluster center using (4.3) may push a given center closer to another one and a redundant cluster may be formed. Therefore, a mechanism to exclude redundancy is needed. One mechanism is to verify whether similar outputs due to distinct rules are produced. In PL clustering, a cluster center is declared redundant whenever its similarity with another center is greater than or equal to a threshold value $\lambda$. If this is the case, then we can either maintain the original cluster center or replace it with the average between the new data and the current cluster center. Similarly to (4.5), the compatibility index among cluster centers is computed as follows:

$$\rho_{v_i}^k = 1 - \sum_{j=1}^{p} |v_i^k - v_j^k| \tag{4.9}$$

Therefore, if

$$\rho_{v_i}^k \geq \lambda \tag{4.10}$$

then the cluster $i$ is declared redundant.

## 4.3.2 Parameter Estimation

After clustering, the fuzzy rule base is constructed using a procedure similar to eTS, described in section 4.2. The cluster centers define the modal values of the Gaussian membership functions while dispersions are chosen to achieve appropriate levels or rule overlapping. Moreover, for each cluster found, the corresponding rules have their linear consequent function parameters adjusted using the recursive least-squares algorithm. The computational details are as follows.

Let $x^k = \lfloor x_1^k, x_2^k, \ldots, x_p^k \rfloor [0, 1]^p$ be the vector of observations and $y_i^k \in [0, 1]$ the output of the $i$th rule, $i = 1, \ldots, c^k$, at $k = 1, 2, \ldots$. Each local model is estimated by a linear equation:

$$Y^k = X^k \gamma^k \tag{4.11}$$

where $\gamma^k \in \Re^{p+1}$ is a vector of unknown parameters defined by

$$(\gamma^k)^T = \begin{bmatrix} \gamma_0^k & \gamma_1^k & \gamma_2^k & \cdots & \gamma_p^k \end{bmatrix}$$

and $X^k = \lfloor 1 \; x^k \rfloor \in [0, 1]^{k \times (p+1)}$ the matrix composed by the $k$th input vector $x^k$ and a constant term; and $Y^k = [y_i^k] \in [0, 1]^k$, $i = 1, \ldots, c^k$ is the output vector.

The model (4.11) gives a local description of the system, but the vector of parameters $\gamma$ is unknown. One way to estimate the values for $\gamma$ is to use the available data. Assume that

$$Y^k = X^k \gamma^k + e^k \tag{4.12}$$

where $\gamma^k$ represents the parameters to be recursively computed and $e^k$ is the modeling error at $k$. The least-squares algorithm chooses $\gamma^k$ to minimize sum-of-squares errors

$$J_k = J(\gamma^k) = (e^k)^T e^k \tag{4.13}$$

Define $X^{k+1}$ and $Y^{k+1}$ as follows:

$$X^{k+1} = \begin{pmatrix} X^k \\ 1 \; x^{k+1} \end{pmatrix}, \quad Y^{k+1} = \begin{pmatrix} Y^k \\ y_i^{k+1} \end{pmatrix} \tag{4.14}$$

where $x^{k+1}$ is the current input data and $y_i^{k+1}$ is the corresponding model output. The vector of parameters that minimizes the functional $J_k$ at $k$ is [32]:

$$\gamma^k = P^k b^k \tag{4.15}$$

where $P^k [(X^k)^t X^k]^{-1}$ and $b^k = (X^k)^T Y^k$. Using the matrix inversion lemma [32]:

$$(A + BCD)^{-1} = A^{-1} - A^{-1} B (C^{-1} + DA^{-1}B)^{-1} DA^{-1}$$

and making

$$A = (P^k)^{-1}, \quad C = I, \quad B = X^{k+1}, \quad D = (X^{k+1})^T$$

we get

$$P^{k+1} = P^k \left[ I - \frac{X^{k+1}(X^{k+1})^{-1} P^k}{1 + (X^{k+1})^T P^k X^{k+1}} \right] \tag{4.16}$$

where $I$ is the identity matrix. After simple mathematical transformations, the vector of parameters is computed recursively as follows:

$$\gamma^{k+1} = \gamma^k + P^{k+1} X^{k+1} \left( Y^{k+1} - (X^{k+1})^T \gamma^k \right) \tag{4.17}$$

Detailed derivation can be found in [10]. For convergence proofs see [16], for example. Expression (4.17) is used to update the rule-consequent parameters at each $k$.

The use of the recursive least-squares algorithm depends on the initial values of the parameters $\hat{\gamma}^0$, and on the initial values of the entries of matrix $P^0$. These initial values are chosen based on the following:

1. Existence of previous knowledge about the system, exploring a database to find an initial rule base, and, consequently, $\hat{\gamma}^0$ and $P^0$.
2. A useful technique when no previous information is available is to choose large values for the entries of matrix $P^0$ [29]. If the initial values of consequent parameters are similar to exact values, then it is enough to choose small values for the entries of $P^0$. A standard choice of $P^0$ is

$$P^0 = sI_m$$

where $I_m$ is the identity matrix of the order $m$, and $m$ is the number of consequent parameters. The value of $s$ usually is chosen such that $s \in [100,10000]$ if large values are required, while for the small values $s \in [1,10]$. More details can be found in [29].

In this chapter, we use the first option; that is, we use a database to choose the initial rule base and its parameters.

### 4.3.3 Evolving Fuzzy Participatory Learning Algorithm

The detailed steps of the evolving fuzzy participatory learning modeling procedure are given by Algorithm 2.

---

**Algorithm 2: ePL Procedure**

*Input:* data samples, $x^k \in [0,1]^p, k = 1, \ldots$
*Output:* model output
Initialize the rule focal points and parameters $\alpha, \beta, \lambda, \tau$:

1. Read new data $x^k$.
2. Compute the compatibility index $\rho_i^k$.
3. Compute the arousal index $a_i^k$:

   *if* $a_i^k \geq \tau, \forall i \in \{1, \ldots, c^k\}$
       $x^k$ is a new cluster center; set $c^{k+1} = c^k + 1$:
   *else* compute (4.3) using (4.5)–(4.8)

4. Compute $\rho_{v_i}^k$ using (4.9):

   *if* $\rho_{v_i}^k \geq \lambda$
       exclude $v_i$
       set $c^{k+1} = c^k - 1$:

5. Update rule-base structure.
6. Compute rules-consequent parameters.
7. Compute firing degree using (4.1).
8. Compute output using (4.2).

---

Detailed guidelines to choose appropriate values of $\alpha$, $\beta$, $\lambda$, and $\tau$ are given in [21], where it is shown that they should be chosen such that:

$$0 < \frac{\tau}{\beta} \le 1-\lambda \le 1$$

where $\tau \le \beta$ and $\lambda \le 1-\tau$. These steps are shown in Figure 4.2.

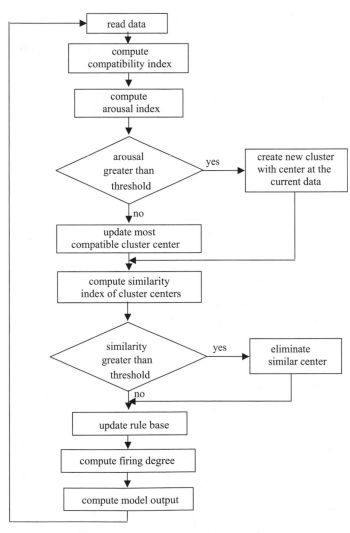

Figure 4.2. Computational steps of ePL.

## 4.4 EXPERIMENTS WITH A BENCHMARK PROBLEM

In this section, the ePL model is used to model and predict the future values of the gas furnace Box & Jenkins time series. The *Box & Jenkins gas furnace* is a well-studied benchmark problem in the literature. It is composed of 290 pairs of input–output data taken from a laboratory furnace [12], emerging from a data set composed of a total 296 values. Each data sample consists of the methane flow rate, the process input variable, $u^k$, and the $CO_2$ concentration in off gas, the process output $y^k$. This is a dynamic process with one input $u^k$ and one output $y^k$. The aim is to predict current output $y^k$ using past input and output values, with the lowest error. Different studies indicate that the best model structure for this system is:

$$\hat{y}^k = f\lfloor y^{k-1}, u^{k-4} \rfloor \tag{4.18}$$

where $\hat{y}^k$ is the model output. We consider the following case: 200 training data examples to initialize the fuzzy rule base and the remaining 90 data pairs to test and validate.

Model evaluation is performed considering the root mean square error (RMSE) and the nondimensional error index (NDEI), which is the ratio between the RMSE and the standard deviation of the target data. These indexes are computed using the following expressions:

$$\text{RMSE} = \left( \frac{1}{N} \sum_{k=1}^{N} (d_k - \hat{y}_k)^2 \right)^{1/2} \tag{4.19}$$

$$\text{NDEI} = \frac{\text{RMSE}}{std(d_k)} \tag{4.20}$$

where $N$ is the number of predictions; $\hat{y}^k$, the model output, is the desired output; and $d_k$ is the desired output and $std$ is the standard deviation function.

Comparison of the ePL model against neural/neuro-fuzzy approaches and evolving models is summarized in Table 4.1. Figure 4.3 shows the actual and forecasted values provided by the ePL model.

T A B L E  4.1.  Modeling Performance for the Box & Jenkins Benchmark

| Model Name and Source | Number of Rules (or Nodes) | RMSE | NDEI |
|---|---|---|---|
| MLP model [27] | 5 | 0.0211 | 0.1319 |
| ANFIS model [14] | 7 | 0.0207 | 0.1294 |
| FuNN model [18] | 7 | 0.0226 | 0.1408 |
| HyFIS model [20] | 15 | 0.0205 | 0.1278 |
| eTS model [4] | 5 | 0.0490 | 0.3057 |
| Simpl_eTS model [4] | 3 | 0.0485 | 0.3023 |
| xTS model [8] | 6 | 0.0375 | 0.2397 |
| ePL current model | 4 | 0.0191 | 0.1189 |

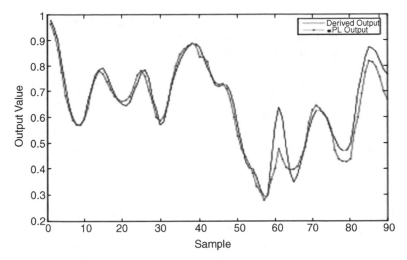

**Figure 4.3.** Box & Jenkins gas furnace forecasting.

The classic approaches considered are a multilayer perceptron neural network (MLP) with one hidden layer with five neurons trained with backpropagation algorithm, and an adaptive neuro-fuzzy inference system (ANFIS) granularized with three fuzzy sets for each input variable and seven fuzzy rules. The MLP network adopted the following scheme for the initialization phase: small weight values randomly assigned; $\alpha = 0.9$ as momentum parameter; 10000 as the maximum number of epochs, and an adaptive learning rate starting from $\eta = 0.01$. The ANFIS has 1000 as the maximum number of epochs, $\eta_i = 0.01$ as initial step size, $s_d = 0.9$ as step-size decrease rate, and $s_i = 1.1$ as step-size increase rate. These two approaches were implemented using the Matlab neural network and fuzzy logic toolboxes.

The xTS model proposed in [8] was chosen to be compared with the ePL. The experiments reported here use the xTS implementation given in [9] with initial value $P^0 = 750$ of the recursive least-squares algorithm.

The results have been also compared with similar ones published in the literature, respectively, the FuNN model [18], HyFIS model [20], eTS model [4], and simpl_eTS model [4].

Table 4.1 suggests that the ePL model performs better than the remaining models. In addition, the ePL model shows the smallest number of rules created. Note also that a small number of rules reduces model complexity and increases interpretability.

## 4.5 ELECTRIC LOAD FORECASTING

Forecasts of load demand are very important in the operation of electrical energy systems, because several decision-making processes, such as system operation planning, security analysis, and market decisions, are strongly influenced by the future values of the load. In this context, a significant error in the load forecast may result in economic losses, security constraints violations, and system operation drawbacks. Accurate and reliable load forecasting models are essential for a suitable system operation.

The problem of load forecasting can be classified as long, medium, and short term, depending on the situation. Long-term forecasting is important for capacity expansion of the electrical system. Medium term is important to organize the fuel supply, in maintaining operations, and in interchange scheduling. Short-term forecasting is generally used for daily programming and operation of the electrical system, energy transfer, and demand management [26].

Particularly in the context of short-term hydrothermal scheduling, load forecasting is important to elaborate the next-day operation scheduling because errors in load forecasting can cause serious consequences, affecting the efficiency and the safety of the system (cost increasing, insufficient electrical energy supply to the existing demand).

The goal of short-term load forecasting is to accurately predict the 24 hourly loads of the next operation day, one-step-ahead. The effectiveness of the ePL approach is illustrated using load data of a major electrical utility located in the Southeast region of Brazil. In evaluating the forecast model, a database consisting of hourly loads from August 1, 2000 to August 31, 2000 is used to develop the model and to produce load forecasts.

Forecasting performance requires an appropriate selection of the input variables of the forecasting model. Here, the number of inputs was found using the partial autocorrelation function. Figure 4.4 shows the first 36 estimated partial autocorrelations

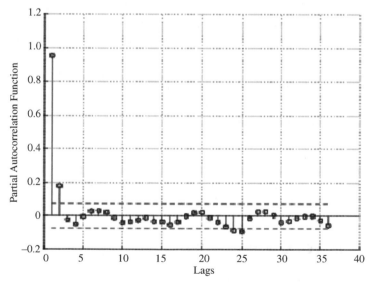

**Figure 4.4.** Estimated partial autocorrelation function and standard error limits.

of the series. The behavior of the function suggests two inputs, respectively, $y_t$ to forecast $y_{t-2}$, $y_{t-1}$. The points between the two dotted lines of Figure 4.4 are within two standard deviations of the estimated partial autocorrelation.

The performance of the ePL is compared with MLP, ANFIS, eTS, and xTS models. The models were developed to forecast hourly loads during the 24-hour period of August 31, 2000. The models were developd using data from August 1, 2000 until August 30, 2000. Data were normalized to fit the unit interval as follows:

$$y_t = \frac{z_t - \min}{\max - \min}$$

where $y_t$ is the normalized data, and min and max denote the minimum and maximum values of $z_t, t = 1, \ldots, N$.

The performance of the forecasting models was evaluated using the root mean square error (RMSE) (4.19) and the nondimensional error index (NDEI) (4.20).

The ePL model adopted the following values: $\beta = \tau = 0.30$, $r = 0.25$, and $\lambda = 0.35$. These are the only parameters of the ePL algorithm that need to be chosen by the user. The ePL found five rules during the 30-day development period. During testing, ePL uses hourly loads data and runs as in online mode.

An MLP with the same structure and initial parameters as that developed for the Box & Jenkins benchmark was used to forecast loads in the period. MLP training also started with small, randomly chosen initial weights and took 5000 epochs to converge.

Load forecasting for the same time period also has been done using ANFIS. The structure and parameters are also the same those used for the Box & Jenkins problem, and the maximum number of epochs was 1000.

The eTS and xTS models were developed considering the first 30 days before the testing period. The value of the cluster radii for the eTS model was $r = 0.4$. Both eTS and xTS models adopted $P^0 = 750$ to initialize the recursive least squares. In the experiments reported here, we ran the eTS and xTS implementation given in [9].

Table 4.2 shows the performance of the models during the testing period (24 hours), considering the two error criteria (4.19) and (4.20). The table also includes the final

TABLE 4.2. Modeling Performance for One-Step-Ahead Load Forecast

| Model Name and Source | Number of Rules (or Nodes) | RMSE | NDEI |
|---|---|---|---|
| MLP model [27] | 5 | 0.0522 | 0.2055 |
| ANFIS model [14] | 9 | 0.0541 | 0.2012 |
| eTS model [4] | 6 | 0.0517 | 0.1922 |
| xTS model [8] | 4 | 0.0562 | 0.2089 |
| ePL current model | 5 | 0.0508 | 0.1888 |

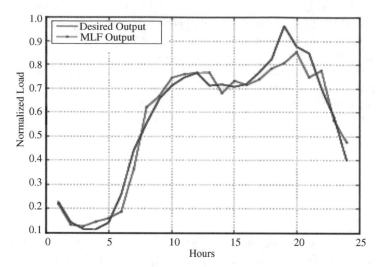

**Figure 4.5.** Load forecast for August 31, 2000—MLP.

number of fuzzy rules (or nodes) achieved by models. Load forecasts are shown in Figures 4.5–4.9.

Notice in Table 4.2 that the ePL approach gives as good results as eTS and xTS, but is simpler and computationally more efficient than eTS and xTS.

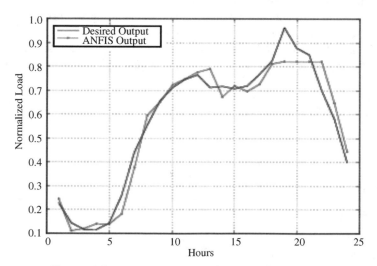

**Figure 4.6.** Load forecast for August 31, 2000—ANFIS.

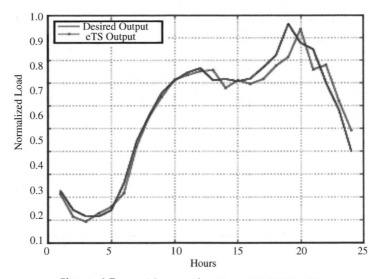

Figure 4.7. Load forecast for August 31, 2000—eTS.

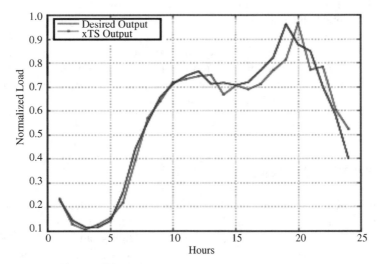

Figure 4.8. Load forecast for August 31, 2000—xTS.

## 4.6 CONCLUSION

This chapter addressed evolving fuzzy participatory learning, a method based on the participatory learning paradigm to develop evolving fuzzy rule-based models. Participatory learning materializes in the evolving fuzzy participatory method in the form of an

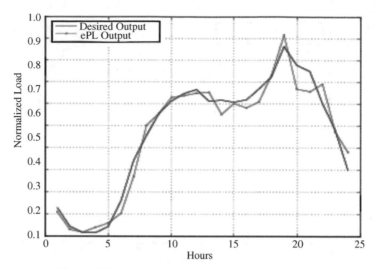

**Figure 4.9.** Load forecast for August 31, 2000—ePL.

unsupervised clustering algorithm. Clustering is a key issue in evolving fuzzy systems because they must dynamically find an appropriate structure in a stream of data. Unsupervised dynamic clustering provides an efficient mechanism to implement a form of self-organization in system modeling. Similarly to eTS, parameters of rule consequents are computed using the least-squares algorithm. Computational experiments with a classic benchmark problem and a real-world application concerning hourly electrical load forecasting show that ePL is a promising approach in the adaptive fuzzy systems modeling area.

## 4.7 ACKNOWLEDGMENTS

This work was supported by the Research Foundation of the State of São Paulo (FAPESP), grants 03/10019-9, 05/58879-1 and 03/05042-1; and by the Brazilian National Research Council (CNPq), grants 305796/2005-4 and 304857/2006-8. The authors also thank Plamen Angelov and the anonymous referees for comments that helped us to improve the chapter.

## 4.8 REFERENCES

1. K. L. Anderson, G. L. Blackenship, L. G. Lebow, "A Rule-Based Adaptive PID Controller." *Proc. 27th IEEE Conf. Decision Control,* New York, 1988, pp. 564–569.
2. P. Angelov, *Evolving Rule-Based Models: A Tool for Design of Flexible Adaptive Systems.* Heidelberg, New York; Springer-Verlag, 2002, ISBN 3-7908-1457-1.

3. P. Angelov, D. Filev. "An Approach to On-line Identification of Evolving Takagi-Sugeno Fuzzy Models." *IEEE Trans. on Systems, Man and Cybernetics,* part B, 34 (1): 484–498, 2004.

4. P. Angelov, D. Filev. "Simpl_eTS: A Simplified Method for Learning Evolving Takagi-Sugeno Fuzzy Models." *Proc. 2005 Int. Conf. on Fuzzy Systems,* FUZZ-IEEE, May 2005, pp. 1068–1073.

5. P. Angelov, R. Guthke, "A GA-Based Approach to Optimization of Bioprocesses Described by Fuzzy Rules," *Journal Bioprocess Engineering,* 16: 299–301, 1997.

6. P. Angelov, N. Kasabov, "Evolving Intelligent Systems—eIS." *IEEE SMC NewsLetter,* June 2006, pp. 1–13.

7. P. Angelov, C. Xydeas, D. Filev, "On-line Identification of MIMO Evolving Takagi-Sugeno Fuzzy Models." *Int. Joint Conference on Neural Networks and International Conference on Fuzzy Systems,* Budapest, Hungary, July 2004, IJCNN-FUZZ-IEEE, pp. 55–60.

8. P. Angelov, X. Zhou, "Evolving Fuzzy Systems from Data Streams in Real-Time." *Proc. Int. Symposium on Evolving Fuzzy Systems,* 2006, pp. 29–35.

9. P. Angelov, X. Zhou,"Online Identification of Takagi-Sugeno Fuzzy Models DeMO," 2006, http://194.80.34.45/eTS/.

10. K. J. Astrom, B. Wittenmark. *Adaptive Control,* 2nd ed. Boston: Addison-Wesley-Longman, 1994.

11. R. Babuska, *Fuzzy Modeling for Control.* Boston: Kluwer Academic Publishers, 1998.

12. G. E. P. Box, G. M. Jenkins, *Time Series Analysis—Forecasting and Control,* 2nd ed. Holden Day, CA, 1976.

13. S. L. Chiu, "Fuzzy Model Identification Based on Cluster Estimation," *Journal of Intelligence and Fuzzy System,* 2: 267–278, 1994.

14. J. S. R. Jang, "ANFIS: Adaptative Network-Based Fuzzy Inference Systems." *IEEE Trans. on Systems, Man and Cybernetics,* 23: 665–685, June 1993.

15. T. A. Johanson, R. Murray-Smith, "Operating Regime Approach to Nonlinear Modeling and Control." In *Multiple Model Approaches to Modeling and Control,* ( R. Murray-Smith, T. A. Johanson, eds.). Hants, UK: Taylor Francis, 1998, pp. 3–72.

16. C. R. Johnson, *Lectures and Adaptive Parameter Estimation.* Upper Saddle River, NJ: Prentice-Hall, 1988.

17. N. Kasabov, *Evolving Connectionist Systems: Methods and Applications in Bioinformatics, Brain Study and Intelligent Machines.* London: Springer-Verlag, 2002.

18. N. Kasabov, J. Kim, M. Watts, A. Gray, "FuNN/2—A Fuzzy Neural Network Architecture for Adaptive Learning and Knowledge Acquisition," *Information Sciences,* 3–4 (101): 155–175, October 1997.

19. N. Kasabov, Q. Song, "DENFIS: Dynamic Evolving Neural-Fuzzy Inference System and Its Application for Time Series Prediction." *IEEE Trans. on Fuzzy Systems,* 10 (2): 144–154, 2002.

20. J. Kim, N. Kasabov, "HyFIS: Adaptive Neuro-Fuzzy Inference Systems and Their Application to Nonlinear Dynamical Systems," *Neural Networks,* 12: 1301–1319, June 1999.

21. E. Lima, "Modelo Takagi-Sugeno Evolutivo Participativo," PhD thesis, Faculty of Electrical and Computer Engineering, State University of Campinas, 2008.

22. F. J. Lin, C. H. Ln, P. H. Shen, Self-Constructing Fuzzy Neural Network Speed Controller for Permanent-Magnet Synchronous Motor Drive. *IEEE Trans. on Fuzzy Systems,* 5(9): 751–759, 2001.

23. O. Nelles, Nonlinear System Identification. Heidelberg: Springer, 2001.

24. F. Hoffmann, L. Magdalena, O. Cordon, F. Herrera. *Generic Fuzzy Systems: Evolutionary Tuning and Learning of Fuzzy Knowledge Bases.* Singapore: World Scientific Publishing, 2001.

25. W. Pedrycz, F. Gomide, *Fuzzy Systems Engineering: Toward Human-Centric Computing.* Hoboken, NJ: Wiley Interscience/IEEE, 2007.

26. S. Rahman, O. Hazim, "A Generalized Knowledge-Based Short-Term Load-Forecasting Technique." *IEEE Trans. on Power Systems*, 8 (2), 1993.

27. D. Rumelhart, G. Hinton, R. Williams, *Learning Internal Representation by Error Propagation.* London: Nature, 1986.

28. L. Silva, F. Gomide, R. R. Yager, "Participatory Learning in Fuzzy Clustering." *2005 IEEE Int. Conf. on Fuzzy Systems,* May 2005, FUZZ-IEEE, pp. 857–861.

29. P. E. Wellstead, M. B. Zarrop, *Self-Tuning Systems: Control and Signal Processing.* New York: John Wiley & Sons, 1995.

30. R. Yager, D. Filev, "Approximate Clustering via the Mountain Method." *IEEE Trans. on Systems, Man and Cybernetics*, 24 (8): 1279–1284, August 1994.

31. R. R. Yager, "A Model of Participatory Learning." *IEEE Trans. on Systems, Man and Cybernetics*, 20: 1229–1234, 1990.

32. P. C. Young, *Recursive Estimation and Time-Series Analysis.* Berlin: Springer-Verlag, 1984.

# 5

# TOWARD ROBUST EVOLVING FUZZY SYSTEMS

Edwin Lughofer

**Abstract:** In this chapter, methodologies for more robustness and transparency in evolving fuzzy systems will be demonstrated. After outlining the evolving fuzzy modeling approaches, FLEXFIS (FLEXible Fuzzy Inference Systems) for fuzzy regression models and FLEXFIS-Class (FLEXible Fuzzy Inference Systems for Classification) for fuzzy classification models, robustness improvement strategies during the incremental learning phase will be explained, including regularization issues for overcoming instabilities in the parameter estimation process, overcoming the unlearning effect, dealing with drifts in data streams, ensuring a better extrapolation behavior, and adaptive local error bars serving as local confidence regions surrounding the evolved fuzzy models. The chapter will be concluded with evaluation results on high-dimensional real-world data sets, where the impact of the new methodologies will be presented.

## 5.1 INTRODUCTION

### 5.1.1 Purpose of Robust Evolving Models

Nowadays, automatic adaptation techniques and evolving schemes for data-driven models, that is, models that are fully built up from data, measurement data, or online

*Evolving Intelligent Systems: Methodology and Applications,* Edited by Plamen Angelov, Dimitar P. Filev, and Nikola Kasabov

data streams, are becoming more and more an essential point in industry. Today's quality control systems need to achieve high accuracies when doing clustering respectively, grouping of data, prediction of future system states, or system identification, or when classifying new production items. For instance, in a fault detection or decision support system a hit rate of 95% or even higher is required; otherwise the throughput of broken items or wrongly classified objects would raise significant customer complaints or may even lead to failures in the system, and finally to severe breakdowns of components in a system or the whole production cycle.

A large amount of samples is needed to set up an initial model framework in offline mode that should achieve a high accuracy and guarantee a safe production. This is because usually not all possible operating conditions can be covered by offline simulated or recorded data in advance; sometimes, a completely new system behavior may demand feedback from a model in its extrapolation space, which is always quite precarious and risky to follow. It is thus a requirement that the models are refined, extended, and evolved online during normal production. Now, the amount of data and the cycle times for such processes usually do not allow postprocessing of batches of data. Consequently, this is an online processing of tasks, which requires an update of some components of the models in the form of incremental learning steps with new data (i.e., the models are evolved sample per sample). An alternative complete rebuilding of the models from time to time with all the data samples, recorded online so far, would yield an unacceptable computational effort as not terminating in real-time.

One important aspect when doing evolving modeling is to guarantee a *robust* learning behavior in order to assure models with high prediction, classification, and control performance. Hereby we see two basic aspects for assuring robustness during online learning and high-performance models:

1. Doing incremental and evolving learning in a way such that the performance of the evolved models is close to the (hypothetical) batch solution (achieved by collecting all the data and loading them at once into the training algorithm). From a mathematical point of view, this means that a kind of convergence of some parameters to an optimality criterion is achieved.

2. Implementing approaches for assuring high performance of the models with respect to accuracy and correctness also in specific cases such as (a) instabilities during parameter estimation, (b) situations causing an unlearning effect, (c) drifts in online data streams, (d) extrapolation situations for new samples to be predicted (i.e., new data samples to be classified appearing outside the previously estimated feature space), and (e) uncertainties in the models due to high noise levels. These approaches include (a) regularization, (b) a strategy for when to update, (c) detection of drifts and gradual forgetting, (d) avoidance of a reactivation of inner fuzzy sets, and (e) adaptive local error bars serving as confidence regions surrounding the evolved models and hence delivering a kind of plausibility criterion of the models' decisions.

Both definitions of *robustness* will be addressed in subsequent sections for a specific type of model architecture: *evolving fuzzy systems.*

## 5.1.2 Fuzzy Systems

Fuzzy systems play an important role for the automatization of modeling, identification, and classification tasks, as they usually represent a good tradeoff between models with high accuracy and linguistic interpretability and transparency [12, 30]. The latter is because their architecture contains rule bases and therefore may yield a better understanding of some underlying system behaviors than pure black-box models (such as neural networks [25]). Transparency and linguistic interpretability can be used, for instance, for fault analysis and reasoning [28] to trace back faults in the system and find the reasons for them. Another important aspect in modeling is the mimicry of human imprecision and vague knowledge. This can be easily achieved with fuzzy systems, as the inner structure of these yields quite a good direct representation of vague knowledge (in form of rules). They are often applied in areas such as system identification [31] and analysis, control [1, 7], fault detection [44], novelty detection [17], or classification [48].

## 5.1.3 Evolving Fuzzy Systems for Regression

In order to cope with the online demands mentioned in the previous section, various approaches for *evolving fuzzy and neuro-fuzzy systems* were developed in the past decade, such as *eTS* [5] and the simplified version *Simp_eTS* [2] for rule-base simplification, *DENFIS* [33, 34], online *SOFNN* [36], *SAFIS* [21], participatory evolving fuzzy modeling [38], *DFNN* [63] and its successor *GDFNN* [64] or the approach presented in [8].

eTS [5] exploits a Takagi-Sugeno fuzzy model and recursively updates the structure of the model based on the potential of the input data (i.e., it implements a kind of incremental version of subtractive clustering). A new rule is added when the potential of the data is higher than the potential of the existing rules or a new rule is modified when potential of the new data is higher than the potential of the existing rules and the new data are close to an old rule. Its simplified version, Simp_eTS [2] extends eTS [5] by including an online rule-base simplification algorithm based on the population of the rules, determined as the number of data samples belonging to the corresponding clusters. In DENFIS [34] the structure learning is carried out with the help of an evolving clustering method, called *ECM* [32]; that is, whenever a new cluster is found, automatically a new rule is set as well. The antecedent fuzzy sets with fixed width for each dimension are then formed around the corresponding center coordinates and the linear consequent parameters are estimated by a recursive weighted least-squares estimator. SAFIS [21] as a truly sequential learning algorithm uses the idea of functional equivalence between an RBF neural network and a fuzzy inference system by the application of the GAP-RBF neural network proposed by [27]. In online SOFNN [36] the learning is divided into a parameter and a structure learning; the former exploits a modified version of recursive least squares [39] and the structure learning includes new adding and pruning techniques. The adding approach is derived from geometric growing criterion and satisfies the [epsilon]-completeness of fuzzy rules [35]. Participatory evolving fuzzy modeling [38] combines the concept of participatory learning (PL) introduced by Yager [66] with the evolving fuzzy modeling approach eTS [5] (by Angelov & Filev). The PL concept is based on unsupervised clustering and hence is a natural candidate to find rule-base structures in adaptive fuzzy modeling procedures. Another variant is the *FLEXFIS* approach [41] (FLEXible Fuzzy Inference Systems), which exploits an evolving version of vector quantization [40] including an alternative winner selection strategy and a split-and-merge procedure for rule evolution and antecedent update, which is connected with recursive weighted least squares for local learning of rule consequents (achieving a high flexibility and convergence of the consequent parameters).

### 5.1.4 Evolving Fuzzy Systems for Classification

For classification tasks in online systems, incremental learning approaches for fuzzy classifiers were developed, such as [58, 60]. In the latter an incremental learning technique for classical fuzzy classification model architecture [48, 52] is demonstrated, which approximates the regions belonging to different classes with multidimensional rectangles, and a new rule (hidden neuron) is generated whenever a sample is misclassified or not covered by any rule at all. Probably the most famous approach is an evolving fuzzy classifier family called *eClass* [4], which comes with three model architectures [3] (classical single-model architecture with class label in the consequent, single and first-order TSK-type classifier with single and multiple consequents) and is able to evolve new rules and prune older rules (clusters) on demand based on a recursive online calculation of potentials of cluster prototypes and input data. Another variant of this evolving fuzzy classifier is the *FLEXFIS-Class* approach (FLEXible Fuzzy Inference Systems for Classification) [42], which comes with two model architectures, again classical single-model architecture with class label in the consequent (*FLEXFIS-Class SM*) and an architecture based on multiple first-order TSK fuzzy models (*FLEXFIS-Class MM*). The latter evolves separate first-order TSK fuzzy regression models (one for each class) with the usage of FLEXFIS based on indicator vectors and applies a one-versus-rest classification scheme.

### 5.1.5 Structure of the Chapter

In this chapter, we first give a short summary of the principal techniques and algorithms of FLEXFIS [41], applicable for online regression problems, as well as FLEXFIS-Class [42], applicable for building up an evolving fuzzy classifier for online classification problems. *The major novel contribution of this chapter lies in the second part*, where we focus on issues guiding the evolving learning algorithms to more robustness and stability during the learning process and hence achieving higher performance of the evolved models (see also previous section). These issues are indeed implemented in FLEXFIS and respectively FLEXFIS-Class (hence a short summary of these methods and references where appropriate is given beforehand in order to keep the chapter self-contained), but are generically described in the sense that they can be quite easily adopted for most of the evolving fuzzy systems and classifiers approaches mentioned above. Evaluation of the proposed approaches will be done throughout the whole chapter, both on two-dimensional simple examples for visualization to the reader and on higher-dimensional problems from real-world applications (section 5.5).

## 5.2 EVOLVING FUZZY REGRESSION MODELS WITH FLEXFIS

We outline the most important characteristics of the basic FLEXFIS method (for further details see [41]) and mention a stepwise description of the algorithm.

The characteristics of this evolving fuzzy modeling variant can be summarized in the following points:

- It applies an extension of conventional vector quantization (VQ) [18] by incorporating a vigilance parameter, which steers the tradeoff between plasticity and stability during incremental online learning. *Plasticity* is the ability to adapt to new information, whereas *stability* is the ability to converge to an optimal solution. This is motivated in the *adaptive resonance theory network* (ART) approach [11] and is exploited for forming a one-pass incremental and evolving clustering process, called *evolving vector quantization* (*eVQ*) [40]. When doing so, it connects a cluster evolution condition and an alternative distance strategy for samplewise winner selection, which is based on the distance calculation to the surface rather than to the centers (as done in conventional VQ). Hence the surface is calculated incrementally synchronously to the centers.
- Each cluster stands for one rule and the clusters are projected onto the axes in order to form the Gaussian fuzzy sets and the antecedent parts of the rules.
- It uses recursive *local learning* by exploiting *recursive weighted least squares* [39] for the linear consequent parameters in a fuzzy basis function network introduced in [61], that is, a Takagi-Sugeno fuzzy system with Gaussian fuzzy sets and product *t*-norm as conjunction operator, in the case of $C$ rules defined as:

$$\hat{f}_{fuz}(\vec{x}) = \hat{y}_{fuz} = \sum_{i=1}^{C} l_i(\vec{x}) \Psi_i(\vec{x}) \qquad (5.1)$$

with the normalized membership functions

$$\Psi_i(\vec{x}) = \mu_i \frac{(\vec{x})}{\sum_{j=1}^{C} \mu_j(\vec{x})} \qquad (5.2)$$

and $\mu_i$ as rule fulfillment of the $i$th rule

$$\mu_i(\vec{x}) = \exp\left(-\frac{1}{2} \sum_{j=1}^{p} \frac{(x_j - c_{ij})^2}{\sigma_{ij}^2}\right) \qquad (5.3)$$

and consequent functions

$$l_i(\vec{x}) = w_{i0} + w_{i1}x_1 + w_{i2}x_2 + \ldots + w_{ip}x_p \qquad (5.4)$$

where $c_{ij}$ is the center and $\sigma_{ij}$ is the width of the Gaussian function appearing as a fuzzy set in the $j$th antecedent part (i.e., the antecedent part for the $j$th input dimension) of the $i$th rule. In this sense, local linear models $l_i$ are connected through an inference scheme, where the Gaussian functions serve as kernel functions and weight new incoming samples according to their distance to the centers. One major advantage is that with a local learning technique the consequent parameters $\vec{w}$ of each rule can be incrementally trained separately and hence an evolution of a new rule does not disturb the consequent parameter training of the others [5]; this is for more flexibility during the training process. Another major advantage of local learning is that the hyperplanes describing the consequent functions tend to snuggle along the surface [45], which is also the key condition for obtaining reliable local error bars as outlined in section 5.4.5.

- It connects two previous learning issues by taking care that a near-optimal solution is reached that is close to the optimal one in the least-squares sense (deviating from the optimal one by a small constant). This can be shown analytically and empirically; for details see [41].

The final point in the itemization addresses the problem of robustness as outlined in section 5.1. (first itemization point). In fact, correction terms are integrated in the learning procedure, which balance out the nonoptimal situation, appearing during the training process as clusters; hence, rules are shifted and moved. Therefore, the recursive weighed least-squares approach, which would guide the parameter solution to optimality in case of fixed premise parts, is disturbed. The correction terms cannot be calculated in an incremental fashion, but it can be shown that they are forced to a decreasing sequence, leading to a near-optimal solution (for details see [41]). This is achieved on the basis that clusters are forced to evolve into a balanced state. The balanced state is guaranteed by controlling the tradeoff between plasticity (ability to adapt to new information) and stability (ability to converge to an optimal solution) with a *vigilance parameter*: If, for instance, two different main states occur during the online process, two different clusters will evolve automatically in the eVQ process; this will prevent strong fluctuating movements of one cluster, as the cluster centers and surfaces are always adapted within local areas.

Figure 5.1 shows an empirical justification of this point by the dependency of model qualities (maximum quality $= 1$) on the number of data samples each block contains loaded into FLEXFIS. This is done for a practical application example, where 32 different models are trained based on (noisy) measurement data from engine test benches and their average model quality is measured in terms of the average $r$-squared-adjusted measure [23], punishing more complex models by dividing $r$-squared measures with the number of model parameters. The maximum of 960 data samples denotes the whole batch of data collected, and FLEXFIS applied on it in batch mode (complete antecedent learning first and complete consequent estimation afterward)

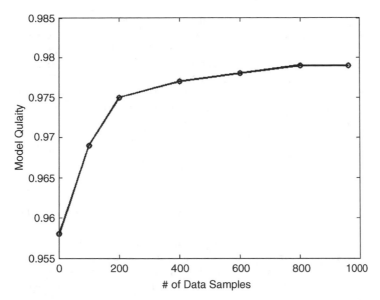

**Figure 5.1.** Dependency between block size and average model quality when training with FLEXFIS; the circles denote the tested block sizes 1, 100, 200, 400, 600, 800, 960 (all points); the difference of model qualities between samplewise incremental training (sample size = 1) and batch training (sample size = 960) is in quite a small range.

delivers the optimal solution in the least-squares sense. It can be seen that the model quality of the samplewise evolved model is not significantly worse than the quality of the model trained in batch mode. This means that the evolved solution comes close to the optimal one.

Integrating all the concepts mentioned previously, the algorithm of FLEXFIS can be summarized as in Algorithm 1 (for further details about the derivation of this algorithm please refer to [41]).

---

## Algorithm 1: FLEXFIS

1. Collect $k$ data points sufficient to yield a good approximation without overfitting; to our best knowledge (from several test-runs with different data streams), a reasonable value for $k$ is $\max(4p, 50)$ with $p$ the number of input variables.
2. From these collected $k$ data points, generate an initial fuzzy model with FLEXFIS *in batch mode*, hence, with clustering by eVQ first and then local learning approach for rules' consequents through weighted least squares. Also estimate the ranges of all input and output variables.
3. Take the next incoming data point: $\vec{x}_{k+1}$.
4. Normalize cluster centers and widths as well as the current data point with the ranges from the previous cycle or from the initial offline step. This has the effect that new incoming (fault-free) data points lying significantly outside the already-estimated range are more likely to cause a new rule.

5. **If** the current data point lies inside any cluster's range of influence:
   (a) Calculate the distance of the selected data point to all those cluster centers belonging to clusters the new sample lies inside by using Euclidian distance measure.
   (b) Elicit the cluster center that is closest to the data point by taking the minimum over all calculated distances → winner cluster $c_{win}$.
   (c) Set $min_{dist} = 0$ (this forces the algorithm that no new cluster is generated).
6. **Else If** the current data point lies outside of all clusters' range of influence:
   (a) Calculate the distance of $\vec{x}$ to the surface of all clusters.
   (b) Elicit the cluster center that is closest to the data point by taking the minimum over all calculated distances → winner cluster $c_{win}$.
   (c) Set $min_{dist}$ as the minimum over all distances.
7. **If** $min_{dist} \geq \rho$:
   (a) Increase the number of clusters from $C$ to $C + 1$.
   (b) Start a new cluster at the $k + 1$th point, hence, $\vec{c}_C = \vec{x}_{k+1}$ with $c$ the center of the new cluster.
   (c) Set the width of the new cluster to zero, hence, $\vec{\sigma}_C = \vec{0}$.
   (d) Transfer cluster centers and widths back to original range.
   (e) Project the new cluster to the axes to from the antecedent part (fuzzy sets) of the new rule; hereby set the width of the fuzzy set in the $i$th dimension to $\varepsilon*range(x_i)$ with $\varepsilon$ a small value.
   (f) Set the linear consequent parameter $\hat{\vec{w}}_C$ of the new rule to $\vec{0}$.
   (g) Set the inverse covariance matrix $P_C$ of the new rule to $\alpha I$.
8. **ELSE:**
   (a) Update the $p$ center components of the winner cluster $c_{win}$ by $c_{win}(new) = c_{win}(old) + \eta_{win}(\vec{x}_{k+1} - c_{win}(old))$ with the choice of an adaptive learning gain $\eta_{win} = \frac{0.5}{k_{win}}$ with $k_{win}$ the number of data samples forming the winning cluster.
   (b) Update the $p$ width components of winner cluster $c_{win}$ by using the recursive variance update formula [51].
   (c) Transfer cluster centers and widths back to original range.
   (d) Project winner cluster onto the axes to update the antecedent part of the rule belonging to the winner cluster; assure that the width of the fuzzy set in the $i$th dimension is equal or bigger than $\varepsilon*range(x_i)$.
   (e) Correct the linear parameter vector of consequent functions and the inverse covariance matrix of the rule corresponding to the winning cluster:

$$\hat{\vec{w}}_{win}(k) = \hat{\vec{w}}_{win}(k) + \vec{\delta}_{win}(k) \quad P_{win}(k) = P_{win}(k) + \Delta_{win}(k) \qquad (5.5)$$

9. Perform recursive weighted least squares for the consequent parameters in all $i = 1, \ldots, C$ rules by

$$\hat{\vec{w}}_i(k+1) = \hat{\vec{w}}_i(k) + \gamma(k)(y(k+1) - \vec{r}^T(k+1)\hat{\vec{w}}_i(k)) \qquad (5.6)$$

$$\gamma(k) = P_i(k+1)\vec{r}(k+1) = P_i(k)\frac{\vec{r}(k+1)}{\frac{1}{\Psi_i(\vec{x}(k+1))} + \vec{r}^T(k+1)P_i(k)\vec{r}(k+1)} \qquad (5.7)$$

$$P_i(k+1) = (I - \gamma(k)\vec{r}^T(k+1))P_i(k) \qquad (5.8)$$

with $\Psi_i(\vec{x}(k+1))$ the normalized membership function value for the $(k+1)$th data sample as weight in the update process, $P_i(k)$ the weighted inverse covariance matrix, and $\vec{r}(k+1) = [1x_1(k+1)x_2(k+1)\ldots x_p(k+1)]^T$ the regressor values of the $(k+1)$th data point, which is the same for all $C$ rules.

10. Update the ranges of all input and output variables.

11. If new data points are processed, set $k = k+1$ and GOTO Step 3, ELSE stop.

From this algorithm it is clear that an initial training phase has to take place. At first glance, this seems to be a drawback versus other approaches that are able to perform incremental learning from the start. However, it should be emphasized that in industrial applications usually an offline modeling step is required in order to get a feeling of the performance of the models and to be able to carry out an analysis of some model components (for examining reliability and reasonability). Furthermore, an initial model building (which is also possible during online mode when carried out on just the first few dozen samples) delivers a good first guess of an appropriate setting of the most important parameter (the vigilance ρ, which guides the number of rules) in FLEXFIS, especially when applied within a best parameter grid search procedure connected with a cross-validation process (see also section 5.5).

## 5.3 EVOLVING FUZZY CLASSIFIERS WITH FLEXFIS-CLASS

FLEXFIS-Class [42] exploits two model architectures:

1. Single-model architecture (usually called the *classical* fuzzy classifier architecture [29, 46, 48, 52]) whose rules are defined in the following way:

$$\text{Rule}_i : \text{IF} \quad x_1 \quad \text{IS} \quad \mu_{i1} \quad \text{AND}\ldots\text{AND} \quad x_p \quad \text{IS} \quad \mu_{ip} \quad \text{THEN} \quad y_i = L_i$$

$$(5.9)$$

where $p$ is the dimensionality of the input space, $\mu_{i1},\ldots,\mu_{ip}$ are the $p$ antecedent fuzzy sets, and $L_i$ is the crisp output class label from the set $\{1,\ldots,K\}$ with $K$ the number of classes. When classifying a new sample $\vec{x}$, the final crisp class label is obtained by taking the class label of the rule with the highest activation degree, that is, by calculating

$$y = L_{i^*} \quad \text{with} \quad i^* = \text{argmax}_{1 \leq i \leq R} \quad \tau_i \qquad (5.10)$$

with $R$ the number of rules and $\tau_i$ the activation degree of rule $i$ defined by a $t$-norm that is usually expressed as a product operator [65]:

$$\tau_i = \underset{j=1}{\overset{p}{T}} \mu_{ij}(x_j)$$

where $\mu_{ij}$ are the membership functions of the antecedent fuzzy sets defined by a Gaussian:

$$\mu_{ij} = e^{-\frac{1}{2}\frac{(x_j - c_{ij})^2}{\sigma_{ij}^2}} \tag{5.11}$$

with $c_{ij}$ signifying the centers and $\sigma_{ij}$ the spread of the membership functions.

2. Multimodel architecture, which is based on $K$ MISO Takagi-Sugeno fuzzy regression models (5.1) using $K$ indicator matrixes for the $K$ classes that are generated from the original classification matrix, containing different features in different columns and a label entry in the last column. This is done for the $i$th matrix by setting each label entry to 1, if the corresponding row belongs to the $i$th class; otherwise it is set to 0, forcing the regression surface always between 0 and 1. The overall output from the fuzzy classifier is calculated by inferencing a new multidimensional sample $\vec{x}$ through the $K$ Takagi-Sugeno models and then eliciting that model producing the maximal output and taking the corresponding class as label response, hence

$$y = class(\vec{x}) = \mathrm{argmax}_{m=1,\ldots,K} \hat{f}_m(\vec{x}) \tag{5.12}$$

hence a kind of aggregation procedure over regression surfaces. This is somewhat equivalent to the well-known "one-versus-rest" classification approach [15].

To our best knowledge, the multimodel option significantly outperforms the single-model architecture in terms of predictive accuracy (see also [3] and [42]); as this type of model architecture is quite a new one, we concentrate on the description of this approach, simply called *FLEXFIS-Class MM*.

## 5.3.1 Flexfis-Class MM

In [24] it is maintained that regression by an indicator matrix works well on two-class problems (0/1) only and can have difficulties with multiclass problems, as then a complete masking of one class by two or more others may happen. However, as opposed to linear regression by an indicator matrix [14], the TS fuzzy models are nonlinear, that is, not only the (locally linear) rule consequents but also the (nonlinear) antecedent parts are trained based on the indicator matrix information, by taking the label column as the (regressing) target variable. In this sense, the approximation behavior is nonlinear, which forces the surface of a model $\hat{f}_m$ to go toward 0 more rapidly compared to inflexible linear hyperplanes; therefore, the masking is much weaker than in the pure linear case. This argument is underlined in Figure 5.2, where the upper image visualizes the linear regression surfaces for three classes. It can be realized that the middle class (red Xs) is completely masked out by the left (blue circles) and the right classes (green pluses), as never dominating in the regression surfaces (never achieving the maximum over all surfaces). On the other hand, the lower image displays the results when first-order TSK fuzzy models are applied for regressing on the indicator matrixes. Here, the masking problem is solved.

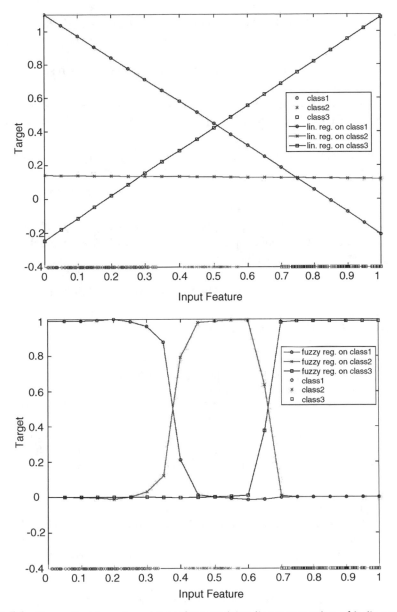

Figure 5.2. *Upper:* Problem of masking when applying linear regression of indicator matrix (light line with Xs is nowhere maximal). *Lower:* Masking problem solved by fuzzy regression of indicator matrix.

For incorporating new classes on demand, FLEXFIS-Class MM possesses the flexibility to simply extend the multimodel structure by opening up a new first-order TSK fuzzy system for this class. The inner structure of the separate first-order TSK fuzzy models is evolved and incrementally adapted with FLEXFIS as described in the previous section (see Algorithm 1). The basic characteristics of FLEXFIS-Class MM can be summarized in the following (for further details please refer to [42]):

- It exploits a multimodel architecture with a one-versus-rest classification approach.
- It performs an evolving regression modeling for each class separately with the usage of FLEXFIS exploiting first-order TSK fuzzy models and based on indicator vectors.
- In this sense, the evolution of every submodel has the same characteristics (with convergence to optimality, etc.), as pointed out in section 5.2.
- It does not suffer from the masking problem in case of multiple classes, as opposed to linear regression by indicator matrix.
- It has the flexibility to include upcoming new classes during online operation mode on demand by opening up a new first-order TSK fuzzy submodel and, hence, without "disturbing" already-trained fuzzy models.

The FLEXFIS-Class MM algorithm can be formulated as in Algorithm 2.

---

**Algorithm 2: FLEXFIS-CLASS MM**

1. Collect $N$ data points sufficient for the actual dimensionality of the problem; estimate the ranges of all features from these $N$ points. As $K$ different first; order TSK models are estimated, $N$ can be estimated as $Kmax(4p, 50)$ (compare Algorithm 1) when assuming equally balanced class distribution; if this is not the case, for each class at least $max(4p, 50)$ number of samples should be collected.
2. Generate $K$ (initial) TS fuzzy models for $K$ classes by using batch-mode FLEXFIS, that is, eVQ and axis-projection on all samples first and LS on all samples afterwards.
3. Take the next sample $\bar{x}$, normalize it in all dimensions using the estimated ranges, and elicit its class label, say $k$.
4. **IF** $k \leq K$, update the $k$th TS fuzzy model by taking $y = 1$ as response (target) value and using FLEXFIS (Algorithm 1).
5. **ELSE**, a new class label is introduced and a new TS-fuzzy model is initiated by using FLEXFIS (Algorithm 1); $K \leftarrow K + 1$.
6. Update all other TS fuzzy models by taking $y = 0$ as response (target) value and using FLEXFIS (Algorithm 1).
7. Update ranges of features.
8. IF new data points are processed, THEN GO TO Step 3; ELSE *stop*.

---

## 5.4 METHODOLOGIES FOR INCREASING ROBUSTNESS AND PERFORMANCE

In the following, we describe approaches for improving the robustness during the incremental training procedure, and for improving the predictive performance of evolving fuzzy classifiers. It will be demonstrated how these approaches can be included into online learning algorithms FLEXFIS resp. FLEXFIS-Class. As FLEX-FIS-Class MM uses FLEXFIS internally for incremental training and evolution of multiple first-order TSK fuzzy models (see Algorithm 2), the implementation of the approaches is mentioned only for the regression case, but also automatically affects the classification case. The issue about adaptive local error bars as demonstrated in section 5.4.5 can be applied only to regression models. All their core aspects will be described in quite a conceptual way, such that they are easily applicable to other evolving fuzzy systems approaches as well. The impact of these issues on the modeling process will be visualized in two-dimensional examples, such that the reader should get a clear impression of what is really improved, and so on. An extensive study on higher-dimensional models will be done in section 5.5.

## 5.4.1 Overcoming Instabilities in the Learning Process with Regularization

Assuming that the complete antecedent part of a TSK fuzzy system is either given or already preestimated with any learning method, we concentrate here on a robust estimation of the consequent parameters with weighted least squares (for an initial offline model building phase as in Step 2 of Algorithm 1) resp. recursive weighted least squares (for the incremental online learning phase as in Step 9). For the offline phase, the problem of instability in the estimation process becomes clear when inspecting the least-squares solution for the whole bunch of consequent parameters:

$$\hat{\vec{w}} = (R^T R)^{-1} R^T \vec{y} \tag{5.13}$$

where the matrix $R$ contains the regression entries for all rules and all dimensions (see, e.g., [7]); hence, $R^T R$ may get rather big and, hence, the likelihood to get singular or at least nearly singular (measured in terms of a high condition) is quite high. In this case, the solution in (5.13) gets unstable, that is, tends to a wrong solution, or is even impossible to calculate. In fact, when applying a weighted least-squares approach for separate local learning of rule consequents (as is done in FLEXFIS and FLEXFIS-Class MM), that is, by

$$\hat{\vec{w}}_i = (R_i^T Q_i R_i)^{-1} R_i^T Q_i \vec{y} \tag{5.14}$$

with $R_i$ containing the regression entry just for one rule (e.g., [67]), the dimensionality is reduced and, hence, the likelihood of singular matrixes is lower. So, local learning already implements an implicit regularization effect, as it divides the original optimization problem into smaller subproblems (for each rule) and hence reduces the size of the matrixes to be inverted. This effect is called *regularization by discretization* [16]; in general, problems of smaller size do not necessarily need to be regularized, because a reasonable lower bound on the singular value of the matrixes can be found. However, in case of high-dimensional input (as will be seen in section 5.5) and also in low-dimensional cases when the noise in the output variable is quite high, the problem is

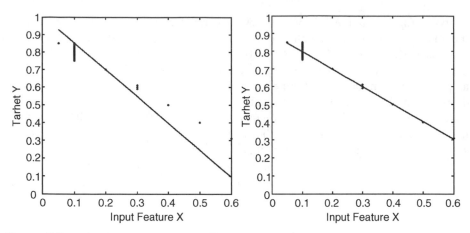

**Figure 5.3.** *Left:* The approximation of a simple 2-dimensional relationship with a not-regularized TS fuzzy regression model with one rule (solid line). *Right:* Regularization is applied → model is correct. In both images the data points are the small dark dots.

still severe. To underline the latter case, in Figure 5.3 a simple first-order TSK fuzzy model with one rule (so, a linear regression model) is a shown as a solid line. Even though the noise in the data and the dimensionality are quite low and the tendency of the functional dependency is obvious (linear), the estimated regression model without regularization gets very inaccurate (left image), where the same model with regularization fits the data quite well (right image). The reason for this unpleasant effect lies in the fact that the data samples appear stepwise, whereas at $x = 0.1$ almost 90% of the data is already covered. This means that in the regression matrix $R$ a lot of rows are identical, causing a covariance matrix $R^T R$, which is nearly singular.

In order to overcome this possible instability problem and avoid a manipulation of the data, we apply Tichonov regularization [16,19,57], which adds a correction term to the covariance matrix $(R_i^T R_i)^{-1}$ in form of $\alpha_i I$ with $I$ the identity matrix; hence, the matrix inversion in (14) becomes $(R_i^T Q_i R_i + \alpha_i I)^{-1}$. The central question is, now, how to choose an appropriate value for $\alpha_i$ when estimating the consequent parameters of the $i$th rule in local learning, in order to stay as close as possible to the optimal least-squares solution while regularizing sufficiently to obtain a stable solution. In this sense, the choice is a matter of a tradeoff between stability and optimality. For achieving an optimal tradeoff, several strategies can be investigated in offline mode, such as Morozov's discrepancy principle [47], sparsity contraints [13, 53], Lepskij balancing principle [37], or hard-balancing [9], each of them motivated by different aspects. While Morozov's discrepancy principle gives a convergent regularization method under the condition that the noise level is known, sparsity constraints have the tendency to force the entries in the vector $\vec{w}_i$ to be zero at best; hence, the resulting regularized vector tends to be sparse without any preassumption to the noise level. Hard-balancing is a new development and can be used for estimating the regularization parameter in cases where the noise level is not known. Here, we concentrate on the demonstration of a heuristic approach, which is applicable for an arbitrary noise level and does not need any past data in its regularization process and, hence, is applicable for samplewise online training. Hereby, the basic aspect is that the condition of the covariance matrix is decreased slightly beneath a threshold by exploiting the fact that the addition of $\alpha_i I$ to $P_i$ influences the small eigenvalues strongly and the larger ones only slightly (Step 3a).

1. Compute (offline) $R_i^T Q_i R_i$ resp. update (online) $(R_i^T Q_i R_i)^{-1}$.
2. Compute the condition of $P_i = R_i^T Q_i R_i$ (offline) resp. $P_i = (R_i^T Q_i R_i)^{-1}$ (online), by applying a singular value decomposition [22] and using the well-known formula $cond(P_i) = \frac{\lambda_{max}}{\lambda_{min}}$ where $\lambda_{min}$ and $\lambda_{max}$ denote the minimal and maximal eigenvalue of $P_i$.
3. If $cond(P_i) > threshold$, the matrix is badly conditioned; hence, do the following:
   (a) Choose $\alpha_i$ in a way such that the condition of $P_i$ gets smaller than the threshold but not too small due to the considerations above. This can be accomplished by exploiting the fact that the addition of $\alpha_i I$ to $P_i$ influences the smallest eigenvalues strongly; therefore, the condition of $threshold/2$, $\alpha_i$ can be approximated by

$$\alpha \approx \frac{2\lambda_{max}}{threshold} \tag{5.15}$$

   (b) Set $(P_i)^{-1} (P_i + \alpha_i I)^{-1}$ (offline); set $P_i = P_i + \alpha_i I$ for further adaptation (online).
4. Apply weighted least-squares approach as in (5.14) (offline) resp., proceed with $P_i$ (online).

*Note:* Setting the threshold can be carried out from experience with badly conditioned matrixes (often a value of $10^{15}$ is suggested) or simply by stepwise trying out which condition level on the inverse leads to unstable results.

In section 5.5 it will be further outlined how necessary a regularization in the initial offline model step of FLEXFIS is in order to gain more predictive accuracy during the incremental learning process. For the online phase, the question remains whether regularization during the update process of the covariance matrix in RWLS helps improve the models further. This means that the question is whether a singular or nearly singular matrix disturbs also the update (not only its inversion, as done in the offline case) of the covariance matrix. This will be also examined in section 5.5; in each incremental learning step it will be checked whether the matrix is nearly singular; if so, it will be corrected by the heuristic regularization approach as described above.

So, in case of FLEXFIS an additional step *between* Steps 8 and 9 in Algorithm 1 is inserted:

*Step 8.5: For all $i = 1, \ldots, C$ rules:*

- Calculate the condition of $P_i$.
- **If** $cond(P_i) < threshold$ elicit $\alpha_i$ by (15); **Else** set $\alpha_i = 0$.
- $P_i = P_i + \alpha_i I$.

## 5.4.2 Overcoming the Unlearning Effect

When performing incremental learning steps of linear rule consequent parameters in TSK fuzzy models, it may happen that the recursive weighted least squares guides the linear parameters to a wrong solution. This would be the case if the newly loaded data points or recently recorded measurements stay (almost) constant for a certain period. To demonstrate this in a simple practical example, see Figure 5.4, where the first 200 data samples (light dots) are indeed well distributed over the whole input space, but the next 1300 samples (represented by the big dark dot) are concentrated around the specific point (1200,2).

Obviously, the car motor was steered with a constant rotation speed; the slight noise variance can be explained by sensor inaccuracies during recording. This example represents the situation whenever a process is in steady state, that is, staying at one specific operating condition for a long time. When doing an initial learning phase with the first 200 points (no matter whether in incremental or batch mode) and performing an adaptation of the fuzzy model with the later 1300 points (in steady state), an undesired *unlearning* effect of already-learned relationships outside this small constant region occurs. This can be recognized in the left image in Figure 5.4, where to the left and right of the small constant region the shape and behavior of the adapted model (dotted line) tend to be completely different from the shape and behavior of the original one (solid line), even though no new measurements were recorded for that area. The reason for these effects is that the parameters of all linear consequent functions are adapted for each incoming data sample, no matter which firing degree the rules have. In fact, rules with a very low firing degree (i.e., rules that are far away from the constant region) are adjusted very slightly for each point, but this sums up with a high amount of data recorded during steady state. Finally, this means that the consequent parameters are

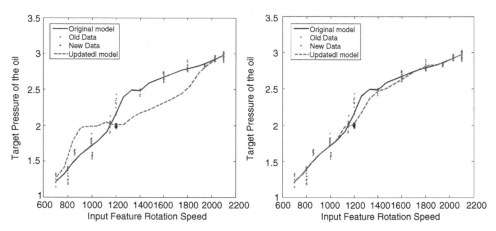

**Figure 5.4.** *Left:* Unlearning effect when adapting all rule consequents for each sample at (1400,2) (dark dot). *Right:* The unlearning effect is prevented when adapting only the significantly firing rules. The dotted light lines represent the updated models. *Note:* The x-axis denotes rotation speed; the y-axis denotes the pressure of the oil.

forced to minimize the error at (1200,2). This causes the linear consequent hyperplanes to go through the point (1200,2). A promising strategy to circumvent this problem lies in the adaptation of only those parameters that correspond to significantly active rules, that is, rules that possess normalized membership function values $\Psi(\vec{x}_{act})$higher than a certain threshold near 0. This guarantees that rules that represent areas not lying near a constant process state remain unchanged and, hence, are not disturbed. In FLEXFIS, this can be accomplished by *replacing* Step 9 in Algorithm 1 with the following condition:

*Step 9:* **If** $\Psi_i(\vec{x}(k+1)) \geq thresh$, perform recursive weighted least squares for the consequent parameters of the $i$th rule by. . . .

This is demonstrated in the right images in Figure 5.4, where a threshold of 0.1 was used. In fact, setting the threshold is a crucial point for a well-performing adaptation: If it is set too close to 0, the unlearning effect remains; if it is set too close to 1, the consequent parameters are hardly updated and may not be able to follow new comming trends in the data.

Another point of view of the unlearning effect is when considering classification problems, where the data distribution of the classes gets quite unbalanced during the incremental learning process, so that one or more classes become significantly more frequent than some others. In this case, the danger is high that the less-frequent classes are simply overwhelmed and do not contribute to a cluster or a rule with majority any longer, causing a bad classification accuracy for these classes [50]. In order to overcome this unpleasant effect, we propose a *timing of update* strategy, where it is not the case that each single new incoming instance is taken into the evolving process of the fuzzy classifiers, but only in the following three situations (here, for two classes):

1. Whenever there is a disagreement between the classifier's decision and the true class ( $\rightarrow$ extending the classifier to this new state).
2. Whenever the relative proportion of samples seen so far and falling into all the classes is equally balanced ( $\rightarrow$ refining the classifier with additional samples is usually advantageous).
3. Whenever the relative proportion of samples seen so far and belonging to the current class into which the sample falls is lower than the relative proportion of the most significant class (class with highest number of representatives—in order to incorporate more samples from less frequent classes and boost up the performance for these).

## 5.4.3 Dealing with Drifts in Data Streams

*Drift* refers to a gradual evolution of the concept over time [59]. A drift in the data set can be caused by a dynamically changing system behavior; that is, the underlying data distribution changes completely [62]. This should be not confused with an upcoming new operating condition, where the data distribution remains the same for the already-learned local dependencies, but the feature/variable space is extended, which requires an extension of the clusters/rules, keeping all the older learned relations—as is usually done in all evolving fuzzy system approaches. The concept of drift concerns the way the data distribution slides smoothly through the feature space from one region to the other. For instance, one may consider a data cluster changing from one position to the other, where the cluster at the older position becomes outdated over time; see Figure 5.5, where the old data distribution is marked with circles, the new one with rectangles. The cluster center (big circle) should move from the left position to the right one. When updating the cluster with standard incremental learning algorithms by taking each sample equally weighted, the updated center would end up somewhere in the middle, causing an inaccurate cluster partition and modeling behavior.

Another viewpoint of a drift, especially appearing in the case of regression modeling, is a shift in the trajectory as shown in Figure 5.6, where the original sinusoidal relationship on the right-hand side changes over time—compare the dark line (samples after the shift) versus the light line (samples before the shift). When applying recursive (weighted) least squares, the regression line would end up somewhere in the middle between the two trajectories, achieving an unsatisfactory accuracy; hence, it is also necessary to forget the older tracking and to change to the new situation as shown in the right-hand image.

***5.4.3.1 Gradual Forgetting.*** In order to track drift occurrences, a mechanism is triggered that incorporates larger weights for the new data samples than for older ones in the incremental/evolving learning process. This is done by a gradual forgetting of older data points over time. For the linear consequent parameters in all Takagi-Sugeno-Kang-type fuzzy models, this can be achieved by introducing a *forgetting* factor $\lambda$ and incorporating it into the *recursive weighted least-squares* formula (here for the $i$th rule of any model):

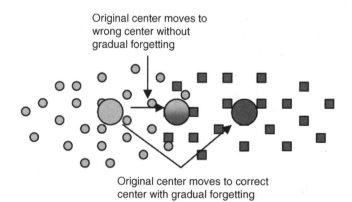

Figure 5.5. *Drifting clusters:* The samples marked with circles represent the underlying data distribution before the drift; the samples marked with rectangles represent the underlying data distribution after the drift; the big circles represent the cluster center for the original data (*left*), the wrongly updated center by standard incremental learning algorithm (*middle*), and the real center for the new data distribution (*right*).

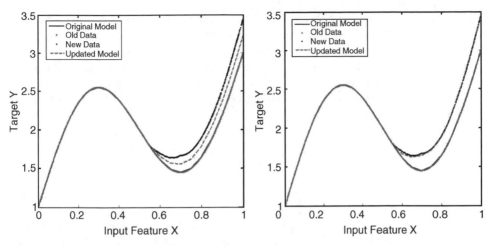

**Figure 5.6.** *Left:* Updated fuzzy model (dashed line) without forgetting. *Right:* Updated fuzzy model with an appropriate forgetting factor (dashed line lying exactly on the trajectory triggered by the dark dots).

$$\hat{\vec{w}}_i(k+1) = \hat{\vec{w}}_i(k) + \gamma(k)(y(k+1) - \vec{r}^T(k+1)\hat{\vec{w}}_i(k)) \qquad (5.16)$$

$$\gamma(k) = \frac{P_i(k)\vec{r}(k+1)}{\frac{\lambda}{\Psi_i(\vec{x}(k+1))} + \vec{r}^T(k+1)P_i(k)\vec{r}(k+1)} \qquad (5.17)$$

$$P_i(k+1) = (I - \gamma(k)\vec{r}^T(k+1))P_i(k)\frac{1}{\lambda} \qquad (5.18)$$

with $P_i(k) = (R_i(k)^T Q_i(k)R_i(k))^{-1}$ the inverse-weighted Hesse matrix and $\vec{r}(k+1) = [1 x_1(k+1) x_2(k+1) \ldots x_p(k+1)]^T$ the regressor values of the $(k+1)$th data point. Please note that in FLEXFIS Algorithm 1, these formulas simply substitute those in Step 9, whenever a drift occurs. In the case of $\lambda = 1$, no forgetting takes place, while with decreasing $\lambda$ the forgetting gets stronger and stronger. An appropriate setting of this parameter depends on the intensity of the drift, which is closely linked to the detection of a drift; see the next paragraph.

For reacting on drifts in the rules' antecedent parts learning of FLEXFIS(-Class), we propose to readjust the parameter in the eVQ [40] clustering algorithm, which steers the learning gain and furthermore a convergence of the centers and surfaces of the cluster over time (with more samples loaded), namely $\eta$ by the following formula (see also Step 8(a) in Algorithm 1):

$$\eta_i = \frac{0.5}{n_i} \qquad (5.19)$$

From formula (5.19) it can be realized that the learning gain decreases with the number of samples forming the $i$th rule ($n_i$), which is a favorable characteristic in order to converge to optimality in the least-squares sense (section 5.2). If a drift occurs in a data stream, this favorable characteristic is not favorable any longer, as then centers and widths of the cluster(s) should change to the new data distribution. Hence, we propose a successive increase of the learning gain with more samples loaded, whenever a drift starts (here, assuming this for the $i$th cluster):

$$\eta_i = \frac{0.5}{n_i - fac * n_{i,drift}} \tag{5.20}$$

where $n_{i,drift}$ denotes the number of data samples forming cluster $i$ since the start of the drift. The factor $fac$ in the denominator depends on $n_i$ and on the speed of the drift from one distribution to the other: Whenever $n_i$ is high, $fac$ should be high as well in order to gain a significant increase, especially at the beginning of the drift; on the other hand, when $n_i$ is low, $fac$ can be kept low, as the already-available cluster is not really distinct and can be easily formed according to the new data distribution. Whenever the speed is high, $fac$ should also be high, as a fast adaptation to the new situation is required. In Figure 5.7 three parameter curves showing the development of $\eta_i$ are visualized when using three different values of $fac$, assuming that a drift starts at $n_i = 600$ and ends at $n_i = 700$.

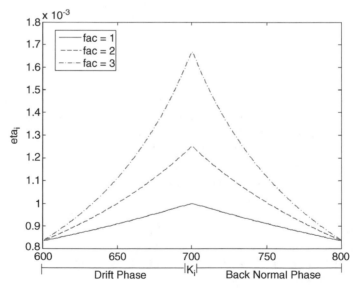

Figure 5.7. Increasing learning gain η during a drift phase (*left-hand side*), decreasing learning gain η when back into normal mode (*right-hand side*), when applying *fac* = 1 (*solid line*), 2 (*dashed line*), and 3 (*dashed dotted line*).

In Section 5.5, we will highlight how a gradual forgetting of consequent resp. antecedent parameters of the rules improves the predictive accuracies of regression models and classifiers.

***5.4.3.2 Drift Detection.*** The remaining central question is how to detect a drift automatically from the data, as only in very rare cases will an external operator give feedback on this issue from outside to the evolving modeling process. The detection is necessary, because the more data, fully and equally weighted, is used in the learning process, the better the accuracies of the models usually become, if no concept drift has occurred since the data arrived. In this sense, a permanent gradual forgetting during the whole online modeling procedure would asymptotically create worse models, when no drift occurs. On the other hand, when a drift occurs, the distribution of the older data differs from the current distribution, so that the older data may be misleading and hence need to be outdated. One possibility for doing drift detection in online data streams when applying evolving rule-based models is by exploiting the "rule age" concept introduced in [2]. The *rule age* tracks how a rule becomes less important and has been used less; that is, it will get "older" quicker than the average rate of ageing. In this sense, the derivatives of the *rule age curves* can be inspected and a detection alarm triggered whenever a significant knee in the smoothed curve can be observed (i.e., by a high second derivative). In this case, a rule is suddenly ageing much faster than before (i.e., a change in the form of a drift or shift in the underlying data distribution is quite likely).

## 5.4.4 Toward Safer Extrapolation Behavior

When doing adaptation of premise parts in fuzzy models with the usage of fuzzy sets with infinite support (especially with the most common Gaussian sets), it usually happens that not all fuzzy sets possess the same width. This is due to the nature of online data streams, where local areas (which are projected onto the axes to form the fuzzy sets) reflect different system behaviors with different ranges. This can lead to undesirable extrapolation effects, when the outermost set is not the broadest one, as a kind of reactivation of an inner membership function in the extrapolation region is caused (see Figure 5.8).

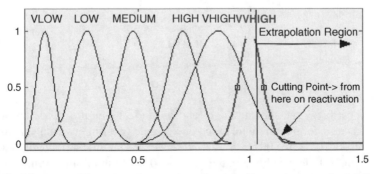

**Figure 5.8.** A fuzzy partition where inner sets are broader than outer ones. Especially compare the two rightmost sets → reactivation of the inner set in the extrapolation region.

Especially compare the two rightmost fuzzy sets; the extrapolation region is based on the range of the input variable in the data set (from 0 to 1.03).

Inner sets can be reactivated, which is a precarious thing, as an outermost set usually stands for the most confidential information in the case of extrapolation as it is the nearest one.

In principle, one may focus on a learning procedure with constraints on the clustering process in order to ensure the same widths for all clusters and consequently fuzzy sets; however, this may cause a severe drop in predictive performance in the normal range as the model may no longer correctly represent the actual data characteristics. Hence, we pursue another possibility for overcoming this drawback, which is simply keeping all inner fuzzy sets as they are and modifying the outermost fuzzy sets by letting them be constant at the membership degree 1 for the second half of their Gaussian membership functions, causing a zero-order extrapolation behavior over the complete range of the variables [49]. Another possibility (which prevents the definition of a twofold membership function) is to transform each outermost Gaussian fuzzy set to a sigmoid function defined by:

$$\mu_{ij}(x_j) = \frac{1}{1 + e^{(-a_{ij}(x_j - b_{ij}))}} \tag{5.21}$$

based on the following two properties (leading to two equations in $a$ and $b$):

1. The position of inflection point of the Gaussian fuzzy set is equal to those of the sigmoid function.
2. At the center position of the Gaussian set the value of the sigmoid function is 0.99 (as 1 is not possible).

The solution gives

$$a_{(right)j} = -\frac{\ln 0.01}{\sigma_{(right)j}}$$
$$b_{(right)j} = c_{(right)j} - \sigma_{(right)j} \tag{5.22}$$

for the rightmost fuzzy set and

$$a_{(left)j} = \frac{\ln 0.01}{\sigma_{(left)j}}$$
$$b_{(left)j} = c_{(left)j} + \sigma_{(left)j} \tag{5.23}$$

for the leftmost fuzzy set, substituting $a_{ij}$ and $b_{ij}$ in (5.21). Figure 5.9 demonstrates the impact of this transformation figure based on a simple two-dimensional example, when trying to regress $10^{-4}\sin(0.001x^2)x^3 + \varepsilon_2$ with $\varepsilon_2$ a normally distributed random noise with $\sigma = 5$ on 700 samples lying in the range of 0 to 80; in all images the samplewise mean-squared error is plotted, which is obtained on 100 samples lying in the extrapolation range of 81 to 100 (so, 5 samples between each whole-number pair) and which are

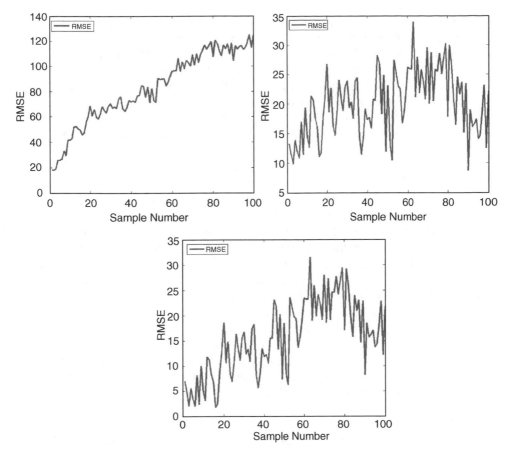

Figure 5.9. *Upper left:* Extrapolation error on 100 (sorted) samples of original fuzzy model when building a regression model for $10^{-4}\sin(0.001x^2)x^3 + \varepsilon_2$; *Upper right:* of improved fuzzy model by applying sigmoid function as in (5.21) with $a$ and $b$ obtained by (5.22) resp. (5.23); *lower:* of further improved fuzzy model by changing outermost fuzzy sets only from inflection point on.

sorted. In the left image, no enhanced extrapolation strategy is applied; the middle image presents a clear improvement of sample-based errors with the abovementioned extrapolation strategy, which is further improved in the right image by the following approach.

For this, the basic consideration is that a Gaussian fuzzy set at the border of a variable's (initial) range represents a reasonable guess for the data behavior in the extrapolation space until no reactivation takes place. However, with the abovementioned approach, the second half of the set is completely exchanged by an almost constant function (lying between 0.99 and 1.0), whereas this second half still gives a better guess than the constant function. This can be circumvented by eliciting the cutting points of the second half of an outermost fuzzy set to all the broader inner sets and taking that cutting point with maximum $y$-value and adding this $y$-value to the function value of the outermost fuzzy set from the cutting point on. The right image in Figure 5.9 clearly underlines the improvement of this strategy for this example.

Please note that this approach can be applied to any TSK fuzzy model using Gaussian fuzzy sets that is trained in batch mode or evolved during online mode. Especially, the third approach can be easily applied by adapting the original Gaussian fuzzy sets further but always virtually extending the outermost sets (in the same manner as pointed out earlier) when producing a prediction value or classification statement for a new incoming point lying outside the range estimated from the previous learning cycles.

## 5.4.5 Modeling Uncertainties with Adaptive Local Error Bars

Models' decisions may be uncertain due to a high noise level in the training data or in extrapolation regions. In these cases, it is reliable or even necessary to provide confidence regions surrounding the trained models, which should provide an insight as to how trustworthy a model is within a certain region. This is essential to judge the quality of the models' predictions. These can be directly weighted with their confidence, or a separate confidence value can be given as feedback to the user or to the system as additional information. Error bars are quite a useful technique to model such confidence bands and, hence, can be seen as an additional contribution to more process safety and robustness. Furthermore, error bars serve as an important component in many fault detection applications, in order to be able to compare a residual between a new incoming point and the error bars of an already-trained (regression) model. As in case of noisy (real-world) data, new incoming points do not exactly lie on the approximation surfaces. The deviation to the error bars is then used in order to gain a final decision as to whether the current point is faulty. This will be pointed out in more detail in section 5.5.2 (refer also to [43]).

One simple possibility to obtain error bars for a regression model lies in (incrementally) calculating the mean-squared error on the past samples and taking the double of the mean-squared error as an error bar. This would have the effect that the error bar denotes a global error band surrounding the model and has the same width throughout the whole model's range. This is shown in the left image of Figure 5.10.

However, usually the data distribution and density as well as the noise intensity are not equally balanced throughout the whole input–output space: In fact, in some regions fewer data may occur than in others. See, for instance, the region between 1300 and 1500, where no data sample appears. In this region, as well as in the extrapolation region from value 2200 on, the model's predictions are obviously less confident than in the region where sufficient training data were available. Hence, the error bars should be wider in these unconfident regions and narrower in the more confident ones, as shown in the right image of Figure 5.10. We call these error bars *local error bars* as they change their width locally. Please also note that in the extrapolation region on the right-hand side the further away the curve is from the data points, the wider the error bars get. This is exactly what somebody usually wants to achieve, as there the model gets more and more untrustworthy.

In order to obtain such local error bars for (evolving) TSK fuzzy models, we first consider local error bars for linear regression models and then extend these to the nonlinear TSK fuzzy regression model case. *Local error bars* for pure linear (regression)

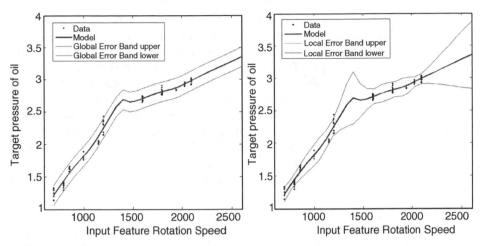

**Figure 5.10.** *Left:* Global model error band (light lines surrounding the darker line = fuzzy model). *Right:* Local error bars giving more precise local information about the confidence of the model (taking into account holes in the data and extrapolation regions).

models

$$\hat{f}(\vec{x}) = \hat{y} = \sum_{i=1}^{deg} w_i * reg_i(\vec{x}) \qquad (5.24)$$

with $reg_i$ the $i$th regressor term applied to input variables $x_1, ..., x_p$, whose linear parameters $\hat{w}$ were estimated by solving the least-squares optimization function, can be calculated through the following formula [14]:

$$\hat{y} \pm \sqrt{diag(cov\{\hat{y}\})} \qquad (5.25)$$

where $\hat{y}$ is the estimated output value from (5.24) and

$$cov\{\hat{y}\} = X_{act} cov\{\sigma^2 (X^T X)^{-1}\} X_{act}^T \qquad (5.26)$$

The noise variance $\sigma$ can be estimated by

$$\hat{\sigma}^2 = \frac{2 \sum_{j=1}^{N} (y(j) - \hat{y}(j))^2}{N - deg} \qquad (5.27)$$

where $N$ is the number of data points, $deg$ is the number of degrees of freedom (the number of parameters in the linear case), $X$ is the regression matrix, $X_{act}$ is the matrix containing the actual data points for which the error bars should be calculated, and $y(j)$ are the measured values of the target. Note that the smaller the number of data points and/ or the higher the noise in the data, the higher the noise variance gets.

Now, the usage of the error bars as in (5.25) can be exploited for evolving (and also nonevolving) TSK fuzzy systems, as long as the linear parameters of the consequent functions in (5.4) are estimated by the local learning approach (e.g., as done in FLEXFIS and FLEXFIS-Class or eTS [5]). Then, a snuggling of the consequent hyperplanes along the model's surface can be observed; see [45]. Hence, this circumstance yields a good approximation of the global model with local linear pieces. In this sense, it is reliable to calculate error bars for each rule consequent function (as one local linear piece) separately, and then connect them with weights to form an overall smooth error bar for the whole fuzzy model. Obviously, the rule-fulfillment degrees are a feasible choice for the weights, as the degrees are getting smaller at the borders of each rule. Thus, in case of $C$ rules, the error bar of an evolving (TS) fuzzy model for a specific sample $\vec{x}_{act}$ can be calculated by

$$\hat{y}_{fuz} \pm \sqrt{cov\{\hat{y}_{fuz}\}} = \hat{y}_{fuz} \pm \frac{\sum_{i=1}^{C} \mu_i(\vec{x}_{act})\sqrt{cov\{\hat{y}_i\}}}{\sum_{i=1}^{C} \mu_i(\vec{x}_{act})} \tag{5.28}$$

where $\hat{y}_i$ is the estimated value of the $i$th rule consequent function, for which $cov$ is calculated as in (5.26) by using inverse weighted matrix $(X_i^T Q_i X_i)^{-1}$ corresponding to the $i$th rule and the noise variance as in (5.27). The symbol $\mu_i(\vec{x}_{act})$ denotes the membership degree of the actual point to the $i$th rule and $\hat{y}_{fuz}$ the output value from the TS fuzzy model (see (5.1)) for the actual input point $\vec{x}_{act}$.

The remaining question is how to calculate the local error bars incrementally and synchronously to the evolving TS fuzzy models, in order to obtain the so-called *adaptive local error bars*. The incremental calculation is already guaranteed through (5.28) and (5.26), as the inverse-weighted matrix $(X_i^T Q_i X_i)^{-1}$ is updated through the incremental learning process (by RWLS, see (5.18)), anyway, and $X_{act}$ usually contains just the actual point for which a prediction statement or classification decision is desired. The only open issue is how to update $\hat{\sigma}^2$ in (5.27). This is done with $m \geq 1$ new points by:

$$\hat{\sigma}^2(\text{new}) = \frac{(N-deg(\text{old}))\hat{\sigma}^2(\text{old}) + 2\sum_{j=N}^{N+m}(y(j)-\hat{y}_{fuz}(j))^2}{N+m-deg(\text{new})}$$

where $deg(\text{new})$ is the new number of parameters, if changed in the model due to an evolution of the structure. So, the squared error on the $m$ new samples is added to the squared error on the $N$ previous samples and normalized with the whole number of samples seen so far minus the new degrees of freedom.

## 5.5 EVALUATION

We evaluate the issues for improving robustness of evolving fuzzy systems that were mentioned in the previous section. This will be done within the scope of FLEXFIS and

FLEXFIS-Class MM approaches. We exploit three different online data sets, that is, data sets that were collected within an online production process and stored onto hard disc exactly in the same order as they appeared during the online process. In this sense, we could simulate online mode in an offline program by simply taking sample by sample from the data collection (row per row from a data matrix) and sending these for incremental learning to FLEXFIS and FLEXFIS-Class respectively. We examine three application cases:

1. Building an online prediction model for the resistance value at rolling mills (applying FLEXFIS).
2. Online fault detection at engine test benches (applying FLEXFIS): This includes a complete online system identification step of several high-dimensional regression models, representing different system dependencies, and together with their adaptive local error bars serving as reference models for detecting faults in the system.
3. Online image classification (applying FLEXFIS-Class MM) for supervising CD imprint production processes and eggs.

In all cases, we are dealing with high-dimensional data (ranging from 32 to 74 input variables/features, so regularization is essential) and in some cases with smaller or bigger drifts in the data streams. In the case of the engine test bench data, there are several steady-state data included (so overcoming the unlearning effect is necessary), always appearing after a significant change in rotation speed and torque was made in order to find the balance for the new operating condition.

*Note:* For an empirical comparison of (conventional) FLEXFIS with other evolving fuzzy systems techniques such as eTS, exTS, DENFIS, MRAN, RANEKF, SAFIS, SOFNN, and GDFNN on both a high-dimensional approximation and a dynamic identification problem, refer to [41]. For a detailed analytical and empirical comparison with eTS, refer to [6]. For an empirical comparison of (conventional) FLEXFIS-Class MM with eClass, refer to [3].

## 5.5.1 Online Prediction at Rolling Mills

The task was to identify a prediction model for the resistance value of a steel plate at a rolling mill. This should be done in a first step with some offline (pre-collected) measurement data in order to obtain a feeling about the achieved quality of the fuzzy model and then to refine the prediction model with newly recorded online data. The latter step was possible as first a prediction for the resistance is given, influencing the whole process at the rolling mill, whereas a few seconds later (after the steel plate is passed) the real value for the resistance is measured, which can then be incorporated into the model adaptation process. In this sense, it is not the predicted (and maybe wrong) value that is taken for further adaptation, but the correct measured value; hence, this can be seen as a potential procedure for improving the models. The initial situation was as follows: An analytical model was already available where some parameters were estimated through linear regression and should be improved by the fuzzy model component FLEXFIS, which was applied purely based on measurement data. The analytical model is physically motivated by material laws that go back to Spittel and Hensel [26]; in modified form, the resistance value can be estimated by an exponential function of the temperature, speed, and thickness of the steel plate. Approximately 6000 training data points and approximately 6000 online data points including 13 system variables (12 inputs, 1 output), such as thickness of the steel plate before and after the rolling mill, average temperature, grain size, and others, were collected during online production. Time delays up to 10 were added for each input variable, leading to 121 input channels. The maximal delay was set to 10, as from the experience of the operators it is known that the resistance value is affected by influence values recorded maximally 8 to 10 passes ago (where one pass delivers one measurement). A 10-fold cross-validation procedure [56] with the training data was conducted for different parameter settings, varying the number of rules in the fuzzy model and varying the input dimension from 1 to 20, whereas the most important inputs were selected using a modified version of forward selection [20]. It turned out that the maximal delay in any of the selected input variables was 8. The best-performing fuzzy models obtained from the cross-validation step (Algorithm 1, Steps 1 and 2) were compared on the independent online data with the analytical model in terms of mean absolute error, the maximal errors from the upper and the lower side (estimated value too high or too low), and the number of values as estimated 20 units too low than the measured one (it was important to keep this error very low). Based on the best-performing parameter setting, the fuzzy model was further adapted and evolved with the online data, where for each sample a prediction was first given and then adapted with the measured value. This was carried out with FLEXFIS (Algorithm 1, from Step 3 on).

The results are demonstrated in Table 5.1. The rows represent the different methods applied, whereas the row "Static fuzzy models" denotes the fuzzy models obtained in the offline CV step and not further updated with the separate online data set (so kept fixed during the whole online prediction process), as opposed to the row "Evolving fuzzy models," where the fuzzy models are further evolved with Algorithm 1 from Step 3 on. The columns represent the different validation measures. From this table it can be realized that the results could be significantly improved when using adaptation/evolution of the models based on new measurements in parallel to the predictions, instead of keeping them static. It is also remarkable that the static fuzzy models could outperform the analytical model in offline mode.

T A B L E  5.1.  Comparison of Evolving Fuzzy Prediction Models Obtained by FLEXFIS with an Analytical and a Static Fuzzy Model for the Resistance Value at Rolling Mills

| Method | MAE | Max MAE Too High/Max MAE Too Low/# MAEs > 20 |
|---|---|---|
| *Analytical* | 7.84 | 63.47 /87.37 /259 |
| *Static fuzzy models* | 5.41 | 38.05 /78.88 /159 |
| *Evolving fuzzy models* | 4.66 | 37.34 /75.43 /97 |
| *Evolving fuzzy models with grad. f.* | 4.34 | 31.99 /74.56 /68 |
| *Evolving fuzzy models no reg.* | 9.88 | 85.23 /151.21 /501 |

Furthermore, based on the feedback from several system specialists, who mention that the online data set is totally independent from the training data set and contains some different system states that may cause a drift resp. shift of the underlying data distribution, gradual forgetting (as outlined in section 5.4.3) was carried out during the evolution of the models on the whole online data. The results are reported in the last-but-one row of Table 5.1 and show a significant increase in the validation measures; especially, the number of big "too low" errors could be reduced by almost one-third. Please also note that for all the mentioned results the heuristic regularization approach was implicitly applied in FLEXFIS; otherwise, the MAE suffers drastically. (See the last line in Table 5.1). This means that regularization is quite necessary in order to achieve reasonable results at all. In Figure 5.11, the evolution of the number of rules is shown for both variants, where the initial number of rules (5.21) is obtained from the initial batch training and cross-validation procedure performed on the training data; four additional rules have emerged during the online phase, which lead to significantly better results, as shown in Table 5.1.

## 5.5.2 Online Fault Detection at Engine Test Benches

The task was to detect as many faults as possible at an engine test bench during the online testing phase of a new engine. Examples of faults are pipe leakages, sensor overheating (usually causing sensor drifts), or interface errors. The detection of such faults at an early stage is strongly recommended, because faults can affect the interpretation of the state of the engine, the measuring and monitoring devices, or the control system (which also modifies the system behavior). This may even lead to breakdowns of components or the whole system. It is assumed that all possibly occurring faults can be recognized in the measurement signals (usually, a few hundred channels), which are recorded during the

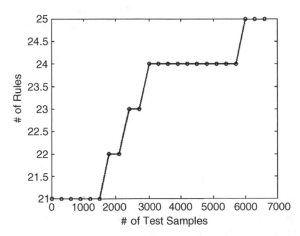

Figure 5.11. Evolution of the number of rules on the online data in steps of 300 data samples.

test phase of an engine, and furthermore that most of the faults appear quite instantaneously. These include measurements of physical variables, such as pressures and temperatures measured from sensors at different positions in the whole test bench cycle (e.g., pressure of the oil is one important factor) and also all kind of emissions ($NO_X$, $CO_2$ etc.) whose values should be quite low in order to be in line with the legally allowed boundary. Faults in the system may spoil these values and mislead the conclusion of an engine under test and evaluation.

Our approach is now to identify high-dimensional relationships and dependencies within the system, serving as (fault-free) reference models, which can be used to calculate the deviation of new samples to these models ($\rightarrow$ residuals). As this identification should be done fully automatically and without prior knowledge within online operating mode in real time, it requires an incremental and evolving learning mechanism for model building. In order not to be restricted to simple linear dependencies, we exploit fuzzy models with highly nonlinear characteristics (and that are also able to model linear dependencies). The noise is usually quite high at such engine test benches, such that the integration of error bands surrounding the models into the fault detection process is necessary.

In the case of global error bands, we exploit the whole model error (including bias and variance error [24]), and the fault condition becomes (for $m$ identified models, see [43]):

$$\exists m : \quad \frac{\hat{f}_{fuz,k,m} - x_{k,m} - \varepsilon_{x_m}}{model\_error_m} > thr \quad \vee \quad \frac{\hat{f}_{fuz,k,m} - x_{k,m} + \varepsilon_{x_m}}{model\_error_m} < -thr \qquad (5.29)$$

with $x_{k,m}$ the actual (the $k$th) measured value of the target variable in the $m$th model and $\hat{f}_{fuz,k,m}$ the estimated output value from the $m$th first-order TSK fuzzy model as defined in (5.1), and $\varepsilon_{x_m}$ the inaccuracy in the target variables (recall: $x_m$ is the output variable in the $m$th model). In this sense, each fuzzy model is checked with (5.29), and, if this condition is fulfilled for at least one fuzzy model, the actual measurement (the $k$th) is classified as faulty, otherwise as nonfaulty. This is quite intuitive, as faults usually appear independently in one or more different measurement channels; hence, one affected measurement channel is sufficient in order to trigger a fault alarm. Note that $thr$ is a threshold, usually set to a value of 2 for taking two times the model error as error band.

As pointed out in section 5.4.5, *local error bars* achieve a good representation of the data distribution in various local regions. In this sense, we extended the condition in (5.29) to

$$\exists m : \quad \frac{\hat{y}_{fuz,k,m} - x_{k,m} - \varepsilon_{x_m}}{\sqrt{cov\{\hat{y}_{fuz,k,m}\}}} > thr \quad \vee \quad \frac{\hat{y}_{fuz,k,m} - x_{k,m} + \varepsilon_{x_m}}{\sqrt{cov\{\hat{y}_{fuz,k,m}\}}} < -thr \qquad (5.30)$$

including the local error bars (as in (5.28)) in the denominator of both conditions. In order to overcome a hard-coded (offline) threshold $thr$ and to achieve an adaptive online thresholding concept, we analyzed the normalized residuals (according to the fault condition)

$$res_{i=1,\ldots,k-1;m} = \frac{\min(|\hat{y}_{fuz,i,m} - x_{i,m} - \varepsilon_{x_m}|, |\hat{y}_{fuz,i,m} - x_{i,m} + \varepsilon_{x_m}|)}{\sqrt{cov\{\hat{y}_{fuz,i,m}\}}} \qquad (5.31)$$

by univariate adaptive statistical methods exploiting a locally sliding regression model for tracking the local trend of the residual signals adaptively over time. If anomalies in these signals are observed (e.g., untypical peaks in case of outliertype faults or unusual transients in case of drift-type faults), a fault alarm is triggered. In this sense, the fault detection approach flexibly adapts to the current residual signal and does not imply one unique threshold, which usually has totally different optimal values for different data sets (engines to be tested). If the fault alarm is not confirmed as correct, the measurement can be assumed to be fault-free and is taken into account for the further evolution of the fuzzy models. On the other hand, if the fault alarm is confirmed as correct, the corresponding residual $res_k$ is not sent into the parameter update of the local trend model and the measurement is not taken into account for the evolution of the fuzzy models.

The evaluation test is performed on measurement data recorded from a BMW diesel engine. Eight different types of possibly occurring faults were simulated at an engine test bench by switching off some components or reproducing leaks in pipes, and so on. In sum, 7180 data points were recorded for 74 different measurement channels. It turned out that 56 measurement channels could be reasonably approximated with maximally five others (reasonably approximated means having a model quality of greater than 0.8 where 1 would denote a perfect model), leading to $m = 1,\ldots,56$ evolving first-order TSK fuzzy models, based on which the fault detection strategy mentioned earlier (i.e., incremental analysis of the residuals) is carried out online and samplewise. The results are reported in Table 5.2, where basic fault detection with global error bands is compared with improved fault detection logic, exploiting adaptive local error bars.

This comparison includes the detection rates on measurement basis (third column); all measurements affected by faults are counted (in sum 80) as well as on the fault basis (fourth column), that is, all different kinds of faults are counted (in sum eight). Column 2 represents the average model quality over all 56 (reasonable) models (as quality measure for the online identification part), which is measured in terms of the $r$-squared-adjusted

T A B L E 5.2. Comparison of Fault Detection Approaches on Real-Occurring Faults at an Engine Test Bench with the Usage of 56 Evolving Fuzzy Models Generated by FLEXFIS

| Method | Average Model Quality | Detection Rate A | Detection Rate B |
|---|---|---|---|
| *Basic* | 0.958 | 71.59% | 6 out of 8 |
| *Improved* | 0.958 | 87.50% | 7 out of 8 |
| *Basic without overcoming unlearning* | 0.913 | 64.23% | 5 out of 8 |
| *Improved without overcoming unlearning* | 0.913 | 72.83% | 6 out of 8 |

measure [23]:

$$R^2_{adjusted} = 1 - \frac{(N-1)(1-R^2)}{N-deg} \tag{5.32}$$

where $deg$ denotes the degrees of freedom (number of rules times the number of inputs) and $N$ the number of data points used for model training and $R^2$ defined by

$$R^2 = \frac{ssreg}{ssreg + ssres} \tag{5.33}$$

where

$$ssreg = \sum_{k=1}^{N} (\hat{y}(k) - \bar{y}(k))^2 \quad ssres = \sum_{k=1}^{N} (y(k) - \hat{y}(k))^2 \tag{5.34}$$

and $\bar{y}$ the mean value of output target channel $y$. This measure is obviously normalized to the unit interval and is nearer to 1 the smaller $ssres$ is. Furthermore, it punishes more complex models as integrating the degrees of freedom in the denominator.

Moreover, improved fault detection using local error bars can significantly outperform the basic one, as two faults more could be detected with the improved approach, where one of these two was a major one and hence mandatory to be detected. Note that rows 2 and 3 represent the results obtained when integrating the approach for overcoming the unlearning effect as outlined in section 5.4.2, that is, only to update the significantly firing rules in Step 9 of FLEXFIS Algorithm 1. This is necessary as the online recorded (dynamic) measurement data contain quite a lot of steady-state samples, that is, samples showing an almost constant behavior in a lot of measurement channels over time (for balancing out a new operating condition to get a valid and robust stationary data sample). Rows 4 and 5 show the results suffering quite a bit when the approach for overcoming the unlearning effect is omitted. The threshold here was set to 0.1, which gave best results over various others (varied between 0 and 0.8 in steps of 0.05). A complete sensitivity analysis of this threshold versus the change in fault detection rate achieved when using adaptive local error bars is shown in Figure 5.12.

It can be seen that varying the threshold between 0.05 and 0.2 does not affect the fault detection rate significantly. The average complexity measured in terms of the number of rules of the finally evolved fuzzy models is 12.2 with a range of between 10 and 22 rules.

### 5.5.3 Online Image Classification Framework

An application example is given that includes an automatically self-reconfigurable and adaptive image classification, which is shown in Figure 5.13.

The framework is able to cope with online operation modes and has a specific component integrated for evolving classifiers based on operator feedback during online production cycles. This human–machine interaction component is highlighted with an ellipsoid in Figure 5.13 and serves as an essential part for improving initially offline-

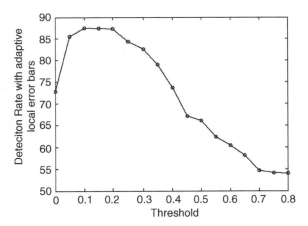

Figure 5.12. Sensitivity analysis for the threshold in FLEXFIS for overcoming the unlearning effect.

trained classifiers further with new incoming images in order to extend classifiers to new operating conditions (e.g., new types of images) and, hence, to prevent extrapolation and a low classification performance. Please note that initially offline-trained classifiers (from prelabeled training data) are mandatory as giving the experts a first hint as to whether the classification task can be reasonably trained at all up to a certain (predefined) level of accuracy, yielding a prediction about the success or failure of the classifier [55].

After preprocessing the images by comparing them with a master to obtain *deviation images*, where each pixel represents a potential candidate for indicating a fault, regions of interest are automatically recognized and for each region a large set of object features are extracted. Examples of object features describing the characteristics of a region of interest are ratio of the principal axis to the secondary axis of a circumscribing ellipse (roundness), perimeter, area, compactness, and statistical values such as curtosis, skew, or different quantiles out of the corresponding gray-level histograms. These are completed with a set of aggregated features characterizing images as a whole, and so, characterizing all pixels and objects joined together. Examples of aggregated features are the number of objects, the maximal density of objects, or the average brightness in an image. Classification of the images is done into good or bad ones, indicating fault-free or

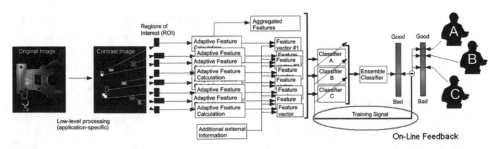

Figure 5.13. Online classification framework for classifying images into good and bad.

faulty situations at the system. Depending on the level of detail the user gives to the system (i.e., labeling only whole images or also single objects), the classification of whole images is done either based on aggregated features plus unsupervised object information (produced by aggregation operators or by clustering approaches on the object features) or by aggregated features plus supervised object information obtained as output from an object-level classifier. (For details see [54].) Here, we report results on the former approach, including 74 features (57 object features plus 17 aggregated features) and based on two different data sets:

1. Online collected CD-imprint data containing 1534 samples that were labeled by four different operators with different experiences (so, we obtained four different classifiers with different accuracies): The task was to distinguish between real faults on CD imprints such as weak colors, wrong palettes, and so on, and pseudo-errors such as shifts of discs in the tray.
2. Online collected egg data containing 4238 samples labeled by just one operator: The task was to discriminate between real faults on eggs, such as scratches or yolks, and nonfaulty appearances on the eggs, such as different kinds of dirt.

In both cases, the online collected data were stored onto hard-disc in the same order as they were recorded; so a valid simulation of the online mode is the case when sending sample per sample into the evolution of the fuzzy models and taking the label entries as a simulation of online operator feedback.

Both data sets were split into a training data set (two-thirds of the data) and a test data set (one-third of the data). The training data was split into two halves, one taken for initial offline training, the other for further evolution of the classifiers. The test data set is for the purpose of evaluating the evolved classifiers on new unseen data. Table 5.3 shows the performance of evolving classifiers obtained by FLEXFIS-Class MM (see Algorithm 2) vs. static classifiers trained in initial offline mode with the first batch of data and not further updated, based on the CD-imprint data. It can be seen that by doing an adaptation during online mode the performance on new unseen samples significantly increases by 10 to 15% over all operators as well as for the egg data. Furthermore, the third row shows us that, when retraining a batch decision-tree classifier on all training samples (the well-known CART algorithm [10], which was the best-performing one on this data set among

T A B L E 5.3. Performance (Accuracy in %) of Evolving Online vs. Static (and Retrained) Batch Classifiers

| Dataset | Op. 1 | Op. 2 | Op. 3 | Op. 4 | Eggs |
|---|---|---|---|---|---|
| Fuzzy classifier static | 68.63 | 85.29 | 85.68 | 78.24 | 76.08 |
| Fuzzy classifier retrained | 86.23 | 89.11 | 90.55 | 87.02 | 93.93 |
| Evolving fuzzy classifier | 84.12 | 88.06 | 89.92 | 86.90 | 93.6 |
| Evolving fuzzy classifier every 5 | 84.05 | 88.01 | 89.44 | 85.99 | 93.11 |
| Decision trees static | 70.94 | 78.82 | 80.00 | 76.08 | 91.73 |
| Decision trees retrained | 82.74 | 90.59 | 90.39 | 88.24 | 96.6 |

SVMs, possibilistic neural networks, k-NN, discriminant analysis, and naive Bayes classifiers), the accuracy for the new unseen samples is just slightly better ($+3\%$) than for the evolving fuzzy classifiers. In this sense, the question remains whether the computationally intensive retraining is a feasible option. This also belongs to the retraining of a fuzzy classifier (row 3), which also here serves as a benchmark of how close the batch solution can be approximated by the incremental/evolving one. The 5th row gives a valuable benchmark on a more realistic online operation mode, where the operator gives a feedback only from time to time (here simulated by taking into account just every 5th sample in the incremental learning phase).

It should be also noted that all the results in Table 5.3 with respect to fuzzy classifiers were produced by including the heuristic regularization approach as mentioned in section 5.4.1. This was even mandatory for the CD-imprint data; an (initial) training without regularization did not terminate correctly at all, as some entries in the inverse covariance matrix even turned out to be 'Inf' due to singularity (hence, no real solution could be obtained in MATLAB). Here, the number of rules in the classifiers for Operator #1 is 65 (35 for class 'good', 30 for class 'bad'), for Operator #2 is 70 (36 for class 'good', 34 for class 'bad'), for Operator #3 is 61 (31 for class 'good', 30 for class 'bad'), and for Operator #4 is 73 (40 for class 'good' and 33 for class 'bad'). Furthermore, it was examined how a gradual forgetting of older samples over time affects the predictive accuracy of new unseen (online) samples. The meaningfulness of the examination of these issues is underlined by the fact that the CD-imprint data was originally recorded for different orders, whereas different orders may contain drifts or shifts in the image data distribution. In this sense, we performed a drift analysis

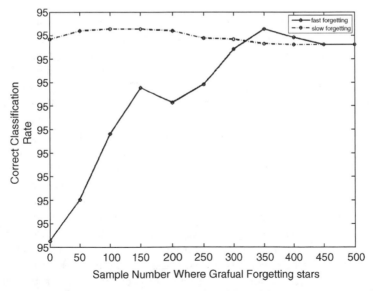

**Figure 5.14.** Drift analysis for the CD-imprint data labeled by Operator #2, applying two different speeds in the gradual forgetting process and starting the "drift phase tracking" at different sample numbers (x-axis); y-axis represents the accuracy on the separate test set.

with different starting points (beginning with gradual evolution at 0, 50, 100, 150, ...,
500 online samples), lasting over 50 samples in the drift phase and with two different
speeds for gradual forgetting. The results for Operator #2 are shown in Figure 5.14,
where the slow gradual forgetting is denoted by the dotted-dashed line and the fast
gradual forgetting by the solid line. The sample number in the second half of the
training set at which the drift is initialized is represented by the $x$-axis; the achieved
accuracies on separate test data when including the gradual forgetting on the rest of the
second half of the training data are represented by the $y$-axis. In fact, the accuracies for
Operator #2 can be boosted up by about 3% (to 91.39% maximum) when initiating a
drift phase at the correct sample number and taking the appropriate speed in the gradual
forgetting process. In our case, this means that a slow forgetting starting between 100
and 150 and a fast forgetting starting at 350 is beneficial, tracking two different types of
drifts. In fact, when combining these two, a classification rate of even over 92% can be
achieved, gaining another 1% accuracy.

Moreover, the class distribution of the CD-imprint data is quite unbalanced as only
around 20% of bad samples could be gathered from the production process. In this sense,
we applied the "timing of update" strategy mentioned at the end of section 5.4.2; that is,
we updated the fuzzy classifier only with samples from the 'good' class in the case of a
disagreement of the classification decision and the true class label of the new sample.
This gave us another 1.4% more accuracy on the CD-imprint data, compared to the 92%
achieved with double drift tracking.

## 5.6 CONCLUSION

In this chapter we demonstrated several issues for obtaining more robustness, process
safety, and higher predictive accuracies when doing an evolution of fuzzy models based
on online data, and underlined the importance of these issues with graphical visualiza-
tions. All of these issues were implemented within the scope of the FLEXFIS and
FLEXFIS-Class approaches which borrow from eTS and eClass approaches, respectively. The evaluation section shows quite promising results when applying some of these
issues for three different real-world applications, including online fault detection at
engine test benches, online image classification based on operator feedback, and online
prediction at rolling mills. Sometimes, some of these issues were even mandatory in
order to obtain any reasonable and robust prediction or classification feedbacks at all. In
most cases, several issues could guide the evolved fuzzy models to more predictive power
in terms of accuracy, especially in the case of steady-state data or a smoothly changing
behavior of the underlying data distribution in the form of a drift. Robustness in terms of
the performance of evolving fuzzy models coming close to the batch performance could
be also shown. The approaches for improving robustness are applicable for other
evolving fuzzy modeling methods as well, especially for those that exploit TSK
(neuro-)fuzzy-type architectures (all issues)—respectively, fuzzy sets with infinite
support (better extrapolation behavior, overcoming unlearning effect) and/or polynomial
consequent functions (adaptive local error bars, regularization, tracking drifts)—but are
not necessarily restricted to these. In this sense, these approaches can be seen as an

important step in the future in order to achieve much richer evolving fuzzy modeling components in intelligent systems.

## 5.7 ACKNOWLEDGMENTS

This work was supported by the European Commission (Project Contract No. STRP016429, acronym DynaVis) and by the the Upper Austrian Technology and Research Promotion. This chapter reflects only the author's view.

## 5.8 REFERENCES

1. J. Abonyi, *Fuzzy Model Identification for Control*. Boston: Birkhäuser, 2003.
2. P. Angelov, D. Filev, "Simpl_eTS: A Simplified Method for Learning Evolving Takagi-Sugeno Fuzzy Models." *Proceedings of FUZZ-IEEE 2005*, Reno, Nevada, 2005, pp. 1068–1073.
3. P. Angelov, X. Zhou, D. Filev, E. Lughofer, "Architectures for Evolving Fuzzy Rule-Based Classifiers." *Proceedings of SMC 2007*, Montreal, Canada, 2007, pp. 2050–2055.
4. P. Angelov, X. Zhou, F. Klawonn, "Evolving Fuzzy Rule-Based Classifiers." *2007 IEEE International Conference on Computational Intelligence Application for Signal and Image Processing*, Honolulu, Hawaii, 2007 pp. 220–225.
5. P.P. Angelov, D. Filev, "An Approach to Online Identification of Takagi-Sugeno Fuzzy Models," *IEEE Trans. on Systems, Man and Cybernetics, Part B*, 34 (1): 484–498, 2004.
6. P. P. Angelov, E. Lughofer, "Data-Driven Evolving Fuzzy Systems Using eTS and FLEXFIS: Comparative Analysis," *International Journal of General Systems*, 37 (1): 45–67, 2008.
7. R. Babuska, *Fuzzy Modeling for Control*. Boston: Kluwer Academic Publishers, 1998.
8. J. C. Barros, A. L. Dexter, "An Evolving Fuzzy Model for Embedded Applications." *Second Int. Symposium on Evolving Fuzzy Systems*, Lake District, UK, 2006, pp. 36–41.
9. F. Bauer, "Some Considerations Concerning Regularization and Parameter Choice Algorithms," *Inverse Problems*, 23: 837–858, 2007.
10. L. Breiman, J. Friedman, C. J. Stone, R. A. Olshen, *Classification and Regression Trees*. Boca Raton: Chapman and Hall, 1993.
11. G. A. Carpenter, S. Grossberg, "Adaptive Resonance Theory (art)." In *The Handbook of Brain Theory and Neural Networks*. (M. A. Arbib, ed.) Cambridge: MIT Press, 1995, pp. 79–82.
12. J. Casillas, O. Cordon, F. Herrera, L. Magdalena, *Interpretability Issues in Fuzzy Modeling*. Berlin, Heidelberg: Springer-Verlag, 2003.
13. D. Donoho, I. Johnstone, "Minimax Estimation via Wavelet Shrinkage," *Annual Statistics*, 26: 879–921, 1998.
14. N. R. Draper, H. Smith, *Applied Regression Analysis: Probability and Mathematical Statistics*. New York: John Wiley & Sons, 1981.
15. R. O. Duda, P. E. Hart, D. G. Stork, *Pattern Classification, Second Edition*. Southern Gate, Chichester, West Sussex PO 19 8SQ, England: Wiley-Interscience, 2000.
16. H. W. Engl, M. Hanke, A. Neubauer, *Regularization of Inverse Problems*. Dordrecht: Kluwer, 1996.

17. D. P. Filev, F. Tseng, "Novelty Detection Based Machine Health Prognostics." *Proc. 2006 Int. Symposium on Evolving Fuzzy Systems*, Lake District, UK, 2006, pp. 193–199.

18. R. M. Gray, "Vector Quantization," *IEEE ASSP*, pages 4–29, 1984.

19. C. W. Groetsch, *The theory of Tikhonov regularization for Fredholm Equations of the First Kind*. Boston: Pitman, 1984.

20. W. Groißböck, E. Lughofer, E. P. Klement, "A Comparison of Variable Selection Methods with the Main Focus on Orthogonalization." In *Soft Methodology and Random Information Systems: Advances in Soft Computing*. (M. Lopéz-Díaz, M. Á. Gil, P. Grzegorzewski, O. Hryniewicz, J. Lawry, ed.) Berlin, Heidelberg, New York: Springer, 2004, pp. 479–486.

21. N. Sundararajan, H.-J. Rong, G.-B. Huang, P. Saratchandran, "Sequential Adaptive Fuzzy Inference System (SAFIS) for Nonlinear System Identification and Prediction," *Fuzzy Sets and Systems*, 157 (9): 1260–1275, 2006.

22. P. C. Hansen, "The truncated svd as a Method for Regularization," *BIT*, 27: 534–553, 1987.

23. F. E. Harrel. *Regression Modeling Strategies*. New York: Springer-Verlag New York, 2001.

24. T. Hastie, R. Tibshirani, J. Friedman, *The Elements of Statistical Learning: Data Mining, Inference and Prediction*. New York, Berlin, Heidelberg: Springer-Verlag, 2001.

25. S. Haykin, *Neural Networks: A Comprehensive Foundation*, 2nd Edition. Upper Saddle River, NJ: Prentice Hall, 1999.

26. A. Hensel, T. Spittel, *Kraft- und Arbeitsbedarf bildsamer Formgebungsverfahren*. VEB Deutscher Verlag für Grundstoffindustrie, 1978.

27. G. B. Huang, P. Saratchandran, N. Sundararajan, "An Efficient Sequential Learning Algorithm for Growing and Pruning RBF (GAP-RBF) Networks," *IEEE Transactions on Systems, Man and Cybernetics, Part B (Cybernetics)*, 34 (6): 2284–2292, 2004.

28. R. Iserman, *Fault Diagnosis Systems: An Introduction from Fault Detection to Fault Tolerance*. Berlin: Springer-Verlag, 2005.

29. H. Ishibushi, T. Nakashima, T. Murata, "Performance Evaluation of Fuzzy Classifier Systems for Multidimensional Pattern Classification Problems," *IEEE Transactions on Systems, Man and Cybernetics, Part B (Cybernetics)*, 29 (5): 601–618, 1999.

30. H. Ishibushi, Y. Nojima, "Analysis of Interpretability-Accuracy Tradeoff of Fuzzy Systems by Multiobjective Fuzzy Genetics-Based Machine Learning," *Int. Journal of Approximate Reasoning*, 44 (1): 4–31, 2007.

31. T. A. Johansen, R. Babuska, "Multiobjective Identification of Takagi-Sugeno Fuzzy Models," *IEEE Transactions on Fuzzy Systems*, 11 (6): 847–860, 2003.

32. N. Kasabov, *Evolving Connectionist Systems: Methods and Applications in Bioinformatics, Brain Study and Intelligent Machines*. London: Springer-Verlag, 2002.

33. N. K. Kasabov, "Evolving Fuzzy Neural Networks for Supervised/Unsupervised Online Knowledge-Based Learning," *IEEE Trans. on Systems, Men and Cybernetics, Part B (Cybernetics)*, 31 (6): 902–918, 2001.

34. N. K. Kasabov, Q. Song, "DENFIS: Dynamic Evolving Neural-Fuzzy Inference System and Its Application for Time-Series Prediction," *IEEE Trans. on Fuzzy Systems*, 10 (2): 144–154, 2002.

35. C. C. Lee, "Fuzzy Logic in Control Systems: Fuzzy Logic Controller, Parts I and II," *IEEE Trans. System, Man, Cybernetics*, 20: 404–435, 1990.

36. G. Leng, T. M.. McGinnity, G. Prasad, "An Approach for On-line Extraction of Fuzzy Rules Using a Self-Organising Fuzzy Neural Network," *Fuzzy Sets and Systems*, 150 (2): 211–243, 2005.

37. O. V. Lepskij, "On a Problem of Adaptive Estimation in Gaussian White Noise," *Theory of Probability and its Applications*, 35 (3): 454–466, 1990.

38. E. Lima, F. Gomide, R. Ballini, "Participatory Evolving Fuzzy Modeling." *Second Int. Symposium on Evolving Fuzzy Systems*, Lake District, UK, 2006, pp. 36–41.

39. L. Ljung, *System Identification: Theory for the User*. Upper Saddle River, NJ: Prentice Hall PTR, Prentice-Hall, 1999.

40. E. Lughofer, "Extensions of Vector Quantization for Incremental Clustering," *Pattern Recognition*, 41 (3): 995–1011, 2008.

41. E. Lughofer, "FLEXFIS: A Robust Incremental Learning Approach for Evolving TS Fuzzy Models," *IEEE Trans. on Fuzzy Systems (Special Issue On Evolving Fuzzy Systems)*, 16 (4): 1–18, 2008.

42. E. Lughofer, P. Angelov, X. Zhou, "Evolving Single- and Multi-Model Fuzzy Classifiers with FLEXFIS-Class." *Proceedings of FUZZ-IEEE 2007*, London, UK, 2007 pp. 363–368.

43. E. Lughofer, C. Guardiola, "Applying Evolving Fuzzy Models with Adaptive Local Error Bars to On-line Fault Detection." *Proceedings of Genetic and Evolving Fuzzy Systems 2008*, Witten-Bommerholz, Germany, 2008, pp. 35–40.

44. E. Lughofer, C. Guardiola, "On-line Fault Detection with Data-Driven Evolving Fuzzy Models," *Journal of Control and Intelligent Systems*, 36 (2), 2008.

45. E. Lughofer, E. Hüllermeier, E. P. Klement, "Improving the Interpretability of Data-Driven Evolving Fuzzy Systems." *Proceedings of EUSFLAT 2005*, Barcelona, Spain, 2005, pp. 28–33.

46. J. G. Qiang Shen Marin-Blazquez, "From Approximative to Descriptive Fuzzy Classifiers," *IEEE Transactions on Fuzzy Systems*, 10 (4): 484–497, 2002.

47. V. A. Morozov, "On the Solution of Functional Equations by the Methdod of Regularization," *Sov. Math. Dokl*, 7: 414–417, 1965.

48. D. Nauck, R. Kruse, "A Neuro-Fuzzy Method to Learn Fuzzy Classification Rules from Data," *Fuzzy Sets and Systems*, 89(3): 277–288, 1997.

49. A. Piegat, *Fuzzy Modeling and Control*. Heidelberg, New York: Physica Verlag, Springer-Verlag, 2001.

50. F. Provost, "Machine Learning from Imbalanced Data Sets." *Proceedings of the AAAI workshop*, Menlo Park, CA, 2000, pp. 1–3.

51. S. J. Qin, W. Li, H. H. Yue, "Recursive PCA for Adaptive Process Monitoring," *Journal of Process Control*, 10: 471–486, 2000.

52. J. A. Roubos, M. Setnes, J. Abonyi, "Learning Fuzzy Classification Rules from Data," *Information Sciences—Informatics and Computer Science: An International Journal*, 150: 77–93, 2003.

53. D. Donoho, S. Chen, M. Saunders, "Atomic decomposition by basis pursuit," *SIAM Rev.*, 43 (1): 129–159, 2001.

54. D. Sannen, M. Nuttin, J. E. Smith, M. A. Tahir, E. Lughofer, C. Eitzinger, "An Interactive Self-Adaptive On-line Image Classification Framework." In, *Proceedings of ICVS 2008, Vol. 5008 of LNCS* ( A. Gasteratos, M. Vincze, J. K. Tsotsos, ed.) Santorini Island, Greece: Springer, 2008 pp. 173–180.

55. J. E. Smith, M. A. Tahir, "Stop Wasting Time: On Predicting the Success or Failure of Learning for Industrial Applications." *Proccedings of the 8th International Conference on Intelligent Data Engineering and Automated Learning (IDEAL'08), Lecture Notes in Computer Science, LNCS 4881*. Birmingham, UK: Springer-Verlag, 2007, pp. 673–683.

56. M. Stone, "Cross-Validatory Choice and Assessment of Statistical Predictions," *Journal of the Royal Statistical Society*, 36: 111–147, 1974.

57. A. N. Tikhonov, V. Y. Arsenin, *Solutions of Ill-Posed Problems*. Washington D.C.: Winston & Sonst, 1977.

58. N. Tschichold-Guerman, "Generation and Improvement of Fuzzy Classifiers with Incremental Learning Using Fuzzy Rulenet." *Proceedings of the 1995 ACM Symposium on Applied Computing*, Nashville, Tennessee, 1995, ACM Press, New York.

59. A. Tsymbal, "*The Problem of Concept Drift: Definitions and Related Work.*" Technical Report TCD-CS-2004-15, Department of Computer Science, Trinity College Dublin, Ireland, 2004.

60. G. C. van den Eijkel, J.C.A. van der Lubbe, E. Backer, "Fuzzy Incremental Learning of Expert Rules for a Knowledge-Based Anesthesia Monitor." *Fourth European Congress on Intelligent Techniques and Soft Computing Proceedings, EUFIT '96*, Verlag Mainz, 1996, pp. 2056–2060.

61. L. X. Wang, J. M. Mendel, "Fuzzy Basis Functions, Universal Approximation and Orthogonal Least-Squares Learning," *IEEE Trans. Neural Networks*, 3(5): 807–814, 1992.

62. G. Widmer, M. Kubat, "Learning in the Presence of Concept Drift and Hidden Contexts," *Machine Learning*, 23(1): 69–101, 1996.

63. S. Wu, M. J. Er, "Dynamic Fuzzy Neural Networks: A Novel Approach to Function Approximation," *IEEE Trans. on Systems, Man and Cybernetics, Part B (Cybernetics)*, 30: 358–364, 2000.

64. S. Wu, M. J. Er, Y. Gao, "A Fast Approach for Automatic Generation of Fuzzy Rules by Generalized Dynamic Fuzzy Neural Networks," *IEEE Trans. on Fuzzy Systems*, 9(4): 578–594, 2001.

65. R. Yager, D. Filev, "*Generation of Fuzzy Rules by Mountain Clustering.*" Technical Report MII-1318R, Machine Intelligence Institute, Iona College, New Rochelle, NY 10801, 1994.

66. R. R. Yager, "A Model of Participatory Learning," *IEEE Trans. on Systems, Man and Cybernetics*, 20: 1229–1234, 1990.

67. J. Yen, L. Wang, C. W. Gillespie, "Improving the Interpretability of TSK Fuzzy Models by Combining Global Learning and Local Learning," *IEEE Trans. on Fuzzy Systems*, 6(4): 530–537, 1998.

# 6

# BUILDING INTERPRETABLE SYSTEMS IN REAL TIME

José V. Ramos, Carlos Pereira, António Dourado

**Abstract:** Building interpretable learning machines from data, incrementally, with the capability for a-posteriori knowledge extraction, is still a big challenge. It is difficult to avoid some degree of redundancy and unnecessary complexity in the obtained models. This work presents two alternative ways for building interpretable systems, using fuzzy models or kernel machines. The goal is to control the complexity of the machine, either the number of rules or the number of kernels, using incremental learning techniques and merging of fuzzy sets. In the first case, online implementation of mechanisms for merging membership functions and rule base simplification, toward evolving first-order Takagi-Sugeno fuzzy systems (eTS), is proposed in this chapter in order to improve the interpretability of the fuzzy models. As a comparative solution, kernel-based methods may also contribute to the interpretability issue, particularly the incremental learning algorithms. The interpretability is analyzed based on equivalence principles between local model networks and Takagi-Sugeno fuzzy inference systems.

A considerable reduction of redundancy and complexity of the models is obtained, increasing the model transparency and human interpretability. The learning technique is developed for large spanned evolving first-order Takagi-Sugeno (eTS) fuzzy models. The benchmark of the Box-Jenkins time-series prediction is used to evaluate the techniques.

*Evolving Intelligent Systems: Methodology and Applications,* Edited by Plamen Angelov, Dimitar P. Filev, and Nikola Kasabov

## 6.1 INTRODUCTION

Every year, more than 1 exabyte ($10^{18}$ bytes) of data is generated worldwide, most of it in digital form [1]. Data-driven methodologies for automatic generation of computational models are probably one of the most important tools needed to be developed to properly process and use that immense quantity of information [2]. In most applications (industry, medicine, finance, business, etc.), these methodologies should be iterative, to process the data as it is being reported in real time, and transparent, building a linguistic model clearly interpretable by humans. eTS (evolving Takagi-Sugeno systems) is one of those methodologies [3]. In the present work, the eTS developed by [4] is improved, increasing the rule-span in state space, and used to build fuzzy systems from data. Traditionally, the most important property of a fuzzy system has been its accuracy in representing the real system (for simulation, prediction, decision making, etc.).

However, the obtained fuzzy systems frequently are without practical utility because it is impossible to give some semantic meaning to the rules due to fuzzy sets superposition, and rules that are sometimes redundant and sometimes contradictory, frequently with high complexity. In [5] a comprehensive collection of papers present several approaches for evolving the fuzzy systems to more interpretability (mainly offline trained or expert-based ones). In recent years, interpretability has been considered to be the key feature of fuzzy models [6, 7], continuing previous important works [8, 9], and can be pursued by rule base simplification and reduction methods. There is actually considerable activity concerning this challenging problem. Several perspectives are being developed, for example, by fuzzy set merging using entropy measures [10], by genetic optimization [11–13], by multiobjective evolutionary algorithms [14–16], by manipulating the cost index [17, 18], or by Radial Basis Function Networks [19]. For a more detailed review and treatment, see [22] or [23]. Most of the known methods have been developed for batch processing for an already-existing rule base.

Kernel-based learning methods, such as Support Vector Machines (SVMs), Relevance Vector Machines (RVMs), or Kernel PCA, have been studied extensively in the machine-learning community, being among the best learning techniques for many benchmark data sets and real-world applications [24]. The basic idea of these methods is to preprocess the data by some nonlinear mapping (using the *kernel trick*) and then apply a linear algorithm in a usually higher-dimensional feature space. Such large feature spaces are handled with the simple computational cost of the kernel function. This approach indicates an alternative point of view to the parameters learning of a fuzzy system, with the membership functions being those examples that are critical to solving the given task. In the traditional forms of automatic learning, the functions are simply regarded as clusters.

The objective of the present chapter is online learning, for developing models in real time for classification problems and dynamic systems. Computational time is a critical issue and simple, efficient techniques are searched for. A pruning technique is developed and tested to reduce the degree of redundancy and unnecessary complexity arising in the automated building of fuzzy rules. This improves the human semantic interpretability and as a consequence the usefulness of the results, allowing the merging of compatible fuzzy sets and possibly reduction of the number of rules and features. The fuzzy system is based on an improved version of the eTS algorithm of [4], strengthening its capability to spread rules over all the reachable state space. Pruning of the rules is based on fusion of the antecedents fuzzy sets subject on a similarity threshold and rule elimination based on similar antecedents. The advantage of similarity measures, principally the geometric ones, is there simplicity from the computational point of view, which is explored in this work.

This chapter is organized as follows. The eTS of [4] is briefly reviewed in section 6.2 and conditions are proposed to increase the span of the rules in the state space. In section 6.3 the pruning technique and merging of fuzzy rules is developed. In section 6.4 the interpretability is analyzed based on equivalence principles between local model networks and Takagi-Sugeno fuzzy inference systems. In addition, methods to improve the interpretability of the support vector machine are briefly discussed. Finally, section 6.5 presents the application to the benchmark problem of Box-Jenkins dynamic time-series prediction. The chapter ends with some conclusions and perspectives.

## 6.2 IMPROVING eTS SPAN IN THE REACHABLE STATE SPACE

Online learning of eTS fuzzy models, which is based on Takagi-Sugeno rules, considers their online identification to be subject to gradually evolving rules. The procedure in the present work includes recursive subtractive fuzzy clustering, for determination of the antecedent parameters, and recursive least-squares estimation, for determination of the consequent parameters. Angelov and Filev [4] developed an interesting technique for recursive clustering and rule creation that is the starting and fulcral point for the present proposal. The procedure can be summarized as follows:

*Step 1:* Initialization of the rule base.
The rule base is initially empty. Rules are created around the centers of the input–output clusters, in the subtractive clustering framework. Let $x_k$ and $y_k$ be the input and output vectors at instant $k$, respectively. When the first input–output data is coming, $z_1 = [x_1, y_1]$, it is the single existing cluster in the input–output space and at the same time its own center $z_1^*$. $P_1(z_1^*)$ is the energy potential of the cluster center $z_1^*$ to be used for subtractive clustering. The cluster center $z_1^*$ is a multidimensional point (the number of dimensions is equal to the number of inputs plus the number of outputs) and each input is an antecedent of each fuzzy rule. To obtain from it a fuzzy set for each antecedent, one needs to project the cluster center into each input dimension, and this projection gives the center of the fuzzy set of each antecedent.
So the rule base is initialized with the first data sample, as in (6.1):

$$k = 1; \ R = 1; \ x_1^* = x_k; \ P_1(z_1^*) = 1 \tag{6.1}$$

where $k$ is the actual sampling point, $R$ is the actual number of rules, $z_1^*$ is the first cluster center; $x_1^*$ is the focal point of the antecedent of first rule, obtained by projecting $z_1^*$ on the input dimensions.
In a mixed-batch–real-time learning approach, the rule base can be initialized by existing expert knowledge or based on previous offline identification, defining

an initial set $z_i^*$ of cluster centers and of initial rules, $R^{ini}$. In this case, we have (6.2):

$$R = R^{ini}; \; P_1(z_i^*) = 1; \; i = 1, \ldots, R^{ini} \qquad (6.2)$$

*Step 2:* Reading the next data sample.

In an online set, each input is coming in fixed successive instants of time. At the next time step, instant $k$, the new data sample $z_k = [x_k, y_k]$ is collected. This new data sample changes all the field energy and as a consequence the potential energy of every existing center; the new potentials must then be calculated.

*Step 3:* Recursive calculation of the potentials of each new data sample (for subtractive clustering).

For online learning, the potentials must be computed recursively, leading to the need of recursive formulas for potentials like the Cauchy function (A1) of the appendix proposed by [4] and adopted in this work.

*Step 4:* Recursive update of the potentials of existing centers taking into account the influence of the new data sample.

This is made according to the method developed by [4].

*Step 5:* Upgrade of the rule base structure: Modify a rule or create a new one.

This is the essential stage in eTS philosophy. The potential of the new data sample is compared to the updated potential of existing centers; then the important decision whether to modify or create a new rule is taken. This is a very sensitive task and different scenarios have been empirically investigated for rule base upgrade and modification. An extensive work undertaken in [17, 18] for a broad set of problems allowed a better understanding about the influence on the creation and modification of the rules and proposed new conditions described in the following, improving the algorithm of [4].

## 6.2.1 Rule Base Upgrade: Improve Span over State Space

Two situations may arise:

1. The new data point spans over new regions of state-space, where previously no point has been reached. This point has a very low potential because it has very few neighbors but it has novelty of information. This means that, although it has a low potential, it must originate a new rule for that particular region of the state-space. A lower-bound threshold must be fixed in order to decide to create a new rule. Let it be fixed by common sense as the minimum of the actual potentials of all the active centers, $\underline{P}_k$. So, we will have the decision (6.3): Create a new rule centered on the new sample if the potential is inferior to the lower bound, that is, if $P_k(z_k) < \underline{P}_k$.

2. The new point is located in a densely populated region and in this way its potential is higher than the maximum potential $\bar{P}_k$ of the existing centers. This means that the point is very meaningful and must generate a new rule, as proposed by [4].

As a consequence, the following procedure is derived, joining cases 1 and 2:

$$\text{If } P_k(z_k) > \overline{P}_k \text{ or } P_k(z_k) < \underline{P}_k \text{ then } \quad R = R+1; x_R^* = x_k; P_k(x_R^*) = P_k(x_k)$$
(6.3)

$$\text{where } \overline{P}_k = \max_{l=1}^{R} P_k(z_l^*) \text{ and } \underline{P}_k = \min_{l=1}^{R} P_k(z_l^*).$$

*Rule base modification:* When the new point has a high potential but is situated near an already-existing center, then a new rule is not created (it would be redundant to some extent), but instead the existing rule is replaced by a new one centered on the new point, since it is more representative than the existing one. In case 1, when the potential of the new point is under the minimum of the potentials of the existing centers but is near an existing center, it will replace this existing center and no new rule is created. The minimum distance of the new point to an existing center is $\delta_{min}$. The threshold is defined as a fraction of the radius r of the clusters of the subtractive clustering method, a simpler technique than that proposed by [4], but proven to be efficient. In our experiments this parameter r has been fixed by experimentation, producing good performance while producing a low number of rules.

The rule for the replacement of an old rule by a new one is then (6.4):

$$\text{If } (P_k(z_k) > \overline{P}_k \text{ or } P_k(z_k) < \underline{P}_k) \text{ and } \delta_{min} < \frac{r}{2} \text{ then } z_j^* = z_k; P_k(z_j^*) = P_k(z_k) \quad (6.4)$$

where $\delta_{min} = \min_{l=1}^{R} \|z_k - z_l^*\|$, r is the constant radii and j is the index of the replaced rule (rule center closest to the new data point).

We return to our step list:

*Step 6:* Recursive calculation of the consequent parameters by modified RLS algorithm for globally optimal parameters or by modified wRLS for locally optimal parameters [4].

When the number of rules increases or decreases, the number of parameters to be optimized increases or decreases as well, and for RLS special care must be taken with the covariance matrix that changes its dimensions in these cases. First-order Takagi-Sugeno rules are used and the number of parameters increases quickly with the number of rules.

*Step 7:* Prediction of the model output for the next time step.

With the rule base as it is, after updating, predict the output for a certain future instant.

The algorithm continues from stage 2 at the next time step (theoretically, an infinite loop in case of online learning). The prediction error will be measured when the future instant arrives and will then be used in the quadratic criterion of the recursive least squares for consequent parameter learning.

## 6.3 PRUNING THE RULE BASE

Fuzzy models obtained with data-driven techniques have already a considerable history, since the pioneers ANFIS [28], LOLIMOT [29], and FMCLUST [30] (for a review of methods see [31]), as in this work, typically contain unnecessary redundancy. When fuzzy clustering algorithms are used to determine the structure of the fuzzy model, redundancy results because the rules, defined in the multidimensional space, overlap in one or more dimensions. In order to reduce that redundancy, rule base simplification and reduction methods must be combined with data-driven modeling tools, resulting in a more transparent fuzzy modeling scheme. Online transparent modeling results from the integration of rule base simplification and reduction procedures in the online learning process. In the online learning procedure of eTS, very few parameters need to be predefined. One of the parameters is the radius of the clusters, and several problems concerning the size, shape, and orientation of the clusters can be considered: same radii for all the input variables, different radii for each of the input variables; different radii for each of the input variables in each cluster (rule); different radii for each of the input variables and orientation in each cluster (rule). This chapter concerns the situation of the same radii for all the input variables.

### 6.3.1 Merging Fuzzy Sets

Merging of fuzzy sets is based on similarity measures [20, 21]. This approach has been adopted because of its simplicity for online learning. A similarity measure S, for this purpose, must satisfy the following conditions:

Nonoverlapping fuzzy sets must have $S = 0$:

$$S(A, B) = 0 \Leftrightarrow \mu_A(x)\mu_B(x) = 0, \forall x \in X \tag{6.5}$$

Overlapping fuzzy sets must have $S > 0$:

$$S(A, B) > 0 \Leftrightarrow \exists x \in X, \mu_A(x)\mu_B(x) \neq 0 \tag{6.6}$$

Only equal fuzzy sets can have $S = 1$:

$$S(A, B) = 1 \Leftrightarrow \mu_A(x) = \mu_B(x), \forall x \in X \tag{6.7}$$

The similarity between two fuzzy sets must not be influenced by scale changes or by displacements in the domain where they are defined:

$$S(A', B') = S(A, B), \mu_{A'}(l + kx) = \mu_A(x), \mu_{B'}(l + kx) = \mu_B(x) \quad k, l \in R, k > 0 \tag{6.8}$$

The last condition guarantees that the particular numerical values in the domain of the variables do not influence the similarity.

Similarity measures are used to detect fuzzy sets in a rule base that represent more-or-less compatible concepts. Similar fuzzy sets express the same region in the universe of discourse of a fuzzy variable—they describe the same concept. The similarity measures are divided in two main groups: geometric and set-theoretic.

Geometric similarity measures represent fuzzy sets as points in a metric space (the centers of the clusters from where the fuzzy sets have been derived) and similarity between the sets is regarded as an inverse of their distance in this metric space. The similarity $S(A,B)$ between fuzzy sets $A$ and $B$ can be written as:

$$S(A, B) = \frac{1}{1 + d(A, B)} \tag{6.9}$$

where $d(A, B)$ is a distance between $A$ and $B$.

Set-theoretic similarity measures achieve the degree of equality of fuzzy sets. The most common similarity measure of fuzzy sets is the *fuzzy Jaccard index* [22], based on the intersection and union operations among fuzzy sets, and defined as (6.10):

$$S(A, B) = \frac{|A \cap B|}{|A \cup B|} = \frac{|A \cap B|}{|A| + |B| - |A \cap B|} \tag{6.10}$$

where $S$ is the similarity measure, $|.|$ designates the cardinality or the size of a set, and intersection and union operators are represented by $\cap$ and $\cup$, respectively.

Geometric similarity measures are best suited for measuring similarity (or dissimilarity) among distinct fuzzy sets, while the set-theoretic measures are the most suitable for capturing similarity among overlapping fuzzy sets. However, the implementation of the fuzzy Jaccard index in a continuous universe of discourse is computationally intensive, particularly for Gaussian membership functions, preventing its use in real time, online, with the current technology.

A simple geometric measure has been searched. The similarity analysis of each pair of fuzzy sets is quite simple since, in this study, all the fuzzy sets have the same size and shape. In this case, a similarity measure based on a distance (6.11) is used:

$$S(A_1, A_2) = \frac{1}{1 + d(A_1, A_2)}; S(.) \in (0, 1] \tag{6.11}$$

For the particular case of Gaussian membership functions, the distinguishing parameters are the centers and the widths of the membership functions. It is then intuitive to define the simple expression (6.12) to approximate the distance between two fuzzy sets [33]:

$$d(A_1, A_2) = \sqrt{(c_1 - c_2)^2 + (\sigma_1 - \sigma_2)^2} \tag{6.12}$$

where $c_i$ is the center and $\sigma_i$ is the width of the Gaussian membership function.

For the problem, since the width is the same for all sets, this equation resumes to (6.13):

$$d(A_1, A_2) = \sqrt{(c_1 - c_2)^2} = |c_1 - c_2| \tag{6.13}$$

If the similarity of two fuzzy sets is greater than a predefined threshold $\lambda \in (0, 1]$, a new fuzzy set is created to replace similar fuzzy sets. The parameters of the new fuzzy set are defined according to (6.14), a weighted average of the parameters of the two original sets:

$$c_{new} = \frac{c_1 \sigma_1 + c_2 \sigma_2}{\sigma_1 + \sigma_2}; \sigma_{new} = \frac{\sigma_1 + \sigma_2}{2} \tag{6.14}$$

Equation (6.14) is simplified as (6.15) since all the fuzzy sets have the same width:

$$c_{new} = \frac{c_1 + c_2}{2}; \sigma_{new} = \sigma_1 = \sigma_2 \tag{6.15}$$

It should be underlined that in formulas (6.11–6.15) we do not need any prior data for this complexity reduction approach; a fully single-pass online algorithm can be performed synchronously to eTS in each incremental learning step demanding a low computational power.

After merging the fuzzy sets, the rule base may contain irrelevant fuzzy sets. For example, if a fuzzy set became similar to the universal set $U$ or to a singleton-like fuzzy set, then it is a candidate to be removed from the rule base. However, this does not happen here, since all the fuzzy sets have the same width before and after fuzzy sets merging.

## 6.3.2 Merging Fuzzy Rules

After the merging of fuzzy sets, the merging of fuzzy rules is likely to happen, particularly when some redundancy is present. In TS fuzzy models, since the consequents of the rules are not fuzzy, the similarity is considered only in the antecedent part of the rules. If the antecedents of two or more rules become equal, these rules can be removed and replaced by one general equivalent rule. The new rule has the same antecedents as the rules that it replaces, but the consequent parameters must be reestimated, since this rule must account for the total contribution of all the rules that it replaces. It may happen that two rules with the same antecedents have different and even contradictory consequents (this is the black side of the data-driven approaches). One possibility is to use the average of the consequents of all the rules with equal premise parts as in (6.12):

$$\theta_{new} = \frac{1}{k} \sum_{i=1}^{k} \theta_i \tag{6.16}$$

where $\theta_i$ is the vector with the parameters of rule $R_i$.

When merging of fuzzy sets occurs, the implications in the online learning algorithm are minimal, but when merging of fuzzy rules occurs the implications are significant, particularly in the covariance matrixes, potential of the cluster centers, and so on. When the membership functions have the same width, from a computational point of view, it is quite simple to accomplish with these implications since basically what happens is that the matrixes are dynamically updated by the elimination of unnecessary information of the removed rules. Unfortunately, the repercussions of this in the learning process of eTS fuzzy models are not completely understood and must be investigated more deeply.

After merging of fuzzy sets and fuzzy rules, the fuzzy model may contain irrelevant inputs. An input is irrelevant if it is not appearing in any rule, and it can be eliminated since it does not contribute to the output.

## 6.4 KERNEL MACHINES

Kernel machines have been highly successful in solving both classification and regression problems. In the particular case of support vector machines, the nonlinear feature space is directly incorporated in the parameter optimization by implicitly mapping the inputs into a new space and finding a suitable linear solution in this feature space. The feature mapping is defined by a positive definite kernel function, given by dot products in the feature space but using only the input space patterns. In classification, the solution is given by the decision surface, which maximizes the margin separating the classes of patterns in the feature space, where the margin is defined as the maximal distance between a training example in the feature space and the separating hyperplane. The solution is given by a set of support vectors lying on the boundary, and basically represents the information required to separate the data. The generalization ability is obtained through the margin maximization. For regression problems, the minimization of the weight vector, with a modified loss function, is used as a criterion. By solving the quadratic optimization problem, one obtains the number of hidden units, their values, and the weights of the output layer.

In the particular case of a support vector machine, a function linear in the parameters is used to approximate the regression in the feature space (6.17):

$$f(\mathbf{x}) = \sum_{j=1}^{m} w_j g_j(\mathbf{x}) \qquad (6.17)$$

where $\mathbf{x} \in \Re^d$ represent the input and $w_j$ the linear parameters, and $g_j$ denotes a nonlinear transformation. The goal is to find a function $f$ with a small test error, based on training data $(x_i, y_i), i = 1, \ldots, n$, by minimizing the empirical risk (6.18):

$$R_{emp}[f] = \frac{1}{n} \sum_{i=1}^{n} L_\varepsilon(y, f(\mathbf{x})) \qquad (6.18)$$

subject to the constraint $\|\mathbf{w}\|^2 \leq c$, where $c$ is a constant. The constrained optimization problem is reformulated by introducing the slack variables $\xi_i \geq 0, \xi_i' \geq 0, i = 1, \ldots, n$ (6.19):

$$
y_i - \sum_{j=1}^{m} w_j g_j(\mathbf{x}) \leq e + \xi_i
$$
$$
\sum_{j=1}^{m} w_j g_j(\mathbf{x}) - y_i \leq e + \xi_i' \tag{6.19}
$$

Assuming this constraint, the problem is posed in terms of quadratic optimization by introducing the following functional (6.20):

$$
Q(\xi_i, \xi_i', \mathbf{w}) = \frac{C}{n} \left( \sum_{i=1}^{n} \xi_i + \sum_{i=1}^{n} \xi_i' \right) + \frac{1}{2} \mathbf{w}^T \mathbf{w} \tag{6.20}
$$

The predetermined coefficient $C$ should be sufficiently large and affects the tradeoff between complexity and the training error. Then this optimization problem is transformed into the dual problem by constructing a Lagrangian and applying the Kuhn-Tucker theorem. The regression function is then given by (6.21):

$$
f(\mathbf{x}) = \sum_{i=1}^{n} (\alpha_i - \beta_i) K(\mathbf{x}_i, \mathbf{x}) \tag{6.21}
$$

where $K(\mathbf{x}_i, \mathbf{x})$ represents the inner product kernel defined in accordance with Mercer's theorem. In the dual problem, the parameters $\alpha_i$ and $\beta_i$ are calculated by maximizing the functional (6.22):

$$
Q(\alpha, \beta) = \sum_{i=1}^{n} y_i(\alpha_i - \beta_i) - e \sum_{i=1}^{n} (\alpha_i + \beta_i)
$$
$$
- \frac{1}{2} \sum_{i=1}^{n} \sum_{j=1}^{n} (\alpha_i - \beta_i)(\alpha_j - \beta_j) K(\mathbf{x}_i, \mathbf{x}) \tag{6.22}
$$

subject to the following constraints (6.23):

$$
\sum_{i=1}^{n} (\alpha_i - \beta_i) = 0
$$
$$
0 \leq \alpha_i \leq \frac{C}{n}, \quad 0 \leq \beta_i \leq \frac{C}{n}, \quad i = 1, \ldots, n \tag{6.23}
$$

Concerning online learning, two main difficulties arise from the use of the kernel methods: (1) the time and memory complexities caused by the growing kernel matrix, and (2) the necessity to overcome the overfitting.

Incremental online algorithms are suitable for large data sets and for problems in which the data becomes available during training. Most of the incremental techniques for kernel-based methods simply modify the decision surface whenever a new training example is either misclassified or classified with an insufficient margin. In that case, the example is inserted into the kernel expansion and a suitable coefficient is chosen. Often this causes significant problems with noisy data sets and overfitting, due to the usually large number of support vectors that are quickly achieved. Thus kernel removal techniques have been suggested to control the complexity of the machine. In particular, Bordes and colleagues proposed LASVM [34], a kernel classifier in which examples from the current kernel expansion can be removed online. It is proved that the algorithm converges to the solution of the quadratic programming problem.

Most of the incremental SVMs are based on the algorithm of Cauwenberghs and Poggio [35]. The key idea of the algorithm is to add the new data point to the solution by varying the margin and at the same time preserving the Kuhn-Tucker conditions for the previous trained examples. The incremental approach identifies three types of patterns:

1. The nonsupport vectors represent the patterns being out of the margins and are irrelevant to training.
2. The support vectors represent patterns that are strictly on the margin.
3. The patterns lying between the two margins are named the error vectors—these patterns are not necessarily wrongly classified.

Only the patterns belonging to the last two classes are critical and should affect directly the incremental training process. In the decremental learning process, a leave-one-out (LOO) error estimation is performed on the relevant vectors. The key idea is unlearning part of the relevant patterns by decrementing its corresponding $\alpha$ coefficients to zero, and computing the output of the resulting SVM [36]. This auxiliary technique helps decrease the complexity of the machine.

Particularly useful for regression problems, an incremental method, the Kernel Recursive Least Squares (KRLS) algorithm, combines the principles of recursive least squares and the benefits of the kernel trick, providing an efficient and nonparametric approach for online regression [37]. In this method, the size of the kernel matrix is limited by mapping the input patterns to a limited set of kernels, admitting into the kernel representation a new input pattern only if its feature space representation cannot be sufficiently well approximated by a combination of the current kernel representation. This technique permits both reducing the order of the feature space and bounding the time and memory complexity of the algorithm. It should be noted that other existing architectures like least-squares support vector machines, RBF neural networks, and TS fuzzy systems are equivalent to a KRLS machine. Recently, kernel least-squares approaches have been successfully applied to different areas such as anomaly detection [38], dynamic systems [39], channel identification [40].

As with any other kernel method, the KRLS output is a predictor of the form (6.24), equivalent to (17):

$$f(\mathbf{x}) = \sum_{j=1}^{m} w_j \langle \phi(\mathbf{x}_j), \phi(\mathbf{x}) \rangle \tag{6.24}$$

To select the kernel representatives, a minimum threshold on the amount of new information of an input vector must be provided in order to be added to the kernel representation.

A given feature vector $\phi(\mathbf{x}_k)$ is said to be approximately linearly dependent on $\{\phi(\mathbf{x}_1), \phi(\mathbf{x}_2), \ldots, \phi(\mathbf{x}_{k-1})\}$, if the projection error defined according to (6.25)

$$\delta_k = \min_a \left\| \sum_{i=1}^{k-1} a_i \cdot \phi(\mathbf{x}_i) - \phi(\mathbf{x}_k) \right\| \tag{6.25}$$

is less than a predefined threshold, $\delta_k < \nu$.

The weights $w_j$ are learned online through successive minimization of prediction errors based on recursive leastsquares.

As a final remark, it can be stated that incremental learning algorithm approaches enable the application of SVMs to large data sets but do not significantly contribute to system interpretability. Additional preprocessing algorithms may help decrease the complexity of the kernel machine. Further studies will follow this research direction. Results of a combination of subtractive clustering with kernel least squares for regression problems are presented in section 6.5.

## 6.4.1 Complexity and Interpretability

The main issue in the kernel-based learning methods is to identify the most suitable kernel function. A number of algorithms have been proposed to automatically learn the kernel function/matrix from the labeled examples. However, some of these methods do not assume any parametric form of the kernel functions and interpretability is not possible. Evolutionary algorithms have also been used to evolve the parameter values for a given kernel function. In particular, [41] proposed a parallel evolutionary algorithm to learn optimal parameters in a Gaussian kernel.

When Gaussian kernels are used, the resulting SVM corresponds to an RBF network. In this case, hidden neurons and support vectors correspond to each other, thus giving interpretability to the learning machine.

### 6.4.1.1 Structure Interpretability. The SVM works by mapping the input space into a high-dimensional feature space using a set of nonlinear basis functions [42]. It can be used either in classification or regression tasks. The framework was originally designed for pattern recognition, but the basic properties carry over to regression by choosing a suitable cost function, for example, the e-insensitive or Vapnik's loss function. Instead of minimizing the empirical training error, like traditional methods, the support vector machine aims at minimizing an upper bound of the generalization error, finding a separating hyperplane and maximizing the margin between the hyperplane and the training data.

An SVM with Gaussian kernels belongs to a general class of local model function estimators and can be interpreted as an output of a fuzzy system. However, the SVM solution does not guarantee real model transparency. It guarantees only that the linear combination of local basis functions accurately approximates the true function. The solution takes the form (6.26):

$$y = \sum_{i=1}^{m} \phi_i(\mathbf{x})\theta_i \tag{6.26}$$

where $\phi_i$ are the basis functions and $\theta_i$ the consequent parameters. These local basis function networks are under certain conditions functionally equivalent to the fuzzy model (6.27) with constant consequent parts:

$$R_i : \quad \text{If } \mathbf{x} \text{ is } A_i \quad \text{then} \quad y = \theta_i, \quad i = 1, 2, \ldots, m. \tag{6.27}$$

where $\mathbf{x}$ is the antecedent linguistic variable, which represents the input to the fuzzy system, and $y$ is the consequent variable representing the output. $A_i$ is the linguistic term defined by the Gaussian multivariable membership function, and $m$ denotes the number of rules.

A major problem of SVMs is their lack of capacity to provide an explanation in a human-comprehensible form. In particular, for medical applications the transparency and explanation of the model is crucial. Considering rule extraction, a measure of its success is the performance of extracted rules as compared to the original SVM model.

Support vector learning in combination with data preprocessing allows reducing the complexity of the problem; however, the SVM solution may not correspond to a set of interpretable local models, which characterizes a fuzzy representation. An approach to reduce the training complexity of the support vector machines using supervised clustering and combining the approximation and generalization ability provided by SVM with the interpretability of fuzzy systems has been proposed in [43]. The learning mechanism proceeds in two phases:

1. *Information complexity reduction*: Estimate relevant data using supervised clustering.
2. *Machine complexity reduction*: Estimate a function from relevant data using support vector learning.

Nowadays there is a wide range of methods to extract comprehensible rules from SVMs. In particular, the eclectic rule-extraction approach [44] includes three stages: training, rule extraction, and rule quality evaluation. After training the SVM (first stage), a data set composed of the examples that became support vectors is built with the target class for these patterns replaced by the class predicted by the SVM. In the final stage, the rules representing the concepts learned by the SVM are extracted using a decision tree learner.

In fact, in support vector machines, only part of the training samples are used as a solution, and if all data points that are not support vectors were discarded from the training data set, the same solution would be found. Based on this property, a definition for information quality has been proposed [35]. A data set has the highest quality if:

1. All the training patterns are support vectors.
2. The generalization ability of the support vector machine is the highest.

**6.4.1.2 Estimation of Relevant Data.** If domain knowledge should become available before applying support vector learning by means of a preliminary analysis of training data, then mechanisms of data clustering arise as natural options to be considered for the preprocessing phase.

The purpose of a clustering algorithm is to classify a set of $N$ data points $\mathbf{X} = \{x_1, x_2, \ldots, x_N\}$ into homogeneous groups of data $\mathbf{P} = \{p_1, p_2, \ldots, p_C\}$ with $1 \leq c \leq N$. (If $c = 1$, all data belongs to the same class, and if $c = N$, each data sample defines a class.) One important drawback that is common to a variety of clustering algorithms is that all of them are considered as completely unsupervised. However, in the context of the support vector learning, it is important that the clustering mechanism establishes groups within the data, assuring that these are also homogeneous with regard to the output variable. Therefore, the vectors to which a clustering algorithm will be applied are obtained by augmenting the input samples with the desired output.

To modify the objective function used by the unsupervised clustering method, the augmented vector in $\mathfrak{R}^{n+1} : \mathbf{X} = [\mathbf{x} \, y]$ is defined. As a result, the positions of the centers are influenced not only by the input sample spread but also by the output values. This will improve of the quality of the training data set (large data sets increase the training complexity and do not always make a better model accuracy or generalization). In [35], the input–output data is clustered according to the subtractive clustering method, a modified form of the *mountain* method [45] for cluster estimation. The advantage of using the subtractive clustering algorithm is that the number of clusters does not need to be a priori specified—the method determines the optimal number of clusters and their positions.

## 6.5 EXPERIMENTAL RESULTS

The approach for online learning and fuzzy rule base simplification is tested on the well-known benchmark of the Box-Jenkins time-series prediction [46].

The Box-Jenkins time-series data set consists of 290 pairs of input–output data taken from a laboratory furnace. Each data sample consists of the methane flow rate, the process input variable $u_k$, and the $CO_2$ concentration in off gas, the process output $y_k$. From different studies, the best model structure for this system is:

$$y_k = f(y_{k-1}, u_{k-4}) \tag{6.28}$$

The learning data set consists of the first 200 pairs and the last 90 pairs from the validation data set. The data is normalized into the domain [0, 1].

*Online learning without interpretability.* The developed approach is applied for online learning without online interpretability; that is, the rule base simplification and reduction procedures are not active. In the online learning process, the following configuration was applied: constant radii, 0.3; initialization parameter for the RLS, the initial diagonal covariance matrix $\Omega = diag(750)$. It is remarkable that for the eTS fuzzy models only two parameters need to be predefined. Figure 6.1 shows the evolution of the online learning process.

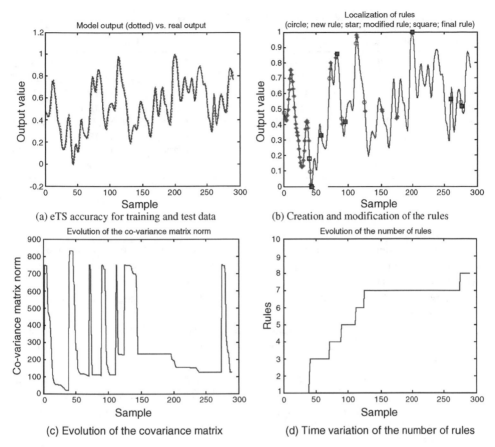

Figure 6.1. Online learning process without rule base simplification and reduction.

From Figure 6.1 it is possible to inspect the evolution of the rule base, particularly the evolution of the number of rules and the exact instants when a rule is created or modified. The final number of fuzzy rules is 8, and this value is strongly dependent on the predefined parameter radii (the most important one) that can be used to control the number of fuzzy rules and inherently the model complexity and accuracy. As a general guidance, too-large values of radii lead to averaging and too-small values lead to overfitting. A value of radii in the range of [0.3, 0.5] is generally recommended.

The *VAF* criterion is used to evaluate the performance of the fuzzy models. The *VAF* criterion represents the percentile "variance accounted for" measured between the real data and the model output. The value of *VAF* equals 100% when the signals $y_r$ and $y_m$ are equal:

$$VAF = 100\% \left[ 1 - \frac{\text{var}(y_r - y_m)}{\text{var}(y_r)} \right] \qquad (6.29)$$

**T A B L E  6.1.** The eTS Fuzzy Rules without Interpretability

| Rule | Input 1 ($y_{k-1}$) | Input 2 ($u_{k-4}$) | Output ($y_k$) |
|------|------|------|------|
| $R_1$ | 0.6730 | 0.3658 | $y^1 = -0.5332y_{k-1} + 0.5193u_{k-4} + 0.5012$ |
| $R_2$ | 0.7432 | 0.2953 | $y^2 = -0.4268y_{k-1} + 0.5587u_{k-4} + 0.3957$ |
| $R_3$ | 0.9960 | 0.0134 | $y^3 = -0.6588y_{k-1} + 0.4629u_{k-4} + 0.6415$ |
| $R_4$ | 0.1748 | 0.8591 | $y^4 = -0.3768y_{k-1} + 0.6073u_{k-4} + 0.4056$ |
| $R_5$ | 0.5966 | 0.3624 | $y^5 = -0.3369y_{k-1} + 0.6585u_{k-4} + 0.3530$ |
| $R_6$ | 0.0695 | 0.9933 | $y^6 = -0.2583y_{k-1} + 0.3958u_{k-4} + 0.6128$ |
| $R_7$ | 0.4939 | 0.4295 | $y^7 = -0.3747y_{k-1} + 0.6243u_{k-4} + 0.3779$ |
| $R_8$ | 0.4834 | 0.5436 | $y^8 = -1.1143y_{k-1} + 1.2395u_{k-4} + 0.3908$ |

The performance of the model is satisfactory and the value for the *VAF* criterion in the validation data is 89.6%.

Table 6.1 details information about the antecedent (centers of the Gaussian membership functions in columns 2 and 3) and consequent parameters of the rules (linear subsystems, column 4).

The width of the antecedent membership functions is the same for all fuzzy sets, $\sigma_i = 0.1061$.

To better understand the interpretability properties of the eTS fuzzy model obtained, we have to inspect the model and look at the membership functions of the input variables, drawn in Figure 6.2.

Most of the membership functions are distinguishable, but it is not possible to assign proper distinct linguistic labels to the fuzzy sets. In fact there are some fuzzy sets with a high degree of overlapping and some of the fuzzy rules are also quite similar in the antecedents (e.g., $R_1$ and $R_5$). This means that the interpretability of the model must be improved.

*Online learning with online interpretability.* The approach is now applied for online learning with online interpretability; that is, the rule base simplification and reduction

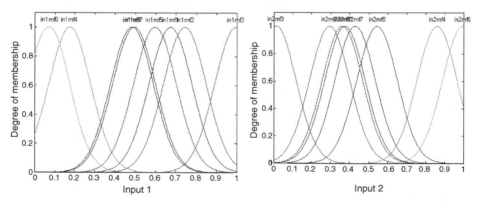

**Figure 6.2.** Membership functions of the input variables without rule base simplification and reduction.

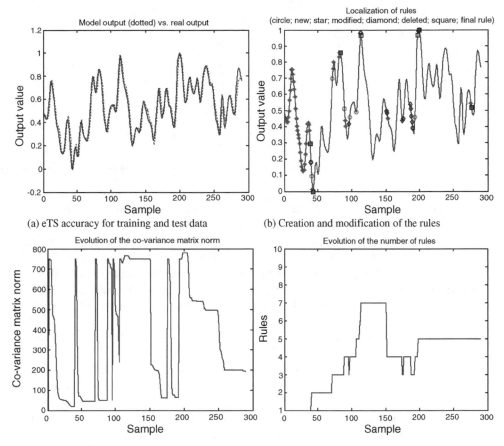

**Figure 6.3.** Online learning process with online interpretability.

procedures are active during the learning process. The configuration for the online learning process is basically the same ($r = 0.3$ and $\Omega = diag(750)$) with the exception of the new parameter for the similarity threshold between fuzzy sets, $\lambda = 0.9$. The merging of similar fuzzy sets takes place when the similarity is greater than $\lambda$. Figure 6.3 shows information about the evolution of the online learning process. Table 6.2 contains

**T A B L E 6.2.** Fuzzy Model Parameters with Online Interpretability

| Rule | Input 1 $(y_{k-1})$ | Input 2 $(u_{k-4})$ | Output $(y_k)$ |
|------|------|------|------|
| $R_1$ | 0.5913 | 0.5005 | $y^1 = -0.3760y_{k-1} + 0.6276u_{k-4} + 0.3743$ |
| $R_2$ | 0.9960 | 0.0134 | $y^2 = -0.5563y_{k-1} + 0.3736u_{k-4} + 0.5482$ |
| $R_3$ | 0.1748 | 0.9471 | $y^3 = -0.3684y_{k-1} + 0.6818u_{k-4} + 0.2577$ |
| $R_4$ | 0.4834 | 0.5005 | $y^4 = -0.4271y_{k-1} + 0.9937u_{k-4} + 0.2577$ |
| $R_5$ | 0.0555 | 0.9471 | $y^5 = -0.3917y_{k-1} + 0.7578u_{k-4} + 0.2649$ |

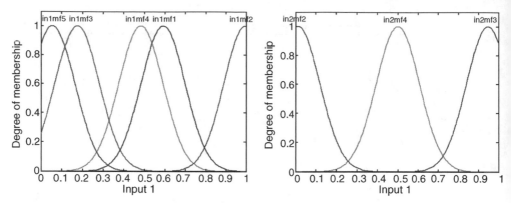

**Figure 6.4.** Membership functions of the input variables with online interpretability.

the antecedent and consequent parameters of the eTS fuzzy model acquired from data. Figure 6.4 presents the membership functions for the input variables at the end of the learning process. The width of the membership functions is the same as in the previous experiment, $\sigma_i = 0.1061$, since the constant radii remains also the same.

The incorporation of the online rule base simplification and reduction methods has a large impact over the online learning process. The number of fuzzy rules attains a maximum of 7 during the learning process and reaches the final number of 5 sooner than in the previous experiment without online interpretability.

The behavior of the approach is now strongly influenced not only by the parameter radii but also by the similarity threshold between fuzzy sets. These two parameters allow the control of the model interpretability, complexity, and precision. The threshold $\lambda$ represents the degree to which the user allows for equality between fuzzy sets used in the model. The lower the value of $\lambda$, the more fuzzy sets are merged, decreasing the term set of the model. It is expected that the numerical accuracy of the model decreases as the parameter $\lambda$ decreases, but it depends on the redundancy of the model. Typical values for parameter $\lambda$ are in the range of [0.65, 0.95], but there is always a tradeoff between accuracy and interpretability, since they act in opposing directions.

The performance of the model is not very different from the one in the previous experiment. The value for the *VAF* criterion in the validation data is 89.4%. The reason for this is that the value for the similarity threshold is quite high, $\lambda = 0.9$. However, the interpretability of the model has improved considerably since now it is possible to assign proper linguistic terms to all the fuzzy sets (Figure 6.4). The number of fuzzy rules reduced from 8 to 5 and for input 2 ($u_{k-4}$) the number of linguistic terms necessary to describe the variable is reduced from 8 to 3. This allows us also to conclude that input 1 ($y_{k-1}$) is more relevant than input 2 in the model.

For input 1 ($u_{k-1}$) the labels are *very low, low, medium, quite high, very high*. For input 2 ($u_{k-4}$) they are *very low, medium, very high*. With these semantic labels the five rules are shown in Table 6.3.

Now the time series is verbally described by a set of five rules with semantic meaning. Of course the fuzzy sets *quite high, low,* and so on, are those of Figure 6.4 and no others. For a lower value of the radii coefficient, more rules are obtained, eventually

TABLE 6.3. The Five Interpretable Rules for the Box-Jenkins Time Series Prediction

| Rule | Syntax |
|---|---|
| $R_1$ | IF $u_{k-1}$ is *quite high* AND $u_{k-4}$ is *medium* |
| | THEN $y_k^1 = -0.3760y_{k-1} + 0.6276u_{k-4} + 0.3743$ |
| $R_2$ | IF $u_{k-1}$ is *very high* AND $u_{k-4}$ is *very low* |
| | THEN $y_k^2 = -0.5563y_{k-1} + 0.3736u_{k-4} + 0.5482$ |
| $R_3$ | IF $u_{k-1}$ is *low* AND $u_{k-4}$ is *very high* |
| | THEN $y_k^3 = -0.3684y_{k-1} + 0.6818u_{k-4} + 0.2577$ |
| $R_4$ | IF $u_{k-1}$ is *medium* AND $u_{k-4}$ is *medium* |
| | THEN $y_k^4 = -0.4271y_{k-1} + 0.9937u_{k-4} + 0.2577$ |
| $R_5$ | IF $u_{k-1}$ is *very low* AND $u_{k-4}$ is *very high* |
| | THEN $y_k^5 = -0.3917y_{k-1} + 0.7578u_{k-4} + 0.2649$ |

with better performance in the training set but with poorer generalization capabilities in the testing set. These five rules produce a good value for *VAF*.

The methodology described in section 6.4, in particular the combination of supervised subtractive clustering [35, 43] with KRLS [37, 39], has been also applied to the Box-Jenkins furnace data set. The estimation of relevant data represents an additional criterion to control machine complexity, that is, nonclustered points will not be included in the kernel representation [43]. As a result of the application of the KRLS with clustering, using a Gaussian width of 0.2 and a threshold of 0.01, the number of kernels achieved was 8. The representation of the multidimensional fuzzy sets for both inputs reveals a satisfactory interpretability of the results (Figures 6.5 and 6.6), while the accuracy has been better than that achieved by the evolving fuzzy system. Comparing the three proposed methodologies, the KRLS with clustering achieved 95.2% for the *VAF* criterion (Table 6.4). Concerning the structure complexity, it is slightly higher than with

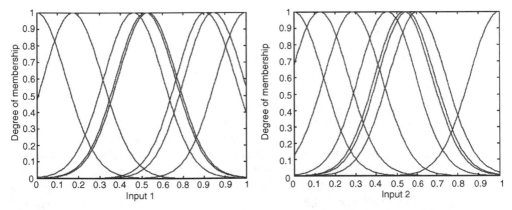

Figure 6.5. Representation of the Gaussian kernels as membership functions of the input variables.

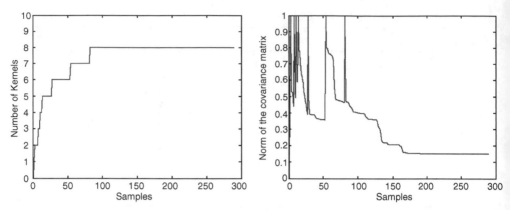

Figure 6.6. Time evolution of the number of kernels and norm of the covariance matrix.

TABLE 6.4. Structure Complexity Analysis

| Method | Structure Complexity (Number of Rules/Kernels) | Accuracy (VAF) |
|---|---|---|
| eTS | 8 | 89.6 % |
| eTS + Interpretability | 5 | 89.4 % |
| KRLS + Clustering | 8 | 95.2 % |

eTS with online interpretability. However, it should be also noted that the kernel model is equivalent to a zero-order TSK fuzzy systems, while the applied evolving fuzzy system has linear consequents that help decrease the number of rules. In an overall conclusion, both methodologies proved to be effective in controlling model complexity, providing a good tradeoff between interpretability and accuracy.

## 6.6 CONCLUSION

The approach for online learning with the integration of online rule base simplification and reduction procedures allows implementing the concept of online transparent modeling in order to improve interpretability and reduce the complexity of fuzzy models acquired with a purely data-driven approach.

The behavior of the approach is strongly influenced by two predefined parameters: the radius of the clusters (radii) and the similarity threshold between fuzzy sets. Parameter radii can be used to control the number of fuzzy rules, and inherently model complexity and precision, while the similarity threshold parameter can be used to balance the interpretability and numerical accuracy of the model. These two parameters together allow the control of model interpretability, complexity, and precision.

The role of the radii of the clusters is also particularly important for the formulation of different problems concerning the size, shape, and orientation of the clusters. When the same radii is used for all the input variables of the model, a relatively simple solution for online transparent modeling can be obtained. The incorporation of the rule base simplification and reduction methods has a great impact in the online learning process, and despite the influence of the predefined parameters in the approach is well understood; the implications of the merging of fuzzy sets and fuzzy rules in the learning process of eTS fuzzy models (covariance matrix, consequent parameters, and potential of the cluster centers) still need to be investigated more deeply.

Procedure (6.16) is a simple way for knowledge fusion to give satisfactory results for the presented benchmark problems. However, alternative and more elaborated methods, for example, the form of an affine combination, might eventually be preferable in other type of problems. But it must be stated that reestimation of the consequent parameters in the reduced rule base using past training data is not possible because the data is no longer available, since we are in the context of online learning, and this is an additional difficulty that cannot yet be resolved.

The work was developed in the MATLAB environment including the Fuzzy Logic Toolbox [47].

## 6.7 ACKNOWLEDGMENTS

The authors express their gratitude to Professor Plamen Angelov, Lancaster University, for the fruitful and interesting discussions concerning online learning and eTS systems. This work is supported by the Portuguese Government, under the program PRODEP III—Acção 5.3, and partially supported by POSI—Programa Operacional Sociedade de Informação—of Portuguese Fundação para a Ciência e Tecnologia under Project ALCINE (POSI/EEI/14155/2001), including FEDER EU financial support, and partially supported by FCT – Fundação para a Ciência e Tecnologia, under Project BIOINK (PTDC/EIA/71770/2006).

## 6.8 REFERENCES

1. D. A. Keim, "Information Visualization and Visual Data Mining," *IEEE Trans. on Visualization and Computer Graphics*, 8(1): **1–8**, Jan–Mar 2002.
2. P. Angelov, "Evolving Rule-Based Models: A Tool for Design of Flexible Adaptive Systems," *Studies in Fuzziness and Soft Computing*, 92, Springer-Verlag, 2002.
3. N. Kasabov, Q. Song, "DENFIS: Dynamic Evolving Neural-Fuzzy Inference System and Its Application for Time-Series Prediction," *IEEE Trans. on Fuzzy Systems*, 10(2): 144–154, 2002.
4. P. Angelov, D. Filev, "An Approach to Online Identification of Takagi-Sugeno Fuzzy Models," *IEEE Trans. on Systems, Man, and Cybernetics—Part B*: Cybernetics, 34(1): 484–498, 2004.

5.  J. Casillas, O. Cordon, F. Herrera, L. Magdalena, *Interpretability Issues in Fuzzy Modeling*, Berlin, Heidelberg: Springer-Verlag, 2003.

6.  C. Mencar, G. Castellano, A. M. Fanelli, "Distinguishability Quantification of Fuzzy Sets," *Information Science*, 177: 130–149, Elsevier, 2007.

7.  R. Mikut, J. Jäkel, L. Gröll, "Interpretability Issues in Data-Based Learning of Fuzzy Systems," *Fuzzy Sets and Systems*, 150: 179–197, 2005

8.  C. Mencar, G. Castellano, A. M. Fanelli, "Some Fundamental Interpretability Issues in Fuzzy Modeling." *Proc. EUSFLAT, Barcelona*, September 7–9, 2005.

9.  M. Setnes, "Complexity Reduction in Fuzzy Systems," PhD Thesis, Delft University of Technology, 2001.

10. S.-M. Zhou, J. Q. Gan, "Constructing Accurate and Parsimonious Fuzzy Models with Distinguishable Fuzzy Sets Based on an Entropy Measure," *Fuzzy Sets and Systems* 157: 1057–1074, 2006.

11. E. V. Broekhoven, V. Adriaenssens, B. De Baets, "Interpretability-Preserving Genetic Optimization of Linguistic Terms in Fuzzy Models for Fuzzy Ordered Classification: An Ecological Case Study," *Int. J. Approximate Reasoning* 44(1): 65–90, 2007.

12. Rafael Alcalá, Jesús Alcalá-Fdez, Francisco Herrera, José Olero, "Genetic Learning of Accurate and Compact Fuzzy Rule-Based Systems Based on the 2-Tuples Linguistic Representation," *Int. J. Approximate Reasoning* 44(1) (33 ref.): 45–64, 2007, Elsevier, **ISSN** 0888-613X.

13. C. Sivapragasam, "Rule Reduction in Fuzzy Logic for better Interpretability in Reservoir Operation Hydrological Processes", Vol. 21, Issue 21, Hoboken: John Wiley &Sons, 2007, pp. 2835–2844.

14. J. González, I. Rojas, H. Pomares, L. J. Herrera, A. Guillén, J. M. Palomares, F. Rojas, "Improving the Accuracy While Preserving the Interpretability of Fuzzy Function Approximators by Means of Multi-objective Evolutionary Algorithms," *Int. J. Approximate Reasoning*, 44(1): 32–44, 2007.

15. A. F. Gómez-Skarmeta, F. Jiménez, G. Sánchez, "Improving Interpretability in Approximative Fuzzy Models via Multiobjective Evolutionary Algorithms," *Int. J. Intelligent Systems*, Vol. 22, Issue 9, Wiley Periodicals, 2007, pp. 943–969.

16. H. Ishibuch, Y. Nojima, "Analysis of Interpretability-Accuracy Tradeoff of Fuzzy Systems by Multiobjective Fuzzy Genetics-Based Machine Learning," *Int. J. Approximate Reasoning*, 44(1): 4–31, 2007.

17. J. L. Díez, J. L. Navarro, A. Sala, "A Fuzzy Clustering Algorithm Enhancing Local Model Interpretability," *Soft Computing, A Fusion of Foundations, Methodologies and Applications*, Vol. 11, pp. 973–983, Springer-Verlag, 2007.

18. Feng Liu, Chai Quek, Geok See Ng, "A Novel Generic Hebbian Ordering-Based Fuzzy Rule Base Reduction Approach to Mamdani Neuro-Fuzzy System," *Neural Comput.* 19(6): 1656–80, June 2007.

19. Y. Jin, B. Sendhoff, "Extracting Interpretable Fuzzy Rules from RBF Networks," *Neural Processing Letters*, Vol. 17(2), pp. 149–164 (16), Springer, 2003.

20. M. Eftekhari, S. D. Katebi, M. Karimi, A. H. Jahanmiri, "Eliciting Transparent Fuzzy Model Using Differential Evolution," *Applied Soft Computing Journal*, Elsevier, in press, 2008.

21. E. Lughofer, E. Hüllermeier, E. P. Klement, "Improving the Interpretability of Data-Driven Evolving Fuzzy Systems." *Proc. EUSFLAT 2005, Barcelona, Spain*, 2005, pp. 28–33.

22. K. P. Ajoy, D. Popovic, "Transparent Fuzzy/Neuro-Fuzzy Modelling in Computational Intelligence in Time Series Forecasting, Theory and Engineering Applications," London: Springer, 2005, pp. 275–303.

23. Plamen Angelov, Edwin Lughofer, "Data-Driven Evolving Fuzzy Systems Using eTS and FLEXFIS: Comparative Analysis," *Int. J. General Systems*, 37(1): 45–67, 2008.

24. J. Victor, A. Dourado, "Evolving Takagi-Sugeno Fuzzy Models," Technical Report, CISUC, 2003, http://cisuc.dei.uc.pt/acg.

25. B. Scholkopf, A. Smola, *Learning with Kernels*. Cambridge, MA: MIT Press, 2001.

26. V. Vapnik, *The Nature of Statistical Learning Theory*. Springer, 1995.

27. J. Victor, A. Dourado, "Online Interpretability by Rule Base Simplification and Reduction." *Proc. Eunite Symposium, Aachen*, 2004.

28. J.-S.R. Jang, ANFIS: "Adaptive-Network-Based Fuzzy Inference Systems," *IEEE Trans. Syst. Man Cybern.*, 23: 665–685, 1993.

29. O. Nelles, "LOLIMOT Local Linear Model Trees for Nonlinear Dynamic System Identification," *Automatisierungstechnik*, 45(4): 163–174, April 1997.

30. R. Babuska, *Fuzzy Modeling for Control*. Boston: Kluwer Academic Publishers, 1998.

31. P. Angelov, C. Xydeas, "Fuzzy Systems Design: Direct and Indirect Approaches," *Soft Computing: A Fusion of Foundations, Methodologies and Applications*, 10: 836–849, Springer Verlag, 2006.

32. M. Setnes, R. Babuska, U. Kaymak, H. R. van Nauta Lemke, "Similarity Measures in Fuzzy Rule Base Simplification," *IEEE Trans. on Systems, Man, and Cybernetics—Part B: Cybernetics*, 28(3): 376–386, 1988.

33. Y. Jin, "Fuzzy Modeling of High-Dimensional Systems: Complexity Reduction and Interpretability Improvement," *IEEE Trans. on Fuzzy Systems*, 8(2): 212–221, 2000.

34. A. Bordes, S. Ertekin, J. Weston, Léon Bottou, "Fast Kernel Classifiers with Online and Active Learning," *J. Machine Learning Research*, 6: 1579–1619, 2005.

35. G. Cauwenberghs, T. Poggio, "Incremental and Decremental Support Vector Machine Learning." In *Advances in Neural Processing Systems*, vol. 10, Cambridge, MA: MIT Press, USA, 2001.

36. C. Diehl, G. Cauwenberghs, "SVM Incremental Learning, Adaptation and Optimization." *Proc. IEEE Int. Joint Conf. Neural Networks (IJCNN'03)*, 2003.

37. Y. Engel, S. Mannor, R. Meir, "The Kernel Recursive Least Squares Algorithm," *IEEE Trans. Signal Proc.*, 52(8): 2275–2285, 2004.

38. T. Ahmed, M. Coates, A. Lakhina, "Multivariate Online Anomaly Detection Using Kernel Recursive Least Squares." *Proc. IEEE Infocom, Anchorage*, 2007.

39. D. Wingate, S. Singh, "Kernel Predictive Linear Gaussian Models for Nonlinear Stochastic Dynamical Systems." *Int. Conf. Machine Learning*, 2006; resources at wcb.mit.edu/~wingated/www/resources.html.

40. S. Van Vaerenbergh, J. Via, I. Santamaria, "A Sliding Window Kernel RLS Algorithm and Its Application to Nonlinear Channel Identification." *IEEE Int. Conf. Acoustics, Speech, and Signal Processing (ICASSP), Toulouse, France, May 2006*.

41. T. Runarsson, S. Sigurdsson, "Asynchronous Parallel Evolutionary Model Selection for Support Vector Machines," *Neural Information Processing—Letters and Reviews*, 3(3): 59–67, 2004.

42. C. Cortes, V. Vapnik, "Support Vector Networks," *Machine Learning*, 20: 273–297, 1995.

43. C. Pereira, A. Dourado, "On the Complexity and Interpretability of Support Vector Machines for Process Modeling. *IJCNN '02—Int. Joint Conference on Neural Networks*, 2002.

44. N. Barakat, J. Diederich, "Eclectic Rule-Extraction from Support Vector Machines," *Int. J. Computational Intelligence*, 2(1): 59–62, 2005.

45. R. Yager, D. Filev, "Learning of Fuzzy Rules by Mountain Clustering." *Proc. SPIE Conf. on Applications of Fuzzy Logic Technology, Boston*, 1994, pp. 246–254.

46. UCI Repository of Machine Learning Databases, University of California, www.ics.uci.edu/~ mlearn/MLRepository.html.

47. MATLAB and Fuzzy Logic Toolbox, Mathworks, Inc.

# 7

# ONLINE FEATURE EXTRACTION FOR EVOLVING INTELLIGENT SYSTEMS

S. Ozawa, S. Pang, N. Kasabov

## 7.1 INTRODUCTION

When we build a classification system or a forecasting system, we sometimes encounter a situation where it is not easy to collect a complete set of training samples. For example, human faces have large variations due to lighting conditions, emotional expression, glasses, makeup, hairstyles, age, and so forth. Taking all these factors into consideration when a face database is constructed is almost impossible. Thus, in many cases, we construct an imperfect system that works well in some limited conditions, and the system is improved whenever the system makes incorrect recognition or prediction. Therefore, in more practical situations, the presentation of training samples becomes sequential, and the learning and prediction have to be alternatively carried out by a system. This type of learning is often called *online learning*. On the other hand, in some practical applications (e.g., stock price forecasting), the property of a data source might be changed over time. In that case, even if a system made a correct prediction for some input at a certain time, the prediction might have to be modified in the future. Then, the learning also has to be online. In online learning circumstances, a system is required to modify only wrong predictions without loosing prediction accuracy for other inputs. In this sense, *incremental learning* has recently received a great deal of attention in many practical applications.

When data are composed of many attributes, feature extraction (or selection) is very important to attain both good generalization performance and fast learning of classifiers.

*Evolving Intelligent Systems: Methodology and Applications,* Edited by Plamen Angelov, Dimitar P. Filev, and Nikola Kasabov

Therefore, the incremental learning should be considered not only for classifiers but also for feature extraction. However, many approaches to incremental learning are aimed at classifiers such as decision trees (Utgoff, 1989; Weng & Hwang, 2007), support vector machines (Shilton et al., 2005), memory-based learning models (Atkeson, 1997), and neural networks (Carpenter & Grossberg, 1988). There have not been proposed many incremental feature extraction methods so far.

As for the incremental learning of feature extraction, Incremental Principal Component Analysis (IPCA) (Hall et al., 1998; Oja & Karhunen, 1985, Sanger, 1989) and Incremental Linear Discriminant Analysis (ILDA) (Weng et al., 2003) have been proposed. Hall and Martin (1998) have devised a smart method to update eigenvectors and eigenvalues incrementally based on eigenvalue decomposition. Ozawa et al. (2004) have extended this IPCA algorithm such that an eigen-axis is augmented based on the accumulation ratio in order to control the dimensionality of an eigenspace easily. On the other hand, Pang et al. (2005) have proposed an incremental LDA (ILDA) algorithm in which a between-class scatter matrix and a within-class scatter matrix are incrementally updated, and then the eigen-axes of a feature space are obtained by solving an eigenproblem. Zhao et al. (2006) have also proposed different ILDA algorithms based on a singular decomposition technique.

Recently, we have proposed a new scheme of incremental learning in which feature extraction and classifier learning are simultaneously carried out online (Ozawa et al., 2004, 2005; Pang et al., 2005). In our previous work, IPCA or ILDA are adopted as feature extraction methods, and $k$-nearest neighbor classifier with Evolving Clustering Method (ECM) (Kasabov, 2002) or Resource Allocating Network with Long-Term Memory (RAN-LTM) (Kobayashi et al., 2001; Ozawa et al., 2005) are adopted as classifiers. A distinctive feature of the proposed scheme is that the learning of feature extraction and a classifier is simultaneously conducted in *one pass*, which means that training samples are passed through a system only once for learning purposes (Kasabov, 2002). One-pass incremental learning is quite important and effective especially when a system has to learn from a large-scale data set with limited computational resources (i.e., CPU performance and memory). It was verified that the classification accuracy of the above classification system was improved constantly even if a small set of training samples were provided at a starting point (Ozawa et al., 2005). To enhance the learning speed, we have proposed an extension of IPCA (Ozawa et al., 2008), called *Chunk IPCA*, in which the update of an eigenspace is completed for a chunk of data by performing single eigenvalue decomposition.

This chapter introduces the above two versions of IPCA as online feature extraction methods and shows how to construct a classification system. Section 7.2 describes the learning algorithm of IPCA in which an eigenspace model is updated for a single training sample at a time. Section 7.3 explains Chunk IPCA, which can update an eigenspace model with a chunk of training samples; in addition, we explain how to combine IPCA with $k$-nearest neighbor classifier, whose prototypes are trained by ECM. In section 7.4, we show the performance evaluation for IPCA and Chunk IPCA using six real data sets. Section 7.5 summarizes the chapter and discusses directions for further work.

## 7.2 INCREMENTAL PRINCIPAL COMPONENT ANALYSIS (IPCA)

### 7.2.1 Learning Assumptions and General Idea in IPCA

Assume that $N$ training samples $\mathbf{x}^{(i)} \in R^n (i = 1, \ldots, N)$ are initially provided to a system and an eigenspace model $\Omega = (\bar{\mathbf{x}}, \mathbf{U}_k, \Lambda_k, N)$ is obtained by applying Principal Component Analysis (PCA) to the training samples. In the eigenspace model $\Omega$, $\bar{\mathbf{x}}$ is a mean vector of $\mathbf{x}^{(i)} (i = 1, \ldots, N)$, $\mathbf{U}_k$ is an $n \times k$ matrix whose column vectors correspond to eigenvectors, and $\Lambda_k = \text{diag}\{\lambda_1, \ldots, \lambda_k\}$ is a $k \times k$ matrix whose diagonal elements are non-zero eigenvalues. Here, $k$ is the number of eigen-axes spanning the eigenspace (i.e., eigenspace dimensionality) and the value of $k$ is determined based on a certain criterion (e.g., accumulation ratio). After calculating $\Omega$, the system holds the information on $\Omega$ and all the training samples are thrown away.

Now assume that the $(N + 1)$th training sample $\mathbf{x}^{(N+1)} = \mathbf{y} \in R^n$ is given. The addition of this new sample results in the changes in the mean vector and the covariance matrix; therefore, the eigenspace model $\Omega = (\bar{\mathbf{x}}, \mathbf{U}_k, \Lambda_k, N)$ should be updated. Let us define the new eigenspace model by $\Omega' = (\bar{\mathbf{x}}', \mathbf{U}'_{k'}, \Lambda'_{k'}, N + 1)$. Note that the eigenspace dimensions might be increased from $k$ to $k + 1$; thus, $k'$ in $\Omega'$ is either $k$ or $k + 1$. Intuitively, if $\mathbf{y}$ includes almost all energy in the current eigenspace spanned by the eigenvectors $\mathbf{U}'_k$, there is no need to increase its dimensions. However, if $\mathbf{y}$ includes certain energy in the complementary eigenspace, the dimensional augmentation is inevitable; otherwise, crucial information on the new sample $\mathbf{y}$ might be lost. Regardless of the necessity in eigenspace augmentation, the eigen-axes should be rotated to adapt to the variation in the data distribution. In summary, there are three main operations in IPCA: (1) mean vector update, (2) eigenspace augmentation, and (3) rotation of eigen-axes.

The first operation is easily carried out based on the following equation:

$$\bar{\mathbf{x}}' = \frac{1}{N+1}(N\bar{\mathbf{x}} + \mathbf{y}) \in R^n \tag{7.1}$$

The other two are explained below.

### 7.2.2 Condition on Eigenspace Augmentation

There are two criteria for deciding whether the dimensional augmentation is needed. One is the norm of a residue vector defined by

$$\mathbf{h} = (\mathbf{y} - \bar{\mathbf{x}}) - \mathbf{U}_k^T \mathbf{g} \quad \text{where} \quad \mathbf{g} = \mathbf{U}_k^T(\mathbf{y} - \bar{\mathbf{x}}) \tag{7.2}$$

Here, $T$ means the transposition of vectors and matrixes. The other is the accumulation ratio whose definition and incremental calculation are shown as follows:

$$A(\mathbf{U}_k) = \frac{\sum_{i=1}^{k} \lambda_i}{\sum_{j=1}^{n} \lambda_j} = \frac{(N+1)\sum_{i=1}^{k} \lambda_i + \left\| \mathbf{U}_k^T(\mathbf{y} - \bar{\mathbf{x}}) \right\|^2}{(N+1)\sum_{j=1}^{n} \lambda_j + \left\| \mathbf{y} - \bar{\mathbf{x}} \right\|^2} \tag{7.3}$$

where $\lambda_i$ is the $i$th largest eigenvalues, and $n$ and $k$ mean the dimensionality of the input space and that of the current eigenspace, respectively. The former criterion in equation (7.2) was adopted by the original IPCA proposed by Hall and Martin (1998), and the latter in equation (7.3) was used in the modified IPCA proposed by the authors (Ozawa et al., 2004). Using these criteria, the condition on the eigenspace augmentation is respectively represented by:

$$[\text{Residue Vector Norm}] \quad \hat{\mathbf{h}} = \begin{cases} \mathbf{h}/\|\mathbf{h}\| & \text{if}\|h\|>\eta \\ 0 & \text{otherwise} \end{cases} \tag{7.4}$$

$$[\text{Accumulation Ratio}] \quad \hat{\mathbf{h}} = \begin{cases} \mathbf{h}/\|\mathbf{h}\| & \text{if } A(\mathbf{U}_k) < \theta \\ 0 & \text{otherwise} \end{cases} \tag{7.5}$$

where $\eta$ (in the original IPCA (Hall & Martin, 1998), $\eta$ is set to zero) and $\theta$ are a positive constant. Note that setting a too-large threshold $\eta$ or too-small $\theta$ would cause serious approximation errors for eigenspace models. Hence, it is important to set proper values to $\eta$ in equation (7.4) and $\theta$ in equation (7.5). In general, finding a proper threshold $\eta$ is easier than doing a proper $\theta$ unless input data are appropriately normalized within a certain range (another difficulty arises for automatic data normalization in online learning environments). On the other hand, since the accumulation ratio is defined by the ratio of input energy in an eigenspace over the original input space, the value of $\theta$ is restricted between 0 and 1. Therefore, it would be easier for $\theta$ to get an optimal value by applying a cross-validation method. The detailed algorithm of selecting $\theta$ in incremental learning settings is described in Ozawa et al. (2008).

## 7.2.3 Eigenspace Rotation

If the condition of equation (7.4) or (7.5) satisfies, the dimensions of the current eigenspace would be increased from $k$ to $k+1$, and a new eigen-axis $\hat{\mathbf{h}}$ should be added to the eigenvector matrix $\mathbf{U}_k$. Otherwise, the dimensionality remains the same. After this operation, the eigen-axes are rotated to adapt to the new data distribution. Assume that the rotation is given by a rotation matrix $\mathbf{R}$; then the eigenspace update is represented by the following equation:

1. If there is a new eigen-axis to be added,

$$\mathbf{U}'_{k+1} = [\mathbf{U}_k, \hat{\mathbf{h}}]\mathbf{R} \tag{7.6}$$

2. Otherwise,

$$\mathbf{U}'_k = \mathbf{U}_k \mathbf{R} \tag{7.7}$$

In order to obtain $\mathbf{R}$, it has been shown that new eigenvectors and the corresponding eigenvalues are obtained by solving the following intermediate eigenproblem (Hall & Martin, 1998):

1. If there is a new eigen-axis to be added,

$$\left\{ \frac{N}{N+1}\begin{bmatrix} \Lambda_k & \mathbf{0} \\ \mathbf{0}^T & 0 \end{bmatrix} + \frac{N}{(N+1)^2}\begin{bmatrix} \mathbf{gg}^T & \gamma\mathbf{g} \\ \gamma\mathbf{g}^T & \gamma^2 \end{bmatrix} \right\}\mathbf{R} = \mathbf{R}\Lambda'_{k+1} \qquad (7.8)$$

2. Otherwise,

$$\left\{ \frac{N}{N+1}\Lambda_k + \frac{N}{(N+1)^2}\mathbf{gg}^T \right\}\mathbf{R} = \mathbf{R}\Lambda'_k \qquad (7.9)$$

Here, $\gamma = \hat{\mathbf{h}}(\mathbf{y}-\bar{\mathbf{x}})$ and $\mathbf{0}$ is a $k$-dimensional zero vector. Here, $\Lambda'_{k+1}$ and $\Lambda'_k$ are the new eigenvalue matrixes whose diagonal elements correspond to $k$ and $k+1$ eigenvalues, respectively. Using the solution $\mathbf{R}$, the new eigenvector matrix $\mathbf{U}'_k$ or $\mathbf{U}'_{k+1}$ is calculated from equation (7.6) or (7.7).

## 7.3 CHUNK INCREMENTAL PRINCIPAL COMPONENT ANALYSIS (CIPCA)

IPCA can be applied to a single training sample at a time, and the intermediate eigenproblem in equation (7.8) or (7.9) must be solved separately for each of the samples even though a chunk of samples is provided for learning. Obviously, this is inefficient from a computational point of view, and the learning may get stuck in a deadlock if a large chunk of training samples is given to learn in a short time. That is, the next chunk of training samples could come before the learning is completed if it takes a long time to update an eigenspace.

To overcome this problem, we extended the original IPCA so that the eigenspace model $\Omega$ can be updated with a chunk of training samples in a single operation (Ozawa et al., 2008). This extended algorithm is called *Chunk IPCA*.

### 7.3.1 Update of Eigenspace

Let us assume that training samples $\mathbf{X} = \{\mathbf{x}^{(1)}, \ldots, \mathbf{x}^{(N)}\} \in R^{n \times N}$ have been given so far and they were already discarded. Instead of keeping actual training samples, a system holds an eigenspace model $\Omega = (\bar{\mathbf{x}}, \mathbf{U}_k, \Lambda_k, N)$ where $\bar{\mathbf{x}}$, $\mathbf{U}_k$, and $\Lambda_k$ are a mean input vector, an $n \times k$ eigenvector matrix, and a $k \times k$ eigenvalue matrix, respectively. Here, $k$ is the number of eigen-axes spanning the current eigenspace. Now, assume that a chunk of $L$ training samples $\mathbf{Y} = \{\mathbf{y}^{(1)}, \ldots, \mathbf{y}^{(L)}\} \in R^{n \times L}$ is presented. The mean vector $\bar{\mathbf{x}}'$ is updated without the past training samples $\mathbf{X}$ as follows:

$$\bar{\mathbf{x}}' = \frac{1}{N+L}(N\bar{\mathbf{x}} + L\bar{\mathbf{y}}) \qquad (7.10)$$

Next, let us derive the update equations for $\mathbf{U}_k$ and $\Lambda_k$. Suppose that $l$ eigen-axes are augmented to avoid loosing essential input information when a chunk of $L$ training samples $\mathbf{Y}$ is provided; that is, the eigenspace dimensions are increased by $l$. Let us denote the augmented eigen-axes as follows:

$$\mathbf{H}_l = \{\mathbf{h}_1, \ldots, \mathbf{h}_l\} \in R^{n \times l}, \quad 0 \le l \le L \tag{7.11}$$

Then, the updated eigenvector matrix $\mathbf{U}'_{k+l}$ is represented by

$$\mathbf{U}'_{k+l} = [\mathbf{U}_k, \mathbf{H}_l]\mathbf{R} \tag{7.12}$$

where $\mathbf{R}$ is a rotation matrix. It has been shown that eigenvectors and the corresponding eigenvalue are obtained by solving the following intermediate eigenproblem (Ozawa et al., 2008):

1. If there are new eigen-axes to be added (i.e., $l \ne 0$),

$$\left\{ \frac{N}{N+L} \begin{bmatrix} \Lambda_k & \mathbf{0} \\ \mathbf{0}^T & 0 \end{bmatrix} + \frac{NL^2}{(N+L)^3} \begin{bmatrix} \bar{\mathbf{g}}\bar{\mathbf{g}}^T & \bar{\mathbf{g}}\bar{\gamma}^T \\ \bar{\gamma}\mathbf{g}^T & \bar{\gamma}\bar{\gamma}^T \end{bmatrix} + \frac{N^2}{(N+L)^3} \sum_{i=1}^{L} \begin{bmatrix} \mathbf{g}'_i\mathbf{g}'^T_i & \mathbf{g}'_i\gamma'^T_i \\ \gamma'_i\mathbf{g}'^T_i & \gamma'_i\gamma'^T_i \end{bmatrix} \right.$$

$$\left. \frac{L(L+2N)}{(N+L)^3} \sum_{i=1}^{L} \begin{bmatrix} \mathbf{g}''_i\mathbf{g}''^T_i & \mathbf{g}''_i\gamma''^T_i \\ \gamma''_i\mathbf{g}''^T_i & \gamma''_i\gamma''^T_i \end{bmatrix} \right\} \mathbf{R} = \mathbf{R}\Lambda'_{k+l} \tag{7.13}$$

2. Otherwise,

$$\left\{ \frac{N}{N+L}\Lambda_k + \frac{NL^2}{(N+L)^3}\bar{\mathbf{g}}\bar{\mathbf{g}}^T + \frac{N^2}{(N+L)^3}\sum_{i=1}^{L}\mathbf{g}'_i\mathbf{g}'^T_i + \frac{L(L+2N)}{(N+L)^3}\sum_{i=1}^{L}\mathbf{g}''_i\mathbf{g}''^T_i \right\} \mathbf{R} = \mathbf{R}\Lambda'_k \tag{7.14}$$

where $\bar{\mathbf{g}} = \mathbf{U}_k^T(\bar{\mathbf{y}}-\bar{\mathbf{x}})$, $\mathbf{g}'_i = \mathbf{U}_k^T(\mathbf{y}^{(i)}-\bar{\mathbf{x}})$, $\mathbf{g}''_i = \mathbf{U}_k^T(\mathbf{y}^{(i)}-\bar{\mathbf{y}})$, $\bar{\gamma} = \mathbf{H}_l^T(\bar{\mathbf{y}}-\bar{\mathbf{x}})$, $\gamma'_i = \mathbf{H}_l^T(\mathbf{y}^{(i)}-\bar{\mathbf{x}})$, $\gamma''_i = \mathbf{H}_l^T(\mathbf{y}^{(i)}-\bar{\mathbf{y}})$.

Solving this intermediate eigenproblem, the rotation matrix $\mathbf{R}$ and the eigenvalue matrix $\Lambda'_{k+l}$ are obtained. Then, the corresponding new eigenvector matrix $\mathbf{U}'_{k+l}$ is given by equation (7.12).

## 7.3.2 A Criterion for Eigen-axis Augmentation

In Chunk IPCA, the number of eigen-axes to be augmented is determined by finding the minimum $k$ such that $A(\mathbf{U}_k) \ge \theta$ holds where $\theta$ is a threshold between 0 and 1. To introduce this criterion, we need to modify equation (7.3) such that the accumulation ratio can be updated incrementally for a chunk of $L$ samples. In Chunk IPCA, we need two types of accumulation ratios. One is the accumulation ratio for a $k$-dimensional eigenspace spanned by $\mathbf{U}'_k = \mathbf{U}_k\mathbf{R}$ and the other is that for a $(k + l)$-dimensional augmented eigenspace spanned by $\mathbf{U}'_{k+l} = [\mathbf{U}_k \, \mathbf{H}_l]\mathbf{R}$. The former is used for checking whether the current $k$-dimensional eigenspace should be augmented. The latter is used for checking whether further eigen-axes are needed for the $(k + l)$-dimensional augmented eigenspace.

The updated accumulation ratio $A'(\mathbf{U}'_k)$ and $A'(\mathbf{U}'_{k+l})$ are calculated as follows:

$$A'(\mathbf{U}'_k) = \frac{\displaystyle\sum_{i=1}^{k}\lambda_i + \frac{L}{N+L}\|\bar{\mathbf{g}}\|^2 + \frac{1}{N}\sum_{j=1}^{L}\|\mathbf{g}''_j\|^2}{\displaystyle\sum_{i=1}^{n}\lambda_i + \frac{L}{N+L}\|\bar{\boldsymbol{\mu}}\|^2 + \frac{1}{N}\sum_{j=1}^{L}\left\|\boldsymbol{\mu}''_j\right\|^2} \tag{7.15}$$

$$A'(\mathbf{U}'_{k+l}) \approx \frac{\displaystyle\sum_{i=1}^{k}\lambda_i + \frac{L}{N+L}\left\|\frac{\bar{\mathbf{g}}}{\bar{\gamma}}\right\|^2 + \frac{1}{N}\sum_{j=1}^{L}\left\|\frac{\mathbf{g}''_j}{\gamma''_j}\right\|^2}{\displaystyle\sum_{i=1}^{n}\lambda_i + \frac{L}{N+L}\|\bar{\boldsymbol{\mu}}\|^2 + \frac{1}{N}\sum_{j=1}^{L}\|\boldsymbol{\mu}''_j\|^2} \tag{7.16}$$

where $\bar{\boldsymbol{\mu}} = \bar{\mathbf{x}} - \bar{\mathbf{y}}$ and $\boldsymbol{\mu}''_j = \mathbf{y}^{(j)} - \bar{\mathbf{y}}$. To update $A'(\mathbf{U}'_k)$, the summation of eigenvalues $\lambda_i (i = 1, \ldots, n)$ is required, and this summation can be held by accumulating the power of training samples. Hence, the individual eigenvalues $\lambda_i$ $(i = k+1, \ldots, n)$ are not necessary for this update. As seen from equations (7.15) and (7.16), we need no past sample $\mathbf{x}^{(j)}$ and no rotation matrix $\mathbf{R}$ to update the accumulation ratio. Therefore, this accumulation ratio is updated with the following information: a chunk of given training samples $\mathbf{Y} = \{\mathbf{y}^{(1)}, \ldots, \mathbf{y}^{(L)}\}$, the current eigenspace model $\Omega = (\bar{\mathbf{x}}, \mathbf{U}_k, \Lambda_k, N)$, the summation of eigenvalues $\sum_{i=1}^{n}\lambda_i$, and a set of augmented eigen-axes $\mathbf{H}_l$, which are obtained through the procedure described next.

### 7.3.3 Selection of Eigen-axes

In IPCA, a new eigen-axis is selected so as to be perpendicular to the existing eigenvectors given by the column vectors of $\mathbf{U}_k$. A straightforward way to get new eigen-axes is to apply Gram-Schmidt orthogonalization to a chunk of given training samples (Hall et al., 2000). If the training samples are represented by $\tilde{L}$ linearly independent vectors, the maximum number of augmented eigen-axes is $\tilde{L}$. However, the subspace spanned by all of the $\tilde{L}$ eigen-axes is redundant in general; in addition, if the chunk size is large, the computation costs to solve the intermediate eigenproblem in equation (7.13) would be considerably expensive. Therefore, we need to find the smallest set of eigen-axes without losing essential information of the given training samples.

The problem of finding an optimal set of eigen-axes is stated below.

*Find the smallest set of eigen-axes $\mathbf{H}^* = \{\mathbf{h}_1, \ldots, \mathbf{h}_{l^*}\}$ for the current eigenspace model $\Omega = (\bar{\mathbf{x}}, \mathbf{U}_k, \Lambda_k, N)$ without keeping the past training samples $\mathbf{X}$ such that the accumulation ratio $A'(\mathbf{U}'_{k+l^*})$ of the given training samples $\{\mathbf{X}, \mathbf{Y}\}$ is larger than a threshold $\theta$.*

Assume that we have a candidate set of augmented eigen-axes $\mathbf{H}_l = \{\mathbf{h}_1, \ldots, \mathbf{h}_l\}$. Since the denominator of equation (7.16) is constant once the mean vector $\bar{\mathbf{y}}$ is calculated, the increment of the accumulation ratio from $A'(\mathbf{U}'_k)$ to $A'(\mathbf{U}'_{k+l})$ is determined by the numerator terms. Thus, let us define the following difference $\Delta\tilde{A}'(\mathbf{U}'_{k+l})$ of the numerator terms between $A'(\mathbf{U}'_k)$ and $A'(\mathbf{U}'_{k+l})$:

$$\Delta\tilde{A}'(\mathbf{U}'_{k+l}) = \frac{L}{N+L}\left\|\mathbf{H}_l^T(\bar{\mathbf{x}}-\bar{\mathbf{y}})\right\|^2 + \frac{1}{N}\sum_{j=1}^{L}\left\|\mathbf{H}_l^T(\mathbf{y}^{(j)}-\bar{\mathbf{y}})\right\|^2 \underset{\text{def}}{=} \sum_{i=1}^{l}\Delta\tilde{A}'_i \qquad (7.17)$$

where

$$\Delta\tilde{A}'_i = \frac{L}{N+L}\left\{\mathbf{h}_i^T(\bar{\mathbf{x}}-\bar{\mathbf{y}})\right\}^2 + \frac{1}{N}\sum_{j=1}^{L}\left\{\mathbf{h}_i^T(\mathbf{y}^{(j)}-\bar{\mathbf{y}})\right\}^2 \qquad (7.18)$$

Equation (7.17) means that the increments of the accumulation ratio are determined by the linear sum of $\Delta\tilde{A}'_i$. Therefore, to find the smallest set of eigen-axes, first find $\mathbf{h}_i$ with the largest $\Delta\tilde{A}'_i$, and put it into the set of augmented eigen-axes $\mathbf{H}_l$ (i.e., $l = 1$ and $\mathbf{H}_l = \mathbf{h}_i$). Then, check whether the accumulation ratio $A'(\mathbf{U}'_{k+l})$ in equation (7.16) becomes larger than the threshold $\theta$. If not, select $\mathbf{h}_i$ with the second-largest $\Delta\tilde{A}'_i$, and the same procedure is repeated until $A'(\mathbf{U}'_{k+l}) \geq \theta$ satisfies. This type of greedy algorithm makes the selection of an optimal set of eigen-axes very simple. Eigen-axis selection is summarized in Pseudo-code 1.

---

**Pseudo-code 1:** *Selection of Eigen-axes*

**Input**: Eigenspace model $\Omega = (\bar{\mathbf{x}}, \mathbf{U}_k, \Lambda_k, N)$, a chunk of $L$ training samples $\mathbf{Y} = \{\mathbf{y}^{(1)}, \ldots, \mathbf{y}^{(L)}\}$, the summation of eigenvalues $\sum_{i=1}^{n}\lambda_i$, and threshold $\theta$ of accumulation ratio.

1. Calculate the mean vector $\bar{\mathbf{y}}$ of the given training samples $\mathbf{Y}$.
2. Calculate the accumulation ratio $A'(\mathbf{U}'_k)$ from equation (7.15).
3. If $A'(\mathbf{U}'_k) \geq \theta$, terminate this algorithm.
4. For $i = 1$ to $L$ do
   Obtain the following residue vectors $\mathbf{h}_i$ using the $i$th training sample $\mathbf{y}^{(i)}$:

$$\mathbf{h}_i = \frac{r_i}{\|r_i\|} \text{ where } r_i = (\mathbf{y}^{(i)}-\bar{\mathbf{x}})-\mathbf{U}_k\mathbf{U}_k^T(\mathbf{y}^{(i)}-\bar{\mathbf{x}}). \qquad (7.19)$$

   End for

5. Define an index set $\Gamma$ of $\mathbf{h}_i$, and initialize $\mathbf{H}$ and $l$.
6. Loop:
   (i) Find the residue vector $\mathbf{h}_{i'}$ that gives the largest $\Delta \tilde{A}'_i$ in equation (7.18):
     $\mathbf{h}_{i'} = \mathrm{argmax}_{i \in \Gamma} \Delta \tilde{A}'_i$.
   (ii) $\mathbf{H} \leftarrow [\mathbf{H}, \mathbf{h}_{i'}]$, $l \leftarrow l+1$, and $\Gamma \leftarrow \Gamma - i'$.
   (iii) If $\Gamma$ is empty, terminate this algorithm.
   (iv) Calculate the updated accumulation ratio $A'(\mathbf{U}'_{k+l})$ from equation (7.16).
   (v) If $A'(\mathbf{U}'_{k+l}) > \theta$, terminate this algorithm.

End loop
   **Output**: Set of augmented eigen-axes: $\mathbf{H}_l = \{\mathbf{h}_1, \ldots, \mathbf{h}_l\}$.

## 7.3.4 Training of Initial Eigenspace

Assume that a set of initial training samples $D_0 = \{(\mathbf{x}^{(i)}, \mathbf{z}^{(i)}) | i = 1, \ldots, N\}$ is given before the learning gets started. To obtain an initial eigenspace model $\Omega = (\bar{\mathbf{x}}, \mathbf{U}_k, \Lambda_k, N)$, the conventional PCA is applied to $D_0$ and the smallest dimensionality $k$ of the eigenspace is determined such that the accumulation ratio is larger than $\theta$. Since a proper $\theta$ is usually unknown and often depends on training data, the cross-validation technique can be applied to determining $\theta$ (Ozawa et al., 2008). However, let us assume that a proper $\theta$ is given in advance. The initial training is shown in Pseudo-code 2.

---

**Pseudo-code 2:** *Training of Initial Eigenspace*

**Input**: Initial training set $D_0 = \{(\mathbf{x}^{(i)}, z^{(i)}) | i = 1, \ldots, N\}$ and threshold $\theta$.
1. Calculate the mean vector $\bar{\mathbf{x}}$ of $\mathbf{x}^{(i)} \in D_0$.
2. Apply PCA to $D_0$ and obtain the eigenvectors $\mathbf{U}_n = \{\mathbf{u}_1, \ldots, \mathbf{u}_n\}$ whose eigenvalues $\Lambda_n = \mathrm{diag}\{\lambda_1, \ldots, \lambda_n\}$ are sorted in decreasing order.
3. Find the smallest $k$ such that the following condition holds: $A(\mathbf{U}_k) \geq \theta$.
**Output**: $\Omega = (\bar{\mathbf{x}}, \mathbf{U}_k, \Lambda_k, N)$ where $\mathbf{U}_k = \{\mathbf{u}_1, \ldots, \mathbf{u}_k\}$ and $\Lambda_k = \mathrm{diag}\{\lambda_1, \ldots, \lambda_k\}$.

---

## 7.3.5 Incremental Learning of a Classifier

Since the eigen-axes spanning a feature space are rotated and sometimes increased over time, it is not simple to build a classifier under such a dynamic environment. For this purpose, we have proposed a nearest-neighbor classifier whose prototypes (reference vectors) are evolved by the Evolving Clustering Method (ECM) (Kasabov, 2002).

    Let the $j$th prototype in the current eigenspace $\Omega = (\bar{\mathbf{x}}, \mathbf{U}_k, \Lambda_k, N)$ be $\tilde{\mathbf{p}}_j (j = 1, \ldots, P)$ and let the corresponding prototype in the original input space be

$\mathbf{p}_j$. Here, $P$ is the number of prototypes. Obviously, the following relation holds between these prototypes:

$$\tilde{\mathbf{p}}_j = \mathbf{U}_k^T(\mathbf{p}_j - \bar{\mathbf{x}}) \tag{7.20}$$

After adding a chunk of $L$ training samples $\mathbf{Y}$, assume that the eigenspace $\Omega$ is updated to $\Omega' = (\bar{\mathbf{x}}', \mathbf{U}'_{(k+l)}, \Lambda'_{(k+l)}, N+L)$. Substituting equations (7.10) and (7.12) into (7.20), the updated prototypes $\tilde{\mathbf{p}}'_j (j = 1, \ldots, P)$ are given by

$$\tilde{\mathbf{p}}'_j = \mathbf{U}'^T_{(k+l)}(\mathbf{p}_j - \bar{\mathbf{x}}') = \mathbf{R}^T \begin{bmatrix} \tilde{\mathbf{p}}_j \\ \mathbf{H}^T(\mathbf{p}_j - \bar{\mathbf{x}}) \end{bmatrix} + \frac{L}{N+L} \mathbf{R}^T \begin{bmatrix} \bar{\mathbf{g}} \\ \bar{\gamma} \end{bmatrix} \tag{7.21}$$

If no dimensional augmentation is needed, $\mathbf{H} = \mathbf{0}$ holds. Hence, equation (7.21) reduces to

$$\tilde{\mathbf{p}}'_j = \mathbf{R}^T \tilde{\mathbf{p}}_j + \frac{L}{N+L} \mathbf{R}^T \bar{\mathbf{g}} \tag{7.22}$$

where no information on $\mathbf{p}_j$ is needed in the prototype update. However, when the dimensional augmentation as well as the rotation occurs, the original prototypes $\mathbf{p}_j$ are necessary for the exact calculation of the new prototype $\tilde{\mathbf{p}}'_j$. That is, unless we keep the original prototypes in memory, it is impossible to carry out this prototype update.

Since the complementary space generally includes only negligible energy of the prototypes, equation (7.21) is approximated by

$$\tilde{\mathbf{p}}'_j \approx \mathbf{R}^T \begin{bmatrix} \tilde{\mathbf{p}}_j \\ \mathbf{0} \end{bmatrix} + \frac{L}{N+L} \mathbf{R}^T \begin{bmatrix} \bar{\mathbf{g}} \\ \bar{\gamma} \end{bmatrix} \tag{7.23}$$

where $[\tilde{\mathbf{p}}_j^T, \mathbf{0}^T]^T$ is a $(k+1)$-dimensional column vector that is given by adding $l$ zeros to the current prototype $\tilde{\mathbf{p}}_j$. This approach is efficient in memory use, but we have to mind the approximation error if the threshold $\theta$ is too small.

## 7.3.6 Incremental Learning Algorithm

In online learning environments, classification and learning in a system are conducted alternatively as follows. First, suppose that $N$ training samples are given to form an initial eigenspace model $\Omega = (\bar{\mathbf{x}}, \mathbf{U}_k, \Lambda_k, N)$. Then, a chunk of query inputs is presented to the system, and the distances between each of the query inputs and all the prototypes are calculated, and then the nearest-neighbor method is applied to determine the class. The misclassified query inputs (and sometimes some of the correctly classified ones) as well as their class labels are stored temporally into a set of training samples $\mathbf{Y} = \{\mathbf{y}^{(1)}, \ldots, \mathbf{y}^{(L)}\}$ where $L$ is the number of training samples. Next, $\mathbf{Y}$ is applied to Chunk IPCA to update the current eigenspace model $\Omega$. The updated eigenspace model $\Omega' = (\bar{\mathbf{x}}', \mathbf{U}'_{(k+l)}, \Lambda'_{(k+l)}, N+L)$ is utilized for transforming $\mathbf{Y}$ into the features, and the feature vectors as well as the prototypes are used to train the classifier.

The main routine for learning and classification is summarized in Pseudo-code 3. Note that the online classification process to select a set of training samples **Y** is omitted here for the sake of simplicity.

---

### Pseudo-code 3: Learning and classification

**Input**: Initial training set $D_0 = \{(\mathbf{x}^{(i)}, z^{(i)})|i = 1, \ldots, N\}$ and the threshold $\theta$ of accumulation ratio.

**Initialization**:

1. Call *Training of Initial Eigenspace* to calculate the initial eigenspace model $\Omega = (\bar{\mathbf{x}}, \mathbf{U}_k, \Lambda_k, N)$ of $D_0 = \{(\mathbf{x}^{(i)}, z^{(i)})|i = 1, \ldots, N\}$.
2. Calculate the projection of each initial training sample $\mathbf{x}^{(i)} \in D_0$ into the eigenspace to obtain the feature vector $\tilde{\mathbf{x}}^{(i)}$. Apply ECM (Kasabov, 2002) to the feature vectors, and obtain the prototypes $\tilde{\mathbf{p}}_j$.
3. Loop:
    (i) Input: A new chunk of training samples $D = \{(\mathbf{y}^{(i)}, z^{(i)})|i = 1, \ldots, L\}$.
    (ii) Apply *Chunk IPCA* to $\mathbf{Y} = \{\mathbf{y}^{(1)}, \ldots, \mathbf{y}^{(L)}\}$:
        (a) Call *Selection of Eigen-axes* to obtain $\mathbf{H}_l$ of the $l$ augmented eigen-axes.
        (b) Solve an intermediate eigenproblem in equation (7.13) or (7.14) to obtain a rotation matrix $\mathbf{R}$ and an eigenvalue matrix $\Lambda'_{k+l}$.
        (c) Update the mean vector $\bar{\mathbf{x}}'$ and the eigenvector matrix $\mathbf{U}'_{k+l}$ based on equations (7.10) and (7.12), respectively.
    (iii) Update the eigenspace model as follows: $\Omega = (\bar{\mathbf{x}}, \mathbf{U}_k, \Lambda_k, N) \leftarrow \Omega' = (\bar{\mathbf{x}}', \mathbf{U}'_{(k+l)}, \Lambda'_{(k+l)}, N+L)$.
    (iv) Calculate the feature vectors $\tilde{\mathbf{Y}} = \{\tilde{\mathbf{y}}^{(1)}, \ldots, \tilde{\mathbf{y}}^{(L)}\}$ of $\mathbf{Y}$ as follows: $\tilde{\mathbf{y}}^{(i)} = \mathbf{U}'_h(\mathbf{y}^{(i)} - \bar{\mathbf{x}})$   $(i = 1, \ldots, L)$.
    (v) Apply ECM to $\tilde{\mathbf{Y}}$, and obtain the updated prototypes $\tilde{\mathbf{p}}'_j (j = 1, \ldots, P)$ where $P$ is the number of prototypes.
    (vi) Predict the classes of $\mathbf{y}^{(i)} (i = 1, \ldots, L)$ based on the nearest-neighbor method.

**Output**: Prediction $z(\mathbf{y}^{(i)})(i = 1, \ldots, L)$.
End loop

---

## 7.4 PERFORMANCE EVALUATION

### 7.4.1 Experimental Setup

We selected six data sets for evaluation from the UCI Machine Learning Repository (see Table 7.1), which have various numbers of data samples and attributes. Since Internet Advertisement, MUSK, and Spambase are not divided into training and test samples, we split them randomly into two halves, and the evaluations are conducted based on twofold cross-validation. Although, the MUSK database includes two data sets, we select the larger one.

**TABLE 7.1.** Evaluated UCI Data Sets

| Database Name | #Attributes | #Classes | #Train. Data | #Test Data |
|---|---|---|---|---|
| Internet Advertisement | 1558 | 2 | 1180 | 1179 |
| Isolet Spoken Letter Recog. | 617 | 26 | 6238 | 1559 |
| MUSK | 166 | 2 | 3299 | 3299 |
| Spambase | 57 | 2 | 2301 | 2300 |
| Image Segmentation | 19 | 7 | 210 | 2100 |
| Vowel | 10 | 11 | 528 | 462 |

To construct an initial eigenspace, 5% of training samples are applied to the conventional PCA. The remaining 95% of training samples are sequentially provided as shown in Figure 7.1. Although the proposed Chunk IPCA algorithm can work even if the chunk size is changed at every learning stage, we assume that the size is fixed with $L$ during the learning. In the first experiment, the chunk size $L$ is set to 10; in the other experiments, the chunk size is fixed with one of the following values: $L = 1, 5, 10, 20, 50$, or 100.

A chunk of training samples is randomly selected and it has no overlap with other chunks; hence, all the training samples are presented only once to learn. Hence, the number of learning stages $S$ is given by $S = \lfloor 0.95N/L \rfloor$, where $N$ is the total number of training samples. Note that the number of training samples in the last chunk can be less than $L$, and it is given by $N - L\lfloor 0.95N/L \rfloor$. Since the performance of incremental learning generally depends on the sequence of training samples, 10 trials with different sequences of training samples are conducted to evaluate the average performance.

## 7.4.2 Classification Performance

The proposed Chunk IPCA is evaluated through a comparison with the following three eigenspace models.

1. **Fixed eigenspace.:** An eigenspace is obtained by applying PCA to an initial training set, and it is fixed during the whole learning stage. This eigenspace model is adopted to see the usefulness of updating a feature space.
2. **Original IPCA.:** An eigenspace model is incrementally updated based on the original IPCA algorithm. The eigenspace model is updated with a single training sample at a time even if the training samples are provided in a chunk. The eigenaxes are augmented based on the criterion in equation (7.4), where $\eta$ is

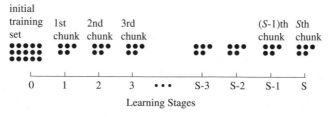

**Figure 7.1.** Presentation of training samples.

determined such that the eigenspace has similar dimensionality to the eigenspace constructed by the proposed Chunk IPCA. Therefore, the main concern in adopting the original IPCA is to evaluate the computation costs.

3. **Batch PCA.:** An eigen-feature space is updated at every learning stage by applying PCA to all the training samples given so far. The computation costs would be more expensive than the incremental learning methods, but an accurate eigenspace is always obtained. The dimensionality of an eigenspace is set to the same value as the proposed Chunk IPCA. Therefore, the classification accuracy of this method gives a target value for the proposed Chunk IPCA.

Table 7.2 shows the experimental results of the above three eigenspace models and the proposed Chunk IPCA ($L = 10$) when the nearest neighbor method combined with ECM is adopted as classifier. As seen in Table 7.2a, the classification accuracy of the fixed eigenspace model is inferior to other models except for the Isolet and MUSK data sets. This result shows that the features extracted from the initial training samples were inappropriate to classify the remaining training samples correctly; therefore, it is effective to update the feature space to adapt to the change of data distributions. As for the Isolet and MUSK data sets, we could not find a clear difference in classification accuracy, and the results suggest that even 5% of training samples include enough information to construct an effective eigenspace. However, even in such a case, the importance of incremental learning is not lost because it is generally impossible to know in advance whether an initial data set includes a sufficient amount of information on future training samples.

On the other hand, there is no significant difference in classification accuracy between the original IPCA and the Chunk IPCA. This is not a negative result because the threshold $\eta$ in equation (7.4) is determined such that the eigenspaces constructed by these

**T A B L E  7.2.** Performance Comparison on (a) Classification Accuracy and (b) CPU Time with Three Eigenspace Models: Fixed Eigenspace, Original IPCA, and Batch IPCA

(a) Classification Accuracy

|                  | Advertisement | Isolet | MUSK | Spambase | Segmentation | Vowel |
|------------------|---------------|--------|------|----------|--------------|-------|
| Fixed Eigenspace | 89.7          | 88.0   | 95.0 | 69.4     | 77.3         | 54.8  |
| Original IPCA    | 93.2          | 88.3   | 95.1 | 78.9     | 87.3         | 57.7  |
| Batch PCA        | 94.2          | 88.5   | 94.8 | 79.2     | 87.3         | 58.6  |
| Chunk IPCA       | 93.4          | 88.0   | 94.9 | 78.9     | 87.3         | 57.2  |

(b) CPU Time

|                  | Advertisement | Isolet | MUSK  | Spambase | Segmentation | Vowel |
|------------------|---------------|--------|-------|----------|--------------|-------|
| Fixed Eigenspace | 13.7          | 1.8    | 0.044 | 0.003    | 0.0003       | 0.001 |
| Original IPCA    | 18.1          | 6379   | 17.4  | 27.4     | 0.073        | 0.109 |
| Batch PCA        | 3000          | 2146   | 37.6  | 3.1      | 0.022        | 0.05  |
| Chunk IPCA       | 18.5          | 265.9  | 1.7   | 0.9      | 0.023        | 0.058 |

two models have as similar a dimensionality as possible; that is, the threshold value is determined such that the two eigenspaces include the same amount of information on training samples. Compared with the Batch PCA, the proposed Chunk IPCA has slightly lower classification accuracy; however, the difference is not significant. This means that the proposed method ensures the quasi-optimality in the construction of eigenspace without keeping past training samples.

The computation costs of the eigenspace update are estimated by measuring the CPU time using a MATLAB function. In Table 7.2b, the CPU time of *Fixed Eigenspace* corresponds to the time required to construct an initial feature space. As you can see in Table 7.2b, the computation costs of Chunk IPCA are significantly reduced against both Original IPCA and Batch PCA, especially for large data sets. However, for the Advertisement data set, Chunk IPCA has no advantage over Original IPCA, in which an intermediate eigenproblem is solved for every training sample. The main reason for this is that the computation costs of the eigen-axis selection could be expensive for large-dimensional data because the large-scale matrix multiplication is needed many times for all eigen-axis candidates. However, this can be alleviated by introducing a more sophisticated search algorithm (e.g., binary search) in the eigen-axis selection. The experimental results here suggest that the proposed method possesses excellent scalability unless the number of attributes is too large.

## 7.4.3 Influence of Chunk Size on System Performance

Since eigen-axes selection is based on a greedy approach, the approximation error of eigen-axes obtained by Chunk IPCA could increase when a large chunk of training samples is given for training at one time. On the other hand, fast learning of an eigenspace is expected for Chunk IPCA. Therefore, it should be interesting for Chunk IPCA to study the influence of chunk size on classification accuracy and learning time.

Figure 7.2 shows the classification accuracy at the final learning stage and the learning time when training samples are provided in various chunk sizes. The relative CPU time is defined as the ratio of the CPU time to that for $L = 1$.

As seen in Figure 7.2a, the classification accuracy is not seriously affected by the chunk size except for the Image Segmentation data set, although the approximation error of eigen-axes could be increased for a larger chunk size. Figures 7.3a, and b, respectively, show the time evolutions of classification accuracy and feature space dimensions when the chunk size $L$ is set to 1, 10, and 20. The data set used here is "Spambase." From the results in Figure 7.3a, it is also confirmed that chunk size does not affect the learning process very much in terms of classification accuracy. Figure 7.3b suggests that the evolution of classification accuracy results from dynamic augmentation of feature spaces. Therefore, one can say that incremental learning not only of classifiers but also of the feature extraction part is very effective in online pattern recognition problems.

As seen in Figure 7.3b, however, the feature space dimensions seem to depend on the chunk size. Although the evolutions of classification accuracy have similar trends among those three cases (see Figure 7.3a), the dimensions are increasing in different ways after around the 200th learning stage. As will be discussed later, since

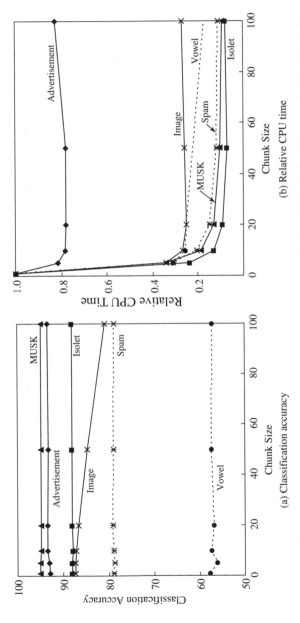

**Figure 7.2.** Final classification accuracy and relative CPU time of Chunk IPCA when the chunk size $L$ is set to 1, 2, 5, 10, 20, 50, and 100.

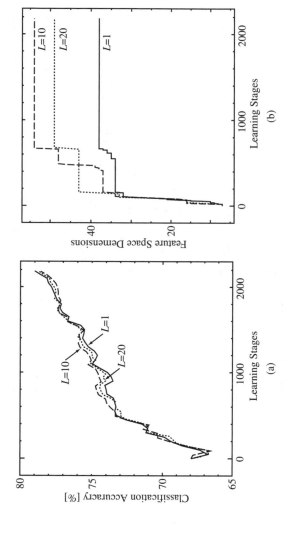

Figure 7.3. Time evolutions of (a) classification accuracy and (b) feature space dimensions when the chunk size L is set to 1, 10, and 20. The data set is "Spambase."

the primary eigenvectors of Chunk IPCA have good approximation to those of Batch PCA for any chunk size, it is considered that the above differences in dimensions originate from the approximation errors for minor eigenvectors. Thus, the differences in feature space dimensions do not usually cause serious problem from a practical point of view.

On the other hand, as seen in Figure 7.2b, computation time is greatly reduced as chunk size becomes large. The reduction in computation time is mainly attained by reducing the repeated times of solving the intermediate eigenproblem. However, the decreasing rate for the Advertise data set is smaller than for the others. This result suggests that the increase in the computation costs of calculating the matrix products in equations (7.13), (7.16), and (7.19) cancels the reduction in the computation costs of solving the intermediate eigenproblem.

### 7.4.4 Accuracy of Updated Eigenvectors

To see whether an appropriate feature space is constructed by Chunk IPCA, the similarity of eigenvectors obtained by Batch PCA and Chunk IPCA is examined. The similarity is measured by the following directional cosine $d_i$:

$$d_i = \frac{1}{M} \sum_{j=1}^{M} \frac{\mathbf{u}_{ji}^{(b)T} \mathbf{u}_{ji}^{(c)}}{\left\| \mathbf{u}_{ji}^{(b)} \right\| \left\| \mathbf{u}_{ji}^{(c)} \right\|} \qquad (7.24)$$

where $\mathbf{u}_{ji}^{(b)}$ and $\mathbf{u}_{ji}^{(c)}$ are respectively the $i$th eigenvector obtained by Batch PCA and Chunk IPCA in the $j$th trial, and $M$ is the number of trials to average the similarity. Obviously, if the similarity is one, it means two eigenvectors are identical.

Figure 7.4 shows the average similarity between the eigenvectors obtained by Batch PCA and Chunk IPCA for the six UCI data sets in Table 7.1. The horizontal axis corresponds to the number of eigenvectors with the largest 25 eigenvalues. Figures 7.4a and b show the similarity when the chunk size $L$ is 10 and 50, respectively.

As seen in Figure 7.4, in almost all cases, the similarity is kept above 0.9 for the major eigenvectors. As for Isolet and MUSK data sets, about 20 major eigenvectors are precisely obtained by Chunk IPCA. Figure 7.5 shows the distribution of the normalized eigenvalues for the 25 major eigenvectors. Here, the $i$th normalized eigenvalue is defined as the eigenvalue for the $i$th eigenvector normalized by the sum of all the eigenvalues. As seen in Figure 7.5, the normalized eigenvalues are going down quickly to zero after around the 5th major eigenvector except for Isolet and MUSK data sets. From the results in Figures 7.4 and 7.5, we can say that the proposed Chunk IPCA gives a good approximation to major eigenvectors with large eigenvalues even if the eigen-axes are selected based on a greedy method.

On the other hand, the approximation to minor eigenvectors, whose normalized eigenvalues are almost zero as shown in Figure 7.5, has a large error. The primary reason for this originates from the approximation error introduced in the derivation of the intermediate eigenproblem in equation (7.13). This approximation error could be small if the threshold for accumulation ratio $\theta$ is set properly. However, it is not easy to know a

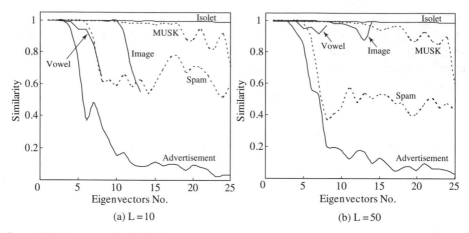

**Figure 7.4.** Average similarity between eigenvectors obtained by Batch PCA and Chunk IPCA for the six UCI data sets when the chunk size *L* is 10 and 50.

proper value of $\theta$ in advance because it depends on the sequence of training samples. In the one-pass learning situation assumed here, a chunk of training samples given sequentially is thrown away after the learning is done at every stage. Therefore, if the sample distributions were largely varied from those at early learning stages, some crucial information would be lost during learning, and the loss would prevent constructing an effective eigenspace. To overcome this problem, we should introduce an adaptive mechanism for $\theta$, but this is left as our future work.

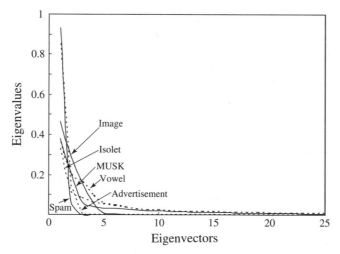

**Figure 7.5.** Average eigenvalues of the major 25 eigenvectors. For "Image Segmentation" and "Vowel" data sets, 19 and 10 eigenvalues are shown.

## 7.5 CONCLUSION AND FUTURE WORK

This chapter introduced an adaptive method for evolving intelligent systems in which Incremental Principal Component Analysis (IPCA) and Evolving Clustering Method (ECM) are effectively combined. This learning scheme gives a new concept for pattern recognition systems: Feature extraction and classifier learning are simultaneously carried out online. One drawback of this approach was scalability in terms of the number of data samples and the number of their attributes. This drawback comes from the limitation of the Original IPCA, where training samples must be applied one by one even if a chunk of training samples is given at one time.

To overcome this problem, the authors developed a new method called Chunk IPCA (Ozawa et al., 2008), in which a chunk of training samples can be applied at one time to update an eigenspace model incrementally. In addition, a nearest-neighbor classifier whose prototypes are adapted to the evolution of a feature space was proposed. This chapter explained the algorithm of eigen-axis selection, the introduction of accumulation ratio as a criterion of eigen-axis augmentation, and the integration of two types of incremental learning for feature space and classifier. The proposed learning scheme enables a classification system to learn incrementally, online, and in one pass. This property provides an efficient method of learning a system in terms of computations and memory.

To evaluate the scalability and the learning efficiency of the proposed Chunk IPCA, we tested the method on six standard data sets with various numbers of data samples and attributes. The experimental results meant that the proposed learning scheme worked quite well regardless of the sizes of chunks of training samples provided at one time. That is to say, chunk size does not affect the final classification accuracy of the system, and the learning time is significantly shortened depending on the chunk size. Furthermore, we examined the approximation error of the eigenvectors obtained by Chunk IPCA. As a result, Chunk IPCA learned major eigenvectors without serious errors, whereas minor eigenvectors have large errors. However, as far as we can see from the experimental results, the errors for minor eigenvectors do not seriously affect classification accuracy.

There remains further work to be done. First, the approximation error to minor eigenvectors may prevent construction of an effective eigenspace if the sample distributions were largely changed over time. This problem can be alleviated by introducing an adaptive selection for the threshold $\theta$. Second, system performance can be greatly enhanced by introducing Incremental Linear Discriminant Analysis (LDA) (Pang et al., 2005) as feature extraction and by introducing other powerful classifiers such as neural networks (Ozawa et al., 2005) and a support vector machine. Therefore, pursuing the optimal combination of feature space learning and classifier learning is another interesting topic. Finally, PCA and LDA transform inputs into linear features, and these features are not always effective for classification purposes. Recently, kernel PCA and kernel LDA have been widely noticed as high-performance feature extraction methods (Scholkopf et al., 1996); hence, the extension of the incremental learning approach to kernel PCA (Takeuchi et al., 2007) and kernel LDA (Cai et al., 2007) is also a promising future work.

## 7.6 REFERENCES

Atkeson, C. G., A. W. Moore, S. Schaal (1997). "Locally Weighted Learning," *Artificial Intelligence Review*, Vol. 11, pp. 75–113.

Cai, D., X. He, J. Han (2007). "Efficient Kernel Discriminant Analysis via Spectral Regression." Proc. Seventh IEEE Int. Conf. on Data Mining, pp. 427–432.

Carpenter, G. A., S. Grossberg (1988). "The ART of Adaptive Pattern Recognition by a Self-organizing Neural Network," *IEEE Computer*, Vol. 21, No. 3, pp. 77–88.

Hall, P., R. Martin (1998). "Incremental Eigenanalysis for Classification." Proc. British Machine Vision Conference, Vol. 1, pp. 286–295.

Hall, P., D. Marshall, R. Martin (2000). "Merging and Splitting Eigenspace Models," *IEEE Trans. on Pattern Analysis and Machine Intelligence*, Vol. 22, No. 9, pp. 1042–1049.

Kasabov, N. (2002). *Evolving Connectionist Systems: Methods and Applications in Bioinformatics, Brain Study and Intelligent Machines.* Springer-Verlag, London, UK.

Kasabov, N. (2007). *Evolving Connectionist Systems: The Knowledge Engineering Approach*, London: Springer.

Kobayashi, M. A. Zamani, S. Ozawa, S.Abe (2001). "Reducing Computations in Incremental Learning for Feedforward Neural Network with Long-term Memory." Proc. Int. Joint Conf. on Neural Networks, Vol. 3, pp. 1989–1994.

Oja, E. J. Karhunen (1985). "On Stochastic Approximation of the Eigenvectors and Eigenvalues of the Expectation of a Random Matrix," *J. Math. Analysis and Application*, Vol. 106, pp. 69–84.

Ozawa, S., S. Pang, N. Kasabov (2004). "A Modified Incremental Principal Component Analysis for On-line Learning of Feature Space and Classifier." In *PRICAI 2004: Trends in Artificial Intelligence*, LNAI, (C. Zhang, H. W. Guesgen, W. K. Yeap, eds.). Springer-Verlag, pp. 231–240.

Ozawa, S., S. L. Toh, S. Abe, S. Pang, N. Kasabov (2005). "Incremental Learning of Feature Space and Classifier for Face Recognition," *Neural Networks*, Vol. 18, No. 5–6, pp. 575–584.

Ozawa, S., S. Pang, N. Kasabov (2008). "Incremental Learning of Chunk Data for On-line Pattern Classification Systems," *IEEE Trans. on Neural Networks*, Vol. 19, No. 6, pp. 1061–1074.

Pang, S., S. Ozawa, N. Kasabov (2005). "Incremental Linear Discriminant Analysis for Classification of Data Streams." *IEEE Trans. on Systems, Man, and Cybernetics, Part B*, Vol. 35, No. 5, pp. 905–914.

Sanger, T. D. (1989). "Optimal Unsupervised Learning in a Single-layer Linear Feedforward Neural Network," *Neural Networks*, Vol. 2, No. 6, pp. 459–473.

Scholkopf, B., A. Smola, K.-R. Muller (1996). "Nonlinear Component Analysis as a Kernel Eigenvalue Problem," MPI Technical Report, No. 44.

Shilton, A., M. Palaniswami, D. Ralph, A. C. Tsoi (2005). "Incremental Training of Support Vector Machines." *IEEE Trans. on Neural Networks*, Vol. 16, No. 1, pp. 114–131.

Takeuchi, Y., S. Ozawa, S. Abe (2007). "An Efficient Incremental Kernel Principal Component Analysis for Online Feature Selection." Proc. Int. Joint Conf. on Neural Networks 2007, CD-ROM.

Thrun S., L. Pratt (1998). *Learning to Learn.* Kluwer Academic Publishers, Boston, MA, USA.

Utgoff, P. E. (1989). "Incremental Induction of Decision Trees," *Machine Learning*, Vol. 4, No. 2, pp. 161–186.

Weng, J., Y. Zhang, W.-S. Hwang (2003). "Candid Covariance-Free Incremental Principal Component Analysis," *IEEE Trans. on Pattern Analysis and Machine Intelligence*, Vol. 25, No. 8, pp. 1034–1040.

Weng, J., W.-S. Hwang (2007). "Incremental Hierarchical Discriminant Regression." *IEEE Trans. on Neural Networks*, Vol. 18, No. 2, pp. 397–415.

Yan, J., Q.-S. Cheng, Q. Yang, B. Zhang (2005). "An Incremental Subspace Learning Algorithm to Categorize Large Scale Text Data." Prof. of 7th Asia-Pacific Web Conference, pp. 52–63.

Zhao, H., P. C. Yuen, J. T. Kwok (2006). "A Novel Incremental Principal Component Analysis and Its Application for Face Recognition." *IEEE Trans. on Systems, Man and Cybernetics, Part B*, Vol. 36, No. 4, pp. 873–886.

# 8

# STABILITY ANALYSIS FOR AN ONLINE EVOLVING NEURO-FUZZY RECURRENT NETWORK

José de Jesús Rubio

## 8.1 OUTLINE

In this chapter, an online *evolving neuro-fuzzy recurrent network (ENFRN)* is proposed. The network is capable of perceiving the change in the actual system and adapting (self-organizing) itself to the new situation. Both structure and parameters learning take place at the same time. The network generates a new hidden neuron if the smallest distance between the new data and all the existing hidden neurons (the winner neuron) is more than a predefined radius. A new pruning algorithm based on the population density is proposed. *Population density* is the number of times each hidden neuron is used. If the value of the smallest density (the looser neuron) is smaller than a prespecified threshold, this neuron is *pruned*. It is proposed to use a modified least-squares algorithm to train the parameters of the network. The major contributions of this chapter are: (1) The stability of the algorithm of the proposed evolving neuro-fuzzy recurrent network was proven; and (2) the bound of the average identification error was found. Three examples are provided to illustrate the effectiveness of the suggested algorithm based on simulations.

---

*Evolving Intelligent Systems: Methodology and Applications,* Edited by Plamen Angelov, Dimitar P. Filev, and Nikola Kasabov

## 8.2 INTRODUCTION

Both neural networks and fuzzy logic are universal estimators; they can approximate any nonlinear function to any prescribed accuracy, provided that sufficient hidden neurons or fuzzy rules are available.

Resent results show that the fusion procedure of these two different technologies seems to be very effective for nonlinear system identification [7]. Over the past few years, the application of fuzzy neural networks to nonlinear system identification has been a very active area [28]. Fuzzy modeling involves structure and parameters identification.

Neural networks can be classified as *feedforward* and *recurrent* [15]. Feedforward networks, for example, multilayer perceptrons (MLPs), are implemented for the approximation of nonlinear functions. The main drawbacks of these neural networks are that the updating of the weights can fall in a local minimum, and the function approximation is sensitive to the training data [30]. Since recurrent networks incorporate feedback, they have powerful representation capability and can successfully overcome disadvantages of feedforward networks [26].

System identification can be classified into two groups: (1) offline identification [4, 9, 18, 32, 38, 41]; (2) online identification [2, 3, 20, 21, 23, 24, 27, 31, 39, 40, 42].

In offline identification, the update of the parameters and the structure takes place only after the whole training data set has been presented, that is, only after each epoch. Structure identification is used to select fuzzy rules. It often relies on a substantial amount of heuristic observation to express proper knowledge of a strategy. It is often tackled by offline, trial-and-error approaches, like the unbiasedness criterion [32]. Several approaches generate fuzzy rules from numerical data. One of the most common methods for structure initialization is uniform partitioning of each input variable into fuzzy sets, resulting in a *fuzzy grid*. This approach is followed in ANFIS [18]. In [4], the Takagi-Sugeno model was used for designing various neuro-fuzzy systems. This approach consists of two learning phases: (1) *structure learning*, which involves finding the main input variables out of all the possible ones specifying the membership functions, the partitioning of the input space, and determining the number of fuzzy rules; and (2) *parameter learning*, which involves the determination of the unknown parameters and the optimization of the existing ones using some mathematical optimization method. The latter phase is based on linguistic information from the human expert and on the numeric data obtained from the actual system to be modeled. The parameter updating is employed after the structure is decided. Most structure identification methods are based on data clustering, such as fuzzy C-means clustering [5], mountain clustering [41], and subtractive clustering [9].

In online identification, model structure and parameter identification are updated immediately after each input–output pair has been presented, that is, after each iteration. Online identification also includes (1) model structure and (2) parameter identification. For structure identification, mainly clustering methods are used. In clustering, to update fuzzy rules, distance from centers of fuzzy rules, potentials of new data sample, or errors from previous steps have been used. Different mechanisms are used in constructing the structure. The *resource allocating network (RAN)* [31] uses a geometric growing criterion to update fuzzy rules. *Evolving fuzzy neural networks (EFuNNs)* [23] use the difference between two membership vectors to update the fuzzy rules. *Dynamic evolving neural fuzzy inference system (DENFIS)* [24], *self-constructing neural fuzzy inference network (SONFIN)* [20], and the *recurrent self-organizing neural fuzzy inference network (RSONFIN)* [21] use the distance to update the fuzzy rules. The *Evolving Takagi-Sugeno model (ETS)* [2] uses potential to update fuzzy rules. The Takagi-Sugeno inference algorithm in [25] considers input and output data to update the rules.

In order to extract fuzzy rules in a growing fashion from a large numerical database, some self-constructing fuzzy networks are presented. In [2] they form new focals of fuzzy rules based on data density, which is calculated recursively (online), and considers whether a new piece of data, which is accepted as a focal point of a new rule, is too close to a previously existing rule. Then the old rule is replaced by the new one, and the self-constructing neural fuzzy networks can be used for online learning. The *dynamic fuzzy neural network (DFNN)* [39] approach is shown to provide good results. The error reduction ratio of each radial basis function neuron is used to decide which radial basis function neurons are important to the network. The less important radial basis function neuron may be deleted. The *general dynamic fuzzy neural network (GDFNN)* proposed in [40] tries to give reasonable explanations for some predefined training parameters in DFNN. These explanations, however, depend on the number of total training data. The *self-organizing fuzzy neural network (SOFNN)* [27] approach proposes a pruning method devised from the *optimal brain surgeon (OBS)* approach [14]. The basic idea of the SOFNN is to use the second derivative information to find the unimportant neuron. The *simplified method for learning evolving Takagi-Sugeno fuzzy models (simpl_eTS)* given in [3] monitors the population of each cluster, and if it amounts to less than 1% of the total data samples at that moment, the cluster is ignored by removing the rule (respectively, neuron) from the rule-based (network) and reducing the size of the covariance matrix. On the other hand, the stability of fuzzy neural networks is important for online training, and the self-constructing neural fuzzy networks mentioned above do not guarantee the stability. The online training is used in online control. It is well known that normal identification algorithms (for example, gradient descent and least squares) are stable in ideal conditions. In the presence of unmodeled dynamics, they may become unstable. The lack of robustness of the parameter identification was demonstrated in [11] and became a hot issue in the 1980s, when some robust modification techniques were suggested in [17]. The learning procedure of fuzzy neural networks can be regarded as a type of parameter identification. Gradient descent and backpropagation algorithms are stable, if fuzzy neural models can match nonlinear plants exactly. However, some robust modifications must be applied to assure stability with respect to uncertainties. The *projection operator* is an effective tool to guarantee that the fuzzy modeling is bounded [17, 38]. In [42] the *input-to-state stability (ISS)* approach is applied to system identification via fuzzy neural networks and gradient descent algorithm. In [33] neural identification uses *double dead-zone* to assure stability of the identification error in the gradient algorithm. In [34] the *Lyapunov* method is used to prove that a double dead-zone Kalman filter training is stable. A *self-constructing* fuzzy-neural network uses different mechanisms of rules/neurons update based on the error in previous steps [20–22].

For example, while evolving fuzzy rule-based models [1–3], use the data density (informative potential) of the new data sample as a trigger to update the rule base. Knowledge-based *evolving intelligent systems* (*EISs*) should be able to do the following [23, 24]:

1. Learn fast from a large amount of data (using fast training).
2. Adapt incrementally in an online mode.
3. Dynamically create new modules with open structure.
4. Memorize information that can be used at a later stage.
5. Interact continuously with the environment in a lifelong learning mode.
6. Deal with knowledge (e.g., rules) as well as with data.
7. Adequately represent space and time.

Developing a computational model, called an *evolving fuzzy neural recurrent network*, that meets these seven requirements is one of the objectives of the current research. In this chapter an online *evolving neuro-fuzzy recurrent network* (*ENFRN*) was proposed to address these problems. Structure and parameters learning are active each time step of the algorithm. It generates a new hidden neuron if the smallest distance between the new data and all the existing hidden neurons (the winner neuron) is more than a given threshold, as in [20–22]. When a new hidden neuron is generated, the center of the membership function of the antecedent part takes the state of the nonlinear system and the center of the consequent part takes the output of the nonlinear system, as in [1], [3], and [25]. A new pruning algorithm is proposed based on the number of data associated to each hidden neuron with its population density. The hidden neuron that has the smallest population density (the looser neuron) is pruned if the value of its population density is smaller than a prespecified threshold. In order to have faster parameter convergence, a modified least-squares algorithm is used to train the centers and the widths in the hidden layer and the centers in the output layer in parameter learning, as in [2] and [24]. The stability of the proposed algorithm was proven and the bound of the average identification error was found theoretically.

## 8.3 EVOLVING NEURO-FUZZY RECURRENT NETWORK FOR NONLINEAR IDENTIFICATION

Let us consider the following discrete-time nonlinear recurrent system:

$$x_i(k) = h_i[x(k-1), u(k-1)] \tag{8.1}$$

where $i = 1, \ldots, n$, $x_i(k)$ is the $i$th state, $x(k-1) = [x_1(k-1), x_2(k-1), \ldots, x_n(k-1)] \in \Re^n$, $u(k-1) \in \Re^{m2}$ is an input vector, $\| u(k) \|^2 \leq \bar{u}$, $\bar{u}$ is the upper bound of $\| u(k) \|^2$, $u(k-1)$ and $x(k-1)$ are known, and $h_i$ is an unknown nonlinear smooth function, $h_i \in C^{\infty}$, $h(\bullet) = [h_1(\bullet), h_2(\bullet), ..., h_n(\bullet)] \in \Re^n$. We use the following series-parallel [29] recurrent neural network to identify the nonlinear plant (8.1):

$$\hat{x}_i(k) = s_i\hat{x}_i(k-1) + \hat{f}_{i,k-1} + \hat{g}_{i,k-1} \tag{8.2}$$

where $i = 1, ..., n, \hat{f}_{i,k-1} = V_{1i,k-1}\sigma(k-1), \hat{g}_{i,k-1}V_{2i,k-1}\phi(k-1)u(k-1), \hat{x}_i(k)$ represents the $i$th state of the neural network, $\hat{x}(k-1) = [\hat{x}_1(k-1), \hat{x}_2(k-1), ..., \hat{x}_n(k-1)] \in \Re^n$. The matrix $S = diag(s_i) \in \Re^{n \times n}$ is a stable matrix. The weights in the output layer are $V_{1i,k} \in \Re^{1 \times m1}$, $V_{21i,k} \in \Re^{1 \times m2}$, $\sigma$ is $m_1$-dimension vector function, and $\phi(\bullet) \in \Re^{m2 \times m2}$ is a diagonal matrix:

$$\sigma(k-1) = [\sigma_1(k-1), \sigma_2(k-1), ..., \sigma_{m1}(k-1)]^T$$
$$\phi(k-1) = diag[\phi_1(k-1), \phi_2(k-1), ..., \phi_{m2}(k-1)]^T \tag{8.3}$$

where $\sigma_i$ and $\phi_i$ are given later. Each input variable $x_i$ has $n$ fuzzy sets. By using product inference, center-average defuzzifier and center fuzzifier, called *Sugeno fuzzy inference system* (FIS), with weighted average can be expressed as [19, 38]:

$$\hat{f}_{i,k-1} = \frac{a_{1i}(k-1)}{b_1(k-1)}$$

$$a_{1i}(k-1) = \sum_{j=1}^{m1} v_{1ij}(k-1)z_{1j}(k-1)$$

$$b_1(k-1) = \sum_{j=1}^{m1} z_{1j}(k-1)$$

$$z_{1j}(k-1) = \exp\left[-\gamma_{1j}^2(k-1)\right]$$

$$\gamma_{1j}(k-1) = \sum_{i=1}^{n} w_{1ij}(k-1)\left[x_i(k-1) - c_{1ij}(k-1)\right]$$

$$\hat{g}_{i,k-1} = \frac{a_{2i}(k-1)}{b_2(k-1)}$$

$$a_{2i}(k-1) = \sum_{j=1}^{m2} v_{21ij}(k-1)z_{2j}(k-1)u_j(k-1)$$

$$b_2(k-1) = \sum_{j=1}^{m2} z_{2j}(k-1)$$

$$z_{2j}(k-1) = \exp\left[-\gamma_{21j}^2(k-1)\right]$$

$$\gamma_{2j}(k-1) = \sum_{i=1}^{n} w_{2ij}(k-1)\left[x_i(k-1) - c_{2ij}(k-1)\right] \tag{8.4}$$

where $x_i(k-1)$ are states of system (8.1), $(i = 1, ..., l, n)$, $c_{1ij}(k-1)$, and $w_{1ij}(k-1) = \frac{1}{\rho_{1ij}(k-1)}$ are the centers and the widths of the membership function of the antecedent part, respectively, and $(j = 1, \ldots, m_1)$, $v_{1ij}(k-1)$ is the center of the membership function of the consequent part. We use $w_{1ij}(k-1)$ inside of $\rho_{1ij}(k-1)$ in order to avoid singularity in the identifier for online training; the online training is used in control. Note that the weighted average *radial basis function (RBFN)* [19] comes to the same expression, (8.4), where $x_i(k-1)$ are the states of the system (8.1), $(i = 1, \ldots, n)$, $c_{1ij}(k-1)$, and $w_{1ij}(k-1)$ are the centers and the widths of the hidden layer, respectively, and $(j = 1, \ldots, m_1)$, $v_{1ij}(k-1)$ are the weights of the output layer. The conditions under which an RBFN and an FIS are functionally equivalent are summarized as follows [19]:

- Both the RBFN and the FIS under consideration use the same aggregation method (namely, either weighted average or weighted sum) to derive their overall outputs.
- The number of receptive field units in the RBFN is equal to the number of fuzzy IF-THEN rules in the FIS.
- Each radial basis function of the RBFN is equal to a multidimensional composite membership function of the antecedent part of a fuzzy rule in the FIS. One way to achieve this is to use Gaussian membership functions with the same variance in a fuzzy rule, and apply product to calculate the firing strength. The multiplication of these Gaussian membership functions becomes a multidimensional Gaussian function—a radial basis function in RBFN.
- Corresponding radial basis function and fuzzy rule should have the same response function. That is, they should have the same constant terms (for the original RBFN and zero-order Sugeno FIS) or linear equations (for the extended RBFN and first-order FIS).

Let us define the functions $\sigma_i(k-1)$ and $\phi_i(k-1)$ from (8.3) as [42]:

$$\sigma_j(k-1) = \frac{z_{1j}(k-1)}{b_1(k-1)}$$

$$\phi_j(k-1) = \frac{z_{2j}(k-1)}{b_2(k-1)} \tag{8.5}$$

Then (8.4) can be written as follows:

$$\hat{f}_{i,k-1} = \sum_{j=1}^{m1} v_{1ij}(k-1)\sigma_j(k-1) = V_{1i,k-1}\sigma(k-1)$$

$$\hat{g}_{i,k-1} = \sum_{j=1}^{m2} v_{2ij}(k-1)\phi_j(k-1)u_j(k-1) = V_{2i,k-1}\phi(k-1)u(k-1) \tag{8.6}$$

where $V_{1i,k-1} = \left[w_{1i1}(k-1) \ldots w_{1im1}(k-1)\right] \in \Re^{m1}$ and $V_{2i,k-1} = [w_{2i1}(k-1) \ldots w_{2im2}(k-1)] \in \Re^{m2}$.

The parameter $m_1$ is changing with the structure of the algorithm (see the next section), while the parameter $m_2$ is fixed and it is given by the dimension of the input $u(k-1)$. The state $x_i(k-1)$ on $\hat{f}_{i,k-1}$ and $\hat{g}_{i,k-1}$ on the right-hand side of (8.2) (this is $x_i(k-1)$ given in (8.4)) can also be $\hat{x}_i(k-1)$, in which case it is called a *parallel model* [29]. By using the

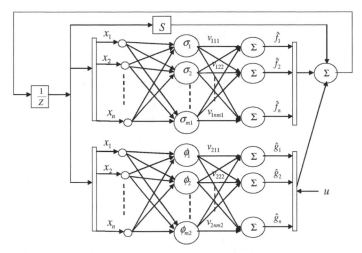

Figure 8.1. The evolving neuro-fuzzy recurrent network used in this chapter.

previous results from [34] it can be demonstrated that the parallel model training has similar results as the series-parallel model (8.2). See Figure 8.1.

According to the Stone-Weierstrass theorem [26], the unknown nonlinear system (8.1) can be written in the following form:

$$x_i(k) = s_i x_i(k-1) + f_{i,k-1} + g_{i,k-1} \tag{8.7}$$

where $f_{i,k-1} = V_{1i}^* \sigma^*(k-1) + \in_{i,k-1}^f$, $g_{i,k-1} = V_{2i}^* \Phi^*(k-1)u(k-1) + \in_{i,k-1}^g$, $\in_{i,k-1}^f + \in_{i,k-1}^g = h_i[x_i(k-1), u(k-1)] - s_i x_i(k-1) - f_{i,k-1} - g_{i,k-1}$ represents unmodeled dynamics. In [26] it was shown that the term $(\in_{i,k-1}^f + \in_{i,k-1}^g)$ can be made arbitrarily small by simply selecting appropriate number of the hidden neurons.

**Remark 8.1:** The structure (8.1) is the discrete time version of the continuous time network given in [26], where a sigmoidal activation function is used. In this chapter we use a Gaussian function and they use the gradient descent algorithm and use the recursive least-squares algorithm introduced in [2] and also used in [23] and [27]. The recursive least-squares algorithm has faster convergence in parameters than the gradient. The stability of the algorithm is proven theoretically.

The unknown nonlinear function $f_{i,k-1}$ of (8.7) is:

$$f_{i,k-1} = \sum_{j=1}^{m1} v_{1ij}^* \sigma_j^*(k-1) + \in_{i,k-1}^f = V_{1i}^* \sigma^*(k-1) + \in_{i,k-1}^f \tag{8.8}$$

where $\sigma_j^*(k-1) = \frac{z_{1j}^*(k-1)}{b_1^*(k-1)}$, $b_1^*(k-1) = \sum_{j=1}^{m1} z_{1j}^*(k-1)$, $z_{1j}^*(k-1) = \exp\left[-\gamma_{1j}^{*2}(k-1)\right]$, $\gamma_{1j}^*(k-1) \sum_{i=1}^{n} w_{1ij}^* \left[x_i(k-1) - c_{1ij}^*\right]$, $v_{1ij}^*$, $w_{1ij}^*$, and $c_{1ij}^*$ are the optimal parameters that can minimize the modeling error $\in_{i,k-1}^f$ [26].

In this section, we linearize the model that will be used to find the parameters updating and to prove the stability of the proposed algorithm. We need the stability of the structure and parameters learning because this algorithm works online. Online learning is used in control.

In the case of three independent variables, a smooth function has a Taylor series as:

$$f(\alpha_1, \alpha_2, \alpha_3) = f(\alpha_0^0, \alpha_{21}^0, \alpha_3^0) + \frac{\partial f(\alpha_1, \alpha_2, \alpha_3)}{\alpha_1}(\alpha_1 - \alpha_1^0) +$$

$$\frac{\partial f(\alpha_1, \alpha_2, \alpha_3)}{\alpha_2}(\alpha_2 - \alpha_2^0) + \frac{\partial f(\alpha_1, \alpha_2, \alpha_3)}{\alpha_3}(\alpha_3 - \alpha_3^0) + R_{i,k-1} \quad (8.9)$$

where $R_{i,\,k-1}$ is the remainder of the Taylor series. Let $\alpha_1$, $\alpha_2$, and $\alpha_3$ correspond to $c_{1ij}(k-1), w_{1ij}(k-1)$, and $v_{1ij}(k-1), \alpha_1^0, \alpha_2^0$, and $\alpha_3^0$ correspond to $c_{1ij}^*, w_{1ij}^*$, and $v_{1ij}^*$. Let us define $\tilde{c}_{1ij}(k-1) = c_{1ij}(k-1) - c_{1ij}^*$, $\tilde{w}_{1ij}(k-1) = w_{1ij}(k-1) - w_{1ij}^*$ and $\hat{v}_{1ij}(k-1) = v_{1ij}(k-1) - v_{1ij}^*$. Then we apply the Taylor series to linearize $V_{1i,k-1}\sigma(k-1)$ of (8.4) and (8.6) as:

$$V_{1i,k-1}\sigma(k-1) = V_{1i}^*\sigma^*(k-1) + R_{i,k-1}^f + \sum_{j=1}^{m1} \frac{\partial v_{1ij}(k-1)\sigma_j(k-1)}{\partial c_{1ij}(k-1)}\tilde{c}_{1ij}(k-1)$$

$$+ \sum_{j=1}^{m1} \frac{\partial v_{1ij}(k-1)\sigma_j(k-1)}{\partial w_{1ij}(k-1)}\tilde{w}_{1ij}(k-1) + \sum_{j=1}^{m1} \frac{\partial v_{1ij}(k-1)\sigma_j(k-1)}{\partial v_{1ij}(k-1)}\tilde{v}_{1ij}(k-1)$$

$$(8.10)$$

Considering (8.4), (8.5), (8.6) and using the chain rule [20, 33, 34, 38], we get:

$$\frac{\partial v_{1ij}(k-1)\sigma_j(k-1)}{c_{1ij}(k-1)} = \frac{\partial v_{1ij}(k-1)\sigma_j(k-1)}{\partial a_{1i}(k-1)}\frac{\partial a_{1i}(k-1)}{\partial z_{1j}(k-1)}\frac{\partial z_{1j}(k-1)}{\partial \gamma_{1j}(k-1)}\frac{\partial \gamma_{1j}(k-1)}{\partial c_{1ij}(k-1)}$$

$$+ \frac{\partial v_{1ij}(k-1)\sigma_j(k-1)}{\partial b_1(k-1)}\frac{\partial b_1(k-1)}{\partial z_{1j}(k-1)}\frac{\partial z_{1j}(k-1)}{\partial \gamma_{1j}(k-1)}\frac{\partial \gamma_{1j}(k-1)}{\partial c_{1ij}(k-1)}$$

$$= 2\gamma_{1j}(k-1)z_{1j}(k-1)w_{1ij}(k-1)\frac{v_{1ij}(k-1)-\hat{f}_{i,k-1}}{b_1(k-1)}$$

$$+ \frac{\partial v_{1ij}(k-1)\sigma_j(k-1)}{w_{1ij}(k-1)} = \frac{\partial v_{1ij}(k-1)\sigma_j(k-1)}{\partial a_{1i}(k-1)}\frac{\partial a_{1i}(k-1)}{\partial z_{1j}(k-1)}\frac{\partial z_{1j}(k-1)}{\partial \gamma_{1j}(k-1)}\frac{\partial \gamma_{1j}(k-1)}{\partial w_{1ij}(k-1)}$$

$$+ \frac{\partial v_{1ij}(k-1)\sigma_j(k-1)}{\partial b_1(k-1)}\frac{\partial b_1(k-1)}{\partial z_{1j}(k-1)}\frac{\partial z_{1j}(k-1)}{\partial \gamma_{1j}(k-1)}\frac{\partial \gamma_{1j}(k-1)}{\partial w_{1ij}(k-1)}$$

$$= 2\gamma_{1j}(k-1)z_{1j}(k-1)[x_i(k-1)-c_{1ij}(k-1)]\frac{\hat{f}_{i,k-1}-v_{1ij}(k-1)}{b_1(k-1)}$$

$$\frac{\partial v_{1ij}(k-1)\sigma_j(k-1)}{v_{1ij}(k-1)} = \sigma_j(k-1)$$

Substituting $\frac{\partial v_{1ij}(k-1)\sigma_j(k-1)}{c_{1ij}(k-1)}$, $\frac{\partial v_{1ij}(k-1)\sigma_j(k-1)}{w_{1ij}(k-1)}$ and $\frac{\partial v_{1ij}(k-1)\sigma_j(k-1)}{v_{1ij}(k-1)}$ in equation (8.10) gives:

$$
\begin{aligned}
V_{1i,k-1}\sigma(k-1) = {}& V_{1i}^*\sigma^*(k-1) + R_{i,k-1}^f + \sum_{j=1}^{m1}\sigma_j(k-1)\tilde{v}_{1ij}(k-1) \\
& + \sum_{j=1}^{m1}2\gamma_{1j}(k-1)z_{1j}(k-1)w_{1ij}(k-1)\frac{v_{1ij}(k-1)-\hat{f}_{i,k-1}}{b_1(k-1)}\tilde{c}_{1ij}(k-1) \\
& + \sum_{j=1}^{m1}2\gamma_{1j}(k-1)z_{1j}(k-1)\big[x_i(k-1)-c_{1ij}(k-1)\big]\frac{\hat{f}_{i,k-1}-v_{1ij}(k-1)}{b_1(k-1)}\tilde{w}_{1ij}(k-1)
\end{aligned}
$$

$$(8.11)$$

Le us define $B_{1ij}^c(k-1)$, $B_{1ij}^w(k-1)$ and $B_{1ij}^v(k-1)$ as:

$$
\begin{aligned}
B_{1ij}^c(k-1) &= 2\gamma_{1j}(k-1)z_{1j}(k-1)w_{1ij}(k-1)\frac{v_{1ij}(k-1)-\hat{f}_{i,k-1}}{b_1(k-1)} \\
B_{1ij}^w(k-1) &= 2\gamma_{1j}(k-1)z_{1j}(k-1)\big[x_i(k-1)-c_{1ij}(k-1)\big]\frac{\hat{f}_{i,k-1}-v_{1ij}(k-1)}{b_1(k-1)} \qquad (8.12) \\
B_{1ij}^v(k-1) &= \sigma_j(k-1)
\end{aligned}
$$

Note that $\sigma_j(k-1)$ is repeated for each $i$ in $B_{1ij}^v(k-1)$. Using the above definitions in (8.11) gives:

$$
\begin{aligned}
V_{1i,k-1}\sigma(k-1) = {}& \sum_{j=1}^{m1}B_{1ij}^c(k-1)\tilde{c}_{1ij}(k-1) \\
& + \sum_{j=1}^{m1}B_{1ij}^w(k-1)\tilde{w}_{1ij}(k-1) + \sum_{j=1}^{m1}B_{1ij}^v(k-1)\tilde{v}_{1ij}(k-1) \qquad (8.13) \\
& + V_{1i}^*\sigma^*(k-1) + R_{i,k-1}^f
\end{aligned}
$$

Let us define $\tilde{f}_{i,k-1}=\hat{f}_{i,k-1}-f_{i,k-1}$, substituting (8.6), (8.8), and $\tilde{f}_{i,k-1}$ in (8.13) gives:

$$\tilde{f}_{i,k-1}=B_{i,k-1}^{fT}\tilde{\theta}_i^f(k-1)+\mu_i^f(k-1) \qquad (8.14)$$

where $i=1,\dots,n$, $B_{i,k-1}^{fT}=\big[B_{1i1}^c(k-1),\dots,B_{1im1}^c(k-1),B_{1i1}^w(k-1),\dots,B_{1im1}^w(k-1),$ $B_{1i1}^v(k-1),\dots,B_{1im1}^v(k-1)\big]\in\Re^{1\times 3m1}$, $\tilde{\theta}_i^f(k-1)=[\tilde{c}_{1i1}(k-1),\dots,\tilde{c}_{1im1}(k-1),\tilde{w}_{1i1}(k-1),$ $\dots,\tilde{w}_{1im1}(k-1),\tilde{v}_{1i1}(k-1),\dots,\tilde{v}_{1im1}(k-1)]^T\in\Re^{3m1\times 1}$. Thus $\tilde{\theta}_i^f(k-1)=\theta_i^f(k-1)-\tilde{\theta}_i^{f*}$, $B_{1ij}^c(k-1)B_{1ij}^w(k-1)$, and $B_{1ij}^v(k-1)$ are given in (8.12), $\mu_i^f(k-1)=R_{i,k-1}^f-\in_{i,k-1}^f$. Similarly in $\tilde{g}_{i,k-1}=\hat{g}_{i,k-1}-g_{i,k-1}$ we have:

$$\tilde{g}_{i,k-1}=B_{i,k-1}^{gT}\tilde{\theta}_i^g(k-1)+\mu_i^g(k-1) \qquad (8.15)$$

where $i = 1, \ldots, n$, $B_{i,k-1}^{gT} = \left[ B_{2i1}^c(k-1), \ldots, B_{2im1}^c(k-1), B_{2i1}^w(k-1), \ldots, B_{2im1}^w(k-1), \right.$
$\left. B_{2i1}^v(k-1), \ldots, B_{2im1}^v(k-1) \right] \in \Re^{1 \times 3m2}$, $\tilde{\theta}_i^g(k-1) = [\tilde{c}_{2i1}(k-1), \ldots, \tilde{c}_{2im1}(k-1), \tilde{w}_{2i1}(k-1),$
$\ldots, \tilde{w}_{2im1}(k-1), \tilde{v}_{2i1}(k-1), \ldots, \tilde{v}_{2im2}(k-1)]^T \in \Re^{3m2 \times 1}$. Thus $\tilde{\theta}_i^g(k-1) = \theta_i^g(k-1) - \tilde{\theta}_i^{g*}$,
$B_{2ij}^c(k-1), = 2u_j(k,-1)\gamma_{2j}(k-1)z_{2j}(k,-1)w_{2ij}(k-1) \frac{v_{2ij}(k-1) - \hat{g}_{i,k-1}}{b_2(k-1)}$, $\quad B_{2ij}^w(k-1) =$
$2u_j(k-1)\gamma_{2j} \quad (k-1)z_{2j}(k-1)\left[x_i(k-1) - c_{2ij}(k-1)\right] \frac{\hat{g}_{i,k-1} - v_{2ij}(k-1)}{b_2(k-1)}$ and $B_{2ij}^v(k-1) =$
$u_j(k-1)\phi_j(k-1)$. Note that $\phi_j(k-1)$ is repeated for each $i$ in $B_{2ij}^v(k-1)$,
$\mu_i^g(k-1) = R_{i,k-1}^g - \in_{i,k-1}^g$. We can define the identification error as:

$$e_i(k-1) = \hat{y}_i(k-1) - y_i(k-1) \tag{8.16}$$

where $\hat{y}_i(k-1) = \hat{f}_{i,k-1} + \hat{g}_{i,k-1} = \hat{x}_i(k) - s_i\hat{x}_i(k-1)$ is the output of the network and
$y_i(k-1) = f_{i,k-1} + g_{i,k-1} = x_i(k) - s_ix_i(k-1)$ is the output of the nonlinear system,
$e_i(k-1) \in \Re$. Then substituting $\hat{y}_i(k-1)$, $y_i(k-1)$, (8.14), and (8.15) in (8.16) gives:

$$e_i(k-1) = B_{i,k-1}^T \tilde{\theta}_i(k-1) + \mu_i(k-1) \tag{8.17}$$

where $i = 1, \ldots, n$, $B_{i,k-1}^T = \left[ B_i^{gT}(k-1), B_i^{gT}(k-1) \right] \in \Re^{1 \times 3(m2+m1)}$, $\tilde{\theta}_i(k-1) = \left[ \tilde{\theta}_i^g(k-1), \right.$
$\left. \tilde{\theta}_i^f(k-1) \right] \in \Re^{3(m2+m1) \times 1}$, $\mu_i(k-1) = \mu_i^f(k-1) + \mu_i^g(k-1) \in \Re$, $\tilde{\theta}_i^f(k-1)$ and $B_{i,k-1}^{fT}$ are
given in (8.14), and $\tilde{\theta}_i^g(k-1)$ and $B_{i,k-1}^{gT}$ are given in (8.15).

We define the state error as $\tilde{x}_i(k) = \hat{x}_i(k) - x_i(k)$. From (8.16) we have $\hat{x}_i(k) = s_i\hat{x}_i(k-1) + \hat{y}_i(k-1)$ and $x_i(k) = s_ix_i(k-1) + y_i(k-1)$; the first equation minus the second one gives $\hat{x}_i(k) - x_i(k) = s_i[\hat{x}_i(k-1) - x_i(k-1)] + [\hat{y}_i(k-1) - y_i(k-1)]$. Substituting $\tilde{x}_i(k)^i$ and $e_i(k-1)$ of (8.16) in the previous equation gives:

$$\tilde{x}_i(k) = s_i\tilde{x}_i(k-1) + e_i(k-1) \tag{8.18}$$

## 8.4 STRUCTURE IDENTIFICATION

Choosing an appropriate number of hidden neurons is important in designing evolving neuro-fuzzy systems, because too many hidden neurons result in a complex evolving system that may be unnecessary for the problem and can cause overfitting [19], whereas too few hidden neurons produce a less powerful neural system that may be insufficient to achieve the objective. We view the number of hidden neurons as a design parameter and determine it based on the input-output pairs and on the number of elements of each hidden neuron. The basic idea is to group the input–output pairs into clusters and use one hidden neuron for one cluster, as in [1–3], [23, 24]; that is, the number of hidden neurons equals the number of clusters.

One of the simplest clustering algorithms is the nearest-neighbor clustering algorithm. In this algorithm, first we put the first data as the center of the first cluster. Then, if the distances of the data to the cluster centers are less than a prespecified value (the radius $r$), put these data into the cluster whose center is the closest to these data; otherwise, set these data as a new cluster center. The details are given as follows.

Let $x(k-1)$ be a newly incoming pattern. Then from (8.4) we get:

$$p(k-1) = \max_{1 \leq j \leq m1} z_{1j}(k-1) \tag{8.19}$$

If $p(k-1) < r$, then a new hidden neuron is generated (each hidden neuron corresponds to each center) and $m_1 = m_1 + 1$ where $r$ is a selected radius, $r \in (0, 1)$. Once a new hidden neuron is generated, the next step is to assign initial centers and widths of the network. A new density with value 1 is generated for this hidden neuron:

$$
\begin{aligned}
c_{1\,im1+1}(k) &= x_i(k) \\
w_{1\,im1+1}(k) &= rand \in (2, 4) \\
v_{1\,im1+1}(k) &= y_i(k) \\
d_{m1+1}(k) &= 1
\end{aligned}
\tag{8.20}
$$

If $p(k-1) \geq r$, then a hidden neuron is not generated. If $z_{1j}(k-1) = p(k-1)$, we have the winner neuron $j^*$. The *winner neuron* is a neuron that increments its importance in the algorithm. Then its population density [3] must be increased and is updated as:

$$d_{j*}(k) = d_{j*}(k) + 1 \tag{8.21}$$

The algorithm above is no longer a practical system if the number of input–output pairs is large because the number of hidden neurons (clusters) grows; some data are even grouped into hidden neurons (clusters). Therefore, one needs a pruning method. In this chapter a new pruning algorithm based on the number associated to each hidden neuron is proposed. From (8.20) one can see that when a new hidden neuron is generated its population density starts at one, and from (8.21) one can see that when a piece of data is associated to an existing hidden neuron, the population density of this hidden neuron is simply increased by one. Thus each cluster (hidden neuron) has its own population density, as introduced in [3]. The least important hidden neuron is the hidden neuron that has the smallest population density. After several iterations ($\Delta L$) one can prune the least important hidden neuron if the value of its population density is smaller than a prespecified threshold ($d_u$). The details are given as follows.

At each $\Delta L$ iterations where $\Delta L \in \mathbb{N}$, we take:

$$d_{\min}(k) = \min_{1 \leq j \leq m1} d_j(k) \tag{8.22}$$

If $m_1 \geq 2$ (if there is one hidden neuron given as $m_1 = 1$), we cannot prune any hidden neuron, and if $d_{\min}(k) \leq d_u$, this hidden neuron is pruned, where $d_u \in \mathbb{N}$ is the minimum selected population density allowed and it is called the *threshold parameter*. Once a hidden, neuron is pruned, the next step is to assign centers and widths of the network. When $d_j(k) = d_{\min}(k)$, we have the looser neuron $j_*$. The looser neuron is the least important neuron of the algorithm. If $j \leq j_*$, do nothing; but if $j > j_*$, we move all the parameters in order to organize them as follows:

$$
\begin{aligned}
c_{1ij-1}(k) &= c_{1ij}(k) \\
w_{1ij-1}(k) &= w_{1ij}(k) \\
v_{1ij-1}(k) &= v_{1ij}(k) \\
d_{j-1}(k) &= d_j(k)
\end{aligned}
\tag{8.23}
$$

In this way we send the looser neuron $j_*$ to the last element $j = m_1$. For $j = m_1$ we prune the looser neuron as follows:

$$
\begin{aligned}
c_{1im1}(k) &= 0 \\
w_{1im1}(k) &= 0 \\
v_{1im1}(k) &= 0 \\
d_{m1}(k) &= 0
\end{aligned}
\tag{8.24}
$$

Then we update $m_1$ as $m_1 = m_1 - 1$ in order to decrease the size of the network: If $d_{\min}(k) > d_u$ or $m_1 = 1$, do nothing.

Finally, we update $L$ as $L = L + \Delta L$.

**Remark 8.2:** The parameters $L$ and $\Delta L$ are needed because the pruning algorithm is not active at each iteration. The initial value of $L$ is $\Delta L$. The pruning algorithm works at the first time when $k = L$; then $L$ is increased by $\Delta L$. The pruning algorithm works every $\Delta L$ iterations. The parameter $\Delta L$ was found empirically as $5d_u$; thus, the pruning algorithm has only $d_u$ as the design parameter.

**Remark 8.3:** The clustering algorithm is somewhat similar to that given in [20–22] but they do not take the max of $z_{1j}(k-1)$ as (8.19). This idea is taken from the competitive learning of ART recurrent neural network [16, 19] in order to get the winner neuron.

**Remark 8.4:** In [27] the second derivative of an objective function is used to find the unimportant hidden neuron. In this chapter we use the population density [3] to find the unimportant neuron.

**Remark 8.5:** You can see that the structure identification of this recurrent network uses the informative potential of the new data sample as a trigger to update the hidden neuron (rule) base as [1–3], and it is able to satisfy the basic features of an *evolving intelligent system (EIS)* as in section 8.2 of this chapter; thus, it is an evolving neuro-fuzzy recurrent network.

## 8.5 STABILITY OF THE IDENTIFICATION

The fuzzily weighted recursive least-squares algorithm proposed in [2] and also used in [24] is modified in this chapter as follows:

$$\theta_i(k) = \theta_i(k-1) - \frac{1}{Q_{i,k-1}} P_{i,k} B_{i,k-1} e_i(k-1)$$

$$P_{i,k} = P_{i,k-1} - \frac{1}{R_{i,k-1}} P_{i,k-1} B_{i,k-1} B_{i,k-1}^T P_{i,k-1} \tag{8.25}$$

where $i = 1, \ldots, n$, $Q_{i,k-1} = 10 + B_{i,k-1}^T P_{i,k} B_{i,k-1}$, $R_{i,k-1} = 2Q_{i,k-1} + B_{i,k-1}^T P_{i,k} B_{i,k-1}$, $B_{i,k-1}^T$ and $\theta_i(k-1)$ are given in (8.17), and $P_{i,k} \in \Re^{3(m2+m1) \times 3(m2+m1)}$ is a positive definite covariance matrix.

Now, we analyze the stability of the algorithm proposed.

***Theorem 8.1:*** The modified least-squares algorithm (8.2), (8.4), (8.20), and (8.25) to train structure and parameters is uniformly stable and the upper bound of the average identification error satisfies:

$$\limsup_{T \to \infty} \frac{(B_{i,k-1}^T P_{i,k-1} B_{i,k-1})^2}{Q_{i,k-1}^2 R_{i,k-1}} e_i^2(k-1) \leq \frac{\bar{\mu}_i}{10} \tag{8.26}$$

$\bar{\mu}_i$ is the upper bound of the uncertainty $|\mu_i(k-1)| < \bar{\mu}_i$.

***Proof:*** Let us define the following Lyapunov function:

$$L_i(k-1) = \tilde{\theta}_i^T(k-1) P_{i,k-1}^{-1} \tilde{\theta}_i(k-1) \tag{8.27}$$

Substituting $\tilde{\theta}_i(k-1)$ of (8.25) in $\Delta L_i(k)$ gives:

$$\Delta L_i(k) = \tilde{\theta}_i^T(k) P_{i,k}^{-1} \tilde{\theta}_i(k) - \tilde{\theta}_i^T(k-1) P_{i,k-1}^{-1} \tilde{\theta}_i(k-1)$$

$$= \left[ \tilde{\theta}_i(k-1) - \frac{1}{Q_{i,k-1}} P_{i,k} B_{i,k-1} e_i(k-1) \right]^T P_{i,k}^{-1} \left[ \tilde{\theta}_i(k-1) - \frac{1}{Q_{i,k-1}} P_{i,k} B_{i,k-1} e_i(k-1) \right]$$

$$- \tilde{\theta}_i^T(k-1) P_{i,k-1}^{-1} \tilde{\theta}_i(k-1) = \tilde{\theta}_i^T(k-1) \left[ P_{i,k}^{-1} - P_{i,k-1}^{-1} \right] \tilde{\theta}_i(k-1)$$

$$- \frac{2}{Q_{i,k-1}} \tilde{\theta}_i^T(k-1) B_{i,k-1} e_i(k-1) + \frac{1}{Q_{i,k-1}^2} B_{i,k-1}^T P_{i,k} B_{i,k-1} e_i^2(k-1) \tag{8.28}$$

Now we apply the matrix inversion lemma [12], [38] to

$$P_{i,k} = P_{i,k-1} - \frac{1}{2Q_{i,k-1} + B_{i,k-1}^T P_{i,k} B_{i,k-1}} P_{i,k-1} B_{i,k-1} B_{i,k-1}^T P_{i,k-1} :$$

$$(A + BCD)^{-1} = A^{-1} - A^{-1} B (DA^{-1}B + C^{-1})^{-1} DA^{-1} \tag{8.29}$$

with $A^{-1} = P_{i,k-1}, B = B_{i,k-1}, C^{-1} = 2Q_{i,k-1}, D = B_{i,k-1}^T$; so we have

$$P_{i,k}^{-1} = P_{i,k-1}^{-1} + \frac{1}{2Q_{i,k-1}} B_{i,k-1} B_{i,k-1}^T \text{ or } P_{i,k}^{-1} - P_{i,k-1}^{-1} = \frac{1}{2Q_{i,k-1}} B_{i,k-1} B_{i,k-1}^T$$

Substituting in (8.28) gives:

$$\Delta L_i(k) = \frac{1}{2Q_{i,k-1}} \tilde{\theta}_i^T(k-1) B_{i,k-1} B_{i,k-1}^T \tilde{\theta}_i(k-1) - \frac{2}{Q_{i,k-1}} \tilde{\theta}_i^T(k-1) B_{i,k-1} e_i(k-1)$$

$$+ \frac{1}{Q_{i,k-1}^2} B_{i,k-1}^T P_{i,k} B_{i,k-1} e_i^2(k-1) \tag{8.30}$$

Considering (8.25), the last term of (8.30) is:

$$\frac{1}{Q_{i,k-1}^2} B_{i,k-1}^T P_{i,k} B_{i,k-1} e_i^2(k-1)$$

$$= \frac{1}{Q_{i,k-1}^2} B_{i,k-1}^T \left[ P_{i,k-1} - \frac{1}{R_{i,k-1}} P_{i,k-1} B_{i,k-1} B_{i,k-1}^T P_{i,k-1} \right] B_{i,k-1} e_i^2(k-1)$$

$$= \frac{B_{i,k-1}^T P_{i,k-1} B_{i,k-1}}{Q_{i,k-1}^2} e_i^2(k-1) - \frac{(B_{i,k-1}^T P_{i,k-1} B_{i,k-1})^2}{Q_{i,k-1}^2 R_{i,k-1}} e_i^2(k-1)$$

So

$$\frac{1}{Q_{i,k-1}^2} B_{i,k-1}^T P_{i,k} B_{i,k-1} e_i^2(k-1) \leq \frac{1}{Q_{i,k-1}} e_i^2(k-1) - \frac{(B_{i,k-1}^T P_{i,k-1} B_{i,k-1})^2}{Q_{i,k-1}^2 R_{i,k-1}} e_i^2(k-1)$$

$$\tag{8.31}$$

Substituting (8.31) in (8.30) gives:

$$\Delta L_i(k) \leq \frac{1}{2Q_{i,k-1}} \tilde{\theta}_i^T(k-1) B_{i,k-1} B_{i,k-1}^T \tilde{\theta}_i(k-1) - \frac{2}{Q_{i,k-1}} \tilde{\theta}_i^T(k-1) B_{i,k-1} e_i(k-1)$$

$$+ \frac{1}{Q_{i,k-1}} e_i^2(k-1) - \frac{(B_{i,k-1}^T P_{i,k-1} B_{i,k-1})^2}{Q_{i,k-1}^2 R_{i,k-1}} e_i^2(k-1) \tag{8.32}$$

Since (8.17) we have $e_i(k-1) = B_{i,k-1}^T \tilde{\theta}_i(k-1) + \mu_i(k-1)$, then $e_i^2(k-1) = \tilde{\theta}_i^T(k-1) B_{i,k-1} B_{i,k-1}^T \tilde{\theta}_i(k-1) + 2\mu_i(k-1) B_{i,k-1}^T \tilde{\theta}_i(k-1) + \mu_i^2(k-1)$. Substituting in the second and in the third elements of (8.32) gives:

$$\Delta L_i(k) \leq \frac{1}{2Q_{i,k-1}} \tilde{\theta}_i^T(k-1)B_{i,k-1}B_{i,k-1}^T\tilde{\theta}_i(k-1)$$

$$+ \frac{1}{Q_{i,k-1}}\left[\tilde{\theta}_i^T(k-1)B_{i,k-1}B_{i,k-1}^T\tilde{\theta}_i(k-1) + 2\mu_i(k-1)B_{i,k-1}^T\tilde{\theta}_i(k-1) + \mu_i^2(k-1)\right]$$

$$- \frac{2}{Q_{i,k-1}}\tilde{\theta}_i^T(k-1)B_{i,k-1}\left[B_{i,k-1}^T\tilde{\theta}_i(k-1) + \mu_i(k-1)\right]$$

$$- \frac{(B_{i,k-1}^T P_{i,k-1} B_{i,k-1})^2}{Q_{i,k-1}^2 R_{i,k-1}} e_i^2(k-1)$$

$$\Delta L_i(k) \leq \frac{1}{2Q_{i,k-1}} \tilde{\theta}_i^T(k-1)B_{i,k-1}B_{i,k-1}^T\tilde{\theta}_i(k-1) - \frac{2}{Q_{i,k-1}}\tilde{\theta}_i^T(k-1)B_{i,k-1}B_{i,k-1}^T\tilde{\theta}_i(k-1)$$

$$- \frac{2}{Q_{i,k-1}}\tilde{\theta}_i^T(k-1)B_{i,k-1}\mu_i(k-1) + \frac{1}{Q_{i,k-1}}\tilde{\theta}_i^T(k-1)B_{i,k-1}B_{i,k-1}^T\tilde{\theta}_i(k-1)$$

$$+ \frac{1}{Q_{i,k-1}}\mu_i^2(k-1) + \frac{2}{Q_{i,k-1}}\tilde{\theta}_i^T(k-1)B_{i,k-1}\mu_i(k-1)$$

$$- \frac{(B_{i,k-1}^T P_{i,k-1} B_{i,k-1})^2}{Q_{i,k-1}^2 R_{i,k-1}} e_i^2(k-1)\Delta L_i(k) \leq - \frac{1}{2Q_{i,k-1}}\tilde{\theta}_i^T(k-1)B_{i,k-1}B_{i,k-1}^T\tilde{\theta}_i(k-1)$$

$$+ \frac{1}{Q_{i,k-1}}\mu_i^2(k-1) - \frac{(B_{i,k-1}^T P_{i,k-1} B_{i,k-1})^2}{Q_{i,k-1}^2 R_{i,k-1}} e_i^2(k-1) \tag{8.33}$$

Considering that $Q_{i,k-1}^2 > 0, R_{i,k-1} > 0, B_{i,k-1}^T P_{i,k} B_{i,k-1} > 0$, so $\frac{(B_{i,k-1}^T P_{i,k-1} B_{i,k-1})^2}{Q_{i,k-1}^2 R_{i,k-1}}$ $e_i^2(k-1) > 0$, and also that $Q_{i,k-1} = 10 + B_{i,k-1}^T P_{i,k} B_{i,k-1} > 0$, so $\frac{1}{Q_{i,k-1}} < \frac{1}{10}$, $|\mu_i(k-1)| < \bar{\mu}_i$ in (8.33), we have:

$$\Delta L_i(k) \leq - \frac{1}{2Q_{i,k-1}}\tilde{\theta}_i^T(k-1)B_{i,k-1}B_{i,k-1}^T\tilde{\theta}_i(k-1) + \frac{1}{Q_{i,k-1}}\mu_i^2(k-1)$$

$$\leq - \frac{1}{2Q_{i,k-1}}\tilde{\theta}_i^T(k-1)B_{i,k-1}B_{i,k-1}^T P_{i,k-1} P_{i,k-1}^{-1}\tilde{\theta}_i(k-1) + \frac{\bar{\mu}_i^2}{10}$$

$$\Delta L_i(k) \leq -\omega_i L_i(k-1) + \frac{\bar{\mu}_i^2}{10} \tag{8.34}$$

where $\omega_i = \frac{\lambda_{\min}[B_{i,k-1}^T P_{i,k-1}^{-1} B_{i,k-1}]}{2Q_{i,k-1}} > 0$ and $\frac{\bar{\mu}_i^2}{10} > 0$. From [17] we know that the modified least-squares algorithm is uniformly stable and $L_i(k-1)$ is bounded.

Using (8.4), (8.6), (8.20), and (8.16), when the algorithm adds a new neuron, for this neuron we have:

$$\hat{y}_i(k-1) = \frac{y_i(k-1)\exp[-\gamma_{im1+1}^2]}{\exp[-\gamma_{im1+1}^2]} = y_i(k-1)$$

$$e_i(k-1) = \hat{y}_i(k-1) - y_i(k-1) = 0 \tag{8.35}$$

Then from (8.25) for this case: $\tilde{\theta}_i(k) = \tilde{\theta}_i(k-1) - \frac{1}{Q_{i,k-1}} P_{i,k} B_{i,k-1} e_i(k-1)$
$= \tilde{\theta}_i(k-1) < \infty$. From (8.17) we have $B_{i,k-1}^T \tilde{\theta}_i(k-1) + \mu_i(k-1) = e_i(k-1) = 0$,
$|B_{i,k-1}^T \tilde{\theta}_i(k-1)| = |-\mu_i(k-1)| = |\mu_i(k-1)| \le \bar{\mu}_i < \infty$. Then $|B_{i,k-1}^T| < \infty$, as $P_{i,k}^{-1} = P_{i,k-1}^{-1} + \frac{1}{2Q_{i,k-1}} B_{i,k-1} B_{i,k-1}^T$, we have $P_{i,k}^{-1} < \infty$. Then in this case $L_i(k-1) = \tilde{\theta}_i^T(k-1) P_{i,k-1}^{-1} \tilde{\theta}_i(k-1)$ is bounded. When the algorithm prunes a neuron, the parameters are updated with the modified least-squares algorithm (8.25). Thus, in all the cases $L_i(k-1)$ is bounded.

The identification error $e_i(k)$ is not the same as the state error $\tilde{x}_i(k) = \hat{x}_i(k) - x_i(k)$, but they are minimized at the same time. From (8.18) we have:

$$\tilde{x}_i(2) = s_i \tilde{x}_i(1) + e_i(1)$$
$$\tilde{x}_i(3) = s_i \tilde{x}_i(2) + e_i(2) = s_i^2 \tilde{x}_i(1) + e_i(2)$$
$$\tilde{x}_i(k+1) = s_i^k \tilde{x}_i(1) + \sum_{j=1}^{k} s_i^{k-j} e_i(j)$$

because $|s_i| < 1$:

$$|\tilde{x}_i(k+1)| \le |\tilde{x}_i(1)| + \sum_{j=1}^{k} |e_i(j)| \tag{8.36}$$

since $|\tilde{x}_i(1)|$ is a constant, the minimization of the training error $e_i(j)$ means the upper bound of the identification error $\tilde{x}_i(k+1)$ is minimized. When $e_i(j)$ is bounded, $\tilde{x}_i(k+1)$ is also bounded.

Using again (8.33) and as $\frac{1}{2Q_{i,k-1}} \tilde{\theta}_i^T(k-1) B_{i,k-1} B_{i,k-1}^T \tilde{\theta}_i(k-1) > 0$, $\frac{1}{Q_{i,k-1}} < \frac{1}{10}$ and $|\mu_i(k-1)| < \bar{\mu}_i$, we have:

$$\Delta L_i(k) \le -\frac{\left(B_{i,k-1}^T P_{i,k-1} B_{i,k-1}\right)^2}{Q_{i,k-1}^2 R_{i,k-1}} e_i^2(k-1) + \frac{\bar{\mu}_i^2}{10} \tag{8.37}$$

Summarizing (8.37) from 2 to T:

$$\sum_{k=2}^{T} \frac{\left(B_{i,k-1}^T P_{i,k-1} B_{i,k-1}\right)^2}{Q_{i,k-1}^2 R_{i,k-1}} e_i^2(k-1) - \frac{T\bar{\mu}_i^2}{10} \le L_i(1) - L_i(T) \tag{8.38}$$

Since $L_i(T) > 0$ is bounded and $L_i(1) > 0$ is constant:

$$\sum_{k=2}^{T} \frac{\left(B_{i,k-1}^T P_{i,k-1} B_{i,k-1}\right)^2}{Q_{i,k-1}^2 R_{i,k-1}} e_i^2(k-1) \le \frac{T\bar{\mu}_i^2}{10} + L_i(1) - L_i(T) \le \frac{T\bar{\mu}_i^2}{10} + L_i(1)$$

$$\frac{1}{T} \sum_{k=2}^{T} \frac{\left(B_{i,k-1}^T P_{i,k-1} B_{i,k-1}\right)^2}{Q_{i,k-1}^2 R_{i,k-1}} e_i^2(k-1) \le \frac{\bar{\mu}_i^2}{10} + \frac{1}{T} L_i(1)$$

$$\limsup_{T \to \infty} \frac{1}{T} \sum_{k=2}^{T} \frac{(B_{i,k-1}^T P_{i,k-1} B_{i,k-1})^2}{Q_{i,k-1}^2 R_{i,k-1}} e_i^2(k-1) \le \frac{\bar{\mu}_i^2}{10} \tag{8.39}$$

Equation (8.26) is established.

**Remark 8.6:** From (8.26) one can see that the final iteration parameter (time) $T$ tends to infinity; thus, the stability of the algorithm proposed is preserved when $T \to \infty$.

**Remark 8.7:** The parameter $m_1$ (number of rules) is bounded because the clustering and pruning algorithms do not let $m_1$ become infinity. The number of rules $m_1$ is changed by the clustering and pruning algorithms, and $m_1$ only changes the dimension of $B_{i,k-1}^T$ and $\theta_i(k-1)$; thus, the stability result is preserved.

## 8.6 THE PROPOSED ALGORITHM

The proposed final algorithm is as follows:

1. Select the following parameters: The parameter of the clustering algorithm is $r \in (0,1)$, and the parameter of the pruning algorithm is $d_u \in \aleph$, $(L = L + \Delta L, \Delta L = 5d_u)$.

2. For the first data $k = 1$, (where $k$ is the number of iterations) $m_1 = 1$ (where $m_1$ is the number of hidden neurons), the initial parameters of the modified least-squares algorithm are $P_{i,1} \in \mathfrak{R}^{3(m2+m1) \times 3(m2+m1)}$ with diagonal elements, $v_{1i1}(1) = y_i(1), c_{1i1}(1) = x_i(1)$, and $w_{1i1}(1) = rand \in (2,4)$, ($v_{1i1}(1)$ is the initial parameter of the consequent part, $c_{1i1}(1)$ and $w_{1i1}(1)$ are the centers and widths of the membership function of the antecedent part, $i = 1, \dots, n$), $v_{21i1}(1) = y_i(1), c_{2i1}(1) = x_i(1)$, and $w_{2i1}(1) = rand \in (2,4)$, $m_2$ is the size of the input $u(k-1)$, and the initial parameter of the clustering and pruning algorithm is $d_1(1) = 1$, (where $d_i$ is the population density parameter).

3. For the other data $k \ge 2$, evaluate the fuzzy network parameters $z_{1j}(k-1)$, $b_1(k-1), z_{2j}(k-1)$, and $b_2(k-1)$ with (8.4); evaluate the output of the fuzzy network $\hat{y}_i(k-1)$ with (8.5), (8.6), and (8.16), evaluate the identification error $e_i(k-1)$ with (8.16), update the parameters of the modified least-squares algorithm $v_{1ij}(k), c_{1ij}(k), w_{1ij}(k), v_{2ij}(k), c_{2ij}(k)$, and $w_{2ij}(k)$ with (8.25) (where $i = 1, \dots, n, j = 1, \dots, m_1$ for $\hat{f}_{i,k-1}$ and $j = 1, \dots, m_2$ for $\hat{g}_{i,k-1}$), and evaluate the parameter of the clustering and pruning algorithm $p(k-1)$ with (8.19).

    The updating of the clustering algorithm is as follows:

4. If $p(k-1) < r$, then a new neuron is generated ($m_1 = m_1 + 1$) (e.g., the number of neurons is increased by one); assign initial values to the new neuron as $v_{1im1+1}(k), c_{1im1+1}(k), w_{1im1+1}(k)$, and $d_{m1+1}(k)$ with (8.20). We assign values for $P_{i,k} \in \mathfrak{R}^{3(m2+m1+1) \times 3(m2+m1+1)}$ from elements $m_2 + 1$ to $m_2 + m_1 + 1$ with diagonal elements, (where $v_{1ij}(k), c_{1ij}(k), w_{1ij}(k)$, and $P_{i,k}$ are the modified

least-square algorithm parameters, $d_j(k)$ is the population density parameter, $i = 1, \ldots, n, j = 1, \ldots, m_1$), go to 3.

5. If $p(k-1) \geq r$, then a neuron is not generated; if $z_{1j}(k-1) = p(k-1)$, we have the winner neuron $j^*$. The value of the population density $d_{j^*}(k)$ of this hidden neuron is updated with (8.21). The winner neuron is a hidden neuron that increments its importance in the algorithm, go to 3.

The updating of the pruning algorithm is as follows:

6. For the case that $k = L$, the pruning algorithm works (the pruning algorithm is not active at each iteration). Evaluate the minimum population density $d_{\min}(k)$ with (8.22) and $L$ is updated as $L = L + \Delta L$.

7. If $m_1 \geq 2$ and if $d_{\min}(k) \leq d_u$, this hidden neuron is pruned. If $d_j(k) = d_{\min}(k)$, we have the looser neuron $j_*$. The looser neuron is the least important neuron of the algorithm. We assign values to $v_{1ij}(k), c_{1ij}(k), w_{1ij}(k)$, and $d_j(k)$ with (8.23) and (8.24) in order to prune the looser neuron $j_*$. We assign values for $P_{i,k} \in \mathfrak{R}^{3(m2+m1-1) \times 3(m2+m1-1)}$ from elements $m_2 + 1$ to $m_2 + m_1 - 1$ with diagonal elements in order to prune the looser neuron $j_*$ (where $v_{1ij}(k), c_{1ij}(k), w_{1ij}(k)$, and $P_{i,k}$ are the modified least-squares algorithm parameters and $d_j(k)$ is the population density parameter, $i = 1, \ldots, n, j = 1, \ldots, m_1$), update $m_1$ as $m_1 = m_1 - 1$ (e.g., the number of neurons is decreased by one), go to 3.

8. If $d_{\min}(k) > d_u$ or $m_1 = 1$, this rule is not pruned, go to 3.

## 8.7 SIMULATIONS

In this section, the suggested online evolving neuro-fuzzy recurrent algorithm is applied to nonlinear system identification based on three synthetic (simulated-based) systems. Note that in this chapter the structure learning and parameters learning work at each time-step and online.

*Example 8.1:* The nonlinear plant to be identified is expressed as [29, 36]:

$$y(k-1) = \frac{y(k)y(k-1)y(k-2)}{1 + y^2(k) + y^2(k-1) + y^2(k-2)} + 0.5y(k-3) + 2u(k) \qquad (8.40)$$

This input–output model can be transformed into the following state-space model:

$$x_1(k) = \frac{x_1(k-1)x_2(k-1)x_3(k-1)}{1 + x_1^2(k-1) + x_2^2(k-1) + x_3^2(k-1)} + 0.5x_4(k-1) + 2u(k-1)$$
$$x_2(k) = x_1(k-1), x_3(k) = x_2(k-1), x_4(k) = x_3(k-1) \qquad (8.41)$$

The input is $T = 0.01$, $u(k-1) = 0.03\sin[3\pi(k-1)T] + 0.01\sin[4\pi(k-1)T] + 0.06\sin[\pi(k-1)T]$. This unknown nonlinear system has the standard form (8.1). We use the recurrent neural network given in (8.2) and (8.4) or (8.2), (8.5), and (8.6) to

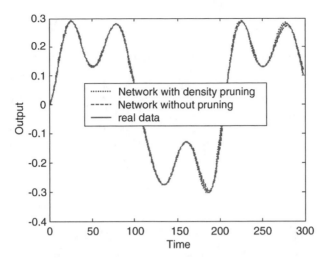

Figure 8.2. Identification results for Example 1.

identify it, where $x(k) = [x_1(k), x_2(k), x_3(k), x_4(k)]^T$, $\hat{x}(k) \in \Re^4$, $S \in \Re^{4 \times 4}$. We select $S = diag(0.1)$, which is a stable diagonal matrix. The parameters of the ENFRN are $P_{i,1} = diag(100) \in \Re^{3(1+1) \times 3(1+1)}$, $r = 0.9$, and $d_u = 4$. We compare the ENFRN without a pruning algorithm with the ENFRN with the pruning algorithm given in this chapter based on the population density [3]. The identification results for $x_1(k)$ are shown in Figure 8.2. If we define the mean squared error for finite time as

$$J(T) = \frac{1}{2T} \sum_{k=1}^{T} e_i^2(k-1),$$ the comparison results for the identification error are shown

in Figure 8.3 and the growth of the hidden neurons is shown in Figure 8.4, denoted by $m_1$. From Figures 8.2 to 8.4, it can be seen that the proposed pruning algorithm provides an improvement to the result with a guaranteed stability, because the result is more compact and the error is smaller.

***Example 8.2:*** Consider the model taken from [8]; which can be represented by the following difference equations:

$$x_3(k) = \frac{x_1^2(k-1) + x_2^2(k-1) + x_3^2(k-1) + \tanh[u(k-1)]}{x_1^2(k-1) + x_2^2(k-1) + x_3^2(k-1) + 1}$$

$$x_1(k) = x_2(k-1), x_2(k) = x_3(k-1) \tag{8.42}$$

The input is $T = 0.01$, $u(k-1) = 0.18 \sin[1.5\pi(k-1)T] + 0.28 \sin[0.5\pi(k-1)T]$.

This unknown nonlinear system has the standard form (8.1). We use the recurrent neural network given in (8.2) and (8.4) or (8.2), (8.5), and (8.6) to identify it, where $x(k) = [x_1(k), x_2(k), x_3(k)]^T$, $\hat{x}(k) \in \Re^3$, $S \in \Re^{3 \times 3}$. We select $S = diag(0.1)$. Which is a stable diagonal matrix. The parameters of the ENFRN are $P_{i,1} = diag(100) \in \Re^{3(1+1) \times 3(1+1)}$, $r = 0.9$, and $d_u = 4$. We compare the ENFRN without a pruning algorithm with the ENFRN with the pruning algorithm given in this

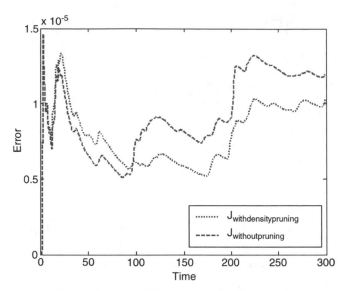

Figure 8.3. Identification error for Example 1.

chapter based on the population density. The identification results for $x_3(k)$ are shown in Figure 8.5. The comparison results for the identification error are shown in Figure 8.6 and the growth of the hidden neurons is shown in Figure 8.7, denoted by $m_1$. In Figures 8.5 through 8.7, it is seen that the proposed pruning algorithm given in this chapter provides an improvement to the result with a guaranteed stability. The result is more compact and the error is smaller.

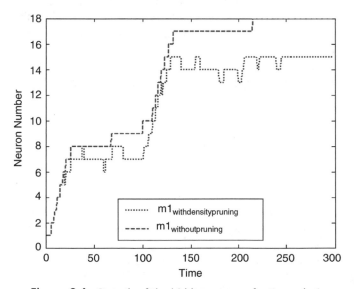

Figure 8.4. Growth of the hidden neurons for Example 1.

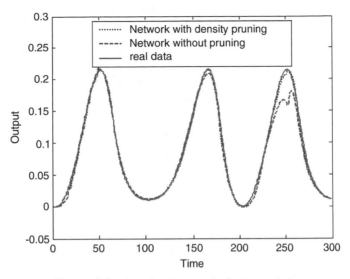

Figure 8.5. Identification results for Example 2.

***Example 8.3:*** The model of experimental population studies of a model of flour beetle population dynamics describes an age-structured population [13]:

$$L_f(k) = b_f A_f(k-1)\exp{-c_{ea}\lfloor A_f(k-1)-c_{el}L_f(k-1)\rfloor}$$
$$P_f(k) = L_f(k-1)[1-\mu_l] \qquad\qquad (8.43)$$
$$A_f(k) = P_f(k-1)\exp[-c_{pa}\,A_f(k-1)] + A_f(k-1)[1-\mu_a]$$

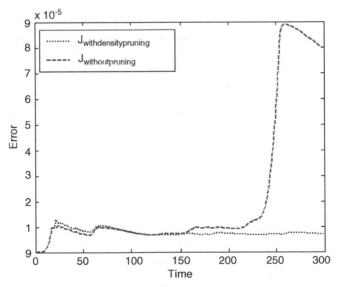

Figure 8.6. Identification error for Example 2.

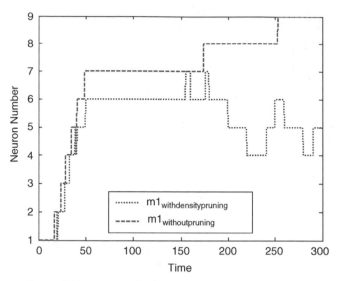

Figure 8.7. Growth of the hidden neurons for Example 2.

where variables and parameters are defined in Table 8.1. Cannibalism is important in this species and is represented in the model as a decrease in the survival rates of the consumed ages in the presence of consuming age. Adults and larvae both consume larvae; pupae do not eat larvae. Adults eat pupae, but not other adults. So, negative exponentials in (8.43) represent the reduction of larval survival as adult or larvae numbers increase. The number of larval recruits increases linearly with the adults number by the rate $b_f$. Thus, the rate equation for larvae is composed of two rate process rates multiplied together: reproduction and mortality. The equation for pupae is simple: Every larva that survives predation becomes a pupae, but pupae die from causes of mortality other than cannibalism at the rate $\mu_l$. Adults have a similar death term. In addition, adult consume pupae, so the number of pupae emerging as adults is the fraction not eaten by the current adult cohort. This survival rate declines as a negative exponential term with

**T A B L E 8.1.** Parameters of the Age-Structured Population

| Variables | | | |
|---|---|---|---|
| $L_f$ | $x_1$ | 250 numbers | Larvae |
| $P_f$ | $x_2$ | 5 numbers | Pupae |
| $A_f$ | $x_3$ | 100 numbers | Adults |
| Parameters | | | |
| $b_f$ | 11.98 numbers | Larvae recruits per adult | |
| $c_{ea}$ | 0.011 unitless | Susceptibility of eggs to cannibalism by adults | |
| $c_{el}$ | 0.013 unitless | Susceptibility of eggs to cannibalism by larvae | |
| $c_{pa}$ | 0.017 unitless | Susceptibility of pupae to cannibalism by adults | |
| $\mu_l$ | 0.513 unitless | Fraction of larvae dying (not cannibalism) | |
| $\mu_a$ | Varied unitless | Fraction of adults dying | |

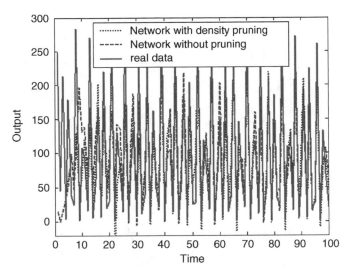

Figure 8.8. Identification results for Example 3.

increasing numbers of adults. For $\mu_a = 0.04$ we have high equilibrium; for $\mu_a = 0.27$ we have two cycles; for $\mu_a = 0.73$ we have low equilibrium; and for $\mu_a = 0.96$ we have an aperiodic behavior [13]. We use $\mu_a = 0.96$ to identify this model.

This unknown nonlinear system has the standard form (8.1) without using input $u(k-1)$. We use the recurrent neural network given in (8.2) and (8.4) or (8.2), (8.5), and (8.6) without using $\hat{g}_{i,k-1}$ to identify it, where $x(k) = [x_1(k), x_2(k), x_3(k)]^T$, $\hat{x}(k) \in \Re^3$, $S \in \Re^{3\times 3}$. We select $S = diag(0.1)$, which is a stable diagonal matrix. The parameters of the ENFRN are $P_{i,1} = diag(1 \times 10^5) \in \Re^{3(1)\times 3(1)}$, $r = 0.9$, and $d_u = 4$. We compare the ENFRN without a pruning algorithm with the ENFRN with the pruning algorithm given in this chapter based on the population density. The identification results for $x_1(k)$ are shown in Figure 8.8. The comparison results for the identification error are shown in Figure 8.9 and the growth of the hidden neurons are shown in Figure 8.10, denoted by $m_1$. In Figures 8.8 through 8.10, it is seen that the proposed pruning algorithm given in this chapter provides an improvement to the result with a guaranteed stability. The result is more compact and the error is smaller.

## 8.8 CONCLUSION

In this chapter a quick and efficient approach for system modeling is proposed using an evolving neuro-fuzzy recurrent network. It is effective, as it does not require retraining of the whole model along the lines of the EIS proposed in [41] and developed in [1–3, 23, 24, 27]. It is based on recursive building of the hidden neuron base by unsupervised and supervised learning, the hidden neuron-based model structure learning, and parameter

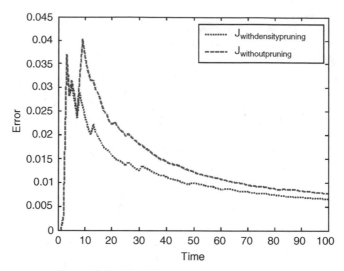

Figure 8.9. Identification error for Example 3.

estimation. The adaptive nature of EIS in addition to the transparent and compact form of hidden neurons makes them promising candidates for online modeling and control of complex processes competitive to neural networks. From a dynamic system point of view, such training can be useful for all neural network applications requiring real-time updating of the weights. The main advantages of the EIS are: (1) It can develop an existing model when the data pattern changes, while inheriting the rule base; (2) it can start to learn a process from a single data sample and improve the performance of the model predictions online; and (3) it is recursive and very effective.

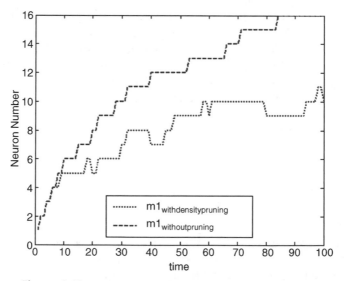

Figure 8.10. Growth of the hidden neurons for Example 3.

The main contribution of this chapter is the theoretical proof of stability of learning based on the modified version of the fuzzily weighted recursive least-squares method for a particular type of evolving fuzzy network (with particular types of consequences).

## 8.9 ACKNOWLEDGMENTS

We express our gratitude to the editors for inviting us to participate in this project and to the reviewers for their valuable comments and suggestions, which helped to improve this research.

## 8.10 REFERENCES

1. P. P. Angelov, R. Buswell, "Identification of Evolving Fuzzy Rule-Based Models," *IEEE Trans. on Fuzzy Systems*, Vol. 10, No. 5, pp. 667–677, 2002.

2. P. P. Angelov, D. P. Filev, "An approach to Online Identification of Takagi-Sugeno Fuzzy Models," *IEEE Trans. on Systems, Man and Cybernetics*, Vol. 32, No. 1, pp. 484–498, 2004.

3. P. P. Angelov, D. P. Filev, "Simpl_eTS: A Simplified Method for Learning Evolving Takagi-Sugeno Fuzzy Models." *Int. Con. on Fuzzy Systems*, 2005, pp. 1068–1072.

4. M. F. Azem, M. Hanmandlu, N. Ahmad, "Structure identification of Generalized Adaptive Neuro-Fuzzy Inference Systems," *IEEE Trans. on Fuzzy Systems*, Vol. 11, No. 6, pp. 666–681, 2003.

5.    J. C. Bezdek, "Fuzzy Mathematics in Pattern Classification," PhD thesis, Applied Math. Center, Cornell University, Ithaca, 1973.

6. E. G. P. Box, G. M. Jenkins, *Time Series Analysis, Forecasting and Control*. San Francisco: Holden Day, 1976.

7. M. Brown, C. J. Harris, *Adaptive Modeling and Control*. New York: Macmillan, Prentice-Hall, 1994.

8. J. B. D. Cabrera, K. S. Narendra, "Issues in the Application of Neural Networks for Tracking Based on Inverse Control," *IEEE Transactions on Automatic Control*, Vol. 44, No. 11, pp. 2007–2027, November 1999.

9. S. L. Chiu, "Fuzzy Model Identification Based on Cluster Estimation," *Journal of Intelligent and Fuzzy Systems*, Vol. 2, No. 3, 1994.

10. G. Cybenco, "Approximation by Superposition of Sigmoidal Activation Function," *Math. Control Sig. System*, Vol. 2, pp. 303–314, 1989.

11. B. Egardt, "Stability of Adaptive Controllers," Springer-Verlag Berlin, *Lecture Notes in Control and Information Sciences*, Vol. 20, 1979.

12. G. C. Goodwin, K. Sang Sin, *Adaptive Filtering Prediction and Control*. Englewood Cliffis, NJ: Prentice Hall, 1984.

13. J. W. Haefner, *Modeling Biological Systems: Principles and Applications*. New York: Springer, 2005, ISBN-10: 0-387-25012-3 (E).

14.    D. Hassibi, D. G. Stork, "Second Order Derivatives for Network Pruning," Advances in Neural Information Processing, Los Altos, CA, Vol. 5, pp. 164-171, 1993.

15. S. Haykin, *Neural Networks. A Comprehensive Foundation*. New York: Macmillan, 1994.

16. J. R. Hilera, V. J. Martines, *Redes Neuronales Artificiales, Fundamentos, Modelos y Aplicaciones*. Addison-Wesley Iberoamericana, 1995.

17. P. A. Ioannou, J. Sun, *Robust Adaptive Control*. Upper Saddle River: NJ: Prentice-Hall, 1996.

18. J. S. R. Jang, "AFNFIS: Adaptive-Network-Based Fuzzy Inference System," *IEEE Trans. on Systems, Man and Cybernetics*, Vol. 23, pp. 665–685, 1993.

19. J. S. R. Jang, C. T. Sun, E. Mizutani, *Neuro-Fuzzy and Soft Computing*. Englewood Cliffs, NJ: Prentice-Hall, 1996.

20. C. F. Juang, C.T. Lin, "An On-line Self-Constructing Neural Fuzzy Inference Network and Its Applications," *IEEE Trans. on Fuzzy Systems*, Vol. 6, No. 1, pp. 12–32, 1998.

21. C. F. Juang, C.T. Lin, "A Recurrent Self-Organizing Fuzzy Inference Network," *IEEE Trans. on Neural Networks*, Vol. 10, No. 4, pp. 828–845, 1999.

22. C. F. Juang, "A TSK-Type Recurrent Fuzzy Network for Dynamic Systems Processing by Neural Network and Genetic Algorithms," *IEEE Trans. on Fuzzy Systems*, Vol. 10, No. 2, pp. 155–169, 2002.

23. N. K. Kasabov, "Evolving Fuzzy Neural Networks for Supervised/Unsupervised Online Knowledge-Based Learning," *IEEE Trans. on Systems, Man and Cybernetics*, Vol. 31, No. 6, pp. 902–918, 2001.

24. N. K. Kasabov, Q. Song, "DENFIS: Dynamic Evolving Neural-Fuzzy Inference System and Its Application for Time-Series Prediction," *IEEE Trans. on Fuzzy Systems*, Vol. 10, No. 2, pp. 144–154, 2002.

25. K. Kim, E. J. Whang, C.-W. Park, E. Kim, M. Park, *A TSK Fuzzy Inference Algorithm for Online Identification*, Berlin, Heidelberg: Springer-Verlag, 2005, pp. 179–188.

26. E. B. Kosmatopoulos, M.M. Polycarpou, M.A. Christodoulou, P.A. Ioannou, "High-order Neural Network Structures for Identification of Dynamic Systems," *IEEE Trans. on Neural Networks*, Vol. 6, No. 2, pp. 422–431, 1995.

27. G. Leng, T. M. McGinnity, G. Prasad, "An Approach for On-line Extraction of Fuzzy Rules Using a Self-Organizing Fuzzy Neural Network," *Fuzzy Sets and Systems*, Vol. 150, pp. 211–243, 2005.

28. C. T. Lin, *Neural Fuzzy Control Systems with Structure and Parameter Learning*. New York: World Scientific, 1994.

29. K. S. Narendra, K. Parthasarathy, "Identification and Control of Dynamic Systems Using Neural Networks," *IEEE Trans. Neural Networks*, Vol. 1, No. 1, pp. 4–27, 1990.

30. A. G. Parlos, S. K. Menon, A. F. Atiya, "An Algorithm Approach to Adaptive State Filtering Using Recurrent Neural Network," *IEEE Trans. Neural Networks*, Vol. 12, No. 6, pp. 1411.1432, 2001.

31. J. Platt, "A Resource-Allocating Network for Function Interpolation," *Neural Computation*, Vol. 3, No. 2, pp. 213–225, 1991.

32. I. Rivals, L. Personnaz, "Neural Network Construction and Selection in Nonlinear Modeling," *IEEE Trans. on Neural Networks*, Vol. 14, No. 4, pp. 804–820, 2003.

33. J. J. Rubio, W. Yu, "A New Discrete-Time Sliding-Mode Control with Time-Varying Gain and Neural Identification," *Int. J. Control*, Vol. 79, No. 4, pp. 338–348, April 2006.

34. J. J. Rubio, W. Yu, "Nonlinear System Identification with Recurrent Neural Networks and Dead-Zone Kalman Filter Algorithm," *Neurocomputing*, Vol. 70, pp. 2460–2466, 2007.

35. J. J. Rubio, W. Yu, "Dead-Zone Kalman Filter Algorithm for Recurrent Neural Networks." *44th IEEE Conf. on Decision and Control, Spain*, 2005, pp. 2562–2567.

36. P. S. Sastry, G. Santharam, K. P. Unnikrishnan, "Memory Neural Networks for Identification and Control of Dynamic Systems," *IEEE Trans. Neural Networks*, Vol. 5, pp. 306–319, 1994.

37. S. G. Tzafestas, K. C. Zikidis, "On-Line Neuro-Fuzzy ART-Based Structure and Parameter Learning TSK Model," *IEEE Trans. on Systems, Man and Cybernetics*, Vol. 31, No. 5, pp. 797–803, 2001.

38. L. X. Wang, *A Course in Fuzzy Systems and Control*. Englewood Cliffs, NJ: Prentice-Hall, 1997.

39. S. Wu, M. J. Er, "Dynamic Fuzzy Neural Networks: A Novel Approach to Function Approximation," *IEEE Trans. on Systems, Man and Cybernetics—Part B*, Vol. 30, pp. 358–364, 2000.

40. S. Wu, M. J. Er, "A Fast Approach for Automatic Generation of Fuzzy Rules by Generalized Dynamic Fuzzy Neural Networks," *IEEE Trans. on Fuzzy Systems*, Vol. 9, pp. 578–594, 2001.

41. R. R. Yager, D. P. Filev, "Learning of Fuzzy Rules by Mountain Clustering." *Proc. SPIE Conf. on Application of Fuzzy Logic Technology, Boston*, 1993, pp. 246–254.

42. W. Yu, X. Li, "Fuzzy Identification Using Fuzzy Neural Networks with Stable Learning Algorithms," *IEEE Trans. on Fuzzy Systems*, Vol. 12, No. 3, pp. 411–420, 2004.

# 9

# ONLINE IDENTIFICATION OF SELF-ORGANIZING FUZZY NEURAL NETWORKS FOR MODELING TIME-VARYING COMPLEX SYSTEMS

G. Prasad, G. Leng, T.M. McGinnity, D. Coyle

**Abstract:** Fuzzy neural networks are hybrid systems that combine the theories of fuzzy logic and neural networks. By incorporating in these hybrid systems the ability to self-organize their network structure, self-organizing fuzzy neural networks (SOFNNs) are created. The SOFNNs have enhanced ability to identify adaptive models, mainly for representing nonlinear and time-varying complex systems, where little or insufficient expert knowledge is available to describe the underlying behavior. Problems that arise in these systems are large dimensions, time-varying characteristics, large amounts of data, and noisy measurements, as well as the need for an interpretation of the resulting model.

This chapter presents an algorithm for online identification of a self-organizing fuzzy neural network. The SOFNN provides a singleton or Takagi-Sugeno (TS)-type fuzzy model. It therefore facilitates extracting fuzzy rules from the training data. The algorithm is formulated to guarantee the convergence of both the estimation error and the linear network parameters. It generates a fuzzy neural model with high accuracy and compact structure. Superior performance of the algorithm is demonstrated through its applications for function approximation, system identification, and time-series prediction in both industrial and biological systems.

*Evolving Intelligent Systems: Methodology and Applications,* Edited by Plamen Angelov, Dimitar P. Filev, and Nikola Kasabov

## 9.1 INTRODUCTION

In order to effectively handle the complexity and dynamics of real-world problems, there is often the need to model online nonlinear and time-varying complex systems. Such a need arises in both industrial and biological systems, for example, models for market forecasts, optimal manufacturing control, and administering anesthesia optimally. The complexity of modeling these systems is exacerbated due to the fact that there is often very little or insufficient expert knowledge available to describe the underlying behavior. Additional common problems that arise in these systems are large dimensions, large amounts of data, and noisy measurements. In such cases, it is thus an obvious requirement that an appropriate modeling algorithm should have a much higher level of autonomy in the modeling process as well as being capable of providing an interpretation of the resulting model. In order to meet these stringent modeling requirements, an algorithm developed using a hybrid intelligent systems approach is reported in this chapter. The algorithm is basically a *fuzzy neural network* (*FNN*) identification procedure, in which fuzzy techniques are used to enhance certain aspects of the neural network's learning and adaptation performance. FNNs are usually represented as multilayer feedforward networks and are used to learn fuzzy membership functions and explain the rules that are used to make decisions. A good review about FNNs can be found in Buckley and Hayashi (1994) and Nauck (1997). Some authors make a distinction between FNNs and neuro-fuzzy systems. However, no differentiation is made in this chapter. The algorithm we are discussing is based on a self-organizing fuzzy neural network (SOFNN) approach, in which the FNN possesses an ability to self-organize its structure along with associated premise parameters. A type of *recursive least-squares* (*RLS*) algorithm (Astrom & Wittenmark, 1995) forms an integral part of the approach. This is used to identify consequent parameters of a *singleton* or *Takagi-Sugeno* (*TS*)-*type* (Takagi & Sugeno, 1985) fuzzy model. Thus, the main purpose of the SOFNN approach here is to devise a hybrid fuzzy neural network architecture to create self-adaptive fuzzy rules for online identification of a singleton or TS-type fuzzy model of a nonlinear time-varying complex system. The associated algorithm therefore aims to create a self-organizing neural network that is designed to approximate a fuzzy algorithm or a process of fuzzy inference through the structure of neural networks and thus create a more interpretable hybrid neural network model making effective use of the superior learning ability of neural networks and easy interpretability of fuzzy systems. The twin main issues associated with the identification of a singleton or TS-type fuzzy model are: (1) structure identification, which involves partitioning the input–output space and thus identifying the number of fuzzy rules for the desired performance, and (2) parameter estimation, which includes identifying parameters of premises and consequences.

With sufficient good-quality training data, there are several supervised training approaches (Mitra & Hayashi, 2000; Wang & Lee, 2001) proposed in the literature for an adaptive fuzzy neural model identification. The main difference lies in the method adopted for the partitioning of input–output space for the structure identification. As suggested in Wang and Lee (2001), the methods proposed in the literature can be placed into two broad categories: (1) the *static* adaptation method, where the number of input–output partitions are fixed, while their corresponding fuzzy rule configurations are adapted through optimization to obtain the desired performance, and (2) the *dynamic adaptation* method, where both the number of input–output space partitions and their corresponding fuzzy rule configurations are simultaneously and concurrently adapted. The main focus of the SOFNN algorithm is the design of an approach for dynamic adaptation of the structure of the hybrid network, so that the underlying behavior of a nonlinear time-varying complex system could be captured in a model that is more accurate, compact, and interpretable.

For similar performance, the number of fuzzy partitions, and thereby fuzzy rules, can be greatly reduced by cluster-based partitioning of the input–output space (Zadeh, 1994). Therefore, for identifying a more compact structure, input–output space partitioning based on the traditional clustering approaches, such as hard $c$-means (HCM) and fuzzy $c$-means (FCM) (Gonzalez et al., 2002; Klawonn & Keller, 1998; Wang & Lee, 2001), has been proposed. The number of partitions, however, needs to be fixed by *a priori* expert knowledge in these approaches. The final configuration of the clusters and the corresponding fuzzy rule parameters are obtained by a nonlinear optimization. However, there is no guarantee of convergence to an optimal solution, as the final solution greatly relies on the selection of initial locations of cluster centers. Also, it is difficult and time consuming to visualize the optimal number of partitions required for modeling a complex system, particularly if the underlying structural behavior of the system is time-varying and inadequately known.

Under the dynamic adaptation method, the training may start with a single fuzzy rule or neuron or none at all (Er & Wu, 2002; Kasabov & Song, 2002; Rizzi et al., 2002; Wang & Lee, 2001; Wu & Er, 2000; Wu et al., 2001). During training, the network structure grows and concurrently the parameters of antecedents and consequents are adapted to obtain the desired modeling accuracy.

A constructive approach for creating on ANFIS-like network is proposed in (Mascioli & Martinelli, 1998; Mascioli et al., 2000; Rizzi et al., 2002) based on Simpson's *min-max* technique (Simpson, 1992;1993). The input space is partitioned by constructing hyperboxes using the min-max procedure. The hyperbox-based framework facilitates application of different types of fuzzy membership functions. To decrease the complexity of the network, a pruning method, called *pruning adaptive resolution classifier (PARC)*, is developed in Rizzi et al. (2002). This consists of deleting some negligible hyperboxes and a fusion procedure to make actual coverage complete. This constructive approach is, however, basically developed for batch learning to create a structure-adaptive network with a significantly higher degree of automation.

A *dynamic fuzzy neural network (DFNN)* architecture reported in Wu and Er (2000) and Er and Wu (2002) is another notably relevant work. It makes use of a hierarchical learning approach and an orthogonal least-squares-based pruning technique (Chen et al., 1991). In the DFNN architecture, fuzzy rules are represented by radial basis function (RBF) neurons in the first hidden layer. However, the representation is restrictive in the sense that widths of the membership functions belonging to various inputs that create an RBF neuron of the DFNN have the same value. An enhanced version of DFNN is *GDFNN* (Wu et al., 2001). It introduces width vectors in RBF neurons, so that the Gaussian membership functions within a neuron can be assigned appropriate widths separately. The GDFNN also attempts to provide explanations for selecting the values of width parameter of the Gaussian fuzzy membership functions based on the concept of $\varepsilon$-*completeness* (Wang, 1992). However, the hierarchical learning approach proposed for training GDFNN is dependent on the total number of training data patterns. This implies that the GDFNN approach is primarily designed for batch training using a fixed number of training data patterns.

The *dynamic evolving neuro-fuzzy system* (*DENFIS*) is another notable approach (Kasabov & Song, 2002) that employs a dynamic adaptation method and can be applied in online TS-type model identification. The input space partitioning in DENFIS is accomplished online using an *evolving clustering method* (*ECM*) that creates new clusters as new data vectors arrive, based on a distance threshold. The fuzzy inference and thereby the consequent parameters are estimated based on only the nearest $m$ fuzzy rules. Although this approach implements the concept of local learning by limiting the learning in the region nearest to the current data vector, it has no provision to ensure that network size remains compact while ensuring higher generalization accuracy.

SOFNN is in the same category of approaches as eTS (Angelov and Filev, 2004). In order to model a time-varying nonlinear system, a truly online training algorithm is required so that the desired accuracy as well as network size can be obtained. Ensuring convergence of the network parameters and the estimation error is also essential for an online training algorithm. Based on the dynamic adaptation method, this chapter presents an algorithm for creating a self-organizing fuzzy neural network that identifies a singleton or TS-type fuzzy model online. A modified recursive least-squares (RLS) algorithm derived to guarantee the convergence of the estimation error and the linear network parameters is used for estimating consequent parameters. For structure learning, the algorithm makes use of a procedure to decide how to create a new *ellipsoidal basis function* (*EBF*) neuron with a center vector and a width vector. The EBF neuron represents a fuzzy rule formed by AND logic (or $T$-norm) operating on Gaussian fuzzy membership functions. The elements of center vector and width vector of the EBF neurons are the centers and widths of the Gaussian membership functions. The structure learning approach consists of a combination of system error and firing strength–based criteria for adding new EBF neurons using the concepts from statistical theory and the $\varepsilon$-completeness of fuzzy rules (Lee, 1990). This ensures that the membership functions have the capability to cover more data. The SOFNN approach uses a pruning method based on the *optimal brain surgeon* (*OBS*) approach (Hassibi & Stork, 1993; Leung et al., 2001). This method is computationally very efficient for online implementation, as it does not involve any significant additional computation because it makes direct use of the Hermitian matrix obtained as a part of the RLS algorithm. These two features of adding and pruning neurons automatically enable the SOFNN to have an adaptive structure to model nonlinear and time-varying systems online. The structure learning and parameter learning methods are very simple and more efficient and yield a fuzzy neural model with high accuracy and compact structure.

In the next section, the architecture of the SOFNN is described. The structure learning of the SOFNN that presents the approach of adding and pruning neurons is organized in Section 9.2. It also describes the modified RLS algorithm and the analysis of the properties of this algorithm for the parameter learning. Typical applications and a performance evaluation of the SOFNN algorithm are discussed in Section 9.3. Finally, conclusions are summarized in Section 9.4.

## 9.2 ALGORITHMIC DETAILS

### 9.2.1 Architecture of the SOFNN

The architecture of the self-organizing fuzzy neural network is a five-layer fuzzy neural network, shown in Figure 9.1. The five layers are the *input* layer, the *ellipsoidal basis function* (*EBF*) layer, the *normalized* layer, the *weighted* layer, and the *output* layer. Some of the interconnections are shown by dotted lines. This is to indicate that the SOFNN has the ability to self-organize its own neurons in the learning process for implementing singleton or Takagi-Sugeno (TS)-fuzzy models.

In the EBF layer, each neuron is a *T*-norm of Gaussian fuzzy membership functions belonging to the inputs of the network. Every membership function (MF) thus has its own distinct center and width, which means every neuron has both a center vector and a width vector and the dimensions of these vectors are the same as the dimension of the input vector. Figure 9.2 illustrates the internal structure of the *j*th neuron, where $\mathbf{x} = [x_1 \quad x_2 \quad \ldots\ldots \quad x_r]$ is the input vector, $\mathbf{c_j} = [c_{1j} \quad c_{2j} \quad \ldots\ldots \quad c_{rj}]$ is the vector of centers in the *j*th EBF neuron, and $\mathbf{s_j} = [\sigma_{1j} \quad \sigma_{2j} \quad \ldots\ldots \quad \sigma_{rj}]$ is the vector of widths in the *j*th neuron. Here, *multi-input, single-output* (*MISO*) systems are considered. However, all results could also be applied to *multi-input, multi-output* (*MIMO*) systems. A layerwise mathematical description of the network follows.

*Layer 1* is the input layer. Each neuron in this layer represents an input variable, $x_i, i = 1, 2, \ldots, r$.

*Layer 2* is the EBF layer. Each neuron in this layer represents an *if-part* (or *premise*) of a fuzzy rule. The outputs of EBF neurons are computed by products of the grades of

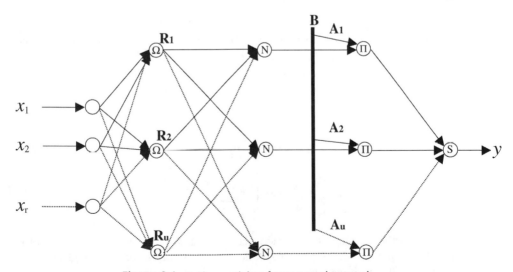

Figure 9.1. Self-organizing fuzzy neural network.

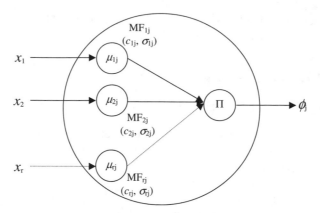

**Figure 9.2.** Structure of the $j$th neuron $R_j$ with $\mathbf{c}_j$ and $\sigma_j$ in the EBF layer.

MFs. Each MF is in the form of a Gaussian function,

$$\mu_{ij} = \exp\left[-\frac{(x_i - c_{ij})^2}{2\sigma_{ij}^2}\right]$$  (9.1)

$$i = 1, 2, \ldots, r; \, j = 1, 2, \ldots, u$$

where $\mu_{ij}$ is the $i$th membership function in the $j$th neuron; $c_{ij}$ is the center of the $i$th membership function in the $j$th neuron; $\sigma_{ij}$ is the width of the $i$th membership function in the $j$th neuron; $r$ is the number of input variables; and $u$ is the number of neurons.

For the $j$th neuron, the output is

$$\phi_j = \exp\left[-\sum_{i=1}^{r} \frac{(x_i - c_{ij})^2}{2\sigma_{ij}^2}\right]$$  (9.2)

$$j = 1, 2, \ldots, u$$

*Layer 3* is the normalized layer. The number of neurons in this layer is equal to that of layer 2. The output of the $j$th neuron in this layer is

$$\psi_j = \frac{\phi_j}{\sum_{k=1}^{u} \phi_k}$$

$$= \frac{\exp\left[-\sum_{i=1}^{r} \frac{(x_i - c_{ij})^2}{2\sigma_{ij}^2}\right]}{\sum_{k=1}^{u} \exp\left[-\sum_{i=1}^{r} \frac{(x_i - c_{ik})^2}{2\sigma_{ik}^2}\right]}$$  (9.3)

$$j = 1, 2, \ldots, u$$

*Layer 4* is the weighted layer. Each neuron in this layer has two inputs and the product of these inputs as its output. One of the inputs is the output of the related neuron in layer 3 and the other is the weighted bias $w_{2j}$ obtained as the dot product of the bias vector

**B** and the row vector $\mathbf{A_j}$. For the Takagi-Sugeno (TS) model (Takagi & Sugeno, 1985), the bias is the column vector $\mathbf{B} = [1\ x_1\ x_2 \ldots x_r]^T$. For the singleton fuzzy model, $\mathbf{B} = [1\ 0\ 0 \cdots 0]^T$. The dimension of the column vector $\mathbf{B}$ is $r+1$. The row vector $\mathbf{A_j} = [a_{j0}\ \ a_{j1}\ \ a_{j2}\ \ \ldots\ldots\ \ a_{jr}]$ represents the set of parameters corresponding to the *then-part* (or *consequent*) of the fuzzy rule $j$. The weighted bias $w_{2j}$ is

$$w_{2j} = \mathbf{A_j} \cdot \mathbf{B} = a_{j0} + a_{j1}x_1 + \cdots + a_{jr}x_r$$
$$j = 1, 2, \ldots, u \tag{9.4}$$

This is thus the then-part (or consequent) of the $j$th fuzzy rule of the fuzzy model. The output of each neuron is $f_j = w_{2j}\psi_j$.

*Layer 5* is the output layer. Each neuron in this layer represents an output variable as the summation of incoming signals from layer 4. The output of a neuron in layer 5 is

$$y(\mathbf{x}) = \sum_{j=1}^{u} f_j$$
$$= \frac{\displaystyle\sum_{j=1}^{u} w_{2j} \exp\left[-\sum_{i=1}^{r} \frac{(x_i - c_{ij})^2}{2\sigma_{ij}^2}\right]}{\displaystyle\sum_{k=1}^{u} \exp\left[-\sum_{i=1}^{r} \frac{(x_i - c_{ik})^2}{2\sigma_{ik}^2}\right]} \tag{9.5}$$

where $y$ is the value of an output variable.

Suppose $u$ EBF neurons are generated from the $n$ training patterns of the input vector $\mathbf{x_t}$ and the corresponding desired output $d_t(t = 1, 2, \ldots, n)$. Rewrite the output of the network as

$$\mathbf{Y} = \mathbf{W_2}\Psi \tag{9.6}$$

where, for the TS model,

$$\mathbf{Y} = [y_1\ \ y_2\ \ \cdots\ \ y_n] \tag{9.7}$$

$$\mathbf{W_2} = [a_{10}\ \ a_{11}\ \ \cdots\ \ a_{1r}\ \ \cdots\ \ a_{u0}\ \ a_{u1}\ \ \cdots\ \ a_{ur}] \tag{9.8}$$

$$\Psi = \begin{bmatrix} \psi_{11} & \cdots & \psi_{1n} \\ \psi_{11}x_{11} & \cdots & \psi_{1n}x_{1n} \\ \vdots & \vdots & \vdots \\ \psi_{11}x_{r1} & \cdots & \psi_{1n}x_{rn} \\ \vdots & \vdots & \vdots \\ \psi_{u1} & \cdots & \psi_{un} \\ \psi_{u1}x_{11} & \cdots & \psi_{un}x_{1n} \\ \vdots & \vdots & \vdots \\ \psi_{u1}x_{r1} & \cdots & \psi_{un}x_{rn} \end{bmatrix} \tag{9.9}$$

where $\mathbf{W}_2$ is the parameter matrix, and $\psi_{jt}$ is the output of the $j$th neuron in the normalized layer when the $t$th training pattern enters the network.

## 9.2.2 The SOFNN Learning Algorithm

The learning process of the SOFNN includes the structure learning and the parameter learning. The structure learning attempts to achieve an economical network size with a self-organizing approach. As a result of this, neurons in the EBF layer are augmented or pruned dynamically in the learning process. The parameter learning makes the network converge quickly through an online recursive least-squares algorithm.

### 9.2.2.1 Adding a Neuron.
There are two criteria to judge whether to generate an EBF neuron. One is the *system error* criterion, and the other is the *coverage* or the *if-part* criterion. The error criterion considers the generalization performance of the overall network. The if-part criterion evaluates whether existing fuzzy rules or EBF neurons can cover and cluster the input vector suitably.

*The Error Criterion:* Consider the $n$th observation $(\mathbf{x_n}, d_n)$, where $\mathbf{x_n}$ is the input vector and $d_n$ is the desired output. The output of the network with the current structure is $y_n$. The system error $\varepsilon(n)$ is defined as

$$|\varepsilon(n)| = |d_n - y_n| \tag{9.10}$$

If

$$|\varepsilon(n)| > \delta \tag{9.11}$$

where $\delta$ is the predefined error tolerance, a new EBF neuron should be considered either for addition to the structure or to modify the widths of some membership functions.

*The Coverage Criterion:* Every EBF neuron in the EBF layer represents an if-part of a fuzzy rule. For the nth observation $(\mathbf{x_n}, d_n)$ with $r$ as the dimension of input vector, the firing strength or the output of each EBF neuron is

$$\phi_j = \exp\left[-\sum_{i=1}^{r} \frac{(x_{in} - c_{ij})^2}{2\sigma_{ij}^2}\right] \quad j = 1, 2, \ldots, u \tag{9.12}$$

The input vector $\mathbf{x_n}$ would be assumed to have been appropriately clustered by existing fuzzy rules or EBF neurons if the firing strength of at least one neuron is greater than 0.1354. This condition would ensure that no individual input can have a fuzzy membership grade less than 0.1354, and thus the $\varepsilon$-completeness of fuzzy rules (Lee, 1990), with $\varepsilon = 0.1354$, would be satisfied. It is also to be noted that for a Gaussian membership function $MF(c_{ij}, \sigma_{ij})$ the membership grade is 0.1354 for the inputs at $c_{ij} \pm 2\sigma_{ij}$. Assuming a normal input data distribution, 95% of input data belonging to this membership function will lie within the input range $[c_{ij} - 2\sigma_{ij}, c_{ij} + 2\sigma_{ij}]$.

Now define

$$\phi(n) = \max_{j=1.....u} (\phi_j) \tag{9.13}$$

If $\phi(n) < 0.1354$, it means no neuron in this structure can cluster this input vector. So, the width should be modified to cover the input vector suitably or a new EBF neuron should be considered for adding into the structure. Keeping the neuron output threshold constant, the capability of membership functions for covering input vectors may be increased by enlarging the widths of membership functions.

When the first training pattern $(\mathbf{x_1}, d_1)$ enters the network, the structure of the first neuron is defined as

$$\mathbf{c_1} = \mathbf{x_1^T} \tag{9.14}$$

$$\mathbf{s_1} = \begin{bmatrix} \sigma_0 & \sigma_0 & \cdots & \sigma_0 \end{bmatrix}^T \tag{9.15}$$

where $\mathbf{c_1}$ is the center vector whose dimension is $r \times 1$, $\mathbf{s_1}$ is the width vector whose dimension is $r \times 1$, and $\sigma_0$ is a predefined initial width.

For the $n$th training pattern, the following scenarios are possible:

1. $|\varepsilon(n)| \leq \delta$ and $\phi(n) \geq 0.1354$: This means that the network has good generalization and some neurons can cluster this input vector. The fuzzy neural network can thus accommodate the observation. Either nothing should be done or only the parameters should be adjusted.

2. $|\varepsilon(n)| \leq \delta$ and $\phi(n) < 0.1354$: In this case, the network has good generalization, but no neuron can cluster this input vector. To ensure the $\varepsilon$-completeness of fuzzy rules, the widths of this EBF neuron should be enlarged to make its output match the threshold 0.1354. So, the width of the membership function that has the least value in this neuron should be enlarged to cover the input vector suitably using (9.21), described later.

3. $|\varepsilon(n)| > \delta$ and $\phi(n) \geq 0.1354$: This means that the network has poor generalization performance but a neuron can cluster the current input vector. Thus, despite proper coverage of the current input by the existing neurons, the generalization performance of the network is poor. A new EBF neuron is therefore required to be added to the current structure to improve the performance.

Suppose the $k$th new neuron is to be added to the structure. For every neuron in the EBF layer except the $k$th new neuron, find the minimum distance vector,

$$\mathbf{Dist_k} = \begin{bmatrix} dist_{1n}(h_{m1}) \\ dist_{2n}(h_{m2}) \\ \vdots \\ dist_{rn}(h_{mr}) \end{bmatrix} = \begin{bmatrix} \displaystyle\min_{j=1,\cdots,k-1} (|x_{1n} - c_{1j}|) \\ \displaystyle\min_{j=1,\cdots,k-1} (|x_{2n} - c_{2j}|) \\ \vdots \\ \displaystyle\min_{j=1,\cdots,k-1} (|x_{rn} - c_{rj}|) \end{bmatrix} \tag{9.16}$$

where $dist_{in}(h_{mi})$ is the distance between the $i$th input of the $n$th observation $\mathbf{x_n} = [x_{1n} \quad x_{2n} \quad \ldots\ldots \quad x_{rn}]$ and the center of the $h_{mi}$th membership function in the $m_i$th neuron. The center $c_{ih_{mi}}$ of the $h_{mi}$th membership function is the nearest center from $x_{in}$. Here $i = 1, 2, \ldots\ldots r$. Let the center vector $\mathbf{c_k}$ and the width vector $\mathbf{s_k}$ of the $k$th new neuron be

$$\mathbf{c_k} = \begin{bmatrix} c_{1k} & c_{2k} & \ldots & c_{rk} \end{bmatrix}^T \tag{9.17}$$

and

$$\mathbf{s_k} = \begin{bmatrix} \sigma_{1k} & \sigma_{2k} & \ldots & \sigma_{rk} \end{bmatrix}^T \tag{9.18}$$

If $dist_{in}(h_{mi}) \leq k_d(i)$, where $k_d(i)$ is a predefined distance threshold of the $i$th input, $i = 1, 2, \ldots r$, then

$$\begin{aligned} c_{ik} &= c_{ih_{mi}} \\ \sigma_{ik} &= \sigma_{ih_{mi}} \end{aligned} \tag{9.19}$$

and if $dist_{in}(h_{mi}) > k_d(i)$, then

$$\begin{aligned} c_{ik} &= x_{in} \\ \sigma_{ik} &= dist_{in}(h_{mi}) \end{aligned} \tag{9.20}$$

The parameters of the current network should be updated to minimize the system error $\varepsilon(n)$ since there is a new neuron added in this situation.

4. $|\varepsilon(n)| > \delta$ and $\phi(n) < 0.1354$: This shows that the network has poor generalization and no neurons can cluster this input vector. The strategy for this case is to try improving the entire performance of the current network by enlarging some of the widths to cover the current input vector. Suppose $\phi(n)$ is the output of the $j$th EBF neuron. The width of the $i$th membership function that has the least value in this neuron should be enlarged to cover the input vector suitably:

$$\sigma_{ij}^{new} = k_\sigma \sigma_{ij}^{old} \tag{9.21}$$

where $k_\sigma$ is a predefined constant that is larger than 1. For simulations in this chapter, $k_\sigma = 1.12$. The width enlargement process is continued until $\phi(n) \geq 0.1354$. If the network still has bad generalization, that is, $|\varepsilon(n)| > \delta$, the old widths are maintained and a new EBF neuron is added to the structure using the same procedure as described in the scenario 3. The parameters of the new network also should be updated.

### 9.2.2.2 The Linear Parameter Learning Method. 
The SOFNN model could be rewritten as a special case of a linear regression model

$$d(t) = \sum_{i=1}^{M} p_i(t)\theta_i + \varepsilon(t) \tag{9.22}$$

where $d(t)$ is the desired output; $p_i(t)$ is the $i$th regressor, which is a fixed function of input vector $\mathbf{x_t} = [x_{1t} \quad x_{2t} \quad \dots \quad x_{rt}]$, that is, $p_i(t) = p_i(\mathbf{x_t})$; $\theta_i$ is the $i$th linear parameter; $\varepsilon(t)$ is the error signal; and $M$ is the dimension of the parameters, here, $M = u \times (r + 1)$.

Using (9.6) through (9.9), (9.22) can be written in matrix form at time $t = n$ as

$$\mathbf{D(n)} = \mathbf{P(n)}\Theta(\mathbf{n}) + \mathbf{E(n)} \tag{9.23}$$

where, $\mathbf{D(n)} = [d(1) \quad d(2) \quad \dots \quad d(n)]^T \in R^n; \mathbf{P(n)} = \Psi^T = [\mathbf{p}^T(1) \quad \mathbf{p}^T(2) \dots \mathbf{p}^T(n)]^T \in R^{n \times M}$, and $\mathbf{p}^T(\mathbf{i}) = [p_1(i) \quad p_2(i) \quad \dots \quad p_M(i)]$, $1 \leq i \leq n$; $\Theta(\mathbf{n}) = \mathbf{W}_2^T = [\theta_1 \quad \theta_2 \quad \dots \quad \theta_M]^T \in R^M$; and $\mathbf{E(n)} = [\varepsilon(1) \quad \varepsilon(2) \quad \dots \quad \varepsilon(n)]^T \in R^n$.

Using the linear least-squares method, the parameter of the regression model is given by

$$\hat{\Theta}(t) = [\mathbf{P}^T(t)\mathbf{P}(t)]^{-1}\mathbf{P}^T(t)\mathbf{D}(t) \tag{9.24}$$

Based on the RLS algorithm (Astrom & Wittenmark, 1995) at time $t$, an online weight learning algorithm is developed for the parameter learning. Define an $M \times M$ Hermitian matrix $\mathbf{Q}$ as

$$\mathbf{Q(t)} = [\mathbf{P}^T(t)\mathbf{P}(t)]^{-1} \tag{9.25}$$

Using the matrix $\mathbf{Q}$, the final update equations of the standard RLS algorithm can be written as

$$\mathbf{L(t)} = \mathbf{Q(t)}\mathbf{p(t)} = \mathbf{Q(t-1)}\mathbf{p(t)}[1 + \mathbf{p}^T(t)\mathbf{Q(t-1)}\mathbf{p(t)}]^{-1} \tag{9.26}$$

$$\mathbf{Q(t)} = [\mathbf{I} - \mathbf{L(t)}\mathbf{p}^T(t)]\mathbf{Q(t-1)} \tag{9.27}$$

$$\hat{\Theta}(\mathbf{t}) = \hat{\Theta}(\mathbf{t-1}) + \mathbf{L(t)}[d(t) - \mathbf{p}^T(t)\hat{\Theta}(\mathbf{t-1})] \tag{9.28}$$

In order to ensure convergence, a variation of the above standard recursive least-squares algorithm is used. At time $t$, when the estimation error $|e(t)|$ is less than the approximation error $|\varepsilon(t)|$, the parameters of the network are not adjusted and the structure is also not modified. Thus, the online learning algorithm is modified to:

$$\mathbf{L(t)} = \mathbf{Q(t)}\mathbf{p(t)} = \mathbf{Q(t-1)}\mathbf{p(t)}[1 + \mathbf{p}^T(t)\mathbf{Q(t-1)}\mathbf{p(t)}]^{-1} \tag{9.29}$$

$$\mathbf{Q(t)} = [\mathbf{I} - \alpha\mathbf{L(t)}\mathbf{p}^T(t)]\mathbf{Q(t-1)} \tag{9.30}$$

$$\hat{\Theta}(\mathbf{t}) = \hat{\Theta}(\mathbf{t-1}) + \alpha\mathbf{L(t)}[d(t) - \mathbf{p}^T(t)\hat{\Theta}(\mathbf{t-1})] \tag{9.31}$$

$$\alpha = \begin{cases} 1, & |e(t)| \geq |\varepsilon(t)| \\ 0, & |e(t)| < |\varepsilon(t)| \end{cases} \tag{9.32}$$

where $e(t) = [d(t) - \mathbf{p}^T(t)\hat{\Theta}(t-1)]$, $\quad \varepsilon(t) = [d(t) - \mathbf{p}^T(t)\hat{\Theta}(t)]$.

This modification ensures that the above modified algorithm guarantees an asymptotic convergence of the estimation error to zero and the convergence of the parameter to finite values. The proof of the convergence is detailed in Leng et al. (2004).

**9.2.2.3 Pruning a Neuron.** In the learning process, the network reaches a local minimum in error. The cost function is defined as the squared error, $E(\Theta, t) = \frac{1}{2}\sum_{i=1}^{t}[d(i) - \mathbf{p}^\mathbf{T}(i)\Theta]^2$. At time $t$, using the functional Taylor series of the error with respect to parameters $\Theta$, it can be shown that (Gang et al., 2004):

$$\Delta E(\Theta, t) \approx \frac{1}{2}\Delta\Theta^\mathbf{T}\mathbf{H}\Delta\Theta \qquad (9.33)$$

where

$$\mathbf{H} = \frac{\partial^2 E(\Theta, t)}{\partial\Theta^2} = \sum_{i=1}^{t}\mathbf{p}(i)\mathbf{p}^\mathbf{T}(i) = \mathbf{P}^\mathbf{T}(\mathbf{t})\mathbf{P}(\mathbf{t}) = \mathbf{Q}^{-1}(\mathbf{t}-1) + \mathbf{p}(\mathbf{t})\mathbf{p}^\mathbf{T}(\mathbf{t}) = \mathbf{Q}^{-1}(\mathbf{t})$$

$$(9.34)$$

Deleting a neuron is equivalent to setting the values of the related parameters to zero. The smaller the value of the change in the squared error, the less important is the neuron. Based on these twin concepts, the pruning method is designed using the following steps:

1. Calculate the training root mean squared error $E_{rmse}$ at time $t$.
2. Define the tolerance limit for the root mean squared error as $\lambda E_{rmse}$, where $\lambda$ is a predefined value and $0 < \lambda < 1$. For simulations in this chapter, $\lambda = 0.8$.
3. Calculate the change of the squared error $\Delta E$ for every neuron. The smaller the value of $\Delta E$ is, the less important is the neuron.
4. Choose $E = \max(\lambda E_{rmse}, k_{rmse})$, where $k_{rmse}$ is the expected training root mean squared error, which is a predefined value.
5. Select the least important neuron, delete this neuron, and then calculate the training root mean squared error $(E_{RMSE})$ of this new structure. If $E_{RMSE} < E$, this neuron should be deleted. Then do the same thing for the second least important neuron, and so on. Otherwise, stop and do not delete any more neurons.

**9.2.2.4 Combining Membership Functions and Rules.** If some membership functions are very similar to each other, they can be in the same group and combined into one new membership function as in Wang (1997). In the SOFNN algorithm, the membership functions that have the same center are combined into one new membership function. Consider $n$ membership functions that have the same center $c_s$ and different widths $\sigma_{s1}, \sigma_{s2}, \ldots\ldots, \sigma_{sn}$. The new membership function is defined with the center

$$c_{new} = c_s \qquad (9.35)$$

and the width

$$\sigma_{new} = \frac{\sigma_{s1} + \sigma_{s2} + \cdots \cdots + \sigma_{sn}}{n} \tag{9.36}$$

Owing to the elimination of redundant membership functions, fewer membership functions are generated and the complexity of the network is reduced. After combining similar membership functions, it is possible that some neurons have the same center vector and width vector. This requires replacing all these similar rules with a single rule. Suppose there are $i$ neurons having the same membership functions and the consequent parts are $\mathbf{W}_{21}, \mathbf{W}_{22}, \ldots, \mathbf{W}_{2i}$. The new consequence part $\mathbf{W}_{2new}$ can be combined into

$$\mathbf{W}_{2new} = \frac{\mathbf{W}_{21} + \mathbf{W}_{22} + \cdots + \mathbf{W}_{2i}}{i} \tag{9.37}$$

### 9.2.2.5 Computational Complexity.
After pruning or addition of a neuron, the structure has to be updated. This requires updating the matrix $\mathbf{Q(t)}$ using (9.25). The time required is therefore of the order $O(nUM^2)$ and the memory required is of the order $O(nM)$, where $n$ is the number of training data, $U$ is the number of times the structure needs to be updated by adding or pruning a neuron, and $M = u \times (r+1)$, in which $r$ is the number of input variables and $u$ is the number of EBF neurons in the network structure. Compared with other dynamic adaptation method–based algorithms used in DFNN (Er & Wu, 2002; Wu & Er, 2000) and GDFNN (Wu et al., 2001) that use the *linear least-squares (LLS)* algorithm in batch mode, the computational complexity of SOFNN is significantly reduced. In DFNN and GDFNN, the time required in the approach based on the LLS algorithm is of the order $O(n^2M^2)$. Usually, $n \gg U$, so the time required for SOFNN is better than that of DFNN and GDFNN.

A complete flowchart for the learning strategy, including the structure learning and parameter learning, is given in Figure 9.3.

## 9.3 CASE STUDIES

The performance of the SOFNN algorithm has been thoroughly evaluated through its application in dynamic system identification (Leng et al., 2005), function approximation, and time-series predictions required for foreign exchange forecasting (Leng et al., 2004) and devising an EEG-based brain-computer interface (Coyle et al., 2007). For purposes of comparative evaluation and demonstration here, the algorithm's application is illustrated in the following in two typical problems: multistep-ahead Mackey-Glass time-series prediction, and continuous foreign exchange forecasting.

***Example 1: Mackey-Glass (MG) Time-Series Predictions:*** The MG time series is created with the use of the MG time-delay differential equation, defined as

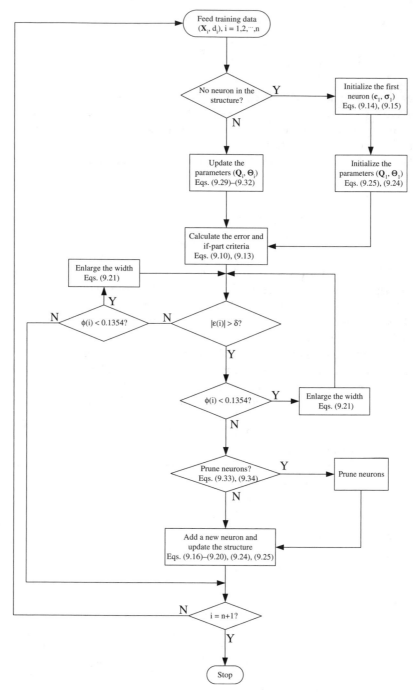

**Figure 9.3.** Flowchart for the learning strategy.

$$\frac{dx}{dt} = \frac{bx(t-\tau)}{1 + x^{10}(t-\tau)} - 0.1x(t) \qquad (9.38)$$

$$b = 0.2, \ \tau = 17, \ x(0) = 1.2$$

To obtain values at integer time points, the fourth-order Runge-Kutta method was used to find the numerical solution to the MG equation (9.38). Here, we assume that time step is 0.1. The task is to predict the values from input vectors for any value of the time. For the purpose of a comparative analysis, we list the performance of existing online learning models neural gas (Fritzke, 1995), RAN (Platt, 1991), and DENFIS (Kasabov & Song, 2002) applied for the same task and reported in (Kasabov, 2007). Here, the performance is evaluated in terms of the *nondimensional error index* (*NDEI*), which is defined as the *root mean-square error* (*RMSE*) divided by the standard deviation of the target series.

In order to obtain the multistep-ahead predictive model, 3000 input-target data between $t = 201$ and 3200 are used as the training data, and another 500 input-target data between $t = 5001$ and 5500 are used as the testing data. The prediction model is given by

$$\hat{x}(t+85) = f(x(t), x(t-6), x(t-12), x(t-18)) \qquad (9.39)$$

It is thus used to predict the value of the next, 85th step. There are four inputs and one output. The values of the training parameters are $\delta = 0.15$, $\sigma_0 = 0.1$, $k_{rmse} = 0.05$, $k_d(1) = 0.1, k_d(2) = 0.1, k_d(3) = 0.1, k_d(4) = 0.1$. The results are shown in Table 9.1 and Figures 9.4 to 9.8. One neuron is pruned in the learning process as seen in Figure 9.7. From Table 9.1, it is clear that the application of SOFNN results in a network of much smaller size and relatively favorable generalization performance. It is possible to further improve the generalization performance by selecting more stringent training parameters. Also, compared to DFNN and GDFNN approaches, the SOFNN provides favorable performance, when applied in chaotic time-series prediction as discussed in (Leng et al. 2004).

***Example 2:*** *Currency Exchange Rate Prediction:* A set of real data is applied in the investigation for the forecasting problem and to demonstrate the effectiveness of the proposed algorithm. The data represent the daily averaged exchange rates between the UK pound and the U.S. dollar during the period from January 3, 1986 to May 31, 2002. There

T A B L E 9.1. Results of Mackey-Glass Time-Series Prediction

| Methods | Number of Neurons/Fuzzy Rules | NDEI for Testing Data |
|---|---|---|
| Neural gas (Fritzke, 1995) | 1000 | 0.062 |
| RAN (Platt, 1991) | 113 | 0.373 |
| DENFIS (Kasabov & Song, 2002) | 58 | 0.276 |
| DENFIS (Kasabov & Song, 2002) | 883 | 0.042 |
| SOFNN | 12 | 0.2159 |

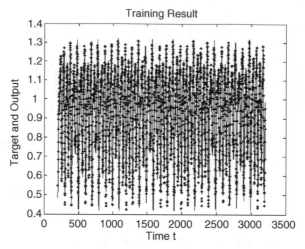

Figure 9.4. Training result (– desired output, · network output).

are 4281 observations. These data are divided into two sets. The first 3000 data are the training data and other data are the testing data. In the $N$-step-ahead predictive model

$$\hat{y}(t+N) = f(y(t), y(t-\tau), \ldots, y(t-(n-1)\tau)) \qquad (9.40)$$

defining $N = 6$, $\tau = 1$, and $n = 6$, the prediction model is given by

$$\hat{y}(t+6) = f(y(t), y(t-1), y(t-2), y(t-3), y(t-4), y(t-5)) \qquad (9.41)$$

This model thus has six inputs and one output and is used to predict the value of the next, 6th step. The values of the training parameters are $\delta = 0.05$, $\sigma_0 = 0.4$,

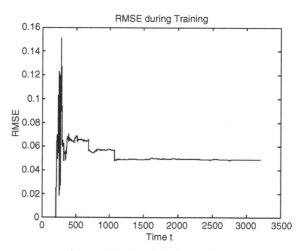

Figure 9.5. RMSE during training.

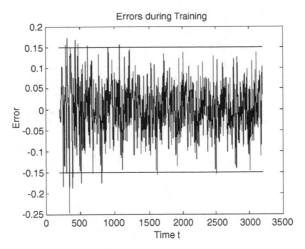

Figure 9.6. Errors during training.

$k_{rmse} = 0.01$, $k_d(1) = 0.2$, $k_d(2) = 0.2$, $k_d(3) = 0.2$, $k_d(4) = 0.2$, $k_d(5) = 0.2$, $k_d(5) = 0.2$, $k_d(6) = 0.2$. The results are shown in Figures 9.9 to 9.14. The fuzzy rules extracted during the training are listed in the appendix of the end of the chapter.

Thus, a 25-EBF-neuron network is generated. The RMSE of training data is 0.0266. The RMSE of testing data is 0.0183. Figure 9.15 shows a frequency distribution of prediction errors for 6-step-ahead prediction. This histogram gives a Gaussian distribution. The mean is $-0.0044$ and the standard deviation is 0.0177. As the average of errors is near 0 and the spread of errors is small, this figure shows that the obtained network is a valid model. The coefficient of correlation for the testing target and testing output is 0.9824.

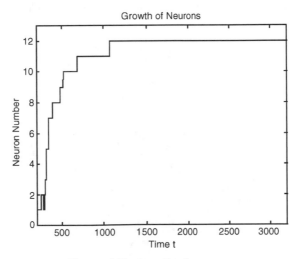

Figure 9.7. Growth of neurons.

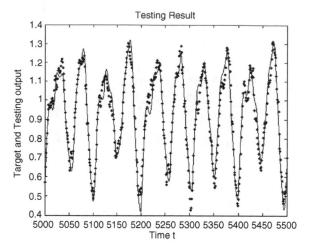

**Figure 9.8.** Testing result (– desired output, · network output).

It is, however, to be noted that currency exchange rate forecasting is a time-variant problem requiring predictions on the ongoing basis. To apply the SOFNN to a real time-variant problem, a sliding window can be used to decay the effect of the old training data when the new ones are available. One way of accomplishing this is discussed in the following.

The training data, the testing data, and the training parameters are the same as before. Based on the training model (41), a first-in, first-out (FIFO) sliding window is applied. Let $L_w$ be the width of this sliding window. When the $n$th $(n > L_w)$ observation enters this window, the oldest one is deleted from this window and the data in the window are thus continuously updated. Three different widths of FIFO sliding window are chosen to check the performances of the obtained networks. Table 9.2 presents the results of the obtained networks. Table 9.3 shows the results of statistical analysis for the prediction

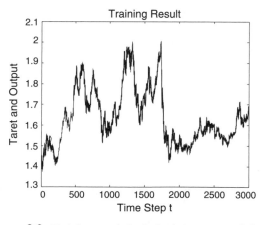

**Figure 9.9.** Training result (– desired data, · actual data).

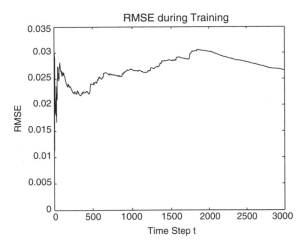

Figure 9.10. RMSE during training.

errors. The distribution of the testing errors for the sliding window whose width is 120 is depicted in Figure 9.16.

Considering the complexity and statistical analysis of the obtained networks using the three sliding windows, the sliding window whose width is 120 has the best coefficient of correlation and yields a smaller structure. This size of the width for the sliding window may thus be a satisfactory choice.

## 9.4 CONCLUSION

The chapter has discussed an algorithm for creating a self-organizing fuzzy neural network (SOFNN) that can identify a singleton or TS-type fuzzy model online. Based on

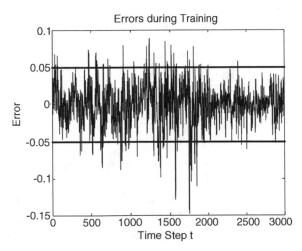

Figure 9.11. Errors during training.

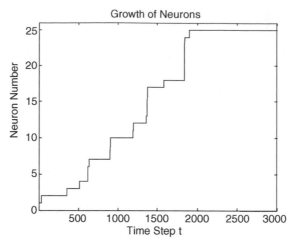

Figure 9.12. Growth of neurons.

the dynamic adaptation method, both the number of input–output space partitions and their corresponding fuzzy rule configurations are simultaneously and concurrently adapted by the SOFNN algorithm. The architecture of the SOFNN consists of ellipsoidal basis function (EBF) neurons with a center vector and a width vector in the first hidden layer. The EBF neuron represents the premise part of a fuzzy rule formed by AND logic (or $T$-norm) operating on Gaussian fuzzy membership functions. The elements of center vector and width vector of the EBF neuron are the centers and widths of the Gaussian membership functions. The structure learning approach combines the system error criterion and firing strength-based coverage criterion for adding new EBF neurons using

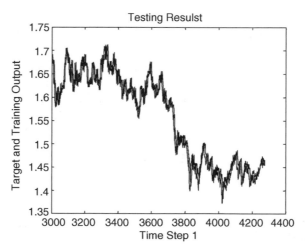

Figure 9.13. Testing result (– desired data, · actual data).

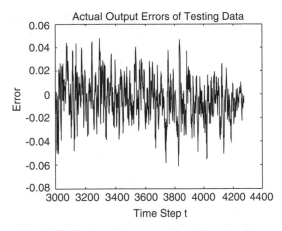

Figure 9.14. Actual output error of testing data.

concepts from statistical theory and the ε-completeness of fuzzy rules. The algorithm includes a pruning method that is based on the optimal brain surgeon (OBS) approach. This method is computationally very efficient for online implementation, as it does not involve any significant additional computation because it makes direct use of the

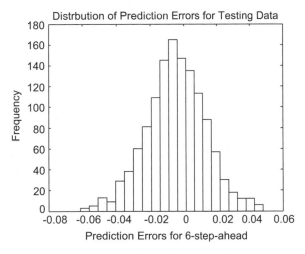

Figure 9.15. Distribution of prediction error for testing data.

TABLE 9.2. Results of the Obtained Networks with Different Windows

| Width of Windows | Number of Neurons | RMSE of Training | RMSE of Testing |
|---|---|---|---|
| 60 | 2 | 0.0221 | 0.0480 |
| 120 | 18 | 0.0229 | 0.0221 |
| 360 | 21 | 0.0247 | 0.0309 |
| No window | 25 | 0.0266 | 0.0183 |

TABLE 9.3. Results of Statistical Analysis for the Prediction Errors with Different Windows

| Width of Windows | Mean | Standard Deviation | Coefficient of Correlation |
|---|---|---|---|
| 60 | −0.0269 | 0.0397 | 0.9518 |
| 120 | −0.0085 | 0.0204 | 0.9804 |
| 360 | −0.0141 | 0.0275 | 0.9722 |
| No window | −0.0044 | 0.0177 | 0.9824 |

Hermitian matrix obtained as a part of the proposed RLS algorithm. A modified recursive least-squares algorithm is derived through the proof of convergence. The proofs of the convergence of the estimation error and the linear network parameters provide conditions for guaranteed convergence in the proposed RLS parameter learning algorithm. Since the new EBF neurons are created based on both the approximation error and the coverage criteria, the SOFNN architecture is less sensitive to the sequence of training data pattern. Moreover, the SOFNN algorithm is superior in time complexity to the other dynamic adaptation method–based algorithms. Through several case studies, it has been shown that the SOFNN algorithm is suitable for application to the area of function approximation with less effort from the designer and has the capability of self-organization to determine the structure of the network automatically. It results in models that provide superior accuracy while ensuring very compact structure.

One difficulty with the SOFNN algorithm is that it has a number of free training parameters. However, based on detailed experimental analysis (Leng, 2004), a general rule for selecting these training parameters can be suggested. The smaller the error tolerance ($\delta$) and the expected training RMSE ($k_{rmse}$), the better the performance of the resulting network, but the more expensive the structure. By choosing about 10–20% of the input data range as the distance threshold ($k_d$), good performance is obtained in most cases. Usually, the smaller the percentage, the more EBF neurons are generated, and

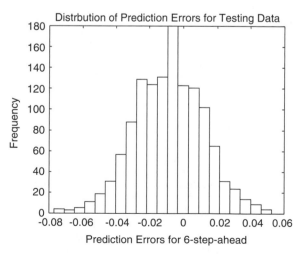

Figure 9.16. Distribution of prediction error for testing data (width is 120).

the performance of the obtained network may be better. Generally, the initial width $(\sigma_0)$ of about twice the smallest value of the input distance thresholds is observed to be an appropriate value. Free parameters can also be obtained through a detailed sensitivity analysis of all of the free parameters, as discussed in Mascioli et al. (2000), wherein a method to measure the automaticity of an algorithm by relying on its sensitivity to the training parameters is outlined. The goal is to find how sensitive the performance is to changes in the predefined parameters. For example, if a slight change in a free parameter results in a large change in the prediction error, then this parameter is critical. This approach has been successfully investigated while applying SOFNN for identifying neural time-series prediction models needed in devising an EEG-based brain–computer interface (Coyle et al., 2006). Further work is ongoing to enhance the autonomy of the algorithm by making the model identification process more robust against outliers and noisy signals.

## 9.5 APPENDIX

The following fuzzy rules are extracted from the training data to create a 6-step-ahead currency exchange prediction model.

*Rule 1.* If $y(t)$ is $A(1.4380, 0.4000)$ and $y(t-1)$ is $A(0, 1.7454)$ and $y(t-2)$ is $A(0, 1.7454)$ and $y(t-3)$ is $A(0, 1.7454)$ and $y(t-4)$ is $A(0, 1.5584)$ and $y(t-5)$ is $A(0, 1.5584)$, then $y(t+6) = 2.9702 - 1.6946y(t) - 1.6159y(t-1) - 2.5043y(t-2) + 4.6495y(t-3) + 3.8791y(t-4) + 4.6954y(t-5)$.

*Rule 2.* If $y(t)$ is $A(1.4380, 0.4000)$ and $y(t-1)$ is $A(1.4178, 1.4178)$ and $y(t-2)$ is $A(1.4100, 1.4100)$ and $y(t-3)$ is $A(1.4092, 1.4092)$ and $y(t-4)$ is $A(1.4120, 1.4120)$ and $y(t-5)$ is $A(1.3940, 1.3940)$, then $y(t+6) = 2.0723 + 7.2870y(t) + 4.0797y(t-1) - 0.9831y(t-2) - 3.6191y(t-3) - 1.9742y(t-4) - 8.0081y(t-5)$.

*Rule 3.* If $y(t)$ is $A(1.6820, 0.2440)$ and $y(t-1)$ is $A(1.6810, 0.2632)$ and $y(t-2)$ is $A(1.6805, 0.2705)$ and $y(t-3)$ is $A(1.6693, 0.2601)$ and $y(t-4)$ is $A(1.6675, 0.2555)$ and $y(t-5)$ is $A(1.6615, 0.2675)$, then $y(t+6) = 0.4681 - 0.6359y(t) - 1.1152y(t-1) - 0.2191y(t-2) - 0.6299y(t-3) + 0.5832y(t-4) + 2.0233y(t-5)$.

*Rule 4.* If $y(t)$ is $A(1.8870, 0.2050)$ and $y(t-1)$ is $A(1.6810, 0.2632)$ and $y(t-2)$ is $A(1.6805, 0.2705)$ and $y(t-3)$ is $A(1.6693, 0.2601)$ and $y(t-4)$ is $A(1.6675, 0.2555)$ and $y(t-5)$ is $A(1.6615, 0.2675)$, then $y(t+6) = -1.4851 - 4.8189y(t) - 0.7613y(t-1) + 1.9410y(t-2) + 2.0636y(t-3) + 4.7936y(t-4) + 1.7146y(t-5)$.

*Rule 5.* If $y(t)$ is $A(1.8870, 0.2050)$ and $y(t-1)$ is $A(1.6810, 0.2632)$ and $y(t-2)$ is $A(1.6805, 0.2705)$ and $y(t-3)$ is $A(1.6693, 0.2601)$ and $y(t-4)$ is $A(1.6675, 0.2555)$ and $y(t-5)$ is $A(1.8665, 0.2050)$, then $y(t+6) = -0.1423 - 1.4870y(t) + 1.6411y(t-1) + 0.7526y(t-2) + 2.1964y(t-3) + 0.4385y(t-4) - 2.8673y(t-5)$.

*Rule 6.* If $y(t)$ is $A(1.8870, 0.2050)$ and $y(t-1)$ is $A(1.6810, 0.2632)$ and $y(t-2)$ is $A(1.6805, 0.2705)$ and $y(t-3)$ is $A(1.6693, 0.2601)$ and $y(t-4)$ is $A(1.8685, 0.2010)$ and $y(t-5)$ is $A(1.8665, 0.2050)$, then $y(t+6) = 0.3998 - 2.5860y(t) + 2.2463y(t-1) + 1.4929y(t-2) + 1.3186y(t-3) - 1.2658y(t-4) - 4.1081y(t-5)$.

*Rule 7.* If $y(t)$ is $A(1.6820, 0.2440)$ and $y(t-1)$ is $A(1.6810, 0.2632)$ and $y(t-2)$ is $A(1.6805, 0.2705)$ and $y(t-3)$ is $A(1.6693, 0.2601)$ and $y(t-4)$ is $A(1.8685, 0.2010)$ and $y(t-5)$ is $A(1.8665, 0.2050)$, then $y(t+6) = -2.3948 - 1.6585y(t) + 1.6235y(t-1) - 3.1106y(t-2) - 4.1815y(t-3) + 1.0034y(t-4) + 5.2777y(t-5)$.

*Rule 8.* If $y(t)$ is $A(1.6820, 0.2440)$ and $y(t-1)$ is $A(1.4178, 1.4178)$ and $y(t-2)$ is $A(1.6805, 0.2705)$ and $y(t-3)$ is $A(1.6693, 0.2601)$ and $y(t-4)$ is $A(1.6675, 0.2555)$ and $y(t-5)$ is $A(1.6615, 0.2675)$, then $y(t+6) = 2.4617 - 1.6756y(t) - 1.7724y(t-1) - 0.3653y(t-2) + 0.5775y(t-3) + 1.8644y(t-4) + 2.4504y(t-5)$.

*Rule 9.* If $y(t)$ is $A(1.4380, 0.4000)$ and $y(t-1)$ is $A(1.6810, 0.2632)$ and $y(t-2)$ is $A(1.6805, 0.2705)$ and $y(t-3)$ is $A(1.6693, 0.2601)$ and $y(t-4)$ is $A(1.6675, 0.2555)$ and $y(t-5)$ is $A(1.6615, 0.2675)$, then $y(t+6) = 3.8904 + 3.6036y(t) + 0.6532y(t-1) - 0.3136y(t-2) - 0.0174y(t-3) - 1.1595y(t-4) - 0.0073y(t-5)$.

*Rule 10.* If $y(t)$ is $A(1.4380, 0.4000)$ and $y(t-1)$ is $A(1.4178, 1.4178)$ and $y(t-2)$ is $A(1.6805, 0.2705)$ and $y(t-3)$ is $A(1.6693, 0.2601)$ and $y(t-4)$ is $A(1.6675, 0.2555)$ and $y(t-5)$ is $A(1.6615, 0.2675)$, then $y(t+6) = 4.3341 + 3.0301y(t) + 0.3956y(t-1) - 1.7438y(t-2) - 1.4548y(t-3) - 2.3981y(t-4) - 2.7462y(t-5)$.

*Rule 11.* If $y(t)$ is $A(1.8870, 0.2050)$ and $y(t-1)$ is $A(1.6810, 0.2632)$ and $y(t-2)$ is $A(1.6805, 0.2705)$ and $y(t-3)$ is $A(1.8715, 0.2022)$ and $y(t-4)$ is $A(1.8685, 0.2010)$ and $y(t-5)$ is $A(1.8665, 0.2050)$, then $y(t+6) = 1.3026 + 0.3954y(t) + 4.4722y(t-1) + 3.7180y(t-2) + 2.1874y(t-3) - 2.2567y(t-4) - 2.6959y(t-5)$.

*Rule 12.* If $y(t)$ is $A(1.8870, 0.2050)$ and $y(t-1)$ is $A(1.8990, 0.2180)$ and $y(t-2)$ is $A(1.8820, 0.2015)$ and $y(t-3)$ is $A(1.8715, 0.2022)$ and $y(t-4)$ is $A(1.8685, 0.2010)$ and $y(t-5)$ is $A(1.8665, 0.2050)$, then $y(t+6) = -7.2540 - 2.1435y(t) - 7.1385y(t-1) + 0.4498y(t-2) + 6.7225y(t-3) + 2.2576y(t-4) + 9.7282y(t-5)$.

*Rule 13.* If $y(t)$ is $A(1.6820, 0.2440)$ and $y(t-1)$ is $A(1.6810, 0.2632)$ and $y(t-2)$ is $A(1.6805, 0.2705)$ and $y(t-3)$ is $A(1.8715, 0.2022)$ and $y(t-4)$ is $A(1.8685, 0.2010)$ and $y(t-5)$ is $A(1.8665, 0.2050)$, then $y(t+6) = -1.2048 - 0.6483y(t) + 3.3214y(t-1) - 2.0228y(t-2) - 3.7937y(t-3) + 0.0485y(t-4) + 5.1957y(t-5)$.

*Rule 14.* If $y(t)$ is $A(1.8870, 0.2050)$ and $y(t-1)$ is $A(1.6810, 0.2632)$ and $y(t-2)$ is $A(1.8820, 0.2015)$ and $y(t-3)$ is $A(1.6693, 0.2601)$ and $y(t-4)$ is $A(1.8685, 0.2010)$ and $y(t-5)$ is $A(1.8665, 0.2050)$, then $y(t+6) =$

2.0090 − 0.8164$y(t)$ + 2.0942$y(t − 1)$ + 2.4415$y(t − 2)$ + 4.1190$y(t − 3)$ + 0.4264$y(t − 4)$ − 2.1817$y(t − 5)$.

*Rule 15.* If $y(t)$ is $A(1.8870, 0.2050)$ and $y(t − 1)$ is $A(1.6810, 0.2632)$ and $y(t − 2)$ is $A(1.8820, 0.2015)$ and $y(t − 3)$ is $A(1.8715, 0.2022)$ and $y(t − 4)$ is $A(1.8685, 0.2010)$ and $y(t − 5)$ is $A(1.8665, 0.2050)$, then $y(t + 6) =$ −0.3215 − 1.0764$y(t)$ + 0.0705$y(t−1)$ + 0.1660$y(t − 2)$ + 0.7547$y(t − 3)$ − 4.2133$y(t − 4)$ − 3.6794$y(t − 5)$.

*Rule 16.* If $y(t)$ is $A(1.8870, 0.2050)$ and $y(t − 1)$ is $A(1.8990, 0.2180)$ and $y(t − 2)$ is $A(1.6805, 0.2705)$ and $y(t − 3)$ is $A(1.8715, 0.2022)$ and $y(t − 4)$ is $A(1.8685, 0.2010)$ and $y(t − 5)$ is $A(1.8665, 0.2050)$, then $y(t + 6) = −0.6878$ − 4.1172$y(t)$ − 4.0004$y(t−1)$ + 2.6210$y(t − 2)$ + 4.6924$y(t − 3)$ − 0.8018$y×$ $(t − 4)$ + 1.2282$y(t − 5)$.

*Rule 17.* If $y(t)$ is $A(1.6820, 0.2440)$ and $y(t − 1)$ is $A(1.6810, 0.2632)$ and $y(t − 2)$ is $A(1.8820, 0.2015)$ and $y(t − 3)$ is $A(1.8715, 0.2022)$ and $y(t − 4)$ is $A(1.8685, 0.2010)$ and $y(t − 5)$ is $A(1.8665, 0.2050)$, then $y(t + 6) =$ 1.0696 + 2.8785$y(t)$ + 4.9632$y(t − 1)$ + 0.0680$y(t − 2)$ − 1.9631$y(t − 3)$ − 0.1113$y(t − 4)$ − 0.2044$y(t − 5)$.

*Rule 18.* If $y(t)$ is $A(1.6820, 0.2440)$ and $y(t − 1)$ is $A(1.8990, 0.2180)$ and $y(t − 2)$ is $A(1.8820, 0.2015)$ and $y(t − 3)$ is $A(1.8715, 0.2022)$ and $y(t − 4)$ is $A(1.8685, 0.2010)$ and $y(t − 5)$ is $A(1.8665, 0.2050)$, then $y(t + 6) =$ 2.4530 + 2.6305$y(t)$ − 0.1678$y(t − 1)$ − 0.5804$y(t − 2)$ − 0.0308$y(t − 3)$ − 2.0911$y(t − 4)$ − 4.9579$y(t − 5)$.

*Rule 19.* If $y(t)$ is $A(1.4380, 0.4000)$ and $y(t − 1)$ is $A(1.4178, 1.4178)$ and $y(t − 2)$ is $A(1.4100, 1.4100)$ and $y(t − 3)$ is $A(1.6693, 0.2601)$ and $y(t − 4)$ is $A(1.4120, 1.4120)$ and $y(t − 5)$ is $A(1.6615, 0.2675)$, then $y(t + 6) = − 0.8160 − 0.8992y(t)$ + 1.1975$y(t − 1)$ − 0.0167$y(t − 2)$ + 1.2892$y(t − 3)$ + 2.8390$y(t − 4)$ + 0.3297$y(t − 5)$.

*Rule 20.* If $y(t)$ is $A(1.4380, 0.4000)$ and $y(t − 1)$ is $A(1.4178, 1.4178)$ and $y(t − 2)$ is $A(1.4100, 1.4100)$ and $y(t − 3)$ is $A(1.6693, 0.2601)$ and $y(t − 4)$ is $A(1.6675, 0.2555)$ and $y(t − 5)$ is $A(1.6615, 0.2675)$, then $y(t + 6) =$ 3.5789 + 1.8287$y(t)$ + 0.6149$y(t − 1)$ − 2.0083$y(t − 2)$ − 1.4587$y(t − 3)$ − 2.5421$y(t − 4)$ − 3.2149$y(t − 5)$.

*Rule 21.* If $y(t)$ is $A(1.4380, 0.4000)$ and $y(t − 1)$ is $A(1.6810, 0.2632)$ and $y(t − 2)$ is $A(1.4100, 1.4100)$ and $y(t − 3)$ is $A(1.4092, 1.4092)$ and $y(t − 4)$ is $A(1.6675, 0.2555)$ and $y(t − 5)$ is $A(1.6615, 0.2675)$, then $y(t + 6) =$ 4.5656 − 1.2014$y(t)$ − 1.6341$y(t − 1)$ − 2.3921$y(t − 2)$ − 1.2630$y(t − 3)$ − 0.1076$y(t − 4)$ + 0.7582$y(t − 5)$.

*Rule 22.* If $y(t)$ is $A(1.4380, 0.4000)$ and $y(t − 1)$ is $A(1.4178, 1.4178)$ and $y(t − 2)$ is $A(1.6805, 0.2705)$ and $y(t − 3)$ is $A(1.4092, 1.4092)$ and $y(t − 4)$ is $A(1.4120, 1.4120)$ and $y(t − 5)$ is $A(1.6615, 0.2675)$, then $y(t + 6) =$ − 0.0823 − 1.8718$y(t)$ + 0.0403$y(t − 1)$ − 0.5319$y(t − 2)$ − 0.3908$y(t − 3)$ + 3.7132$y(t − 4)$ + 0.5153$y(t − 5)$.

*Rule 23.* If $y(t)$ is $A(1.4380, 0.4000)$ and $y(t-1)$ is $A(1.4178, 1.4178)$ and $y(t-2)$ is $A(1.4100, 1.4100)$ and $y(t-3)$ is $A(1.6693, 0.2601)$ and $y(t-4)$ is $A(1.4120, 1.4120)$ and $y(t-5)$ is $A(1.3940, 1.3940)$, then $y(t+6) = -1.2382 - 5.5875y(t) - 1.8131y(t-1) - 1.3073y(t-2) - 0.0610y(t-3) + 3.6037y(t-4) + 7.3688y(t-5)$.

*Rule 24.* If $y(t)$ is $A(1.4380, 0.4000)$ and $y(t-1)$ is $A(1.4178, 1.4178)$ and $y(t-2)$ is $A(1.4100, 1.4100)$ and $y(t-3)$ is $A(1.4092, 1.4092)$ and $y(t-4)$ is $A(1.6675, 0.2555)$ and $y(t-5)$ is $A(1.6615, 0.2675)$, then $y(t+6) = 0.1478 + 2.0104y(t) + 3.3299y(t-1) + 1.0922y(t-2) + 0.1780y(t-3) + 0.3262y(t-4) - 2.8788y(t-5)$.

*Rule 25.* If $y(t)$ is $A(1.4380, 0.4000)$ and $y(t-1)$ is $A(1.4178, 1.4178)$ and $y(t-2)$ is $A(1.6805, 0.2705)$ and $y(t-3)$ is $A(1.6693, 0.2601)$ and $y(t-4)$ is $A(1.6675, 0.2555)$ and $y(t-5)$ is $A(1.3940, 1.3940)$, then $y(t+6) = 2.2146 - 4.9791y(t) - 2.9356y(t-1) - 1.9422y(t-2) - 0.0269y(t-3) + 2.4106y(t-4) + 9.1815y(t-5)$.

## 9.6 REFERENCES

P. Angelov, D. Filev, (2004). "An Approach to On-line Identification of Takagi-Sugeno Fuzzy Models," *IEEE Trans. on Systems, Man, and Cybernetics, Part B: Cybernetics*, Vol. 35, No. 3, pp. 275–289.

K. J. Astrom, B. Wittenmark, (1995). *Adaptive Control*, 2nd ed. Addison-Wesley.

M. Berthold, K. P. Huber, (1999). Constructing Fuzzy Graphs from Examples," *Int. J. Intelligent Data Analysis*, 3, pp. 37–53.

J. J. Buckley, Y. Hayashi, (1994). "Fuzzy Neural Networks: A Survey," *Fuzzy Sets & Systems*, 66, pp. 1–13.

C. T. Chao, Y. J. Chen, C. C. Teng,(1995). "Simplification of Fuzzy-Neural Systems Using Similarity Analysis." *IEEE Trans. on Systems, Man, and Cybernetics, Part B: Cybernetics*, 26, pp. 344–354.

S. Chen, C.F.N. Cowan, Grant P. M.,(1991). "Orthogonal Least Squares Learning Algorithm for Radial Basis Function Network," *IEEE Trans. on Neural Networks*, 2, pp. 302–309.

K.B. Cho, B. H. Wang, (1996). "Radial Basis Function Based Adaptive Fuzzy Systems and Their Applications to Identification and Prediction," *Fuzzy & Systems*, 83, pp. 325–339.

D. H. Coyle, G. Prasad, T. M. McGinnity, (2006), "Enhancing Autonomy and Computational Efficiency of the Self-Organizing Fuzzy Neural Network for a Brain Computer Interface." Proc. 2006 *IEEE International Conference on Fuzzy Systems, World Congress on Computational Intelligence*, Ontario, Canada, pp. 2270–2277.

M. J. Er, S. Wu, (2002). "A Fast Learning Algorithm for Parsimonious Fuzzy Neural Systems," *Fuzzy Sets & Systems*, 126, pp. 337–351.

G. F. Franklin, J. D. Powell, M. L. Workman, (1990). *Digital Control of Dynamic Systems*, 2nd ed. Addison-Wesley.

B. Fritzke, (1995), "A Growing Neural Gas Network Learns Topologies," *Adv. Neural Inform. Processing System*, Vol. 7.

J. Gonzalez, I. Rojas, H. Pomares, J. Ortega, A. Prieto, (2002). "A New Clustering Technique for Function Approximation," *IEEE Transactions on Neural Networks*, 13, pp. 132–142.

B. Hassibi, D. G. Stork, (1993). "Second-Order Derivatives for Network Pruning: Optimal Brain Surgeon," *Advances in Neural Information Processing*, 4, pp. 164–171. Morgan Kaufman.

K. Hornik, M. Stinchcombe, H. White, (1989). "Multilayer Feedforward Networks Are Universal Approximators," *Neural Networks*, 2, pp. 359–366.

J. S. R. Jang,, (1993). "ANFIS: Adaptive-Network-Based Fuzzy Inference System," *IEEE Trans. on Systems, Man, and Cybernetics*, 23, pp. 665–684.

N. Kasabov, (2007). *Evolving Connectionist Systems: The Knowledge Engineering Approach*, 2nd ed. London: Spinger-Verlag.

N. Kasabov, Q. Song, (2002). "DENFIS: Dynamic Evolving Neural-Fuzzy Inference System and Its Applications to Time-Series Predictions," *Transactions on Fuzzy Systems*, Vol. 10, No. 2, pp. 144–154.

F. Klawonn, A. Keller, (1998). "Grid Clustering for Generating Fuzzy Rules." European Congress on Intelligent Techniques and Soft Computing (EUFIT98), Aachen, Germany, pp. 1365–1369.

C. C. Lee, (1990). "Fuzzy Logic in Control Systems: Fuzzy Logic Controller—Parts I and II," *IEEE Trans. on Systems, Man, and Cybernetics*, 20, pp. 404–435.

G. Leng, (2004). "Algorithmic Developments for Self-Organising Fuzzy Neural Networks," PhD thesis, University of Ulster, UK.

G. Leng, G. Prasad, McGinnity T. M. (2004). "An On-line Algorithm for Creating Self-Organising Fuzzy Neural Networks," *Neural Networks*, Vol. 17, pp. 1477–1493, Elsevier.

G. Leng, T. M. McGinnity, Prasad G. (2005). "An Approach for On-Line Extraction of Fuzzy Rules Using a Self-Organising Fuzzy Neural Network," *Fuzzy Sets & Systems*, Vol. 150, pp. 211–243, Elsevier.

C. S. Leung, K. W. Wong, P. F. Sum, L. W. Chan, (2001). A Pruning Method for the Recursive Least Squared Algorithm," *Neural Networks*, 14, pp. 147–174.

C. T. Lin, (1995). "A Neural Fuzzy Control System with Structure and Parameter Learning," *Fuzzy Sets & Systems*, 70, pp. 183–212.

Mascioli, F.M.F., G. Martinelli, (1998). "A Constructive Approach to Neuro-Fuzzy Networks," *Signal Processing*, 64, pp. 347–358.

F.M.F. Mascioli, A. Rizzi, M. Panella, G. Martinelli, (2000). Scale-Based Approach to Hierarchical Fuzzy Clustering," *Signal Processing*, 80, pp. 1001–1016.

S. Mitra, Y. Hayashi, (2000). "Neuro-Fuzzy Rule Generation: Survey in Soft Computing Framework," *IEEE Trans. on Neural Networks*, 11, pp. 748–768.

D. Nauck, (1997). "Neuro-Fuzzy Systems: Review and Prospects." *Proc. Fifth European Congress on Intelligent Techniques and Soft Computing (EUFIT'97)*, pp. 1044–1053.

D. Nauck, R. Kruse, (1999). "Neuro-Fuzzy Systems for Function Approximation," *Fuzzy Sets & Systems*, 101, pp. 261–271.

J. Platt, (1991). "A Resource Allocating Network for Function Interpolation," *Neural Comp.*, Vol. 3, pp. 213–225.

A. Rizzi, M. Panella, Mascioli, F.M.F. (2002). "Adaptive Resolution Min-Max Classifiers," *IEEE Trans. on Neural Networks*, 13, pp. 402–414.

I. Rojas, H. Pomares, J. Ortega, A. Prieto, (2000). "Self-Organized Fuzzy System Generation from Training Examples," *IEEE Trans. on Fuzzy Systems*, 8, pp. 23–36.

P. K. Simpson, (1992). "Fuzzy Min-Max Neural Networks—Part 1: Classification," *IEEE Trans. on Neural Networks*, 3, pp. 776–786.

P. K. Simpson, (1993). "Fuzzy Min-Max Neural Networks—Part 1: Classification," *IEEE Trans. on Fuzzy Systems*, 1, pp. 32–45.

T. Takagi, M. Sugeno, (1985). "Fuzzy Identification of Systems and Its Applications to Modeling and Control," *IEEE Trans. on Systems, Man, and Cybernetics*, 15, 116–132.

L. X. Wang, (1992). "Fuzzy Systems are Universal Approximators." *Proc. Int. Conf. Fuzzy Syst.*, pp. 1163–1170, 1992.

W. J. Wang, (1997). "New Similarity Measures on Fuzzy Sets and on Elements," *Fuzzy Sets & Systems*, 85, pp. 305–309.

J. S. Wang, Lee, C.S.G. (2001). "Efficient Neuro-Fuzzy Control Systems for Autonomous Underwater Vehicle Control." *Proc. 2001 IEEE Int. Conf. on Robotics and Automation*, pp. 2986–2991.

S. Wu, M. J. Er, (2000). "Dynamic Fuzzy Neural Networks: A Novel Approach to Function Approximation," *IEEE Trans. on Systems, Man, and Cybernetics, Part B: Cybernetics*, 30, pp. 358–364.

S. Wu, M. J. Er, Y. Gao, (2001). "A Fast Approach for Automatic Generation of Fuzzy Rules by Generalized Dynamic Fuzzy Neural Networks," *IEEE Trans. on Fuzzy Systems*, 9, pp. 578–594.

L. A. Zadeh, (1994). "Soft Computing and Fuzzy Logic," *IEEE Soft.*

# 10

# DATA FUSION VIA FISSION FOR THE ANALYSIS OF BRAIN DEATH

L. Li, Y. Saito, D. Looney, T. Tanaka, J. Cao, D. Mandic

**Abstract:** Information *fusion* via signal *fission* is addressed in the framework of empirical mode decomposition (EMD) to determine brain death in deep coma patients. In this way, a general nonlinear and nonstationary brain signal is decomposed into its oscillatory components (fission); the components of interest are then combined in an ad-hoc or automated fashion in order to provide greater knowledge about a process in hand (fusion). This chapter illustrates how the *fusion via fission* methodology can be used to retain components of interest in electroencephalography (EEG), thus highlighting the absence or presence of brain death. Additionally, it is shown how complex extensions of the algorithm can be used to detect phase synchronization by simulations and applications to EEG signals.

## 10.1 INTRODUCTION

As modern society evolves, there is an ever-growing requirement for more focused information rather than superfluous data. The ability to take measurements and gather data is generally well developed. But optimizing data gathering and information production, which is vital for economic and social progress, are in their infancy. For example, it is difficult via conventional means to characterize signals that display highly

*Evolving Intelligent Systems: Methodology and Applications,* Edited by Plamen Angelov, Dimitar P. Filev, and Nikola Kasabov
Copyright © 2010 Institute of Electrical and Electronics Engineers

complex nonlinear and nonstationary behavior caused by either the measurement equipment or the interconnection of data from different sources.

Data analysis methods, which are not limited to linear, deterministic, or stationary signals, are needed for the analysis of real-world data. Recently, *information fusion via fission* has been realized [15] by decomposing input signals into a set of their components using *empirical mode decomposition* (*EMD*) (originally introduced in [10]) and then fusing these components using suitable criteria. In this chapter, we apply this methodology to the area of analyzing electroencephalogram (EEG) data recorded from the brain. We illustrate, through experimental results, how the characteristics of the underlying data can be extracted via EMD.

## 10.2 DATA FUSION VIA FISSION

Time-domain analysis illustrates amplitude changes with time. However, by examining data in the frequency domain, it is often possible to extract more useful information, especially when examining signals obtained from the brain. Fourier-based analysis is the traditional data analysis method and regarded as the best-established tool for the processing of linear and stationary data. In the real world, data are nonlinear and nonstationary, for which Fourier analysis is not well suited, it is required to resort to time-frequency analysis techniques such as the *short time fourier transform* (*STFT*) and *wavelet transform* (*WT*). Despite the power of these techniques, they still rely on some kind of projection on a set of predefined bases; this makes some areas of their application, particularly when focusing on high-frequency content, rather limited [10]. Therefore, empirical mode decomposition [10] was first introduced as a fully data-driven technique that makes no assumptions on the underlying data being analyzing. It decomposes the signal into a set of zero mean components, which are called *intrinsic mode functions* (*IMFs*).

EMD has enormous appeal for nonlinear and nonstationary signals because it makes no prior assumptions about the data and, as such, it belongs to the class of *exploratory data analysis* (*EDA*) techniques [20]. The original algorithm was successfully applied to a number of problems that require high resolution but are separable in the time–frequency domain, such as in ocean engineering [6], biomedical signal processing [18] and seismics [23]. Although EMD has primarily been used for time–frequency analysis, it is clear that the IMFs represent the oscillation modes embedded in the data and therefore has potential within the framework of data fusion and feature extraction [12, 13].

Data and information fusion is the approach whereby data from multiple sensors or components are combined to achieve improved accuracies and more specific inferences that could not be achieved by the use of only a single sensor [9]. Its principles have been employed in a number of research fields, including information theory, signal processing, and computing [7, 9, 21, 22]. Recent work [14] demonstrates that the decomposition nature of EMD provides a unifying framework for information fusion via fission, where fission is the phenomenon by which observed information is decomposed into a set of its components. More specifically, the stages of *signal processing, feature extraction*, and *situation assessment* from the waterfall model (a well-established fusion model given in Figure 10.1) can all be achieved by EMD.

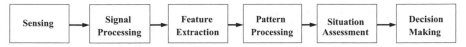

Figure 10.1. *Waterfall model* of information fusion.

A simple example of the fission and feature extraction properties of EMD is its ability to separate original input components from a signal composed of linear sinusoids, as shown in Figure 10.2. The signal "U" shown at the top of the figure is a linear sum of three sinusoids, with individual frequencies of 0.1 Hz, 1 Hz, and 10 Hz, represented below as:

$$U(t) = \sin(0.2\pi t) + \sin(2\pi t) + \sin(20\pi t) \qquad (10.1)$$

The above signal is decomposed into its IMFs with EMD. The IMFs are denoted by $C_i(k)$, $i = 1, 2, \ldots, M$ in the subsequent panels on Figure 10.2. Note that the IMFs represent the original sinusoidal components used to create U. Most importantly, though, EMD has distinct advantages over other decomposition techniques in analyzing real-world signals as it does not make unrealistic assumptions about the data.

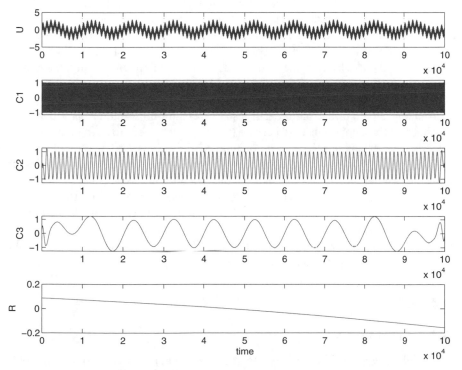

Figure 10.2. Example of data fission via EMD.

*Principal component analysis (PCA)*, for example, assumes linearity and stationarity. As a result, PCA performs poorly when processing real-world signals that display nonlinear and nonstationary behavior such as biomedical data [18]. Similar criticisms can be made of *independent component analysis (ICA)*, which requires that input components be statistically independent. This issue is highlighted by the ability of EMD to decouple noisy recordings in the problem of blood volume estimation [18].

## 10.3 BRAIN DEATH DETECTION

The investigation of the brain's consciousness, especially the state of brain death, is highly important. Brain death is currently used as a definition for death among the legal and medical communities. It is for this reason that brain death needs to be determined precisely so as not to cause patients potential risk.

The legal definition of brain death is an irreversible loss of forebrain and brainstem functions [2]; however, it is very difficult to realize brain death diagnosis precisely due to clinical difficulties. Specialized personnel and technology are needed to perform a series of tests that are expensive and time consuming and can sometimes bring risk to the patient. In this chapter, brain death means an initial diagnosis.

Some of the tests require that medical care instruments be removed. Further, some tests require that the patient be transported out of the intensive care unit (ICU) and others (confirmatory test) need to be performed several times at an interval of up to 10 hours and can take as long as 30 minutes. After initial documentation of the clinical signs of brain death, repetition of clinical testing is required by a number of countries. Although the diagnosis criteria are different from country to country, these tests can bring the patient a potential medical risk of less medical care due to the requirements of implementing test and stress to the already compromised organ [16].

To overcome these difficulties, a preliminary EEG test has been proposed [3] to determine whether further brain death tests, especially those requiring patients to be disconnected from important medical care (the respirator), need to be implemented. This is clearly of great benefit as it reduces potential complications and stress for patients. The test is not trivial, however, as interference to the EEG signal is caused by various other medical instruments in the ICU. As a result, these interferences can contaminate the EEG signal we want to investigate. In the past, ICA has been used to perform the preliminary test [3]. But, for reasons explored earlier, ICA is limited by its unrealistic assumptions. Therefore, *data fusion via fission through empirical mode decomposition* is introduced in this chapter to analyze EEG signals and extract useful information without making assumptions of the input EEG signal.

## 10.4 EEG DATA

### 10.4.1 Introduction

*Electroencephalography (EEG)* is regarded as a vital clinical monitoring tool in understanding the brain activity by recording the voltage differences between different parts of brain using electrodes placed on the scalp, subdurally or in the cerebral cortex. Essentially, EEG can detect brain activities by highlighting the voltage differences generated by neurons in the brain.

## 10.4.2 EEG Data Acquisition

The standardized 10–20 system for collecting EEG data was originally described by Jasper in 1958 [11] for placement of electrodes. There are also other systems such as the 10–10 system, an extension to the original 10–20 system with a higher channel density of 81, suggested by [4]. But the 10–20 system has also been accepted as the standard of the American Clinical Neurophysiology Society (formerly the American Electroen-cephalographic Society) and the International Federation of Clinical Neurophysiology (formerly the International Federation of Societies for Electroencephalography and Clinical Neurophysiology). The 10–20 system was used to collect the EEG data for our experiments.

In our analysis of brain death, the patients involved were all lying in bed facing up with eyes closed, and the data was obtained via nine electrodes on the forehead with channels based on the 10–20 system. That is, electrodes were placed at positions F3, F4, F7, F8, Fp1, Fp2, as well as GND, and also two were placed on the ears (denoted by A1 and A2 respectively). The electrodes placed on the ears act as a reference for the measurements, which can be calculated as (A1 + A2)/2. The measured voltage signal is then digitalized via a portable EEG recording instrument with a sampling frequency of 1000 Hz. The position of the electrodes and its output signal can be seen in Figure 10.3.

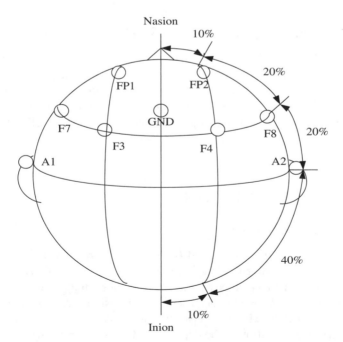

**Figure 10.3.** Electrode placement.

TABLE 10.1. Experimental Data

| Type of Patient | Coma | Quasi-Brain-Death | Male | Female | Total |
|---|---|---|---|---|---|
| Number of Patients | 19 | 18 | 20 | 16 | 36 |

## 10.4.3 Patients' Data

The experimental data shown in Table 10.1 was obtained from 36 patients (16 female, 20 male) of ages ranging from 17 to 85 years old from 2004 until 2006. Nineteen of the patients were in a state of coma, 18 of them need a further test to determine its status, and the consciousness of one patient was clinically in a state of uncertainty. Total recordings of EEG signals from these 36 patients with an average signal length of five minutes were stored and analyzed.

To illustrate, two sets of EEG signals are shown here: Figure 10.4 is the EEG signal of patient 1: a 64-year-old male patient in a deep coma state. The patient regained consciousness. Figure 10.5 is the EEG signal of patient 2: a 48-year-old male patient who lost consciousness on October 18, 2005.

The signal shown in Figure 10.4 is the time–amplitude plot of the EEG signal from patient 2 in a deep coma status. In the figure, from top to bottom, the six EEG channels are shown individually with the same time slot of 40,000 seconds. Figure 10.5 presents the EEG signal of the same patient in a brain-death status.

## 10.4.4 EEG Frequency Band and Its Relative Behavior

EEG signals are typically nonlinear and nonstationary data that are composed of frequency components of interest up to 40 Hz. The basic EEG frequencies are summarized briefly in Table 10.2, with regard to their typical distribution on the scalp and subject states [5]. The EEG signal is closely related to the level of consciousness of the person. As the brain activity increases, the higher frequency bands of the EEG become more dominant.

## 10.5 EMPIRICAL MODE DECOMPOSITION

## 10.5.1 The EMD Algorithm

The empirical mode decomposition and *Hilbert–Huang transform* (*HHT*) were introduced specifically for analyzing data from nonlinear and nonstationary processes by Huang et al. [10]. The EMD method adaptively decomposes the signals into a set of zero-mean components. As these components, called intrinsic mode functions (IMFs), are band-limited signals, the Hilbert transform can be applied to determine a unique time–frequency representation of the data. The decomposition of a signal into a set of IMFs is achieved using the *sifting algorithm*:

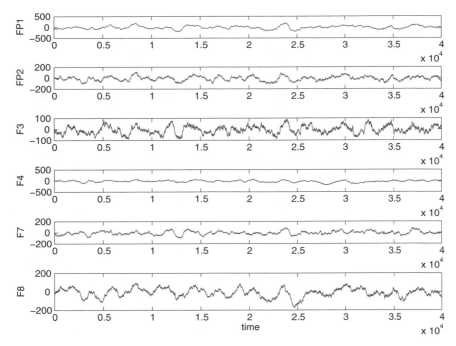

Figure 10.4. Coma signal.

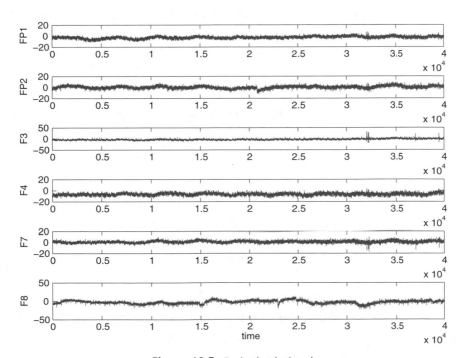

Figure 10.5. Brain death signal.

TABLE 10.2. EEG Signal Frequency Band

| Frequency Band | Frequency (Hz) | Consciousness Level | Distribution |
|---|---|---|---|
| Delta | 0.5–4 | Low level of arousal | Generally broad, diffused |
| Theta | 4–8 | Distracted | Regional, involves many lobes |
| Alpha | 8–12 | Relaxed, meditation | Regional, involves entire lobe |
| Low Beta | 12–15 | Relaxed, yet focused | By side and lobe (frontal, occipital, etc.) |
| Midrange Beta | 15–18 | Alert, active, not agitated | Localized, over various areas |
| High Beta | > 18 | Very focused, alertness | Very localized, maybe very focused |
| Gamma | 40 | High-level info processing | Very localized |

**Sifting Algorithm**

1. Find the local maxima and connect the maxima with interpolation (max envelope). Also extract the minima and connect them by interpolation (min envelope).
2. Take the average of the max envelope and the min envelope to determine the signal mean.
3. Subtract the signal mean obtained from step 2 from the original signal.
4. Repeat steps 1, 2, and 3 until the signal satisfies the IMF criteria defined by Huang [10].
5. Subtract the IMF signal from the original signal; a new signal is then obtained. Again, steps 1, 2, 3, 4, and 5 should be implemented to extract IMFs until the residual is a monotonic function.

The decomposition of a signal x(t) into IMFs can be summarized by the following equation:

$$x(t) = \sum_{i=1}^{n} (C_i(t)) + r(t) \tag{10.2}$$

where $C_i(t)$ is the $i$th IMF, $n$ is the total number of IMFs, and $r(t)$ is the residue.

The criteria of an IMF are as follows. The first condition is that the number of local extrema and the number of zero crossings must either be equal or differ at most by one. The second condition is that at any point the mean of the signal defined by the local maxima and the local minima is zero.

## 10.5.2 The Hilbert Spectrum and Instantaneous Frequency

The monocomponent nature of the IMFs facilitates a unique time–frequency representation of the original signal—the *Hilbert–Huang spectrum*. The Hilbert transform is given by [8]:

$$\tilde{x}(t) = \mathcal{H}[x(t)] = \int_{-\infty}^{\infty} \frac{x(u)}{\pi(t-u)} du \qquad (10.3)$$

where $x(t)$ is a time domain signal. $\mathcal{H}[\cdot]$ is the Hilbert operator. The analytic signal $z(t)$ is related to the Hilbert transform of $x(t)$, represented below as:

$$z(t) = x(t) + j\tilde{x}(t) \qquad (10.4)$$

Given the analytic representation, the magnitude function $a(t)$ and phase function $\theta(t)$ can be obtained from $z(t)$ as:

$$a(t) = \sqrt{x^2(t) + \tilde{x}^2(t)} \quad and \quad \theta(t) = arctan\left(\frac{\tilde{x}(t)}{x(t)}\right) \qquad (10.5)$$

$$z(t) = a(t)e^{j\theta(t)} \qquad (10.6)$$

where $a(t)$ describes the envelope of the original signal $x(t)$, in the other words, the instantaneous amplitude of the signal [8]. $\theta(t)$ describes the instantaneous phase of $x(t)$. Therefore, the instantaneous frequency of $x(t)$ can be defined as the derivative of the phase of the signal as:

$$\omega(t) = \frac{d}{dt}\theta(t) \qquad (10.7)$$

Thus, the Hilbert spectrum is given by [10]:

$$x(t) = \sum_{i=1}^{n} a_i(t)exp\left(j\int \omega_i(t)\right)dt \qquad (10.8)$$

Given the above representation equation, a three-dimensional plot with the amplitude, instantaneous frequency as a function of time can be obtained in a straightforward fashion. This is the Hilbert spectrum.

## 10.5.3 Importance of Complex EMD

The extension to the complex domain $\mathbb{C}$ is particularly important for the analysis of phase-dependent processes [15]. This applies not only to naturally occurring complex data, but also to multi-channel real data. In this way, it is possible to analyze mutual phase information between real-valued signals.

The first method of employing EMD in the complex domain, *complex empirical mode decomposition*, was introduced in 2007 [19]. The method is rigorously derived, based on the inherent relationship between the positive and negative frequency components of a complex signal and the properties of the Hilbert transform. The idea behind this approach is rather intuitive: first note that a complex signal has a two-sided, asymmetric spectrum. The complex signal can therefore be converted into a sum of analytic signals by a straightforward filtering operation that extracts the opposite sides of the spectrum. Direct analysis in $\mathbb{C}$ can be subsequently achieved by applying standard EMD to both the positive and negative frequency parts of the signal. Given a complex signal $x(k)$, real-valued components corresponding to the positive and negative sides of the spectrum can be extracted as

$$
\begin{aligned}
x_+(k) &= \mathcal{R}\mathcal{F}^{-1}\{X(e^{j\omega}) \cdot H(e^{j\omega})\} \\
x_-(k) &= \mathcal{R}\mathcal{F}^{-1}\{X(e^{j\omega}) \cdot H(e^{-j\omega})\}
\end{aligned}
\tag{10.9}
$$

where $\mathcal{F}^{-1}$ is the inverse Fourier transform, $\mathcal{R}$ is an operator that extracts the real part of a signal, and $H(e^{j\omega})$ is an ideal filter with the transfer function

$$
H(e^{j\omega}) = \begin{cases} 1, & \omega > 0 \\ 0, & \omega < 0 \end{cases}
$$

Given that $x_+(k)$ and $x_-(k)$ are real valued, standard EMD can be applied to obtain a set of IMFs for each analytic signal. This can be expressed as

$$
\begin{aligned}
x_+(k) &= \sum_{i=1}^{M_+} x_i(k) + r_+(k) \\
x_-(k) &= \sum_{i=-M_-}^{-1} x_i(k) + r_-(k)
\end{aligned}
\tag{10.10}
$$

where $\{x_i(k)\}_{i=1}^{N_+}$ and $\{x_i(k)\}_{i=-N_-}^{i=1}$ denote sets of IMFs corresponding, respectively, to $x_+(k)$ and $x_-(k)$, whereas $r_+(k)$ and $r_-(k)$ are the respective residuals. The original complex signal can be reconstructed by

$$
x[(k)] = (x_+(k) + j\mathcal{H}[x_+(k)]) + (x_-(k) + j\mathcal{H}[x_-(k)])^*
\tag{10.11}
$$

where $\mathcal{H}$ is the Hilbert transform operator. To conclude the derivation, a single set of complex IMFs corresponding to the complex signal $x(k)$ is given by

$$
x(k) = \sum_{i=M_-, i \neq 0}^{M_+} y_i(k) + r(k)
\tag{10.12}
$$

where $r(k)$ is the residual and $y_i(k)$ is defined by

$$
y_i(k) = \begin{cases} (x_+(k) + j\mathcal{H}[x_+(k)]), & i = 1, \ldots, M_+, \\ (x_-(k) + j\mathcal{H}[x_-(k)])^*, & i = -M_-, \ldots, -1 \end{cases}
$$

Although the two time series ($x_1(k)$ and $x_2(k)$) are real valued, a complex signal, $z(k) = x_1(k) + jx_2(k)$, is constructed with the signals representing the real and imaginary parts, respectively. To its advantage, it has a straightforward, intuitive mathematical derivation. As an example of its mathematical robustness, it preserves the dyadic filter property of standard EMD. In other words, the algorithm acts as dyadic filter bank when processing complex noise [19].

*Rotation-invariant EMD*, introduced in [1], proposes a way of extending EMD theory so that it operates fully in $\mathbb{C}$. This is achieved through the use of complex splines. Unlike complex EMD, by design this method generates an equal number of IMFs for the real and imaginary parts; these can be given physical meaning, thus retaining an important property of real-valued EMD. A critical aspect of the derivation of EMD in $\mathbb{C}$ is the definition of an *extremum*. Several possible approaches are suggested in [1], such as the extrema of the modulus and the locus where the angle of the first-order derivative (with respect to time) changes sign; this way it can be assumed that local maxima will be followed by local minima (and vice versa). This definition is equivalent to the extrema of the imaginary part, that is, for a complex signal $Z(t)$ (for convenience we here use a continuous time index $t$):

$$\angle \dot{Z}(t) = 0 \Rightarrow \angle \{ \dot{x}(t) + j \cdot \dot{y}(t) \} = 0$$
$$\Rightarrow tan^{-1} \frac{\dot{y}(t)}{\dot{x}(t)} = 0 \Rightarrow \dot{y}(t) = 0 \tag{10.13}$$

Because of its aforementioned advantages over complex EMD, namely the physical meaning of its IMFs, rotation-invariant EMD is the extension of choice to perform analysis on complex data.

## 10.5.4 Experiments and Results

As stated previously, an EEG signal can reflect brain activities; therefore, it is regarded as a powerful tool to analyze cerebral consciousness status (e.g., coma and quasi-brain-death). We distinguish cerebral consciousness status by analyzing EEG frequency components within the frequency range from 0 Hz to 30 Hz; in particular, we are interested (See Table 10.2) in the delta range (0.5 to 4 Hz), theta range (4 to 8 Hz), alpha wave (8 to 12 Hz), and 13 Hz components within the low beta range. This is because the patients are in a state of coma, as noted before, and this means that the brain activity of interest dominates lower-frequency ranges.

We consider two patients (patient 1 and patient 2) in a coma state. EEG data for each patient has been provided by [3]. Since these recordings were collected, patient 1 has awakened from coma while patient 2 has died. It is proposed to apply EMD to extract the relevant features from the EEG data and to illustrate how these features can be used to detect inevitable brain death in patient 2. Time–amplitude plots of length one second for each of the six EEG channels (FP1, FP2, ..., etc.) for patient 1 and patient 2 are given in the left columns of Figures 10.6 and 10.7, respectively. EMD was applied to each of the channels to decompose them into their IMFs and the resulting Hilbert spectrum was computed. The Hilbert spectrum of each channel within the range 0 to 30 Hz is given in Figures 10.6 and 10.7, respectively. The third column of each figure shows the frequency–amplitude plots for each channel obtained by averaging the corresponding Hilbert spectrum plots.

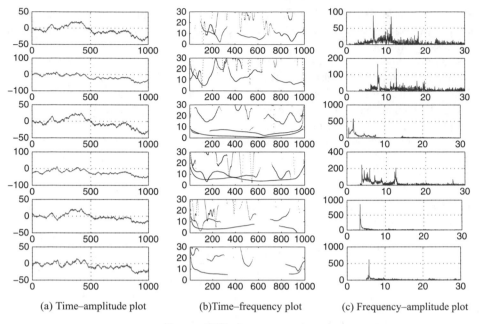

(a) Time–amplitude plot          (b)Time–frequency plot          (c) Frequency–amplitude plot

Figure 10.6.  Coma to awake.

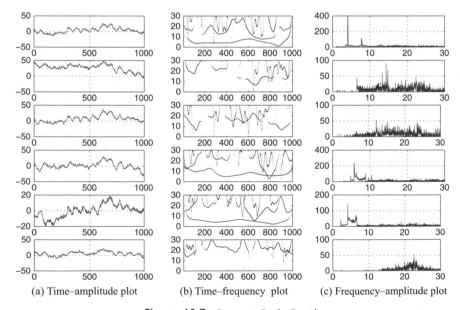

(a) Time–amplitude plot          (b) Time–frequency  plot          (c) Frequency–amplitude plot

Figure 10.7.  Coma to Brain Death.

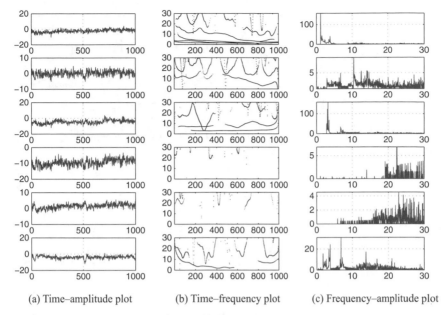

(a) Time–amplitude plot        (b) Time–frequency plot        (c) Frequency–amplitude plot

**Figure 10.8.** Brain Death.

There are several important points to note regarding the features obtained using EMD. First, it is clear that by comparing the frequency–amplitude plots for patient 1 and patient 2, the brain activity within the range of 0 to 13 Hz is significantly weaker for patient 2. As mentioned earlier, activity within this range is related to the low level and meditative brain activity. It can therefore be suggested that there is little or no activity within this crucial range and that it can be used as an indication of inevitable brain death. Also note that the same observations can be made from the data given in Figure 10.8, patient 2 at a later date. The second point to note is that there exists strong similarity between the spectra obtained from EEG channels of patient 1. For example, compare the frequency–amplitude plots of FP1 and FP2 in Figure 10.6. However, it is clear that this is not the case for patient 2. It can be thus concluded that strong similarities in the range 0 to 13 Hz (particularly in channel FP1 and FP2) indicate that the patient will not succumb to brain death.

### 10.5.4.1 EEG Phase Analysis using EMD.
It is clear that if similarities exist between specific frequency ranges (8 to 13 Hz) among different EEG channels (FP1 and FP2), then this is an indication that the patient will not succumb to brain death. For this reason, it is proposed to extract relevant channel features using EMD and to compare these features using complex extensions of the algorithm.

The EEG data from channel FP1 and FP2 for each patient were decomposed into their IMFs and their instantaneous amplitude and frequencies were calculated. Features within the desired frequency range were retained by [17], fusing instantaneous amplitudes that corresponded to instantaneous frequencies within 8 to 13 Hz. All other

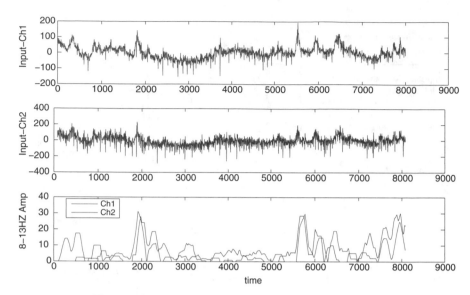

**Figure 10.9.** Filtered EEG deep coma patient 1 to awake.

instantaneous amplitudes were omitted from the fusion process. The data was subsequently denoised [17] by zeroing the underlying signal if in a certain period, unless the signal continuously has non-zero value in this period. The results of this fusion process for FP1 andFP2 are given in the bottom panel of Figure 10.9 for patient 1. Similarly, the fusion result for FP1 and FP2 for patient 2 is given in the bottom panel of Figure 10.10

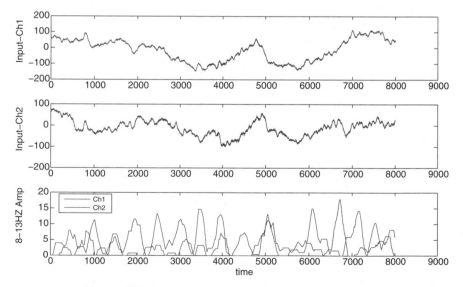

**Figure 10.10.** Filtered EEG deep coma patient 2 to death.

as FP1′ and FP2′, respectively. Note that among the features extracted for patient 1, there is much synchronization between the extrema. This is not the case for patient 2.

Complex extensions of EMD were then applied to the features so as to highlight any synchronizations that were present. By decomposing the complex signal (FP1′ + $j$FP2′) using rotation-invariant EMD, it was possible to monitor the phase relationship accurately between the two channels. Taking the first complex IMF, it can be assumed extracting the high-frequency information, which can suggest the spikes of the original signal. By design, if the variations of two signals are similar, the phase of the complex signal is approximately π/4. As is shown in Figure 10.11, the panel represents the absolutely value of the first complex IMF. The amplitude peaks when FP1′ and FP2′ both have a peak. The third plot in Figure 10.11 is a digitalized phase information. If the phase of the first complex IMF is near to π/4, the value was set to one; otherwise, the value was set to zero. Then the extracted phase and amplitude information was combined together by multiplying the absolute value of the first IMF with the digitalized phase information. The combined amplitude–phase information can be seen from the plot at the bottom of Figure 10.11. This is regarded as an index for detecting the amplitude–phase similarity of the two signals. The result of the same method applied to the filtered signals FP1′ and FP2′ is shown at the bottom of Figure 10.12.

By comparing the index derived from the coma signals of patient 1 and patient 2, it can be seen that patient 1 is likely to recover. Note that the interval in the digitalized phase information of patient 1 is longer than the interval in the digitalized phase information of patient 2. This can suggest a quicker phase change in patient 2. Therefore, the patient should be treated by medical care rather than having further diagnosis tests for braindeath.

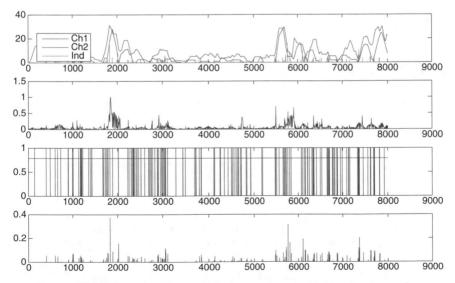

Figure 10.11. Complex EEG analysis deep coma patient 1 leading to awake.

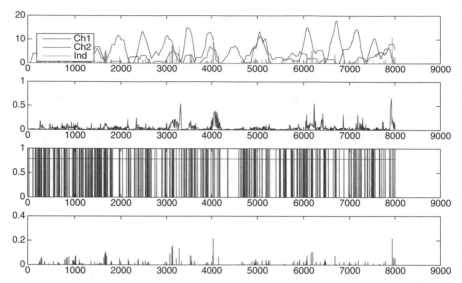

**Figure 10.12.** Complex EEG analysis deep coma patient 2 leading to brain death.

## 10.6 CONCLUSION

The data fusion via fission concept is introduced in this chapter. Using EMD as the methodology of data fission, then fusing the information of interest, provides a powerful tool for analyzing data. By extending EMD fusion via fission to the complex domain, it can be seen that the methodology is not limited to complex signals, but is also useful when the phase information between two signals is important. It has been illustrated in the area of quasi-brain-death preliminary diagnosis.

## 10.7 REFERENCES

1. M. U. B. Altaf, T. Gautama, T. Tanaka, D.P. Mandic, "Rotation Invariant Complex Empirical Mode Decomposition." *Proc. International Conference on Acoustics, Speech and Signal Processing (ICASSP)*, 2007, Vol. 3, pp. 1009–1012.

2. H. K. Beecher, "A Definition of Irreversible Coma: Report of the Ad Hoc Committee of the Harvard Medical School to Examine the Definition of Brain Death," *JAMA: Journal of the American Medical Association*, 205: 337–340, 1968.

3. J. Cao, "Analysis of the Quasi-Brain-Death EEG Data Based on a Robust ICA Approach," *LNAI 4253*, Part III: 1240–1247, KES 2006.

4. G. E. Chatrian, E. Lettich, P. L. Nelson, "Ten Percent Electrode System for Topographic Studies of Spontaneous and Evoked EEG Activity," *American Journal of EEG Technology*, 25: 83–92, 1985.

5. T. F. Collura, "The Five Percent Electrode System for High-Resolution EEG and ERP Measurements," *Clinical Neurophysiology*, 112: 713–719, 1997.

6. M. Datig, T. Schlurmann, "Performance and Limitations of the Hilbert-Huang Transformation (HHT) with an Application to Irregular Water Waves," *Ocean Engineering*, 31: 1783–1834, October 2004.

7. D.F. Group,"Functional Description of the Data Fusion Process," Technical Report, Office of Naval Technology, 1992.

8. S. L. Hahn, *Hilbert Transforms in Signal Processing*. Artech House, 1996.

9. D. L. Hall, J. Llinas, "An introduction to Multisensor Data Fusion." *Proc. IEEE*, 1997, 85 (1): 6–23.

10. N. E. Huang, Z. Shen, S. R. Long, M. L. Wu, H. H. Shih, Z. Quanan, N. C. Yen, C. C. Tung, H. H. Liu, "The Empirical Mode Decomposition and the Hilbert Spectrum for Nonlinear and non-stationary Time Series Analysis," *Proc. Royal Society A*, 1998, 454: 903–995.

11. H. H. Jasper. "Report of the Committee on Methods of Clinical Examination in electro-encephalography," *Electroencephalography and Clinical Neurophysiology*, (10): 370–375, 1958.

12. D. Looney, D. P. Danilo, "A Machine Learning Enhanced Empirical Mode Decomposition (Accepted)." *Proc. IEEE Int. Conf. on Acoustics, Speech, and Signal Processing (ICASSP'O8)*, 2008.

13. D. Looney, L. Li, T. Rutkowski, D. P. Mandic, A. Cichocki, "Ocular Artifacts Removal from EEG Using EMD." *First Int. Conf. Cognitive Neurodynamics*, Shanghai, China, November 2007.

14. D. P. Mandic, M. Golz, A. Kuh, D. Obradovic, T. Tanaka, *Signal Processing Techniques for Knowledge Extraction and Information Fusion*. Springer, 2008.

15. D. P. Mandic, G. Souretis, W. Leong, D. Looney, M. Hulle, T. Tanaka, *Signal Process ing Techniques for Knowledge Extraction and Information Fusion*. Springer, 2007.

16. A. Paolin, A. Manuali, F. Di Paola, F. Boccaletto, P. Caputo, R. Zanata, G. P. Bardin, G. Simini, "Reliability in diagnosis of brain death," *Intensive Care Med*, 21: 657–662, 1995.

17. Y. Saito, T. Tanaka, J. Cao, D. P. Danilo, "Quasi-Brain-Death EEG Data Ayalysis by Empirical Mode Decomposition." *Proc. ICCN* 2007.

18. G. Souretis, D. P. Mandic, M. Griselli, T. Tanaka, M. M. Van Hulle, "Blood Volume Signal Analysis with Empirical Mode Decomposition." *Proc. 15th International DSP Conference*, 2007, pp. 147–150.

19. T. Tanaka, D. P. Mandic, "Complex Empirical Mode Decomposition," *IEEE Signal Processing Letters*, 14(2): 101–104, February 2007.

20. J. W. Tukey, *Exploratory Data Analysis*. Reading, MA: Addison-Wesley, 1977.

21. L. Wald, "Some Terms of Reference in Data Fusion." *IEEE Trans. Geosciences and Remote Sensing*, 37(3): 1190–1193, 1999.

22. E. Waltz, J. Llinas, *Multisensor Data Fusion*. Artech House, 1990.

23. R. R. Zhang, S. Ma, E. Safak, S. Hartzell, "Hilbert-Huang Transform Analysis of Dynamic and Earthquake Motion Recordings. *J. Engineering Mechanics*, 129: 861–875, 2003.

# 11

# SIMILARITY ANALYSIS AND KNOWLEDGE ACQUISITION BY USE OF EVOLVING NEURAL MODELS AND FUZZY DECISION

Gancho Vachkov

**Abstract:** This chapter proposes a computational scheme for fuzzy similarity analysis and classification of large data sets and images that first uses an information granulation procedure followed by a subsequent fuzzy decision procedure. A special new version of the growing unsupervised learning algorithm for information granulation is introduced in the chapter. It reduces the original *raw data* (the RGB pixels) of the image to a considerably smaller number of information granules (neurons). After that, two features are extracted from each image: the *center of gravity* and the *weighted average size* of the image. These features are further used as inputs of a special fuzzy inference procedure that numerically computes the similarity degree for a given pair of images. Finally, a sorting procedure with a predefined threshold is used to obtain the classification results for all available images. The proposed similarity and classification scheme is illustrated using the example of 18 images of flowers. The chapter also emphasizes that the appropriate tuning of the parameters of the fuzzy inference procedure is quite important for obtaining plausible, humanlike results. Therefore, a simple empirical process for selection of these parameters is also suggested. Finally, the iterative computation scheme for knowledge acquisition by using a gradually enlarging image base is also presented and analyzed.

*Evolving Intelligent Systems: Methodology and Applications,* Edited by Plamen Angelov, Dimitar P. Filev, and Nikola Kasabov
Copyright © 2010 Institute of Electrical and Electronics Engineers

## 11.1 INTRODUCTION

During the daily operation of many industrial systems and complex machines, such as chemical and metallurgical plants, trucks, hydraulic excavators, and other construction machines, large data sets can be collected from a number of sensors. These data sets are later used by maintenance engineers and experts to discover any significant difference or change in the operating conditions, which points to a possible faulty condition of the machine or system. If this is the case, quick countermeasures by the operator are needed to prevent further deterioration in the system performance.

The above is only a small example of the many typical cases in which the human operator is faced with the problem of similarity analysis of large multidimensional data sets. Evaluating the similarity between a given set or pairs of large data sets and discovering the differences between them is a very fundamental step that is used for further classification and extracting a kind of knowledge about the system.

The complexity of the problem of similarity analysis arises from the fact that we have to analyze and compare directly the large data sets to each other rather than just classifying single patterns (single data points) in the predefined feature space, as in the standard classification problem.

The problem of similarity exists also when different types of pictorial information should be properly compared and classified. Here, the similarity analysis of a large number of images is considered to be a very important step in the more general procedure for unsupervised classification [1, 2] and knowledge acquisition from many types of pictorial information.

This is a very specific and important task, where humans still perform better than the currently available computerized systems. Among the reasons for such results are the obvious complexity and the vagueness (subjective nature) of the problem itself, as well as the various possible criteria that could be used for the similarity analysis. Nevertheless, a "good" (i.e., true and plausible) solution to the problem of similarity evaluation is a key factor for success in many applications, such as fast visual search through a large amount of image information for proper sorting and classification.

In this chapter, we present a special fuzzy rule-based scheme for similarity analysis. The results from this analysis, in the form of *similarity degrees*, can be later used for unsupervised classification of images. After investigating several possible features for a plausible similarity analysis, we have finally selected two of them as inputs of the fuzzy decision procedure. These are the *center of gravity* of the image and the *weighted average size* of the image, computed in two versions. The features are extracted from the "raw" pixel data information through respective algorithms. Especially, the image volume is approximately evaluated as the number of *information granules* (*neurons*) that represent the original raw data set (*pixels*). The number of neurons, as well as their proper locations in the three-dimensional RGB space, is automatically defined by a specially introduced *growing unsupervised learning algorithm*.

Finally, extended simulations are performed over a test example, consisting of 18 images of different flowers. They show the merits of the proposed fuzzy rule-based similarity analysis, which can be successfully applied to solving real-world classification problems that include much larger numbers of images. An iterative computation scheme for knowledge acquisition based on a given image base with *core images* is also presented and discussed in the chapter.

## 11.2 BASICS OF INFORMATION GRANULATION

Normally, the large data sets and images are stored in the original "raw" form that keeps all the measurements or all pixels. In the case of image information, it is usually stored as respective BMP or JPG file, where each pixel is represented by three integer numbers within the range [0,255] that correspond to the intensity of the three basic colors *Red*, *Green* and *Blue*. Thus the whole image information is saved as a three-dimensional RGB data set $\mathbf{x}_i = [x_{i1}, x_{i2}, \ldots, x_{iK}], i = 1, 2, \ldots, M$, where $K = 3$ is the dimension number and $M$ represents the total number of pixels in this image.

However, it is obvious that directly using the original large raw RGB data set for further processing is not the best idea from the point of view of efficient computation. Therefore, we propose here another idea, according to the general concept of information granulation in [3]. It is to replace the original large number of raw data with a smaller number of "information granules," by an appropriate *unsupervised learning* algorithm [4–7]. The reduced set of *information granules* (called also *neurons* in this chapter) is obtained by using the appropriate unsupervised learning algorithm, as will be shown in the next sections. As a result of this learning, the set of neurons that is produced should resemble as much as possible the density distribution, shape, and the volume of the original set of RGB pixels in the three-dimensional space. This process is also called *information compression* and the trained set of neurons is regarded as a kind of *compressed information model* (*CIM*) or *granulation model* (*GM*) of the original (raw) data set. It should be mentioned that such an approach to information compression (granulation) that uses any of the unsupervised learning algorithms is a *lossy compression* in the sense that it would be not possible to fully recover the original information from the obtained compressed model.

From a theoretical viewpoint, the *information granulation* can be considered as a kind of unsupervised learning process that uses the original large three-dimensional data set (containing $M$ pixels): $\mathbf{x}_i = [x_{i1}, x_{i2}, x_{i3}], i = 1, 2, \ldots, M$ in order to determine the locations of $N$ *information granules* (neurons) in the same space, that is, $\mathbf{c}_i = [c_{i1}, c_{i2}, c_{i3}], i = 1, 2, \ldots, N, N \ll M$ with $CR = M/N$, called the *compression ratio*.

An illustrative example for information granulation is shown in the next two figures. Figure 11.1 shows the original RGB data set (4200 pixels) from a small image (not shown here), whereas Figure 11.2. depicts the result of the information granulation, by using the fixed number of $N = 62$ information granules (neurons) obtained after the end of the unsupervised learning process.

Generally, the available unsupervised learning algorithms for information granulation can be divided into three big groups:

> *Group 1,* which consists of *standard offline unsupervised learning* algorithms with the assumption of preliminary *fixed* number of neurons (granules) $N$, as in [5–7].

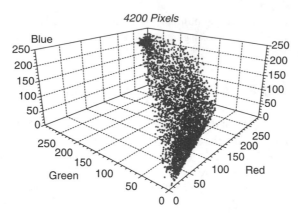

Figure 11.1. Three-dimensional plot of a small image, containing 4200 pixels used as "raw" RGB data set for information granulation.

*Group 2,* which uses the idea of the *growing learning* algorithm [8–10] with variable (adjustable) number of neurons in order to fit a prespecified *granulation quality.*

*Group 3,* in which the concept of *on-line* unsupervised learning is used. Here it is assumed that all data are not available at once but rather come "one by one" in a finite (or even endless) sequence of data points. Then all neurons from the set of assumed core neurons are gradually adjusting their locations in the space, according to the newly arriving data. Our recent research results on this type of online learning algorithm can be found in [10, 11].

Among the most popular standard offline learning algorithms from *Group 1* are the *self-organizing (Kohonen) maps* [4] and the *neural gas learning algorithm* [5]. One modification of the offline neural gas learning algorithm is presented in Section 11.3.

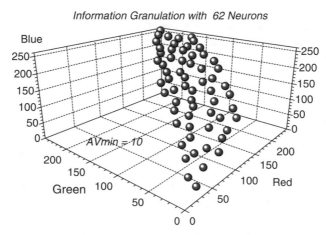

Figure 11.2. Information granulation with $N = 62$ neurons of the original RGB data set from Figure 11.1.

Another popular modification of the standard competitive learning, called the *frequency-sensitive competitive learning(FSCL) algorithm*, has been introduced in [6, 7]. The main advantage of the FSCL algorithm is that it avoids as much as possible (with an appropriate tuning) the cases of so-called *dead units* [6, 7] or *idling neurons* [8–11]. These are neurons that cannot become *winning neurons* for a long subsequent number of learning iterations because of their inappropriate initial location in the space. As a result, they do not update sufficiently during the learning and eventually get stalled in the data space. In order to prevent this, they are "encouraged" by the FSCL algorithm to become winners by gradually suppressing the pace of the other winning neurons. More details about this algorithm can be found, for example, in [6].

The most significant drawback of the *fixed-type* algorithms from *Group 1* is that the number of neurons $N$ should be fixed prior to the learning process, based on some heuristic or guess about the possible granulation quality of the obtained model.

In order to prevent this, the algorithms from *Group 2* use the concept of *growing learning*. They usually start the learning with a small *initial number* of neurons (e.g., $No = 2,3$) and monitor the granulation quality of the current model at each learning epoch. If it is still not sufficient, a new neuron is inserted in the area in the space with the "worst performance." The learning epochs terminate after the predefined granulation quality is achieved. In Section 11.4, two growing learning algorithms are presented and compared.

As a measure of the granulation quality of the model, the *average minimal distance* $AVmin$ [8–11] is introduced, as follows:

$$AV\,min = \frac{1}{M} \sum_{i=1}^{M} \sqrt{\sum_{j=1}^{K} (c_{n*j} - x_{ij})^2} \qquad (11.1)$$

It is seen from this equation that $AVmin$ is computed as the mean value of the Euclidean distances between all $M$ data points and their respective winning neurons $n^*$. By definition, the neuron $n^*$ that has the shortest distance to a given data point $\mathbf{x}_i$ is called the winning neuron for this data point [5–9].

Then the *granulation quality*, computed as $AVmin$, is a parameter that shows *how well* the trained set of information granules represents the structure, the density, and the shape of the original data set. Therefore, it is natural that a smaller $AVmin$ means a better (finer) information granulation, which is achieved with a larger number of information granules (neurons).

## 11.3 THE FIXED UNSUPERVISED LEARNING ALGORITHM FOR INFORMATION GRANULATION

The essential part of any unsupervised learning algorithm is the *updating rule* for the neuron centers $\mathbf{c}_i, i = 1, 2, \ldots, N$ in the $K$-dimensional space ($K = 3$ in the case of processing image information). As mentioned before, this fixed-type algorithm uses a predetermined number of neurons $N$ and the updating rule is performed for a preliminary fixed number of $T$ iterations ($t = 0, 1, 2, \ldots, T$), as follows:

$$\mathbf{c}_i(t) = \mathbf{c}_i(t-1) + \Delta\mathbf{c}_i(t), i = 1, 2, \ldots, N \qquad (11.2)$$

Here the computation way of the update $\Delta\mathbf{c}_i(t)$ varies according to the version of the unsupervised algorithm, such as [4–8]. We use here a special simplified version [8–10] of the original neural gas learning algorithm [5], where the amount of the update is computed as:

$$\Delta\mathbf{c}_i(t) = R(t)H_s(t, r_i)[\mathbf{x}_s - \mathbf{c}_i(t-1)],$$
$$i = 1, 2, \ldots, N; s = 1, 2, \ldots, M \qquad (11.3)$$

The parameter $R(t), 0 \leq R(t) \leq 1, t = 0, 1, 2, \ldots, T$ in (11.3) is a monotonically decreasing *learning rate*, which guarantees the convergence and stability of the learning process:

$$R(t) = R_0 \exp(-t/T_C), t = 0, 1, \ldots, T \qquad (11.4)$$

The *neighborhood function* $0 \leq H_s(t, r_i) \leq 1$ in (11.3) also decreases exponentially with the iterations. It is used to compute the dynamic *activity* of all neurons, which decreases exponentially with the iterations and depends also on the current ranking order of the neuron at this iteration. In [4–8], we proposed a simple way to compute the monotonically decreasing neighborhood function as follows:

$$H_s(t, r_i) = \exp[-(r_i - 1)/B(t)],$$
$$t = 0, 1, \ldots, T; s = 1, 2, \ldots, M; i = 1, 2, \ldots, N \qquad (11.5)$$

where

$$B(t) = \exp(-t/T_W), t = 0, 1, \ldots, T \qquad (11.6)$$

Here $r_i \in [1, 2, \ldots, N]$ is an integer number for the *ranking order* of the $i$th neuron ($i = 1, 2, \ldots, N$) to the $s$th data point ($s = 1, 2, \ldots, M$). This ranking order is defined by the Euclidean distance between the $i$th neuron and the $s$th data point. The closest neuron (in the sense of minimal *Euclidean* distance) is called the *winning* neuron and gets ranking order $r = 1$. The second closest neuron gets $r = 2$, and so on.

The *initial learning rate* $R_0$ and the *steepness* parameters $T_C$ and $T_W$ have to be preset before the learning. In the further simulation we use the following settings: $T = 500; R_0 = 0.15$ and $T_C = T_W = T/5$. One typical example for information compression of a raw data set containing $M = 800$ data by using $N = 60$ neurons is given in Figure 11.3.

The unsupervised learning algorithm described above is referred to as algorithm *Fixed* when compared to the next two learning algorithms presented in Section 11.4.

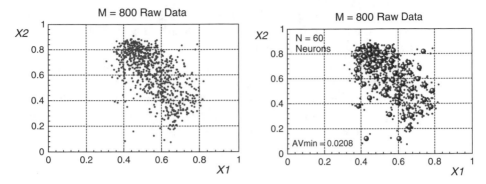

Figure 11.3. Example for creating a compressed information model (CIM) with $N = 60$ neurons (granules) from a raw data set with $M = 800$ data by unsupervised learning.

## 11.4 GROWING LEARNING ALGORITHMS FOR INFORMATION GRANULATION

As mentioned in Section 11.2, the most distinctive point of the *growing unsupervised learning algorithms* is that they start the learning with a small number of *initial* neurons *No* (usually *No* $= 2$ or 3). Then, at each learning *epoch*, they gradually increase the number of the neurons until a predetermined *granulation quality*, taken in the form of average minimal distance $AVmin0(11.1)$, is achieved.

In [8–10], we proposed and analyzed a growing version of the unsupervised learning algorithm, which will be referred to as the *Grow1* algorithm. In the sequel, we propose another version of the growing learning algorthm, which will be called the *Grow2* algorithm. Algorithms *Grow1* and *Grow2* differ in the way in which the decision for including another (new) neuron is made. In order to better understand the difference between them, the two algorithms will be explained by steps in a parallel way, as follows:

*Step 1.* For each learning epoch with a current number of $n \leq N$ neurons, compute the current granulation quality for all $n$ local models, called *Voronoi polygons* [5, 8–10]. By definition, the $p$th Voronoi polygon ($p = 1, 2, \ldots, n$) consists of the sub-area of all raw data points for which this neuron is a *winning neuron*. The quality of the local models is computed in different ways in the two algorithms, as follows:

(A) In the *Grow1* algorithm, the *mean distance $MD_p$* is computed for all $n$ sub-areas (Voronoi polygons) in the following way:

$$MD_p = \frac{1}{m}\sum_{i=1}^{m}\sqrt{\sum_{j=1}^{K}(c_{pj}-x_{ij})^2}, p = 1, 2, \ldots, n \qquad (11.7)$$

Here $m$ represents the number of all data points within the $p$th Voronoi polygon. It is obvious that this distance should be kept smaller in order to achieve a better quality of this local model.

(B) In the newly proposed *Grow2* algorithm, the *cumulative errorCE$_p$* is computed for each Voronoi polygon $p$ $(p = 1, 2, \ldots, n)$. The idea here is first to compute the distances between the data points within the $p$th Voronoi polygon and the respective $p$th neuron and after that to *sum up* all overshoots above the predetermined quality *AVmin 0*. The computations are performed in the following three steps:

$$D_i = \sqrt{\sum_{j=1}^{3} (c_{pj} - x_{ij})^2}, i = 1, 2, \ldots, m \qquad (11.8)$$

$$E_i = \begin{cases} D_i - V\, min\, 0, & \text{if } D_i > AVmin\, 0; \\ 0, \text{otherwise}; & i = 1, 2, \ldots, m \end{cases} \qquad (11.9)$$

$$CE_p = \sum_{i=1}^{m} E_i, p = 1, 2, \ldots, n \qquad (11.10)$$

Here also a smaller cumulative error (11.10) corresponds to a more accurate local model.

*Step 2.* Find the local model (the Voronoi polygon) $p^*$ that has the worst information granulation. It is done in the following way for both algorithms:

(A) In the *Grow1* algorithm, the deviation between the mean distance (11.8) and the desired granulation quality *AVmin* is computed as follows:

$$DEV_p = \begin{cases} MD_p - AVmin\, 0, & \text{if } MD_p > AVmin\, 0; \\ 0, \text{otherwise}; & p = 1, 2, \ldots, n \end{cases} \qquad (11.11)$$

Then the Voronoi polygon $p^*$ with the biggest *deviation $DEV_{p^*} = DEV_{\max}$* corresponds to the sub-area of data with the worst information granulation.

(B) In the *Grow 2* algorithm, the Voronoi polygon with the biggest *cumulative error $CE_{p^*} = CE_{\max}$* corresponds to the sub-area with the worst information granulation.

*Step 3.* Improve the granulation quality in the worst Voronoi polygon $p^*$ by *adding* one *new neuron* (granule) to it: $n \leftarrow n + 1$.

*Step 4.* Perform any standard competitive unsupervised learning algorithm, such as in [4–6], in order to properly tune the locations of the only *two neurons* within this Voronoi polygon, namely the newly added neuron and the previous (old) one.

For the unsupervised learning of the two neurons in the current Voronoi polygon, we use here the FSCL algorithm from [6], for reasons mentioned in Section 11.2.

*Step 5*. Check the granulation quality (11.1) of the whole model, achieved by the current number of $n$ neurons. If $AVmin \leq AVmin0$, then the predetermined quality is achieved with $N = n$ neurons and the algorithm terminates. If $AVmin > AVmin0$, the algorithm continues the learning process with the next epoch from step 1.

## 11.5 COMPARISON OF THE GROWING AND THE FIXED LEARNING ALGORITHMS FOR INFORMATION GRANULATION

It is worth noting that the learning process of the growing algorithms is much faster (as computation time) compared with the fixed-type learning algorithm from Section 11.3. There are two reasons for this. The first one is that, here, instead of the whole data set containing all $M$ data, a much smaller subset of only $m < M$ data is used for the learning at each epoch. This subset consists of the data points that belong to the current, worst sub-area $p^*$. The second reason for the faster performance is that at each learning epoch, only two neurons are used, instead of the whole set of N neurons, as in the case of the algorithm *Fixed*.

We compared all three learning algorithms, namely *Fixed*, *Grow1*, and *Grow2*, in the same example of a large data set, consisting of $M = 49152$ three-dimensional data. This data set was actually the RGB pixels matrix from an image (*image* 4 from Figure 11.6) with resolution $256 \times 192$ pixels. For a predetermined granulation quality of $AVmin = 12$, number of iterations $T = 350$, and learning rate $R_0 = 0.11$, the CPU time (using the same compiler) was as follows: 119 sec for *Grow1*, 177 sec for *Grow2*, and 257 sec for *Fixed*. At the end of the learning, the number of all generated neurons was as follows: $N = 109$ for *Grow1* and $N = 169$ for *Grow2*. The algorithm *Fixed* was run with a predetermined number of $N = 109$ neurons. Figure 11.4 shows the convergence of the $AVmin$ for both algorithms. It becomes clear that *Grow2* is the fastest among the three

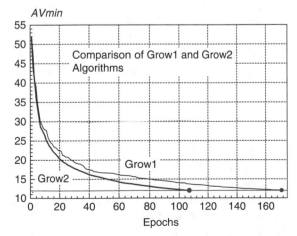

Figure 11.4. Convergence of the granulation quality *AVmin* for *Grow1* and *Grow2*.

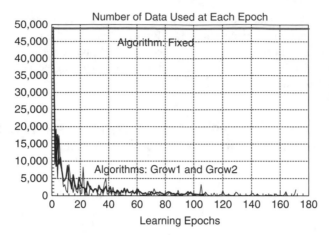

Figure 11.5. Number of data used for learning at each epoch for algorithms *Grow1* and *Grow2* compared with algorithm *Fixed*.

algorithms and, additionally, it produces a more *economical model* with the same granulation quality *AVmin* by using a smaller number of neurons than *Grow1*.

Figure 11.5 shows the amount of data that are used for learning at each epoch for both growing learning algorithms: *Grow1* and *Grow2*. Note that after the first epoch that uses the full set of $M = 49152$ data, all other epochs use only a fraction of these data, located in the worst sub-area of the data space. In addition, this number tends to decrease exponentially with the growing number of epochs. This fact explains the speed of the growing algorithms, compared with the algorithm *Fixed*, which always uses the full set of data.

However, the algorithm *Fixed* produces a granulation model (gm) with a slightly better granulation quality *AVmin*, compared with any of the growing algorithms that use the same number of neurons. For example, algorithm *Grow1* produces a model with $AVmin = 11.987$ by using $N = 109$ neurons. At the same time, algorithm *Fixed* creates a granulation model with the same fixed number of $N = 109$ neurons, but with a better granulation quality of $AVmin = 11.463$. Even if the difference is not so significant, it is a matter of a trade-off (CPU time against the model quality) when making a decision about the proper algorithm for information granulation.

Finally, the growing learning algorithms *Grow1* and *Grow2* can be considered to be a kind of *adaptive algorithms* that gradually adjust both the number and the position of the neurons so as to reach the predetermined model quality *AVmin*. From such a point of view, these algorithms gradually build *evolving models,* during the learning process. Since we use an *offline* data set with a fixed number of data ($M = const$), this allows us to perform iterations over the whole available data set and to *evolve* the models during the iterations. As a result, the final models that are produced will be fitted to the concrete training data set but cannot be used for another data set with different characteristics. From such a point of view, the models produced by the offline data set cannot be regarded as fully evolving models.

## 11.6 SELECTION OF FEATURES FOR THE SIMILARITY ANALYSIS

The unsupervised classification of images [1, 2] can be viewed as a simple computational procedure that uses the results of the preliminary similarity analysis, namely the computed *similarity degrees* between the *new* (unknown) image and all existing images from the *image base*. For classification purposes, these results have to be sorted in descending order of the similarity degrees for each pair of images. Then, according to a preliminary, assumed reasonable *threshold* for the similarity degree, the new (unknown) image is classified as "belonging" to the class of the "most similar" image or rejected as "non-belonging" to any known class of images.

Now it becomes clear that in order to achieve a satisfactory solution to this problem we first need to extract the most representative characteristics (*features*) from the original images in appropriate numerical form that corresponds to the specific of this image.

We can view each separate image as a kind of *data cloud* in the three-dimensional RGB space, which has its specific *density distribution, shape*, and *location* in this space. All three correspond in some indirect way to the diversity and the overall ratio of the colors in the original two-dimensional image. Therefore, the problem of computing the *similarity degree* between a given pair of images becomes a problem of evaluating the *difference* between the respective features of the three-dimensional data clouds in the RGB space.

It seems natural to assume that the *first* (and probably the most important) *feature* that can be extracted from a given data cloud is its center of gravity (*COG*), defined as the vector $\mathbf{CG} = [CG_1, CG_2, CG_3]$, which can be directly computed from the original raw data as follows:

$$CG_j = \sum_{i=1}^{M} x_{ij}/M, j = 1, 2, 3 \tag{11.12}$$

If the original raw data are already not available (after the information granulation), then the center of gravity can be also approximately evaluated by using the parameters of the obtained granulation model, in the following way:

$$CG_j = \sum_{i=1}^{N} c_{ij}g_i / \sum_{i=1}^{N} g_i, j = 1, 2, 3 \tag{11.13}$$

Here, $0 < g_i \le 1, i = 1, 2, \ldots, N$ are the *normalized weights* of the neurons, computed as:

$$g_i = m_i/M; i = 1, 2, \ldots, N \tag{11.14}$$

and $m_i \le M, i = 1, 2, \ldots, N$ is the number of the data points: $\mathbf{x}_s, s = 1, 2, \ldots, m_i$ for which the $i$th neuron is a winning neuron.

It is obvious that there will be a slight difference between the real *COG* computed by (11.12) and its evaluated value, computed by (11.13). This discrepancy is related to the preliminary chosen granulation quality *AVmin0* and will gradually decrease with decreasing the value of *AVmin0*.

For a given pair *(A,B)* of images, the *center-of-gravity-distance (COGD)* between the *image A* and *image B* can be easily computed and used as one parameter for the similarity analysis procedure, namely:

$$COGD_{AB} = \sqrt{\sum_{j=1}^{K} [CG_j^A - CG_j^B]^2} \qquad (11.15)$$

Other parameters of the granulation model that is produced can be used as features that indirectly estimate the *shape, density*, and overall *volume* (size) of the data cloud in the three-dimensional space. For example, the number of the neurons (information granules) *N*, obtained after the end of the growing unsupervised learning algorithm, can be successfully used as a possible feature that estimates the *image volume (VOL)* of a given image. Then, the difference between the image volumes of a given pair *(A,B)* of images is denoted by *VOLD* and can be used as another parameter for the similarity analysis, as follows:

$$VOLD_{AB} = |VOL_A - VOL_B| \qquad (11.16)$$

This new feature along with the feature *COG* from (11.12) and (11.13) have been already used for similarity analysis of images in our previous work [12]. However, our experience shows that the image volume *VOL* has a drawback, namely that it does not represent properly the internal structure (the density distribution of the data) from the original image. Therefore, there are some cases of classification of complex images when the use of *VOLD* from (11.16) leads to a deviation from the true results.

In order to correct this deficiency, we propose here two other features that represent the *weighted average size (WAS)* of the granulation model, taking into account the normalized weights of the neurons from (11.14). These two new features are named *WAS* and *WAS2*, respectively. They differ in the way of computing the *connection weights w* and *w2* between all pairs of neurons, as seen from the following equations:

$$WAS = \sum_{p=1}^{N-1} \sum_{q=p+1}^{N} ED_{pq} \bigg/ \sum_{p=1}^{N-1} \sum_{q=p+1}^{N} w_{pq} \qquad (11.17)$$

and

$$WAS2 = \sum_{p=1}^{N-1} \sum_{q=p+1}^{N} ED_{pq} \bigg/ \sum_{p=1}^{N-1} \sum_{q=p+1}^{N} w2_{pq} \qquad (11.18)$$

Here

$$w_{pq} = \min(g_p, g_q) \quad \text{and} \quad w2_{pq} = g_p \times g_q \qquad (11.19)$$

denote the connection weights for a given pair $\{p, q\}$ of neurons, and $ED_{pq}$ in (11.17) and (11.18) is the *Euclidean Distance* between the neurons in this pair.

The differences *WASD* and *WAS2D* between the respective weighted average sizes (11.17) and (11.18) for a given pair $(A,B)$ of images can be used as two other parameters for the similarity analysis, as follows:

$$WASD_{AB} = |WAS_A - WAS_B| \qquad (11.20)$$

$$WAS2D_{AB} = |WAS2_A - WAS2_B| \qquad (11.21)$$

Performance analysis of the classification, made by using all four parameters, computed by (11.15), (11.6) and (11.20), (11.21), is shown and discussed in the next sections.

## 11.7 EXAMPLE OF SIMILARITY ANALYSIS OF IMAGES

In order to illustrate the whole proposed process for image classification, based on similarity analysis, later we use the following test example of 18 images, representing different flowers, as shown in Figure 11.6.

As mentioned in Section 11.2, first the BMP files with the original images have been preprocessed in order to obtain the respective RGB files with the raw data in the form of three-dimensional matrixes containing the pixel values within the range of 0–255.

The center of gravity **CG** of all 18 images from Figure 11.6. have been computed from the raw pixel data by using equation (11.12). Their locations in the three-dimensional RGB space are shown in Figure 11.7. They almost coincide with the locations of the **CG** obtained from the respective granulation models and computed by (11.13).

It is easy to see in Figure 11.7 that the CGs for many of the images are quite close to each other, that is, they can be considered to be very similar. However, this differs from the reality, as seen from the original images in Figure 11.6. Therefore, a conclusion can be made that the use of only one feature (the center of gravity in this case) is not sufficient for a true and precise similarity analysis and classification.

The image volumes *VOL* for all 18 images have been computed by both learning algorithms, *Grow1* and *Grow2*, and for three desired values of the granulation quality, as follows: $AVmin0 = 12$, 13, and 14. The results from using the *Grow2* algorithm are shown in Figure 11.8. It is seen from this figure that the ratio between the image volumes of the different images remains almost unchanged with increasing or decreasing granulation quality *AVmin0*. This means that even larger (faster-computed) values of *AVmin0* could be used with the same success for the similarity analysis.

A direct comparison between algorithms *Grow1* and *Grow2* is shown in Figure 11.9 for the same granulation quality $AVmin0 = 12$. Note that the *Grow2* algorithm reaches the same (predetermined) granulation quality *AVmin0* by using fewer neurons; that is, it produces a more economical solution to the granulation problem. The general reason for such a result is that the cumulative error (11.10) gives a more precise characteristic of the model than the mean distance (11.7).

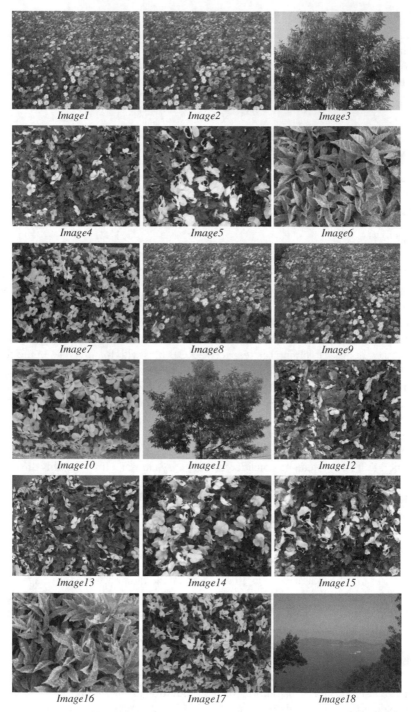

**Figure 11.6.** Images of 18 different flowers, used as test example for unsupervised classification by the fuzzy similarity analysis.

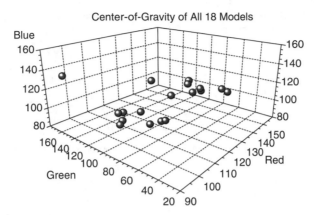

Figure 11.7. Centers of gravity **CG** of all 18 Images from Figure 11.6, computed by (11.12). They almost coincide with the **CG** computations by (11.13).

Figure 11.10 depicts the next two features, namely the weighted average sizes *WAS* (11.17) and *WAS2*(11.18) for all 18 test images. In the figure, these two features follow the same (increase–decrease) tendency, which means that we expect similar results from them for the similarity analysis.

Each of the above four features have been used separately for similarity analysis and classification, by computing the respective distances: (11.15), (11.16), (11.20), and (11.21). The results are shown in Table 11.1. Here *N1* and *N2* denote the most similar and the second-most-similar image.

It is easy to note the discrepancy between the results produced by each feature separately.

The results from this similarity analysis lead to the conclusion that using each of the four single features separately does not produce plausible results for all test examples

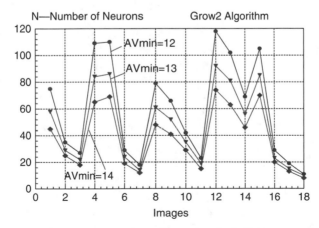

Figure 11.8. Image volumes *VOL* (number of neurons *N*) of all 18 Images from Figure 11.6, computed by learning algorithm *Grow2*.

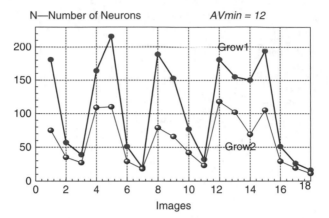

**Figure 11.9.** Image volumes *VOL* of all 18 Images from Figure 11.6, computed by both learning algorithms: *Grow1* and *Grow2*. Note that the *Grow2* algorithm produces a more efficient model for the same desired *AVmin*.

T A B L E 11.1. Four Different Classifications of All 18 Images, Performed by Using Separately All Four Single Features

| | Four "Single-Feature" Classifications | | | | | | | |
|---|---|---|---|---|---|---|---|---|
| | *COGD* (11.15) | | *VOLD* (11.16) | | *WASD* (11.20) | | *WAS2D* (11.21) | |
| Image | *N1* | *N2* | *N1* | *N2* | *N1* | *N2* | *N1* | *N2* |
| 1 | 9 | 8 | 8 | 14 | 2 | 9 | 8 | 2 |
| 2 | 10 | 6 | 6 | 16 | 9 | 1 | 9 | 1 |
| 3 | 14 | 15 | 6 | 16 | 11 | 13 | 13 | 18 |
| 4 | 13 | 12 | 5 | 15 | 12 | 18 | 12 | 18 |
| 5 | 15 | 14 | 4 | 15 | 15 | 7 | 11 | 14 |
| 6 | 16 | 10 | 16 | 3 | 16 | 9 | 16 | 9 |
| 7 | 17 | 15 | 17 | 11 | 17 | 11 | 17 | 15 |
| 8 | 9 | 1 | 1 | 14 | 10 | 1 | 1 | 2 |
| 9 | 1 | 8 | 14 | 1 | 2 | 1 | 2 | 1 |
| 10 | 2 | 16 | 2 | 6 | 8 | 18 | 8 | 4 |
| 11 | 12 | 4 | 3 | 17 | 17 | 3 | 5 | 15 |
| 12 | 4 | 13 | 5 | 4 | 4 | 18 | 18 | 13 |
| 13 | 4 | 12 | 15 | 4 | 4 | 3 | 18 | 12 |
| 14 | 3 | 15 | 9 | 1 | 15 | 5 | 5 | 11 |
| 15 | 5 | 17 | 13 | 4 | 5 | 14 | 7 | 17 |
| 16 | 6 | 10 | 16 | 3 | 6 | 9 | 6 | 9 |
| 17 | 7 | 15 | 7 | 11 | 11 | 7 | 7 | 15 |
| 18 | 13 | 4 | 7 | 17 | 12 | 4 | 12 | 13 |

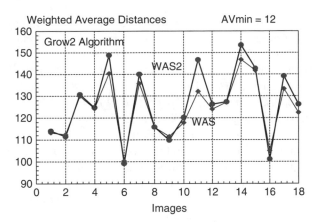

Figure 11.10. Weighted average sizes, *WAS* and *WAS2*, computed for all 18 test images from Figure 11.6 by learning algorithm *Grow2*.

from Figure 11.6. This means that a single feature is not sufficient for a true similarity analysis. Obviously, we have to combine two or more features in a reasonable (human-knowledge-based) decision-making scheme. Such a scheme could be, for example, a fuzzy rule-based decision procedure, as explained in the next section.

## 11.8 TWO-PARAMETER FUZZY RULE-BASED SIMILARITY ANALYSIS

We propose to combine two of the above four features in a standard two-input (two-parameter) *fuzzy rule-based decision procedure* for similarity analysis of a given pair (*A,B*) of images, as we did in [13]. The expectations are that because of the flexibility and nonlinearity of the general fuzzy decision procedure, we could obtain more plausible, humanlike results from the similarity analysis.

As is well known in the research area of fuzzy modeling, decision, and control [1], here we also follow the three standard computation steps in the proposed fuzzy rule-based decision procedure:

1. *Fuzzyfication* (using triangular membership functions)
2. *Fuzzy inference* (using the product operation)
3. *Defuzzification* (using the weighted mean average)

From a theoretical viewpoint, this fuzzy rule-based procedure is a two-input/one-output fuzzy system, as follows: $D = \mathbf{F}(P1, P2)$. Here, $0.0 \leq D \leq 1.0$ is the *difference degree* (also called *dissimilarity degree*). $D = 0$ denotes *identical* (equal) images, while $D = 1$ means that the selected images A and B are *completely different*. All other cases of similarity are somewhere within this range.

As parameter (input) *P1*, we use the center-of-gravity distance, computed by (11.15) for a given pair (*A,B*) of images, that is, $P1 = COGD$. As for parameter (input) *P2*, we use the weighted average size differences, computed by (11.20) and also by (11.21). Since the results obtained from the similarity analysis using *WASD* and those using *WAS2D* were similar, we will display the results by using *P2 = WAS2D*.

For each of the inputs *P1* and *P2*, we have assumed *five triangular membership functions* for the *fuzzification step*. Their respective linguistic variables are: *VS = Very Small*; *SM = Small*; *MD = Medium*; *BG = Big*; and *VB = Very Big*.

It is well known that the general problem in fuzzy modeling, control, and decision is the proper tuning of the locations (centers) of all membership functions. Here different optimization techniques could be applied to successfully tune the membership function locations, with a preliminary defined *optimization criterion*.

In this chapter we are not dealing with the problem of *precise tuning* and the choice of the optimization criterion. We are rather interested in investigating and showing *how sensitive* are the preliminary chosen parameters *P1* and *P2* to the final results from the similarity analysis. For this purpose in the sequel we propose a kind of simple heuristic (and approximate) computational procedure for finding the *range* and the *centers* of the membership functions for *P1* and *P2*.

First, we compute the ranking lists *P1min* → *P1max* and *P2min* → *P2max* for each image separately, compared to all other images. The results from these computations for the test example with 18 images is shown in Figure 11.11 for parameter *P1 = COGD* and in Figure 11.12 for parameter *P2 = WAS2D*.

After that, the centers of each linguistic variable are computed according to the following (heuristic) rule:

*VS = 0.0*

*SM* = Mean value of *Rank No. 2* for all images

*MD* = Mean value of *Rank No. 5* for all images

*BG* = Mean value of *Rank No. 9* for all images

*VB* = Mean value of *Rank No. 17* (the most different image)

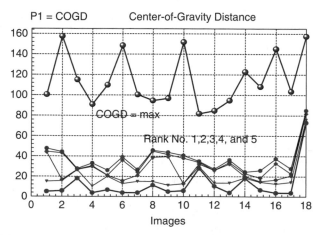

**Figure 11.11.** Ranking list for all 18 images, using parameter *P1 = COGD*(11.15).

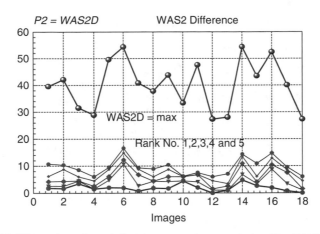

Figure 11.12. Ranking list of all 18 images, using parameter $P2 = WAS2D$(11.21).

The computed centers of the triangular membership functions for parameters $P1$ and $P2$ are shown in the three charts in Figure 11.13.

The next important block in the fuzzy decision procedure is the *fuzzy rule base*. As shown in Figure 11.14, it consists of 25 human-experience-based fuzzy rules, with singleton-type (numerical) outputs denoted by $U_1, U_2, \ldots, U_9$.

The following numerical values for all nine singletons $U_1, U_2, \ldots, U_9$ have been assumed in this simulation:

$$U_1 = 0.0; U_2 = 0.125; U_3 = 0.250;$$
$$U_4 = 0.375; U_5 = 0.500; U_6 = 0.625; \qquad (11.22)$$
$$U_7 = 0.750; U_8 = 0.875; U_9 = 1.0$$

It is worth noting that any changes in their values could produce different final results from the similarity analysis, so these are important tuning parameters, too.

The response surface of the fuzzy inference procedure that uses the fuzzy rule base from Figure 11.14 and the membership functions from Figure 11.13 is shown in Figure 11.15.

This response surface is computed by the following *defuzzification* procedure:

$$D = \sum_{i=1}^{L} u_i v_i \bigg/ \sum_{i=1}^{L} v_i \qquad (11.23)$$

Here, $0 \le v_i \le 1, i = 1, 2, \ldots, L$ is the *firing (activation) degree* of the $i$th fuzzy rule and $L = 25$ is the total number of fuzzy rules. $u_i \in [U_1, U_2, \ldots, U_9]$ represents the actual singleton value of the $i$th fuzzy rule, according to the fuzzy rule base in Figure 11.14, for example, $u_8 = U_4 = 0.375$, since *fuzzy rule 8* as seen from Figure 11.14

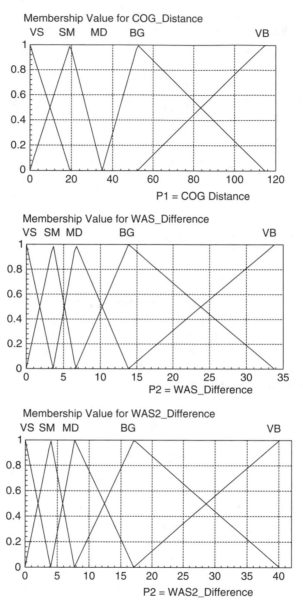

Figure 11.13. Five triangular membership functions assumed for inputs *P1* and *P2*.

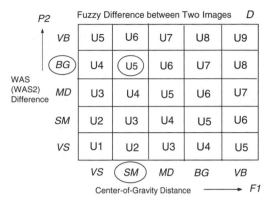

**Figure 11.14.** Proposed fuzzy rule base (FRB) with 25 fuzzy rules, used for similarity analysis.

is as follows:

$$\text{IF}(F1 \text{ is } \textbf{SM} \text{ AND } F2 \text{ is } \textbf{MD}) \text{ THEN } D = U4 \qquad (11.24)$$

The results from the similarity analysis based on the above-proposed fuzzy decision procedure are discussed below.

Table 11.2 shows the three most similar results ranked as no.1, no. 2, and no. 3, for each of the 18 test images. Here, the two input parameters used for the fuzzy decision are $P1 = COGD$ and $P2 = WAS2D$. $N1$, $N2$, and $N3$ denote the code numbers of the image and $FD1$, $FD2$, and $FD3$ are the fuzzy difference degrees $D$ computed by (11.23).

A detailed look at the results shows that, in most cases, the images that are ranked as no. 1 (the most similar images) represent the correct similarity decision, which coincides with the human decision. However, there are also some cases, such as the similarity decisions for images 3 and 13, that do not look correct from a human viewpoint. These two images represent different parts of the same *tree* and, according to the commonsense human decision, this pair of images should be considered to be the most similar images. However, the fuzzy decision procedure shows different results in Table 11.2.

This fact also shows that a proper human-defined criterion for similarity should be established prior to running a respective optimization procedure that tunes the parameters of the fuzzy decision procedure, namely, the centers of the membership functions and the values of the singletons. Then, the computer fuzzy decision procedure should be able to closely simulate the human similarity decision. Our future research goal lies in this direction.

Another important finding from Table 11.2 is that even if an image has been classified as no. 1 (i.e., the most similar image to a given one), the final decision for acceptance or rejection of this result should be made using a prespecified *threshold, Th.* For example, if the preset threshold is $Th = 0.33$, then the solutions for the similarity analysis of images nos. 3, 10, 11, and 18 would be discarded as nonplausible, that is, image no. 18 is not similar to image no. 12, even if it is ranked as no. 1.

TABLE 11.2. Similarity Analysis of All 18 Images by the Fuzzy Decision Procedure

| Image | FD_WAS2 Similarity Analysis | | | | | |
|---|---|---|---|---|---|---|
| | No. 1 | | No. 2 | | No. 3 | |
| | *N1* | *FD1* | *N2* | *FD2* | *N2* | *FD3* |
| 1 | 8 | 0.153 | 9 | 0.165 | 2 | 0.551 |
| 2 | 10 | 0.301 | 16 | 0.395 | 6 | 0.413 |
| 3 | 12 | 0.445 | 17 | 0.454 | 7 | 0.456 |
| 4 | 13 | 0.104 | 12 | 0.114 | 18 | 0.470 |
| 5 | 15 | 0.239 | 14 | 0.282 | 11 | 0.345 |
| 6 | 16 | 0.085 | 2 | 0.413 | 10 | 0.480 |
| 7 | 17 | 0.049 | 15 | 0.181 | 5 | 0.403 |
| 8 | 1 | 0.153 | 9 | 0.266 | 12 | 0.565 |
| 9 | 1 | 0.165 | 8 | 0.266 | 2 | 0.517 |
| 10 | 2 | 0.301 | 16 | 0.469 | 6 | 0.480 |
| 11 | 5 | 0.345 | 15 | 0.407 | 7 | 0.461 |
| 12 | 4 | 0.114 | 13 | 0.120 | 18 | 0.441 |
| 13 | 4 | 0.104 | 12 | 0.120 | 18 | 0.449 |
| 14 | 5 | 0.282 | 15 | 0.413 | 17 | 0.492 |
| 15 | 7 | 0.181 | 17 | 0.201 | 5 | 0.239 |
| 16 | 6 | 0.085 | 2 | 0.395 | 10 | 0.469 |
| 17 | 7 | 0.049 | 15 | 0.201 | 5 | 0.412 |
| 18 | 12 | 0.441 | 13 | 0.449 | 4 | 0.470 |

## 11.9 UNSUPERVISED CLASSIFICATION FOR KNOWLEDGE ACQUISITION

The above-proposed computation scheme for similarity analysis can be incorporated into a larger computation scheme for classification of new (unknown, test) images to a given *image base* that contains the group of currently known *core images*. These images are considered to be available current pieces of knowledge about the process under investigation. The block diagram of this computation scheme is shown in Figure 11.16. Then the process of knowledge acquisition is done in the following relatively simple way.

With a predetermined threshold *Th*, for example, *Th* = 0.33, any newly submitted image could be classified as being similar to a given *core image* from the image base or could be rejected as an unknown image. In the latter case, the new image is added to the image base as a new piece of *knowledge* about the process, thus enlarging the number of the core images in the image base.

Figures 11.17 and 11.18 show the classification results of images nos. 6,7,..., 18 from Figure 11.6 under the assumption that the image base in Figure 11.16 consists of the following five core images, namely nos. 1,2,3,4, and 5. It is seen from the figures that six images (nos. 6, 7, 11, 16, 17, and 18) are rejected by the classification.

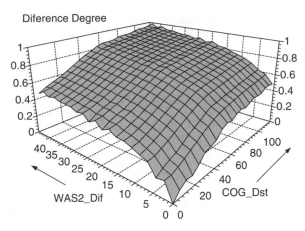

Figure 11.15. Nonlinear response surface using the fuzzy rule base from Figure 11.14. Membership functions for *P1* and *P2* are tuned as shown in Figure 11.13.

This classification procedure can be performed iteratively by adding at each iteration the most strongly rejected image as a new member (new core image) of the image base. Then, after three iterations, three new images will be added to the image base as new pieces of information, namely, image nos. 6, 7, and 18. Finally, the image base would consist of eight pieces of knowledge, as follows: nos. 1, 2, 3, 4, 5, 6, 7, and 18.

Then, image no. 16 will be classified as "similar" to image no. 6 and image no. 17 will be classified as "similar" to image no. 6.

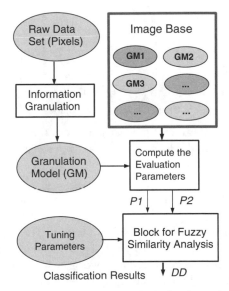

Figure 11.16. Block diagram of the proposed classification scheme for knowledge acquisition, based on the fuzzy similarity analysis.

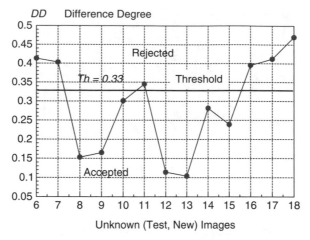

Figure 11.17. Computed difference degrees of the new images that are used for the classification decision (*accepted—rejected*) based on the predefined threshold $Th = 0.33$.

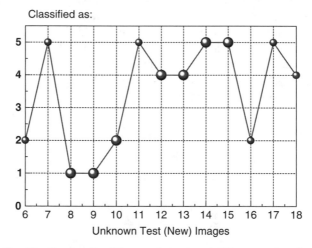

Figure 11.18. Classification results of the remaining (new) 13 images using the image base with the first 5 Images. The accepted results are shown as large ball symbols.

## 11.10 CONCLUSION

In this chapter a special unsupervised classification scheme for large data sets and images is proposed, based on a two-input fuzzy rule-based similarity procedure. In order to extract the inputs for this fuzzy procedure, two growing-type unsupervised learning algorithms are presented and compared. They convert the original "raw" data set (the RGB data set from the image) into the so-called granulation (compressed) model with a smaller number of neurons.

It is shown that the *Grow2* algorithm has the advantage over the *Grow1* algorithm because it produces a granulation model with fewer neurons than *Grow1* within the same granulation quality *AVmin*. Both algorithms *Grow1* and *Grow2* are much faster in computation time compared to the standard offline learning algorithm *Fixed*, which uses the same predetermined number of neurons.

The two parameters used in the fuzzy decision procedure for similarity analysis are extracted from the obtained granulation model as follows. The first parameter *P1* is the center-of-gravity distance *COGD* between a given pair of data sets (images), and parameter *P2* represents the weighted average size difference, computed in two versions, namely *WASD* and *WAS2D*.

The performance of the proposed fuzzy decision procedure for similarity analysis is demonstrated in a test example of 18 images. In addition, the same example is used for the more general computation scheme for knowledge acquisition under the assumption that the first 5 images are used as core images in the initial image base. The iterative process of classification leads to adding 3 new core images to the image base. The proposed procedure could be used as an evolving computation scheme for knowledge acquisition from a large (or even unlimited) number of images or other data sets.

Further development of the above computation schemes is considered in the following two directions. The first one is to establish a proper human-defined criterion for optimizing the parameters of the fuzzy similarity procedure, in order to achieve more plausible humanlike results from the similarity analysis and classification. The second direction is to further refine the iterative (evolving) procedure for knowledge acquisition in order for it to be successfully used for knowledge extraction from online processes and data streams.

## 11.11 REFERENCES

1. J. C. Bezdek, *Pattern Recognition with Fuzzy Objective Function Algorithms*. New York: Plenum Press, 1981.
2. Ch. M. Bishop, *Neural Networks for Pattern Recognition*. Oxford University Press, 2003.
3. W. Pedrycz, *Knowledge-Based Clustering: From Data to Information Granules*. Wiley-Interscience, 2005, p. 316.
4. T. Kohonen, *Self-Organizing Maps*, 3rd ed. Springer Series in Information Sciences. Berlin: Springer, 2001.
5. T. Martinetz, S. Berkovich, K. Schulten, "Neural-Gas Network for Vector Quantization and Its Application to Time-Series Prediction," *IEEE Trans. Neural Networks*, Vol. 4, No. 4, pp. 558–569, 1993.
6. Lei. Xu, A. Krzyzak, E. Oja, "Rival Penalized Competitive Learning for Clustering Analysis, RBF Net and Curve Detection," *IEEE Trans. Neural Networks*, Vol. 4, No. 4, pp. 636–649, 1993.
7. S. C. Ahalt, A. K. Krishnamurty, P. Chen, D. E. Melton, "Competitive Learning Algorithms for Vector Quantization," *Neural Networks*, Vol. 3, pp. 277–291, 1990.
8. G. Vachkov, "Growing Neural Models for Process Identification and Data Analysis," *Int. J. Innovative Computing, Information and Control, IJICIC*, Vol. 2, No. 1, pp. 101–123, February 2006.

9. G. Vachkov, "Classification of Machine Operations Based on Growing Neural Models and Fuzzy Decision," CD-ROM. *Proc. 21st European Conf. on Modelling and Simulation, ECMS 2007*, Prague, Czech Republic, June 4–6, 2007, pp. 68–73.

10. G. Vachkov, H. Ishihara, "Learning Algorithms for Compression and Evaluation of Information from Large Data Sets," CD-ROM. *Proc. SICE Annual Conference 2007,* Takamatsu, Japan, September 17–20, 2007, pp. 1837–1844.

11. G. Vachkov, H. Ishihara, "On-Line Unsupervised Learning for Information Compression and Similarity Analysis of Large Data Sets," CD-ROM. *Proc. 2007 IEEE Int. Conf. on Mechatronics and Automation*, ICMA 2007, Harbin, China, August 5–8, 2007, pp. 105–110.

12. G. Vachkov, "Classification of Images Based on Fuzzy Similarity Analysis," CD-ROM. *Proc. 5th Int. Symposium on Management Engineering, ISME 2008*, Graduate School on Information, Production and Systems, Waseda University, Hibikino, Kitakyushu City, Japan, paper R09, March, 15–17, 2008, pp. 162–169.

13. G. Vachkov, "Classification of Images Based on Information Granulation and Fuzzy Rule Based Similarity Analysis," CD-ROM. *Proc. 2008 World Congress on Computational Intelligence, WCCI 2008*, FUZZ-IEEE 2008, Hong Kong, China, paper FS0528, June 1–6, 2008, pp. 2326–2332.

# 12

# AN EXTENDED VERSION OF THE GUSTAFSON-KESSEL ALGORITHM FOR EVOLVING DATA STREAM CLUSTERING

Dimitar Filev, Olga Georgieva

**Abstract:** The chapter deals with a recursive clustering algorithm that enables a real-time partitioning of data streams. The proposed algorithm incorporates the advantages of the Gustafson-Kessel clustering algorithm of identifying clusters with different shape and orientation while expanding its area of application to the challenging problem of real-time data clustering. The algorithm is applicable to a wide range of practical evolving system–type applications, such as diagnostics and prognostics, system identification, real-time classification, and process quality monitoring and control.

## 12.1 INTRODUCTION

Cluster analysis is one of the challenging theoretical and practical problems in data mining, signal processing, diagnostics and prognostics, and information retrieval in numerous other application areas. Most of the clustering methods are based on the concept of *batch clustering*; that is, the data set is assumed to be available before the clustering analysis is carried out. In a wide range of applications, however, the data is presented to the clustering algorithm in real time.

Recently, we have obseyrved a growing interest toward methods for real-time clustering streams of data [7, 18, 19]. Among them are the methods for single-pass

*Evolving Intelligent Systems: Methodology and Applications,* Edited by Plamen Angelov, Dimitar P. Filev, and Nikola Kasabov

clustering, for example, [15, 21, 23], comprising techniques that find clusters by executing one pass through the data set, in contrast to the iterative strategies like K-means clustering. A prototypical representative of the one-pass evolving algorithms is the *evolving clustering method* (*ECM*) [19]. It is a distance-based clustering method where the cluster centers are represented by evolving nodes that are continuously updated through changing their centers' positions and adjusting their cluster radii. Alternatively, new clusters are created.

The approach of single-pass clustering is also applied in the *dynamic data assigning algorithm* (*DDAA*) [13]. It is a heuristic clustering method that detects a single (good) cluster among noisy data, applying the concept of *noise clustering* [8, 9]. The aim is to discover an interesting pattern in terms of a specific group that might cover only a small proportion of the full data set, rather than to partition the whole data set into clusters. The evolving version of the algorithm [13, 14] is suitable for dealing with data streams. It assigns every new data point to an already-determined good cluster or alternatively to the noise cluster. The assignment can be done in a crisp or fuzzy sense.

Alternative clustering algorithms, for example, DBSCAN [10] or its incremental version [11], take noise into account as well. DBSCAN defines clusters in terms of a homogeneous minimum density; that is, the user must specify two parameters *Eps* and *MinPts*. For each point in a cluster, the *Eps*-neighborhood must contain at least *MinPts* points; otherwise, the point is considered to be noise. This means that the definition of *noise* is homogeneous in the whole data space, and the decision as to whether points are to be marked as noise or as outliers strongly depends on the setting of these parameters. The algorithm is applicable to image analysis.

Some of the clustering methods are widely used as a foundation for structure identification of fuzzy rule-based models [3, 6, 22]. Examples of clustering algorithms that are used in model identification procedures include the *mountain* clustering algorithm [22] and its modification—the *subtractive* clustering algorithm [6]. The *online* extension of mountain/subtractive clustering utilizes recursive and noniterative techniques for calculating the potential of the new data point in order to update the existing clusters or to discover new ones [1, 2]. The method is targeted to real-time modeling and classification tasks.

A new methodology for dynamic data mining based on fuzzy clustering is proposed in [7]. It continuously updates the structure and parameters of a fuzzy classifier by incorporating a *Fuzzy-C-Means* (FCM) clustering algorithm [4].

In a number of real problems, such as performance analysis of dynamic systems, and time-series data, as well as some forecasting and modeling tasks, the identified clusters are not spherical as they are presumed to be by the commonly used FCM clustering method and its derivatives, but are characterized with a different shape and orientation in the space. Several clustering algorithms extend the original FCM method to the case of clusters with a general shape [3, 12, 17, 20]. The Gustafson-Kessel (GK) clustering algorithm [16] is commonly used in most of the cases as a powerful clustering technique with numerous applications in various domains, including image processing, classification, and system identification. By contrast to the FCM algorithm, its main feature is the local adaptation of the distance metric to the shape of the cluster by estimating the cluster covariance matrix and adapting the distance-inducing matrix. In addition, it is relatively insensitive to the data scaling and initialization of the partition matrix.

In this chapter, we propose a new clustering algorithm called the *evolving GK-like (eGKL) algorithm* that builds on the advantages of the GK algorithm as a valuable clustering technique that is able to identify clusters with a generic shape and orientation. We discuss the idea of expanding the original GK algorithm to the problem of clustering data streams. We also address the issues of estimation of the number of clusters and recursive updating and adaptation of their parameters to the data.

The chapter is organized as follows. The second section presents the necessary background on cluster analysis based on the GK algorithm. The idea of the evolving GK-like algorithm and a simplified version are presented in the third section. The further necessary methodological and computational considerations related to the evolving GK concept are presented in the fourth and fifth sections, respectively. The evolving GK-like algorithm is developed in the sixth section. Final conclusions are provided in the seventh section.

## 12.2 CLUSTER ANALYSIS BY GK ALGORITHM

Objective function-based clustering aims at minimization of an objective function $J$ that represents the fitting error of the clusters with respect to the data. In this objective function, the number of clusters has to be fixed in advance. The underlying objective function for most of the clustering algorithms is [4]:

$$J(V, U, F) = \sum_{i=1}^{c} \sum_{k=1}^{N} (u_{ik})^m d_{ik}^2 \tag{12.1}$$

where $N$ is the number of data points, $c$ is the number of clusters given in advance, $u_{ik}$ and $d_{ik}$ denote correspondingly the membership degree and distance between the $k$th data point $x_k = [x_{k1}, x_{k2}, \ldots, x_{kn}], k = 1, \ldots, N$ and the $i$th cluster prototype, $i = 1, \ldots, c$, and $n$ is the number of features describing each data point. $U = \{u_{ik}\}$ is $c \times N$ partition matrix. In the simplest case, the cluster prototype is a single vector called, a *cluster center*, which for the $i$th cluster is $v_i = [v_{i1}, v_{i2}, \ldots, v_{in}]$; $V = \{v_i\}$ is $c \times n$ prototype matrix. The fuzzifier $m \in [1, \infty)$ is the weighted exponent coefficient that determines how much clusters may overlap. In most of cases, satisfactory results are obtained at $m = 2$.

The distance $d_{ik}$ used by the GK algorithm is a squared inner-product distance norm that depends on a positive definite symmetric matrix $A_i$ as follows:

$$d_{ik}^2 = \|x_k - v_i\|_{A_i}^2 = (x_k - v_i) A_i (x_k - v_i)^T \tag{12.2}$$

The matrix $A_i$, $i = 1, \ldots, c$ determines the shape and orientation of the selected cluster. Thus, the GK algorithm employs an adaptive distance norm unique for every cluster as the norm-inducing matrix $A_i$ is calculated by estimates of the data covariance:

$$A_i = [\rho_i \det(F_i)]^{1/n} F_i^{-1} \tag{12.3}$$

where $\rho_i$ is the cluster volume of the $i$th cluster and $F_i$ is the fuzzy covariance matrix calculated as follows:

$$F_i = \frac{\sum_{k=1}^{N} (u_{ik})^m (x_k - v_i)^T (x_k - v_i)}{\sum_{k=1}^{N} (u_{ik})^m} \tag{12.4}$$

Without any prior knowledge, the cluster volumes $\rho_i$, $i = 1, \ldots, c$ are simply fixed at one for each cluster.

Knowing the distances (12.2), the membership degree $u_{ik}, i = 1, \ldots, c$, $k = 1, \ldots, N$ of each data to every cluster is calculated as a relative value:

$$u_{ik} = \frac{1}{\sum_{j=1}^{c} (d_{ik}/d_{jk})^{2/(m-1)}} \tag{12.5}$$

and the cluster centers are defined as a weighted mean:

$$v_i = \frac{\sum_{k=1}^{N} (u_{ik})^m x_k}{\sum_{k=1}^{N} (u_{ik})^m} \tag{12.6}$$

where m > 1 is a parameter defining the fuzziness of the clusters. In order to avoid the trivial solution assigning no data to any cluster by setting all $u_{ik}$ to zero, and to avoid empty clusters, the following constraints are introduced:

$$u_{ik} \in [0, 1], \qquad 1 \leq i \leq c, \quad 1 \leq k \leq N \tag{12.7i}$$

$$\sum_{i=1}^{c} u_{ik} = 1, \qquad 1 \leq k \leq N \tag{12.7ii}$$

$$0 < \sum_{i=1}^{N} u_{ik} < N, \qquad 1 \leq i \leq c \tag{12.7iii}$$

The GK algorithm, as do other FCM-based clustering algorithms, uses the Lagrange multiplier method to minimize the cost functional (12.1). It iteratively determines the membership degree $u_{ik}$ and cluster parameters—cluster center $v_i$ and the fuzzy covariance matrix $F_i$—which finally define the distance value $d_{ik}$. The optimization scheme of the GK clustering is given in the appendix at the end of this chapter.

The obtained clusters are hyperellipsoids with arbitrary orientation. This generalized set of clusters well suits a variety of practical problems.

## 12.3 EVOLVING CLUSTERING BASED ON GK SIMILARITY DISTANCE

Although the GK algorithm possesses a great advantage over the other clustering algorithms as it adapts the clusters according to their real shape, the algorithm is not able to deal with streams of data and limits its scope to batch clustering due mainly to three obstacles. These shortcomings have nothing to do with the GK procedure itself but with the attempt to expand all FCM-type clustering algorithms to cases that deal with streaming data—a basic characteristic of an evolving-system-type application. First, it processes only a fixed data set. Second, the algorithm assumes that the number of clusters is known in advance. Finally, it determines the clusters by an iterative optimization scheme. Thus, in practice, the new incoming data cannot be processed by the original algorithm scheme as the stream of incoming data changes over time.

The idea of an alternative recursive clustering algorithm that is similar to the concept of the GK algorithm in the sense of using clusters with general data structure is presented in the following. Our solution is inspired by two of the most common recursive clustering algorithms—the k-*nearest neighbor* (k-*NN*) [24] and the *linear vector quantization* (*LVQ*) [25] algorithms. We do not consider the proposed algorithm an evolving version of the GK algorithm but a rather recursive complement that uses the same Mahalanobis distance—like metrics and the norm-inducing matrix—while avoiding the aforementioned drawbacks.

One simplified solution could be formulated according to the direct implementation of the $k$-NN approach. Originally, we will be assuming that the GK has been applied to identify an initial set of $c$ clusters of the previously collected data. Each of those clusters is defined by its center $v_i$ and fuzzy covariance matrix $F_i$. This assumption is realistic given the fact that in almost all evolving applications some initial knowledge about the data being processed is available.

We assume that the boundary of each cluster is defined by the cluster radius, which is calculated from the membership degrees (12.5). The radius $r_i$ of the $i$th cluster is equal to the maximal distance between the cluster center $v_i$ and the points belonging to this cluster with membership degree larger than or equal to a given threshold membership degree $u_h$:

$$r_i = \max_{\forall x_j \in \text{ } i\text{th cluster and } u_{ij} > u_h} \left\| v_i - x_j \right\|_{A_i} \qquad (12.8)$$

where $\| \cdot \|_{A_i}$ is the GK distance norm determined according to equation (12.2) and the data $x_j$ belongs to the $i$th cluster with membership degree $u_{ij}$ such that $u_{ij} > u_h$.

Suppose $x_k$ is a new data point coming in currently. Three possibilities should be evaluated. First, the data belongs to an existing cluster if it is within the cluster boundary. This case imposes just clusters' update. If the data point is not within the boundary of any existing cluster, it may define a new cluster. Alternatively, $x_k$ could be an outlier, which does not affect the data structure. These three possibilities for assigning $x_k$ are considered in detail in the following.

The similarity between the new data point $x_k$ and each of the existing $c$ clusters is evaluated by checking the Mahalanobis-like distances using equations (12.2) and (12.3),

$$d_{ik} = \sqrt{(x_k-v_i)[(det(F_i))^{1/n}F_i^{-1}](x_k-v_i)^T} \qquad (12.9)$$

and assuming that each cluster volume $\rho_i$'s is fixed at one. The minimal distance $d_{pk}$ determines the closest cluster $p$ as

$$p = \underset{i=1,\ldots,c}{\arg\min}(d_{ik}) \qquad (12.10)$$

The data point $x_k$ is assigned to the cluster $p$ if the distance $d_{pk}$ is less than or equal to the radius $r_p$, that is, if the condition

$$d_{pk} \leq r_p \qquad (12.11)$$

is satisfied. If this is the case, we can apply the Kohonen rule [25] to update the $p$th cluster parameters—cluster center and covariance matrix:

$$v_{p,new} = (1-\alpha)v_{p,old} + \alpha x_k = v_{p,old} + \alpha(x_k-v_{p,old}) \qquad (12.12)$$

$$\begin{aligned} F_{p,new} &= (1-\alpha)F_{p,old} + \alpha(x_k-v_{p,old})^T(x_k-v_{p,old}) = \\ &= F_{p,old} + \alpha((x_k-v_{p,old})^T(x_k-v_{p,old})-F_{p,old}) \end{aligned} \qquad (12.13)$$

where $\alpha = [0.05\ 0.3]$ is a learning rate; $v_{p,new}$ and $v_{p,old}$ denote the new and old values of the center; and $F_{p,new}$ and $F_{p,old}$ denote the new and old values of the covariance matrix. If condition (12.11) fails, a new potential cluster is created and the number of clusters is incremented:

$$c := c+1 \qquad (12.14)$$

Then, the incoming data $x_k$ is accepted as a center $v_{new}$ of the new cluster,

$$v_{new} = x_k \qquad (12.15)$$

and its covariance matrix $F_{new}$ is initialized with the covariance matrix of the closest cluster:

$$F_{new} = F_{p,old} \qquad (12.16)$$

In order to quantify the credibility of the estimated clusters, a parameter $P_i, i = 1,\ldots,c$ is introduced to assess the number of points belonging to $i$th cluster. Its lower bound is estimated from the minimal number of data points necessary to learn the parameters of the covariance matrix. It is determined by the dimensionality $n$ of the data vector as:

$$P_{min} = n(n+1)/2 \qquad (12.17)$$

Apparently, a high value of $P_i$ not only guarantees the validity of the covariance matrixes but improves the robustness of the algorithm with respect to outliers. That is why we suggest a larger threshold $P_{tol}$, $P_{tol} > P_{min}$ that corresponds to the desired minimal amount of points falling within the $r_i$ boundary of each cluster. The threshold value is context determined due to the specificity of the considered data set.

The simplified online GK-like clustering that summarizes the ideas presented above is given in the following step-by-step description:

1. *Initialization:* Calculate the initial number of clusters $c$ and the corresponding matrixes $V$, $U$ and $F_i$, $i = 1, \ldots, c$ by the offline GK algorithm. Choose in advance: $u_h$, $\alpha$, $P_{tol}$.
   **Repeat** for every new data point $x_k$.
2. Calculate $d_{ik}$, $i = 1, \ldots, c$:

$$d_{ik} = \sqrt{(x_k - v_i)[(det(F_i))^{1/n} F_i^{-1}](x_k - v_i)^T}$$

3. Determine the closest cluster $p$:

$$p = \arg\min_{i=1,\ldots,c}(d_{ik})$$

4. Calculate the radius $r_p$ of the closest cluster:

$$r_p = \max_{\forall x_j \in\, p\text{th cluster and } u_{pj} > u_h} \|v_p - x_j\|_{A_p}$$

5. If $d_{pk} \leq r_p$:

```
Update the center vp and matrix Fp:
    vp,new = vp,old + α (xk−vp,old)
    Fp,new = Fp,old + α ( (xk−vp,old) T (xk−vp,old) −Fp,old)
    Recalculate the partition matrix U.
else  dpk>rp
        Create a new cluster: vc+1 := xs; Fc+1 :− Fp
        Calculate the number Pc+1.
        If Pc+1≥Ptol
            Accept the new cluster, c:= c+1.
        else
            Refuse the new cluster and keep the old structure.
        end
end
```

The choice of the parameters $u_h$, $\alpha$, and $P_{tol}$ is of real importance for the clustering results. The membership threshold $u_h$ is difficult to determine in advance and depends on the density of the data set and the level of cluster overlapping. The default value of $u_h$ is 0.5, but being stricter in the identification of proper clusters the prescribed threshold membership degree should be chosen larger. For a more tolerant identification it should be chosen smaller. The learning rate $\alpha$ determines the step of searching and, thus, a large value guarantees sparsely selected clusters. However, in some cases the large step is not preferred as it leads to large changes that could ignore a valuable cluster. It might be beneficial to use two different threshold membership values as $u_h$ is used to determine the cluster radius of the existing clusters and $u_{h\_new}$ to calculate the radius of the newly created cluster. If we set $u_h > u_{h\_new}$, we give more freedom in the new cluster selection, whereas we remain strict in the assessment of the points belonging to the existing clusters.

The algorithm is validated in two examples based on an artificial data set and the benchmark electroencephalography (EEG) data set [36].

## 12.3.1 Application of the Algorithm to an Artificial Data Set

The clustering capability of the simplified evolving GK-like clustering algorithm is demonstrated on an artificial data set generated by an unvaried nonlinear function [3]:

$$y_k = 10^{-4}\sin(0,001\,k^2)k^3 + e \qquad (12.18)$$

where $e$ is normally distributed random noise. The dynamics simulated by this function present a typical behavior of a certain nonlinear process. The generated data set is organized in a $200 \times 2$ data matrix, whose first column is formed by the values of the vector $k = [1 : 0.5 : 100]$ and the second column by the corresponding values of the vector $y_k$.

The off-line GK algorithm with parameters $m = 2$ and $tol = 0.01$ was applied to the first 100 data points in order to initialize the simplified evolving algorithm (Figure 12.1a) while the remaining data was treated as a data stream. Due to the lack of a priori information the default value of the threshold membership degree $u_h = 0.5$ and a low boundary level of the learning rate $\alpha = 0.05$ were considered. The parameter $P_{tol} = 10$ was determined to guarantee robustness of the clusters. The third cluster was created after the 33-th incoming data had been added. Simultaneously, the second cluster center was updated (Figure 12.1b). After the creation of the forth cluster (Figure 12.1c) the rest of the data only updated the previously identified data structures (Figure 12.1d).

Results comparable to the batch GK clustering application are obtained when we are strict in the assessment of the existing clusters as $u_h = 0.95$ but more free in the evaluation of the newly created cluster as $u_{h\_new} = 0.8$ (Figure 12.2). In both cases, five valuable clusters are selected.

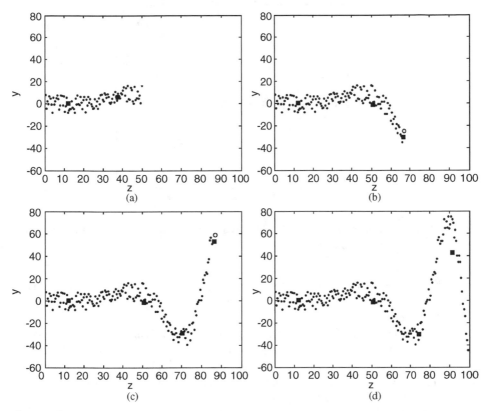

Figure 12.1. Clustering results: dots are data; squares are cluster centers; the circle is the current data point: (a) initial clusters; (b) the third selected cluster at 33rd incoming data; (c) the fourth cluster selected at 173rd data point. (d) The last cluster is slightly updated until the rest of the data have been accumulated.

## 12.3.2 Application of the Algorithm to a Benchmark Data Set

Multiple electrode time-series EEG recordings of control and alcoholic subjects are provided by UC Irvine Machine Learning Repository [36]. This data arises from a large study to examine EEG correlation to genetic predisposition to alcoholism. It contains measurements from 64 electrodes placed on the scalp sampled at 256 Hz (3.9 ms epoch) for 1 second.

Notwithstanding the EEG data set provides a large amount of data series, here we are interested in a single series as a subject of online partitioning. Initially, the first 100 points are clustered by the batch GK algorithm in four clusters. For the rest of the data, the evolving clustering is accomplished through a parameter set close to the default values as $u_h = 0.6$ and $\alpha = 0.05$. The parameter $P_{tol} = 10$ was context defined. As a result, five new clusters are selected that fit the changes in the signal shape (Figure 12.3a).

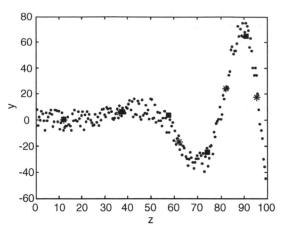

**Figure 12.2.** Squares are cluster centers of the evolving algorithm and stars are the centers of the batch GK algorithm application.

If we reduce the threshold $P_{tol}$ to the minimal value $P_{tol} = P_{min} = 3$ according to equation (12.17), we are able to detect all peaks provided in the data series, obtaining in total 18 clusters (Figure 12.3b).

The simulation results show that the developed evolving algorithm discovers relatively well the changes in the data structure. However, in some cases the cluster centers are not precisely defined and their shape and orientation are not correctly determined (Figure 12.2). The simplified evolving reasoning does not provide a reliable procedure for initiation and adjustment of the newfound cluster. In the next section, these drawbacks are overcome by applying a more sophisticated concept inspired by the theory of *statistical process control* (*SPC*) and the idea to account for older observations within a moving window length.

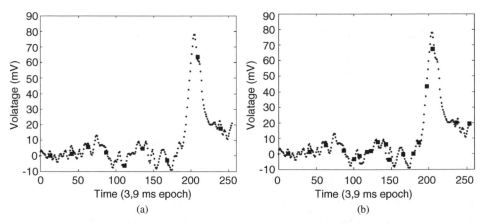

**Figure 12.3.** Evolving clustering of EEG data.

## 12.4 METHODOLOGICAL CONSIDERATIONS

Some additional methodological and computational considerations related to the evolving GK-like (eGKL) concept that concern the definition of the clusters' radii and recursive updating of the cluster parameters will be addressed in the preliminaries.

The main challenge is the determination of the cluster radius. The objective function-based clustering algorithms establish the radius based on data as the value of the cost function (12.1) can be seen as a measure of the total variance of $x_k$ from $v_i$. However, this assumption is not acceptable for an evolving data set due to the growing amount of points coming in as a stream. In the following we propose a new approach for determining a generic cluster radius that can be applicable independently of the data. This approach is inspired by statistical process control as a powerful methodology for identifying variations in monitored output variables that are due to actual input changes rather than process noise.

The main reason to seek to transfer some of the concepts and techniques from the established SPC methodology to the (new) field of evolving clustering is the similarity between the streams of data that are the result of the process monitoring and the data in evolving clustering. In both cases, we deal with data that is generated by a specific system (e.g., device, machine, process), that is, governed by certain model of physical law defining some similarity relationships between the data over time. In the evolving system concept, the data has a temporal dimension that defines a mechanism of ordering the data points/samples. This type of data is different than the type of data considered in conventional clustering, where the temporal dimension is missing and the data is regarded as different objects.

The process variable $y$ could be associated with its current mean $y_i^*$ if the monitored process is in statistical control; that is, the variable $y$ is within the process control limits that are usually set at $y_i^* \pm 3\sigma_{yi}$ according to the following condition:

$$|y - y_i^*| < 3\sigma_{yi} \qquad (12.19)$$

where $y_i^*$ and $\sigma_{yi}$ are the process mean and standard deviation corresponding to the $i$th particular process condition. When $y$ exceeds the process control band (12.19), the system is considered out of control.

In practice, the process control condition (12.19) defines a similarity relation as all values of $y$ within the process control band $y_i^* \pm 3\sigma_{yi}$ are considered similar and could be represented by the mean $y_i^*$. This reasoning could be extended from the perspective of considering a single-dimensional similarity relation clustering of the process variable $y$ into clusters with centers $y_i^*$'s and respective radii $3\sigma_{yi}$'s. If the process variable takes values that are out of the process control limits (12.19), this is an indication of a substantial variable change, which could be additionally indicated by a trend over time, or multiple points below or above the mean. When the process is out of statistical control, the process control parameters are recalculated, resulting in a new mean value $y_j^*$ and standard deviation $\sigma_{yj}$ (Figure 12.4).

The statistical process control condition for an $n$ dimensional process variable $y_k = [y_{k1}, y_{k2}, \ldots, y_{kn}]$ is defined through the squared Mahalanobis distance $D$ between

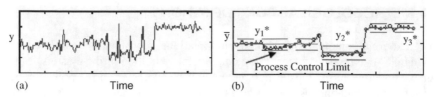

Figure 12.4. Process variable (a) and its SPC (Shewhart) chart (b).

the current vector $y_k$ and the population mean [26, 27], where the population mean and covariance are approximated by the sample mean $y^*$ and covariance $S$ of the certain process control condition:

$$D^2 = (y-y^*)S^{-1}(y-y^*)^T \qquad (12.20)$$

where

$$y^* = \frac{1}{N}\sum_{k=1}^{N} y_k \qquad (12.21\text{i})$$

$$S = \frac{1}{N}\sum_{k=1}^{N}(y_k-y^*)^T(y_k-y^*) \qquad (12.21\text{ii})$$

The process vector $y_k$ is considered in statistical control when $D^2$ is upper bounded by the chi-square distribution, that is,

$$D^2 < \chi^2_{n,\beta} \qquad (12.22)$$

where $\chi^2_{n,\beta}$ is the $(1 - \beta)$th value of the chi-square distribution with $n$ degrees of freedom and $\beta$ is the probability of a false alarm. Several low-dimensional values of the distribution for the well-known $\pm 3\sigma$ and $\pm 2\sigma$ limits are given in Table 12.1. It could be seen that the condition (12.22) covers the single-dimensional case (12.19) for the case of a single process value $n = 1$ [28].

The multidimensional process control condition (12.22) defines a relation of similarity for all vectors $y_k$ that are within the (squared) radius $\chi^2_{n,\beta}$. The data points within this region could be viewed as a cluster with center $y^*$ and shape defined by the covariance matrix $S$. The vectors $y_k$ that are characterized with large values of the

TABLE 12.1.

| | | β | |
|---|---|---|---|
| $\chi^2_{n,\beta}$ | | 0.0027 | 0.0455 |
| | 1 | 9 | 4 |
| $n$ | 2 | 11.8290 | 6.1801 |
| | 3 | 14.1563 | 8.0249 |

distance $D^2$ are far away from the center of the cluster $y^*$ and are less likely to belong to that particular cluster.

The squared radius of the cluster is independent of the data as it is determined by the chi-square distribution constant $\chi^2_{n,\beta}$ that remains the same for a given probability $\beta$ and dimensionality $n$ of the vector $y_k$. The constant $\chi^2_{n,\beta}$ defines the maximal distance $D^2$ for a given probability threshold $1 - \beta$. Beyond that distance, we reject the null hypothesis that the process is in control. Thus, vectors $y_k$ that fail condition (12.22) are considered not to belong to the specific cluster.

The other challenge is to transfer the concepts of the SPC to the problem of evolving GK-like clustering. Some additional specifications related to the application of the SPC condition (12.22) to the evolving clustering features have to be given. In order to calculate the radii of the eGKL clusters that are induced by the Mahalanobis-like distance (12.2), we modify expression (12.22) by multiplying the left and right sides of the inequality with the nonnegative (the covariance matrix $S$ is always positive semidefinite) constant $(det(S))^{1/n}$:

$$(y-y^*)S^{-1}(y-y^*)^T (det(S))^{1/n} < \chi^2_{n,\beta}(det(S))^{1/n} \qquad (12.23)$$

Therefore, for a given probability $\beta$ and dimensionality $n$ of the vectors $y_k$, the radii of the Mahalanobis-like distance (12.2), the induced eGKL clusters are dependent on the determinant of the covariance matrix:

$$R^2 = \chi^2_{n,\beta}(det(S))^{1/n}$$

and the similarity measure that is associated with the Mahalanobis-like distance clusters is:

$$d^2 < R^2 \qquad (12.24)$$

where

$$d^2 = (y-y^*)(det(S))^{1/n}S^{-1}(y-y^*)^T \qquad (12.25)$$

From expression (12.23), it is easy to see that GK-like clusters are identical to the clusters generated by the similarity measure (12.22). Therefore, we can use either (12.22) or (12.24) to determine the clusters. In the next section, we will introduce the similarity measure (12.22) as a criterion for deciding whether a data vector belongs to a cluster in the process of creating the eGKL clusters. Further, we will employ the distance measure (12.25) in order to calculate the degrees of membership of the individual data vectors similarly to the GK clustering algorithm.

Nevertheless, condition (12.22) provides a natural and objective way to define the cluster radii. Its application is connected with restrictions for a normal distribution. If this assumption is not valid, the vectors $y_k$ can be wrongly associated with process control situations or can be identified as outliers. Several authors, for example, Thissen et al. [29] and Fraley and Raftery [31], have explored the idea of using the multivariate process control of modeling nonnormally distributed process control regions by combining Gaussian mixture clusters. However, all these works have been focused on batch-type application of the *expectation-maximization* (*EM*) clustering method to estimate a mixture of Gaussian functions and could not be directly transferred to the streaming data set. The other restriction is in the ability of the SPC condition (12.22) to detect anomalies as this capacity is significantly reduced with increasing process dimensionality [27]. Third, the calculation of (12.22) is considered tedious and impractical since it involves updating the covariance matrix and calculation of its inverse for every new observation vector $y_k$ [30]. The last drawback could be compensated by a recursive computational scheme.

## 12.5 RECURSIVE COMPUTATIONAL ASPECTS

Though conditions (12.22) and (12.24) guarantee that the cluster radii are reliably identified, the problem with the correct and exact adjustment of the newfound cluster is still open. Conventional distance definition (12.20) through the sample mean and covariance matrix (12.21) is not convenient for real-time implementation since it requires buffering of data and does not support recursive evaluation of the similarity measure (12.22). On the other hand, experience shows (see section 12.3) that one-step update does not provide exact results. In order to compensate for these shortcomings we apply the *exponentially weighted moving average* (*EWMA*) procedure. The mean value (12.21i) is replaced with its exponentially weighted moving average version:

$$y^*_{new} = (1-\alpha)y^*_{old} + \alpha y_k = y^*_{old} + \alpha(y_k - y^*_{old}) \tag{12.26}$$

where the constant forgetting factor $0 \leq \alpha \leq 1$ controls the rate of updating the new mean $y^*_{new}$ by assigning a set of exponentially decreasing weights to the older observations $y^*_{old}$. Thus, for a constant $\alpha$, expression (12.26) recursively generates a vector of positive weights:

$$W = [(1-\alpha)^k \alpha (1-\alpha)^{k-1} \alpha (1-\alpha)^{k-2} \cdots \alpha] \tag{12.27}$$

with a unit sum. The vector $W$ forms a weighted average–type aggregating operator with exponentially decreasing weights that depend on $\alpha$. The key question in EWMA application is the memory depth (moving window length) of the aggregating operator. It can be shown that the memory depth $K_\alpha$ is approximately reciprocal to the forgetting factor $K_\alpha = 1/\alpha$. The moving window length is calculated for indexes belonging to the soft interval:

$$s \in \{k - K_\alpha + 1, k] \tag{12.28}$$

where the symbol { indicates a soft lower interval limit that includes values with lower indexes than $(k - K_\alpha)$, which have relatively low contribution [32, 33]. For a variable parameter $\alpha = 1/k$, expression (12.26) equals the recursive form of the arithmetic mean in (12.21).

Analogously to the recursive calculation of the mean values, we can apply the EWMA SPC chart to derive an alternative exponentially weighted recursive expression for the covariance matrix $S$:

$$S_{new} = (1-\alpha)S_{old} + \alpha(y_k - y_{old}^*)^T (y_k - y_{old}^*) \qquad (12.29)$$

where $S_{old}$ and $S_{new}$ are the old and updated versions of the covariance matrix $S$. It is easy to see that expression (12.29) is a weighted form of the average-based conventional covariance matrix (12.21ii). For $\alpha = 1/k$, the exponentially weighted covariance matrix (12.29) is identical to the recursive form of the covariance matrix (12.21ii).

However, the recursive calculations of the covariance matrix have to tackle another problem as well. Although the recursive expression (12.29) significantly simplifies the calculation of the covariance matrix, it does not resolve the problem with the calculation of its inversion. This problem is further complicated by the possible singularity of the covariance matrix—a valid concern in cases of correlated data.

The algorithm for recursive calculation of the inverse covariance matrix follows from the *woodbury matrix inversion lemma* [34]:

$$(A + BCD)^{-1} = A^{-1} - A^{-1}B(C^{-1} + DA^{-1}B)^{-1}DA^{-1} \qquad (12.30)$$

that is valid for any nonsingular square matrixes $A$, $C$, and $(C^{-1} + DA^{-1}B)$. If we denote

$$A = (1-\alpha)S_{old}; \quad B = \delta^T; \quad C = \alpha; \quad D = \delta; \quad \delta = (y_k - y_{old}^*)$$

we can obtain the recursive inversion of the covariance matrix (12.29) as follows:

$$\begin{aligned}
S_{new}^{-1} &= ((1-\alpha)S_{old} + \alpha(y_k - y_{old}^*)^T (y_k - y_{old}^*))^{-1} \\
&= (1-\alpha)^{-1} S_{old}^{-1} - (1-\alpha)^{-1} S_{old}^{-1} \delta^T (\alpha^{-1} + \delta(1-\alpha)^{-1} S_{old}^{-1} \delta^T)^{-1} \delta(1-\alpha)^{-1} S_{old}^{-1} \\
&= (1-\alpha)^{-1} S_{old}^{-1} - G \delta(1-\alpha)^{-1} S_{old}^{-1} = (I - G\delta)S_{old}^{-1}(1-\alpha)^{-1}
\end{aligned}$$

$$\qquad (12.31)$$

where

$$G = (1-\alpha)^{-1} S_{old}^{-1} \delta^T (\alpha^{-1} + \delta(1-\alpha)^{-1} S_{old}^{-1} \delta^T)^{-1} \qquad (12.32)$$

and $S_{old}^{-1}$ and $S_{new}^{-1}$ are the old and updated inverses of the covariance matrix $S$.

The nonsingularity requirements of the Woodbury matrix inversion lemma are satisfied if $S_{old}^{-1}$ is initialized as a diagonal matrix with sufficiently large elements and $0 < \alpha < 1$.

By applying the determinant identity [35]:

$$det(A + xy^T) = det(A)(1 + y^T A^{-1} x)$$

where $x$ and $y$ are vectors with dimensionality equal to the rank of the squared matrix $A$, to the expression for the updated covariance matrix (12.29):

$$det(S_{new}) = det((1-\alpha)S_{old} + \alpha(y_k - y_{old}^*)^T(y_k - y_{old}^*))$$

we can calculate the recursive version of the determinant of the covariance matrix. With this aim, let us denote by $detS_{new}$ and $detS_{old}$ the updated and the old values of the covariance determinant, and also denote $x = \alpha(y_k - y_{old}^*)^T, y = (y_k - y_{old}^*)^T$. A recursive form of calculation of the determinant of the covariance matrix can be recursively expressed as follows:

$$
\begin{aligned}
detS_{new} &= det((1-\alpha)S_{old} + \alpha(y_k - y_{old}^*)^T(y_k - y_{old}^*)) \\
&= det((1-\alpha)S_{old})(1 + \alpha(y_k - y_{old}^*)(1-\alpha)^{-1}S_{old}^{-1}(y_k - y_{old}^*)^T) \\
&= (1-\alpha)^n det(S_{old})(1 + \alpha(1-\alpha)^{-1}(y_k - y_{old}^*)S_{old}^{-1}(y_k - y_{old}^*)^T) \\
&= (1-\alpha)^{n-1} detS_{old}(1 - \alpha + \alpha(y_k - y_{old}^*)S_{old}^{-1}(y_k - y_{old}^*)^T) \quad (12.33)
\end{aligned}
$$

where $S_{old}^{-1}$ is the old inverse of the covariance matrix $S$. Since the inverse covariance is initialized as a diagonal matrix with sufficiently large elements, the initial value of the determinant, $detS_{old}$, of the initial covariance is easily obtained.

The previous equations show that covariance matrix (12.31) and its determinant (12.33) could be easily recursively updated by using their previously estimated values from the previous step. Both expressions will be further incorporated in the formulation of the evolving GK-like algorithm.

## 12.6 EVOLVING GK-LIKE (eGKL) CLUSTERING ALGORITHM

If there is no initially collected data set, we can suppose that vector $x_1$ represents the first data point of the data stream $x_k, k = 1, 2, \dots$. We associate the first cluster center with that point

$$v_1 = x_1$$

and initialize its inverse covariance matrix and determinant, and the counter $M_1$ of the vectors belonging to the cluster:

$$F_{1,new}^{-1} = F_0^{-1}; \quad detF_{1,new} = det(F_0); \quad M_1 = 1 \quad (12.34)$$

where $F_0$ is an initial estimate of the covariance matrix. The initial covariance matrix could be evaluated as an sample covariance of the already-collected data. If such information does not exist, the matrix is initialized as a diagonal matrix $F_0^{-1} = \gamma I$, where $I$ is an identity matrix of size $n$ and $\gamma$ is a sufficiently large positive number. This initialization corresponds to assigning a small ball-type cluster around the first cluster center.

Suppose we have $c$ cluster centers when the $k$th data vector is presented. The similarity between $x_k$ and each of the existing $c$ clusters is evaluated by checking the similarity relation (i.e., the process control condition) (12.22):

$$D_{ik}^2 < \chi_{n,\beta}^2, i = [1, c] \tag{12.35}$$

where

$$D_{ik}^2 = (x_k - v_i)F_i^{-1}(x_k - v_i)^T \tag{12.36}$$

$D_{ik}$ is the Mahalanobis distance of $x_k$ to each of the already-identified $c$ cluster centers. The minimal distance $D_{pk}$:

$$p = \underset{i=[1,c]}{\arg \min}(D_{ik}), D_{ik}^2 < \chi_{n,\beta}^2, i = [1, c] \tag{12.37}$$

determines the $p$th cluster that is closest to the $k$th data vector $x_k$ that simultaneously satisfies condition (12.35). In this case the vector $x_k$ is assigned to the $p$th cluster, for which we apply updating expressions (12.26), (12.31), (12.32), (12.33) to recalculate the $p$th cluster's characteristics—cluster center, inverse covariance matrix, and its determinant—as follows:

$$v_{p,new} = (1-\alpha)v_{p,old} + \alpha x_k = v_{p,old} + \alpha(x_k - v_{p,old}) \tag{12.38}$$

$$F_{p,new}^{-1} = (I - G_p(x_k - v_{p,old}))F_{p,old}^{-1}\frac{1}{1-a} \tag{12.39}$$

where

$$G_p = F_{p,old}^{-1}(x_k - v_{p,old})^T \frac{\alpha}{1-\alpha + \alpha(x_k - v_{p,old})F_{p,old}^{-1}(x_k - v_{p,old})^T} \tag{12.40}$$

$$detF_{p,new} = (1-\alpha)^{n-1}detF_{p,old}(1-\alpha + \alpha(x_k - v_{p,old})F_{p,old}^{-1}(x_k - v_{p,old})^T)$$

As the parameter $M_p$ counts the number of data points that fall within the boundary of each cluster, its value is increased by assigning a point to the closest cluster:

$$M_{p,new} = M_{p,old} + 1 \tag{12.41}$$

Simultaneously, we update in the opposite direction the remaining cluster centers in an attempt to move them away from the $p$th cluster:

$$v_{q,new} = v_{q,old} - \alpha(x_k - v_{q,old}), q = [1, c], q \neq p \tag{12.42}$$

The parameter $M_i, i = [1, c]$ assesses the credibility of the estimated clusters. Its minimal value corresponds to the minimal number of data points needed to learn the parameters of the $i$th inverse covariance matrix $F_i^{-1}$ that is estimated by the dimensionality $n$ of the data vector:

$$M_{min} = n(n+1)/2$$

However, from a practical point of view, the algorithm needs a more conservative value of the $M_{min}$ parameter to ensure the cluster significance:

$$M_{min} = Q\,n(n+1)/2$$

where $Q$ is a credibility parameter with default value $Q = 2$. A high value of $M_{min}$ not only guarantees the validity of covariance matrixes $F_i$'s but improves the robustness of the algorithm with respect to outliers.

In the opposite case, condition (12.35) fails. The vector $x_k$ is not similar to any of the cluster centers and it could not be assigned to any of the existing clusters. So, the natural decision is to create a new cluster. However, before implementing that step we check whether that fact is not due to the lack of credible clusters surrounding $x_k$, that is, whether the condition:

$$M_{p'} < M_{min} \qquad (12.43)$$

where

$$p' = \arg \min_{i=[1,c]}(D_{ik})$$

applies. If this is the case, we have to fulfill the updates (12.38)–(12.42) to the closest cluster $p'$. Note that for cluster $p'$ the similarity condition is not satisfied. Otherwise, a new cluster is created and the number of clusters is incremented:

$$c_{new} = c_{old} + 1$$

The center of the new cluster is initialized with the new data point $x_k$. The covariance matrix of the newly formed cluster is initialized with the sample covariance matrix of the population:

$$v_{c,new} = x_k; \; F_{c,new}^{-1} = F_0^{-1}; \; detF_{c,new} = det(F_0); \; M_{c,new} = 1 \qquad (12.44)$$

As the parameter $M_i$ accounts for the number of points that form a given cluster, it could be used to control the value of the learning rate $\alpha$. The inequality $M_i < M_{min}$ presents a situation when the estimated $i$th cluster is sparse and its covariance matrix $F_i$ is not completely estimated. Obviously, we should not allow for any forgetting of the data, and the true sample inverse covariance is calculated by considering:

$$\alpha = 1/(M_{min}+1)$$

For dense clusters that contain points exceeding the minimal number of $M_{min}$, we consider a learning rate

$$\alpha \geq 1/M_{min} \qquad (12.45)$$

that guarantees that the memory depth (the length of the moving window) will not be less than the minimum $M_{min}$. This ensures credible estimation of the inverse covariance and also that the clusters will be continually updated with new data.

The clusters defined by the similarity relationship (12.35) can be viewed as sets of points that are characterized with their sample means, covariance matrices, and radii $\chi^2_{n,\beta}$. We can extend those clusters by assigning additional data points that belong to them with degrees of fuzzy membership corresponding to their similarities to the identified cluster centers. We can use either the Mahalanobis distance (12.36) or the Mahalanobis-like distance as in the original GK algorithm:

$$d^2_{ik} = (x_s - v_i)[(det(F_i))^{1/n} F_i^{-1}](x_s - v_i)^T i = [1, c] \qquad (12.46)$$

to determine the membership grades of all points to each core cluster. In the first case, we get degrees of membership that are calculated from the distances $D_{ik}$'s by (12.36):

$$U_{ik} = \frac{1}{\sum_{j=1}^{c} (D_{ik}/D_{jk})^2}, \forall i, M_i > M_{min}, i = [1, c] \qquad (12.47)$$

or alternatively, if the Mahalanobis-like distances $d_{ik}$'s from expression (12.46) are determined, another set of membership functions could be calculated:

$$u_{ik} = \frac{1}{\sum_{j=1}^{c} (d_{ik}/d_{jk})^2}, \forall i, M_i > M_{min}, i = [1, c] \qquad (12.48)$$

For every vector $x_k$, the memberships of any of the credible clusters yield a set of membership functions that is similar to the one used in the GK clustering algorithm. We'll call the clusters with membership functions according to (12.48) the eGKL clusters because of their similarity to the ones used in the GK clustering algorithm.

Next we summarize the eGKL algorithm. We assume no prerequisite information about the clusters.

### Summary of the eGKL Algorithm

1. Choose the probability of a false alarm $\beta$ and define the $\chi^2_{n,\beta}$ according to Table 12.2. We consider a default probability of false alarm $\beta = 0.0455$ that relates to the $2\sigma$ process control band in the single-variable SPC. Estimated values of $\chi^2_{n,\beta}$ for different sizes of the data vector $x$ are given in Table 12.1:

TABLE 12.2.

| $n$ | 2 | 3 | 4 | 5 | 6 | 7 | 8 | 9 | 10 |
|---|---|---|---|---|---|---|---|---|---|
| $\chi^2_{n,0.0455}$ | 6.1801 | 8.0249 | 9.7156 | 11.3139 | 12.8489 | 14.3371 | 15.7891 | 17.2118 | 18.6104 |

2. Choose the initialization parameter $\gamma$ for the inverse covariance matrix (we consider default values $\gamma = 50$):

$$F_0^{-1} = \gamma I$$

3. Choose the cluster credibility parameter $Q$ (default value $Q = 2$) and establish $M_{min}$:

$$M_{min} = Q n(n+1)/2$$

4. Read the first data point $x_1$ and set $c = 1$.
5. Initialize the first cluster as follows:

$$v_c = x_1; \quad F_{c,new}^{-1} = F_0^{-1}; \quad \det F_{c,new} = \det(F_0); \qquad M_c = 1$$

6. Read the next data point $x_k$.
7. Calculate the membership of $x_k$ in all credible clusters:

$$u_{ik} = \frac{1}{\sum_{j=1}^{c} (d_{ik}/d_{jk})^2}, \forall i, M_i > M_{min}, i = [1, c]$$

where

$$d_{ik}^2 = (x_k - v_i)[(\det(F_i))^{1/n} F_i^{-1}](x_k - v_i)^T < R^2, i = [1, c]$$

8. Check the similarity of $x_k$ to the existing clusters:

$$D_{ik}^2 < \chi_{n,\beta}^2, \quad i = [1, c]$$

where

$$D_{ik}^2 = (x_k - v_i) F_i^{-1} (x_k - v_i)^T$$

9. Identify the closest cluster:

$$p = \arg \min_{i=[1,c]} (D_{ik})$$

10. If $D_{pk}^2 < \chi_{n,\beta}^2$ or $M_p < M_{min}$, then do the following:

10.1. Update the parameters of the $p$th cluster:

$$v_{p,new} = v_{p,old} + \alpha(x_k - v_{p,old})$$

$$F_{p,new}^{-1} = (I - G_p(x_k - v_{p,old})) F_{p,old}^{-1} \frac{1}{1-\alpha}$$

where

$$G_p = F_{p,old}^{-1}(x_k - v_{p,old})^T \frac{\alpha}{1 - \alpha + \alpha(x_k - v_{p,old})F_{p,old}^{-1}(x_k - v_{p,old})^T}$$

$$\det F_{p,new} = (1-\alpha)^{n-1} \det F_{p,old}(1 - \alpha + \alpha(x_k - v_{p,old})F_{p,old}^{-1}(x_k - v_{p,old})^T)$$

$$M_{p,new} = M_{p,old} + 1$$

10.2. Move away the centers of remaining clusters:

$$v_{q,new} := v_{q,old} - \alpha(x_k - v_{q,old}), q = [1, c], q \neq p$$

10.3. Go to step 6.

11. If none of the conditions $D_{pk}^2 < \chi_{n,\beta}^2$ or $M_p < M_{min}$ applies, then do the following:

11.1. Increment $c$.

11.2. Initialize the next cluster as follows:

$$v_c = x_k; \quad F_{c,new}^{-1} = F_0^{-1}; \quad \det F_{c,new} = \det(F_0); \quad M_c = 1;$$

11.3. Go to step 6.

Without a loss of generality, the eGKL algorithm could be applied if a set of clusters has been already identified with the conventional batch GK algorithm. In this case, the algorithm starts from step 6.

The application of the eGKL algorithm to the problem of real-time clustering streams of data is illustrated in the example data set generated by (12.18). However, the data stream data set was extended to 994 data points. This new data set shows a large difference in the magnitude of the elements of the two-dimensional row data vectors. In order to ensure that the two data vectors are within the same magnitude in their variations independently of the different physical meanings, the raw vectors $y$'s are replaced by their standardized values

$$Y_k = (y_k - y^*)(diag(s))^{-0.5}$$

where $y^*$ and $s$ are the sample mean and covariance matrix. This preprocessing standardization is a realistic assumption that can be easily implemented as a process of recursive learning of the means and the variances of the components of the raw data $x$:

$$y_k^* = \frac{k-1}{k} y_{k-1}^* + \frac{1}{k} y_k; y_1^* = 0$$

$$s_k^2 = \frac{k-1}{k} s_{k-1}^2 + \frac{1}{k-1} diag((y_k - y_k^*)^T (y_k - y_k^*)); s_1^2 = 0$$

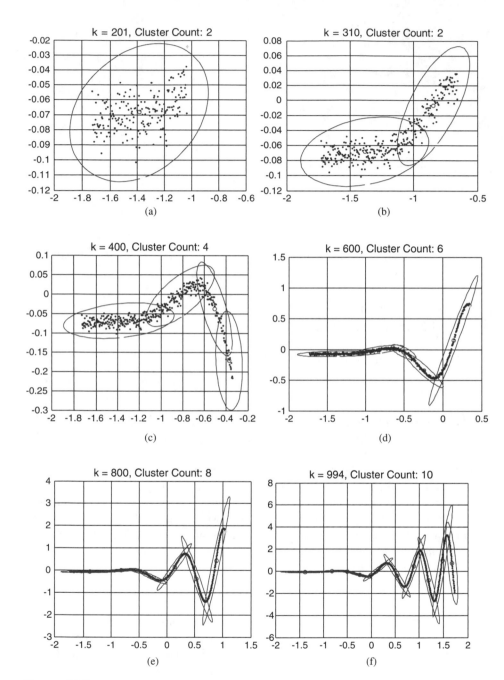

**Figure 12.5.** Snapshots of the evolving core clusters after 201 (a), 310 (b), 400 (c), 600 (d), 800 (e), and 994 (f) data points.

The eGKL clustering algorithm is applied with the following initial parameters:

$$\beta = 0.0455, Q = 2, \gamma = 50$$

The first cluster center is initialized with the first data vector $x_1 = [-1.7294 - 0.0396]$. Its initial inverse covariance matrix is $F_1^{-1} = diag([50\ 50])$. The first 200 data points are shown in Figure 12.5a. All the points are contained in the first core cluster. The first core cluster continues to evolve until the 201st data point. Its center now is at $v_1 = [-1.3846\ 0.0681]$ with inverse covariance matrix $F_1^{-1} = 10^3 \begin{bmatrix} 0.03 & -0.08 \\ -0.08 & 3.16 \end{bmatrix}$ and determinant $detF_1 = 0.13*10^{-4}$. The next cluster is initiated with the arrival of the 201st point $x_{201} = [-1.0328 - 0.0241]$ since it does not satisfy similarity condition (12.35):

$$D_{1,201} > 6.1801$$

where

$$v_1 - x_{201} = [-1.3846 - 0.0681] - [-1.0328 - 0.0241] = [-0.3518 - 0.0440]$$

$$D_{1,201} = [-0.3518 - 0.0440] * 10^3 \begin{bmatrix} 0.03 & -0.07 \\ -0.07 & 3.08 \end{bmatrix} * [-0.3518 - 0.0440]^T = 6.87$$

Figure 12.5b shows the evolution of the first two core clusters during the first 310 data points. The next diagrams depict the evolution of the core clusters after the 400th (Figure 12.5c), 600th (Figure 12.5d), 800th (Figure 12.5e), and 994th (Figure 12.5f) data point.

Figure 12.6a represents the membership functions to the eGKL clusters identified from the first 800 data points. Figure 12.6b depicts the membership functions to all 10

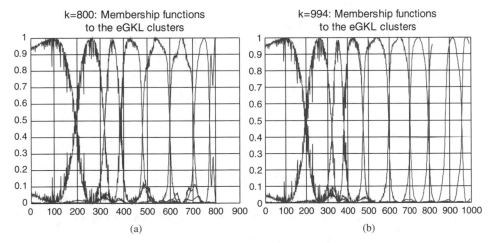

Figure 12.6. Evolution of eGKL membership functions calculated for $k = 800$ (a) and $k = 994$ (b).

clusters identified from that data stream. Membership functions are calculated using the Mahalanobis-like distance.

## 12.7 CONCLUSION

This chapter presents one approach to the challenging problem of discovering structures of streaming data in real time. The proposed evolving Gustafson-Kessel-like (eGKL) clustering algorithm is a step toward the problem of online evolving clustering of streams of data. Although inspired by the generic cluster shape and orientation of the Gustafson-Kessel algorithm, the new algorithm is closer to the spirit of the $k$-NN and LVQ clustering methods. It provides a methodology for adaptive, step-by-step identification of clusters that are similar to the GK clusters. The algorithm is based on a new approach to the problem of estimation of the number of clusters and their boundaries that is motivated by the identified similarities between the concept of evolving clustering and the well-established multivariate SPC techniques. The proposed algorithm addresses some of the basic problems of the new field of evolving systems, for example, recursive estimation of the cluster centers, inverse covariance matrixes, covariance determinants, Mahalanobis distance-type similarity relations that are enablers for computationally efficient implementation in real-time identification, classification, prognostics, process modeling, and anomaly detection, and other embedded-system types of applications.

---

### Appendix: GK Algorithm

**Initialization**: Choose in advance the number of clusters $c$, the weight exponent $m$ (default $m = 2$), and the termination tolerance $tol$ (default $tol = 0,01$) and volumes $\rho_i$ (default $\rho_i = 1$, $i = 1, \ldots, c$).

1. Initialize randomly partition matrix $U^{(o)}$ according to the membership constrains.
   **Repeat for** $l = 1, 2, \ldots$.
2. Compute the cluster centers:

$$v_i^{(l)} = \frac{\sum_{k=1}^{N} \left(u_{ik}^{(l-1)}\right)^m x_k}{\sum_{k=1}^{N} \left(u_{ik}^{(l-1)}\right)^m}, \quad \text{for } i = 1, \ldots, c$$

3. Compute the cluster covariance matrixes:

$$F_i = \frac{\sum_{k=1}^{N} \left(u_{ik}^{(l-1)}\right)^m \left(x_k - v_i^{(l)}\right)^T \left(x_k - v_i^{(l)}\right)}{\sum_{k=1}^{N} \left(u_{ik}^{(l-1)}\right)^m}, \quad \text{for } i = 1, \ldots, c$$

4. Compute the distances between the current point $x_k$ and the cluster centers $v_i$:

$$d_{ik}^2 = \left(x_k - v_i^{(l)}\right)\left[(\rho_i det(F_i))^{1/n} F_i^{-1}\right]\left(x_k - v_i^{(l)}\right)^T, \quad i = 1, \ldots, c, \ k = 1, \ldots, N$$

5. Update the partition matrix:

$$\text{If}\quad d_{ik} > 0 \quad \text{for}\quad i = 1, \ldots, c \quad k = 1, \ldots, N$$

$$u_{ik}^{(l)} = \frac{1}{\sum_{j=1}^{c} (d_{ik}/d_{jk})^{2/(m-1)}}$$

$$\text{otherwise } u_{ik}^{(l)} = 0 \text{ if } d_v > 0, \text{ and } u_{ik}^{(l)} \in [0,1] \text{ with} \sum_{i=1}^{c} u_{ik}^{(l)} = 1.$$

**until** $\left\| U^{(l)} - U^{(l-1)} \right\| < tol.$

## 12.8 ACKNOWLEDGMENTS

The research of the second author was partly supported by the project "SISTER: Strengthening the IST Research Capacity of Sofia University" of 7FP-PEGPOT-2007-1 program of the European Union.

## 12.9 REFERENCES

1. P. P. Angelov, *Evolving Rule-Based Models: A Tool for Design of Flexible Adaptive Systems.* Heidelberg, Germany: Springer-Verlag, 2002.

2. P. P. Angelov, D. P. Filev, "An Approach to Online Identification of Takagi-Sugeno Fuzzy Models," *IEEE Trans. on SMC—Part B: Cybernetics*, Vol. 34, No. 1, pp. 484–498, 2004.

3. R. Babuska, *Fuzzy Modeling for Control.* Boston: Kluwer Academic Publishers, 1998.

4. J. C. Bezdek, *Pattern Recognition with Fuzzy Objective Function Algorithms.* New York: Plenum Press, 1981.

5. J. C. Bezdek, "A Convergence Theorem for the Fuzzy ISODATA Clustering Algorithms," IEEE Trans. Pattern Analysis and Machine Intelligence, Vol. 2, pp. 1–8, 1980.

6. S. L. Chiu, "Fuzzy Model Identification Based on Cluster Estimation," *J. Intelligent and Fuzzy Systems*, Vol. 2, pp. 267–278, 1994.

7. F. Crespo, R. Weber, "A Methodology for Dynamic Data Mining Based on Fuzzy Clustering," *Fuzzy Sets and Systems*, Vol. 150 pp. 267–284, 2005.

8. R. H. Davé, "Characterization and Detection of Noise in Clustering," *Pattern Recognition Letters*, Vol. 12, pp. 657–664, 1991.

9. R. H. Davé, R. Krishnapuram, "Robust Clustering Methods: A Unified View," *IEEE Trans. on Fuzzy Systems*, Vol. 5 pp. 270–293, 1997.

10. M. Ester, H.-P. Kriegel, J. Sander, X. Xu, "A Density-Based Algorithm for Discovering Clusters in Large Spatial Databases with Noise." *Proc. 2nd Int. Conf. on Knowledge Discovery and Data Mining, Portland, OR*, 1996, pp. 226–231.

11. M. Ester, H.-P. Kriegel, J. Sander, M. Wimmer, X. Xu, "Incremental Clustering for Mining in a Data Warehousing Environment." *Proc. 24th Int. Conf. Very Large Databases, VLDB*, 1998, pp. 323–333.

12. I. Gath, A. B. Geva, "Unsupervised Optimal Fuzzy Clustering," *IEEE Trans. on Pattern Analysis and Machine Intelligence*, Vol. 7, pp. 773–781, 1989.

13. O. Georgieva, F. Klawonn,"Dynamic Data Assigning Assessment Clustering of Streaming Data, *Applied Soft Computing*—Special Issue on Dynamic Data Mining (in press), 2008.

14. O. Georgieva, F. Klawonn, "Evolving Clustering via the Dynamic Data Assigning Assessment Algorithm." *Proc. 2006 International Symposium on Evolving Fuzzy Systems*, Ambleside, UK, September 7–9, 2006, pp. 95–100, IEEE Catalog Number: 06EX1440; ISBN: 0-7803-9718-5.

15. C. Gupta, R. L. Grossman, "GenIc: A Single Pass Generalized Incremental Algorithm for Clustering." *2004 SIAM Int. Conf. on Data Mining, SDM 04 (SIAM)*, Philadelphia, 2004, pp. 137–153.

16. D. E. Gustafson, W. C. Kessel, "Fuzzy Clustering with a Fuzzy Covariance Matrix." *Proc. IEEE CDC (IEEE)*, San Diego, 1979, pp. 761–766.

17. F. Höppner, F. Klawonn, R. Kruse, T. Runkler, *Fuzzy Cluster Analysis*. Chichester, New York: John Wiley & Sons, 1999.

18. G. Hulten, L, Spencer, P. Domingos, "Mining Time-Changing Data Streams." *Proc. of KDD 2001*. New York: ACM Press, 2001, 97–106.

19. N. K. Kasabov, Q. Song, "DENFIS: Dynamic Evolving Neuro-Fuzzy Inference System and Its Application for Time-Series Prediction," *IEEE Trans. Fuzzy Systems*, Vol. 10, pp. 144–154, 2002.

20. A. Keller, F. Klawonn, "Adaptation of Cluster Sizes in Objective Function Based Fuzzy Clustering." *Intelligent Systems: Technology and Applications, Vol. IV: Database and Learning Systems* ( C. T. Leondes,ed.) Boca Raton: CRC Press, 2003, pp. 181–199.

21. R. Papka, J. Allan, "On-Line New Event Detection Using Single Pass Clustering," UMASS Computer Science Technical Report 98-21, 1998.

22. R. Yager, D. Filev, *Essentials of Fuzzy Modeling and Control*. New York: John Wiley & Sons, 1994.

23. J. Yang, "Dynamic Clustering of Evolving Streams with a Single Pass." *Proc. 19th Int. Conf. on Data Engineering, ICDE'03*, Bangalore, 2003, pp. 695–697.

24. J. Keller, M. Gray, J. Givens, "A Fuzzy k-Nearest Neighbor Algorithm," *IEEE Trans. on Systems, Man, and Cybernetics*, Vol. 15, pp. 580–585.

25. T. Kohonen, *Self-Organization and Associative Memory*, 3rd ed. Berlin: Springer-Verlag.

26. T. Ryan, *Statistical Methods for Quality Improvement*. New York: John Wiley & Sons, 1989.

27. N. Ye, C. Borror, D. Parmar, "Scalable Chi-Square Distance versus Conventional Statistical Distance for Process Monitoring with Uncorrelated Data Variables," *Quality and Reliability Engineering International*, Vol. 19, pp. 505–515.

28. N. Ye, Q. Chen, S. M. Emran, S. Vilbert, " Hotelling's$T^2$ Multivariate Profiling for Anomaly Detection." *Proc. 1st IEEE SMC Inform. Assurance and Security Workshop*, 2000.

29. U. Thissen et al., "Multivariate Statistical Process Control Using Mixture Modeling," *J. Chemometrics*, Vol. 19, pp. 23–31, 2005.

30. N. Ye et al., "Probabilistic Techniques for Intrusion Detection Based on Computer Audit Data," *IEEE Trans. on Systems, Man and Cybernetics, Part A*, Vol. 31, pp. 266–274, 2001.

31. C. Fraley, A. Raftery, "Model-Based Clustering, Discriminant Analysis, and Density Estimation," *J. Am. Statist. Assoc.*, Vol. 97, pp. 611–631, 2002.

32. A. Beex, J. Zeidler, "Non-Wiener Effects in Recursive Least Squares Adaptation," *Proc. 7th Int. Symposium on Signal Processing and Its Applications*, Vol. 2, 2003, pp. 595–598.

33. D. Erdogmus et al., "Recursive Principal Components Analysis Using Eigenvector Matrix Perturbation," *EURASIP J. Applied Signal Processing*, Vol. 13, pp. 2034–2041, 2004.

34. M. Woodbury, "Inverting Modified Matrices: Memorandum Rept. 42,"Statistical Research Group, Princeton University, Princeton, NJ, p. 4, 1950.

35. M. Brookes, *The Matrix Reference Manual*. London: Imperial College, 2005.

36. UC Irvine Machine Learning Repository, http://archive.ics.uci.edu/ml/databases/eeg/eeg.data.html.

# 13

# EVOLVING FUZZY CLASSIFICATION OF NONSTATIONARY TIME SERIES

Ye. Bodyanskiy, Ye. Gorshkov, I. Kokshenev, V. Kolodyazhniy

**Abstract:** The problem of adaptive segmentation of time series changing their properties at a priori unknown moments is considered. The proposed approach is based on the idea of indirect sequence clustering, which is realized with a novel robust evolving recursive fuzzy clustering algorithm that can process incoming observations online (possibly in real-time mode) and is stable with respect to outliers that are often present in real data. An application to the segmentation of a biological time series confirms the efficiency of the proposed algorithm.

## 13.1 INTRODUCTION

Recent years have witnessed a growing interest in the analysis of nonstationary time series changing their properties at a priori unknown moments. The problems of time-series analysis are quite typical in speech processing, text and web mining, robot sensor analysis, and especially in medical and biological diagnostics. It is important to note that these problems often need to be solved online as new data become available.

In the process of solving such problems, the time series is partitioned (segmented) into internally homogeneous (homomorphic) parts, which are subsequently represented via some more compact description for further diagnosis.

*Evolving Intelligent Systems: Methodology and Applications,* Edited by Plamen Angelov, Dimitar P. Filev, and Nikola Kasabov

Such problems in some cases were solved using the approach based on the methods of properties change detection in signals and systems [1]. However, the known algorithms are usually oriented to the detection of abrupt changes, and are not well suited for the detection of slow variations in characteristics.

In real situations, especially in biomedical applications, internal changes in the monitored object are usually quite slow, and the stable states of an organism usually overlap in many of their characteristics. Besides that, transient states exist that simultaneously have characteristics of several stable ones.

In this situation, the methods of fuzzy clustering of time series are preferable because of the ability to find parameters of the overlapping clusters or segments. They are based on the widely used techniques of fuzzy cluster analysis [2–4]. These methods have proved to be effective in solving many problems in batch mode, but their use in real time is complicated by a number of difficulties. One can overcome some of these difficulties using the fast evolving methods of recursive cluster analysis [5–9]. However, the methods mentioned earlier are capable of efficient data clustering when the clusters are overlapping only with the assumption that the clusters are compact, that is, they do not have abrupt (anomalous) outliers. Whereas real data sets usually contain up to 20% outliers [10–12], the assumption of cluster compactness may sometimes become inadequate.

Thus, the problem of cluster analysis of data with heavy-tailed distributions has received more and more attention in recent years. Various modifications of the clustering methods mentioned earlier were proposed in papers [13–15] to process data containing outliers.

At the same time, most of the proposed robust fuzzy clustering algorithms are not suitable for real-time or sequential operation. So, it is advisable to develop recursive algorithms for robust fuzzy clustering of time series, having evolving properties and suitable for the sequential processing of incoming data, when the characteristics of the system generating the data are changing with time.

## 13.2 PREPROCESSING OF TIME SERIES AND INDIRECT SEQUENCE CLUSTERING

In the problems of segmentation of time series $Y = \{y(1), y(2), \ldots, y(k), \ldots, y(T)\}$, the indirect sequence clustering approach [14] is used quite often. It consists in the extraction of some characteristic features from the time series and their subsequent mapping onto a transformed feature space, where known space-based clustering algorithms can be used to form clusters. Such features can be the correlation, regression, and spectral characteristics of the time series, which in our case should be computed with adaptive iterative procedures.

For this purpose, such estimates as mean, variance, and autocorrelation coefficients can be used. To provide adaptive properties, these estimates can be computed via exponential smoothing [1]. The mean value can be estimated as

$$S(k) = \alpha\, y(k) + (1-\alpha)S(k-1), \quad 0 < \alpha < 1 \qquad (13.1)$$

where $\alpha = 2/(N+1)$ corresponds to smoothing on a moving window of width $N$.

The variance of the time series can be estimated as

$$\sigma^2(k) = \alpha(y(k){-}S(k))^2 + (1{-}\alpha)\sigma^2(k{-}1) \tag{13.2}$$

and the autocorrelation coefficients as

$$\rho(k,\tau) = \alpha(y(k){-}S(k))(y(k{-}\tau){-}S(k)) + (1{-}\alpha)\rho(k{-}1,\tau) \tag{13.3}$$

where $\tau = 1, 2, \ldots, \tau_{max}$.

Thus, a feature vector $x(k) = (s(k), \sigma^2(k), \rho(k,1), \rho(k,2), \ldots, \rho(k,\tau_{max}))^T$ of dimensionality $2 + \tau_{max}$ is computed at every instant $k$, such that a set of T $n$-dimensional feature vectors $X = \{x(1), x(2), \ldots, x(T)\}$ is formed, where $x(k) \in R^n$, $k = 1$, $2, \ldots, T$. The output of a fuzzy clustering algorithm should be the separation of the source data into $m$ clusters with some degrees of membership $w_j(k)$ of the $k$th feature vector $x(k)$ to the $j$th cluster, where $m$ in the common case is unknown and can change over time.

In what follows, we make an attempt to derive an adaptive computationally simple robust fuzzy clustering algorithm for recursive data processing in the online mode as more and more data become available.

## 13.3 RECURSIVE FUZZY CLUSTERING APPROACH

The approach that we use belongs to the class of the objective function–based algorithms [2] that are designed to solve the clustering problem via the optimization of a certain predetermined clustering criterion, and are, in our opinion, the best grounded from the mathematical point of view.

We consider the objective function

$$E(w_j(k), c_j) = \sum_{k=1}^{T} \sum_{j=1}^{m} w_j^{\beta}(k)D(x(k), c_j) \tag{13.4}$$

subject to constraints

$$\sum_{j=1}^{m} w_j(k) = 1, \quad k = 1, \ldots, T \tag{13.5}$$

$$0 < \sum_{k=1}^{T} w_j(k) \leq T, \quad j = 1, \ldots, m \tag{13.6}$$

Here $w_j(k) \in [0, 1]$ is the degree of membership of the vector $x(k)$ to the $j$th cluster, $c_j$ is the prototype (center) of the $j$th cluster, $\beta$ is a nonnegative parameter, referred to as a *fuzzifier* (usually $\beta = 2$), and $D(x(k), c_j)$ is the distance between $x(k)$ and $c_j$ in the adopted metrics. The result of the clustering is assumed to be a $T \times m$ matrix $W = \{w_j(k)\}$, referred to as the *fuzzy partition matrix*.

Note that since the elements of the matrix $W$ can be regarded as the probabilities of the hypotheses of data vectors' membership in certain clusters, the procedures generated from (13.4) subject to constraints (13.5), (13.6) can be referred to as "probabilistic clustering algorithms" [4]. Note that it is also possible to remove the probabilistic constraints (13.5) and (13.6) using the *possibilistic* approach to fuzzy clustering [9, 16, 17], but this approach is not considered here.

The distance function $D(x(k), c_j)$ is usually assumed to be the Minkowski $L^p$ metrics [1]

$$D(x(k), c_j) = \left( \sum_{i=1}^{n} |x_i(k) - c_{ji}|^p \right)^{\frac{1}{p}}, \quad p \geq 1 \tag{13.7}$$

where $x_i(k)$, $c_{ji}$ are $i$th components of $(n \times 1)$-vectors $x(k)$, $c_j$ respectively. Assuming $\beta = p = 2$ leads us to the most popular, simple, and quite effective Bezdek's fuzzy c-means algorithm [2]:

$$w_j(k) = \frac{\|x(k) - c_j\|^{-2}}{\sum_{l=1}^{m} \|x(k) - c_l\|^{-2}} \tag{13.8}$$

$$c_j = \frac{\sum_{k=1}^{T} w_j^2(k) x(k)}{\sum_{k=1}^{T} w_j^2(k)} \tag{13.9}$$

## 13.4 ROBUST RECURSIVE FUZZY CLUSTERING ALGORITHM

The estimates connected with the quadratic objective functions are optimal when the processed data belong to the class of distributions with bounded variance. The most important representative of this class is the Gaussian distribution. Varying the parameter $p$, we can improve the robustness property of the clustering procedures. However, the estimation quality is determined by the distribution of data. Indeed, the estimates corresponding to $p = 1$ are optimal for the Laplacian distribution, but obtaining them requires a lot of computations.

Using the following construct as the robust metrics (see Figure 13.1)

$$D^R(x(k), c_j) = \sum_{i=1}^{n} (1 - \text{sech}^2(x_i(k) - c_{ji}))(x_i(k) - c_{ji})^{\frac{2}{3}} \tag{13.10}$$

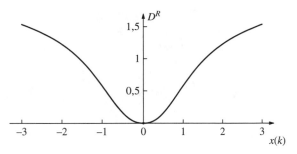

Figure 13.1. Plot of the robust metrics function (13.10).

we can introduce an objective function for robust fuzzy clustering

$$
E^R(w_j(k), c_j) = \sum_{k=1}^{T}\sum_{j=1}^{m} w_j^\beta D^R(x(k), c_j)
$$

$$
= \sum_{k=1}^{T}\sum_{j=1}^{m} w_j^\beta \sum_{i=1}^{n}(1-\mathrm{sech}^2(x_i(k)-c_{ji}))(x_i(k)-c_{ji})^{\frac{2}{5}}
$$

(13.11)

and a corresponding Lagrange function

$$
L(w_j(k), c_j, \lambda(k)) = \sum_{k=1}^{T}\sum_{j=1}^{m} w_j^\beta(k)\sum_{i=1}^{n}(1-\mathrm{sech}^2(x_i(k)-c_{ji}))(x_i(k)-c_{ji})^{\frac{2}{5}}
$$

$$
+ \sum_{k=1}^{T}\lambda(k)\left(\sum_{j=1}^{m} w_j(k)-1\right)
$$

(13.12)

where $\lambda(k)$ is an undetermined Lagrange multiplier that guarantees the fulfillment of the constraints (13.5, 13.6).

The saddle point of the Lagrange function (13.12) can be found solving the following system of Kuhn-Tucker equations:

$$
\begin{cases}
\dfrac{\partial L(w(k), c_j, \lambda(k))}{\partial w_j(k)} = 0, \\[2ex]
\dfrac{\partial L(w_j(k), c_j, \lambda(k))}{\partial \lambda(k)} = 0, \\[2ex]
\nabla_{c_j} L(w_j(k), c_j, \lambda(k)) = 0
\end{cases}
$$

(13.13)

Solving the first and the second equation of the system (13.13) leads to the well-known result [4] (13.14)–(13.15)

$$w_j(k) = \frac{(D^R(x(k), c_j)^{\frac{1}{1-\beta}}}{\sum_{l=1}^{m}(D^R(x(k), c_l))^{\frac{1}{1-\beta}}} \tag{13.14}$$

$$\lambda(k) = -\left(\sum_{l=1}^{m}(\beta D^R(x(k), c_l))^{\frac{1}{1-\beta}}\right)^{1-\beta} \tag{13.15}$$

but the third one

$$\nabla_{c_j}L(w_j(k), c_j, \lambda(k)) = \sum_{k=1}^{T} w_j^{\beta}\nabla_{c_j}D^R(x(k), c_j) = 0 \tag{13.16}$$

obviously has no analytical solution. The solution of (13.15) could be computed with the use of a local modification of the Lagrange function [5] and the recursive fuzzy clustering algorithms [9]. Furthermore, the search for the saddle point of the local Lagrange function

$$L_k(w_j(k), c_j, \lambda(k)) = \sum_{j=1}^{m} w_j^{\beta}(k)D^R(x(k), c_j) + \lambda(k)\left(\sum_{j=1}^{m} w_j(k) - 1\right) \tag{13.17}$$

with the help of the Arrow-Hurwitz-Uzawa procedure [18] leads to algorithm (13.17), where $\eta(k)$ is the learning rate parameter, and $c_{ji}(k)$ is the $i$th component of the $j$th prototype vector calculated at the $k$th step:

$$w_j(k) = \frac{(D^R(x(k), c_j)^{\frac{1}{1-\beta}}}{\sum_{l=1}^{m}(D^R(x(k), c_l))^{\frac{1}{1-\beta}}} \tag{13.18}$$

$$c_{ji}(k+1) = c_{ji}(k) - \eta(k)\frac{\partial L_k(w_j(k), c_j, \lambda(k))}{\partial c_{ji}} = c_{ji}(k)$$

$$+ \eta(k)w_j^{\beta}(k)\left(2\operatorname{sech}^2(x_i(k) - c_{ji}(k))\tanh(x_i(k) - c_{ji}(k))|x_i(k) - c_{ji}(k)|^{\frac{2}{5}}\right.$$

$$\left. + 0.4(1 - \operatorname{sech}^2(x_i(k) - c_{ji}(k)))|x_i(k) - c_{ji}(k)|^{\frac{-3}{5}}\operatorname{sign}(x_i(k) - c_{ji}(k))\right) \tag{13.19}$$

Cluster centers $c_{ji}(k)$ and membership values $w_j(k)$ can be initialized with random values uniformly distributed over the data set range.

The considered robust recursive method (13.18)–(13.19) could be used in the batch clustering mode as well as in the online mode. The computational complexity is of the same order as that of the known recursive fuzzy clustering algorithms [7–9], and depends linearly on the number of samples in the data set.

## 13.5 EXPERIMENTS

The data set is a time series of a hamster's heartbeat intervals (the *R-R intervals* between *R* wave peaks of the QRS complexes on the electrocardiogram, ECG) in the process of evolving and awaking from an artificial hypometabolic state. The time series preseg-mented by expert biologists and projection of the data set after the preprocessing stage to the first two principal components are shown in Figure 13.2.

The comparison of the clustering-based segmentation of this time series using the proposed robust clustering algorithm to the other conventional recursive clustering methods based on different objective functions is presented in this section. We compare it to the well-known Bezdek's fuzzy c-means [2] and Gustafson-Kessel [19] clustering algorithms.

Clustering is performed in a single pass over the data set. For better results, the data set is randomly shuffled. There are only three features computed at the preprocessing stage: $s(k)$, $\sigma^2(k)$, and $\rho(k, 2)$ with $\alpha = 0.095238$ (20 samples window). This subset of features was selected experimentally as the minimum subset of (13.1)–(13.3) that provided meaningful and stable results. The number of prototypes $m = 5$ was chosen experimentally. Smaller numbers of clusters ($m < 5$) led to unstable results, heavily dependent on the initialization. For $m > 5$, some of the generated clusters became indistinguishable. Thus, we assumed that there are five different clusters connected with the changing of the animal's functional condition.

### 13.5.1 Robust Recursive Fuzzy Clustering Algorithm (13.18)–(13.19)

The parameters of the algorithm (13.18)–(13.19) were as follows: fuzzifier $\beta = 2$, learning rate $\eta = 0.01$. The projections of the data and cluster prototypes onto the first two principal components of the feature space are shown in Figure 13.3 and the time-series segmentation obtained with this algorithm is shown in Figure 13.4. Crisp segments of the time series shown on the plots correspond to the data samples with maximal degrees of membership in the computed clusters.

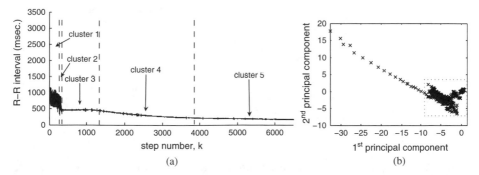

**Figure 13.2.** Hamster's heartbeat intervals: (a) segmentation of the time series made by expert biologists; (b) projection of the preprocessed data set onto the first two principal components.

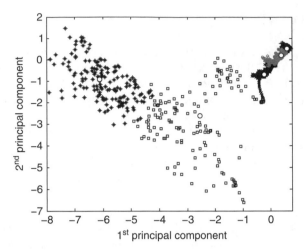

**Figure 13.3.** Projection of the data set and cluster centers onto the principal components for robust recursive clustering algorithm.

## 13.5.2 Fuzzy C-Means Clustering Algorithm

The parameters of the algorithm [2] were as follows: fuzzifier $\beta = 2$, termination tolerance $\varepsilon = 10^{-3}$. The projections of the data and cluster prototypes onto the first two principal components of the feature space are shown in Figure 13.5 and the time-series segmentation obtained with this algorithm is shown in Figure 13.6.

## 13.5.3 Gustafson-Kessel Clustering Algorithm

The parameters of the algorithm [19] were as follows: fuzzifier $\beta = 2$, termination tolerance $\varepsilon = 10^{-6}$, predetermined cluster volumes $\rho_j = 1$, $j = 1, 2, \ldots, m$, maximal

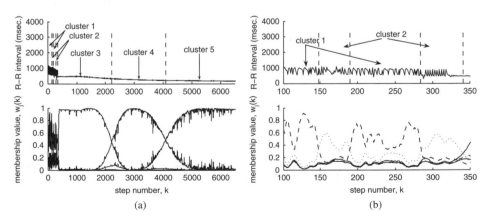

**Figure 13.4.** Segmentation of heartbeat intervals time series with robust recursive fuzzy clustering algorithm: (a) full time-series range; (b) fragment of the time series on a range $k = 0, \ldots, 350$.

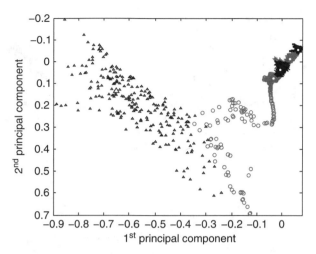

**Figure 13.5.** Projection of the data set and cluster centers onto the principal components for fuzzy c-means clustering algorithm.

ratio between the maximum and minimum eigenvalue of the covariance matrix $\vartheta = 10^{15}$, and weighting parameter $\lambda = 0$. The projections of the data and cluster prototypes onto the first two principal components of the feature space are shown in Figure 13.7 and the time-series segmentation obtained with this algorithm is shown in Figure 13.8.

Without any other direct criteria for determination of the changes in the animal's organism condition, the following interpretation can be assumed [20].

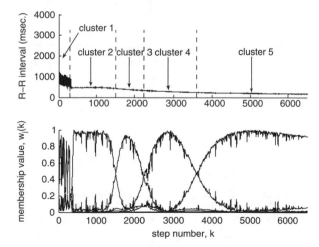

**Figure 13.6.** Segmentation of heartbeat intervals time series with fuzzy c-means clustering algorithm.

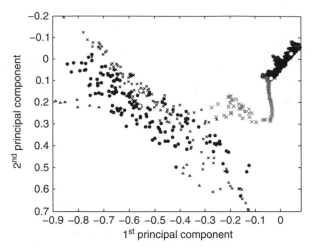

Figure 13.7. Projection of the data set and cluster centers onto the principal components for Gustafson-Kessel clustering algorithm.

The first part of the curve (time steps $k = 0, \ldots, 350$), which is characterized by the simultaneous presence of two clusters, may reflect some degree of imbalance in the heart rhythm control system caused by the initiation of the artificial hypometabolic state.

The most probable reason for such a disturbance may be connected with the drastic deceleration of breathing frequency (to 1 per min) that consequently results in the disturbance of the modulating effect on the heart rhythm by breathing.

Reaching a stable hypometabolic state with reversible reduction of the main vital functions (body temperature near 15°C) is represented in the second part of the curve. The corresponding cluster combined two different stages: both the stable hypometabolic condition and the initial stage of the animal's rewarming taking place on the background

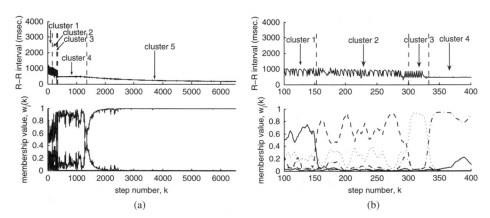

Figure 13.8. Segmentation of heartbeat intervals time series with Gustafson-Kessel clustering algorithm: (a) full time-series range; (b) fragment of the time series on a range $k = 0, \ldots, 350$.

of gradual activation of the thermoregulation system. Rapid activation of the latter with maximal activation of the shivering thermogenesis leads to changing the cluster.

Normalization of temperature homeostasis of the organism that is typical for the last part of the curve of heat rate distribution results in the appearance of the last cluster. Its domination may reflect the emergence of a relatively stable functional state, which, as one may suppose, is connected with the finishing of the most power-consuming period in temperature homeostasis restoration.

Thus, the results of solving the clustering problem in unsupervised mode do not contradict the facts of the laboratory animal's condition.

## 13.6 CONCLUSION

In this chapter, an evolving robust recursive fuzzy clustering algorithm based on the objective function of a special form, suitable for time-series segmentation, is discussed. The algorithm could be used in a wide range of applications, such as medical diagnosis and monitoring, data mining, fault diagnosis, and pattern recognition in self-organizing mode when the size of the data set is not known a priori, there are outliers in the data, and the processing must be done in real time.

Due to its adaptive sequential form, the clustering algorithm proposed in this chapter is related to evolving fuzzy systems [21], and can be used for the online tuning of their rule bases.

## 13.7 REFERENCES

1. L. F. Pau, *Failure Diagnosis and Performance Monitoring*. New York: Marcel Dekker, 1981.
2. J. C. Bezdek, *Pattern Recognition with Fuzzy Objective Function Algorithms*. New York; Plenum Press, 1981.
3. F. Höppner, F. Klawonn, R. Kruse, *Fuzzy-Klusteranalyse. Verfahren für die Bilderkennung, Klassifikation und Datenanalyse*. Braunschweig: Vieweg, 1996.
4. F. Klawonn, R. Kruse, H. Timm, "Fuzzy Shell Cluster Analysis," In *Learning, Networks and Statistics* (G. Della Riccia, H. J. Lenz, R. Kruse, eds.). Wien: Springer-Verlag, 1997, pp. 105–120.
5. C. G. Looney, "A Fuzzy Clustering and Fuzzy Merging Algorithm," Technical Report, Computer Science Department, University of Nevada, Reno, NV, 1999. Available at http://sherry.ifi.unizh.ch/looney99fuzzy.html.
6. C. G. Looney, "A Fuzzy Classifier Network with Ellipsoidal Epanechnikovs," Technical Report, Computer Science Department, University of Nevada, Reno, NV, 2001. Available at http://sherry.ifi.unizh.ch/looney01fuzzy.html.
7. F. L. Chung, T. Lee, "Fuzzy Competitive Learning," *Neural Networks*, Vol. 7, pp. 539–552, 1994.
8. D. C. Park, I. Dagher, "Gradient Based Fuzzy C-Means (GBFCM) Algorithm," *Proc. IEEE Int. Conf. on Neural Networks*, 1984, pp. 1626–1631.

9. Ye. Bodyanskiy, V. Kolodyazhniy, A. Stephan, *"Recursive Fuzzy Clustering Algorithms."* Proc. 10th East–West Fuzzy Colloquium, Zittau, Germany, 2002, pp. 276–283.

10. V. Barnett, T. Lewis, *Outliers in Statistical Data.* Chichester-New York-Brisbane-Toronto: John Wiley & Sons, 1978.

11. W. J. J. Rey, "Robust Statistical Methods," *Lecture Notes in Mathematics*, Vol. 690. Berlin-Heidelberg-New York: Springer-Verlag, 1978.

12. P. J. Huber, *Robust Statistics*, New York: John Wiley & Sons, 1981.

13. K. Tsuda, S. Senda, M. Minoh, K. Ikeda, "Sequential Fuzzy Cluster Extraction and Its Robustness Against Noise," *Systems and Computers in Japan*, Vol. 28, pp. 10–17, 1997.

14. F. Höppner, F. Klawonn, *"Fuzzy Clustering of Sampled Functions,"* Proc. 19th Int. Conf. of the North American Fuzzy Information Processing Society (NAFIPS), Atlanta, USA, 2000, pp. 251–255.

15. O. Georgieva, F. Klawonn, "A Clustering Algorithm for Identification of Single Clusters in Large Data Sets." *Proc. 11th East–West Fuzzy Colloquium,* Zittau, Germany, 2004, pp. 118–125.

16. R. Krishnapuram, J. Keller, "A Possibilistic Approach to Clustering," *IEEE Trans. on Fuzzy Systems*, Vol. 1, pp. 98–110, 1993.

17. R. Krishnapuram, J. Keller, "Fuzzy and Possibilistic Clustering Methods for Computer Vision," *Neural Fuzzy Systems*, Vol. 12, pp. 133–159, 1994.

18. K. Arrow, L. Hurwitz, H. Uzawa, *Studies in Nonlinear Programming.* Stanford: Stanford University Press, 1958.

19. E. E. Gustafson, W. C. Kessel, "Fuzzy Clustering with a Fuzzy Covariance Matrix." *Proc. IEEE CDC,* San Diego, California, 1979, pp. 761–766.

20. Ye. Gorshkov, I. Kokshenev, Ye. Bodyanskiy, V. Kolodyazhniy, O. Shylo, "Robust Recursive Fuzzy Clustering-Based Segmentation of Biological Time Series." *Proc. 2006 Int. Symp. on Evolving Fuzzy Systems,* Ambleside, UK, 2006, pp. 101–105.

21. P. Angelov, *Evolving Rule-Based Models.* Heidelberg-New York: Physica-Verlag, 2002.

# 14

# EVOLVING INFERENTIAL SENSORS IN THE CHEMICAL PROCESS INDUSTRY

Plamen Angelov, Arthur Kordon

## 14.1 INTRODUCTION

This chapter presents a new and promising technique for design of inferential sensors in the chemical process industry that has a broad range of applicability. It is based on the concept of *evolving fuzzy rule-based systems* (*EFSs*). Mathematical modeling was used to infer otherwise-difficult-to-measure variables such as product quality since the 1980s, including in online mode. The challenge today is to develop such adaptive, flexible, self-calibrating online inferential sensors that reduce maintenance costs while keeping high precision and interpretability/transparency. The methodology of fuzzy rule-based models of the Takagi-Sugeno type (Takagi-Sugeno, 1985), which have flexible, open structure and are therefore called *evolving* (see also Chapter 2), is particularly suitable for addressing this challenge. The basic concept is described from the point of view of the implementation of this technique in self-maintaining and self-calibrating inferential sensors for several chemical industry processes. The sensitivity analysis (input variables selection) was performed online and this was compared to the offline input variables selection using genetic programming. A case study based on four different inferential sensors for estimating chemical properties is presented in more detail, while the methodology and conclusions are valid for the broader area of the chemical and process industry in general. The results demonstrate that easily interpretable inferential sensors

*Evolving Intelligent Systems: Methodology and Applications,* Edited by Plamen Angelov, Dimitar P. Filev, and Nikola Kasabov
Copyright © 2010 Institute of Electrical and Electronics Engineers

with simple structure can be designed automatically from the data stream in real time to provide estimation of the real values of process variables of interest. The proposed approach can be used as a basis for development of a new generation of inferential sensors that can address the challenges of the modern advanced process industry.

## 14.2 BACKGROUND

Inferential sensors (also called *soft* sensors) aim to provide accurate real-time estimates of otherwise-difficult-to-measure parameters or to replace expensive measurements (such as emissions, biomass, melt index, etc.), based on available cheap sensors for physical variables like temperatures, pressures, and flows. The commercial offerings are based on black-box models derived by artificial neural networks. Several vendors, such as Pavilion Technologies, Aspen Technologies, Honeywell, Siemens, Gensym Corporation, and so on, have applied hundreds of soft sensors in almost every industry. The benefit from improved quality and reduced process upsets is estimated in the hundreds of millions of dollars (Kordon et al., 2003).

Model-based techniques for process quality monitoring often provide a valuable advantage over the conventional approaches that rely on manual intervention and laboratory tests. Such models, however, are costly to build and maintain since the environment in which the industrial process takes place is dynamically changing, and the equipment is getting older and contaminated or being replaced; the complexity of the processes leads to a number of aspects of the process being ignored by the models. Raw materials often alter in quality. To maintain the quality of the products in the chemical and process industry, in general, it is a routine practice to take samples from the product during the processing (fermentation, rectification, etc.) due to the lack of or difficulties related to the measurements of some variables such as concentrations, product quality, and so on. (Fortuna et al., 2007; Macias et al., 2003). Samples are usually taken in several-hour intervals and analyzed in a laboratory environment. The main aim is to certify the process by monitoring the deviation from a specification. Another scenario includes modeling at the design and process planning stage—the inference between certain measurable process variables and a certain target value (product quality, for example)—is of great importance (Macias et al., 2003).

A crucial weakness of model-based approaches for design of inferential sensors is that significant efforts must be made based on batch sets of data to develop and maintain these models/sensors offline. Even minor process changes outside the conditions used for offline model development can lead to performance deterioration of the model-based (including advanced NN-based and statistical) inferential sensors, which require maintenance and recalibration.

## 14.2.1 Modes of Operation of Inferential Sensors

After installing a preselected and pretrained offline inferential sensor in a real dynamic environment, it can be used in different modes of operation, dependent on the level of process changes. The first alternative is when the inferential sensor predicts reliably with the chosen *fixed* structure and parameters. The industrial experience from the chemical industry, however, shows that the inferential sensors that have been applied demonstrate acceptable performance in this mode only if the process changes are very minor, that is, on average less than 5% outside the offline model development range. In case of more significant process changes (i.e., on average, 5–20% outside the offline model development range), the sensor starts to provide a higher number of errors and needs recalibration or retraining. The most frequent solution is offline refitting of the model parameters to the new process conditions. However, in case of frequent changes, a continuous adaptation to the new conditions is needed through parameter estimation within the fixed structure. The third possible mode of operation of inferential sensors handles the most difficult case of major process changes (i.e., on average, > 20% outside the offline model development range) when the predictive model changes automatically its structure and corresponding parameters in order to adjust to the new data pattern. We call the latter mode *evolving* self-calibrating inferential sensor, or briefly, *eSensor*. In this chapter we will describe an approach particularly suitable for this mode of operation (although it can also work in any of the former modes, too).

## 14.2.2 Need for Evolving Inferential Sensors

Different empirical methods, such as *statistical models* (Hastie et al., 2001), *neural networks* (*NN*) (Rallo et al., 2004), partial least squares (PLS) (Fortuna et al., 2007), *support vector machines* (*SVM*) (Yan et al., 2004), and *genetic programming* (*GP*) (Kordon & Smits, 2001), have been used for inferential sensor development. In order to prevent future extrapolation, during offline model development the broadest possible ranges of the inputs and outputs are selected from the available historical data. However, for different reasons such as operating regime fluctuations, due to different product demand, control system readjustment, or equipment changes, the online operating conditions for at least 30% of the applied inferential sensors in the chemical industry exceed the initial offline model development ranges (on average, > 20% outside the offline model development range). This extrapolation level is very high and is a challenge for any of the usual empirical modeling techniques. Unfortunately, the high extrapolation level requires model redesign, including derivation of an entirely new structure. In this case, modeling expertise is needed and, as a result, maintenance cost is increased.

An alternative that we propose is to use evolving/adaptive inferential sensors that are flexible in the sense that they can adapt/evolve their structure as well as their parameters in order to follow the data pattern, to retrain, and recalibrate, in brief, to be *self-maintaining* (autonomous). This alternative is appealing to the industry because it saves time and computational and human resources. If the evolving inferential sensors are based on fuzzy rule-based models, they have another important advantage—they are transparent and interpretable (Hopner & Klawonn, 2000; Victor & Dourado, 2004). The gradual evolution of the model structure (fuzzy rules) will mean that a retraining of the sensor when required will modify (add or replace) only one or a few fuzzy rules (Angelov, 2002). Ideally, we would require inferential sensors that can automatically recalibrate, detect and *shifts* and *drifts* in the data stream (Klinkenberg & Joachims, 2000; Widmer & Kubat, 1996). One such methodological framework is presented by the evolving Takagi-Sugeno fuzzy models (eTS) (Angelov and Filev, 2004; Angelov & Zhou, 2006; see also Chapter 2).

### 14.2.3 Input Variables Selection

A key issue in inferential sensor development is input variables selection. The dominant approach in the offline case is the dimensionality reduction by principal component analysis (PCA) and building linear models with projections to latent structures by means of partial least squares (PLS). This approach, however, has two key problems: (1) The model interpretation is difficult, and (2) it is limited to linear systems. One approach to extend this to nonlinear systems is to use neural networks. The variables selection algorithm in this case is based on gradually reducing the number of inputs until an optimal structure is obtained (Saltelli et al., 2001). However, this process is coupled with the hidden layer structure selection and requires high-quality data sets, which are not always available for real processes. An alternative is to apply genetic programming (GP), which has a built-in mechanism to select the variables that are related to the problem during the simulated evolution and to gradually ignore variables that are not (Kordon & Smits, 2001). In this way, a different type of nonlinear input variables selection can be used for dimensionality reduction that could be appropriate for industrial data analysis in general and inferential sensor development in particular. A more efficient procedure for online input variables selection applicable in real time is provided by eTS + (see Chapter 2 and also Angelov & Zhou, 2008).

## 14.3 STATE OF THE ART OF INDUSTRIAL INFERENTIAL SENSORS

Soft sensors can infer important process variables (called *outputs*) from available hardware sensors (called *inputs*). Usually the outputs are measured infrequently by laboratory analysis, material property tests, expensive gas chromatograph analysis, and so forth. Very often the output measurement is performed offline and then introduced into the online process monitoring and control system. It is assumed that soft sensor inputs are available online, either from cheap hardware sensors or from other soft sensors.

Different inference mechanisms can be used for soft sensor development. If there is a clear understanding of the physics and chemistry of the process, the inferred value can be derived from a fundamental model. Another option is to estimate the parameters of the fundamental model via *Kalman filter* or *extended Kalman filter*. There are cases when the input–output relationship is linear and can be represented either by linear regression or by multivariate model; additionally, Kalman filter assumes Gaussian distribution and stationary signals (Kalman, 1960). The most general representation of the soft sensor, however, is a form of nonlinear empirical model, and the signal is, generally, nonstationary.

### 14.3.1 Assumptions for Industrial Inferential Sensor Development

As with any model, the inferential sensor is derived under certain assumptions that define its validity limits. The first assumption for soft sensor design is that the developed input–output relationship could be nonlinear. This assumption broadens the implementation areas, especially in the chemical industry. However, it imposes challenges typical for nonlinear empirical models, such as unpredictable extrapolation, lack of model confidence limits, and multiplicity of model solutions. The second assumption is that the derived empirical model will guarantee reliable performance with acceptable accuracy of prediction inside the range of input data used for model development (also called *training data*). The excellent interpolation qualities of machine learning approaches, in general, and the universal approximator property of neural networks, in particular (Hornik, 1990) form the basis underlying this assumption. It is critical for industrial applications of inferential sensors because it gives the necessary theoretical basis for reliable predictions and to support the investment for model development. The third assumption is the expectations of performance deterioration in new operating conditions (i.e., outside the range of training data), which is a logical consequence from the previous two assumptions. As a result, model retraining or even a complete redesign is recommended. Since the process and operating condition variations are rather a rule than an exception, increased robustness in these circumstances becomes the central issue of inferential sensor design.

## 14.3.2 Economic Benefits from Industrial Inferential Sensors

The assumptions formulated above define the requirements and the realistic expectations for industrial implementation of inferential sensors. However, the key issue that can turn the technical capabilities of this modeling approach into a successful application is the potential for *value creation*. The sources of economic benefits from inferential sensors are as follows:

- Soft sensors allow tighter control of the most critical parameters for final product quality and, as a result, product consistency is significantly improved.
- Online estimates of critical parameters reduce process upsets through early detection of problems.
- Inferential sensors improve working conditions by reducing or eliminating laboratory measurements in a dangerous environment.
- Very often soft sensors are at the economic optimum. Their development and maintenance cost is lower in comparison with the alternative solutions of expensive hardware sensors or more expensive first-principles models.
- One side effect of the implementation of inferential sensors is the optimization of the use of expensive hardware; that is, they reduce capital investments.
- Soft sensors can be used not only for parameter estimation but also for running *what-if* scenarios in production planning.

These economic benefits have been realized rapidly by the industry, and from the early 1990s a spectacular record of successful applications is reported by the vendors and in the literature. We will illustrate the large range of applications with several typical cases.

### 14.3.3 Inferential Sensor Application Areas

The poster child of inferential sensor applications is environmental emission monitoring (Kordon et al., 2003; Qin et al., 1997). Traditionally, emission monitoring is performed by expensive analytical instruments with costs ranging between $100,000 and $200,000 and maintenance costs of at least $15,000/year. The inferential sensor alternative, implemented as a "classical" neural network, is much cheaper and has accuracy acceptable by federal, state, and local regulations in the U.S. and similarly in the EU. $NO_x$ emissions in burners, heaters, incinerators, and so on, are inferred by associated process variables—mostly temperatures, pressures, and flows. According to one of the leading vendors in soft sensors for emission monitoring, Pavilion Technologies, more than 250 predictive emission monitors (PEMs) have been installed in the United States alone since the mid-1990s.

Another area of successful inferential sensor implementation is biomass estimation in different continuous and fed-batch bioprocesses (Chen et al., 2000; Kordon et al., 2003). Estimating the biomass is of critical importance for successful control of fermenters, especially during the growth phase of organisms. Usually, the biomass concentrations are determined offline by laboratory analysis every two to four hours. However, the low measurement frequency can lead to poor control. This can be compensated by online estimates.

One of the first popular applications of inferential sensors was estimation of product composition in distillation columns (Kordon et al., 2003). However, the most widespread implementation of soft sensors in the chemical industry is for prediction of polymer quality (Kordon et al., 2003). Several polymer quality parameters such as *melt index*, *average molecular weight*, *polymerization rate,* and *conversion* are inferred from *reactor temperature*, *jacket inlet* and *outlet temperatures*, and the *coolant flow rate* through the jacket. It is also possible to estimate online the amount of reactor impurities during the initial stage of polymerization. Of special interest is the nonlinear controller developed by Pavilion Technology, called Process Perfecter, which optimizes the *transition* between different polymer products.

In summary, inferential sensors fill the growing need in industry for sophisticated nonlinear models of process quality parameters. For several years, a number of well-established vendors, such as Pavilion Technologies, Aspen Technology, Siemens, Honeywell, and so on, have implemented thousands of soft sensors in almost every industry. The benefit from improved quality and reduced process upsets is estimated in hundreds of millions of dollars, but the potential market is much bigger.

## 14.4 OPTIONAL OFFLINE PREPROCESSING USING GENETIC PROGRAMMING

### 14.4.1 Inferential Sensors Generated by Genetic Programming

One modeling approach that is increasingly being used in the industry is genetic programming (GP). GP is of special interest to soft sensor development due to its capability for symbolic regression (Koza, 1992). GP-generated *symbolic regression* is a result of simulation of the natural evolution of numerous potential mathematical expressions. The final result is a list of "the best and the brightest" analytical forms according to the selected objective function. Of special importance to the industry are the following unique features of GP (Kordon & Smits, 2001):

- No a priori modeling assumptions
- Derivative-free optimization
- Few design parameters
- Natural selection of the most important process inputs
- Parsimonious analytical functions as a final result

The final feature has double benefit. On one hand, a simple soft sensor often has the potential for better generalization capability and increased robustness, and needs less frequent retraining. On the other hand, process engineers and developers prefer to use non-black-box empirical models and are much more open to the risk of implementing inferential sensors based on functional relationships. An additional advantage is the low implementation cost of such soft sensors. They can be incorporated directly into the existing distributed control systems (DCSs), avoiding the additional specialized software packages that are typical for NN-based inferential sensors.

At the same time, there are still significant challenges in implementing industrial soft sensors generated by GP, such as (1) function generation with noisy industrial data; (2) dealing with time delays; and (3) sensitivity analysis of large data sets, to name a few. Of special importance is the main drawback of GP: the *low speed* of model development due to the *inherently high computational requirements* of this method. For real industrial applications, the calculation time is in the order of several hours, even with the current high-end PCs.

## 14.4.2 Pareto-Front Method for Parsimonious Inferential Sensor Selection

Several thousand empirical models are generated in a typical GP run with at least 20 simulated evolutionary processes of 200 generations. Most of the generated models have similar performance and proper model selection is nontrivial. The direct approach is to use the $r^2$-statistic (Hastie et al., 2001) as the model selection criterion and to select the best model based on the fitness measure at the end of the run. However, the fitness measure does not take *complexity* or *smoothness* of the function into account. Furthermore, it is possible that for a slight decrease in the measure a far less complex function may be obtained that may have higher robustness. Therefore, the experience of the analyst is needed to inspect a manageable number of models that have been extracted.

One indicator of the complexity of the models in a GP run is the number of nodes used to define the model. This measure may be misleading because it does not discern between the types of operators used in each node. For example, no distinction is made between an operator that is additive and an operator that is an exponential function. Clearly, there is a huge difference in complexity. However, using the number of nodes as an indicative measure can help reduce the number of models to inspect to a reasonable size.

In order to find the right tradeoff between complexity and accuracy, the Pareto-front is constructed. The *Pareto-front* is a concept commonly used in multiobjective optimization (Zitzler & Thiele, 1999). In *multiobjective optimization*, apart from the solution space, which is constructed by the constraints in terms of the input variables, there is also an objective space. The objective space is a mapping of the solution space onto the objectives. In classical multiobjective optimization, the problem is cast onto a single-objective optimization problem by defining an a priori weighted sum. Each solution of the single-objective optimization problem represents a single point in the objective space. However, as the optimal weighted sum is seldom known a priori, it is often better to make the final decision from a set of solutions that is independent of the weights. This set of solutions is given by the Pareto-front (Zitzler & Thiele, 1999). The Pareto-front thus represents a surface in the objective space of all possible weighted combinations of the different objectives that satisfy the constraints.

Since the model selection task is, in principle, a multiobjective problem (i.e., accuracy vs. complexity), one can apply the fundamentals of the Pareto-front. Using the Pareto-front for GP-generated models has many advantages (Smits & Kotanchek, 2004). First, it effectively displays the tradeoff between the measures, which enables the analyst to make an unbiased decision. Second, as only a small fraction of the generated models in GP will end up on the Pareto-front, the number of models that need to be inspected individually is decreased tremendously. Finally, additional considerations such as variety in input variables used for ensemble construction can be taken into account. For example, if a Pareto-optimal model uses an undesirable transformation or input variable, one could look for an alternative model among the models close to the Pareto-front.

In Figure 14.1 the Pareto-front is displayed for a set of GP-generated models in terms of two objectives: (1) ratio of nodes (RN), and (2) the $r^2$ value. The *ratio of nodes* is

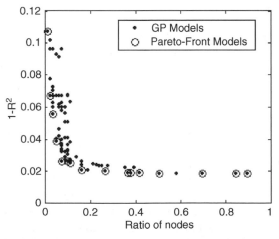

Figure 14.1. Pareto-front of predictive models, generated by GP.

a measure of complexity and needs to be minimized. The second objective, $r^2$, is a measure of the performance of the models. Using $(1 - r^2)$ instead of $r^2$ allows easier interpretation as both objectives are minimized. The Pareto-front models provide *nondominated solutions* for which no improvement on one objective can be obtained without deteriorating another objective. The optimal model will, therefore, lie somewhere on the Pareto-front. Its position will depend on the problem at hand. For example, if complexity and performance have equal importance, then the optimal model would lie in the lower-left corner of the Pareto-front.

Recall that another advantage of using the Pareto front is the reduced number of models to inspect. This is clearly seen in Figure 14.1, where 88 models in total are depicted. However, only 18 of them are identified as Pareto-front models. Furthermore, one can clearly see that using models with a ratio of nodes higher than 0.3 does not result in a significant improvement of $r^2$. Therefore, the number of models to consider may be even less. Generally, Pareto-front does not provide a unique solution/model structure, but rather a small subset of solutions. One way to extract a unique solution is to minimize the distance to the origin of the coordinate system. In Figure 14.1, this means to minimize the vector:

$$\vec{p} = \sqrt{(1 - r^2)^2 + (RN)^2} \tag{14.1}$$

## 14.4.3 Input Variable Selection Using Pareto-Front GP

As mentioned earlier, one of the potential applications of symbolic regression via genetic programming is sensitivity analysis of nonlinear problems with a potentially large set of candidate input variables. These kinds of problems are frequently encountered in the chemical processing industry. *Sensitivity analysis* is also called the *problem of input variables selection* in machine learning terminology. Many problems in the chemical industry are of this type. Usually, there are a large number of measurements available at a plant, many of which are redundant or not relevant to the problem that one is trying to solve.

Engineering knowledge about the problem is usually the first step in trying to narrow down the number of inputs. Sensitivity analysis generates a ranking of all the input variables in terms of how important they are in modeling a certain unknown process. In linear problems the sensitivity of an input variable is related to the derivative of the output with respect to that variable. In nonlinear problems, however, the derivative becomes a local property and has to be integrated over the entire input domain to qualify as sensitivity. Since this approach is not really practical in a genetic programming context, the sensitivity of a given input variable can be related to its fitness in the population of equations. The rationale is that important input variables will be used in equations that have a relatively high fitness. So, the fitness of input variables is related to the fitness of the equations they are used in. There is, however, a question with respect to credit assignment, that is, what portion of the fitness goes to which variable in the equation. The easiest approach is to distribute the credit (the fitness of the equation) equally over all variables present. Provided the population size is large enough, we can take the fitness of each equation in the population, distribute this fitness in equal amounts over the input variables present in that equation, and sum all these contributions for each input variable over the entire population.

We already mentioned that when variables accumulate fitness from the entire population there is a chance that we get somewhat of a distorted picture because unimportant variables that happen to be part of equations with a relatively high fitness will also pick up fitness from those. To compensate for this, we introduced a modification where variables accumulate fitness only from equations that reside in the archive. Since the archive contains the Pareto-front of all of the high-fitness equations relative to their complexity, this modification is expected to make input variables selection more robust.

## 14.4.4 Example of Variables Selection Based on Pareto-Front GP

An example of variables selection from an inferential sensor for emissions prediction based on eight potential inputs relative to the emissions is given in Smits et al. (2006). Pareto GP was used for variables selection and nonlinear model generation. The results from the variables selection are shown in Figure 14.2.

The results are based on 5 independent runs of 10 cascades with 50 generations. The average sensitivities with their standard deviations for each input, as defined in the previous section, for a population size of 100 are shown in Figure 14.3. It is clearly seen that four inputs (x2, x5, x6, and x8) have been consistently selected in the generated functions during the simulated evolution. For comparison, a linear variable selection, based on the PCA-PLS model with two principal components, is shown in Figure 14.3. The inputs ranking is represented by a *variable importance in the projection* (VIP) (Eriksson et al., 2001); variables with VIP $> 1$ are treated as important.

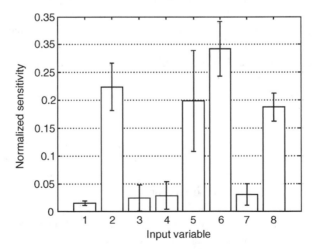

Figure 14.2. Nonlinear sensitivity of all models generated by GP for emissions inferential sensor at the last generation.

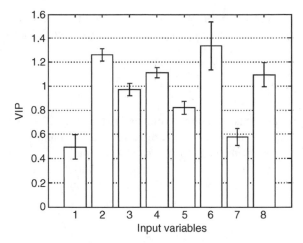

**Figure 14.3.** Variable importance in the projection (VIP) of the 8 inputs based on a two-principal-components PCA-PLS model of the emissions soft sensor.

One of the differences between linear and GP-based variables selection is that input x5 is insignificant from the linear point of view. However, it is one of the most significant inputs, according to nonlinear sensitivity analysis and process experts. The experts also selected two models for the final implementation, which included the four most influential inputs from GP variables selection—x2, x5, x6, and x8. The application details are given in Kordon et al. (2003).

## 14.5 INPUT VARIABLES SELECTION USING eTS +

Selecting informative inputs is a critical task for an automatic modeling system such as an inferential (soft) sensor. The complexities of this task are rooted in the inherent relationships between input physical variables and input–output relationships/dependencies, which are (normally) highly nonlinear and nonstationary. Conventionally, this task is performed as part of preprocessing offline before the modeling of the real system. In classification- and data mining–related literature it is called *feature selection* or *sensitivity analysis*. Typical approaches used to address this problem include *principal component analysis* (PCA) (Fukunaga, 1990; Li et al. 2000), *genetic programming* (Kordon & Smits, 2001), and *partial least squares* (Fortuna et al., 2007). It is difficult, however, to obtain appropriate training samples.

The method for online input variables selection (see Chapter 2) allows us to evaluate online the importance of input variables based on the sensitivity of the output, $\frac{\partial y^i}{\partial x_j}$; $i = 1, 2, \ldots R; j = 1, 2, \ldots, n$ because of the (partially) linear consequences in terms of the inputs (Angelov, 2006):

$$\frac{\partial y^i}{\partial x_j} = a_j^i \qquad (14.2)$$

When accumulated over the period of training (or retraining), these weights indicate the relative contribution of the respective input variables (Angelov, 2006):

$$\omega_j^i = \left| \sum_{l=1}^k \frac{\partial y^i(l)}{\partial x_j(l)} \right| \tag{14.3}$$

Note that the inputs and the output are normalized in the range [0;1] or standardized and therefore the consequent parameters are comparable. Also, note that absolute values are taken to ignore the role of the sign and to avoid cancellations.

One can define the weight $\bar{\omega}_j^i$ of a particular input variable $x_j$ as a proportion of the contribution of this particular variable to the contributions of the other variables (Angelov, 2006):

$$\bar{\omega}_j^i = \frac{\omega_j^i}{\sum_{l=1}^n \omega_l^i} \tag{14.4}$$

The inputs can be ranked based on their relative weight $\bar{\omega}_j^i$ and inputs with *low* value of $\bar{\omega}_j^i$, which do not contribute significantly to the output and can be removed.

## 14.6 CASE STUDIES—INFERENTIAL SENSORS FOR THE CHEMICAL PROCESS INDUSTRY

The capabilities of the proposed evolving inferential sensors will be explored on four different industrial data sets for chemical properties estimation. All four cases include operating regime changes with different impacts on the specific chemical properties. However, all the changes create a challenge to existing inferential sensors with a fixed structure. As a basis for comparison, a robust inferential sensor with a simple structure, generated by GP, will be used.

The first case (*Case1*) is based on product composition estimation in a distillation tower. The selected 6 inputs are the most statistically significant process variables related to this composition. The measurements are based on laboratory analysis, taken every 8 hours, and are noisy. Process data are the hourly averaged values for the time when the grab sample for the laboratory measurement has been taken. The data includes 309 records (samples) where a significant change in the operating conditions has been introduced after sample 127. The time series of the measured composition is shown in Figure 14.4.

The second case (*Case2*) is based on product composition estimation in the bottom of a distillation tower. Using 47 process variables the measurements are based on laboratory analysis, taken every 8 hours, and are not as noisy as in the other cases. Process data are the hourly averaged values for the time instances when the sample for the laboratory measurement has been taken. The data includes 308 records (samples) where a significant change in the operating conditions has been introduced after sample 113. The time series of the output is shown in Figure 14.5.

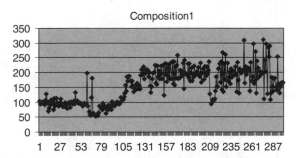

**Figure 14.4.** Time series for Case1.

The third case (*Case3*) is based on product composition estimation in the top of the same distillation tower as Case2. In this case, the same 47 process variables are used as inputs in the model development. The data includes 308 records (samples) where a significant change in the operating conditions has been introduced in the same place (after sample 113). The difference from the previous case is the higher level of output noise, as is seen in Figure 14.6.

The final case (*Case4*) is based on propylene evaluation in the top of a distillation tower. In this case, 22 process variables are potentially related to propylene and are used as inputs in the model development. The propylene measurements are based on gas chromatograph analysis, taken every 15 minutes. Process data are the snapshot minute values for the time when the gas chromatograph measurement has been taken. The data includes 3000 records (samples) with a very broad range of operating conditions and the time series of the measured propylene is shown in Figure 14.7.

These four test cases cover most of the real issues in applying inferential sensors in industry, such as noisy data, changing operating conditions, need for variable selection, and so forth. Case 4 is in operation at the Dow Chemical plants since May 2004.

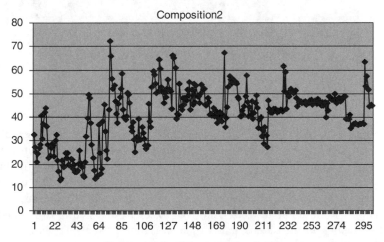

**Figure 14.5.** Time series for Case2.

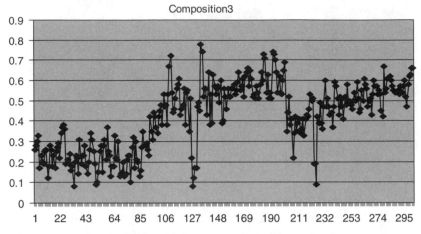

Figure 14.6. Time series for Case3.

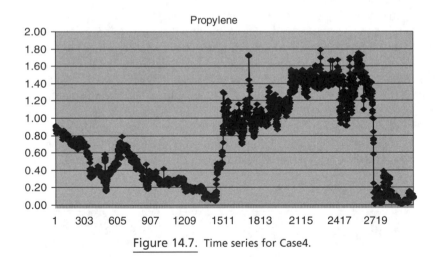

Figure 14.7. Time series for Case4.

## 14.7 EXPERIMENTAL RESULTS AND ANALYSIS

The experiments for the evolving inferential sensor are carried out on the real data from the four cases described in section 14.6. The main aim was to generate interpretable, simple-to-understand models that are flexible and adaptive (evolving in time and following the dynamics of the data) and are robust to noise and imprecise measurement data starting with no a priori information. The precision was measured using *root mean squares* (*RMSE*) (Hastie et al., 2001). All four cases were tested in two experimental settings: (1) using all measured input variables (features) that may have a potential effect on the output, and (2) using selected input variables (features) as described in section 14.4. The data in all experiments were normalized based on the estimated range as described in Hastie et al. (2001) and Angelov and Zhou (2006). Both experiments are conducted in a simulated online manner. eSensor starts with an empty fuzzy rule base and generates it on-the-fly based on the data that are provided sample-by-sample and disregarded from the memory once processed. Based on the data spatial distribution, eSensor evolves the structure of the fuzzy rule base on-the-fly and optimizes the parameters as detailed in Chapter 2. The output prediction is calculated for every data sample and can be used at any time instant. Training samples are provided when they are available. The experimental results indicate that the selection of most important input variables significantly improves the performance of the inferential sensor in both precision and interpretability (simplicity) terms.

## 14.7.1 Offline Preselection of Input Variables Using Genetic Programming

The first part of the experimental study includes the nonadaptive model generation by GP. The summary of the results from the inputs or features selection are represented in Table 14.1.

The GP-based variables selection significantly reduced the number of relevant inputs in all four cases. The selected analytical functions with optimal balance between accuracy and complexity, lying on the Pareto-front, for the four cases are given below, where $x_i$ are the corresponding input indexes:

$$Case1: y = -6.45 + 324075e^{\frac{x_1 - x_6}{3.05}} \tag{14.5}$$

$$Case2: y = -635 + 732.5\frac{x_{30}}{x_{29}} \tag{14.6}$$

$$Case3: y = -4.94 + 0.06\left(\frac{x_{29}}{x_{47}} + \log(x_{42}) + x_{32} - x_{43}\right) \tag{14.7}$$

$$Case4: y = -0.175 + 0.00292\left(\frac{x_{11}^2}{x_{11} - x_8}\right) \tag{14.8}$$

TABLE 14.1. Results of Offline Features Selection by GP

| inputs | Case1 | | Case2 | | Case3 | | Case4 | |
|---|---|---|---|---|---|---|---|---|
| | Initial | Selected | Initial | Selected | Initial | Selected | Initial | Selected |
| Number | 6 | 2 | 47 | 2 | 47 | 5 | 22 | 2 |
| Selection | $[x_1; x_6]$ | $x_1, x_6$ | $[x_1; x_{47}]$ | $x_{29}, x_{30}$ | $[x_1; x_{47}]$ | $x_{29}, x_{32},$ | $[x_1; x_{22}]$ | $x_8, x_{11}$ |
| | | | | | | $x_{42}, x_{43}, x_{47}$ | | |

T A B L E  14.2. Performance of the Nonadaptive Inferential Sensor Based on (14.5)–(14.8)

| | Case1 | | Case2 | | Case3 | | Case4 | |
|---|---|---|---|---|---|---|---|---|
| | Offline Training | Testing | Offline Training | Testing | Offline Training | Testing | Offline Training | Testing |
| RMSE | 11.596 | **19.73** | 1.628 | **2.636** | 0.054 | **4.59** | 0.027 | **0.21** |

All the selected equations are very simple and have been accepted and interpreted by process engineers. A summary of the performance of these models is given in Table 14.2.

The performance of the nonadaptive sensor deteriorates dramatically in the new operating conditions in all four experiments. The effect is very strong in Case3, where the nonadaptive sensor gives very unreliable estimates.

## 14.7.2  eSensor with All Features

In this experiment, no feature selection was applied and thus all available measured input variables were used. The summary of the result is shown in Table 14.3.

As soon as there are data samples that include the measured output, eSensor can start to generate its structure or to update (recalibrate). It evolves its fuzzy rule base from the very first input for which the output is also measured (a supervision is provided). The automatically generated rule-base is in the following form:

---

**Final Rule Base for Case2:**

$R_1$:  **IF** $(x_1$ is close to 42.00) **AND** $(x_2$ is close to 64.37) ...... **AND** $(x_{47}$ is close to 20.83) **THEN** $(\bar{y} = 0.019 - 0.016\bar{x}_1 + \ldots - 0.109\bar{x}_{47})$

$R_2$:  **IF** $(x_1$ is close to 42.05) **AND** $(x_2$ is close to 56.33) ...... **AND** $(x_{47}$ is close to 36.70) **THEN** $(\bar{y} = 0.813 - 0.004\bar{x}_1 + \ldots - 0.113\bar{x}_{47})$

$R_3$:  **IF** $(x_1$ is close to 43.42) **AND** $(x_2$ is close to 34.21) ...... **AND** $(x_{47}$ is close to 66.20) **THEN** $(\bar{y} = 0.712 - 0.007\bar{x}_1 + \ldots - 0.206\bar{x}_{47})$

$R_4$:  **IF** $(x_1$ is close to 40.078) **AND** $(x_2$ is close to 34.209) ...... **AND** $(x_{47}$ is close to 32.17) **THEN** $(\bar{y} = 0.432 - 0.150\bar{x}_1 + \ldots - 0.094\bar{x}_{47})$

---

where $\bar{y}, \bar{x}$ denote the normalized values of the output $y$ and inputs $x$, respectively.

T A B L E  14.3. Results Using eSensor with All Features Online

| | Case1 | Case2 | Case3 | Case4 |
|---|---|---|---|---|
| RMSE | **18.015** | **4.5968** | **0.095961** | **0.16903** |
| Correlation | **0.94959** | **0.91931** | **0.83202** | **0.94769** |
| # of Rules | 2 | 4 | 3 | 4 |
| # of features | 6 | 47 | 47 | 23 |

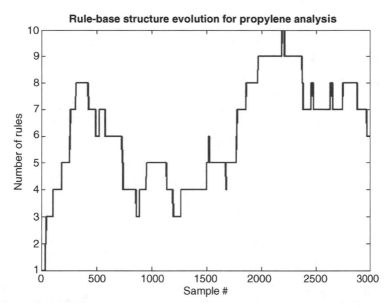

**Figure 14.8.** Evolution of the fuzzy rule base for propylene using eTS-based eSensor.

This is, for example, the result of training eSensor for Case2 with all the data available. The evolution of the fuzzy rule base is provided for Case4 in Figure 14.8. One can see that the number of fuzzy rules is growing but also reducing (due to, for example, *ageing* and a shift of the concept as described in Chapter 2).

Due to the large number of input variables (features), especially for Case2 and Case3 (47 inputs!) and propylene (23 inputs!), the antecedent (linguistic) part of the fuzzy rules becomes very long and therefore difficult to understand. The high dimensionality of the inputs and input–output data space leads also to computational problems. Note that in the rule base shown above, some fuzzy sets from different rules have values that are very close in a particular dimension (e.g., in dimension $x_1$, rule 1 and rule 2 have a very close definition of the fuzzy sets: *IF($x_1$is close to 42.00/42.05)*. This is also seen in Figure 14.9.

In order to increase the interpretability of the rule base, such very close fuzzy sets can be merged by using one of the focal points (the one that represents a *younger* rule) to represent the similar fuzzy sets. Note that the approach proposed in Victor and Dourado (2004) and applied to eTS for online fuzzy rule base and fuzzy sets simplification based on arithmetic averaging suffers from the following problems: (1) The averaged result may be infeasible; and (2) the nonlinearity of the input–output relation leads to introducing an error. The approach described in more detail in Chapter 2 does not suffer from these limitations and leads to simpler and more accurate models as illustrated in this section.

Looking into the consequent part of the rules, the absolute values of some parameters on one dimension (feature) are significantly higher than the parameters on the other dimensions (features). These features therefore have more impact on the output of the rules and are therefore more important.

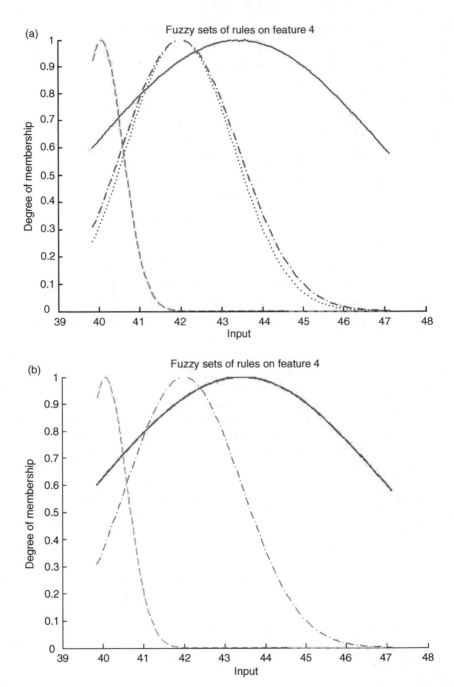

Figure 14.9. Membership functions of fuzzy sets for input 4: (a) before simplification; (b) after simplification by removing the older fuzzy set.

TABLE 14.4. Results for the Online Experiment Using Feature Selection

|  | Case1 | Case2 | Case3 | Case4 |
|---|---|---|---|---|
| RMSE | 18.907 | 4.7494 | 0.09067 | 0.071866 |
| Correlation | 0.94435 | 0.92143 | 0.84721 | 0.98937 |
| # of Rules | 3 | 3 | 3 | 6 |
| # of Features | 2 | 2 | 4 | 2 |

Estimation can be retrieved from the sensor when necessary. As shown in Table 14.3, prediction accuracy is acceptably high and the rule base generated automatically has a small number of fuzzy rules (2 to 6 rules generated over the whole data set).

### 14.7.3 Results for the Experiment Including Online Feature Selection

In the second experiment, the input variables were selected automatically online as described in section 14.5 using eTS-based eSensor. As seen in Table 14.4, a significantly smaller number of input variables (features) were used, which leads to very clearly interpretable models.

The results show that eSensor is able to produce very high rates of precision with simpler models (see Figure 14.10).

This leads to models extracted automatically from the data that are robust, flexible, and yet understandable by the operator of the process. That means that the fuzzy rule

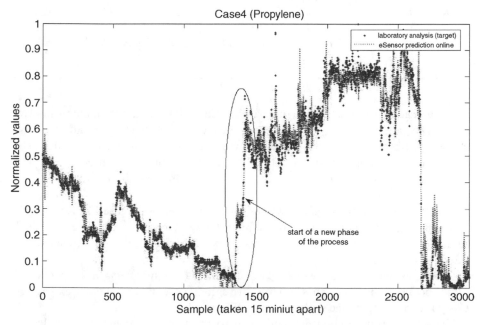

Figure 14.10. Prediction of the output by eSensor.

base that can be extracted and stored can be directly presented to the operators without postprocessing.

The fuzzy rule bases generated automatically are:

---

**Final Rule Base for Case2:**

$R_1$:  **IF** (*$x_1$ is around 183.85*) **AND** (*$x_2$ is around 170.31*) **THEN** ($\bar{y} = 0.84 - 0.96\bar{x}_1 + 0.61\bar{x}_2$)

$R_2$:  **IF** (*$x_1$ is around 178.09*) **AND** (*$x_2$ is around 166.84*) **THEN** ($\bar{y} = 0.87 - 0.98\bar{x}_1 + 0.54\bar{x}_2$)

$R_3$:  **IF** (*$x_1$ is around 172.70*) **AND** (*$x_2$ is around 166.01*) **THEN** ($\bar{y} = 0.87 - 1.02\bar{x}_1 + 0.64\bar{x}_2$)

---

**Final Rule Base for Case4:**

$R_1$:  **IF** (*$x_1$ is around 24.6*) **AND** (*$x_2$ is around 26.3*) **THEN** ($\bar{y} = -0.039 + \bar{x}_1 - 0.324\bar{x}_2$)

$R_2$:  **IF** (*$x_1$ is around 39.0*) **AND** (*$x_2$ is around 43.5*) **THEN** ($\bar{y} = -0.615 + 4.77\bar{x}_1 - 0.340\bar{x}_2$)

$R_3$:  **IF** (*$x_1$ is around 46.2*) **AND** (*$x_2$ is around 49.5*) **THEN** ($\bar{y} = -0.679 + 1.090\bar{x}_1 + 0.450\bar{x}_2$)

$R_4$:  **IF** (*$x_1$ is around 45.9*) **AND** (*$x_2$ is around 49.9*) **THEN** ($\bar{y} = -1.340 + 5.570\bar{x}_1 - 3.320x_2$)

$R_5$:  **IF** (*$x_1$ is around 36.2*) **AND** (*$x_2$ is around 43.5*) **THEN** ($y = -0.002 + 0.320\bar{x}_1 - 0.065\bar{x}_2$)

$R_6$   **IF** (*$x_1$ is around 31.6*) **AND** (*$x_2$ is around 38.7*) **THEN** ($\bar{y} = -0.007 + 0.366\bar{x}_1 - 0.129\bar{x}_2$)

---

Note that the fuzzy sets in the rule base for Case2 for the features/inputs $x_1$ and $x_2$, respectively, are very close to each other. They were further merged into one fuzzy rule as described earlier, leaving rule 3 as *younger* rules between similar rules. This leads to the interesting conclusion that for Case2 a linear model may be sufficient. This fact is automatically detected by eSensor analyzing the data in a simulated online regime.

The interpretability of the fuzzy rules can also be seen in Figure 14.11, where the consequent part of the fuzzy rules for the propylene experiment are depicted alongside the membership functions of the fuzzy sets for two of the input variables (features), $x_1$ and $x_2$, respectively.

This illustrates the rate at which a particular input (feature) affects the output in each of the local regions. One can see the local regions generated in another experiment (Case1) represented by the dashed lines in Figure 14.12.

It is interesting to note that, compared to the first experiment, fewer rules are generated, whereas, instead of dropping down, the prediction rate is higher for all four

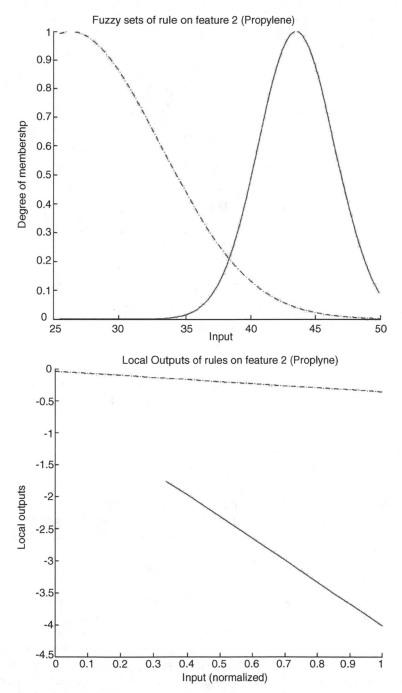

Figure 14.11. *Top plot:* Membership functions of fuzzy sets for the input/feature 2. *Bottom plot:* Consequents of two of the fuzzy rules in Case4 in respect to (projection on) input variable (feature) 1 (the other input variable is assumed to be equal to zero (2D cut).

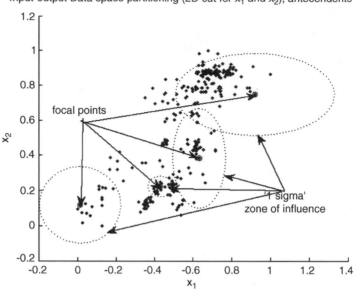

**Figure 14.12.** Antecedents that represent local regions in the data space for Case1.

scenarios. This is because the less relevant information in the data is removed along with the removed inputs/features, and the fuzzy rules that are generated are more generic.

## 14.8 CONCLUSION

A new type of adaptive, self-calibrating, and self-developing inferential sensor that is based on evolving fuzzy systems of the Takagi-Sugeno type (eTS) is described in this chapter and tested on a range of case studies from real chemical processes. The proposed eSensors can be trained on-the-fly, either starting from scratch or being primed with an initial rule base. Also optionally, eSensor can select online the most relevant and important input variables. The results with data from real chemical processes demonstrate that the proposed adaptive and evolving inferential sensor is very flexible (it develops its model structure and adapts to sudden changes such as the introduced change of operating condition after sample 127 for Case1 and after sample 113 for Case2 automatically). It does not need any pretraining and specific maintenance and thus reduces the life-cycle costs of the inferential sensors significantly. The structure of the proposed eSensor is transparent as it is composed of linguistic fuzzy rules. The proposed evolving inferential sensor is also very robust, which was demonstrated for Case3. The proposed eSensor is suitable for a range of process industries including, but not limited to, chemical, biotechnology, oil refining, and so forth.

## 14.9 ACKNOWLEDGMENT

The authors would like to thank Mr. Xiaowei Zhou for performing the numerical experiments.

## 14.10 REFERENCES

Angelov P. (2002). *Evolving Rule Based Models: A Tool for Design of Flexible Adaptive Systems.* Heidelberg, New York: Springer-Verlag, ISBN 3-7908-1457-1.

Angelov P., D. Filev (2004). "An Approach to On-line Identification of Takagi-Sugeno Fuzzy Models," *IEEE Trans. on System, Man, and Cybernetics, Part B—Cybernetics*, Vol. 34, No. 1, pp. 484–498, ISSN 1094-6977.

Angelov, P. (2006). "Machine Learning (Collaborative Systems)," patent (WO2008053161, priority date—November 1, 2006).

Angelov, P., X. Zhou (2006). "Evolving Fuzzy Systems from Data Streams in Real-Time." *Proc. 2006 Int. Symposium on Evolving Fuzzy Systems, Ambleside, UK,* September 7–9, 2006, IEEE Press, pp. 29–35, ISBN 0-7803-9719-3.

Angelov, P., X. Zhou (2008). "On-Line Learning Fuzzy Rule-based System Structure from Data Streams." *Proc. World Congress on Computational Intelligence, WCCI-2008,* Hong Kong, June 1–6, 2008, IEEE Press, pp. 915–922, ISBN 978-1-4244-1821-3/08.

Chen L., O. Bernard, G. Bastin, P. Angelov (2000). "Hybrid Modelling of Biotechnolo-gical Process Using Neural Networks," *Control Eng. Practice*, Vol. 8, No. 7, pp. 821–827.

Eriksson, L., E. Johansson, N. Wold, S. Wold (2001). *Multi- and Megavariate Data Analysis: Principles and Applications.* Umea, Sweden: Umetrics Academy.

Fortuna L., S. Graziani, A. Rizzo, M. G. Xibilia (2007). "Soft Sensor for Monitoring and Control of Industrial Processes." In *Advances in Industrial Control Series* (M. J. Grimble, M.A. Johnson eds.). Springer Verlag: Berlin, Germany.

Fukunaga K. (1990). *Introduction to Statistical Pattern Recognition*, 2nd edition, Academic Press, San Diego, CA, USA, ISBN 0-12-269851-7.

Hastie T., R. Tibshirani, & J. Friedman (2001). *The Elements of Statistical Learning: Data Mining, Inference and Prediction.* Heidelberg, Germany: Springer-Verlag.

Hopner F., F. Klawonn (2000). "Obtaining Interpretable Fuzzy Models from Fuzzy Clustering and Fuzzy Regression." *Proc. 4th Int. Conf. on Knowledge Based Intelligent Engineering Systems and Allied Technologies (KES)*, Brighton, UK, pp. 162–165.

Hornik K. (1990). "Approximation Capabilities of Multilayer Feedforward Neural Networks," *Neural Networks*, Vol. 4, pp. 251–257.

Kalman R. (1960). "A New Approach to Linear Filtering and Prediction Problems," *Transactions of the ASME—Journal of Basic Engineering*, Vol. 83, pp. 95–107.

Klinkenberg R., T. Joachims (2000). "Detection Concept Drift with Support Vector Machines." *Proc. 7th Int. Conf. on Machine Learning (ICML)*, Morgan Kaufman, pp. 487–494.

Kordon A., G. Smits (2001). "Soft Sensor Development Using Genetic Programming." *Proc. GECCO'2001,* San Francisco, pp. 1346–1351.

Kordon A., G. Smits, A. Kalos, E. Jordaan (2003). "Robust Soft Sensor Development Using Genetic Programming." In *Nature-Inspired Methods in Chemometrics* (R. Leardi ed.). Amsterdam, Holland: Elsevier, pp. 69–108.

Koza J. (1992). *Genetic Programming: On the Programming of Computers by Means of Natural Selection*. Cambridge, MA: MIT Press.

Li W., H. H. Yue, S. Valle-Cervantes, S. J. Qin (2000). "Recursive PCA for Adaptive Process Monitoring," *Journal of Process Control*, Vol. 10, No. 5, pp. 471–486.

Macias, J., Feliu, J., Bosch, A. (2003). "Simulation Workbench between HYSYS Rigorous Model and Its NN Extension: Case Study of a Complex Simulation with Re-circulation." *Proc. 4th European Congress on Chemical Engineering, ECCE 4*, ISBN: 84-88233-31-0.

Qin, S. J., H. Yue, R. Dunia (1997). "Self-Validating Inferential Sensors with Application to Air Emission Monitoring," *Industrial Engineering Chemistry Research*, Vol. 36, pp. 1675–1685.

Rallo R., J. Ferre-Gine, A. Arena, F. Girault (2004). "Neural Virtual Sensor for the Inferential Prediction of Product Quality from Process Variables," *Computers and Chemical Engineering*, Vol. 26, pp. 1735–1754.

Saltelli, A., K. Chan, E. Scott (2001). *Sensitivity Analysis*, John Wiley and Sons Ltd., Chichester, West Sussex, UK, ISBN 0-471-99892-3.

Smits G., M. Kotachenek (2004). "Pareto-Front Exploitation Symbolic Regression," In *Genetic Programming Theory and Practice II* (U. M. O'Reiley, T. Yu, R. Riolo, B. Worzel, eds). New York: Springer, pp. 283–300.

Smits, G., A. Kordon, E. Jordaan, C. Vladislavleva, M. Kotanchek (2006). "Variable Selection in Industrial Data Sets Using Pareto Genetic Programming." In *Genetic Programming Theory and Practice III* (T., Yu, R. Riolo, B. Worzel,eds). New York: Springer, pp. 79–92.

Takagi T., M. Sugeno (1985). "Fuzzy Identification of Systems and Its Applications to Modeling and Control," *IEEE Trans. on Systems, Man and Cybernetics*, Vol. 15, No. 1, pp. 116–132.

Victor J., A. Dourado (2004). On-line Interpretability by Fuzzy Rule Base Simplification and Reduction," *European Symposium on Intelligent Technologies, Hybrid Systems and Their Implementation on Smart Adaptive Systems, EUNITE2004*, Aachen, Germany.

Widmer G., M. Kubat (1996). "Learning in the Presence of Concept Drift and Hidden Contexts," *Machine Learning*, Vol. 23, No. 1, pp. 69–101.

Yan W., H. Shao, X. Wang (2004). "Soft Sensing Modelling Based on Support Vector Machine and Bayesian Model Selection," *Computers and Chemical Engineering*, Vol. 28, pp. 1489–1498.

Zitzler E., L. Thiele (1999). "Multiobjective Evolutionary Algorithms: A Comparative Case Study and the Strength Pareto Approach," *IEEE Trans. on Evolutionary Computation*, Vol. 3, No. 4, pp. 257–271.

# 15

# RECOGNITION OF HUMAN GRASP BY FUZZY MODELING

R. Palm, B. Kadmiry, B. Iliev

## 15.1 INTRODUCTION

Over the past decade, the field of humanlike robotic hands has attracted significant research efforts aiming at applications such as service robots and prosthetic hands, as well as industrial applications. However, such applications are relatively few so far due to the lack of appropriate sensor systems and some unsolved problems with human–robot interaction. One reason is the difficult programming procedure due to the high dimensionality of grasping and manipulation tasks. An approach to solve this problem is *programming by demonstration (PbD)*, which is used in complex robotic applications such as grasping and dexterous manipulation.

In PbD, the operator performs a task while the robot captures the data by a motion-capture device or a video camera and analyzes the demonstrated actions. Then the robot has to recognize these actions and replicate them in the framework of a complex application. One of the most complicated tasks is the recognition procedure because of the ambiguous nature of human grasp. One of the techniques to cope with the recognition problem is to use *evolving fuzzy systems (EFSs)* that are able to learn parameters online in a self-developing and self-adapting manner. Important research has been done in the fields of identification of TS-fuzzy models [1] and the adaptation of fuzzy rule bases using online clustering methods [2]. A robotic application for mobile robots in a dynamic environment can be found in [3]. Different techniques for grasp recognition have been

*Evolving Intelligent Systems: Methodology and Applications,* Edited by Plamen Angelov, Dimitar P. Filev, and Nikola Kasabov

applied in PbD. Kang et al. [4] describe a system that observes, recognizes, and maps human grasp to a robot manipulator using a stereo vision system and a data glove. Zoellner et al. [5] use a data glove with integrated tactile sensors where the recognition is based on *support vector machines (SVMs)*. Ikeuchi et al. [6] apply *hidden Markov models (HMMs)* to segment and recognize grasp sequences. Ekvall and Kragic [7] also use HMM methods and address the PbD problem using arm trajectory as an additional feature for grasp classification. Li et al. [8] use *singular value decomposition (SVD)* for the generation of feature vectors of human grasp and SVMs, which are applied to the classification problem. Aleotti and Caselli [9] describe a virtual-reality-based PbD system for grasp recognition where only final grasp postures are modeled based on finger joint angles. Palm and Iliev presented two methods based on fuzzy models [10] and [11]. These two methods can be seen as evolving fuzzy systems as they are able to learn robotic behaviors or task primitives from experience. However, looking at the rich variety of cited methods, it is evident that they do not provide equally successful results.

Therefore, three methods are compared with one another, two of them being already described in detail in [10] and [11] and the third one being a hybrid method of fuzzy clustering and HMM methods. All three methods start with fuzzy time clustering. The first method, which is the simplest one, classifies a given test grasp using the distances of the time clusters between the test grasp and a set of model grasps [10]. The second method, which is more complex, is based on qualitative fuzzy recognition rules and solves the segmentation problem and the recognition problem at once [11]. The third method deals with fuzzy time clustering and grasp recognition using HMMs [12]. All three methods are tested on the same set of grasp data in order to provide a fair comparison of the methods.

This chapter is organized as follows: Section 15.2 describes the experimental platform consisting of a data glove and a hand simulation tool. Section 15.3 discusses the learning of grasps by time-clustering and the training of model grasps. Section 15.4 describes the three recognition methods. Section 15.5 presents the experimental results and gives a comparison of the three methods. Finally, section 15.6 draws some conclusions and directions for future work.

## 15.2 AN EXPERIMENTAL PLATFORM FOR PBD

Robotic grasping involves two main tasks: *segmentation* of human demonstrations and *grasp recognition*. The first task is to partition the data record into a sequence of episodes, where each one contains a single grasp. The second task is to recognize the grasp performed in each episode. Then the demonstrated task is (automatically) converted into a program code that can be executed on a particular robotic platform (see Figure 15.1). If the system is able to recognize the corresponding human grasps in a demonstration, the robot will also be able to perform the demonstrated task by activating respective grasp primitives (see Figure 15.2). The experimental platform consists of a hand-motion-capturing device and a hand simulation environment. The motions of the human operator are recorded by a data glove (CyberGlove), which measures 18 joint angles in the hand and the wrist (see [13]). Since humans mostly use a limited number of grasp types, the recognition process can be restricted to certain grasp taxonomies, such as those

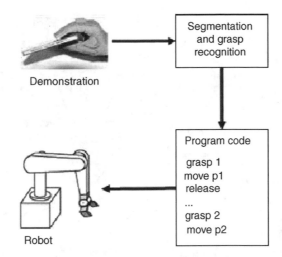

Figure 15.1. Programming by demonstration of grasping tasks.

developed by Cutkosky [14] and Iberall [15]. Here, we use Iberall's human grasp taxonomy (see Figure 15.3).

To test the grasp primitives, we developed a simulation model of a five-fingered hand with three links and three joints in each finger. The simulation environment allows us to perform a kinematic simulation of the artificial hand and its interaction with modeled objects.

Moreover, we can simulate recorded demonstrations of human operators and compare them with the result from the execution of corresponding grasp primitives. We tested the grasping of 15 different objects (see Figure 15.4), some of them belonging to the same class in terms of an applied type of grasps. For example, *cylinder* and *small bottle* correspond to *cylindrical grasp*, and *sphere* and *cube* to *precision grasp*, and so on.

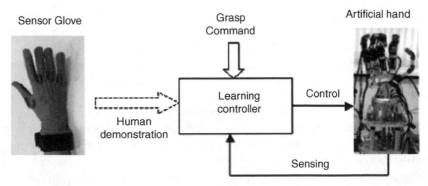

Figure 15.2. Learning of grasp primitives from human demonstrations.

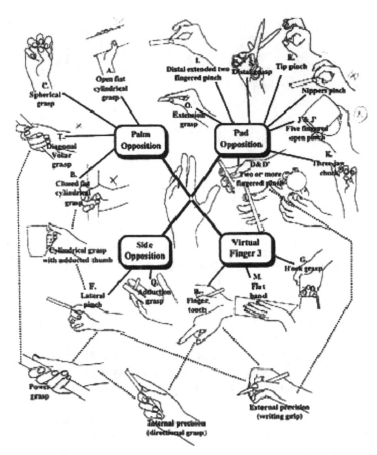

Figure 15.3. Grasp taxonomy by Th. Iberall [15].

## 15.3 MODELING OF GRASP PRIMITIVES

### 15.3.1 Modeling by Time-Clustering

The recognition of a grasp type is achieved by a model that reflects the *behavior of the hand in time*. In the following, an approach to learning human grasps from demonstrations by *time-clustering* [10] is briefly described. The result is a set of grasp models for a selected number of human grasp motions. According to section 15.2, a number of experiments were performed in which time sequences for 15 different grasps were collected using a data glove with 18 sensors (see [13]).

Each demonstration has been repeated several times to collect enough samples of every particular grasp. The time period for a single grasp is about 3 seconds. From those data, models for each individual grasp have been developed using fuzzy clustering and Takagi-Sugeno fuzzy modeling [16].

The basic idea is described in the following [10]. We consider the time instants as model inputs and the three finger joint angles as model outputs (for fingertip coordinates,

1. *cylinder;*
2. *big bottle;*
3. *small bottle;* ──────────────
4. *hammer;*
5. *screw driver;*
6. *small ball;*
7. *big ball;* ──────────────
8. *precision grasp (sphere);*
9. *precision grasp (cube);*
10. *plane (1 CD-ROM);* ────────
11. *plane (3 CD-ROMs);*
12. *fingertrip grasp (small ball);*
13. *fingertrip grasp (big ball);*
14. *fingertrip grasp (can);*
15. *penholder grasp;*

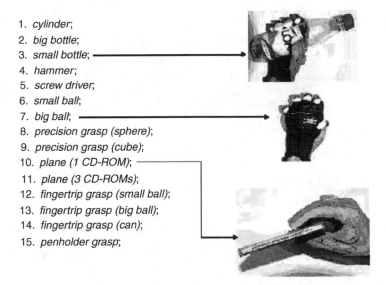

Figure 15.4. Grasp primitives.

see Figures 15.5 and 15.6). Let the angle trajectory of a finger be described by

$$\mathbf{q}(t) = \mathbf{f}(t) \tag{15.1}$$

where $\mathbf{q} \in R^3, \mathbf{f} \in R^3, t \in R^+$. Linearization of (15.1) at selected time points $t_i$ yields

$$\mathbf{q}(t) = \mathbf{q}(t_i) + \left.\frac{\Delta \mathbf{f}(t)}{\Delta t}\right|_{t_i} \cdot (t - t_i) \tag{15.2}$$

which is a linear equation in $t$:

$$\mathbf{q}(t) = \mathbf{A}_i \cdot t + \mathbf{d}_i \tag{15.3}$$

where

$$\mathbf{A}_i = \left.\frac{\Delta \mathbf{f}(t)}{\Delta t}\right|_{t_i} \in R^3 \text{ and } \mathbf{d}_i = \mathbf{q}(t_i) - \left.\frac{\Delta \mathbf{f}(t)}{\Delta t}\right|_{t_i} \cdot t_i \in R^3$$

Using (15.3) as a local linear model one can express (15.1) in terms of a Takagi-Sugeno fuzzy model [17]:

$$\mathbf{q}(t) = \sum_{i=1}^{c} w_i(t)(\mathbf{A}_i \cdot t + \mathbf{d}_i) \tag{15.4}$$

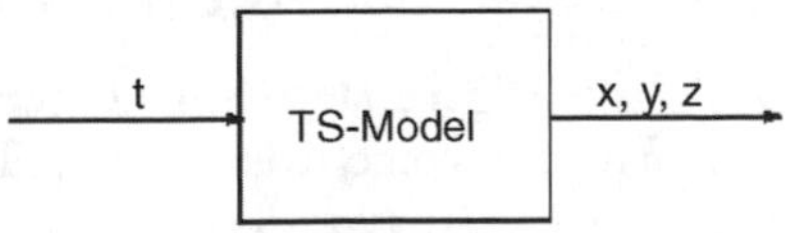

```
        t  ┌─────────┐  x, y, z
  ─────────│ TS-Model│──────────►
           └─────────┘
```

Figure 15.5. Block scheme of grasp modeling.

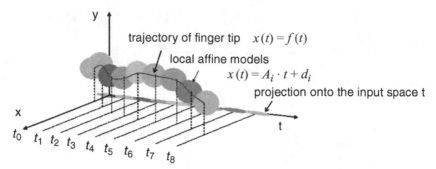

**Figure 15.6.** Time-clustering principle for one fingertip and its motion in (x,y).

where $w_i(t) \in [0, 1]$ is the degree of membership of the time point $t$ to a cluster with the cluster center $t_i$, $c$ is the number of clusters, and $\sum_{i=1}^{c} w_i t) = 1$. Let $t$ be the time and $\mathbf{q} = (q_1, q_2, q_3)^T$ the finger angle coordinates. Then the principal clustering and modeling steps are:

1. Choose an appropriate number $c$ of local linear models (data clusters).
2. Find $c$ cluster centers $(t_i, q_{1i}, q_{2i}, q_{3i}), i = 1 \ldots c$ in the product space of the data quadruples $(t, q_1, q_2, q_3)$ by *fuzzy-c-elliptotype clustering*.
3. Find the corresponding fuzzy regions in the space of input data $t$ by projection of the clusters in the product space into Gustafson-Kessel clusters (GK) onto the input space [18].
4. Calculate $c$ local linear (affine) models (15.4) using the GK clusters from step 2. The degree of membership $w_i(t)$ of an input data point $t$ in an input cluster $C_i$ is determined by

$$w_i(t) = \cfrac{1}{\sum_{j=1}^{c} \left( \cfrac{(t-t_i)^T M_{i\,proj}(t-t_i)}{(t-t_j)^T M_{i\,proj}(t-t_j)} \right)^{\frac{1}{\tilde{m}_{proj}-1}}} \tag{15.5}$$

The projected cluster centers $t_i$ and the induced matrixes $M_{i\,proj}$ define the input clusters $C_i$, $i = 1 \ldots, c$. The parameter $\tilde{m}_{proj} > 1$ determines the fuzziness of an individual cluster.

## 15.3.2 Training of Time Cluster Models Using New Data

Once a particular grasp model has been generated it might become necessary to take new data into account. These data may have come from different human operators to cover several ways of performing the same grasp type. The old model is represented by input cluster centers $t_i$ and output cluster centers $\mathbf{q}_i$ ($i = 1 \ldots c$). It is also described by parameters $\mathbf{A}_i$ and $\mathbf{b}_i$ of the local linear models. The old model was built by a time sequence $[t_1, t_2, \ldots, t_N]$ and a respective angle sequence $[\mathbf{q}_1, \mathbf{q}_2, \ldots, \mathbf{q}_N]$. A new model using new data $[\tilde{t}_1, \tilde{t}_2, \ldots, \tilde{t}_M]$ and $[\tilde{\mathbf{q}}_1, \tilde{\mathbf{q}}_2, \ldots, \tilde{\mathbf{q}}_M]$ can be built by combining the sequences $[t_1, t_2, \ldots, t_N, \tilde{t}_1, \tilde{t}_2, \ldots, \tilde{t}_M]$ and $[\mathbf{q}_1, \mathbf{q}_2, \ldots, \mathbf{q}_N, \tilde{\mathbf{q}}_1, \tilde{\mathbf{q}}_2, \ldots, \tilde{\mathbf{q}}_M]$. The result is a model that involves properties of the old model and the new data. If the old sequence of data is not available, a corresponding sequence can be generated by running the old model with the time instants $[t_1, t_2, \ldots, t_N]$ as inputs and the joint angles $[\mathbf{q}_1, \mathbf{q}_2, \ldots, \mathbf{q}_N]$ as outputs.

## 15.3.3 Modeling of Inverse Kinematics

In a similar way, the inverse kinematics of each finger for a particular grasp is modeled. Let

$$\mathbf{x}(t) = \mathbf{f}(\mathbf{q}); \qquad \mathbf{q}(t) = \mathbf{f}^{-1}(\mathbf{x}) \qquad (15.6)$$

be the nonlinear direct and inverse transformation for a single finger where the inverse transformation is not necessarily unique for the existing finger kinematics. From (15.6) one can easily obtain the differential transformations

$$\dot{\mathbf{x}}(t) = \mathbf{J}(\mathbf{q})\dot{\mathbf{q}}; \qquad \dot{\mathbf{q}}(t) = \mathbf{J}^+(\mathbf{x})\dot{\mathbf{x}} \qquad (15.7)$$

where $\mathbf{J}(\mathbf{q}) = \frac{\partial \mathbf{q}}{\partial \mathbf{x}}$ is the Jacobian and $\mathbf{J}^+(\mathbf{x})$ is the pseudo-inverse Jacobian. Since $\mathbf{x}(t)$ or $\dot{\mathbf{x}}(t)$, respectively, are already known from (15.4), the inverse kinematics in (15.7) remains to be computed.

In order to avoid the time-consuming calculation of the inverse Jacobian at every time instant, the inverse differential kinematics is approximated by a TS model

$$\dot{\mathbf{q}}(t) = \sum_{i=1}^{c} w_i(\mathbf{q}) \mathbf{J}_i^+(\mathbf{x}_i) \dot{\mathbf{x}} \qquad (15.8)$$

where $w_i(\mathbf{q}) \in [0, 1]$ is the degree of membership of the angle vector $\mathbf{q}$ to a cluster with the cluster center $\mathbf{q}_i$, and $\mathbf{J}_i^+(\mathbf{x}_i)$ are the pseudo-inverse Jacobians in the cluster centers $\mathbf{x}_i$. Due to the errors $\Delta \mathbf{x} = \mathbf{x}(t) - \mathbf{x}_m(t)$ between the desired position $\mathbf{x}(t)$ and the real position $\mathbf{x}_m(t)$, a correction of the angles is done using the analytical forward kinematics $\mathbf{x}_m = \mathbf{f}(\mathbf{q}(t))$ of the finger (see Figure 15.7). This changes (15.8) into

$$\dot{\mathbf{q}}(t) = \sum_{i=1}^{c} w_i(\mathbf{x}) \mathbf{J}_i^+(\mathbf{x}_i)(\dot{\mathbf{x}} + K \cdot (\mathbf{x}(t) - \mathbf{x}_m(t))) \qquad (15.9)$$

where $K$ is a scalar that has to be determined so that the optimization loop is stable. It has to be emphasized that the correction or optimization loop using the forward kinematics $\mathbf{f}(\mathbf{q}(t))$ is started at every new time instant and stops when either a lower bound $||\Delta \mathbf{x}|| < \varepsilon$ is reached or a given number of optimization steps is executed. The general control scheme is shown in Figure 15.8. Kawato [19] used a related technique that suggests that

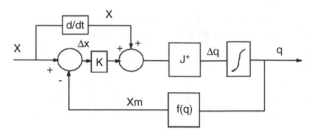

Figure 15.7. Inverse kinematics with correction.

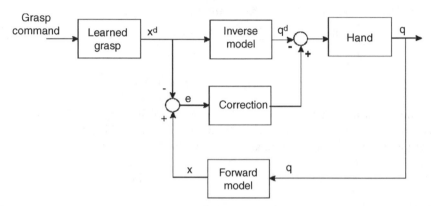

Figure 15.8. Control architecture.

humans use both kinematical and dynamical internal models in movement planning and control. In our implementation, a grasp command activates the respective forward dynamic model of type (15.6) to generate the desired trajectory in Cartesian space. The desired joint space trajectories are obtained using the inverse kinematical model (15.8). The grasping motion continues until contact with the object is established.

## 15.4 RECOGNITION OF GRASPS—THREE METHODS

In the previous section we showed that TS fuzzy models can be successfully used for modeling and imitation of human grasp behaviors. Now, we will show that they can also be used for classification of grasps from recorded human demonstrations. If we just observe captured motions of a human arm while executing several grasp actions it is difficult to identify the exact moment when a grasp sequence starts and ends. Related research shows that this task can be solved efficiently only by fusion of additional information sources such as tactile sensing and vision (see [6] and [7]).

In the following, we present three different recognition methods, all of them based on the time clustering of human grasps. The first method classifies a test grasp by comparing the time clusters of the test grasp and a set of model grasps. The second method uses fuzzy recognition rules for segmentation and recognition. The third method classifies a test grasp using HMMs, which are applied to the output cluster centers of the grasp models. It should be stressed that methods 1 and 2 are related; both of them use distances between fuzzy clusters for recognition. Method 3 is a completely different approach using a probability method for recognition and classification.

## 15.4.1 Recognition of Grasps Using the Distance between Fuzzy Clusters

Let the model of each grasp have the same number of clusters $i = 1 \ldots c$ so that each duration $T_l(l = 1 \ldots L)$ of the $l$th grasp is divided into $(c-1)$ time intervals $\Delta t_i = t_i - t_{i-1}, i = 2 \ldots c$, of the same length. Let the grasps be executed in an environment comparable to the modeled grasp in order to avoid calibration and rescaling procedures. Furthermore let

$$V_{model\,l} = [V_{index}, V_{middle}, V_{ring}, V_{pinkie}, V_{thumb}]_l$$
$$V_{index\,l} = [\mathbf{q}_1, \ldots, \mathbf{q}_i, \ldots, \mathbf{q}_c]_{index\,l}$$
$$\vdots \qquad\qquad\qquad (15.10)$$
$$V_{thumb\,l} = [\mathbf{q}_1, \ldots, \mathbf{q}_i, \ldots, \mathbf{q}_c]_{thumb\,l}$$
$$\mathbf{q}_i = (q_{1i}, q_{2i}, q_{3i})^T$$

where matrix $V_{model\,l}$ includes the output cluster centers $\mathbf{q}_i$ of every finger for the $l$th grasp model. $\mathbf{q}_i$ is the vector of joint angles of each finger. A model of the grasp to be classified is built by the matrix

$$V_{grasp} = [V_{index}, V_{middle}, V_{ring}, V_{pinkie}, V_{thumb}]_{grasp} \qquad (15.11)$$

A decision on the type of grasp is made by applying the Euclidean matrix norm

$$N_l = \|V_m - V_{grasp}\|_l \qquad (15.12)$$

The unknown grasp is classified to the grasp model with the smallest norm $\min(N_l)$, $l = 1 \ldots L$, and the recognition of the grasp is finished.

## 15.4.2 Recognition Based on Qualitative Fuzzy Recognition Rules

The identification of a grasp from a combination of grasps is based on a recognition model. This model is represented by a set of recognition rules using the model grasps mentioned in the previous section. The generation of the recognition model is based on the following steps:

1. Computation of distance norms between a test grasp combination and the model grasps involved
2. Computation of extrema along the sequence of distance norms

3. Formulation of a set of fuzzy rules reflecting the relationship between the extrema of the distance norms and the model grasps

4. Computation of a vector of similarity degrees between the model grasps and the grasp combination

**15.4.2.1 Distance Norms.** Let, for example, $\text{grasp}_2$, $\text{grasp}_5$, $\text{grasp}_7$, $\text{grasp}_{10}$, $\text{grasp}_{14}$ be a combination of grasps taken from the list of grasps shown in Figure 15.4. In the training phase, a time series of these grasps is generated using the existing time series of the corresponding grasp models. Then, each of the model grasps $i = 2,5,7,10,14$ is shifted along the time sequence of the grasp combination and compared with parts of it while taking the norm2 $\|\mathbf{Q}_{ci} - \mathbf{Q}_{mi}\|$ between the difference of the finger angles

$$\mathbf{Q}_{mi} = (\mathbf{q}_m(t_1), \ldots, \mathbf{q}_m(t_{nc}))_i^T$$

of a $\text{grasp}_i$ and the finger angles of the grasp combination

$$\mathbf{Q}_{ci} = (\mathbf{q}_{ci}(\tilde{t}_1), \ldots, \mathbf{q}_{ci}(\tilde{t}_{nc}))_i^T$$

The vectors $\mathbf{q}_m$ and $\mathbf{q}_c$ include the three finger angles for each of the five fingers. For scaling reasons, the norm of the difference is divided by the norm $\|\mathbf{Q}_{mi}\|$ of the model grasp. Then we obtain for the scaled norm

$$n_i = \frac{\|\mathbf{Q}_{ci} - \mathbf{Q}_{mi}\|}{\|\mathbf{Q}_{mi}\|} \tag{15.13}$$

where $n_i$ are functions of time. With this, for each grasp $i = 2, 5, 7, 10, 14$ a time sequence $n_i(t_1)$ is generated. Once the model grasp starts to overlap a grasp in the grasp combination, the norms $n_i$ reach an extremum at the highest overlap, which is either a minimum or a maximum (see Figure 15.9).

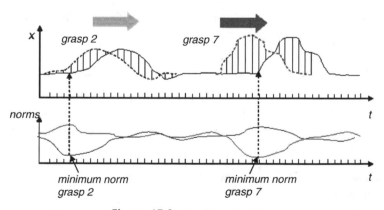

Figure 15.9. Overlap principle.

**15.4.2.2 Extrema in the Distance Norms.** For our example grasp combination, it can be expected that for each model grasp a minimum or a maximum of the norm $n_i$ occurs at five particular time points. In order to find the local extrema in $n_i$, the whole time period $T$ is partitioned into $l$ time slices; the length $T_{slice}$ is bounded by

$$T_{grasp,\min} < T_{slice} < T_{dist,\min}/2$$

where $T_{grasp,\min}$ is the minimum time length of a grasp, and $T_{dist,\min}$ is the minimum time distance between two grasps. This search yields two vectors whose elements are the absolute values of the minima of $n_i$

$$\mathbf{z}_{\min,i} = \left(z_{1\ \min,i}, \ldots, z_{1\ \min,i}\right)^T$$

and the absolute values of the maxima of $n_i$

$$\mathbf{z}_{\max,i} = \left(z_{1\ \max,i}, \ldots, z_{1\ \max,i}\right)^T$$

in each time slice.

**15.4.2.3 Set of Fuzzy Rules.** The two sets of vectors $\mathbf{z}_{\min,i}$ and $\mathbf{z}_{\max,i}$ build *fingerprint patterns* for each of the grasps in a specific grasp combination. On the basis of these patterns, a set of rules decide whether a special combination of minima and maxima by consideration of their absolute values belong to a certain grasp or to another one. Obviously, for a selected grasp, these patterns change with the change of a grasp combination. For example, the pattern for grasp$_2$ in the grasp combination $(2, 5, 7, 10, 14)$ differs significantly from the pattern in grasp combination $(1, 2, 3, 4, 5)$, etc. This is taken into account by the formulation of an individual set of rules for each grasp combination. In order to recognize a model grasp$_i$ from a specific grasp combination, a set of 5 rules is formulated, one rule for each grasp in the combination. A general recognition rule for grasp$_i$ to be identified from the combination reads

$$
\begin{aligned}
&IF \quad (n_j \quad is \quad ex_{ji}) \\
&\ldots \\
&AND \quad (n_k \quad is \quad ex_{ki}) \\
&THEN \quad grasp \quad is \quad grasp_i
\end{aligned}
\tag{15.14}
$$

Rule (15.14), for example, can be read

IF (norm $n_2$ of *model grasp$_2$ is* max$_{2,5}$

$\ldots$

AND (norm $n_{14}$ of model *grasp$_{14}$ is* max$_{14,5}$)

THEN *grasp is grasp$_5$*

The full rule to identify *grasp₅* reads

$$
\begin{array}{llll}
IF & (n_2 & is & \max_{2,5}) \\
AND & (n_5 & is & \min_{5,5}) \\
AND & (n_7 & is & \max_{7,5}) \\
AND & (n_{10} & is & \min_{10,5}) \\
AND & (n_{14} & is & \min_{14,5}) \\
THEN & grasp & is & grasp_5
\end{array}
\tag{15.15}
$$

$j = 2 \ldots 14$ are the indexes of the grasps in the grasp combination; $i$ is the index of *grasp$_i$* to be identified; $ex_{ij}$ indicate fuzzy sets of local extrema, which can be either minima $\min_{ij}$ or maxima $\max_{ij}$. Extrema appear at the time points $\tilde{t} = t_j$ at which *model grasp$_i$* meets *grasp$_j$* in the grasp combination with a maximum overlap.

Let the total extremum $z_{ex, tot}$ be either a total minimum $z_{min, tot}$ or a maximum $z_{max, tot}$ over all 5 rules and all time slices (see Figure 15.10):

$$
z_{min, tot} = \min(z_{j_{min,i}}), \quad z_{max, tot} = \max(z_{j_{max,i}})
$$
$$
j = 1 \ldots l; \quad i = 2, 5, 7, 10, 14
\tag{15.16}
$$

Then a local extremum $z_{j_{ex,i}}$ can be expressed by the total extremum $z_{ex, tot}$ and a weight $w_{ji} \in [0, 1]$:

$$
z_{j_{ex,i}} = w_{ji} \cdot z_{ex, tot}, \quad z_{j_{min,i}} = w_{ji} \cdot z_{min, tot}
$$
$$
z_{j_{max,i}} = w_{ji} \cdot z_{max, tot}, \quad j, i = 2, 5, 7, 10, 14
\tag{15.17}
$$

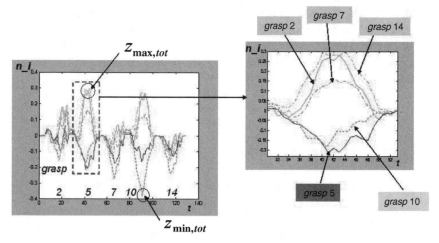

Figure 15.10. Norms of a grasp sequences.

**15.4.2.4 Similarity Degrees.** From the time plots in Figure 15.10 of the norms $n_i$ for the training sets, the analytical form of (15.15) for the identification of $grasp_i$ is chosen as follows:

$$\mathbf{a}_i = \prod_j \mathbf{m}_{ji},$$

$$\mathbf{m}_{ji} = Exp(-|w_{ji} \cdot \mathbf{z}_{ex,tot} - \mathbf{z}_{ex\,i}|)$$

$$\mathbf{z}_{ex\,i} = (z_{1ex,i}, \ldots, z_{1ex,i})^T$$

$$j = 2, 5, 7, 10, 14 \tag{15.18}$$

$\mathbf{a}_i = (a_{1i}, \ldots, a_{li})^T$, $a_{mi} \in [0,1]$, $m = 1, \ldots, l$ is a vector of *similarity degrees* between the *model grasp$_i$* and the individual grasps 2, 5, 7, 10, 14 in the grasp combination at the time point $t_m$. The vector $\mathbf{z}_{ex,i}$ represents the vector of either minima $\mathbf{z}_{min,i}$ or maxima $\mathbf{z}_{max,i}$ of the norms $n_i$, respectively.

The product operation in (15.18) represents the AND-operation in rules (15.15). The exponential function in (15.18) is a *membership function* indicating the distance of a norm $n_i$ to a local extremum $w_{ji} \cdot \mathbf{z}_{ex,tot}$. With this, the exponential function reaches its maximum at exactly that time point $t_m$ when $grasp_i$ in the grasp combination has its local extremum (see, e.g., Figure 15.11). Since we assume the time points for the occurrence of the particular grasps in the combination to be known, we also know the similarity degrees $a_{m,i}$ between the *model grasp$_i$* and grasps 2, 5, 7, 10, 14 at these time points. If, for

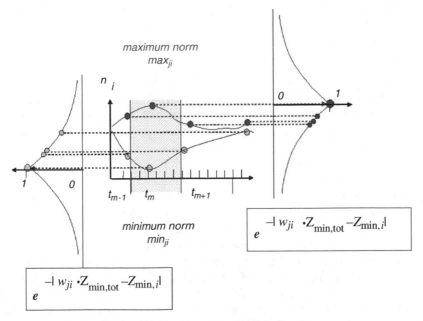

**Figure 15.11.** Grasp membership functions.

example, $grasp_5$ occurs at time point $t_m$ in the grasp combination, then we obtain for $a_{m,5} = 1$.

All the other grasps lead to smaller values of $a_{k,i} = 1$, $k = 2, 7, 10, 14$. With this, the type of grasp is identified and the grasp recognition is finished.

## 15.4.3 Recognition Based on Time-Cluster Models and HMM

The task is to classify an observation sequence of a test grasp given a set of observation sequences of model grasps using HMMs. The HMMs used here are of discrete nature, which requires the formulation of a number discrete states and discrete observations. One condition for the use of HMMs in our approach is that all model grasps and the test grasp to be recognized are modeled by the time-clustering described earlier.

The elements of a discrete HMM can be described in the compact notation [20]:

$$\lambda = (A, B, \pi, N, M) \tag{15.19}$$

where $N$ is the number of states $S$, $M$ is the number of observations $O$, $A = \{a_{ij}\}$ is the matrix of state transition probabilities, $B = \{b_{ij}\}$ is the observation symbol probability of symbol $O_k$ in state $j$, and $\pi$ is the initial state distribution vector. To prepare the HMM for the recognition, a number of steps have to be done:

**Step 1:** Determine a number $N$ of states $S$. The states need not be directly connected with a physical meaning, but it is of great advantage to do so.
Therefore, $M = 5$ states are chosen, getting the following labels:
State S1: open hand
State S2: half-open hand
State S3: middle position
State S4: half-closed hand
State S5: closed hand

**Step 2:** Generate a number $M$ of discrete observations $O$. To generate discrete observations, one first has to deal with the continuous observations, meaning the output cluster centers in $V_{grasp}$ and the corresponding joint angles $\mathbf{q}_i$. It should be mentioned that the clustering process leads to vectors of cluster centers whose elements, although being "labelled" by a time stamp, are not sorted in increasing order of time. Since clustering of several grasps is done independently of each other, the orders of time stamps of the cluster centers are in general different. This makes a comparison of test clusters $V_{grasp}$ and model clusters $V_{model}$ impossible. Therefore, after time clustering has been performed, the output clusters have to be sorted in increasing order of time. In the following, cluster centers are assumed to be sorted in that way. Next, one has to transform the continuous output cluster centers $V_{model}$ (i), $i = 1 \ldots 10$ of the model into discrete numbers or labels. If one attached to each cluster center an individual label, one would obtain $M = 10 \times 15 = 150$ observation labels (10-number of clusters, 15-number of grasps). This number of observations is unnecessarily high because some of the cluster centers form almost identical hand poses. Therefore, two observations are reserved for the starting pose and ending pose of all grasps since it can be assumed that every grasp starts and ends with nearly the same pose. Three poses for each grasp are then chosen at cluster numbers (3,5,6), which makes $M = 3 \times 15 + 2 = 47$ observations. The result is obviously a set of possible observations labeled by the numbers $1 \ldots 47$, representing 47 poses of 15 time-clustering models of grasps. In order to label a specific pose of a given grasp, one finds the minimal norms

$$I_j(i) = \min(\|V_{grasp_j}(i) - out_1\|, \ldots, \|V_{grasp_j}(i) - out_{47}\|), \quad i = 1 \ldots 10 \quad (15.20)$$

where $I_j(i) \in [1 \ldots 47]$ is the observation label, $i \in [1 \ldots 10]$ is the number of a time cluster for test grasp $j \in [1 \ldots 15]$, $O(k) = V_{model\,m}(l)$, $k \in [1 \ldots 47]$ is the $k$th observation, $m \in [1 \ldots 15]$ is a corresponding model grasp, and $l \in [2, 3, 5, 6, 9]$ is a corresponding number of a time cluster in model grasp $m$. This procedure is done for all model grasps $V_{model}$ with the result of 15 sequences $I_j(i)$ of 10 observations each, and for the test grasp $V_{grasp}$ to be recognized.

**Step 3:** Determine the initial matrixes $A \in R^{M \times M}$, $B \in R^{N \times M}$ and the initial state distribution vector $\pi \in R^{1 \times N}$. Since in the experiments the hand always starts to move from almost the same pose and keeps on moving through the states defined above, we can estimate both the initial matrixes $A$ and $B$, and the initial state distribution vector $\pi$ easily.

**Step 4:** Generate 15 observation sequences $O_{train} \in R^{10 \times 15}$ for the 15 model grasps according to step 2.

**Step 5:** Generate 1 observation sequence $O_{test} \in R^{10 \times 1}$ for the test grasp according to step 2.

**Step 6:** Train the HMM with every model sequence $O_{train}$ separately, using the iterative *expectation-modification (EM)*, procedure, also known as the *Baum-Welch method*. The training process evaluates a log-likelihood $LL$ of the trained model during iteration and stops as the change of $LL$ undergoes a certain threshold. Observe here that $LL \le 0$.

**Step 7:** Classify the observation sequence $O_{test}$ by evaluating the log-likelihood $LL$ of the $m$th trained HMM for a model grasp $m$ given the test data $O_{test}$. In addition, the most probable sequence of states using the Viterbi algorithm is computed.

**Step 8:** Compute the most probable model grasp number $m$ to be closest to the test model by computing $\max(LL_i)$, $i = 1 \ldots 15$. With step 8, the grasp recognition is completed.

## 15.5 EXPERIMENTS AND SIMULATIONS

In this section, we present the experimental evaluation of the proposed approach for modeling and classification of grasps. We tested 15 different grasps:

1. Cylinder
2. Big bottle
3. Small bottle
4. Hammer
5. Screwdriver
6. Small ball
7. Big ball
8. Precision grasp (sphere)
9. Precision grasp (cube)
10. Plane (1 CD-ROM)
11. Plane (3 CD-ROMs)
12. Fingertip grasp (small ball)
13. Fingertip grasp (big ball)
14. Fingertip grasp (can)
15. Penholder grasp

and recorded five instances for each one to perform the modeling. Here, three of the tested grasps and their simulations are shown. The motion trajectories are generated according to the scheme in Figure 15.8.

The grasp is completed when the fingers establish contact with the object as in the demonstrations:

- Grasp a CD-ROM (plane; see Figures 15.12, 15.13)
- Grasp a small bottle (cylinder; see Figures 15.14, 15.15)
- Grasp a big ball (sphere; see Figures 15.16, 15.17)

## 15.5.1 Modeling of the Fingertip Trajectories

For each grasp and finger, 10 fingertip position models with 10 cluster centers have been generated from the collected data. Furthermore, 3 inverse Jacobian models for each grasp

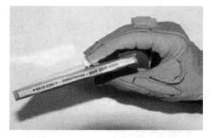

Figure 15.12. CD-ROM grasp.

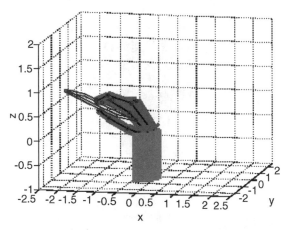

Figure 15.13. CD-ROM grasp simulation.

Figure 15.14. Small bottle grasp.

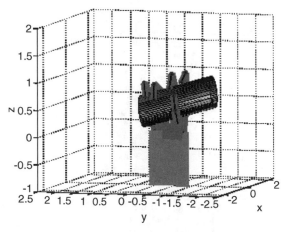

Figure 15.15. Small bottle grasp simulation.

Figure 15.16. Big ball grasp.

behavior and finger with 3 cluster centers have been built. Since there are 33 time steps for the whole motion, time clustering results in the cluster centers

$$t_1 = 2.04,\ 5.43,\ 8.87,\ 12.30,\ 15.75,\ 19.19,\ 22.65,\ 26.09,\ 29.53,\ 32.94$$

These are complemented by the corresponding cluster centers for the x,y,z coordinates of the fingertips. This equidistant spacing can be found for every individual grasp primitive as a result of the time clustering. Figures 15.18 and 15.19 present the example of the index finger performing the task "grasp CD-ROM." Figures 15.20–15.23 show the modeling results for the middle, ring, and pinkie finger, and the thumb. All results show a good or even excellent modeling quality.

## 15.5.2 Grasp Segmentation and Recognition

In this subsection, we present the experimental evaluation of the three proposed approaches for recognition of human grasp behaviors.

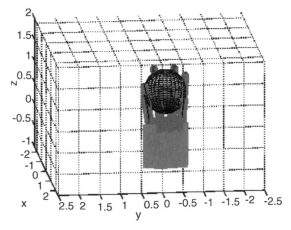

Figure 15.17. Big ball grasp simulation.

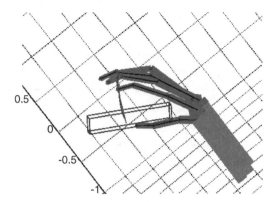

Figure 15.18. Trajectories of index finger.

***15.5.2.1 Method 1: Distance between Fuzzy Clusters.*** The experimental results are divided into three groups of recognition rates:

1. Grasps with a recognition rate $\geq 75\%$
2. Grasps with a recognition rate $< 75\% \ldots \geq 50\%$
3. Grasps with a recognition rate $< 50\%$

Table 15.1 shows the recognition rates for method 1. The first group with a recognition rate $\geq 75\%$ is the largest one, where 4 of 7 grasps show a recognition rate 100%. The equally large groups 2 and 3 follow. The experimental results confirm the assumption that distinct grasps can be discriminated quite well from each other, whereas the discrimination between similar grasps is difficult. Therefore, merging of similar grasps and

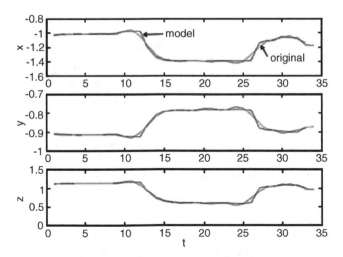

Figure 15.19. Index finger time plots.

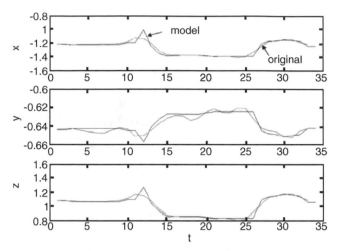

Figure 15.20. Middle finger time.

building of larger classes can improve the recognition process significantly. Examples of such classes are grasps (4, 5, 15), grasps (10, 11), and grasp (8,9).

**15.5.2.2 Method 2: Qualitative Fuzzy Recognition Rules.** In this experiment, 12 grasp combinations of 5 grasps each from the set of grasps shown in Figure 15.4 have been tested. In the following, a grasp combination with grasps 2, 5, 7, 10, 14 will be discussed. For the training phase, a sequence of model grasps 2, 5, 7, 10, 14 is generated. Then, according to (15.13), with the help of the same model grasps, the norms $n_i = n_i(\tilde{t})$ are computed. Based on the resulting curves in Figure 15.24 (see details in Figure 15.25), the weights for rule model (15.15) are determined.

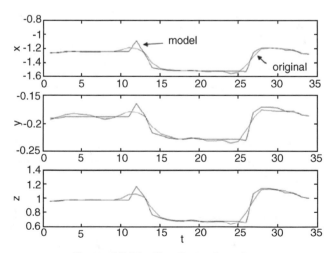

Figure 15.21. Ring finger time plots.

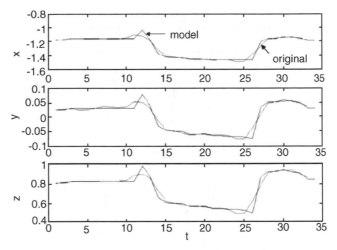

Figure 15.22. Pinkie finger time plots.

The training results in the table in Figure 15.26 show that both the starting points and the types of grasps 5, 7, 10, and 14 can be reliably recognized. Grasp 2, however, shows rather high numbers at other time points, too, meaning that the recognition of this grasp is less reliable. A test sample of the same grasp combination confirms this assumption: There are good results for grasps 5, 7, 10, and 14 but a different (wrong) result for grasp 2 (see Figure 15.27). Many tests with other grasp combinations have shown that some grasps can be more reliably recognized than others. Grasps with distinct maxima and minima in their $n_i$ patterns can be recognized better than those grasps without this feature. In addition to the above example, another combination with a high recognition rate is grasp(1,13,12,8,10), where grasps 1, 12, 8, and 10 are reliably recognized. In the

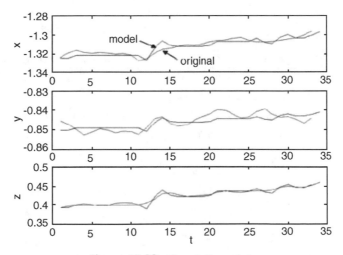

Figure 15.23. Thumb time plots.

TABLE 15.1. Recognition Rates, Method 1

| Class | Grasp | Percentage |
|---|---|---|
| ≥ 75% | 4. Hammer | 100% |
| | 8. Precision grasp sphere | 87% |
| | 10. Small plane | 100% |
| | 11. Big plane | 85% |
| | 12. Fingertip small ball | 100% |
| | 14. Fingertip can | 100% |
| | 15. Penholder grip | 85% |
| < 75%, ≥ 50% | 1. Cylinder | 71% |
| | 2. Big bottle | 57% |
| | 3. Small bottle | 57% |
| | 13. Fingertip big ball | 71% |
| < 50% | 5. Screwdriver | 0% |
| | 6. Small ball | 14% |
| | 7. Big ball | 28% |
| | 9. Precision grasp cube | 42% |

combination grasp(11,12,13,14,15) only grasps 11, 14, and 15 could be well recognized, where other combinations show even lower recognition rates.

Here we notice again that bulding larger classes of grasps may improve the recognition results. The final decision about the recognition of a grasp within a class may be made on the basis of the technological context.

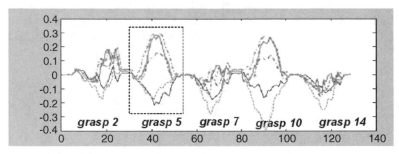

**Weights for the combination "grasp 2 5 7 10 14"**

| grasp | big bottle | screw driver | big ball | s. plane | b.plane |
|---|---|---|---|---|---|
| 2 | 0.6 | 0.3 | 0.3 | 0.5 | 0.4 |
| 5 | 1.0 | 0.5 | 0.6 | 0.3 | 1.0 |
| 7 | 0.1 | 0.4 | 0.4 | 0.7 | 0.1 |
| 10 | 0.8 | 0.3 | 0.4 | 1.0 | 0.8 |
| 14 | 0.05 | 0.2 | 0.2 | 0.5 | 0.2 |

Figure 15.24. Grasp combination.

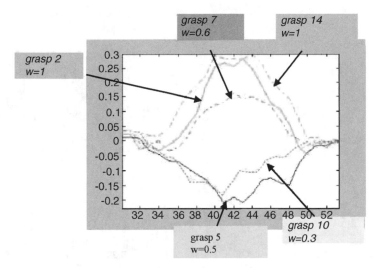

Figure 15.25. Details of grasp 5.

Table 15.2 shows the recognition rates for method 2. It could be shown that grasps with distinct maxima and minima in their $n_i$ patterns can be recognized better than grasps without this feature. Reliable grasps are also robust against variations in the time span of an unknown test grasp compared to the time span of the respective model grasp. Our results show that this method can handle a temporal difference up to 20%. The first group

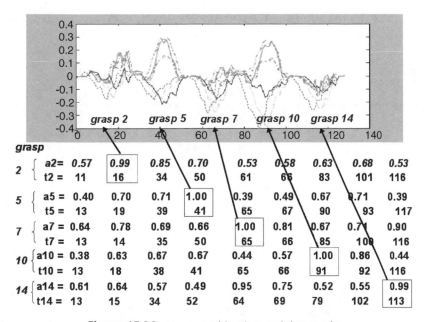

Figure 15.26. Grasp combination, training results.

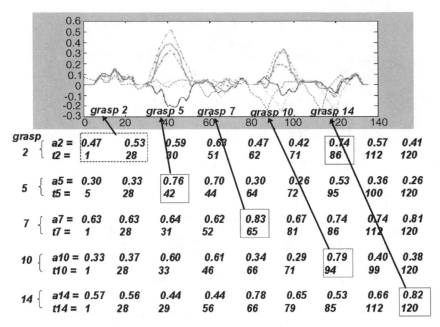

Figure 15.27. Grasp combination, test results.

with recognition rate $\geq 75\%$ is again the largest one, where 3 of 8 grasps show recognition rate 100%.

**15.5.2.3 Method 3: Time Cluster Models and HMM.** The detailed choice of the number of states and observations has already been described in steps 1 and 2 of the

TABLE 15.2. Recognition Rates, Method 2

| Class | Grasp | Percentage |
|---|---|---|
| $\geq 75\%$ | 4. Hammer | 100% |
| | 5. Screwdriver | 93% |
| | 8. Precision grasp sphere | 80% |
| | 9. Precision grasp cube | 100% |
| | 10. Small plane | 100% |
| | 11. Big plane | 88% |
| | 13. Fingertip big ball | 75% |
| | 15. Penholder grip | 75% |
| $< 75, \geq 50\%$ | 1. Cylinder | 55% |
| | 2. Big bottle | 60% |
| | 3. Small bottle | 66% |
| | 6. Small ball | 55% |
| $< 50\%$ | 7. Big ball | 16% |
| | 12. Fingertip small ball | 33% |
| | 14. Fingertip can | 33% |

TABLE 15.3. Recognition Rates, Method 3

| Class | Grasp | Percentage |
|---|---|---|
| ≥ 75% | 4. Hammer | 100% |
| | 9. Precision grasp cube | 85% |
| | 10. Small plane | 85% |
| | 14. Fingertip can | 85% |
| | 15. Penholder grip | 100% |
| < 75%, ≥ 50% | 1. Cylinder | 71% |
| | 2. Big bottle | 57% |
| | 3. Small bottle | 71% |
| | 5. Screwdriver | 71% |
| | 6. Small ball | 57% |
| | 11. Big plane | 57% |
| | 12. Fingertip small ball | 57% |
| | 13. Fingertip big ball | 71% |
| < 50% | 7. Big ball | 0% |
| | 8. Precision grasp sphere | 28% |

description of the algorithm. The recognition rates for method 3 are shown in Table 15.3. Here, the second group is the largest one, with recognition rate $<75\%$, $\geq 50\%$, followed by the first group, where 2 of 5 grasps show recognition rate 100%, and then by the third one.

**15.5.2.4 Comparison of the Three Methods.** For more than half of the grasp primitives, all three methods provide similar results. This is true for grasps 1, 2, 3, 4, 7, 8, 10, and 15. However, similarities between grasps may give space for misinterpretations, which explains the low percentages for some grasps (e.g., grasps 5 and 9 in method 1 or grasps 5 and 8 in method 3). Looking at the first groups in Tables 15.1, 15.2, and 15.3, group 1, method 1 is the most successful, and is also a solution with the easiest implementation. Then follows method 2, with quite a high implementation effort, and finally method 3, based on HMM. It should be stated that the HMM principle may allow some improvement of the results, especially in the case of an extended sensory in the experimental setup.

## 15.6 CONCLUSION

The goal of grasp recognition is to develop an easy way of programming by demonstration of grasps for a humanoid robotic arm. One promising way to cope with the recognition problem is to use evolving fuzzy systems, which are self-developing and self-adapting systems. In this chapter, three different methods of grasp recognition are presented. Grasp primitives are captured by a data glove and modeled by TS-fuzzy models. Fuzzy clustering and modeling of time-and-space data are applied to the modeling of the finger joint angle trajectories (or fingertip trajectories) of grasp primitives. The first method, being the simplest one, classifies a human grasp by computing the minimum distance between the time clusters of the test grasp and a set of model grasps. In the second method, a qualitative fuzzy model is developed, with the help of which both a segmentation and a grasp recognition can be achieved. These first two methods can be seen as evolving fuzzy systems, whereas the third method uses hidden Markov models for grasp recognition. A comparison of the three methods shows that the first method is the most effective method, followed by the second and third approaches.

To improve the PbD process, these methods will be further developed for the recognition and classification of operator movements in a robotic environment using more sensory information about the robot workspace and the objects to be handled.

## 15.7 REFERENCES

1. P. Angelov, D. Filev, "An approach to On-line Identification of Takagi-Sugeno Fuzzy Models," *IEEE Trans. on Syst., Man, and Cyb., part B*, Vol. SMC-34, No. 1, pp. 484–498, January/February 2004.
2. P. Angelov, R. Buswell, "Identification of Evolving Rule-Based Models," *IEEE Trans. on Fuzzy Systems*, Vol. SMC-34. No. 1, pp. 667–677, October 2002.
3. N. Kubota, Y. Nojima, F. Kojima, "Local Episode-Based Learning of a Mobile Robot in a Dynamic Environment," *IEEE Trans. on Fuzzy Systems*, Dynamic Systems Approach for Embodiment and Sociality—From Ecological Psychology to Robotics. Int. Series on Advanced Intelligence, pp. 318–322, 2003.
4. S. B. Kang, K. Ikeuchi, "Towards Automatic Robot Instruction from Perception: Mapping Human Grasps to Manipulator Grasps," *IEEE Trans. on Robotics and Automation*, Vol. 13, No. 1, 1997.
5. R. Zoellner, O. Rogalla, R. Dillmann, J.M. Zoellner, "Dynamic Grasp Recognition within the Framework of Programming by Demonstration." *Proc. Robot and Human Interactive Communication, 10th IEEE International Workshop, Bordeaux*, Paris, France, September 18–21, 2001, IEEE.
6. K. Ikeuchi, K. Bernardin, K. Ogawara, R. Dillman, "A Sensor Fusion Approach for Recognizing Continuous Human Grasp Sequences Using Hidden Markov Models," *IEEE Trans. on Robotics*, Vol. 21, No. 1, February 2005.
7. S. Ekvall, D. Kragic, "Grasp Recognition for Programming by Demonstration." *Proc. Int. Conf. Robotics and Automation, ICRA 2005*, Barcelona, Spain, 2005.
8. Ch. Li, L. Khan, B. Prabhaharan, "Real-Time Classification of Variable Length Multi-attribute Motions," *Knowledge and Information Systems*, DOI 10.1007/s10115-005-0223-8, 2005.
9. J. Aleotti, S. Caselli, "Grasp Recognition in Virtual Reality for Robot Pregrasp Planning by Demonstration." *ICRA 2006—Int. Conf. on Robotics and Automation*, Orlando, Florida, May 2006, IEEE.
10. R. Palm, B. Iliev, "Learning of Grasp Behaviors for an Artificial Hand by Time Clustering and Takagi-Sugeno Modeling." *Proc. FUZZ-IEEE 2006—IEEE Int. Conf. on Fuzzy Systems*, Vancouver, BC, Canada, July 16–21, 2006, IEEE.
11. R. Palm, B. Iliev. "Segmentation and Recognition of Human Grasps for Programming-by-Demonstration Using Time Clustering and Takagi-Sugeno Modeling." *Proc. FUZZ-IEEE 2007—IEEE Int. Conf. on Fuzzy Systems*, London, UK, July 23–26, 2007, IEEE.

12. R. Palm, B. Iliev, "Grasp Recognition by Time-Clustering, Fuzzy Modeling, and Hidden Markov Models (HMM): A Comparative Study." *Proc. FUZZ-IEEE 2008—IEEE Int. Conf. on Fuzzy Systems*, Hong Kong, June 1–6, 2008, IEEE.

13. H. H. Asada, J. R. Fortier, "Task Recognition and Human–Machine Coordination through the Use of an Instrument-Glove," Progress Report No. 2–5, pp. 1–39, March 2000.

14. M. Cutkosky, "On Grasp Choice, Grasp Models, and the Design of Hands for Manufacturing Tasks," *IEEE Trans. on Robotics and Automation*, Vol. 5, No. 3, 1989.

15. Thea Iberall, "Human Prehension and Dexterous Robot Hands," *Int. J. Robotics Research*, Vol. 16, pp. 285–299, 1997.

16. R. Palm, Ch. Stutz, "Generation of Control Sequences for a Fuzzy Gain Scheduler," *Int. J. Fuzzy Systems*, Vol. 5, No. 1, pp. 1–10, March 2003.

17. T. Takagi, M. Sugeno, "Identification of Systems and Its Applications to Modeling and Control." *IEEE Trans. on Syst., Man, and Cyb.*, Vol. SMC-15, No. 1, pp. 116–132, January/February 1985.

18. D. E. Gustafson, W. C. Kessel, "Fuzzy Clustering with a Fuzzy Covariance Matrix." *Proc. 1979 IEEE CDC*, pp. 761–766, 1979.

19. M. Kawato, "Internal Models for Control and Trajectory Planning," *Current Opinion in Neurobiology*, No. 9, pp. 718–727, 1999.

20. L. R. Rabiner, "A Tutorial on Hidden Markov Models and Selected Applications in Speech Recognition." *Proc. IEEE*, Vol. 77, No. 2, pp. 257–286, February 1989.

# 16

# EVOLUTIONARY ARCHITECTURE FOR LIFELONG LEARNING AND REAL-TIME OPERATION IN AUTONOMOUS ROBOTS

R. J. Duro, F. Bellas, J. A. Becerra

## 16.1 CHAPTER OVERVIEW

This chapter deals with evolution in the creation of a cognitive architecture for robots to be able to learn and adapt throughout their lifetime. The emphasis of the architecture is placed on modularity, progressive construction, and real-time adaptation to changes in the environment, in the robot itself or in its motivations. As in other explicit cognitive architectures, there is a part dealing with models (of the world, of the robot itself, of its satisfaction...) and another part dealing with the generation of actions. Models must adapt to changing circumstances and they must be remembered and generalized in order to be reused. Actions and sequences of actions, on the other hand, must be generated in real time so that the robot can cope with the environment and survive. In this line, the basic idea of the system involves modular and incremental neural network–based architectures for robot controllers that are in charge of the actions and reactions of the robots, and a cognitive mechanism, based on evolutionary techniques, that permits learning about the world and the robot itself and using this information to provide a framework for selecting and modifying the controllers through lifelong interaction with the world, leading to the ability of the robots to adapt to changing environments, goals, and circumstances. With this combination, an evolutionary architecture is proposed for autonomous robots to create complex behavior controllers that provide quick real-time response and that can be

*Evolving Intelligent Systems: Methodology and Applications,* Edited by Plamen Angelov, Dimitar P. Filev, and Nikola Kasabov

adjusted or even developed during the robot's lifetime. Several examples of the use of these types of architectures and their elements are presented and discussed.

## 16.2 INTRODUCTION

When dealing with the problem of robots that are supposed to be autonomous, and leaving aside the whole discussion on body–mind interaction (for this topic, see the excellent review in [1]), a question arises on how to obtain the complex adaptive control system that is required. A control system such as the one that is necessary for autonomy is really something that goes beyond traditional control in terms of the specifications or requirements. These additional requirements imply the ability to learn the control function from scratch, the ability to change or adapt it to new circumstances, and the ability to interact with the world in real time while performing the aforementioned processes and, in some instances, even to change the objectives that guide the control system.

Consequently, and to differentiate it from traditional control systems, these structures are usually called *cognitive systems* or *mechanisms* and in this chapter we will be dealing with ways to apply evolution as an intrinsic element within these structures.

*Cognition*, as defined in [2], is "The mental process of knowing, including aspects such as awareness, perception, reasoning, and judgment." According to [3], cognitive systems can be taken as "a collection of emerging information technologies inspired by the qualitative nature of biologically based information processing and information extraction found in the nervous system, human reasoning, human decision-making, and natural selection." To this we think it is very pertinent to add that a cognitive system makes no sense without its link to the real (or virtual) world in which it is immersed and which provides the data to be manipulated into information, requiring, consequently, the capability of acting and sensing.

It is from these broad definitions that the actual implementations of cognitive systems must arise, and there are several elements that should be taken into account. On one hand we have the mental process of knowing, that is, in more mathematical terms, of extracting models from data. These models can be employed in the process of decision making so that appropriate actions may be taken as a function of sensing and motivation. On the other, we have the decision-making process itself, and, in robotics, a decision is always related to an action or sequence of actions. In a sense, the models must be used in order to decide the appropriate actions so as to fulfill the agent's motivations. It is in how the model-making process and the action determination process takes place that cognitive mechanisms differ from each other.

To select actions is to explore the action space trying to fulfill the motivations or objectives, that is, to find the optimal action for the agent. To create models is to try to minimize the difference between the reality that is being modeled and the predictions provided by the model. Consequently, it is clear that a cognitive mechanism must involve some type of optimization strategy or algorithm. One of the most promising avenues in this line, especially as the search spaces are not really known beforehand and are usually very complex, is to employ stochastic multipoint search techniques, in particular, *artificial evolution*.

In the field of autonomous robotics, evolutionary algorithms have been widely applied to obtain controllers due to their adequateness for providing robust solutions while minimizing the knowledge imposed by the designer. In fact, over the past two decades, *evolutionary robotics* [4] has been one of the most active fields in the area of autonomous robotics in terms of the number of publications on this topic.

However, most approaches presented take a static point of view regarding the controllers or cognitive mechanisms obtained. That is, evolution is used as a tool to obtain different types of data and information processing structures that are adapted to a particular robot, environment, and tasks, and, once obtained, these structures hardly change during the operation of the robot; they are mostly static [4]. In this chapter we consider a different problem: how to obtain a cognitive mechanism that uses evolution intrinsically to allow the robot cognitive system to adapt throughout its lifetime to changing circumstances in terms of environment, objectives, and even of the robot itself. Obviously, the ideal situation with respect to designer work would be for the robot to start interacting with the world with no information and for it to be able to autonomously construct its models and behaviors.

In the literature dealing with this problem, solutions may be found that use evolution in a sort of lifelong learning process that starts from scratch, without any initial knowledge provided to the robot. That is, the evolutionary algorithm is executed in real time in the real robot, so that the improvement of the controller occurs in the genetic algorithm's time scale. Relevant examples of this approach are Watson et al. and their *embodied evolution* system [5], where the authors use a population of physical robots that autonomously reproduce while situated in their task environment; Nehmzow's *PEGA algorithm* [6], where the author presents experiments with a group of autonomous mobile robots that learn to perform fundamental sensory-motor tasks through a collaborative learning process, or Floreano et al.'s *coevolution* system [7], where two Khepera robots, one a predator and one the prey, interact with each other in a competitive way, so that changes in the behavior of one agent drive further adaptation in the other. However, few examples can be found following a pure lifelong-learning approach, mainly because the evolutionary techniques applied in real robots that learn from scratch require a very robust and complex learning system. The main problem is that initial solutions are poor and the real robot could be damaged when using these initial controllers to select an action. In addition, the learning system must be designed minimizing the interference of the evolutionary process on the task; that is, the robot must work in real time without pauses or speed limitations as a consequence of the time taken up by evolution.

To minimize these problems, different authors have proposed, as an alternative to lifelong learning, the application of an initial training stage where the robot works in a controlled fashion and learns a limited number of tasks prior to real-time operation. This way, when the robot starts with its task in the real world, it has a knowledge base in terms of simple controllers that can be improved or adapted during its lifetime, if needed. Within this approach, the solutions that can be found in the literature could be divided into two main groups: authors that use the real robot for the training stage and authors that use a simulator. In the first case, the real robot is used to estimate the fitness of the individuals in the evolutionary algorithm for a particular task. Once the task is learned, the controller obtained is stored and a new learning process starts with the aim of learning another. Obviously, this is a very designer-dependent approach where the teaching process is highly time consuming. On the other hand, the solutions obtained are very robust because they have been created in the same conditions the robot will find during its real-time operation. Examples of this approach are Horny et al.'s [8] project to develop efficient gaits in an AIBO robot or Marocco et al.'s [9] *active vision* system for mobile robots.

Many more authors can be found that have used some kind of simulation stage to obtain the controllers, mainly because this procedure permits complete control over the environment, as well as carrying out a larger number of tests, avoiding in both cases all the problems derived from the use of real robots. Within this approach we must point out the work of Wilson et al. [10], where the evolution in simulation and the real world are interleaved. Initially, the authors produced primitive behaviors in simulation that were tested on the physical robot. In later stages, these basic behaviors were randomly concatenated to create sequences of behaviors. Another relevant approach is the application of *anytime learning* [11] to hexapod robots, developed by Parker et al. [12], where evolution took place in simulation and the best solution was sent to the physical robot periodically. The information provided by the real robot application was used to modify the genetic algorithm itself.

Finally, Walker [13] et al. have developed an approach to investigate the relative contributions to robot performance of the training stage and lifelong learning. In this case, the authors make use of a standard genetic algorithm for the training phase and an evolutionary strategy for the real-time application stage. In their work, they conclude that the real application stage improves the performance of a trained robot controller in dynamic environments, and that the initial knowledge is very important for the performance of the lifelong phase. In this line, in a recent review paper [14], Walker has noted the observed advantages of using a combination of an initial training phase where a knowledge base is created and a lifelong learning phase where the robot can adapt this knowledge to the dynamics of real operation.

All of the aforementioned research, however, is based on consideration of the autonomous robot as a system to be controlled and not really a cognitive system in terms of having an internal structure that allows it to autonomously train and retrain itself—a structure that allows the robot to have some type of modifiable internal representation of its world, itself, and its objectives so that it can really apply cognitive strategies to solving the problems it encounters throughout its lifetime as opposed to just following a set of cleverly obtained recipes for particular situations in which it has been trained.

In this chapter, we provide an overview of what would be required as a first step toward a cognitive robot and, in this line, one that can learn throughout its lifetime in an adaptive manner. In particular, we will describe an approach that considers evolution an intrinsic part of the cognitive system and that allows a robot to be able to learn different tasks and objectives. Taking the process one step further, we will incorporate the concept of *controller* and *controller architecture* into cognition as a way to implement actions and behaviors on the part of the robot; in particular, behaviors that are repeatedly and successfully used will become reflex in terms of not having to go through the whole cognitive process in order to activate them under particular circumstances. It is important to note that a controller architecture that can be used within a cognitive system must verify a series of requirements in order to be able to fully exploit its potential. The architecture must be modular so that different behaviors may be combined to create new ones, thus generating a structure that can grow depending on requirements without having to relearn all from scratch, and parts of which may be reused as needed. In addition there must be a mechanism to gradually go from one behavior to another, so that combinations of behaviors may be regulated.

The chapter is organized as follows: Section 16.3 describes the basic evolutionary cognitive system and explains its general operation, including some comments on the requirements for the evolutionary algorithms employed. Section 16.4 provides an introduction to the behavior-based controller architecture that will act as a base for the actuation part of the cognitive mechanism. Section 16.5 is devoted to the presentation of some examples of the application of the cognitive architecture to real robots and a discussion of its operation. Finally, Section 16.6 provides some conclusions and comments on future work that is necessary in this line.

## 16.3 LIFELONG LEARNING EVOLUTIONARY ARCHITECTURE: THE MULTILEVEL DARWINIST BRAIN

The *multilevel Darwinist brain* (MDB) is a general *cognitive architecture* first presented in [15], that permits automatic acquisition of knowledge in a real agent through interaction with its environment, so that it can autonomously adapt its behavior to achieve its design objectives. To achieve this requirement, we have resorted to classical biopsychological theories by Changeaux [16], Conrad [17], and Edelman [18] in the field of cognitive science relating the brain and its operation through a Darwinist process. All of these theories lead to the same concept of cognitive structure based on the brain adapting its neural connections in real time through evolutionary or selectionist processes.

The MDB can be formalized through a cognitive model, which is a particularization of the standard *abstract architectures* for agents [19]. In this case, a utilitarian cognitive model was adopted that starts from the premise that, to carry out any task, a motivation (defined as the need or desire that makes an agent act) must exist that guides the behavior as a function of its degree of satisfaction. From this basic idea, the concepts of *action, world,* and *internal* models (*W* and *I*), *satisfaction* model (*S*) and *action–perception pairs* (sets of values made up by the sensorial inputs and the satisfaction obtained after the execution of an action in the real world) are used to construct a cognitive mechanism. Two processes must take place in a real non-preconditioned cognitive mechanism: (1) models *W*, *I*, and *S* must be obtained as the agent interacts with the world, and (2) the best possible actions must be selected through some sort of internal optimization process using the models available at that time to determine fitness.

Thus, formalizing in general, the external perception $e(t)$ of an agent is made up of the sensory information it is capable of acquiring through its sensors from the environment in which it operates. The environment can change due to the actions of the agent or to factors uncontrolled by the agent. Consequently, the external perception can be expressed as a function of the last action performed by agent $A(t-1)$, the sensory perception it had of the external world in the previous time instant $e(t-1)$, and a description of the events occurring in the environment that are not due to its actions $X_e(t-1)$ through a function $W$:

$$e(t) = W[e(t-1), A(t-1), X_e(t-1)]$$

The internal perception $i(t)$ of an agent is made up of the sensory information provided by its internal sensors, its *proprioception*. Internal perception can be written in terms of the last action performed by the agent, the sensory perception it had from the internal sensors in the previous time instant $i(t-1)$, and other internal events not caused by the agent action $X_i(t-1)$ through a function $I$:

$$i(t) = I[i(t-1), A(t-1), X_i(t-1)]$$

The satisfaction $s(t)$ of the agent can be defined as a magnitude or vector that represents the degree of fulfilment of the motivation or motivations of the agent and it can be related to its internal and external perceptions through a function $S$. As a first approximation, we are going to ignore the events over which the agent has no control and reduce the problem to the interactions of the agent with the world and itself. Thus, generalizing:

$$s(t) = S[e(t), i(t)] = S[W[e(t-1), A(t-1)], I[i(t-1), A(t-1)]]$$

The main objective of the cognitive architecture is the satisfaction of the motivation of the agent, which, without any loss of generality, may be expressed as the maximization of the satisfaction $s(t)$ in each instant of time. Thus:

$$\max\{s(t)\} = \max\{S[W[e(t-1), A(t-1)], I[i(t-1), A(t-1)]]\}$$

To solve this maximization problem, the only parameter the agent can modify is the action it performs, as the external and internal perceptions should not be manipulated. That is, the cognitive architecture must explore the possible action space in order to maximize the resulting satisfaction. To obtain a system that can be applied in real time, the optimization of the action must be carried out internally (without interaction with the environment), so $W$, $I$, and $S$ are theoretical functions that must be somehow obtained. These functions correspond to what are traditionally called:

*World model (W)*: function that relates the external perception before and after applying an action

*Internal model (I)*: function that relates the internal perception before and after applying an action

*Satisfaction model (S)*: function that provides a predicted satisfaction from predicted perceptions provided by the world and internal models

As mentioned before, the main starting point in the design of the MDB was that the acquisition of knowledge should be automatic, so we establish that these three models must be obtained during execution time as the agent interacts with the world. To perform this modeling process, information can be extracted from the real data the agent has after each interaction with the environment. These data will be called action–perception pairs and are made up of the *sensorial data* in instant *t*, the *action applied* in instant *t*, the *sensorial data* in instant $t + 1$, and the *satisfaction* in $t + 1$.

Summarizing, for every interaction of the agent with its environment, two processes must be solved:

1. The modeling of functions *W*, *I*, and *S* using the information in the action perception pairs. As we will explain later, these are learning processes.
2. The optimization of the action using the models available at that time.

Figure 16.1 displays a block diagram of the MDB with arrows indicating the flow of execution. The operation of the architecture can be summarized by considering that the selected action (represented by the current action block) is applied to the environment through an acting stage obtaining new sensing values. These acting and sensing values provide a new action–perception pair that is stored in *short-term memory* (*STM*). After this, the model learning processes start (for world, internal, and satisfaction models) trying to find functions that generalize the real samples stored in the STM. The best models in a given instant of time are taken as current world, internal, and satisfaction models and are used in the process of optimizing the action with regard to the predicted satisfaction of the motivation. After this process finishes, the best action obtained (current action) is applied again to the environment through an acting stage obtaining new sensing values. These steps constitute the basic operation cycle of the MDB, and we will call it *one iteration*. As more iterations take place, the MDB acquires more information from the real environment (new action–perception pairs) and thus the model learning processes have more information available and, consequently, the action chosen using these models is more appropriate.

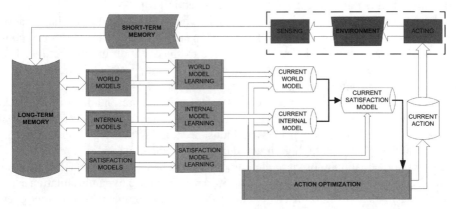

Figure 16.1. Block diagram of the multilevel Darwinist brain.

Finally, we must point out that the block labeled *long-term memory* (*LTM*) in Figure 16.1 stores those models that have provided successful and stable results on their application to a given task in order to be reused directly in other problems or as seeds for new learning processes. This memory element provides a quick adaptation in dynamic environments where the robot returns to a previously learned situation, because it avoids the need to relearn the models. The LTM is a highly relevant element in the performance of the MDB and its interplay with the STM is very important in the learning process, as we will explain in the next section.

## 16.3.1 Short- and Long-Term Memory

The management of short-term memory is critical in the real-time learning processes we are using in the MDB, because the quality of the learned models depends on what is stored in this memory and the way it changes. On the other hand, long-term memory is necessary if model knowledge is to be stored. As this chapter is aimed at describing the application of evolutionary algorithms to the creation of cognitive models for lifelong learning, and the mechanisms governing STM and LTM are not evolutionary, we will not dwell too much on the details of short- and long-term memory and will just provide an overview of their participation in the MDB.

The STM stores action–perception pairs that are taken as the input and target values for the evolution of the world, internal, and satisfaction models. The data stored in the STM are acquired in real time as the system interacts with the environment; obviously, it is not practical or even useful to store all the samples acquired in the agent's lifetime. A dynamic replacement strategy was designed that labels the samples using four basic features (*distance, complexity, initial relevance*, and *time*) related to saliency of the data and their temporal relevance. These four terms are weighted and, depending on the storage policy (depending on the motivation), the information stored in the STM may be different. For example, while the agent is exploring the environment or wandering (the motivation could be just to explore), we would like the STM to store the most general and salient information of the environment, and not necessarily the most recent. This can be achieved by simply adjusting the parameters of the replacement strategy. Details about the management strategy for the STM can be found in [20].

Long-term memory is a higher-level memory element, because it stores information obtained after the analysis of the real data stored in the STM. From an operational point of view, the LTM stores the knowledge acquired by the agent during its lifetime. This knowledge is represented in the MDB as models (world, internal, and satisfaction models) and their context. Thus, the LTM stores the models that were classified by the agent as relevant in certain situations (context) and stores a representation of the context by storing the contents of the STM in a given instant of time for that model. As an initial approach we have considered that a model must be stored in the LTM if it predicts the contents of the STM with high accuracy during an extended period of time.

From a practical point of view, the introduction of the LTM in the MDB avoids the need of relearning the models in a problem with a real agent in a dynamic situation every time the agent changes into different states (different environments or different operational schemes). The models stored in the LTM in a given instant of time are introduced in the evolving populations of MDB models as seeds, so that if the agent returns to a previously learned situation, or to a similar one, the model will be present in the population and the prediction soon will be accurate. Obviously, for LTM to work adequately, unless it is infinite in size, it is necessary to introduce some type of replacement strategy. This strategy will determine when a model is good enough to go into LTM and what model in the LTM should be erased to leave room for the new one. The process is not evident, as models are generalizations of situations and, in the present case, where they are implemented as artificial neural networks, it is not easy to see whether a model is the same or similar to another one. This is the reason for storing the context together with the model as it allows the MDB to test how good models are in predicting other models' contexts and thus provide a measure of similarity among models in terms of their application. In [21] there is formal presentation of the LTM in the MDB.

In addition, as explained earlier, the replacement strategy of the STM favors the storage of relevant samples. But, in dynamic environments, what is considered relevant could change during time, and consequently the information that is stored in the STM should also change so that the newly generated models correspond to the new situation. If no regulation is introduced, when situations change, the STM will be polluted by information from previous situations (there is a mixture of information) and, consequently, the models generated will not correspond to any one of them. These intermediate situations can be detected by the replacement strategy of the LTM as it is continuously testing the models to be stored in the LTM. Thus, if it detects a model that suddenly and repeatedly fails in the predictions of the samples stored in the STM, it is possible to assume that a change of context has occurred. This detection will produce a regulation of the parameters controlling the replacement in the STM so that it will purge the older context. A more in-depth explanation of the interaction between short- and long-term memory can be found in [22].

## 16.3.2 Some Comments on the Evolutionary Mechanisms Necessary for the MDB

The main difference of the MDB with respect to other architectures lies in the way the process of modeling functions $W$, $I$, and $S$ is carried out by exploring different actions and observing their consequences. The models resulting from this exploration are usually complex due to the fact that the real world is dynamic and the robot state, the environment, and the objective may change in time. To achieve the desired neural adaptation through evolution established by the Darwinist theories that are the basis for this architecture, it was decided to use *artificial neural networks* (*ANNs*) as the representation for the models and *evolutionary algorithms* as modeling techniques. Consequently, the acquisition of knowledge in the MDB is basically a neuroevolutionary process.

*Neuroevolution* is a reference learning tool due to its robustness and adaptability to dynamic environments and nonstationary tasks [23]. In our case, the modeling is not an optimization process but a learning process taking into account that we seek the best generalization for all times, or, at least, an extended period of time, which is different from minimizing an error function in a given instant $t$ [24]. Consequently, the modeling technique selected must allow for gradual application, as the information is known progressively and in real time. Evolutionary techniques permit this gradual learning process by controlling the number of generations of evolution for a given content of the STM. Thus, if evolutions last just a few generations per iteration (interactions with the environment), gradual learning by all the individuals is achieved.

To obtain general modeling properties in the MDB, the population of the evolutionary algorithm must be maintained between iterations (represented in Figure 16.1 through the world, internal, and satisfaction model blocks that are connected with the learning blocks), leading to a sort of inertia learning effect where what is being learned is not the contents of the STM in a given instant of time, but of sets of STMs that were previously seen. In addition, the dynamics of the real environments where the MDB will be applied imply that the architecture must be intrinsically adaptive. This strategy of evolving for a few generations and maintaining populations between iterations permits a quick adaptation of models to the dynamics of the environment, as we have a collection of possible solutions in the populations that can be easily adapted to the new situation.

In the first versions of the MDB, the evolution of the models was carried out using standard canonic genetic algorithms where the ANNs were represented by simple two-layer perceptron models. These tools provided successful results when dealing with simple environments and tasks, but as soon as real-world learning problems were faced, they were insufficient. Standard *genetic/evolutionary* algorithms, when applied to these tasks, tend to converge toward homogeneous populations, that is, populations where all of the individuals are basically the same. In static problems this would not be a drawback if this convergence took place after reaching the optimum. Unfortunately, there is no way to guarantee this, and diversity may be severely reduced long before the global optimum is achieved. In dynamic environments, where even the objective may change, this is quite a severe drawback. In addition, the episodic nature of real-world problems implies that whatever perceptual streams the robot receives could contain information corresponding to different learning processes or models that are intermingled (periodically or not), that is, learning samples need not arise in an orderly and appropriate manner. Some of these sequences of samples are related to different sensorial or perceptual modalities and might not overlap in their information content; others correspond to the same modalities but should be assigned to different models. The problem that arises is how to learn all of these different models, the samples of which are perceived as partial sequences that appear randomly intermingled with those of the others.

Most traditional learning algorithms fail in this task as they have mostly been designed for learning a single model from sets of data that correspond to that model and, at most, some noisy samples or outliers within the training set. This problem becomes even more interesting if we consider that it would be nice to be able to reuse some of the models, or at least parts of them, that have been successful in previous tasks in order to produce models for more complex tasks in an easier and more straightforward manner.

The existing approaches for applying evolutionary algorithms to dynamic problems, mainly optimization, can be grouped into two types [25]: memory-based approaches and search-based approaches. In the first group, the algorithm includes some kind of memory structure that stores information that can be used in the future to improve the optimization. This memory may be internal, that is, included in the chromosomes [26, 27] and evolved, or external, storing successful individuals that are usually introduced in the population as seeds [28, 29]. External memory-based approaches perform better in periodic dynamic environments, with predictable changes or when the changes are easy to detect, where the individuals can be associated to a given objective function and stored. For problems where the changes are not predictable or are hard to detect, most authors have resorted to search-based techniques, enhancing their ability for continuously searching, usually by trying to preserve a high level of diversity in the population [25, 30]. These techniques have had success to some degree in the case of quasi-stationary changes, but when abrupt changes occur they are basically starting neuroevolution from scratch.

With regard to learning with ANNs, the most relevant neuroevolutionary methods presented in last few years are SANE [31], a cooperative coevolutionary algorithm that evolves a population of neurons instead of complete networks; ESP [32], similar to SANE, but which allocates a separate population for each of the units in the network, and where a neuron can be recombined only with members of its own subpopulation; and NEAT [33], nowadays the most-used neuroevolutionary algorithm. It can evolve networks of unbounded complexity from a minimal starting point and is based on three fundamental principles: employing a principled method for the crossover of different topologies, protecting structural innovation through speciation, and incrementally growing networks from a minimal structure. Some of these neuroevolutionary techniques have been tested in nonstationary periodic tasks using external memory elements [29, 32].

In order to deal with the particularities of the learning processes involved in the MDB, we were confronted with the need of developing a new neuroevolutionary algorithm able to deal with general dynamic problems, that is, combining both memory elements and the preservation of diversity. This algorithm was called the *promoter-based genetic algorithm (PBGA)*. In this algorithm the chromosome is endowed with an internal or genotypic memory and tries to preserve diversity using a genotype–phenotype encoding that prevents the loss of relevant information throughout the generations. An external memory is added to improve the adaptive capabilities of the algorithm. The basic operation and the main features of this algorithm within the MDB are presented in the next section.

### 16.3.3 PBGA: Promoter-Based Genetic Algorithm

There are two basic biologically based approaches to gene expression: diploid representations and promoter-based mechanisms. *Diploid* genotypes are made up of a double chromosome structure where each strand contains information for the same functions. In this work, however, we concentrate on the use of gene promoters. *Gene promoters* are important regulatory structures that control the initiation and level of transcription of a gene. They sit upstream of the gene and dictate whether, or to what extent, that gene is turned on or off.

An initial approach to the introduction of promoter genes was implemented in the *structured genetic algorithm (sGA)*, developed by Dasgupta and McGregor [26] as a general hierarchical genetic algorithm. They applied a two-level interdependent genetic algorithm for solving the knapsack problem and developing application-specific neural networks [34]. A two-layer sGA was used to represent the connectivity and weights of a feedforward neural network. Higher-level genes (connectivity) acted as a switch for sections of the lower-level weight representation. Sections of the weight level, whose corresponding connectivity bits were set to one, were expressed in the phenotype. Those whose corresponding bits had the value of zero were retained, but were not expressed. The main difference between the sGA applied to neuroevolution and the PBGA, is that the activation genes in the sGA act at the connection level, whereas the PBGA works with neuron units, that is, functional units. This is a very relevant difference as, even though to enable/disable a neuron may seem much more disruptive, it permits preserving complex functional units.

To demonstrate the potential of these types of structures when applied to neuroevolution, we have considered a GA that evolves the weights of feedforward artificial neural networks (any other evolutionary algorithm with a similar type of encoding could have been chosen). These neural networks are encoded into sequences of genes for constructing a basic ANN unit. Each of these blocks is preceded by a gene promoter acting as an on/off switch that determines whether that particular unit will be expressed. For example, the genotypic representation used in the PBGA corresponding to the simple feedforward ANN shown in Figure 16.2 (top) is:

$$[1\,1\,1\,W_{13}\,W_{23}\,1\,W_{14}\,W_{24}\,1\,W_{15}\,W_{25}\,1\,W_{36}\,W_{46}\,W_{56}\,1\,W_{37}\,W_{47}\,W_{57}\,1\,W_{38}\,W_{48}\,W_{58}\,1\,W_{69}\,W_{79}\,W_{89}]$$

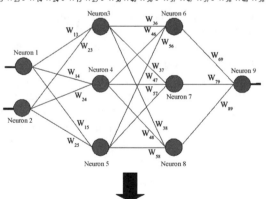

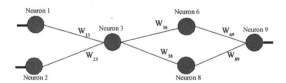

Figure 16.2. Genotypic (top) and phenotypic (bottom) representation of an ANN with two input neurons, two hidden layers, with a maximum of three neurons and one output neuron corresponding to a PBGA example chromosome.

where all the genes of value 1 are promoter genes. Thus, the first two genes represent that the two input neurons are enabled, the third gene represents that neuron 3 is enabled (controlling weights $W_{13}W_{23}$), and so on. Continuing with the same example, Figure 16.2 (bottom) shows the phenotypic representation of the PBGA chromosome:

$$[1\,1\,1\,W_{13}\,W_{23}\,0\,W_{14}\,W_{24}\,0\,W_{15}\,W_{25}\,1\,W_{36}\,W_{46}\,W_{56}\,0\,W_{37}\,W_{47}\,W_{57}\,1\,W_{38}\,W_{48}\,W_{58}\,1\,W_{69}\,W_{79}\,W_{89}]$$

where the promoter genes of neurons 4, 5, and 7 are disabled and, consequently, these three neurons and their inbound and outbound connections are not shown on the phenotype.

We have considered a neuron with all of its inbound connections as represented in Figure 16.3 as the basic unit of the PBGA. Consequently, the genotype of a basic unit is a set of real-valued weights followed by the parameters of the neuron (in this case, a traditional sigmoid, but it could be any other) and controlled by an integer-valued field that determines the promoter gene value and, consequently, the expression of the unit. By concatenating units of this type we can construct the whole network. With this encoding we want the information that is not expressed to still be carried by the genotype in evolution but shielded from direct selective pressure, preserving in this way the diversity in the population. Therefore, a clear difference is established between the search space and the solution space, permitting information learned and encoded into the genotypic representation to be preserved by disabling promoter genes.

As a consequence, in order to maintain previously learned information in the chromosomes when dealing with nonstationary problems and taking into account that the information is in the structure of the ANN, the genetic operators must be tailored toward preserving these topological relationships. Although other approaches are possible, the same topology was used for the genotypic representation of all the ANNs in the population to avoid complexities such as a continuous growth in the ANN size (which results in CPU-intensive tasks) or the high number of parameters that are needed to

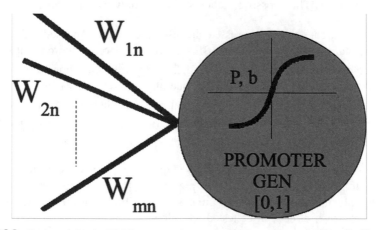

**Figure 16.3.** Basic unit in the PBGA genotypic representation: a neuron with all of its inbound connections.

control the combination of the different topologies, associated to other approaches where the topology is completely free, as in NEAT [33]. This way, all the ANN genotypes have the same number of total neurons, in this case, within a two-layer feedforward representation. The designer simply imposes a maximum number of neurons per hidden layer, and all the ANNs are created with the same chromosome length. This does not mean that the ANNs resulting from the genotype–phenotype transformation have the same topology, as this depends on what functional units are enabled by the promoters. The PBGA usually starts with minimal phenotypical ANNs (just one neuron enabled per hidden layer) and evolution makes different types of ANNs (in terms of enabled neurons) coevolve.

## 16.3.4 Genetic Operators

The main problem that had to be dealt with in the implementation of the algorithm is how to perform crossover and mutation without being extremely disruptive or generating a bias in the evolution of what genes are expressed. Bear in mind that not only weight values, but also the neurons that conform the topology of the network are being crossed over. Consequently, it is necessary to be careful about how disruptive crossover or mutation are on the information units found in the genotype. If two parent chromosomes are taken at random, they will probably not have the same expressed neurons, and these are the ones that directly affect the fitness of the individual when implemented in the phenotype. Thus, we find two types of information in the parent genotypes that must be recombined in order to produce an offspring: genes corresponding to expressed neuron units, which are responsible for fitness, and genes for unexpressed neurons, about which we have little information.

The crossover is panmitic in the PBGA, that is, one child chromosome is created from two parent chromosomes. This process implies crossing over whole neuron units. To be statistically neutral regarding the expression of the genes, crossover must be performed carefully taking into account the promoter genes that control the expression of the gene sequences. This crossover adheres to the following three rules:

1. If both parent units are expressed, the offspring unit is expressed and the weights are obtained applying a simple BLX-$\alpha$ crossover to the neuron unit's weights.
2. If both parent units are not expressed, the offspring unit is not expressed and the weights are directly inherited from one of the parents (50% chance).
3. When one unit is expressed and the other is not, there is a 50% chance of the offspring unit being expressed and the weights are inherited from the corresponding parent.

Thus, on average, the number of expressed units is preserved and a bias in this term prevented. In addition, the strategy of preserving the disabled neuron units and performing information crossover only in cases when both neurons are active, that is, where the crossover effect can be tested, is followed.

Regarding mutation, things are simpler, and the only consideration that needs to be made is that gene promoters must be mutated at a different rate from that of regular genes.

Note that mutating gene promoters may be very disruptive as it affects in a very serious way the composition of the phenotype, whereas mutation of the rest of the genes is, on average, much more gradual on the resulting phenotype. Consequently, we decided to use different mutation rates on the gene promoters (structural mutation) and on the real-valued genes (parametric mutation). The structural mutation operator simply inverts the activation value from 0 to 1 or from 1 to 0, and the parametric mutation operator applies a nonlinear cubed random mutation mechanism ($f(x) = f(x) + \text{rand}(0,1)^3$) only to genes belonging to active neurons. As will be shown in the examples presented later, the values for these mutation probabilities are quite critical for the performance of the algorithm.

## 16.3.5 Working Cycle

The PBGA is a genetic algorithm and follows the basic scheme of this type of algorithm, performing crossover and mutation over a selected pool of individuals that represent ANNs. The working cycle of the PBGA is very standard:

1. Creation of a random population of $N$ individuals using the representation mentioned earlier.
2. Fitness calculation over the whole population.
3. Selection of $2N$ individuals using a tournament selection operator.
4. Panmitic crossover with a probability $P_c$ over the $2N$ population. The crossover operator is applied twice over the same parents and the offspring with highest fitness is selected.
5. After crossover, an $N$ individual offspring population is produced.
6. Mutation with probabilities $P_{sm}$, $P_{pm}$ over the offspring population.
7. Fitness calculation over the offspring population.
8. Elitism that substitutes the worst individuals of the offspring population with the best individuals of the original population.
9. Return to step 3 for $n$ generations.

Six parameters must be established by the user in the PBGA: (1) maximum number of neurons of the ANNs, (2) population size, (3) crossover probability, (4) structural mutation probability, (5) parametric mutation probability, and (6) number of generations of evolution. All of these are problem dependent but, as we will show in the next section, their values are intuitively easy to set up.

## 16.3.6 Simple Application of the PBGA

To test the PBGA in the conditions used for its design and development, we take inspiration from the type of task that a real robot must perform when learning in a dynamic environment. Thus, we assume that a robot is executing a given task in an environment that changes due to several possible reasons, like a change in the ambient conditions or because the robot moves to another environment, and as a consequence, the model of the environment that the robot is learning changes, too. To simulate this change of objective functions to be learned, we have used two different 3D functions that the PBGA must learn and that are cycled periodically and nonperiodically:

$$F1(x,y) = (x+y)/2 \qquad x,y \in [-10, 10]$$
$$F2(x,y) = \sin(4x) + y\sin(y) \quad x,y \in [-10, 10]$$

To show the basic features of the PBGA as a consequence of its architecture, in a first experiment we used a given fitness function (F1) for 100 generations of evolution and a different one (F2) for the next 100 generations and kept cycling between them, simulating thus a periodic change of the environment. It is important to note that even though the change occurred periodically, this information is not known to the algorithm and what it is experimenting is an unpredictable change. We expect the PBGA to converge faster as the iterations (fitness function switch cycles) progress, because some of the previously learned information has a chance of remaining in the unexpressed part of the genotype. Figure 16.4 displays the root mean squared error (RMSE) for the first 2000 generations (20 cycles) of evolution (top graph). Function F1 is learned with a lower error rate than function F2, as expected due to its simpler nature. The RMSE decreases during each 100-generation cycle as expected for a typical error evolution. When a change of objective function occurs, there is an error peak that is larger in the cycle from F1 to F2 due to the higher complexity of the second function. This peak rapidly decreases as the networks adapt to the new function. In addition, it can be observed how the error level at the end of each 100-generation cycle decreases in both functions along the cycles until it stabilizes.

Figure 16.5 displays the number of generations required by the PBGA in order to achieve a given error value, for example, 1.5 RMSE for the F2 function, when, as in the

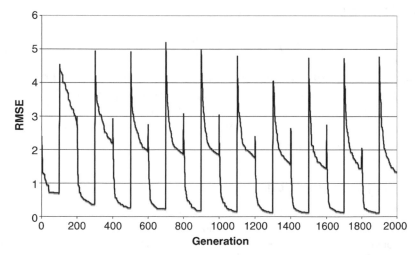

**Figure 16.4.** Evolution of the RMSE for the first 2000 generations obtained using the PBGA cycling between functions to be learned $F_1$ and $F_2$ every 100 generations.

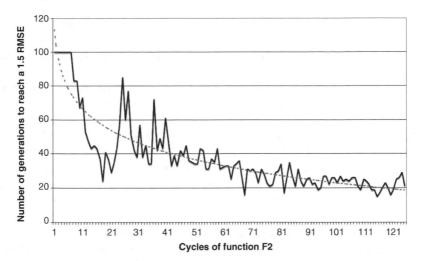

Figure 16.5. Number of generations required by the PBGA to achieve an RMSE error value of 1.5 for function $F_2$ when this function appeared interspersed with $F_1$ every 100 generations. The dashed gray line represents a logarithmic trend line of the points.

previous case, this function appeared interspersed with F1 every 100 generations. The $x$ axis represents the number of cycles when the F2 function was learned. It is clear from the graph that, except in the 8 initial cycles where the PBGA is not able to reach the desired error level of 1.5 RMSE in the 100 generations, there is a decreasing tendency in the error level (represented in the figure with a pointed gray logarithmic trend line). This is the main property of the PBGA and clearly indicates that the preservation of information in the unexpressed part of the genotype really leads to improvements in the speed of evolution toward a solution the system has seen totally or partially before.

To conclude this section, we must point out that the PBGA has been tested in real-world modeling tasks within the MDB [35], providing successful results with real data.

## 16.4 ACTIONS AND BEHAVIORS

The description of the MDB presented in the previous sections provides an overview of how a general cognitive mechanism and, in particular, this implementation of it, operates. As commented before, the tasks to be performed when running a cognitive mechanism can be divided into two main processes:

1. Generating and maintaining appropriate models of the world, of the agent itself, and of the relationship between sensing and satisfaction
2. Obtaining the most adequate action or actions for the achievement of the agent's objectives

The process of generating and maintaining the models has already been mentioned and the implications for the evolutionary algorithms required for this task analyzed. In this section we will concentrate on the part of the mechanism that obtains the actions the robot must perform.

In its most simple form, a cognitive mechanism produces just one action as output each iteration. The selection of the action is also an optimization process whose aim is to produce the action that results in the highest possible predicted satisfaction value for the agent within the time constraints of the operation of the mechanism. Thus, we have an optimization process whose fitness function is given by running the world and internal models with the information present in the STM on the latest perceptions of the robot and the actions to be evaluated. The world and internal models will produce the predicted perceptions of the robot for the next instant of time and, by feeding these data to the satisfaction model, a predicted satisfaction value is obtained. Obviously, if the number of possible actions to be performed is very small (i.e., the robot can go only left, right, forward, or backward), all of the options can be tested on the models and the one predicted as most satisfying chosen and executed. However, if the action space is large and high dimensional (lots of actuators with lots of possible states), some type of search and optimization algorithm must be employed in order to choose the resulting action within the allowed time constraints.

This action-by-action approach is not very efficient; many tasks in the world require more than one action to be carried out as a sequence in order to achieve the objective and it would make the operation of the robot smoother if sequences of actions could be generated as a response. Extending this concept, one could think of generalizing the concept of action to that of whole behaviors. That is, the action selection part of the MDB, instead of producing an action as a result of its processing, could produce or select a behavior controller (in the same sense as in behavior-based robotics) that would be applied until one that offered a better predicted satisfaction was available.

In this case, instead of testing actions in order to obtain their fitness and thus try to decide on the best one, the process would consist in testing behavior based controllers on a simulated world constructed through the world and internal models and assigning them fitness values with respect to the predicted satisfaction. The idea is simple: An action is the most basic representation of behavior, so, if the appropriate structures are created, more complex behaviors can be constructed incrementally by interacting with the world.

These behaviors will come into play whenever the MDB verifies that they are the ones that will predictably produce the best results for the agent's current motivation or objective and, as long as they fulfil their purpose, the MDB will be liberated from the task of constantly having to produce an action as these behavior modules can operate autonomously. The concept is very similar to learning skills. Initially one has to pay a lot of attention to every detail of the actions that come together to do something and to the decision of what action to take (hit a tennis ball with a racket, punch the keyboard typing something that makes sense, etc.). As more practice or experience is gathered performing the task, the behavior becomes more automatic and in some cases even reflex.

To achieve this objective, one needs a structured manner of constructing any type of behavior-based module or structure and an algorithm that will achieve the task of doing so autonomously. As the process of constructing the architecture must be incremental and, for the sake of efficiency, parts should be reusable, it is obvious that a modular behavior-based architecture should be considered. Additionally, it would be interesting to be able to regulate behaviors so that smooth transitions from one behavior to another can occur and intermediate behaviors between any two can be obtained without having to create new modules. To fulfill all of these requirements, a behavior-based architecture using ANNs and the concept of modulation has been developed and is presented in the next section.

## 16.4.1 Behavior-Based Architecture

As stated earlier, the three main requirements behind the design of the behavior architecture presented here are reusability, smooth transitions, and the possibility of obtaining it incrementally. These requirements have led to the following characteristics: Controllers implementing behaviors may consist of one or several modules. These modules are other controllers that were previously obtained. This way, the fact that in order to learn something we usually reuse previously obtained behaviors and skills is reflected, and controllers are combined to obtain other more complex controllers.

Modules are grouped into two classes: action and decision. Action modules can establish values for actuators, whereas decision modules cooperate to select what action modules have to be activated. Of course, an architecture where every module is able to do both things is possible, but this function separation allows for the reuse of some modules (decision modules) even between different kinds of robots. It also makes the process of obtaining the modules easier (there are fewer possible interactions compared to the case where every module can do everything) and, finally, makes the whole process and the final controller easier to understand from a human point of view.

From a designer viewpoint, modules are coupled into a hierarchical structure where the lowest-level modules are action modules and modules at higher levels are decision modules that govern modules below them. Again, this makes the process of obtaining it easier to carry out and to understand as compared to distributed architectures.

There are three types of decision modules, each one with its particular capabilities: actuator modulators, sensor modulators, and selectors. *Actuator* modulators regulate how the action modules at the bottom of the hierarchy take control of actuators, dismissing, augmenting, and combining their values before applying them to the actuators. *Sensor* modulators regulate how modules below them in the hierarchy perceive the world by modifying the data coming from the sensors. Finally, *selectors* just activate one module in the level immediately below, preventing execution of the remaining modules.

The process used to obtain a controller is the following. If the desired behavior is very simple, an action module is obtained. If the desired behavior is more complex, or something that is already present may be reused, a decision module is obtained that can use any of the other modules present (irrespective of its type, as decision modules may be organized hierarchically).

In a formal way, the components of the architecture can be described as follows:

- A module $X$ is an ancestor of a module $Y$ if there is a path from $X$ to $Y$.
- $X$ is a descendant of $Y$ if there is a path from $Y$ to $X$.

- $X$ is a direct descendant of $Y$ if there is a path of length 1 from $Y$ to $X$.
- $X$ will be called a *root* node (denoted as R) if it has no ancestors. Every controller has at least one R node. Whenever the controller has to be executed, the control flows starting from its R node(s).
- $X$ is an *actuator node* (A) if its outputs establish values for the actuators.
- $X$ is an *actuator modulating node* (AM) if its outputs modify (multiplying by a value between 0 and 2) the outputs of its descendant nodes of type A. Assuming that an AM modulates the values of $n$ actuators, its number of outputs is n∗number of direct descendants, as the modulation propagated to each descendant is different. An AM does not necessarily modulate all the actuators over which the set of nodes acts, just any subset of them. If between R and A there is more than one AM that modulates one output of A, the resulting modulating value will be the product of the individual modulations in the path. When more than one node A provides values for the same actuator, the actuator receives the sum of these values.
- $X$ is a *sensor modulating node* (SM) if its outputs modify (multiplying by a value between 0 and 2) the inputs of its descendant nodes. Assuming that an SM modulates the values of $n$ sensors, its number of outputs is n∗number of direct descendants, as the modulation propagated to each descendant is different. An SM does not necessarily modulate all the sensors over which the nodes act, just any subset of them. If between R and $Y$ there is more than one SM that modulates one input of $Y$, the resulting modulating value will be the product of the individual modulations in the path.
- $X$ is a *selector node* (S) if its output selects one of its direct descendants as the branch to follow, short-circuiting the others. An S is just a particular case of an AM that always modulates the actuators of a single descendant with a value of 1 and the actuators of the other descendants with a value of 0. The descendant modulated by 1 can be different for each input values combination, but it is always unique.
- $X$ is a *virtual sensor* (VS) if it defines a mapping function from a sensor space to another sensor, real or not, space, which is used by some action or decision module. The only requisite of this function is that it has to be defined for every possible value of the original sensor space.
- $X$ is a *virtual actuator* (VA) if it defines a mapping function from an actuator, real or not, space used by some action or decision module to another actuator space. The only requisite on this function is that it has to be defined for every possible value of the original actuator space.

The global architecture is shown in Figures 16.6 and 16.7. The first one displays an example with every possible element where we notice that the controller is graph-shaped and not tree-shaped as a given module can be used by more than one higher-level module. The second figure provides a global vision of the architecture from a type of module perspective. With this figure, considering the fact that modulations lead us to situations where more than one subtree is in execution, we see how the architecture is not really different from a distributed architecture where modules are categorized into different groups because actuator modulators can be put together in the same level and sensor

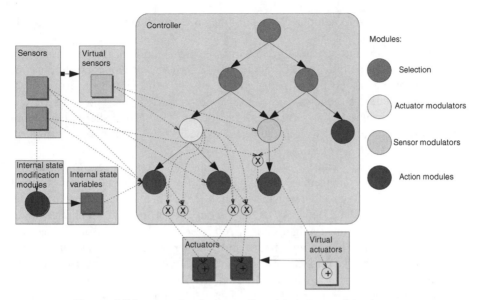

Figure 16.6. Example of a controller with every possible element.

modulators can be set aside from the hierarchy and attached to the appropriate inputs where necessary.

Modulations are the key element in the way modules are connected in this architecture as it provides the possibility of obtaining a broad range of new behaviors from a small set of previously obtained modules. When using actuator modulators, actuator values become at the end a linear combination of those individually produced by action modules, which, in practice, means that by just adding a new module (an actuator modulator) a continuous range of behaviors for the transitions between those determined by the individual controllers may be obtained. On the other hand, sensor modulators permit changing how a module, or set of modules, reacts under a given input pattern,

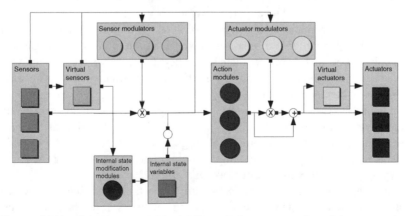

Figure 16.7. Global vision of the architecture from a type of module perspective.

transforming it to a different one. This simplifies making changes in the reactions to already-learned input patterns.

Virtual sensors and actuators permit transferring controllers from one robot to another. This can be done at two different levels. The whole behavior controller may be transferred between robots by designing virtual sensors and actuators for every sensor and actuator needed, or action modules may be reobtained in the new platform and decision modules reused using virtual sensors on them. The second alternative implies a little more work but it usually leads to better results if the target robot platform has a better sensors/actuators set [36].

Regarding two important aspects that remain unmentioned, how to implement modules and how to obtain them, even though nothing in the architecture limits the tools used in both cases, to be coherent with the rest of the MDB, in a similar way as in the case of models, artificial neural networks (ANNs) were chosen for the implementation of the modules and evolutionary algorithms (EAs) for obtaining them. Both choices are very common in behaviour-based robotics and jointly permit automating that process so the robot can obtain the behavior by itself, without human intervention. However, the problem we are coping with here is quite different from the general problem evolutionary behavior-based roboticists face due to the fact that, even though the behaviors are operating in a real robot, their evolution is taking place using models of the real world and robot instead of fitness functions and precalculated models. This implies that evolution is taking place within a simulator, but unlike the case of traditional evolutionary robotics studies on obtaining behaviors in simulated environments [37], here the simulator is functional and is changing in time as the models adapt to the incoming perceptual stream from the dynamic environment the robot is operating in. Thus, it is a more realistic simulator (at least once good models have been obtained) and we have a situation that is closer to operation in reality.

What is clear is that the process of obtaining these behavior controllers can be carried out either starting from scratch (that is, the initial controllers are randomly generated) or having an initial population of modules that have been seeded with previous controllers obtained online or offline. These seeds may be modified during evolution to adapt them to the current circumstances or new decision modules may be created that combine some of these seeds in order to achieve new behaviors.

From a purely behavior-based perspective and when obtaining modules offline in order to seed the populations, simulations have the problem of not being perfect and, consequently, the evaluation of candidate controllers has to be treated as a noisy process applying the correct techniques to minimize differences between behavior in simulation and the resulting behavior in the real world. In addition, in order to make the controllers robust, a broad range of possible variations or possible environments must be used.

Regarding these problems, Jakobi [37] established a set of conditions to be fulfilled in an evolutionary process using simulation to guarantee that the behaviors obtained in evolution work adequately in the real robot. Santos et al. [38] have reported some ideas on the types of noise needed to fulfill Jakobi's criteria.

These latest considerations are relevant only for obtaining offline behaviors. When carrying out online evolution to improve existing behaviors or to obtain new ones, the process relies on the world and internal models instead of precalculated models. In online evolution we just use the world models being evolved as a reflection of the environment as it is being observed by the robot at that given moment. That is, the environment itself adjusts the robot's behaviors.

In terms of the evolutionary algorithms to employ in this behavior-generation part of the MDB, the problem is very similar to that faced by traditional evolutionary roboticists but with some constraints. It is a neuroevolution problem that takes place in a very complex solution space, but in the case of the MDB populations must be small as real-time operation is required. J. A. Becerra et al. [39] observe that when carrying out evolution to obtain robot controllers very hard search spaces arise, with sparse hyperdi-mensional peaks, representing good solutions, separated by large hyperdimensional areas with an almost constant fitness value (Figure 16.8). This situation is not predictable at all, especially in the type of online evolution required here, where the search space is changing continuously due to the adapting world models, implying a changing optimal strategy.

As a consequence of all this, what is usually sought is a very robust EA in terms of minimizing the probability of falling into local optima that is capable of operating reasonably well with limited populations and that presents a low computational

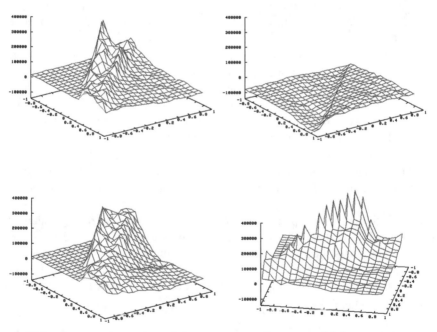

Figure 16.8. Example of a hard search space corresponding to a wall following behavior with a Pioneer 2DX robot. Each view is a snapshot of an animation that plots the fitness landscape. In the animation, 4 genes out of 70 of the chromosome change in the whole range of possible values and the other genes remain fixed with the values of the best solution obtained in evolution. Regarding the 4 genes that change, one of them changes in the x-axis, another one changes in the y-axis, and the other two change in time. Therefore, it is clear in the pictures that just changing two genes by a small amount makes a huge difference in the fitness of the solution.

complexity. The *macroevolutionary algorithm* (*MA*) [40], which is the algorithm selected here, seems to be an appropriate choice [39]. The main difference between MAs and other kinds of EAs is how selection for mating is performed. For the majority of EAs, more fitness means more probability of mating and transmitting information to the next generation. In MAs, fitness plays a role together with distance between individuals in order to determine who survives and, once an individual is tagged as a survivor, it has the same probabilities of reproducing as any other survivor. The MA's dynamics can be summarized as follows:

1. An initial population is randomly generated. In MAs, the term *species* is used instead of *individuals* in order to provide a better analogy with nature, although in current implementations each species corresponds to a single individual.
2. The population is evaluated.
3. A survival coefficient is calculated for each species $i$ as the sum of $(f(i) - f(j))/d(i - j)$, where $j$ is every other species, $f$ the fitness function, and $d$ the distance in the search space. If that sum is positive, the species survives; otherwise, it becomes extinct. That is, a species survives if its fitness is better than a weighted average that takes into account the distance between species. Consequently, a species can survive with a relatively poor fitness value if it is far from the rest of the species.
4. Each extinct species is substituted by another species that can be randomly generated or derived from a combination of itself and a randomly chosen survivor depending on the value of a $t$ parameter. This parameter is usually set up so that in the first generations most of the new species are random, and, in the last generations, most of the new species are derived from combining extinct species with survivors, going from almost pure exploration to almost pure exploitation as generations evolve.
5. The population is evaluated again and the algorithm loops until a stopping criterion (number of generations or a given fitness value) is reached.

This particular way of performing selection, taking into account distance in the search space and maintaining a low evolutionary pressure, produces a niching effect in the population; that is, individuals tend to organize themselves into clusters in the search space simultaneously exploring different areas, which helps to avoid falling into local optima. Finally, MAs also present a low computational complexity for low populations, which is the case in online evolution.

## 16.5 SOME APPLICATION EXAMPLES

In this section, we are going to present some application examples. The objective is to provide an indication of the possibilities of the different elements that go into the MDB. Initially, an example is described where a complete behavior-based control architecture is obtained for a Pioneer 2 DX robot in order to demonstrate the versatility and capabilities of modulation-based architectures as a base for the action part of the global cognitive mechanism. In fact, the complex controller obtained is an example of the base controllers that can be inserted as initial material to be refined by the cognitive mechanism when in real-time operation. After this, we describe an example where the whole MDB cognitive mechanism is used, showing its ability to adapt and readapt to different environments and/or tasks through a process of interacting with teachers.

## 16.5.1 Training a Modulation Architecture

The following example [41] illustrates the offline process for obtaining controllers with the aim of showing how the behavior-based architecture used for the action part of the cognitive mechanism obtains complex behaviors from combinations of simple modules and modulation. The example shows many of the architecture components, including both input and output modulation.

In this behavior, the robot has to catch a prey avoiding a predator. Prey and predator are also mobile objects. The robot gains energy as it goes near the prey and loses energy as it goes near the predator. There are two internal values that also affect the robot energy: the energetic cost associated with each step and the anxiety level of the robot that makes it lose energy (the higher the anxiety level, the higher the energy loss). The objective is to catch the prey, maximizing energy. That means that if the energetic cost in each step or the anxiety is very high, the robot should go straight to the prey, without worrying about being near the predator. Otherwise, the robot should try to catch the prey while avoiding the predator by a long distance.

The controller has 4 modules: 2 low-level modules (go straight to the prey and escape straight from the predator), 1 actuator modulator (which modulates outputs of the 2 low-level modules depending on distance to prey and predator and the energetic cost associated with each step) and 1 sensor modulator (which modulates inputs of the actuator modulator depending on anxiety). Figure 16.9 shows the controller structure.

The ANN of the sensor modulator has 2 inputs, 2 hidden layers with 6 neurons each, and 2 outputs. The ANN of the actuator modulator has 3 inputs (two of them modulated by the sensor modulator), 2 hidden layers with 6 neurons each, and 2 outputs. To simplify the problem, the only output of the low-level modules is the angular velocity (which will be between $-40°$/sec and $40°$/sec). Linear velocity is set to a fixed value (200 mm/sec). The prey escapes from the robot and the predator tries to get between the prey and the robot. A *macroevolutionary algorithm* [40] was used in every evolution with a very small number of individuals (for instance, the sensor modulator's evolution was performed with a population of 100 individuals, during 100 generations, and each individual was evaluated 200 times with a life of 300 steps).

The process was carried out as follows. First, the lowest-level modules were obtained. Then, the actuator modulator was evolved and we had a behavior that allowed the robot to catch the prey avoiding the predator by a distance that depends on the energetic penalization for each step. Finally, a sensor modulator was obtained so that the robot could take into account not only the energetic penalization but also its anxiety level when deciding how far away the predator had to be.

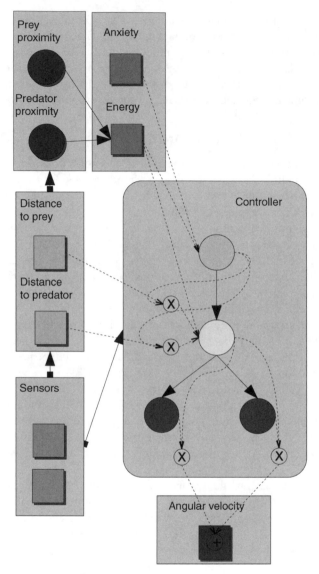

Figure 16.9. Controller diagram.

Figures 16.10 and 16.11 show some example runs. In the controllers resulting from evolution, the actuator modulator regulates only the "escape from predator" module, maintaining the modulation of the "go to prey" module constant. The sensor modulator evolves in a similar way and it maintains the modulation of the sensor that indicates the distance to the prey constant and modulates only the sensor that indicates the distance to the predator. The constant modulation applied to the "distance to prey" sensor is in fact a "0", so the ANN corresponding to the actuator modulator can be pruned. This makes

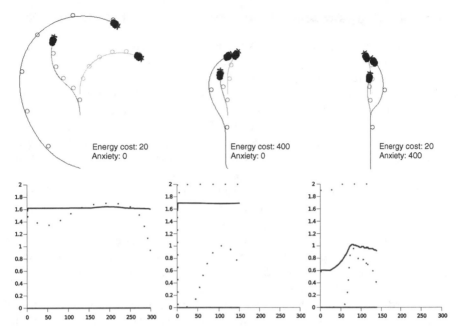

Figure 16.10. Some examples of the global behavior in the simulator. Graphics represent modulation levels. Dashed lines = actuator modulator outputs; continuous lines = sensor modulator outputs.

sense; the actuator modulator activates the "go to prey" module by default and only when it is near the predator does it activate the "escape from predator" module. It is also really interesting to see that the sensor modulator changes the actuator modulator behavior only when anxiety is higher than the amount of energy lost in each step; otherwise, the actuator modulator already behaves correctly.

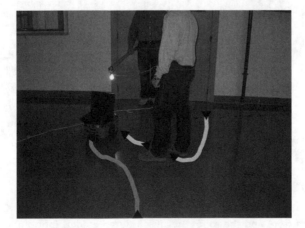

Figure 16.11. Example in the real robot.

## 16.5.2 Online Adaptation

The online learning capabilities of the MDB have been tested in different experiments using real robots [42, 43]. The example we present here [44] employs the main features of the architecture: real-time learning, real-time operation, physical agent operation, and adaptive behavior. In order to emphasize the robustness of the MDB, we have carried out the experiment using the Pioneer 2 robot and Sony's AIBO robot.

The task the robot must carry out is simple: Learn to obey the commands of a teacher that, initially, guides the robot toward an object located in its neighbourhood. In Figure 16.12, we show the experimental setup for both robots. In the case of the Pioneer 2 robot (left image of Figure 16.12), the object to reach is a black cylinder, and in the case of the AIBO robot the object is a pink ball (right images of Figure 16.12). The Pioneer 2 robot is a wheeled robot that has a sonar sensor array around its body and a laptop placed on its top platform. The laptop provides two more sensors, a microphone, and the numerical keyboard, and the MDB runs on it. The AIBO robot is a doglike robot with a larger range of sensors and actuators. In this example, we use the digital camera, the microphones, and the speaker. The MDB is executed remotely on a PC and communicates with the robot through a wireless connection.

Figure 16.13 displays a schematic view of the current world and satisfaction models (with their respective numbers of inputs and outputs) that arise in this experiment in a given instant of time. The sensory meaning of the inputs and outputs of these models in both physical agents is summarized in Table 16.1. In this example, we do not take into account internal sensors in the agent and, consequently, internal models are not used. The flow of the learning process is as follows: The teacher observes the relative position of the robot with respect to the object and provides a command that guides it toward the object.

**Figure 16.12.** Left images show a sequence of real actions in the Pioneer 2 robot when the teacher is present (top) and the robot uses the induced models (bottom). Middle and right images correspond to the same situation, but in the case of the AIBO robot.

T A B L E 16.1. Inputs and Outputs Involved in the Models of the MDB for the Two Physical Agents Used in the Experiment

|  | Pioneer 2 robot | AIBO robot |
|---|---|---|
| Command (1 input) | • Group of seven possible values according to the seven musical notes. | • Group of seven possible values according to seven spoken words: hard right, medium right, right, straight, left, medium left and hard left. |
|  | • Provided by the teacher through a musical keyboard. | • The teacher speaks directly. |
|  | • Sensed by the robot using the microphone of the laptop. | • Sensed using the stereo microphones of the robot. |
|  | • Translated to a discrete numerical range from −9 to 9. | • Speech recognition using Sphinx software translated into a discrete numerical range from −9 to 9. |
| Action (1 input) | • Group of seven possible actions: turn hard right, turn medium right, turn right, follow straight, turn left, turn medium left and turn hard left that are encoded with a discrete numerical range from −9 to 9. | • Group of seven possible actions: turn hard right, turn medium right, turn right, follow straight, turn left, turn medium left and turn hard left that are encoded with a discrete numerical range from −9 to 9. |
|  | • The selected action is decoded as linear and angular speed. | • The selected action is decoded as linear speed, angular speed and displacement. |
| Predicted human feedback (1 output/ input) | • Discrete numerical range that depends on the degree of fulfillment of a command from 0 (disobey) to 5 (obey). | • Group of five possible values according to five spoken words: well done, good dog, ok, pay attention, bad dog. |
|  | • Provided by the teacher directly to the MDB using the numerical keyboard of the laptop. | • The teacher speaks directly |
|  |  | • Sensed using stereo microphones of the robot. |
|  |  | • Speech recognition using Sphinx software translated into a discrete numerical range from 0 to 5 |
| Satisfaction (1 output) | • Continuous numerical range from 0 to 11 that is automatically calculated after applying an action. It depends on:<br>  o The degree of fulfillment of a command from 0 (disobey) to 5 (obey). | • Continuous numerical range from 0 to 11 that is automatically calculated after applying an action. It depends on:<br>  o The degree of fulfillment of a command from 0 (disobey) to 5 (obey). |

(continued)

TABLE 16.1 (*Continued*)

|  | Pioneer 2 robot | AIBO robot |
|---|---|---|
|  | o The distance increase from 0 (no increase) to 3 (max).<br>o The angle with respect to the object from 0 (back turned) to 3 (robot frontally to the object) | o The distance increase from 0 (no increase) to 3 (max).<br>o The angle with respect to the object from 0 (back turned) to 3 (robot frontally to the object). |
| Distance and angle (2 outputs/inputs) | • Sensed by the robot using the sonar array sensor.<br><br>• Measured from the robot to the black cylinder and encoded directly in cm and degrees. | • Sensed by the robot using the images provided by the colour camera.<br>• Colour segmentation process and area calculation taken from Tekkotsu software.<br>• Encoded in cm and degrees.<br>• Measured from the robot to the pink ball. |

Initially, the robot has no idea of what each command means in regard to the actions it applies. After sensing the command, the robot acts and, depending on the degree of obedience, the teacher provides a reward or a punishment as a pain or pleasure signal. The motivation of the physical agent in this experiment is to maximize pleasure, which basically means being rewarded by the teacher.

To carry out this task, the robot just needs to follow the commands of the teacher, and a world model with that command as sensory input is obtained (top world model of Figure 16.13) to select the action. From this point forward, we will call this model *communication model*. The satisfaction model (top satisfaction model of Figure 16.13) is trivial as the satisfaction is directly related to the output of the communication model, that is, the reward or punishment.

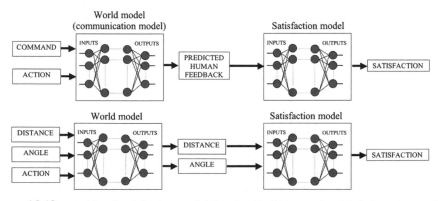

**Figure 16.13.** World and satisfaction models involved in this example with their corresponding sensory inputs and outputs.

The interesting thing here is what happens to the models corresponding to other sensors. We assume that, in general, to design the models needed in the MDB for a particular task, no simplifications are made and world models are generated to cover the sensory capabilities of the physical agent. In this case, a second world model was simultaneously obtained (bottom world model of Figure 16.13) that uses distance and angle to the object as sensory inputs. Obviously, this model is relating information other than the teacher's commands during the performance of the task. If the commands produce any regularities in the information provided by other sensors in regard to the satisfaction obtained, these models can be applied when operating without a teacher. That is, if in a given instant of time, the teacher stops providing commands, the communication model will not have any sensory input and cannot be used to select the actions, leaving this task in the hands of other models that do have inputs. For this second case, the satisfaction model is more complex, relating the satisfaction value to the distance and angle, directly related to rewards or punishments.

In this particular experiment, the four models are represented by multilayer perceptron ANNs (with the number neurons 2-3-3-1 for the communication model, 3-6-6-2 for the world model, and 2-3-3-1 for the second satisfaction model). They were obtained using the PBGA genetic algorithm presented earlier that automatically provides the appropriate size of the ANNs. Thus, in this case, the MDB executes four evolutionary processes over four different model populations every iteration. The STM has a size of 20 action–perception pairs in all the experiments.

Figure 16.14 displays the evolution of the mean squared error provided by the current models (communication, world, and satisfaction) predicting the STM as iterations of the MDB take place in both physical agents. The error clearly decreases in all cases and in a very similar way for both agents (except at the beginning, where the STM is being filled up).

This means that the MDB works similarly on two very different real platforms and that the MDB is able to provide real modeling of the environment, the communication, and the satisfaction of the physical agent. As the error values show in Figure 16.14, both robots learned to follow teacher commands in an accurate way in about 20 iterations (from a practical point of view, this means about 10 minutes of real time) and, what is more relevant, the operation without a teacher was successful using the world and satisfaction models. In these kinds of real robot examples, the main measure we must take into account in order to decide the goodness of an experiment is the time consumed in the learning process to achieve perfect obedience. Figure 16.12 displays a real execution of actions in both robots. In the pictures with a teacher, the robot is following commands; otherwise, it is performing the behavior without any commands, just using its induced models. It can be clearly seen that the behavior is basically the same although a little less efficient without teacher commands (as it has learned to decrease its distance to the object but not the fastest way to do it).

Consequently, an induced behavior was obtained in the physical agents based on the fact that every time the robot applies the correct action according to the teacher's commands, the distance to the object decreases. This way, once the teacher disappears, the robot can continue with the task because it developed a satisfaction model related to the remaining sensors telling it to perform actions that reduce the distance.

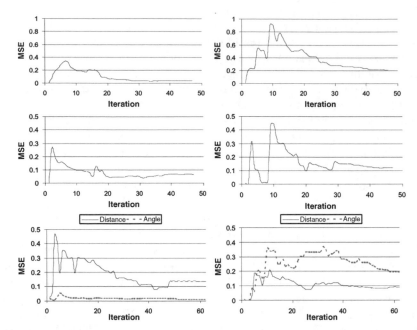

**Figure 16.14.** Evolution of the mean squared error of the current communication model (top), satisfaction model (middle), and world model (bottom) predicting the STM as iterations of the MDB take place in the Pioneer 2 robot.

To show the adaptive capabilities of the MDB, in Figure 16.15 (left) we have represented the evolution of the MSE provided by the current communication model during 200 iterations for the example with the Pioneer 2 robot. In the first 70 iterations, the teacher provides commands using the same encoding (language) applied in the previous experiment. This encoding is not preestablished and we want the teacher to make use of any correspondence it wants. From iteration 70 to iteration 160, another teacher appears using a different language (different and more complex relation between musical notes for the Pioneer robot), and, finally, from iteration 160 to iteration 200, the original teacher returns. As shown in the figure, in the first 70 iterations the error

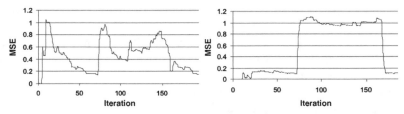

**Figure 16.15.** Evolution of the MSE provided by the current communication model (left) and satisfaction model (right) predicting the STM as iterations of the MDB take place. The left graph corresponds to a dynamic language and the right graph to a dynamic satisfaction.

decreases fast to a level (1.6%) that results in a very accurate prediction of the rewards. Consequently, the robot successfully follows the commands of the teacher. When the second teacher appears, the error level increases because the STM starts to store samples of the new language and the previous models fail in the prediction. At this point, as mentioned before, the LTM management system detects this mixed situation (detects an unstable model) and induces a change in the parameters of the STM replacement strategy to a FIFO strategy. As displayed in Figure 16.15 (left), the increase in the value of the error stops in about 10 iterations and, once the STM has been purged of samples from the first teacher's language, the error decreases again (1.3% at iteration 160). The error level between iterations 70 and 160 is not as stable as in the first iterations. This happens because the language used by the second teacher is more complex than the previous one and, in addition, we must point out that the evolution graphs obtained from real robots oscillate, in general, much more than in simulated experiments due to the broad range of noise sources of the real environments. But the practical result is that about iteration 160 the robot follows the new teacher's commands successfully again, adapting itself to teacher characteristics. When the original teacher returns using the original language (iteration 160 of Figure 16.15, left), the adaptation is very fast because the communication models stored in the LTM during the first iterations are introduced as seeds in the evolutionary processes.

In Figure 16.15 (right) we have represented the evolution of the MSE for the current satisfaction model in another execution of this second experiment. In this case, the change occurs in the rewards provided by the teacher. From iterations 0 to 70, the teacher rewards reaching the object and, as we can see in the graph, the error level is low (1.4%). From iteration 70 to 160, the teacher changes its behavior and punishes reaching the object, rewarding escaping from it. There is a clear increase of error level due to the complexity of the new situation (high ambiguity of possible solutions, that is, there are more directions of escaping than reaching the object). In iteration 160, the teacher returns to the first behavior and, as expected, the error level decreases to the original levels, quickly obtaining a successful adaptive behavior.

## 16.6 CONCLUSION

An approach based on the simultaneous use of a reactive modular ANN-based robot architecture and a more deliberative lifelong-learning mechanism for autonomous robots is presented here. These two approaches to the implementation of the complete control system for an autonomous robot can be combined through the use of the reactive-based modular structure as the action-generation part of an evolutionary-based cognitive mechanism. The cognitive mechanism is in charge of obtaining and managing world and internal models of the environments and the robot as well as satisfaction models, which are used in its action-generation part to evolutionarily adapt the control structure of the robot. One of the advantages of this approach is that some reactive architectures can be roughly pretrained in simulation, as it is more efficient, and then introduced in the real robot so that the cognitive mechanism can refine them to the level required by the task.

This procedure greatly simplifies the task of the cognitive mechanism, as it does not have to start from a clean slate and also facilitates the production of the reactive control architectures, which do not have to be perfectly trained at the beginning. In fact, this approach can be equated to the one used by nature, where a rough set of competencies are preloaded in animal or human brains, which are then tuned to the particular environments and circumstances each individual will face through adaptation by interacting with the world.

Further work is necessary to assess the level of complexity that may be achieved using these strategies, especially in terms of the size of the modular structures that are manageable. But what is more important is to be able to elucidate a methodology that allows for the automatic decomposition of large behaviors into coherent subparts that can be reused by the cognitive mechanism when adapting. This is the main line we are now working on.

## 16.7 REFERENCES

1. R. Pfeifer, J.C. Bongard, *How the Body Shapes the Way We Think*. MIT Press, 2006.
2. *The American Heritage® Dictionary of the English Language*, 4th ed. Houghton Mifflin, 2000.
3. L. M. Brasil, F. M. Azevedo, J. M. Barreto, M. Noirhomme-Fraiture, "Complexity and Cognitive Computing," *IEA/AIE*, Vol. 1, pp. 408–417, 1998.
4. S. Nolfi, S. & D. Floreano, *Evolutionary Robotics: The Biology, Intelligence and Technology of Self-Organizing Machines*. Cambridge, MA: MIT, 2000.
5. R. A. Watson, S. G. Ficici, J. B. Pollack, "Embodied Evolution: Distributing an Evolutionary Algorithm in a Population of Robots," *Robotics and Autonomous Systems*, 39, pp 1–18, 2002.
6. U. Nehmzow, "Physically Embedded Genetic Algorithm Learning in Multi-Robot Scenarios: The PEGA Algorithm." *Proc. 2nd Int. Workshop on Epigenetic Robotics: Modelling Cognitive Development in Robotic Systems*, 2002.
7. D. Floreano, J. Urzelai, "Evolution of Plastic Control Networks," *Autonomous Robots*, 11, pp. 311–317, 2001.
8. G. Hornby, S. Takamura, J. Yokono, O. Hanagata, T. Yamamoto, M. Fujita, "Evolving Robust Gaits with AIBO." *IEEE Int. Conf. on Robotics and Automation*, 2000, pp. 3040–3045.
9. D. Marocco, D. Floreano, "Active Vision and Feature Selection in Evolutionary Behavioural Systems. *From Animals to Animats: Proceedings of the Seventh Int. Conf on the Simulation of Adaptive Behaviour (SAB'02)*, 2002, pp. 247–255.
10. M. Wilson, "Preston: A System for the Evaluation of Behaviour Sequences," *Interdisciplinary Approaches to Robot Learning*, In (Demmiris, J. and Birk, A.,eds.) *Would Scientific*, 24(9), pp. 185–208, 2000.
11. J. Grefenstette, C. Ramsey, "An Approach to Anytime Learning." *Proc. 9th Int. Machine Learning Conference*, 1992, pp 189–195.
12. G. Parker, "Co-evolving Model Parameters for Anytime Learning in Evolutionary Robotics," *Robotics and Autonomous Systems*, 33, pp. 13–30, 2000.
13. J. Walker,"Experiments in Evolutionary Robotics: Investigating the Importance of Training and Lifelong Adaptation by Evolution, PhD thesis, University of Wales, 2003.

14. J. Walker, S. Garret, M. Wilson, "Evolving Controllers for Real Robots: A Survey of the Literature," *Adaptive Behavior*, 11(3), pp. 179–203, 2006.

15. R. J. Duro, J. Santos, F. Bellas, A. Lamas, "On Line Darwinist Cognitive Mechanism for an Artificial Organism." *Proc. Supplement Book SAB2000*, 2000, pp. 215–224.

16. J. Changeux, P. Courrege, A. Danchin, "A Theory of the Epigenesis of Neural Networks by Selective Stabilization of Synapses." *Proc. Nat. Acad. Sci. USA*, 70, 1973, pp. 2974–2978.

17. M. Conrad, "Evolutionary Learning Circuits," *J. Theoretical Biology*, 46, 1974.

18. G. Edelman, *Neural Darwinism: The Theory of Neuronal Group Selection*. Basic Books, 1987, pp. 167–188.

19. M. R. Genesereth, N. Nilsson, *Logical Foundations of Artificial Intelligence*. Morgan Kauffman, 1987.

20. F. Bellas, R. J. Duro, "Multilevel Darwinist Brain in Robots: Initial Implementation." *ICINCO2004 Proceedings Book*, Vol. 2, 2004, pp. 25–32.

21. F. Bellas, R. J. Duro, "Introducing Long Term Memory in an ANN-Based Multilevel Darwinist Brain," *Lecture Notes in Computer Science*, Vol. 2686, 2003, pp. 590–598.

22. F. Bellas, J. A. Becerra, R. J. Duro, "Construction of a Memory Management System in an On-line Learning Mechanism." *ESANN 2006 Proceedings Book*, 2006.

23. X. Yao, "Evolving Artificial Neural Networks." *Proc. IEEE*, 87(9), 1999, 1423–1447.

24. K. Trojanowski, Z. Michalewicz, "Evolutionary Approach to Non-stationary Optimisation Tasks." *Lecture Notes in Computer Science*, Vol. 1609, 1999, pp. 538–546.

25. N. Mori, H. Kita, Y. Nishikawa, "Adaptation to a Changing Environment by Means of the Feedback Thermodynamical Genetic Algorithm." *LNCS*, Vol. 1498, pp. 149–158, 1998.

26. D. Dasgupta, D. R. MacGregor, "Nonstationary Function Optimization Using the Structured Genetic Algorithm." *Proc. Parallel Problem Solving from Nature* 2, 1992, pp. 145–154.

27. C. Ryan, J. J. Collins, D. Wallin, "Non-stationary Function Optimization Using Polygenic Inheritance." *Lecture Notes in Computer Science*, Vol. 2724, pp. 1320–1331, 2003.

28. J. Eggermont, T. Lenaerts, "Non-stationary Function Optimization Using Evolutionary Algorithms with a Case-Based Memory," Technical Report TR 2001-11, 2001.

29. T. D'Silva, R. Janik, M. Chrien, K. Stanley, R. Miikkulainen, "Retaining Learned Behavior During Real-Time Neuroevolution." *Proc. AIIDE 2005*, 2005.

30. H. G. Cobb, "An Investigation into the Use of Hypermutation as an Adaptive Operator in Genetic Algorithms Having Continuous, Time-Dependent Nonstationary Environments," NRL Memorandum Report 6760, pp. 523–529, 1990.

31. D. E. Moriarty, "Symbiotic Evolution of Neural Networks in Sequential Decision Tasks," PhD Thesis, University of Texas at Austin, Tech. Rep. UT-AI97-257, 1997.

32. F. Gomez, D. Burger, R. Miikkulainen, "A Neuroevolution Method for Dynamic Resource Allocation on a Chip Multiprocessor." *Proc. Int. Joint Conf. on Neural Networks*, 2001.

33. K. O. Stanley, R. Miikkulainen, "Evolving Neural Networks through Augmenting Topologies," *Evolutionary Computation*, 10, pp. 99–127, 2002.

34. D. Dasgupta, D. McGregor, "Designing Application-Specific Neural Networks Using the Structured Genetic Algorithm." *Proc. COGANN-92*, 1992, pp. 87–96.

35. F. Bellas, R. J. Duro, "Modelling the World with Statiscally Neutral PBGAs: Enhancement and Real Applications." *Proc. 9th Int. Conf. on Neural Information Processing*, Vol. 1, 2002, IEEE Press, pp. 2093–2098.

36. R. J. Duro, J. A. Becerra, J. Santos, "Behavior Reuse and Virtual Sensors in the Evolution of Complex Behavior Architectures," *Theory in Biosciences*, Vol. 120, pp. 188–206, 2001.

37. N. Jakobi, P. Husbands, I. Harvey, "Noise and the Reality Gap: The Use of Simulation in Evolutionary Robotics," *Lecture Notes in Artificial Intelligence*, Vol. 929, pp. 704–720, 1995.

38. J. Santos, R. J. Duro, J. A. Becerra, J. L. Crespo, F. Bellas, "Considerations in the Application of Evolution to the Generation of Robot Controllers," *Information Sciences*, Vol. 133, pp. 127–148, 2001.

39. J. A. Becerra, J. Santos, R. J. Duro, "MA vs. GA in Low Population Evolutionary Processes with Mostly Flat Fitness Landscapes." *Proc. 6th Joint Conf. on Information Sciences*, 2002, pp. 626–630.

40. J. Marín, R.V. Solé, "Macroevolutionary Algorithms: A New Optimization Method on Fitness Landscapes," *IEEE Trans. on Evolutionary Computation*, Vol. 3, No. 4, pp. 272–286, 1999.

41. J. A. Becerra, F. Bellas, J. Santos, R. J. Duro, "Complex Behaviours through Modulation in Autonomous Robot Control," *LNCS* 3512, pp. 717–724, 2005.

42. F. Bellas, A. Lamas, R. J. Duro, "Adaptive Behavior through a Darwinist Machine," *Lecture Notes on Artificial Intelligence*, 2159, pp 86–89, 2001.

43. F. Bellas, R. J. Duro, "Multilevel Darwinist Brain in Robots: Initial Implementation." *ICINCO2004 Proceedings Book*, Vol. 2, 2004, pp. 25–32.

44. F. Bellas, J. A. Becerra, R. J. Duro, "Induced Behaviour in a Real Agent Using the Multilevel Darwinist Brain," *Lecture Notes in Computer Science*, Vol. 3562, pp. 425–434, 2005.

# 17

# APPLICATIONS OF EVOLVING INTELLIGENT SYSTEMS TO OIL AND GAS INDUSTRY

José Macías-Hernández, Plamen Angelov

## 17.1 BACKGROUND

The oil and gas (O&G) industry has a variety of characteristics that make it suitable for application of evolving intelligent systems (EISs). One can summarize these as:

- The need for constant product monitoring
- Low margin and high throughput
- A regulated market for the products and a free market for the crude
- High process complexity
- Expensive process investment
- High number of process variables
- High number of process products

The raw material for refineries is crude oil. There are a vast variety of crudes with different properties that will give different cuts and yields when processing. The price of crude depends on several factors, ranging from its intrinsic chemical properties to political stability in the country of supply and short- and long-term market behavior. The crude oil purchase department has to balance spot market and long-term contracts to maintain a

*Evolving Intelligent Systems: Methodology and Applications,* Edited by Plamen Angelov, Dimitar P. Filev, and Nikola Kasabov

stable crude supply to their refineries. Yields in crude have to fit refineries' complexity to balance the local consumption. Any violation of the balance is normally undesirable.

Oil refining activities are characterized by *low margin* and *high throughput*. The international energy market is free, but the local market is normally highly regulated. Therefore, lowering production costs is the best option for refineries to survive; they have to produce as many intermediate materials as possible. Importing intermediate components is not optimal. For a process industry with such characteristics, online process monitoring and control is very important.

The processes in an oil refinery generate huge volumes and *streams* of data that are routinely stored in huge databases. The operator of a typical *distributed control system* (DCS) in a complex contemporary oil refinery controls and monitors several process units and has responsibility for more than 400 valves! A typical oil refinery database can contain as many as 10,000–12,000 continuous data points. Laboratory samples are routinely analyzed and more than 2000 characteristics are reported every day. The process operators continuously (in real time) make decisions based on *previous experience* to drive the process toward targets. With evolving intelligent sensors, this process can be automated.

An oil refinery usually produces a very *high number of products*, which ranges from light hydrocarbons to heavy fuels. There are a high number of legal specifications that impact the process economics. It is normal practice to blend several intermediate products and recipes in various combinations in order to produce different final products. All of these combinations have to meet legal specifications. The balance between *specifications* and product *components* gives the degrees of freedom and emphasizes the need for online monitoring of the quality of the products.

## 17.2 APPLICATION OPPORTUNITIES

An oil refinery is a complex industrial installation from the point of view that the number of interconnected processes is large, but also from the point of view of the work organization (White, 2001, 2003). In general, different implementations of evolving intelligent systems (EISs) can be applied in different departments of a typical oil refinery. Table 17.1 shows the possible areas and problems that can be addressed by different

TABLE 17.1. Potential Application Areas for EIS in O&G Industry

| Departments/Areas | Application Type |
|---|---|
| Operations | Alarm monitoring, operator advisory, emergency management |
| Price Prediction | Regression and time-series prediction models (e.g., eTS + ) |
| Process Engineering | Process diagnostics (e.g., eClustering + ) |
| Information Systems | Mining data streams (e.g., eTS + ) (Angelov & Filev, 2004; Angelov & Zhou, 2006; see also Chapter 2) |
| Predictive Maintenance | Machine health monitoring and prognostics (e.g., eClustering and eTS) (Filev & Tseng, 2006) |
| Control Engineering | eControl, guided rule-base adaptation (Filev et al., 2000) |
| Soft Sensors | eSensor (Angelov et al., 2008) |

realizations of EISs. The majority of these departments can be found in any complex industrial system. Therefore, some of the general ideas shown in the table can be applied to any industrial plant.

## 17.2.1 Planning and Scheduling

The complexity and the opportunities to apply EIS to oil refineries begin with the purchase of crude oil. As we have shown, there are tradeoffs among quality, yields, spot and long-term deals, and international policies that impact refinery economics. The purchase of oil (amount and quality) and the products that are being produced have to balance the market demands. *Planning and scheduling* departments have to deal with this problem. There is, therefore, an opportunity to have a complex nonlinear, nonstationary model that takes into account all of this highly uncertain information (ERTC, 2004;Goel & Prashant, 1999). Some companies have reported commercial products that address these problems (e.g., Aspentech®, GenSym®, but clearly there is an opportunity for more advanced solutions in this area that take the dynamics of the economic processes into account.

## 17.2.2 Operations

Complex industrial plants running different types of crude assays are difficult to analyze in real time. *Operations and process engineering* departments have to deal with short-term process troubleshooting, security, and quality management. Process operators have to deal with problems associated with the process security, stability, quality, and optimization targets of the plant. Therefore, there are various opportunities to apply EISs to the field of process operations:

**Operator advisory applications.** It is required to help operators in the real-time decision-making process aiming to maintain security, stability, and process optimization (Macías-Hernández, 2001).

**Alarm monitoring and rationalization.** The main goal is to detect and identify abnormal behavior. Tools that can be useful and efficient for online implementation include eClustering+, eTS + (Angelov, 2006; see also Chapter 2).

**Emergency manager.** This is related to the previous item, but here the goal is to help the operator to manage emergency situations.

## 17.2.3 Process Engineering

The responsibilities of the process engineering department are process design and troubleshooting. Traditionally, process engineers use steady-state simulators to create virtual plants to calculate yields, and so on. Neural networks and neuro-fuzzy models provide an efficient alternative for a rigorous steady-state simulation (Barsamian & Macías, 1998). Process troubleshooting is related to short-term analysis of the process behavior. Most instrument providers have very efficient software for basic instrumentation troubleshooting. Process diagnostics, however, is a more complex problem. Currently, there is no commercial software to accomplish this task in an automatic fashion. A possible solution might be the use of eClustering and eTS (Filev & Tseng, 2006).

## 17.2.4 Maintenance

Predictive maintenance is a key activity to reduce total maintenance cost. The challenge is to detect when and how equipment is going to fail based on vibration analysis, *mean time between failures (MTBF)*, process variables, corrosion indicators, and so forth. This is a very good opportunity to apply an EIS. An early sensor failure detection is, in general, an open problem. There are successful applications where this is the case, such as vibration analysis, but cross-correlation between process operating data and equipment failure is not done in an automatic fashion. eClustering and eTS are very promising tools for this problem (Filev & Tseng, 2006).

## 17.2.5 Process Control

*Control engineering* has several general challenges:

**Software sensors.** There are a lot of successful applications of *soft* sensors (Barsamian et al., 1998; Bhat et al., 2003; Fortuna et al., 2007; Kordon and Smits, 2001; Rallo et al., 2004; Smits et al., 2006, etc.). Most of them, however, are based on offline, black-box-type models. These are not able to recalibrate, or to provide an insight to the process (are not transparent), and do not take into account environmental dynamics and internal changes in the plant (different operating modes, ageing, contamination), and so on. As a result, the life-cycle costs of conventional soft sensors are high.

**Dynamic model identification.** Classical control theory provides a solid theoretical basis for linear cases and a limited number of nonlinear ones. Data mining is suitable for offline cases, and dynamic model identification is a very promising area; but for general nonlinear cases, there are practically no ready solutions apart from EISs.

**Detecting *drift* and *shift*.** in the data pattern in streaming data (Angelov & Zhou, 2008a).

**Hybrid controllers.** (multivariable predictive control [MPC] + fuzzy techniques). MPC tools are mature; however, their utilization depends on a properly designed controller and the selection of variables (Camacho & Bordons, 1999). The first part is usually done in practice using the Lyapunov theory, or linear matrix inequalities (LMI) by the design engineer. Variables selection is an important task that can be done automatically.

## 17.2.6 Information Systems

Modern DCSs have huge volumes of data that are processed and stored by sophisticated information systems. It is common to find, including in the DCS, high-resolution history (snap values) with a limited timeframe. In the majority of cases, there is low-resolution history (average data values) with probably several years of data history. All this data feeds several corporate applications, such as data reconciliation packages, oil movements, product balance, and so forth. The results of these applications permit monitoring of the overall refinery performance and support the planning, accounting, and operations departments.

However, the data is usually highly correlated, so the useful information that is contained there is much less than the overall amount of information stored and collected online. Moreover, the successive events encountered in the plant are not specified in the database, so sometimes the diagnosis of a problem in the operation or in the performance of the plant is very difficult. Therefore, this volume of data alone in the majority of cases is not useful for a deep understanding of the process unit. Because of this, the diagnosis of any plant operation problem is made when it is fully developed, and with the use of raw data and the immediate knowledge of the operations of the plant.

The main characteristic of the database is to have a lot of variables but a short operating window. Because there are different crude types, it is highly noisy. Care should be taken to design models with high information content and robustness.

It is clearly necessary to have more tools to manipulate the data and convert it to information in industrial processes so that it can be used to help in diagnosis and process follow-up. For instance, information can be used to help operators, and aid in diagnosis and better control of processes. Process engineers can improve process performance and planners can select the best feed for each process and plant status. Control engineers can design more robust advanced control applications and solve unconventional process control problems.

To do this effectively, advanced tools for mining data streams are required (e.g., the eTS + approach described in Chapter 2). Figure 17.1 shows a summary of functionality, decision levels, and timeframe data.

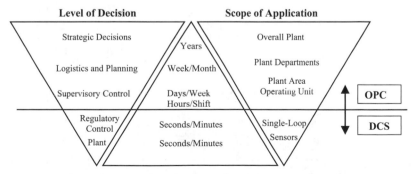

Figure 17.1. Information and decision-making pyramid showing decision levels and application areas for the O&G industry. (DCS denotes *digital control system*; OPC denotes *OLE for process control*.)

## 17.3 REFINERY

An oil refinery consists of an industrial installation where crude oil is separated on its fraction, and then those fractions are treated to produce other fine products. The commercial products are blended mixtures of intermediate refinery products to meet legal specifications (See Figure 17.2).

In this section, the refining process will be briefly described, emphasizing the opportunities for application of EISs to improve the quality of the products and the efficiency.

### 17.3.1 Raw Material

The crude qualities (apart from the yield of each fraction) that are present and have the most impact on refinery economics are *sulfur, density, parafinicity* or *pour point, carbon residue, salt content, nitrogen content*, and *metals*. Sulfur impacts the refinery economics because hydro-treating is required for most of the petroleum fractions. Sour crudes are cheaper than sweet crudes. Low-density crudes correlate to lighter crudes and produce a lower amount of fuel oil, which is one of the cheapest fractions. Upgrading naphtha to gasoline requires the increase of aromaticity of the fraction and that uses energy and requires processing. Therefore, lower parafinicity crudes are cheaper. The carbon residue is related to asphalt content, which is the cheapest fraction. Salt produces corrosion in the process units. The more salts it contains, the cheaper the crude. Nitrogen and sulphur are catalyst poisoning and should be removed. Metals produce catalyst poisoning and severe deactivation.

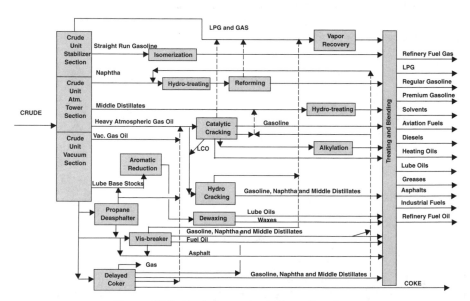

Figure 17.2. Typical complex refinery flowsheet.

## 17.3.2 Process Units

Opportunities for the use of EIS technology in process units can be analyzed from the point of view of quality monitoring and control. Because there are numerous processes, we select only the most typical ones. The same ideas can be extrapolated to others. The principal operations required in a typical refinery are discussed in the following subsections.

*17.3.2.1 Distillation.* **Process Description.** It is the first unit in the flowsheet, and its mission is to separate by distillation the different crude fractions by means of boiling the crude and condensing (see Figure 17.3). Steam is added to improve the separation. The fractions obtained normally are:

- Naphtha
- Kerosene
- Gas oil
- Fuel oil

If there is a vacuum tower, it will be fed with fuel oil from the main distillation tower and this second distillation will produce vacuum gas oil and asphalt.

**Process Key Variables.** The key operating variables are:

- Furnace temperature
- Top reflux

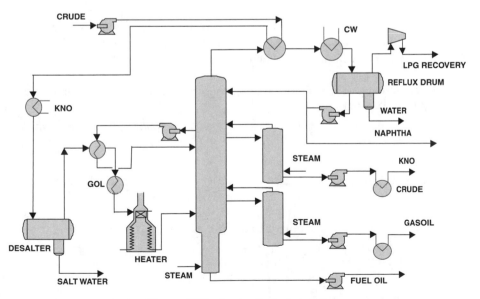

Figure 17.3. Crude distillation unit.

- Side tower heat removal
- Process side-stream flows

These variables produce different ranges of side-stream qualities. It is important these qualities are right because there are no further opportunities to correct them.

**Opportunities for EIS.** The opportunities to apply an EIS are mainly in soft sensors—for example, *soft analyzers* for side-stream cut-point calculations. These are used instead of real distillation analyzers, which are expensive and highly maintenance dependent. Currently used technologies are offline neural networks (NNs), but there are successful applications using partial least squares, *PLS* and *bias update* (Macías, 1998). The latter is especially important for close-loop soft control due to its robustness. There are other soft sensors required for tower-loading calculations.

- **Crude switch.** Each time the process unit changes crude, the unit should be adjusted to maintain qualities. The transient response of the unit is different from normal operation. Therefore, the transient should be detected and corrected in advance so the time-off specification is reduced to a minimum. Detection of the transient is not precisely specified and represents an open problem.

- **Feed properties and operation conditions.** Crude tower behaviors differ from one crude type to another. The unit should be adjusted to the new optimum settings. This is typically accomplished by analyzing the process database to find the best operating conditions of the unit or using *case-based reasoning*. An alternative would be to use an EIS for online update to the new conditions. A good example of an EIS is the guided rule-base initialization applied to advanced manufacturing (Filev et al., 2000).

A case study based on development of evolving intelligent sensors (eSensor) for estimation of different quality parameters of the distillation process will be described in more detail in section 17.4. Four different quality parameters will be of interest:

1. *Thn*,°C: temperature of the heavy naphtha when it evaporates 95% liquid volume, ASTM D86-04b
2. *Tk*,°C: temperature of the kerosene when it evaporates 95% liquid volume, ASTM D86-04b
3. *A*,°C: Abel inflammability analysis of the kerosene
4. *Tgol*,°C: temperature of the gas oil when it evaporates 85% liquid volume, ASTM D86-04b

The inputs of interest for predicting *Thn* are (Maciàs et al., 2003):

- $p$,kg/cm$^2$g: pressure of the tower
- $P$,%: amount of the product taking off
- $d$,g/l: density of the crude

- $Tco$,°C: temperature of the column overhead
- $Tne$,°C: temperature of the naphtha extraction

The inputs of highest relevance for predicting $Tk$ are (Maciàs et al., 2003):

- $p$,kg/cm$^2$: pressure of the tower
- $P$,%: amount of product taking off
- $d$,g/l: density of the crude
- $Tco$,°C: temperature of the column overhead
- $SGK$,kg/h: steam introduced in GOL stripper
- $Tke$,°C: temperature of the kerosene extraction
- $Tne$,°C: temperature of the naphtha extraction

The inputs suggested for predicting the Abel inflammability index of the Kerosene are:

- $p$,kg/cm$^2$g: pressure of the tower
- $P$,%: amount of the product taking off
- $d$,g/l: density of the crude
- $Tco$,°C: temperature of the column overhead
- $Tne$,°C: temperature of the naphtha extraction
- $SK$,kg/h: steam introduced in kerosene stripper

The inputs selected for predicting the temperature of the GOL when it evaporates 85% liquid volume are (Maciàs et al., 2003):

- $p$,kg/cm$^2$g: pressure of the tower
- $P$,%: amount of product taking off
- $d$,g/l: density of the crude
- $Tco$,°C: temperature of the column overhead
- $SG$,kg/h: steam introduced in GOL stripper
- $Tke$,°C: temperature of the kerosene extraction
- $Tne$,°C: temperature of the naphtha extraction

***17.3.2.2 Hydro-treating.* Process Description.** Hydro-treaters process a feed in the presence of hydrogen to convert sulfur combined to $SH_2$. This component will have to be removed in a stripper tower. This unit is used for treatment of naphtha, kerosene, and gas oil (Figure 17.4). This reaction takes place in the presence of a catalyst at high temperature and pressure. Metals are not allowed because they destroy the catalyst. During the process, coke is formed due to cracking. Hydrogen is used to minimize cracking in the reactor.

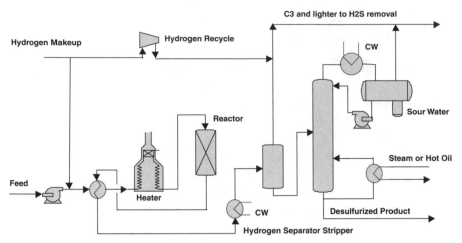

Figure 17.4. Hydro-treating unit.

**Process Key Variables.** The key variables that control the severity of the reaction are:

- Reactor temperature
- Spatial velocity

Recycling hydrogen controls the length of the run. To remove the $SH_2$ dissolved in the reactor, effluent vapor or bottom temperature in the stripper are controlled.

**Opportunities.** Reactor models are only approximated and should be adjusted to process variables. Also, the activity of the catalyst changes and therefore a long-term adjustment should be made. This calls for *evolving recalibrating* models. The difficulty arises due to the fact that the feed is not perfectly characterized. This requires the use of fuzzy sets. eTS + is thus perfectly placed to be used as a backbone technology for the development of advanced evolving soft sensors (eSensors) to address this problem.

***17.3.2.3 Reforming.*** **Process Description.** Reforming is a catalytic process designed to increase the aromatic and isoparafinic content of naphtha, producing high-octane gasoline (Figure 17.5). This process takes place in several reactors in series, using hydrogen to protect the catalyst. Hydrogen is produced as well in the unit due to dehydrogenation reactions. Some cracking takes place, producing liquefied petroleum gas (LPG) and refinery gas.

**Process Key Variables.** Temperature and spatial velocity are again the key variables. A post-fractionation control separates the LPG and gas from the reformed naphtha. The operation variables in that tower are the *reflux ratio* and the *boil-up temperature*. Control variables normally are the *octane number* and the *Reid vapor pressure* of the reformed naphtha.

**Opportunities.** An EIS can be derived to model the operation of the unit to accomplish octane number and yields. Such a model should take into account the

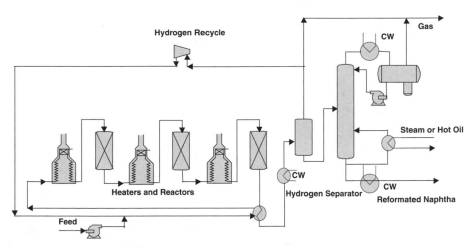

Figure 17.5. Catalytic reforming unit.

deactivation process of the catalyst. Ideally, it should be able to recalibrate and retrain automatically. It is not usual to have octane analyzer at the bottom of the fractionation, so an EIS-based soft sensor can be designed based on operating conditions and type of feed. This latter characteristic should be derived upstream in crude and naphtha hydro-treating units.

**17.3.2.4 Catalytic Cracking.** **Process Description.** Fluid catalytic cracking is a technology to break the gas oil into gasoline and lighter fractions (Figure 17.6). Due to the very high speed of deactivation of the catalyst because of the severe operating conditions, the regeneration process takes place simultaneously in a second regenerator reactor. The catalyst moves from the reactor to the regenerator. The catalyst coke is burned in the regenerator using air.

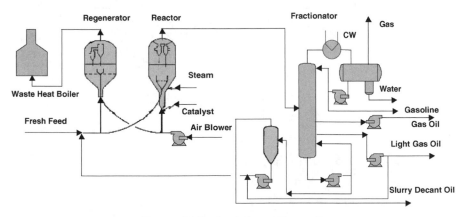

Figure 17.6. Catalytic cracking unit.

**Process Key Variables.** With the fixed type of feedstock, the major operating variables that affect the conversion and product distribution are:

- Cracking temperature
- Catalyst-to-feed ratio
- Space velocity
- Type of catalyst
- Recycle ratio

To increase the conversion, we must increase reaction temperature, catalyst-to-feed ratio, catalyst activity, and reaction time. The limitations come from the limit on burning activity, limit in the air compressor, and the limitation of temperature in the regenerator. Sometimes, oxygen is added to increase the burning capability of the regenerator reactor.

**Opportunities.** This is a strong case for EIS-based *soft analyzers* to calculate octane number of the gasoline and product distribution. There is also a case for hybrid models to simulate the reaction and regeneration sections in a mixed approach to rigorous simulation of the main fractionation to balance catalyst activity with ageing and severity using, for instance, eTS +. A difficult and challenging task is to *detect early* different types of feed to facilitate a faster move to unit limits. There is a large scope to address this using techniques such as *eClustering +* and *age* of the clusters.

***17.3.2.5 Thermal Cracking.* Process Description.** *Vis-breaking* is a type of thermal cracking that reduces the viscosity of a heavier feed to a lower-viscosity fuel by means of breaking higher-molecular-weight molecules into gasoline, kerosene, gas oil, and lower-viscosity fuel (Figure 17.7). The reaction takes place by temperature and space

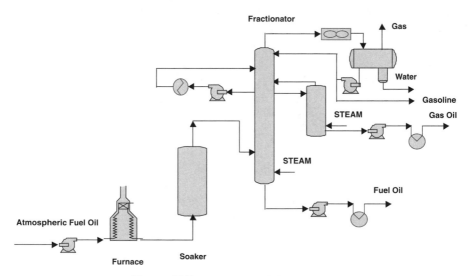

Figure 17.7. Vis-breaking of soaker type.

velocity in the furnace (coil vis-breakers) or a soaker drum (soaker vis-breaker). The first one gets product yields by temperature, the second one by the space velocity. As a result, soaker drum vis-breakers get longer run times than coil vis-breakers. The reactor effluent is separated in fractions in fractionation and stabilizer towers. Run length is controlled by coke deposition in the furnace, which limits the skin temperature.

**Process Key Variables.** The key process variables are the temperature and the spatial velocity. There are other operating variables in the fractionation, such as steam, reflux ratio, and heat distribution in the tower. The key variable is the *stability* of the fuel oil bottoms of the fractionation. A major practical obstacle is the lack of analyzers for stability. Manipulating the extraction side streams and the stripping steam should control side-stream cut point. Some types of feed are more sensitive to coke lay-down than others. Prediction of coke lay-down is important to optimize the run length.

**Opportunities.** There are great opportunities for EIS-based soft analyzers to predict the stability of the cracked fuel oil, that is the key variable for profit in this process unit. There is also an opportunity for a flexible *vis-breaking reaction model* possibly mixed with rigorous steady-state tower simulation into a hybrid model. There is also a need to characterize the cracking ability and stability with the aim to predict coke lay-down and run length. This information can be used to manipulate operating variables when switching from one feed type to another.

## 17.4 CASE STUDY: eSENSOR FOR QUALITY-OF-PRODUCT ONLINE MONITORING

In this section, a particular application of a soft sensor that is based on eTS +, called *eSensor*, will be presented for monitoring the quality of oil products online. Soft sensors and eSensors in particular can contribute to increasing the level of automation and to bringing down life-cycle costs of the exploitation of these sensors in the O&G industry. Due to the extremely high throughput of the oil refinery process, any improvement in product quality has significant impact on the cost and the final profit. The process is complex; a large number of internal variables and many process products (outputs) are involved. Operational environment may also affect the process. Due to the complexity and high setting requirement, the data is usually collected on a daily basis. Considering the high throughput, interrupts of the process are very costly. The continuous running of such a process is very important. As described in the previous sections, the crude oil distillation tower is the first and most important part of the oil refinery. Crude oil is separated into several major cuts (contents) in the distillation tower according to their density and temperature after being heated. These contents are extracted from the distillation tower with lateral pipes and in the consequent processes are refined and blended into gasoline, gas oil, and other commercial products.

The specification for distillation usually is very strict (Macias et al., 2003). The quality of this initial separation of crude oil has a fundamental impact on the efficiency of the later refining process. The *95% ASTM distillation curve* (Macias et al., 2003) specifies the relation between the distilled products and the temperature of the corresponding side vapor stream from the tower (see Figure 17.3). Normally, the products that come from the top end of the distillation tower, have a lower boiling point and higher quality and price. The economic goal of the distillation is to obtain the maximum amount of higher-quality product (Maciàs et al. 2003).

Based on the analysis of the samples and measurements, the operators can adjust the equipment settings and input crude oil, aiming to reduce the deviation of the product quality from the specification. Conventionally, samples are taken for laboratory analysis, which is a costly and slow manual procedure. Another problem with the laboratory analysis is that there are a lot of errors due to the different sampling method, the arbitrarily determined error compensation, and so on. Another issue is that the laboratory analysis usually has hourly or daily delay, which leads to additional error. Attempts to use soft sensors to predict the quality of the crude oil distillation started some 20 years ago using *principal component analysis (PCA)* (Keinosuke, 1990; Li et al., 2000), *partial least squares (PLS)* (Kaspar, 1993), and *genetic programming* (Kordon et al., 2003; Smits et al., 2006). More recently, with the development of more advanced modeling techniques, such as *neural networks* (Rodriguez et al., 1997) and *support vector machines (SVMs)* (Yan et al., 2004), a significant improvement in prediction accuracy has been achieved. The practice shows that this kind of soft sensor is able to maintain acceptable prediction accuracy *when the process is stable.*

However, in real industrial plants, it is usually not possible to maintain the consistent stability of the processes. Once the *shifts* and *drifts* take place in the data pattern that describes the process, the pretrained models have to be retrained (soft sensors have to be recalibrated). Therefore, there is a clear demand for online adaptive/evolving models that are able to cope with the concept of shifts and drifts in the dynamic process, and to self-calibrate and adapt to the dynamic changes in the environment and the plant (EC, 2007; Qin et al., 1997). Applying evolving intelligent models such as eTS + will significantly increase the level of automation of the refining process.

## 17.4.1 Description of the Case Study

The plant used for this case study is a crude distillation installation with a design capacity of 80,000 bbl/d of crude oil from the Middle East (Maciàs et al., 2003). It has 47 valve trays with a diameter of 5.2 m in its top section and 2.4 m at the bottom section. The tower has two cold pumps (kerosene oil [KNO] and gas oil [GOL]) and a hot pump.

From the top to the bottom, the six side streams are (Maciàs et al., 2003):

1. Heavy naphtha (HN)
2. Kerosene (KN)
3. Light gas oil (LGO)
4. Medium gas oil (MGO)
5. Heavy gas oil (HGO)
6. Bottom product, atmospheric residue (RES)

The data for online training and validating of the proposed evolving intelligent sensor are the instrument readings and the output data, including the information on emergencies, shutdowns, process and instrument malfunction, and so on. They are taken on a daily basis. In order to test the performance of the proposed evolving intelligent sensor in conditions close to the reality, the raw data has not been filtered out. The inputs for the modeling are:

- Temperatures
- Flow rates
- Pressures of the tower
- Stream injections
- Unit throughput
- Crude density

Four different eSensors were designed, one for each of the variables of interest to be estimated (see section 17.3.2.1). Note that alternatively one can design also a single eSensor with four outputs using the property of eTS + to be suitable for multi-input-multi-output (MIMO) problems (Angelov et al., 2004). In this study we have developed four separate eSensors using *all* available measurable variables and letting eSensor select the most suitable input variables online. Note that the tests were performed in a simulated online mode, but real-life experiments are currently taking place at the CPESA.

In Figure 17.8, eSensor predicts the value of *Thn* (respectively the other quality parameters) based on the measured online (by hard sensors) temperatures, pressures, and so forth. The input variables selection block automatically reduces the number of input

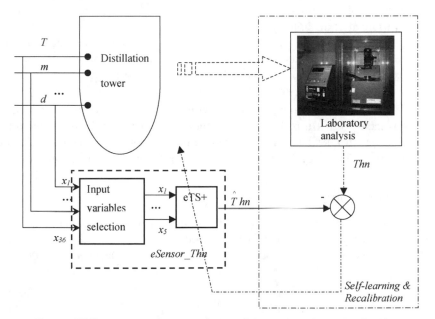

**Figure 17.8.** Schematic representation of the proposed eSensor for *Thn*.

variables based on their contribution as described in Chapters 2 and 14 (section 14.5) into a smaller number of inputs that contribute most to the prediction. From time to time, recalibration of eSensor is needed (the right-hand side of Figure 17.8). This is done automatically without retraining of the model in terms of a change of the structure, but rather as a smooth correction. This process (recalibration) also does not require human involvement and expertise and thus reduces the maintenance and life-cycle costs significantly.

The proposed evolving inferential sensors have two main modes of operation: (1) prediction or estimation, and (2) recalibration (self-learning). Initially, the second mode is active to build (evolve) the structure (fuzzy rule base) of the sensor automatically online. This requires a relatively small number of training samples.

The experiment includes a simulated online mode of operation with initial sensor design stage (learning the rule base) based on a certain limited number of samples (90 samples that correspond to three months of work of the refinery) and a recalibration phase of 60 samples (two months of operation of the refinery) starting at sample 271 (that is, after half a year of prediction with a fixed model). The whole data set consists of 447 daily measurements taken at CEPSA Oil Refinery, Santa Cruz de Tenerife, a few years ago. The results compare three modes:

1. A limited period of learning (90 samples) followed by fixing the structure of the soft sensor (fuzzy rule base) for the remaining period. In this mode, laboratory samples are used for a limited period only (90 samples) and the error is calculated in the remaining period (when only inputs are measured, that is, for samples 91-447).

2. A limited learning period as described above, followed by recalibration with duration of 60 samples starting at sample 271 and predictions with a fixed structure after the initial learning period up to sample 270 and after sample 330 (until sample 447). In this mode, laboratory samples are used for two limited periods (the first 90 samples and 60 samples after half a year of operation with a fixed model). The errors are also calculated in two separate periods (B1, errors for samples 91–270; B2, errors for samples 331–447).

3. Continuous recalibration, which always uses laboratory samples. The benefit of this mode is that it makes one-step-ahead (one day) prediction of the quality parameter in question, but it does not save the laborious work of taking laboratory samples. This mode can also be used as a benchmark for performance.

## 17.4.2 Results and Analysis

The performance of the proposed evolving inferential sensor was validated using an error criterion commonly used in the industry, based on the standard deviation over the absolute errors between the real outputs and the prediction (Macias et al., 2003):

$$\varepsilon^2 = \frac{1}{N-1} \sum_{i=1}^{N-1} (e-|e|)^2 \qquad (17.1)$$

**T A B L E 17.2.** Results for Prediction of Crude Oil Distillation

| Output | Mode | # Rules | # Inputs | $\varepsilon$ |
|--------|------|---------|----------|---|
| *Thn*,°C | A | 4 | 5 | 3.8680 |
|          | B1 | 4 | 5 | 3.6798 |
|          | B2 | 4 | 5 | **3.7335** |
|          | C | 5 | 5 | 3.6927 |
| *Tk*,°C | A | 5 | 9 | 2.5346 |
|         | B1 | 5 | 9 | 2.7671 |
|         | B2 | 3 | 9 | **1.7298** |
|         | C | 3 | 8 | 2.5398 |
| *A*,°C | A | 2 | 6 | 2.4888 |
|        | B1 | 2 | 6 | 2.6546 |
|        | B2 | 3 | 6 | **2.2785** |
|        | C | 2 | 5 | 2.3370 |
| *Tgol*,°C | A | 3 | 7 | 3.6108 |
|           | B1 | 3 | 7 | 4.3209 |
|           | B2 | 3 | 7 | **3.0100** |
|           | C | 3 | 7 | 4.1041 |

where *e* is the value of the error, *N* is the number of samples taken into account, and $|e|$ is the absolute error. The results are summarized in Table 17.2.

Mode A is the typical way of using inferential sensors where a period of design (in this experiment, 90 samples) is followed by a period of usage of the sensor with a fixed structure and no retraining. The proposed evolving inferential sensor can work in this mode as a self-learning fuzzy rule-based sensor benefiting from the automatic way of developing its own structure (fuzzy rule base) from the data stream alone.

After a period of usage (in this experiment, 180 samples, i.e., half a year of exploitation), a recalibration of the sensor may be required. The proposed eSensor can recalibrate automatically, which corresponds to mode B2 (in this experiment, for a period of 60 samples the target values were provided based on laboratory analysis). eSensor was able to evolve its structure as demonstrated in Figure 17.9 and change the number of rules (as seen in the cases of *Tk* and *A* in Table 17.2 and in the latter case of Figure 17.10) using the mechanisms described in more detail in Chapter 2 and also in Angelov (2006). As a result, the performance of the proposed evolving inferential sensor in mode B2 improved in comparison to mode A, as seen in the last column in Table 17.2, most notably for the case of *Tk*.

Finally, an alternative mode (mode C) is also possible where the target value is provided each time (the way this mode is assumed to work is similar to the adaptive control systems) (Astrom & Wittenmark, 1989); namely, at each instant in time a prediction of the quality parameter is made based on the respective inputs, and at the next time instant (in this experiment, the next day) the target value of the output is provided to the model/sensor (in this experiment, based on the laboratory analysis) for training the sensor before the prediction of the next value. The downside of this mode is that it assumes that laboratory analysis goes in parallel with the use of the inferential sensor, which obviously is not cost

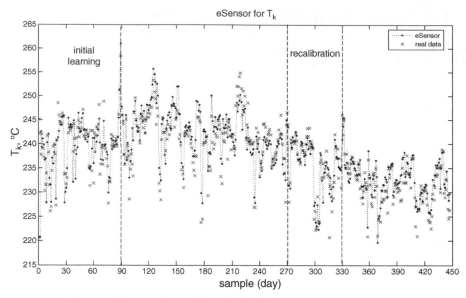

**Figure 17.9.** Evolving inferential sensor of the Abel inflammability index.

effective. As seen in Table 17.2, however, the evolving inferential sensor working in mode B can achieve without using laboratory analysis (apart from the short periods of learning and recalibration) almost the same or even better (as for B2 for *Tk, A,* and *Tgol*) results in terms of precision. Additionally, the proposed evolving inferential sensor has a very

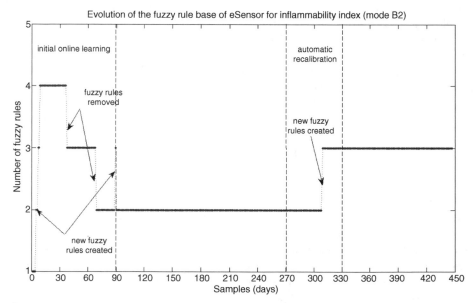

**Figure 17.10.** Evolution of the fuzzy rule base for eSensor of the Abel inflammability index.

intuitive and transparent structure with a small (two to five) number of fuzzy rules. The fuzzy rule base after the end of the learning (90th sample) for the estimation of the Abel inflammability index of the kerosene looks like this:

R1: *IF* (*P is* 5.4%) *AND* (*Tco is* 323.3 °*C*) *AND* . . . *AND* (*Tne is* 126.8 °*C*)*THEN* (A1 = 20.01 + 10.20*P* + 0.05*Tco* + 0.12*Tne*)

R2: *IF* (*P is* 11.7%) *AND* (*Tco is* 365.0 °*C*) *AND* . . . *AND* (*Tne is* 147.6 °*C*)*THEN* (A2 = 39.33 + 19.10*P* + 0.09*Tco* + 0.18*Tne*)

## 17.5 DISCUSSION

The implementation of EISs has a huge potential for applications in the O&G industry at different stages of the process and management. Due to market pressure, they have to use better tools oriented to quality monitoring, prediction, and diagnosis. In the specific case of refining, our proposal is to identify the key applications that can be solved successfully using EISs and others that may be interesting to test in the near future.

The oil refining industry is very complex. Because of the nature of this complexity there are numerous opportunities for implementation of EIS. The information available in the oil refinery has several inherent characteristics: a high number of variables and a small range of variation, and highly collinear and noisy data. Most of the time, there is no clear relation between the data and type of feed. These factors increase uncertainty and noise.

The tools that are most commonly used include soft analyzer, model building, and time-series predictors. The use of fuzzy rule-based systems is suitable for operator advisory systems in normal and emergency situations. An alarm management tool can be a special case of this application. Control engineering is one of the activities with the highest number of opportunities for implementation of EISs. It is very well suited for hybrid control, mixing between conventional control theory and fuzzy systems.

Essentially, opportunities for application of EISs exist in nearly every department of the O&G industry, namely, in plant operations, process engineering, control engineering, predictive maintenance, price prediction, information management, and advanced intelligent sensors.

## 17.6 CONCLUSION

Various EISs offer numerous opportunities such as:

- Fault detection and machine health monitoring and prognostics (e.g., by eClustering + and eTS +, as reported in Filev and Tseng (2006))
- Time-series prediction (price, variables of interest, etc), e.g., by eTS +)
- Classification (e.g., products) by eClass (Angelov & Zhou, 2008b))
- Adaptive intelligent control (e.g., by eControl) (Angelov, 2002)
- Adaptive rule-base of initial conditions (e.g., as described in Filev et al., (2000)).

In this chapter, an overall analysis and overview of all the opportunities is given and a more detailed study of the special case of the evolving intelligent eSensor for oil refining product-quality monitoring is presented. The approach for online input selection has also been demonstrated to provide an automatic selection of a small subset of important input variables. The proposed eSensor is just one possible implementation of EIS techniques to the O&G industry, which provides an automatic, low-maintenance (in fact, self-maintaining), high-performance technical solution.

## 17.7 ACKNOWLEDGMENT

The authors would like to thank Mr. Xiaowei Zhou for his assistance in performing part of the numerical experiments.

## 17.8 REFERENCES

Angelov, P. (2002). *Evolving Rule-Based Models: A Tool for Design of Flexible Adaptive Systems*. Heidelberg, New York: Springer-Verlag, ISBN 3-7908-1457-1.

Angelov, P., D. Filev (2004). "An Approach to On-line Identification of Takagi-Sugeno Fuzzy Models," *IEEE Trans. on System, Man, and Cybernetics, Part B—Cybernetics*, Vol. 34, No. 1, pp. 484–498, ISSN 1094-6977.

Angelov, P., C. Xydeas, D. Filev (2004). "On-line Identification of MIMO Evolving Takagi-Sugeno Fuzzy Models." *Int. Joint Conf. on Neural Networks and Int. Conf. on Fuzzy Systems, IJCNN-FUZZ-IEEE*, Budapest, Hungary, July 25–29, pp. 55–60, ISBN 0-7803-8354-0.

Angelov, P. (2006). "Machine Learning (Collaborative Systems)," patent WO2008053161 (priority date—November 1, 2006).

Angelov, P., X. Zhou (2006). "Evolving Fuzzy Systems from Data Streams in Real-Time." *Proc. 2006 Int. Symp. on Evolving Fuzzy Systems,* Ambleside, UK, September 7–9, IEEE Press, pp. 29–35, ISBN 0-7803-9719-3.

Angelov, P., X. Zhou (2008a). "On Line Learning Fuzzy Rule-based System Structure from Data Streams." *Proc. World Congress on Computational Intelligence, WCCI-2008*, Hong Kong, June 1–6, IEEE Press, pp. 915–922, ISBN 978-1-4244-1821-3/08.

Angelov, P., X. Zhou (2008b). "Evolving Fuzzy Rule-Based Classifiers from Data Streams," *IEEE Trans. on Fuzzy Systems*, ISSN 1063-6706, special issue on evolving fuzzy systems, Dec. 2008, Vol. 16, No. 6, pp. 1462–1475.

Angelov, P., A. Kordon, X. Zhou (2008). "Evolving Fuzzy Inferential Sensors for Process Industry." *Proc. 3rd Int. Workshop on Genetic and Evolving Fuzzy Systems,* Witten-Bomerholz, Germany, March 4–7, IEEE Press, pp. 41–46, ISBN 978-1-4244-1613-4.

Astrom, K. J., B. Wittenmark (1989). *Adaptive Control*. Reading, MA: Addison-Wesley.

Barsamian, A., Macías, J. (1998). "Neural Network-Based Inferential Property Predictors," *Hydrocarbon Processing*, Vol. 77, No. 10, pp. 107–116.

Bhat, S., D. Chatterjee, N. Saraf (2003). "On-line Data Processing and Product Properties Prediction for Crude Distillation Units." *AIChe 2003 Spring National Meeting*, New Orleans, LA, pp. 1–19.

Camacho, E. F., C. Bordons (1999). *Model Predictive Control*. London: Springer, ISBN 3-540-76241-8.

EC (2007). "NMP-2008-3.2—2 Self-Learning Production Systems: Work Programme on Nano-sciences, Nanotechnologies, Materials, and New Production Technologies," available at ftp://ard.huji.ac.il/pub/251/NMP_Fiche_small__2008_02.pdf.

ERTC (2004). *Conf. Proc. ERTC 2004, London, May 2004.*

Filev, D. P., T. Larsson, L. Ma (2000). "Intelligent Control for Automotive Manufacturing—Rule-Based Guided Adaptation." *IEEE Conf. IECON-2000*, Nagoya, Japan, October, pp. 283–288.

Filev, D., T. Tseng (2006). "Novelty Detection-Based Machine Health Prognostics." *Proc. 2006 Int. Symp. on Evolving Fuzzy Systems*, IEEE Press, pp. 193–199.

Fortuna, L., S. Graziani, A. Rizzo, M. G. Xibilia (2007). "Soft Sensor for Monitoring and Control of Industrial Processes." *Advances in Industrial Control Series* ( M. J. Grimble, M. A. Johnson, eds.). Berlin: Springer-Verlag.

Goel, K., Prashant, Y. (1999). "Leveraging Knowledge Capital in Oil Refineries through Intelligent Systems." *Proc. Int. Conf. PETROTECH 99.*

Kordon, A., G. Smits (2001). "Soft Sensor Development Using Genetic Programming." *Proc. GECCO'2001*, San Francisco, pp. 1346–1351.

Kordon, A., G. Smits, A. Kalos, E. Jordaan (2003). "Robust Soft Sensor Development Using Genetic Programming." *Nature-Inspired Methods in Chemometrics* ( R. Leardied.). Amsterdam: Elsevier, pp. 69–108.

Li, W., H. H. Yue, S. Valle-Cervantes, S. J. Qin (2000). "Recursive PCA for Adaptive Process Monitoring. *J. Process Control*, Vol. 10, No. 5, pp. 471–486.

Macías, J. (1998). "Application de la técnica de calibración PLS al control y modelado de Processos". PhD Thesis. University of La Laguna, Tenerife, Spain.

Macías-Hernández, J. (2001). "Design of a Production Expert System to Improve Refinery Process Operations. *European Symposium on Intelligent Technologies, Hybrid Systems, and Their Implementation on Smart Adaptive Systems*, Puerto de la Cruz, Tenerife, Spain, December 13–14, EUNITE 2001, pp. 63–68.

Macias, J., J. Feliu, A. Bosch (2003). "Simulation Workbench between HYSYS Rigorous Model and Its NN Extension: Case Study of a Complex Simulation with Re-circulation," *Proc. 4th European Congress on Chemical Engineering, ECCE 4*, ISBN: 84-88233-31-0.

Qin, S. J., H. Yue, R. Dunia (1997). "Self-Validating Inferential Sensors with Application to Air Emission Monitoring," *Industrial Engineering Chemistry Research*, Vol. 36, pp. 1675–1685.

Rallo, R., J. Ferre-Gine, A. Arena, F. Girault (2004). "Neural Virtual Sensor for the Inferential Prediction of Product Quality from Process Variables, *Computers and Chemical Engineering*, Vol. 26, pp. 1735–1754.

Rodriguez, M., J. J. Rubio, A. Jimenez (1997). "Naphta Cut Point Inference Using Neural Networks." In *Neural Networks in Engineering Systems* (A. B. Bulsari, S. Kallio,eds.), Stockholm, Sweden, June, www.diquima.upm.es/recursos/docs/homme.pdf.

Smits, G., A. Kordon, E. Jordaan, C. Vladislavleva, M. Kotanchek (2006). "Variable Selection in Industrial Data Sets Using Pareto Genetic Programming." In *Genetic Programming Theory and Practice III* (T. Yu, R. Riolo, B. Worzel,eds.). New York: Springer, pp. 79–92.

White, D. C. (2001). "The 'Smart Plant' Refinery: Economics and Technology." *NPRA Annual Meeting*, San Antonio, Texas, March 23–25, AM-03-19.

White, D. C. (2003). "Creating the 'Smart Plant.'" *Hydrocarbon Processing*, October 2003, pp. 41–50.

Yan, W., H. Shao, X. Wang (2004). "Soft Sensing Modelling Based on Support Vector Machine and Bayesian Model Selection," *Computers and Chemical Engineering*, Vol. 28, pp. 1489–1498.

# EPILOGUE

The aim of this edited volume is to set the stage and to outline the methodology and potential for applications of the emerging area of research that targets intelligent systems that can adapt and evolve in response to the dynamics of the environment and data patterns. No doubt more publications will follow that will detail various aspects of this new research discipline, which lies on the crossroads of well-established branches of science and technology such as machine learning, fuzzy logic systems, system identification, control, classification, clustering, and neural networks.

The first part of the book provides a systematic outline of the current state of the art in the main pillars of the new discipline of *evolving intelligent systems*, namely;

- Evolving fuzzy rule-based systems
- Evolving neuro-fuzzy systems
- Evolving clustering and classification

Part II barely touches the surface of the vast area of potential industrial applications. There are already a large number of papers and applications of *evolving intelligent systems* in areas as diverse as car manufacturing, robotics (self-learning and mapping, navigation, image processing), biomedical data processing, brain science, and speech processing. For various reasons, not all of them have been included, but our belief is that this aspect will be growing and will become the engine of further development in this newly emerging field of research, posing new problems and bringing new followers. For example, problems of user behavior modeling, autonomous systems, and intruder detection are some areas in great need of further development of adaptive, self-learning, yet intelligent approaches where the adaptation is not simply limited to model parameter tuning. This new concept reflects the fact that new behavior, new features of the environment or autonomous systems (e.g. machine health), new tactics of intruders, and new states of a system may develop, or that previously existing ones can change/evolve. Thus, it goes far beyond the well-known and exploited concepts of adaptive (primarily linear) systems and learning in the sense of tuning a prespecified fixed structure model.

*Evolving Intelligent Systems: Methodology and Applications,* Edited by Plamen Angelov, Dimitar P. Filev, and Nikola Kasabov
Copyright © 2010 Institute of Electrical and Electronics Engineers

The firm belief of the editors is that although this book is merely a step in the direction of development of this new field, yet it provides readers with a solid background of methodological and applied knowledge and fresh ideas that are needed for innovation and progress.

*Lancaster, UK*
*Detroit, Michigan, USA*
*Auckland, New Zealand*
*February 2010*

# ABOUT THE EDITORS

**Plamen Angelov** is a Senior Lecturer (Associate Professor) at Lancaster University, UK. Prior to that he spent over 10 years as a researcher working on computational intelligence and advanced modeling and control problems. He holds an MEng in Electronics and Automation (1989), and a PhD in Optimal Control (1993). He has been a visiting researcher at the Catholic University of Leuvain-la-neuve, Belgium (1997) and Hans Knoell Institute, Jena, Germany (1995/6). He was a research fellow at Loughborough University from 1998 to 2003, when he was appointed at Lancaster University. He authored and co-authored over 120 peer-reviewed publications, including a research monograph, "Evolving Rule-based Models: A Tool for Design of Flexible Adaptive Systems" (Springer, 2002), two edited volumes (IEEE Press, 2002 and 2006), over 30 journal papers, and a patent (2006). He is Co-Editor-in-Chief of Springer's Journal on Evolving Systems and on the editorial board of three other international scientific journals. He is senior member of IEEE and a member of the Technical Committee on Fuzzy Systems, chair of two and a member of two more task forces within the IEEE Computational Intelligence Society. He is also a member of the Autonomous Systems Working Group of the North-West Science Council of UK (a business-academia advisory group to the regional development agency, and on the National Technical Committee, UK on Autonomous Systems). He serves regularly on the technical/program committees of leading international conferences on different aspects of computational intelligence (over 60 for the last 5 years) and holds a portfolio of research projects, including a participation in a £32 million program ASTRAEA, with funding from industry, EU, UK Research Council, and so on. He supervises, a number of postdoctoral researchers and PhD students. His research interests are in adaptive and evolving (self-organizing) systems that posses computational intelligence. He is especially interested in and has pioneered online and real-time identification and design of systems with evolving (self-developing) structure and intelligent data processing, particularly in evolving fuzzy rule-based models, self-organizing and autonomous systems, intelligent (inferential) sensors, and optimization and optimal control in a fuzzy environment.

**Dimitar P. Filev** is Senior Technical Leader, Intelligent Control & Information Systems, with Ford Research & Advanced Engineering, specializing in intelligent systems and technologies for control, diagnostics, and decision making. He has published three books, and over 180 articles in refereed journals and conference proceedings. He holds 14 granted U.S. patents and numerous foreign patents in the area of industrial intelligent

*Evolving Intelligent Systems: Methodology and Applications,* Edited by Plamen Angelov, Dimitar P. Filev, and Nikola Kasabov
Copyright © 2010 Institute of Electrical and Electronics Engineers

systems. Dr. Filev is a recipient of the 1995 Award for Excellence of MCB University Press and was four times awarded the Henry Ford Technology Award for development and implementation of advanced technologies. He is associate editor of *International Journal of General Systems, International Journal of Approximate Reasoning*, and *International Journal of Applied Mathematics and Computer Science*. He is president of the North American Fuzzy Information Processing Society (NAFIPS). He is a fellow of IEEE and served on the board of the IEEE Systems, Man & Cybernetics Society. He is a vice chair of the IEEE CIS Technical Committee on Fuzzy Systems. Dr. Filev received his PhD. in Electrical Engineering from the Czech Technical University in Prague in 1979. Prior to joining Ford in 1994, he was with the Bulgarian Academy of Sciences—Sofia, Bulgaria, and Iona College and the Machine Intelligence Institute—New Rochelle, New York.

**Nikola Kasabov** is founding director and chief scientist of the Knowledge Engineering and Discovery Research Institute (KEDRI), Auckland (www.kedri.info/). He holds a Chair of Knowledge Engineering at the School of Computing and Mathematical Sciences at Auckland University of Technology. He is a fellow of the Royal Society of New Zealand, fellow of the New Zealand Computer Society, and a senior member of IEEE. He is the president of the International Neural Network Society (INNS) and the immediate president of the Asia Pacific Neural Network Assembly (APNNA). He is a member of several technical committees of the IEEE Computational Intelligence Society and of the IFIP AI TC12. Kasabov is associate editor of several international journals, including *Neural Networks, IEEE TrNN, IEEE TrFS, Information Science, and J. Theoretical and Computational Nanosciences*. He chairs a series of international conferences, ANNES/NCEI in New Zealand. Kasabov holds MSc and PhD from the Technical University of Sofia, Bulgaria. His main research interests are in the areas of neural networks, intelligent information systems, soft computing, neurocomputing, bioinformatics, brain study, speech and image processing, novel methods for data mining, and knowledge discovery. He has published more than 400 publications, including 15 books, 120 journal papers, 60 book chapters, 32 patents, and numerous conference papers. He has extensive academic experience at various academic and research organizations: University of Otago, New Zealand; University of Essex, UK; University of Trento, Italy; Technical University of Sofia, Bulgaria; University of California at Berkeley; RIKEN and KIT, Japan; University Kaiserslautern, Germany, and others. Among the awards received by Professor Kasabov are the RSNZ Science and Technology Medal, the 2007 Bayer Science Innovator Award, the APNNA Excellent Service Award, and two IEEE conferences best paper awards. More information on Professor Kasabov can be found on the KEDRI web site: www.kedri.info.

# ABOUT THE CONTRIBUTORS

## CHAPTER 1

**Ronald R. Yager** has worked in the area of fuzzy sets and related disciplines of computational intelligence for over 25 years. He has published over 500 papers and 15 books. He was the recipient of the IEEE Computational Intelligence Society Pioneer award in fuzzy systems. Dr. Yager is a fellow of the IEEE, the New York Academy of Sciences, and the Fuzzy Systems Association. He was given an award by the Polish Academy of Sciences for his contributions. He served at the National Science Foundation as program director in the Information Sciences program. He was a NASA/Stanford visiting fellow and a research associate at the University of California—Berkeley. He has been a lecturer at NATO Advanced Study Institutes. He received his undergraduate degree from the City College of New York and his PhD from the Polytechnic University of New York. Currently, he is director of the Machine Intelligence Institute and Professor of Information and Decision Technologies at Iona College. He is editor and chief of the *International Journal of Intelligent Systems*. He serves on the editorial board of a number of journals, including the *IEEE Transactions on Fuzzy Systems, Neural Networks, Data Mining and Knowledge Discovery, IEEE Intelligent Systems, Fuzzy Sets and Systems*, the *Journal of Approximate Reasoning*, and the *International Journal of General Systems*. In addition to his pioneering work in the area of fuzzy logic, he has made fundamental contributions to decision making under uncertainty and the fusion of information.

## CHAPTER 3

**Witold Pedrycz** received his M.Sc., PhD, and DSc all from the Silesian University of Technology, Gliwice, Poland. He is a Professor and Canada Research Chair (CRC) in Computational Intelligence in the Department of Electrical and Computer Engineering, University of Alberta, Edmonton, Canada. He is also with the Polish Academy of Sciences, Systems Research Institute, Warsaw, Poland.

His research interests encompass computational intelligence, fuzzy modeling, knowledge discovery and data mining, and fuzzy control, including fuzzy controllers, pattern recognition, knowledge-based neural networks, granular and relational computing, and software engineering. He has published numerous papers in these areas. He

*Evolving Intelligent Systems: Methodology and Applications,* Edited by Plamen Angelov, Dimitar P. Filev, and Nikola Kasabov

has also authored 12 research monographs. Witold Pedrycz has been a member of numerous program committees of IEEE conferences in the area of fuzzy sets and neurocomputing. He serves as editor-in-chief of *IEEE Transactions on Systems, Man, and Cybernetics*—Part A, and associate editor of *IEEE Transactions on Fuzzy Systems*. He is also editor-in-chief of *Information Sciences*. Dr. Pedrycz is a recipient of the prestigious Norbert Wiener award from the IEEE Society of Systems, Man, and Cybernetics and an IEEE Canada Silver Medal in computer engineering.

## CHAPTER 4

**Rosangela Ballini** received her BSc in Applied Mathematics from the Federal University of São Carlos (UFSCar), SP, Brazil, in 1996. In 1998, she received an MSc in Mathematics and Computer Science from the University of São Paulo (USP), SP, Brazil, and a PhD in Electrical Engineering from the State University of Campinas (UNICAMP), SP, Brazil, in 2000. Currently, she is Professor at the Department of Economic Theory, Institute of Economics (IE), UNICAMP. Her research interests include time-series forecasting, neural networks, fuzzy systems, and nonlinear optimization. She is a member of the IEEE Task Force on Adaptive Fuzzy Systems.

**Fernando Gomide** received a BSc in Electrical Engineering from the Polytechnic Institute of the Pontifical Catholic University of Minas Gerais (IPUC, PUC-MG), Belo Horizonte, Brazil, an MSc in Electrical Engineering from the University of Campinas (UNICAMP), Campinas, Brazil, a PhD in Systems Engineering from Case Western Reserve University (CWRU), Cleveland, Ohio. He is Professor of the Department of Computer Engineering and Automation (DCA), Faculty of Electrical and Computer Engineering (FEEC) of UNICAMP, since 1983. His interests include fuzzy systems, neural and evolutionary computation, modeling, control and optimization, logistics, multiagent systems, decision making, and applications. He is past vice president of IFSA (International Fuzzy Systems Association), past IFSA secretary, and member of the editorial board of *IEEE Transactions on SMC—B*. Currently, he serves on the board of NAFIPS (North American Fuzzy Information Processing Society) and the editorial boards of *Fuzzy Sets and Systems, Intelligent Automation and Soft Computing, IEEE Transactions on SMC—A, Fuzzy Optimization and Decision Making, International Journal of Fuzzy Systems*, and *Mathware and Soft Computing*. He is a past editor of *Controle & Automação*, the journal of the Brazilian Society for Automatics (SBA), the Brazilian National Member Organization of IFAC, and IFSA. He is on the advisory board of the *International Journal of Uncertainty, Fuzziness and Knowledge-Based Systems, Journal of Advanced Computational Intelligence*, and *Intelligent Automation and Soft Computing*, and member of the IEEE Task Force on Adaptive Fuzzy Systems, IEEE Emergent Technology Technical Committee.

**Michael Hell** received the B.Sc. degree in electrical engineering from the Polytechnic Institute of the Pontifical Catholic University of Minas Gerais (IPUC, PUC-MG)

Belo Horizonte, Brazil, the M.Sc. degree in electrical engineering from the Graduate Program in Electrical Engineering of the Pontifical Catholic University of Minas Gerais (PPGEE, PUC-MG) Belo Horizonte, Brazil. He got his Ph.D. degree in Electrical Engineering from the University of Campinas (Unicamp), Campinas, Brazil. His current research interest areas include nonlinear system modeling, computational intelligence, fault detection and isolation, power systems and electrical devices.

**Elton Lima** received his BSc in Applied Mathematics and Computation from the State University of Campinas (UNICAMP), SP, Brazil, in 2006. In 2008, he received an MSc in Electrical Engineering from the State University of Campinas (UNICAMP), SP, Brazil. His research interests include time-series forecasting and fuzzy systems.

## CHAPTER 5

**Edwin Lughofer** recieved his MS (1997) and PhD degrees (2005) at the Department of Knowledge-Based Mathematical Systems, University of Linz, Austria and is now employed as post-doc and research assistant. During the past five years, he has participated in several research projects, such as EU-project DynaVis and EU-project AMPA (Automatic Measurement Plausibility and Quality Assurance). He has published several journal and conference papers in the fields of evolving fuzzy systems, incremental (online) learning, fault detection, and image processing and clustering, and a monograph "Evolving Fuzzy Models" (published by Verlag Dr. Müller).

Research visits and stays include the following locations: Center for Bioimage Informatics and Departments of Biological Sciences, Biomedical Engineering, and Machine Learning, Carnegie Mellon University, Pittsburgh, Pennsylvania; Faculty for Informatics (ITI) at Otto-von-Guericke-Universität, Magdeburg (Germany); Department of Communications Systems InfoLab21 at Lancaster University, UK; and Institute for Computational Intelligence and Bioinformatics, Phillips University Marburg (Germany). In September 2006, he received the best-paper award for the invited paper, "Process safety enhancements for data-driven evolving fuzzy models" at the International Symposium on Evolving Fuzzy Systems. In February 2007, he visited (Royal Society grant) Lancaster University to study evolving fuzzy systems. In March 2008, he recieved the best finalist award together with co-author Carlos Guardiola, for the paper, "Applying evolving fuzzy models with adaptive local error bars to on-line fault detection" at the Third International Workshop on Genetic and Evolving Fuzzy Systems.

## CHAPTER 6

**António Dourado** is full Professor in the Department of Informatics Engineering of the University of Coimbra and head of the research group in adaptive computation of the Center for Informatics and Systems of the University of Coimbra. He has an Electrical

Engineering degree (1977), PhD in Automatique (LAAS du CNRS and Université Paul Sabatier, Toulouse, 1983), and Pós-Doc degree in Aggregation (University of Coimbra, 1997). He is presently teaching theory of computation, soft computing, systems and control theory, and information processing to Informatics Engineering and Biomedical Engineering students at University of Coimbra. His research interests are soft computing, neural networks, fuzzy systems, data mining, real-time learning, and systems diagnosis and control in biomedical and industrial applications. He has more than 200 publications in refeered international books, journals, and conferences.

**Carlos Pereira** is Assistant Professor in the Department of Informatics Engineering and Systems of the Polytechnic Institute of Coimbra and a member of the research group in adaptive computation of the Center for Informatics and Systems of the University of Coimbra. He has an Informatics Engineering degree, a Master's degree in Systems and Automation, and a PhD in Informatics Engineering from the University of Coimbra. His current research interests are computational intelligence, neural networks, fuzzy systems, kernel machines, and bioinformatics.

**José Victor Ramos** is Assistant professor in the Department of Informatics Engineering of the Polytechnic Institute of Leiria. and a member of the research group in adaptive computation of the Center for Informatics and Systems of the University of Coimbra. He has a BSc and MSc in Informatics Engineering from the University of Coimbra. His research interest is computational intelligence.

## CHAPTER 7

**Seiichi Ozawa** received BE and ME degrees in Instrumentation Engineering from Kobe University, Kobe, Japan, in 1987 and 1989, respectively. In 1998, he received his PhD in computer science from Kobe University. He is currently an associate professor with Graduate School of Engineering, Kobe University. His primary research interests include neural networks, machine learning, intelligent data processing, and pattern recognition.

**Shaoning Pang** is the director of center for adaptive pattern recognition systems, Knowledge Engineering and Discovery research Institute (KEDRI), Auckland University of Technology, New Zealand. His research interests include SVM aggregating intelligence, incremental & multi-task learning, Bioinformatics, and adaptive soft computing for industrial applications. He has been serving as a program member and session chair for several international conferences including ISNN, ICONIP, ICNNSP, IJCNN, and WCCI. He was a best paper winner of IEEE ICNNSP 2003, IEEE DMAI2008, and an invited speaker of BrainIT 2007 and ICONIP2009. He is acting as a guest editor of Journal of Memetic Computing, Springer, and a regular paper reviewer for a number of refeered international journals including IEEE Trans on NN, TKDE, SMC-B. Dr. Pang is a Senior Member of IEEE, and a Member of IEICE, and ACM.

## CHAPTER 8

**José de Jesús Rubio** was born in México City in 1979. He graduated in Electronic Engineering from the Institute Politecnico Nacional in México in 2001. He received his Master's degree in automatic control in the CINVESTAV IPN in México in 2004 and his doctorate in Automic Control in the CINVESTAV IPN in México in 2007. He was Assistant Professor in the Autonomous Metropolitan University—Mexico City from 2006 to 2008. Since 2008, he is Assistant Professor of the Sección de Estudios de Posgrado e Investigación—Instituto Politécnico Nacional—ESIME Azcapotzalco. He has published 6 chapters in international books and 10 papers in international magazines, and he has presented 24 papers in international conferences. He is a member of tne adaptive fuzzy systems task force. His research interests are primarily evolving intelligent systems, nonlinear and adaptive control systems, neural-fuzzy systems, mechatronics, robotics, delayed systems, and modeling.

## CHAPTER 9

**Damien Coyle** received a first class degree in computing and electronic engineering in 2002 and a doctorate in Intelligent Systems Engineering in 2006 from the University of Ulster where he is now a lecturer at the School of Computing and Intelligent Systems and a member of the Intelligent Systems Research Centre. His research and development interests include biosignal processing, bio-inspired cognitive, adaptive systems and brain-computer interface technology. More recently he has been investigating computational models of neural systems and neurodegeneration related to Alzheimer's disease (AD). Dr. Coyle chairs the UKRI chapter of the IEEE Computational intelligence Society (CIS) and is the 2008 recipient of the IEEE CIS Outstanding Doctoral Dissertation Award.

**Gang Leng** received a BS in Engineering from Hangzhou Institute of Electronic Engineering, Hangzhou, China, in 1985, an MS in Engineering from Chongqing University, Chongqing, China, in 1992, and a PhD in Computing and Intelligent Systems from University of Ulster, Londonderry, UK, in 2004.

He is currently Research associate in Lancaster University, Lancaster, UK. From 2005 to 2006, he was a postdoctoral research associate at the University of Manchester, Manchester, UK. His research interests include neural networks, fuzzy logic, genetic algorithms, system modeling, and time-series prediction.

**Martin McGinnity** has been a member of the University of Ulster academic staff since 1992, and holds the post of Professor of Intelligent Systems Engineering within the Faculty of Computing and Engineering. He has a first-class honors degree in Physics, and a doctorate from the University of Durham, and is a fellow of the IET, a member of the IEEE, and a chartered engineer. He has 28 years' experience in teaching and research in electronic and computer engineering and was formerly head of the School of Computing and Intelligent Systems at the University's Magee campus. More recently, he held the post of Acting Associate Dean of the Faculty of Engineering with responsibility for research and development, and knowledge and technology transfer. He was a founding member of the Intelligent Systems Engineering Laboratory at the Magee campus of the University, and is currently director of the Intelligent Systems Research Centre, which encompasses the research activities of over 50 researchers. He is also currently a director of the University's technology transfer company, UUTech. He is the author or co-author of over 180 research papers, and has been awarded both a Senior Distinguished Research Fellowship and a Distinguished Learning Support Fellowship by the university in recognition of his contribution to teaching and research.

His current research interests are computational intelligence and the creation of bio-inspired intelligent computational systems in general, particularly in relation to hardware and software implementations of biologically plausible artificial neural networks, fuzzy systems, genetic algorithms, embedded intelligent systems utilizing reconfigurable logic devices, brain computer interfacing, and intelligent systems in robotics.

**Girijesh Prasad** (M'98-SM'07) received the B.Tech. degree in electrical engineering from Regional Engineering College, Calicut, India, in 1987, the M.Tech. degree in computer science and technology from the University of Roorkee, India, in 1992, and the Ph.D. degree from Queen's University, Belfast, UK in 1997. He has been a member of academic staff at the University of Ulster, Magee Campus, Londonderry, UK since 1999 and holds the post of Reader. He is an executive member of Intelligent Systems Research Centre at Magee Campus where he leads the Brain-Computer Interface and Assistive Technology team. His research interests are in self-organising hybrid intelligent systems, neural computation, fuzzy neural networks, type-1 and type-2 fuzzy logic, local model networks, evolutionary algorithms, adaptive predictive modeling and control with applications in complex industrial and biological systems including brain-computer interface (BCI) and assistive robotic systems. He has published over 90 peer reviewed academic papers in international journals, books, and conference proceedings.

Dr. Prasad is a Chartered Engineer and a member of the Institution of Engineering and Technology, UK.

## CHAPTER 10

**Jianting Cao** received M Eng and PhD degrees from the Graduate School of Science and Technology, Chiba University, Japan, in 1993 and 1996, respectively. From 1996 to 1998, he worked as a researcher at the Brain Science Institute, RIKEN, in Japan. From 1998 to 2002, he was an associate, and an assistant professor, at the Sophia University in Japan. From 2002 to 2006, he was associate professor at the Saitama Institute of Technology in Japan. He is currently a professor at the Saitama Institute of Technology, and a visiting research scientist at the Brain Science Institute, RIKEN, in Japan. His research interests include blind signal processing, biomedical signal processing, neural networks, and learning algorithms.

**Ling Li** received a Bachelor's degree from the Department of Electronic Information Engineering, Tianjin University, China in 2003, and an MSc from the Department of

Electrical and Electronic Engineering, University of Liverpool, in 2004. She then worked in a leading electronic testing company, Forwessun International Ltd., as application engineer, and was later promoted to development manager. From 2006, she has been pursuing her PhD at the Department of Electronic and Electrical Engineering, Imperial College London. She is a student member of IET.

**David Looney** obtained a BEng in Electronic Engineering from University College Dublin (UCD), Ireland, in 2005. He is currently pursuing his PhD at Imperial College London. His research interests are machine learning for signal processing, in particular, the fusion of heterogeneous data sources and multichannel processing.

**Danilo P. Mandic** is a reader in signal processing at Imperial College London. He has been working in the area of nonlinear adaptive signal processing and nonlinear dynamics. His publication record includes two research monographs ("Recurrent Neural Networks for Prediction," and "Complex Valued Nonlinear Adaptive Filters") with Wiley, an edited book, *Signal Processing for Information Fusion* (Springer, 2007), and more than 200 publications in signal and image processing. He has been a member of the IEEE Technical Committee on Machine Learning for Signal Processing, and associate editor of *IEEE Transactions on Circuits and Systems II, IEEE Transactions on Signal Processing, IEEE Transactions on Neural Networks*, and *International Journal of Mathematical Modelling and Algorithms*. Dr. Mandic has produced award-winning papers and products resulting from his collaboration with industry. He is a senior member of the IEEE and member of the London Mathematical Society. Dr. Mandic has been a guest professor in KU Leuven Belgium, TUAT Tokyo, Japan, and Westminster University, UK, and frontier researcher in RIKEN Japan.

**Yuki Saito** received the B.E. and the M.E. degrees from the Tokyo University of Agriculture and Technology, Tokyo, Japan, in 2007 and 2009, respectively. He is currently with Sony, Tokyo.

**Toshihisa Tanaka** received the B.E., the M.E., and the Ph.D. degrees from the Tokyo Institute of Technology in 1997, 2000, and 2002, respectively. From 2000 to 2002, he was a JSPS Research Fellow. From Oct. 2002 to Mar. 2004, he was a Research Scientist at RIKEN Brain Science Institute. In Apr. 2004, he joined Department of Electrical and Electronic Engineering, Tokyo University of Agriculture and Technology, where he is currently an Associate Professor. His research interests include image and signal processing, multirate systems, blind signal separation, brain signal processing, and adaptive signal processing. In 2005, he was a Royal Society Visiting Fellow at the Communications and Signal Processing Group, Imperial College London, U.K. He is a co-editor of "Signal Processing Techniques for Knowledge Extraction and Information Fusion" (with Mandic, Splinger), 2008. He has been a member of the Technical Committee on Blind Signal Processing, IEEE Circuits and Systems Society since 2005 and a member of the Technical Group on Signal Processing, IEICE Engineering Science Society since 2006.

## CHAPTER 11

**Gancho Vachkov** graduated from the Technical University in Sofia, Bulgaria; Department of Automation of Industry, in 1970, and obtained his PhD in Analysis of Complex Technological Systems in 1978. From 1970 until 1995, he has been with the Department of Automation of Industry of the University of Chemical Technology and Metallurgy (UCTM) in Sofia, as Associate Professor. Since September 1996 he has been working in Japan with the following three universities: Kitami Institute of Technology: 1996–1998 (Associate Professor, Department of Chemical Systems Engineering); Nagoya University (professor, Department of Micro-System Engineering): 1998–2002; and Kagawa University (Visiting Professor, Department of Reliability-based Information Systems Engineering): 2002–present.

Gancho Vachkov has long-term research interests, works, and achievements in the broad area of computational intelligence, including fuzzy and neural modeling and identification, intelligent control algorithms and applications, supervised and unsupervised learning algorithms for information compression, intelligent fault diagnosis and performance evaluation of complex machines and systems, and evolving models for performance analysis and evaluation.

He has achieved original research results in solving such problems as reducing the dimensionality problem in fuzzy modeling, simplified local learning of fuzzy models, dynamic cause–effect relation-based modeling, fuzzy model-based predictive control, learning algorithms for radial basis function neural networks (RBF NN), growing and adaptive neural models for process identification, and data analysis and performance evaluation of machines and systems.

Gancho Vachkov is a member of IEEE, the Computational Intelligence Society and SMC Society, and of SOFT, the Japanese Society for Fuzzy Theory and Intelligent Informatics, as well as a member of several other Japanese scientific societies. He is also a regular program committee member and active reviewer of many worldwide international conferences and symposia on computational intelligence, soft computing, and system modeling. He has published more than 130 papers on the above topics in different journals and proceedings of various international conferences.

His most recent research results are in the area of learning algorithms for information compression and image similarity analysis, with applications for predictive maintenance and performance evaluation of complex machines and industrial systems.

## CHAPTER 12

**Olga Georgieva** received an MS in Industrial Automation from the Technical University—Sofia, Bulgaria, in 1986, and a PhD from the Institute of Control and System Research (ICSR), Bulgarian Academy of Sciences, in 1995. Since 1994, she is a researcher with the ICSR, where in 2000 she was promoted to Associate Professor. She is also a Lecturer at the Sofia University and Technical University—Sofia. Her interests include intelligent systems, process modeling, data mining, and artificial intelligence applications.

## CHAPTER 13

**Yevgeniy Bodyanskiy** received his engineer's degree in Electrical Engineering, PhD in Technical Cybernetics and Information Theory, and DSc in Control in Technical Systems, all from Kharkiv National University of Radio-Electronics, Ukraine, in 1971, 1980, and 1990, respectively. Currently he is Professor at the Artificial Intelligence department at Kharkiv National University of Radio-Electronics, where he has been since 1994, as well as head of the Control Systems Research Laboratory at the same university. He has published over 400 scientific papers and has authored seven books. His present research interests include hybrid systems of computational intelligence and their technical, medical, and biological applications.

**Yevgen Gorshkov** received his BSc, MSc, and PhD degrees in Computer Science from Kharkiv National University of Radio-Electronics, Ukraine, in 2003, 2004, and 2008, respectively. He is currently a research scientist at the Control Systems Research Laboratory of the same university. His current research interests are hybrid neuro-fuzzy systems, type-2 fuzzy systems, fuzzy clustering, and classification methods.

**Illya Kokshenev** received his BSc and MSc degrees in Computer Science from the Kharkiv National University of Radio-Electronics, Ukraine, in 2003 and 2004, respectively. He is currently a PhD student at the Department of Electronic Engineering, Federal University of Minas Gerais, Brazil. His research interests cover machine learning, neural networks, neuro-fuzzy systems, and multiobjective machine learning.

**Vitaliy Kolodyazhniy** received his MSc and PhD degrees in Control Engineering from Kharkiv National University of Radio-Electronics, Ukraine, in 1998 and 2002, respectively. In 1998–2006, he was with the Control Systems Research Laboratory of the same university, holding positions of research assistant, research scientist, and senior research scientist. In 2002–2003, he was a visiting researcher at the Institute for Automation and System Engineering of the Technical University of Ilmenau, Germany. Since July 2006, he has been a postdoctoral research fellow in pattern recognition and biomedical engineering at the Institute for Psychology of the University of Basel, Switzerland. His current research interests are in computational intelligence techniques for data analysis and nonlinear system modeling, statistics, chronobiology, and psychophysiology.

## CHAPTER 14

**Arthur Kordon** is a data mining and modeling leader in the Data Mining & Modeling Group in Corporate Work Process and Six Sigma Center, The Dow Chemical Company, in Freeport, Texas. He is an internationally recognized expert in applying computational intelligence technologies in industry. Dr. Kordon has successfully introduced several novel technologies for improved manufacturing and new product design, such as robust inferential sensors, automated operating discipline, and accelerated fundamental model building. His research interests include application issues of computational intelligence, robust empirical modeling, intelligent process monitoring and control, and data mining. He has published more than 60 papers, one book and eight book chapters in the area of applied computational intelligence and advanced control. Dr. Kordon holds a Master of Science in Electrical Engineering from the Technical University of Varna, Bulgaria, and a PhD in Electrical Engineering from the Technical University of Sofia, Bulgaria.

## CHAPTER 15

**Boyko Iliev** was born in Sofia, Bulgaria, in 1975. He graduated Technical University in Sofia in 1997 in the field of systems and control engineering. After that, he started working at the Centre for Parallel Information Processing as a research assistant/ programmer. In 1998, he started his PhD studies at Örebro University/Sweden. In February 2004, he defended his PhD thesis, "Minimum-time Sliding Mode Control of Robot Manipulators." He became a senior researcher at AASS and started working on control of robotic hands. Currently, his research interests are humanlike robotic grasping, control of robotic hands, and programming-by-demonstration of industrial robots. Boyko Iliev is author/co-author of three book chapters and/or journal articles, and author/co-author of 10 conference papers.

**Bourhane Kadmiry** is a postdoc at the Department of Technology, Örebro University. He received his PhD in Computer Science at Linköping University—Sweden and a PhD in Robotics and AI at (LAAS) Toulouse University—France. He also holds a Master of Science in Sensor Technology, Control, and AI and a Master of computer Engineering, both from Rouen Technical University—France. His research interests include autonomous helicopter navigation control, visual servoing control for autonomous helicopters, fuzzy control, and control for an artificial (prosthetic) hand. He has authored two journal articles and six fully refereed conference papers, and is a regular reviewer for international conferences. He is also project manager for Airbus aeronautic programs within Soerman Co.—Sweden.

**Rainer Palm** is adjunct professor at the Department of Technology (AASS), Örebro University since 2004. Before 2004, he was a principal research scientist in the Neural Computation Department of the Siemens Corporate Research Technology in Munich, Germany, working both in research projects and industrial applications of automatic control, fuzzy control, modeling of dynamic systems, and distributed systems.

He has been active as a control engineer since 1972, doing research and development in the field of testing machines for electronic devices. He received his Dipl. Ing. degree from the Technical University of Dresden, Germany, in 1975. Since 1982, he worked in robotic research, in particular, the field of sensor-guided robots.

Palm received the Dr. Ing. degree from Humboldt University, Berlin, Germany, in 1981, and the Dr. sc. techn. degree from the Academy of Sciences, Germany, in 1989.

Since 1991, he held a position in the fuzzy logic task force group at Siemens AG. Since 1992, he has had close cooperation with the Department of Computer Science,

Linköping University, and since 1998, with the Department of Technology (AASS), University Örebro.

Palm is author/co-author, editor/co-editor of 15 books or chapters in books, author/co-author of 19 articles in journals, and author/co-author of 35 articles in conference proceedings. He is also author/co-author of 14 patents. His research interests include automatic control, fuzzy control, and robotics. Palm was spokesman of the fuzzy group, 1994–2002, and associate editor of *IEEE Transactions on Fuzzy Systems*, 1994–2004.

## CHAPTER 16

**José Antonio Becerra** received BS and MS degrees in Computer Science from the University of A Coruña, Spain, in 1999, and a PhD in Computer Science from the same university in 2003. He is currently Associated Professor in the Department of Computer Science and member of the Integrated Group for Engineering Research at the University of La Coruña. His research activities are mainly related to autonomous robotics, evolutionary algorithms, and parallel computing.

**Francisco Bellas** is a postdoctoral researcher at the University of A Coruña, Spain. He received BS and MS degrees in Physics from the University of Santiago de Compostela, Spain, in 2001, and a PhD in Computer Science from the University of A Coruña in 2003. He is a member of the Integrated Group for Engineering Research at the University of A Coruña. Current research activities are related to evolutionary algorithms applied to artificial neural networks, multiagent systems, and robotics.

**Richard J. Duro** received an MS in Physics from the University of Santiago de Compostela, Spain, in 1989, and a PhD in Physics from the same university in 1992. He is currently a Professor in the Department of Computer Science and head of the Integrated Group for Engineering Research at the University of La Coruña. His research interests include higher-order neural network structures, signal processing, and autonomous and evolutionary robotics. He is a senior member of the IEEE.

## CHAPTER 17

**José J. Macías-Hernández** is currently manager of the Process Engineering Department at CEPSA Tenerife Oil Refinery and Associate Professor at the University of La Laguna, Tenerife, Spain, where he lectures on simulation and optimization of chemical processes and petroleum technology. He has more than 20 years of experience in oil refining in the areas of process engineering, advanced process control, and operations. During his career he has been in charge of conceptual design, and basic engineering packages for new and revamped projects, and responsible for the design and commissioning of advanced process control applications using both conventional and multivariable techniques. He has published several papers and presented many communications to congresses on steady-state and dynamic simulation, advanced process control, and soft sensors.

# INDEX

*Evolving Intelligent Systems: Methodology and Applications,* Edited by Plamen Angelov, Dimitar P. Filev, and Nikola Kasabov
Copyright © 2010 Institute of Electrical and Electronics Engineers